ENDOGENOUS GROWTH THEORY

ENDOGENOUS GROWTH THEORY

Philippe Aghion and Peter Howitt

Problems and Solutions by Cecilia García-Peñalosa
in collaboration with Jan Boone, Chol-Won Li, and Lucy White

Coordinated by Maxine Brant-Collett

The MIT Press
Cambridge, Massachusetts
London, England

This book was set in Times Roman by Windfall Software using ZzTEX.

Printed and bound in the United States of America.

Library of Congress Cataloging-in-Publication Data

Aghion, Philippe.
  Endogenous growth theory / Philippe Aghion and Peter Howitt ;
  coordinated by Maxine Brant-Collett.
      p. cm.
  "Problems and solutions by Cecilia García-Peñalosa."
  Includes bibliographical references and index.
  ISBN 0-262-01166-2 (alk. paper)
    1. Technological innovations—Economic aspects. 2. Sustainable
development. 3. Economic development. I. Howitt, Peter, 1946–.
II. Brant-Collett, Maxine. III. García-Peñalosa, Cecilia.
IV. Title.
HD45.A47   1998
338.9—dc21   97-29036
                                                                CIP

To Beatriz and Pat,
who made it happen

Contents

Acknowledgments

This book is the result of a ten-year research collaboration that started in the fall of 1987 at MIT, where Philippe Aghion was a first-year assistant professor and Peter Howitt a visiting professor on sabbatical from the University of Western Ontario. During that year we constructed our basic model of growth through creative destruction (later referred to as the "quality-ladder" model), with the purpose of bringing Schumpeter's theory of development back into the mainstream of macroeconomic theory. In those early days of our research project we benefited from numerous conversations with MIT and Harvard colleagues, in particular Robert Solow, and also Olivier Blanchard, Patrick Bolton, Peter Diamond, Zvi Griliches, Elhanan Helpman, and Jean Tirole.

Later, as we extended our basic Schumpeterian framework to address a broader range of issues related to growth (unemployment, business cycles, market structure, income and wage inequality, and so on), we benefited from the constant feedback and encouragement of Robert Barro, Sergio Rebelo, and Xavier Sala-i-Martín. We also received useful comments and suggestions from Bruno Amable, Beatriz Armendariz, Jean-Pascal Benassy, Jess Benhabib, Ricardo Caballero, Daniel Cohen, Russ Cooper, Louis Corriveau, Nick Crafts, Paul David, Steve Davis, Elias Dinopoulos, Steve Durlauf, Joel Fried, Gene Grossman, John Haltiwanger, Rebecca Henderson, Charles Jones, Boyan Jovanovic, Ian King, Pete Klenow, David Laidler, Bev Lapham, Dale Mortensen, Dan Peled, Edmund Phelps, Chris Pissarides, Paul Romer, Bill Scarth, Paul Segerstrom, Luc Soete, Nancy Stokey, and Alwyn Young.

We have been deeply influenced by our collaborations with co-authors and friends, especially Patrick Bolton, with whom we explored the relationships between growth and inequality; Mathias Dewatripont and Patrick Rey, and also Chris Harris and John Vickers, on growth and market structure; Gilles Saint-Paul on growth and business cycles; and finally Jean Tirole on the organization of R&D. The manuscript owes an immensurable debt to their intellectual contributions and also to their moral support over the past ten years.

We have also benefited greatly from our association with the Economic Growth and Public Policy group of the Canadian Institute of Advanced Research, which includes several of those named above. Other members of the group whose comments and suggestions have directly aided the development of the book are George Akerlof, John Baldwin, Paul Beaudry, Pierre Fortin, Rick Harris, Richard Lipsey, David Mowery, Kevin Murphy, Craig Riddell, Nate Rosenberg, Ed Safarian, Scott Taylor, Eric von Hippel, and Michael Wolfson. We wish to thank all of these people, and also Fraser Mustard, the innovator who created the CIAR and whose encouragement and intellectual drive has been an inspiration to us. We have also gained from joining the "Cost of Inequality" group of the MacArthur Foundation, in particular from close interactions with Abhijit Banerjee, Pranab Bardhan, Roland Benabou, Sam Bowles, Michael Kremer, and Thomas Piketty.

The book is also the result of various attempts at presenting a coherent and yet innovative account of endogenous growth theory to graduate students in various academic institutions. This process started in June 1991, when Kenneth Arrow invited us to teach four lectures on new growth theories in his summer school at the Hebrew University in Jerusalem. We built on these lectures when teaching endogenous growth courses at ECARE in Brussels, IDEI in Toulouse, Nuffield College in Oxford, University College London and Paris X—Nanterre. The numerous comments and reactions by students and colleagues in each of these academic centers have contributed significantly to the conception and realization of this book and also, we hope, to its broad accessibility.

We are highly indebted to our former Oxford colleagues, in particular Tony Atkinson, Paul Klemperer, James Mirrlees, and Steve Nickell, for very insightful comments and advice that deeply influenced the development of the book. We are especially grateful to a few outstanding Oxford scholars who have made the realization of this book possible through their considerable effort made in commenting on successive drafts, and when contributing to the design of problem sets and solutions. We are particularly grateful to Cecilia García-Peñalosa, together with Jan Boone, Chol-Won Li, and Lucy White, for having put together a comprehensive set of problems and solutions that can also be used as teaching material. We are highly indebted to Edmund Cannon for contributing to the nontechnical summaries at the end of each chapter, and to him and Lucy White for invaluable help in copyediting the first draft of the manuscript. Jon Temple and Steve Redding have worked as full co-authors on Chapters 11 and 12, and we have greatly enjoyed collaborating with them.

Part of the work on the book was done when we were visitors at the IDEI in Toulouse. We are especially grateful to Jean-Jacques Laffont and Jean Tirole, not only for their hospitality and for the vigorous intellectual atmosphere they have fostered there, but also for numerous conversations on the subject of growth theory. We also benefited greatly from interactions with many others at the IDEI, including Jacques Crémer, André Grimaud, Norbert Laddoux, Michel Moreau, Eric Rénaud, and Jean-Charles Rochet.

The Department of Economics at University College, London (UCL) provided the financial and logistical support necessary for this book to be completed on time. We are particularly grateful to Costas Meghir for invaluable comments on Chapter 10 and to Eve Caroli for helping making the first chapter accessible to UCL undergraduates, for useful work in assembling the references, and for numerous discussions on the content of Section 8.2.2.

We are infinitely indebted to Maxine Brant-Collett, who coordinated and assembled the various bits and pieces of what eventually became a book, transformed our chaotic handwritten notes into a coherent and extremely well-typed manuscript, and sacrificed many weekends and holidays to get the final version ready on time. We are also very grateful to Maxine's husband, Paul Collett, for his patience and constant cooperation.

At the Ohio State University we have benefited from discussions with numerous colleagues, especially Mario Crucini, Paul Evans, Eric Fisher, Amy Glass, and Enrico Spolare. Karen Park offered useful comments on the earlier chapters and allowed us to meet a tight production schedule with her heroic efforts in preparing the index and figures at the last minute. Suchit Arora reviewed a draft of the manuscript and pointed out several errors. Jo Ducey helped type several chapters and provided excellent editorial assistance. We are grateful to all of them.

Terry Vaughn did a superb job in supervising and monitoring the growth process of the book itself and in providing on behalf of The MIT Press the support necessary for its timely realization and completion.

We owe immeasurable thanks to Pierre Katz for designing the beautiful cover of the book and to Roberto Matta for granting us permission to reproduce one of his paintings.

Last but certainly not least, we owe an unrepayable debt to our wives, Beatriz Armendariz and Pat Howitt, for their continuous support and encouragement, especially on those repeated occasions where we were about to give up on what seemed an impossible task. Without their unending patience and their willingness to bear more than should be asked of anyone, this immense undertaking would never have converged.

Introduction

Change and Innovation

The tremendous increase in material well-being that has taken place in advanced economies since the industrial revolution has been characterized by change and innovation. We do not just have more of the same goods and services; we also have new ones that would have been unimaginable to someone in the eighteenth century. People then knew nothing of such modern marvels as personal computers, jet airplanes, satellite communication, microwave ovens, and laser surgery. The knowledge of how to design, produce, and operate these products and processes had to be discovered, through a succession of countless innovations. More than anything else, it is these innovations that have created the affluence of modern times. Beyond making us richer, they have transformed the way we live and work.

Innovations do not fall like manna from heaven. Instead, they are created by human beings, operating under the normal range of human motivations, in the process of trying to solve production problems, to learn from experience, to find new and better ways of doing things, to profit from opening up new markets, and sometimes just to satisfy their curiosity. Innovation is thus a social process; for the intensity and direction of people's innovative activities are conditioned by the laws, institutions, customs, and regulations that affect their incentive and their ability to appropriate rents from newly created knowledge, to learn from each others' experience, to organize and finance R&D, to pursue scientific careers, to enter markets currently dominated by powerful incumbents, to accept working with new technologies, and so forth.

Thus economic growth involves a two-way interaction between technology and economic life: technological progress transforms the very economic system that creates it. The purpose of endogenous growth theory is to seek some understanding of this interplay between technological knowledge and various structural characteristics of the economy and the society, and how such an interplay results in economic growth.

The approach put forward in this book is based on Josef Schumpeter's notion of creative destruction, the competitive process by which entrepreneurs are constantly looking for new ideas that will render their rivals' ideas obsolete. By focusing explicitly on innovation as a distinct economic activity with distinct economic causes and effects, this approach opens the door to a deeper understanding of how organizations, institutions, market structure, market imperfections, trade, government policy, and the legal framework in many domains affect (and are affected by) long-run growth through their effects on economic agent's incentives to engage in innovative (or more generally knowledge-producing) activities.

An earlier strand to endogenous growth theory is the so-called AK approach, according to which technological knowledge is intellectual capital, which can be lumped together with computers, crankshafts, and other forms of capital into a single aggregate K. This point of view obliterates the distinction between technological progress and capital accumulation. And it portrays economic growth as basically a private activity; economies become richer in the same way Robinson Crusoe might—by saving at a rate determined by intertemporal preferences. In spite of its reduced-form representation of the process of knowledge accumulation, the AK formulation appears to be quite useful, especially when discussing government policies from an aggregate perspective. We shall thus explain, and occasionally use, the AK approach, for example when discussing the effects of redistribution policies and school finance on growth.

Why This Book?

There exist several excellent surveys of endogenous growth theory, such as the books by Grossman and Helpman (1991a) and Barro and Sala-i-Martín (1995), the survey articles by Dinopoulos (1993) and Stern (1989), and the symposium in the *Journal of Economic Perspectives* (1994). So why this book? A first reason is that each of the above surveys emphasizes a particular aspect of endogenous growth; for example, Grossman and Helpman focus more on trade-related issues and Barro and Sala-i-Martín more on AK models and convergence. In contrast, this book aims at providing a more comprehensive account of the field.

A second and deeper reason is that we want to show that endogenous growth theory provides a powerful and flexible engine of analysis that can be used for studying not only economic growth but also many other related phenomena. The first models with endogenous innovation that appeared in the literature in the early 1990s were based on special assumptions that restricted their scope and plausibility. In the following chapters we show that these simple models can fruitfully be extended and generalized in many different directions to address many different questions—that in fact they contain the beginnings of a vast and exciting research program.

The vision of economic life that endogenous innovation growth theory projects—a vision of perpetual change and innovation through competition—is a compelling one. As writers like Porter (1990) have emphasized, firms that survive the competitive struggle do so not so much by varying price and quantity as by innovating. Mokyr (1990) has argued that openness to change and innovation is a salient characteristic of the nations that become economic leaders of their time. Davis and Haltiwanger (1992) and others have documented the tremendous rates of turnover, among firms and among jobs, that characterize a dynamic and prosperous economy like that of the United States in the late twentieth century. The adjustments and dislocations that millions of people are experiencing in the current epoch of the information revolution are not historical anomalies; technological progress has been disturbing people's lives ever since the industrial revolution.

Until recently, it has not been possible to capture this vision of economic life using mainstream economic theory. For the general equilibrium theory that has dominated the mainstream is one in which the product space is given, technology is given, firms are mere placeholders for technological possibilities available to everyone, and there is no discernible process of competition, Schumpeterian or otherwise. Thus the neoclassical growth model of Solow and Swan assumed technological progress to be exogenous not because this was a realistic assumption, but because it was the only manageable one. Such writers as Kuznets, Abramowitz, Griliches, Schmookler, Scherer, Rosenberg, and many others, including Schumpeter himself, had long pointed out the importance of endogenous technological progress for growth.[1] Indeed, as we shall point out in more detail in Chapter 1, some of the leading developers of the Solow-Swan model attempted to endogenize the rate of technological progress. But their attempts did not quite succeed, for want of a suitable analytical framework.

The excitement of endogenous growth theory is that it provides the tools to handle endogenous technological change and innovation within a dynamic general equilibrium setting. This allows us to develop tractable and flexible models that embody the vision of economic life as an endless succession of innovation and change wrought by competition. With these tools we can bring to bear all that we have learned in economics about incentives, organizations, and institutions, not only on the problem of economic growth per se but also on the many other economic phenomena that interact with growth. That, in brief, is the research program of endogenous growth theory to which we would like to recruit the reader.

Aspects of Growth

After a review of earlier theory, including the AK model, in Chapter 1, the presentation of a basic Schumpeterian model of growth in Chapter 2, and an elaboration of a fuller model with capital accumulation and population growth in Chapter 3, the book goes on in Chapter 4 to study the interactions between growth and unemployment. This issue has been the subject of controversy ever since the large-scale introduction of machinery in manufacturing, yet the idea that technological progress might contribute to unemployment has until

---

1. Brewer (1991) has even traced the basic ideas of endogenous growth theory back to John Rae (1834).

recently lived only in the underworld of economic theory, with the single no-table exception of the chapter on machinery in the third edition of Ricardo's *Principles*, a chapter that orthodox theorists have commonly regarded as a blemish on an otherwise brilliant book. In this chapter we show how modern economic tools can be used to analyze under what conditions the encourage-ment of more innovation will reduce unemployment and under what conditions the job-destroying effects of new innovations will reverse the effect.

In Chapter 5 we show how introducing environmental limitations into en-dogenous growth theory can clarify the notion of sustainable development. Ever since the debates over Malthusian population theory, economists have routinely pointed to technological progress as the secret to overcoming the limitations of natural resources. With endogenous growth theory we can get a deeper understanding of the issues involved. Indeed, endogenous growth the-ory is ideally suited for studying the problem of sustainable development, in as much as it is primarily concerned with how growth can be sustained in the face of the ever-present threat of diminishing returns.

In Chapter 6 we study how growth affects and is affected by the structure of knowledge, in particular by the fact that some innovations, especially those coming from learning by doing and from development as distinct from re-search, enhance the rents from previous innovations rather than destroy them. These are the secondary innovations that realize the possibilities opened up by more fundamental breakthroughs. We show, for example, how research can be pushed so far, at the expense of learning by doing and of development, as to reduce the steady-state growth rate.

Chapter 7 studies the effects of market structure on economic growth. This chapter is important not only because creative destruction provides a new view of the process of competition, but also because it deals with a misleading and potentially embarrassing implication of simpler endogenous innovation growth models. That is, to the extent that competition limits the ability of a successful innovator to capture monopoly rents from his or her innovations, it will be harmful to growth. The chapter shows that natural extensions of the simple early models produce several different mechanisms through which an opening up of competition can stimulate growth despite this appropriability problem.

Chapter 8 studies the interaction between long-run growth and short-run fluctuations. One of the general implications of endogenous growth theory is that growth and cycles are related phenomena, with causation going in both directions. This chapter gives special emphasis to the phenomenon of "general purpose technologies" (roughly what Mokyr has called "macroinventions"). It analyzes several channels through which the introduction of a general-purpose technology can lead to a deep and prolonged decline in economic activity, even though it will ultimately put the economy on a higher growth path. Many people have come to the conclusion that this is what the world economy has been going through since the mid–1970s with the information revolution.[2]

Chapter 9 examines the related phenomena of income distribution and political economy, and their interrelationships with growth. We first question the view that inequality should always have a positive incentive effect on growth. We then discuss the so-called Kuznets hypothesis, according to which income inequality should taper off in more advanced economies, and in particular we show why growth typically leads to an increase in wage inequality both across and within educational cohorts. That growth generates sustained inequality should not come as a surprise: creative destruction implies that not everyone gains from the innovations that create long-run growth. Because of this, many people have an incentive to use whatever means at their disposal, including political means, to resist change. We provide a simple model of the political economy of resistance to progress, to account for the recurrent periods of stagnation in industrialized economies.

Chapter 10 examines the interactions between growth and education. We explore first the point of view that education and human capital affect productivity under a fixed technology, and study the related phenomena of development traps and stratification. We then take the point of view put forth by Nelson and Phelps (1966) to the effect that education and human capital are more important for producing technological change than for producing output under a given technology, and show among other things how more education can have ambiguous effects on the degree of wage inequality.

Chapter 11 deals with growth and international trade in goods and ideas. There we study the effects of trade on the equilibrium growth rate, pointing out that although international trade widens the market attainable by a successful innovator and thus raises the incentive to do research, it also raises the cost of research by making labor more productive in manufacturing, with effects that tend to offset each other. We also examine the issue of dynamic comparative advantage and the modern learning-by-doing foundations of the infant-industry argument for protecting domestic manufacturers.

Chapter 12 deals with empirical issues. We discuss this chapter at length in the following subsection of this introductory chapter.

Chapters 13 and 14 examine the organization of R&D. In Chapter 13 we study the contractual and financial issues involved in privately funded R&D, involving vertical integration versus joint ventures, employment contracts with R&D workers, and the role of cofinancing by outside investors, whereas Chapter 14 explores various issues involved in publicly supported R&D, including targeted versus untargeted R&D subsidies and the use of the patent system to

---

2. See, for example, Freeman and Perez (1988), David (1990), or Greenwood and Yorukoglu (1996).

encourage optimal R&D levels. Chapter 14 also analyzes some recent proposals for a national technology policy.

Much of the material covered in this book—either in the text or in the numerous problems at the end of the chapters—has only recently come out or is awaiting publication. Our hope is that this book will show that there is a lot of exciting research waiting to be done, and that endogenous growth theory provides a powerful set of tools for doing it.

Theory and Evidence

Another motivation for us in writing the book is empirical rather than theoretical. Because of its explicit emphasis on structural aspects of the innovation process, endogenous growth theory makes it possible to bridge the gap between theory and various strands of empirical and historical literature. For example, as Crafts (1996) has pointed out, endogenous innovation growth theory helps to account for why productivity growth was so low in Britain in the early nineteenth century, and for why the industrial revolution took place in Britain even though many of the "macroinventions" on which it was based took place in France.

Crafts summarizes the likely gains for economic history from exposure to endogenous-innovation growth theory in three points (p. 68):

(i)   Unlike traditional neoclassical growth economics, the new models can readily allow scope for divergence and for a much richer menu of influences on growth outcomes. The dangers of a Panglossian view of the past and a selective and restrictive search for evidence in evaluating growth performance should be much reduced for the next generation of cliometricians. This branch of growth theory offers improved hypotheses to economic historians unhappy with earlier formal models of induced technological change.

(ii)   Institutions (and policymaking) can be placed right at the heart of the growth process in a rigorous way. This should help to focus attention on detailed characteristics of these arrangements and to explain why they really matter. Institutional arrangements will be an intrinsic part of historical accounts of economic growth partly because they exhibit substantial continuity and windows of opportunity for their reform may well be both narrow and infrequent. There is an opportunity to assimilate key arguments of traditional historians which were previously either excluded by assumption or treated at best discursively.

(iii)   There can be a strong justification to resume the detailed consideration of the reasons for differences in TFP growth rather than to abandon the idea as old fashioned or simply a reflection of measurement error. Informed by new ideas, better techniques of measuring real output and imaginative investigation of the notion of "social capability," it may be possible to refine and extend the estimates of the growth accounting pioneers.

Yet endogenous-innovation growth theory has recently come under attack on empirical grounds. For example, Young (1995b) has argued that it sheds little light on the remarkable growth rates of newly industrialized countries in East Asia. And Jones (1995) has argued that the fact that growth has been relatively constant in the face of huge increases in the volume of resources devoted to R&D in advanced economies constitutes a refutation of endogenous-innovation growth theory.

We believe that these attacks fall short of the mark, mainly because what they portray as a characteristic endogenous-innovation model of growth is a very restrictive one, in which labor is the only input to innovation and innovation is the only factor affecting long-term growth. It is not surprising that such highly specialized models are rejected by empirical evidence. But the research program of endogenous-innovation growth theory does not stand or fall with them. Although it is true that the first generation of models made stark assumptions in order to clarify the new mechanisms that constituted their value added, these assumptions do not lie in the theory's hard core. Thus one of our primary motivations in developing the model of Chapter 3 with capital accumulation and population growth is to show that when these other important aspects of growth are taken into account, our approach becomes broadly consistent with the empirical observations that have been adduced to refute it, while retaining the essential feature that structural aspects of the economy affect long-run growth by altering the course of the innovation process.

The object of endogenous growth theory is not to supplant capital accumulation as an explanation of economic growth but to supplement it. As we explain in Chapter 3, innovation is a crucial ingredient to long-run growth, but not the only one; innovation and capital accumulation are *both* necessary ingredients for growth to be sustained. The problem with neoclassical theory is not that it analyzes capital accumulation but that it does *not* analyze technological progress. The purpose of endogenous growth theory is to fill this gap in neoclassical theory—to open up technological progress and innovation to systematic analysis, and to study their effects on growth, not to show that they explain everything.

This is not to say, however, that the theory is so general as to be devoid of empirical content. On the contrary, in Chapter 12, after discussing these empirical criticisms in some detail, we derive from a very general endogenous-innovation growth model many operational implications that can potentially be tested, concerning the relationships between growth and various measures of change such as exit and entry rates, rates of product introduction, and rates of job creation and destruction, and also concerning the impact on growth of various labor market variables that affect the incentive to innovate.

We believe that the theoretical developments described in this book should act as a stimulus to high-quality empirical research. Indeed, this has already begun to happen in the case of the effects of competition on growth analyzed in Chapter 7, which we discussed above in this introduction. For that chapter goes beyond blanket statements to the effect that competition always stimulates growth or that it always retards growth. It analyses *specific mechanisms* through which competition can stimulate growth, and thereby indicates circumstances in which the positive effect of competition on growth are most likely to outweigh the negative appropriability effect. This opens up the possibility of refining empirical investigations so as to test which of the various mechanisms are at work in producing the positive relationship between competition and growth that empirical researchers have tended to find. Nickell et. al. (1997) and Nickell (1996) have already begun to carry out this research, and we expect to see more in the future.

Chapter 12 also contains a long appendix dealing with the important measurement issues that arise in dealing empirically with the growth of technological knowledge. One of those issues in particular is critical to an assessment of the role of endogenous innovations in long-run growth. Specifically, the amount of resources devoted to the creation of technological knowledge is certainly underestimated by standard measures of R&D activity. For these measures exclude many informal activities routinely undertaken by firms and individuals. Many workers that are counted as engaged in production, management, or other nonresearch activities actually spend a considerable amount of their time and energy looking for better ways of producing and selling the output of the enterprise they are employed by. Likewise, the resources spent by firms on training, market research, brainstorming, exploration, sending people to conferences, and so forth are resources devoted to the creation of new technological knowledge, broadly defined, and yet they are not measured as such. To take a familiar example, all the time people have taken, and all the mistakes they have made, in learning to use computers efficiently should be counted as an input to the process of creating technological knowledge.

When it comes to measuring the input to the innovation process, empirical researchers routinely limit themselves to expenditures on formal R&D, thereby missing all these other activities. This results in a substantial underestimation of the scale of resources devoted to innovation. Moreover, as Jones (1995) has acknowledged, the increasing routinization of innovation may have resulted in a exaggerated appearance of rapid growth in the size of this input, because an increasing fraction of the input to innovation has been allocated to the formal R&D inputs that are actually measured. It is important to keep in mind that when we refer to "research" or to "R&D," what we have in mind is the whole range of inputs to innovation, not just that small part that is actually captured in formal R&D statistics.

Notes on Modeling Long-Run Growth

The theory developed in this book relies heavily on the notion of a steady state, in which capital, output, the wage rate, and knowledge (appropriately measured) all grow at the same constant rate. These assumptions were once routinely taken as given by growth economists on the basis of Kaldor's (1961) having labeled them as "stylized facts," but subsequent research has shown that they are easily falsified by a variety of time-series techniques. So they require some justification.

Our main justification is that because innovations often have effects that take decades to work out, we are primarily interested in "the long run," and the steady state is a convenient analytical device for modeling the long run—for distinguishing between effects that last and effects that are transient. It is much easier to discover and interpret the effects of a parameter change on a single variable than on an entire time path. In some cases the steady state may be a misleading device, because "transient" effects might persist for generations before finally disappearing. But it is at least a starting point from which a more complete dynamic analysis might proceed.

We do concern ourselves with out-of-steady-state dynamics in various places in these chapters where they are particularly relevant, most notably in Chapter 8 on growth and cycles, and in Chapter 12 where it is important to go beyond the steady state in interpreting empirical evidence. But for the most part we deal with issues in which the transition to a steady state is not critical, and for those purposes we confine our attention to the steady state. The book is long enough as it is.

A related aspect of these theories that might seem odd to a microeconomist is the use of infinite-horizon dynamic models. Why not do everything more simply in two periods? Again, our answer that we wish to study the long run. Two periods are not enough to distinguish permanent from transitory. Although two periods would simplify some things, they would not simplify the study of the long run nearly as much as does the simplifying device of "the steady state" that is permitted by an infinite horizon.

Finally, because so much attention is paid to microeconomic detail, why not study these details in a simpler partial-equilibrium setting? Here the answer is simple. Growth is a phenomenon affecting the whole economy, and the interactions between the innovation process and the economy work in both directions. For example, when we discuss growth and unemployment we see that there is a reciprocal feedback between the two phenomena that gives rise to a sort of multiplier process magnifying the partial-equilibrium effects. What makes endogenous growth theory so powerful is the simple and tractable models that it provides for taking general equilibrium effects like this into account.

Who Is the Book For?

The book is aimed primarily at students and researchers interested in the new theoretical developments that have been taking place in endogenous growth. More specifically, Chapter 1 could be used to cover growth theory in an upper level undergraduate macro course. Chapters 1, 2, 3, and 12 could be used for the same purpose in a first-year graduate macro course. The other chapters could be used in upper-level graduate courses, not just in growth but in other fields as well. For example, a course in development economics could use Chapters 1–3, 5, 6, 9, and 10. International trade is dealt with to some extent in Chapter 2 and extensively in Chapter 11. A course in industrial organization with emphasis on R&D could use Chapters 7, 13 and 14. A short graduate course on the foundations of growth theory could be based on Chapters 1, 2, 3, 6, and 12. A course on labor markets and human capital could use Chapters 4, 6, 9, and 10. A course on institutional aspects of growth could use Chapters 1, 2, 7, 10, 13, and 14, and a course on growth and cycles could use Chapters 2 and 8 and the last section of Chapter 9. Although the material developed in this book is fully self-contained, the starred sections may appear somewhat technical and may be skipped at first reading.

Most of all, we hope that students and researchers in all of these areas will find lots of unanswered questions and suggestions for how to address them, and that this will stimulate them to do further research. As we have already indicated, we find the vision of economic life portrayed by endogenous-innovation growth theory a compelling one, and the research program of incorporating that vision within the framework of mainstream economics an exciting one. We hope that readers of this book will be encouraged to keep up the technological progress within economics that has made it possible to start this research program, even though we know that further progress will ultimately render the book obsolete.

1 Toward Endogenous Growth

1.1 The Neoclassical Model of Exogenous Growth

The most basic proposition of growth theory is that in order to sustain a positive growth rate of output per capita in the long run, there must be continual advances in technological knowledge in the form of new goods, new markets, or new processes. This proposition can be demonstrated using the neoclassical growth model developed by Solow (1956) and Swan (1956), which shows that if there were no technological progress, then the effects of diminishing returns would eventually cause economic growth to cease.

The basic building block of the neoclassical model is an aggregate production function exhibiting constant returns in labor and reproducible capital. We abstract initially from all issues concerning population growth and labor supply by assuming a constant labor supply normalized to equal unity. Thus the aggregate production function can be written as a function of capital alone: $Y = F(K)$. This function expresses how much output Y can be produced, given the aggregate capital stock K, under a *given* state of knowledge, with a given range of available techniques, and a given array of different capital, intermediate and consumption goods.[1] We assume that all capital and labor are fully and efficiently employed,[2] so $F(K)$ is not only what can be produced but also what will be produced.

A crucial property of the aggregate production function is that there are diminishing returns to the accumulation of capital. If you continue to equip people with more and more of the same capital goods without inventing new uses for the capital, then a point will be reached eventually where the extra capital goods become redundant except as spare parts in the event of multiple equipment failure, and where therefore the marginal product of capital is negligible. This idea is captured formally by assuming the marginal product of capital to be strictly decreasing in the stock of capital: $F'(K) > 0$ and $F''(K) < 0$ for all K, and imposing the Inada conditions:

$$\lim_{t \to \infty} F'(K) = 0, \quad \text{and} \quad \lim_{t \to o} F'(K) = \infty. \tag{1.1}$$

Because we are assuming away population growth and technological change, the only remaining force that can drive growth is capital accumulation. Output will grow if and only if the capital stock increases. To determine whether and at what rate the capital stock will increase in any given situation, we follow Solow and Swan in assuming that people save a constant fraction s of their gross income[3] Y, and that the constant fraction δ of the capital stock disappears

---

1. Of course, K is an aggregate index of the different capital goods, and should be interpreted broadly so as to include human as well as physical capital.

2. In Chapter 4 we deal with the question of unemployed workers.

3. We are assuming no taxes, so that national income and output are identical.

each year as a result of depreciation. Because the rate at which new capital accumulates[4] is sY, and the rate at which old capital wears out is δK, therefore the net rate of increase of the capital stock (i.e., net investment) is:

$$\dot{K} = sF(K) - \delta K. \tag{1.2}$$

The differential equation (1.2) is the fundamental equation of neoclassical growth theory. It indicates how the rate of change of the capital stock at any date is determined by the amount of capital already in existence at that date. Together with the historically given stock of capital, (1.2) determines the entire time path of capital. The time path of output is then determined by substituting this path of capital into the aggregate production function.

Figure 1.1 shows how the fundamental equation (1.2) works. The depreciation schedule shows how the flow of depreciation depends on the stock of capital. It is a straight line through the origin, with a slope equal to the depreciation rate δ. The saving schedule shows how the gross flow of new investment depends on the stock of capital. Because the marginal product $F'(K)$ is positive but diminishes as K increases, therefore the saving schedule has a positive but diminishing slope.

Given any stock of capital, such as K_0 in figure 1.1, the rate of increase of that stock is the vertical distance between the saving schedule and the depreciation schedule. Thus whenever the saving schedule lies above the depreciation schedule, as it does when $K = K_0$ in figure 1.1, the capital stock will be increasing. Moreover, it will continue to increase monotonically, and will converge in the long run to K^*, the capital stock at which the two schedules intersect.[5] Thus K^* is a unique, stable, stationary state of the economy.

The economic logic of this dynamic analysis is straightforward. When capital is scarce it is very productive, so national income will be large in relation to the capital stock, and this will induce people to save more than enough to offset the wear and tear on existing capital. Thus the capital stock K will rise, and hence national income $F(K)$ will rise. But *because of diminishing returns,* national income will not grow as fast as the capital stock, which means that saving will not grow as fast as depreciation. Eventually depreciation will catch up with saving, and at that point the capital stock will stop rising.

Thus, in the absence of population growth and technological change, diminishing returns will eventually choke off all economic growth. For as the capital stock approaches its stationary level K^* national income will approach its stationary level, defined as $Y^* \equiv F(K^*)$, and the growth rate of national output

---

4. Recall that with no taxes, no government expenditures, and no international trade, saving and investment are identical. That is, saving and investment are just two different words for the flow of income spent on investment goods rather than on consumption goods.

5. It will never quite reach K^*, however, for as it approaches K^* its rate of increase will fall to zero.

saving, depreciation

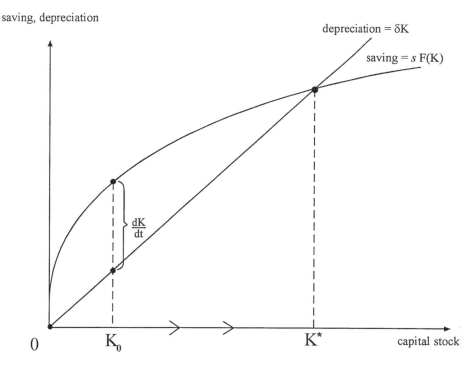

Figure 1.1
The level K* of capital is a unique, stable, stationary state to the Solow-Swan model with no population growth. It is an increasing function of the saving rate s and a decreasing function of the depreciation rate δ.

will fall to zero. According to this model, economic growth is at best a temporary phenomenon.

This means that any attempt to boost growth by encouraging people to save more will ultimately fail. Although an increase in the saving rate s will *temporarily* raise the rate of capital accumulation, it will have no *long-run* effect on the growth rate, which is doomed to fall back to zero. An increase in s will, however, cause an increase in the long-run *levels* of output and capital, by shifting the saving schedule upward in figure 1.1. Likewise an increase in the depreciation rate δ will reduce the long-run levels of output and capital by shifting the depreciation schedule up.

1.1.1 Population Growth

The same pessimistic conclusion regarding long-run growth follows even with a growing population. To see this, suppose that the flow of aggregate output depends on capital and labor according to a constant returns to scale production function $Y = F(K, L)$. (Constant returns to scale makes sense under our assumption that the state of technology is given, for if capital and labor were both to double, then the extra workers could use the extra capital to replicate what was done before, thus resulting in twice the output.) Suppose everyone in the economy inelastically supplies one unit of labor per unit of time, and that there is perpetual full employment. Thus the labor input L is also the population, which we suppose grows at the constant exponential rate n per year.

With constant returns to scale, output per person $y \equiv Y/L$ will depend on the capital stock per person $k \equiv K/L$. To simplify, suppose we consider the Cobb-Douglas case: $Y = L^{1-\alpha} K^\alpha$, $0 < \alpha < 1$, in which the per capita production function can be written as:

$$y = f(k) = k^\alpha. \tag{1.3}$$

The rate at which new saving raises k is the rate of saving per person, sy. The rate at which depreciation causes k to fall is the amount of depreciation per person δk. In addition, population growth will cause k to fall at the annual rate nk. The net rate of increase in k is the resultant of these three forces, which by equation (1.3) is:

$$\dot{k} = sf(k) - (n+\delta)\,k = sk^\alpha - (n+\delta)\,k. \tag{1.4}$$

Note that the differential equation (1.4) governing the capital-labor ratio is almost the same as the fundamental equation (1.2) governing the capital stock in the previous section, except that the depreciation rate is now augmented by the population growth rate, and the per-capita production function f has replaced the aggregate function F. This is because under constant returns to scale the *absolute* size of the economy is irrelevant. All that matters is the *relative* factor proportion k. Moreover, the per capita production function f will have the same shape as the aggregate production function F of the previous section,[6] so that the per capita saving schedule $sf(k)$ in figure 1.2 will look just like the saving schedule in figure 1.1. Although the absolute size of population is irrelevant, its rate of increase is not, because faster population growth will tend to reduce the amount of capital per person in much the same way as faster depreciation would, not by destroying capital but by "diluting" it—by increasing the number of people that must share it. This is why the depreciation rate must be augmented by the population growth rate in equation (1.4).

As figure 1.2 shows, diminishing returns will again impose an upper limit to capital per person. Eventually a point will be reached where all of people's saving is needed to compensate for depreciation and population growth. This

---

6. Constant returns implies that the marginal product of each worker, $f'(k) = f'(K/L)$ is the same as the marginal product in the aggregate production function, $F_1(K, L)$.

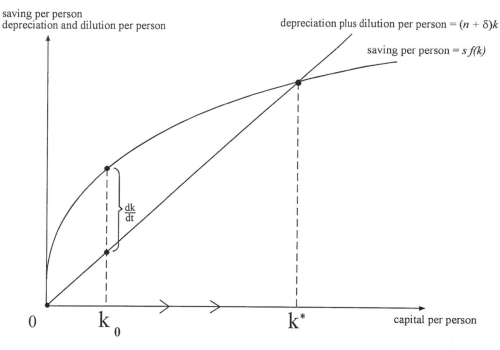

Figure 1.2
The level k* of capital per person is a unique, stable, steady state to the Solow-Swan model with population growth. It is an increasing function of the saving rate s, and a decreasing function of the depreciation rate δ and of the population growth rate n.

point is the "steady-state"[7] value k^*, defined by the condition:

$$sk^\alpha = (n + \delta)\, k$$

The capital stock will converge asymptotically to k^* in the long run, while the level of output per capita converges to the corresponding steady-state value $y^* = f\left(k^*\right)$. In this steady state equilibrium, output and the capital stock will both continue to grow but only at the rate of population growth. Growth as measured by the rate of increase in output *per person* will cease in the long run.

1.1.2   Exogenous Technological Change

It follows that the only way to explain the observed long-run growth in output per person is through technological change that continually offsets the dampening effect of diminishing returns. How this might work can be seen in terms

---

7. The aggregate capital stock is not stationary, but growing at the same steady rate as the work force.

of the Solow-Swan model, by supposing that there is a productivity parameter A in the aggregate production function that reflects the current state of techno-logical knowledge, and that this productivity parameter grows at the constant exponential rate g. The exogenous value of g is assumed to reflect progress in science.

Thus, suppose that the aggregate production function is:

$$Y = (AL)^{1-\alpha} K^{\alpha}. \tag{1.5}$$

This way of writing the production function makes technological progress equivalent to an increase in the "effective" supply of labor AL, which grows not at the rate of population growth n but at the rate of growth of population plus productivity[8]: $n + g$. As before, the rate of increase of the aggregate capital stock is just aggregate saving minus depreciation: $sY - \delta K$.

Formally, the only difference from the model of the previous section is that we have effectively replaced the population L by the "effective" population AL. Wherever L used to appear in the model, now AL appears. The only difference this makes is to raise the "effective" population growth rate from n to $n + g$. Thus by following exactly the same reasoning as before, we see that the supply of capital per "effective person" K/AL will approach a steady state. In this steady state, output and capital will grow at the same proportional rate as the effective population AL. But this means that output and capital *per person* will grow at the exogenous rate of technological progress g.

Intuitively, as capital accumulates, the tendency for the output/capital ratio to fall because of diminishing returns to capital is continually offset by tech-nological progress. The economy approaches a steady state in which the two conflicting forces of diminishing returns and technological progress exactly offset each other and the output/capital ratio is constant. Although the *height* of the steady-state growth path will be determined by such parameters as the saving rate s, the depreciation rate δ, and the rate of population growth n, the only parameter affecting the *growth rate* is the exogenous rate of technological progress g.

1.1.3   Conditional Convergence

The transitional dynamics of the model with population growth are shown diagrammatically in figure 1.2. As long as the economy begins close enough to the steady state k^*, the greater the shortfall of the actual capital/labor ratio

---

8. That A enters the aggregate production function multiplicatively with L is in most cases a very special assumption, amounting to what is sometimes referred to as "Harrod-neutrality," or "purely labor-augmenting technical change." There is no good reason to think that technological change takes this form; it just leads to tractable steady-state results. In the present Cobb-Douglas framework, however, the assumption is innocuous. Because all factors enter multiplicatively in a Cobb-Douglas production function it would make no observable difference if A multiplied L, K, or both.

below k^*, the greater the gap between the two curves in figure 1.2, and hence the higher will be the rate of growth of capital per person.

This implies that the transitional dynamics of the model will exhibit what is called "conditional convergence." That is, consider two economies with the same technologies, and with the same values of the parameters s, δ, and n that determine the steady-state capital/labor ratio. The country that begins with the lower *level* of output per capita must have a higher *growth rate* of output per capita. In that sense the two countries' levels of output per capita will tend to converge to each other.

To see this more clearly, note that the country with the lower initial level of output per person also has the lower level of capital per person (because they share the same production function). As you can see in figure 1.2, this means that the lagging country (as long as it is not too far behind) will have a faster growth rate of the capital/labor ratio. Because, from equation (1.3), $\dot{y}/y = \alpha\dot{k}/k$, and the two countries share the same value of α, therefore the lagging country will also have a faster growth rate of output per capita.

Notice that there would be no tendency to convergence if the countries had different steady states. For example, one country might have the higher initial level of output per person, because of some historical accident, and yet have the lower steady-state level because of a low saving rate. In other words, convergence is *conditional* on the determinants of the countries' steady-state levels of output per person.

In the empirical literature on cross-country growth regressions, authors often estimate equations of the form,

$$\frac{1}{T} \cdot \log\left(\frac{y_{i,t+T}}{y_{i,t}}\right) = \alpha - b.\log(y_{i,t}) + \gamma.X_{i,t} + \epsilon_{i,t}, \tag{1.6}$$

where i indexes economies and $X_{i,t}$ is a vector of variables (such as s, δ and n) that control for the determinants of steady-state output per person. The left-hand side of (1.6) is the growth rate of economy i measured over an interval of T years. Thus, the equation says, growth rates can vary from country to country either because of differences in the parameters determining their steady states (captured in the term $\gamma.X_{i,t}$) or because of differences in initial positions (captured in the term $-b.\log(y_{i,t})$). An estimated value of $b > 0$ is taken as evidence for conditional convergence.

1.2   Extension: The Cass-Koopmans-Ramsey Model

1.2.1   No Technological Progress

As simple hypotheses go, the assumption of a fixed saving rate is not a bad approximation to long run data. But many writers believe that the subtleties of the permanent-income and lifecycle-savings hypotheses should be taken into account, on the grounds that people save with a view to smoothing their consumption over their lifetimes, taking into account their preferences for consumption at different dates and the rate of return that they can anticipate if they sacrifice current consumption in order to save for the future.

Suppose accordingly that we model saving as if it were decided by a representative infinitely lived individual whose lifetime utility function is $W = \int_o^\infty e^{-\rho t} u(c(t)) dt$, where $c(t)$ is the time path of consumption per person, $u(.)$ is an instantaneous utility function exhibiting positive but diminishing marginal utility, and ρ a positive rate of time preference. To simplify the analysis we abstract once again from population growth by assuming a constant labor force: $L = 1$. Then with continuous market clearing, perfect competition, perfect foresight and no externalities, the economy will follow an optimal growth path. That is, it will maximize W subject to the constraint that consumption plus investment must equal net national product:

$$\dot{K} = F(K) - \delta K - c, \tag{1.7}$$

and subject to the historically predetermined value of capital.

Along an optimal growth path, capital should be increasing whenever its net marginal product $F'(K) - \delta$ is greater than the rate of time preference ρ, and decreasing whenever it is less. That is, the rate of time preference can be interpreted as the required rate of return on capital, the rate below which it is not optimal to continue equipping workers with as much capital. This together with the first Inada condition (1.1) implies that growth cannot be sustained indefinitely. For this would require capital to grow without limit, which would eventually drive the net marginal product of capital below the rate of time preference.

To see this more formally,[9] recall that from the theory of optimal control the level of consumption at each point of time must maximize the Hamiltonian:

$$H = u(c) + \lambda[F(K) - \delta K - c],$$

where λ is the shadow value of investment, evaluated in current utils. According to (1.7) the term in square brackets is net investment. Thus the Hamiltonian is analogous to the familiar concept of net national product—consumption plus net investment—the only difference being that the Hamiltonian measures both consumption and net investment in units of utility rather than units of goods.

The necessary first-order condition for maximizing the Hamiltonian is that the marginal utility of consumption equal the shadow value of investment:

$$u'(c) = \lambda. \tag{1.8}$$

---

9. For the mathematical details of optimal growth theory, see Arrow and Kurz (1970). A brief summary of the mathematics of intertemporal optimization in continuous time is provided in the appendix to this chapter.

The shadow value λ is itself determined as the present value of the stream of extra utils that would be created by a marginal unit of capital. Equivalently[10] we can define it in terms of the Euler equation:

$$\rho\lambda = \lambda \left(F'(K) - \delta \right) + \dot{\lambda} \tag{1.9}$$

and the transversality condition:

$$\lim_{t \to \infty} e^{-\rho t} \lambda K = 0. \tag{1.10}$$

The Euler equation (1.9) can be interpreted as an equilibrium asset-pricing condition in a world where the numéraire is current utils and everyone is risk-neutral. The right-hand side of (1.9) shows the incremental flow of income, including capital gain, that can rationally be anticipated by an individual who holds an incremental unit of K.[11] The ratio of this income flow to the "asset price" λ must equal the "competitive rate of interest" ρ. The transversality condition (1.10) is the condition that rules out the kind of inefficiency involved in accumulating capital forever without consuming it.

The stationary state to this growth model is one where both capital K and the shadow value λ are constant. According to the Euler equation (1.9) this stationary-state stock of capital K^* will be the solution[12] to the modified golden rule condition:

$$F'(K^*) = \rho + \delta. \tag{1.11}$$

As in the model with a fixed saving rate, the capital stock will converge asymptotically to the stationary state. Therefore output will also converge to a stationary state and growth will cease in the long run.

Technically, if you invert the optimality condition (1.8) and use it to substitute for c in the law of motion (1.7), then (1.7) and (1.9) constitute a two-dimensional system of differential equations in the two variables K and λ.

---

10. As in standard consumer theory, if we start on an optimal path, then the marginal benefit of having an extra unit of net national product is independent of how that marginal unit is allocated between consumption and investment. Suppose therefore that all the extra NNP resulting from a marginal unit of capital is always exactly consumed. Then the increment to the capital stock will be permanent, and the marginal value will be

$$\lambda(t) = \int_t^\infty e^{-\rho(\tau - t)} u'(c(\tau))(F'(K(\tau) - \delta)d\tau.$$

By routine calculus, this is equivalent to the pair of conditions (1.9) and (1.10) provided that the optimality condition (1.8) can be invoked to replace the marginal utility at each date in the integral. The transversality condition is needed in order to ensure that the intergral converges.

11. That is, the extra K will raise the flow of output by an amount equal to the net marginal product $F'(K) - \delta$, each unit of which has a utility value of λ, and it will also allow the holder to benefit from the increase in the utility value of the unit (or suffer the loss if negative) at the rate $\dot{\lambda}$.

12. The existence of a unique stationary state is guaranteed by the strict concavity of F and the Inada conditions (1.1).

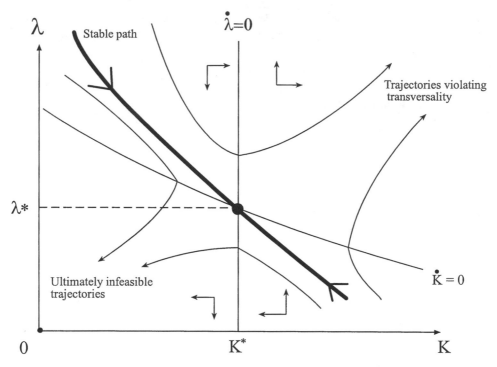

Figure 1.3
The stable path leading to the stationary state (K*, y*) is the optimal growth path in the Cass-Koopmans-Ramsey model.

Although history determines an initial condition for only one of these variables, namely the initial stock of capital, the transversality condition (1.10) determines a terminal condition. Thus there are just enough boundary conditions to determine a unique solution to the dynamic system. That unique solution will be the one that converges asymptotically to the stationary state K^*.

This dynamic system is illustrated by the phase diagram in figure 1.3. According to (1.9), the locus of points along which the shadow value is constant $(\dot{\lambda} = 0)$ is vertical at the modified golden-rule capital stock K^*. To the right of this locus λ must be rising because no one would hold an asset whose current yield $F'(K) - \delta$ is less than the rate of time preference unless he or she were compensated with the prospect of a capital gain $(\dot{\lambda} > 0)$. Likewise, $\dot{\lambda} < 0$ to the left of the locus. According to (1.8), consumption can be expressed as a decreasing function $c(\lambda)$ of the shadow value, because of diminishing marginal utility. The locus of points along which the capital stock is constant $(\dot{K} = 0)$ is defined by the condition that consumption equal net national product: $c(\lambda) = F(K) - \delta K$. This locus is represented in figure 1.3 by a negatively sloped curve,[13] because higher K implies a higher net national product, which permits people to consume more in a steady state, which by diminishing marginal utility requires λ to be lower. Above this locus consumption will be too low to keep K from growing, so $\dot{K} > 0$. Below it consumption will be too high to keep K from falling, so $\dot{K} < 0$.

An optimal growth path can never wander into the "northeast" segment of figure 1.3—above the $\dot{K} = 0$ locus and to the right of the $\dot{\lambda} = 0$ locus—for then the product λK would end up growing too fast to satisfy the transversality condition (1.10). People would be postponing consumption forever. Nor can the optimal growth path ever wander into the "southwest" segment in which consumption is rising ($\dot{\lambda} < 0$) and capital falling, because this would exhaust the capital stock in finite time. There is only one trajectory that avoids both of these forbidden segments. Given any initial K_0 the initial λ_0 must be chosen just right so as to put the economy on this trajectory, which is usually referred to as the "stable path" or the "saddle path."[14] Because the saddle path converges to a stationary point, growth is impossible in the long run.

1.2.2   Exogenous Technological Change

It is possible to add technological progress to the Cass-Koopmans-Ramsey model, just as we did with the Solow-Swan model, and thereby make growth sustainable in the long run. This is typically done by supposing, as in equation (1.5), that the aggregate production function can be written as $F(K, AL)$, where F exhibits constant returns to scale, and where A is an exogenous productivity parameter that grows at the constant exponential rate $g > 0$. As before, the parameter A can be interpreted as the number of "efficiency units" per unit of labor. Because we are assuming for simplicity that $L = 1$, we can write the aggregate production function more economically as $F(K, A)$.

The model is exactly the same as in the case of no technological progress, except that the constant quantity of labor input has been replaced by the growing number of efficiency units A. This change allows the stock of capital to grow indefinitely without driving the marginal product below the rate of time

---

13. This assumes that the net marginal product $F'(K) - \delta$ is positive. The Inada conditions imply, however, that this will cease to be the case when K has risen above K^* by enough. Once that has happened the economy will have "overaccumulated" capital, in the sense that the sacrifice of consumption that was needed to raise K to this level will have yielded a *negative* social return. This sort of "dynamic inefficiency" cannot occur in an optimal growth model, although it can in the Solow-Swan model.

14. This is because mathematically the stationary state (λ^*, K^*) is a "saddle point" to the dynamical system, meaning that while it is not locally stable it is reachable by at least some trajectories. Note, however, that steady state consumption is not maximized at this point (see problem 6).

preference, because the effect of diminishing returns is now offset by the continual rise in productivity.

To characterize the optimal growth rate, assume that the instantaneous utility function belongs to the isoelastic class.[15] Thus

$$u\ (c) = \frac{c^{1-\varepsilon} - 1}{1 - \varepsilon} \text{ for some } \varepsilon > 0 \text{ such that } \varepsilon \neq 1, \text{ or } u\ (c) = \ln\ (c)\ .$$

The class can also be defined by the condition:

$$u'(c) = c^{-\varepsilon} \text{ for some constant } \varepsilon > 0.$$

The parameter ε is the inverse of the intertemporal elasticity of substitution.

With this specification, using equation (1.8) to replace the shadow value in (1.9) yields the modified Euler equation:

$$\frac{\dot{c}}{c} = (1/\varepsilon)[F_1(K, A) - \delta - \rho], \tag{1.12}$$

where the marginal product of capital is now the partial derivative F_1.

The assumption that F exhibits constant return implies that the marginal product F_1 depends only on the ratio K/A. Therefore, K and A can both grow at the exogenous rate g without driving the marginal product below the rate of time preference ρ. According to (1.12), a steady state will exist with positive growth if the ratio K/A satisfies:

$$g = (1/\varepsilon)[F_1(K, A) - \delta - \rho]. \tag{1.13}$$

In this steady state,[16] capital, consumption and GNP all grow at the exogenous rate g. The growth path will be optimal if and only if the following modified transversality condition[17] holds:

$$\rho + (\varepsilon - 1)\ g > 0.$$

1.3   Initial Attempts to Endogenize Technology

Mankiw (1995) has argued that this simple neoclassical model suffices to account for international differences in growth paths if we adopt a broad view of capital that includes human as well as physical capital. We will discuss

---

15. Note that as $\varepsilon \to 1$, $\frac{c^{1-\varepsilon}-1}{1-\varepsilon} \to \ln\ (c)$.

16. Because $\dot{K} = gK$ in the steady state, consumption is given by the law of motion: $gK = F(K, A) - \delta K - c$.

17. This condition is necessary and sufficient for the transversality condition (1.10) to hold in the steady state that we have just described. Although it imposes a direct restriction on the set of allowable parameter values, it is not nearly as arbitrary as it might seem. On the contrary, it is a necessary condition for there to be a finite upper bound to social welfare.

the merits of this point of view later. Meanwhile, it suffices to remark that the model as it stands is incapable of accounting for persistent differences in growth rates across countries because it takes the rate of technological progress g, which uniquely determines the growth rate in each country, as exogenous.

The main problem with basing a theory of sustained growth on *exogenous* technological change is that there is every reason to believe that the growth of technology depends on economic decisions at least as much as does capital accumulation. Various attempts to endogenize technology were made before the recent vintage of endogenous growth models. But the problem facing all such attempts was how to deal with increasing returns in a dynamic general-equilibrium framework. More specifically, if A is to be endogenized, then the decisions that make A grow must be rewarded, just as K and L must be rewarded. But because F exhibits constant returns in K and L when A is held constant, it must exhibit increasing returns in three "factors" K, L, and A. Euler's theorem tells us that with increasing returns not all factors can be paid their marginal products. Thus something other than the usual Walrasian theory of competitive equilibrium, in which all factors are paid their marginal products, must be found to underlie the neoclassical model.

Arrow's (1962) solution to this problem was to suppose that the growth of A is an unintended consequence of the experience of producing new capital goods, a phenomenon dubbed "learning by doing." Learning by doing was assumed to be purely external to the firms who did the producing and to the firms that acquired the new capital goods. Thus K and L could continue to receive their marginal products, because in a competitive equilibrium no additional compensation would be paid to A. Nevertheless the growth of A became endogenous, in the sense that an increased saving propensity would affect its time path. The Arrow model, however, was fully worked out only in the case of a fixed capital/labor ratio and fixed (but vintage-specific) labor requirements. This implied that in the long run the growth of output was limited by growth in labor, and hence was independent of savings behavior, as in the Solow-Swan model.

The idea that investment and technological progress are tightly linked can be rationalized not only by Arrow's assumption of learning by doing, but also by recognizing that new ideas generally need new vintages of capital goods for their implementation. Kaldor (1957) therefore proposed abandoning altogether the notion of an aggregate production function and the distinction between increases in productivity due to capital and those due to technological progress. In their stead, he introduced a "technical progress function," relating the rate of output growth to the rate of investment, the shape and position of which reflected the underlying rate of new ideas and society's adaptability to those new ideas. In Kaldor's model, however, as in Arrow's, the steady state rate of growth was independent of savings behavior and was determined entirely by the exogenous properties of the postulated technical progress function.

Nordhaus (1969) and Shell (1973) built the first growth models in which technological change occurred as a result of deliberate economic choices. Both models assumed that research was motivated by the prospect of monopoly rents. The Nordhaus model, like the above-mentioned Arrow model, did not have enough increasing returns to sustain economic growth in the long run without population growth. The technical difficulties of dealing with increasing returns in a dynamic optimization framework forced Shell to assume strictly decreasing returns, with the result that sustained growth in per capita income was not possible without relying again on an additional, exogenous source of technological progress.

Uzawa (1965) showed how sustained growth at an endogenous rate could be achieved in the neoclassical model. He interpreted A as representing human capital per worker, assumed that its growth required the use of labor services in the form of educational inputs, and analyzed optimal growth paths. Under the additional assumption that the utility function, u, was linear, he showed that the optimal accumulation path was one in which all investment was specialized either in physical or human capital, until some finite time at which a steady state was entered with equal exponential growth in A and K. Uzawa's model was limited, however, to the description of optimal accumulation paths, and therefore did not come to grips with the problem of how the economy would compensate activities that made A grow in a world of increasing returns.

1.4   The AK Approach to Endogenous Growth

Diminishing returns to the accumulation of capital, which plays a crucial role in limiting growth in the neoclassical model, is an inevitable feature of an economy in which the other determinants of aggregate output, namely technology and the employment of labor, are both given. However, there is a class of model in which one of these other determinants is assumed to grow automatically in proportion to capital, and in which the growth of this other determinant counteracts the effects of diminishing returns, thus allowing output to grow in proportion to capital. These models are generally referred to as AK models, because they result in a production function of the form $Y = AK$, with A constant.

1.4.1   The Harrod-Domar Model with Unemployment

An early variant of the AK model was the Harrod-Domar model,[18] which assumes that labor input grows automatically in proportion to capital. To see

---

18. See Harrod (1939) and Domar (1946).

how this works, suppose first that the aggregate production function has fixed technological coefficients:

$$Y = F(L, K) = \min \{AK, BL\},$$

where A and B are the fixed coefficients. Under this technology, producing a unit of output requires $1/A$ units of capital and $1/B$ units of labor; if either input falls short of this minimum requirement there is no way to compensate by substituting the other input.

With a fixed-coefficient technology, there will either be surplus capital or surplus labor in the economy, depending on whether the historically given supply of capital is more or less than (B/A) times the exogenous supply of labor. When $AK < BL$, capital is the limitational factor. Firms will produce the amount $Y = AK$, and hire the amount $(1/B) Y = (1/B) AK < L$ of labor. With a fixed saving rate, the capital stock will grow according to

$$\dot{K} = sAK - \delta K.$$

Thus the growth rate of capital will be:

$$g = \frac{\dot{K}}{K} = sA - \delta.$$

Because output is strictly proportional to capital, g will also be the rate of growth of output, and $g - n$ will be the growth rate of output per person.

In the model as just described, an increase in the saving propensity s will raise the rate of growth g. If output per person is rising, then the increase in growth will not be permanent, because with K growing faster than L, eventually the binding constraint on output will become the availability of labor rather than the availability of capital; beyond that point there will be no more possibility of growth in per capita output. But if output per person is falling, the increase in growth resulting from an increase in saving will be permanent. In this case, diminishing returns will never set in because the faster growth of capital will be accompanied by a permanently faster growth of labor input, which is made possible by the fact that there is always a surplus of unemployed labor in the economy.

1.4.2 The Frankel-Romer Model with Full Employment

The other variant of AK model assumes that technological knowledge, rather than employment, is the factor that grows automatically with capital. It is based on the idea that technological knowledge is itself a kind of capital good. It can be used in combination with other factors of production to produce final output, it can be stored over time because it does not get completely used up whenever it is put into a production process, and it can be accumulated through R&D and other knowledge-creation activities, a process that involves the sacrifice of current resources in exchange for future benefits. In all these respects knowledge is just a kind of disembodied capital good. Because we are interpreting K broadly as an aggregate of different sorts of capital goods, we might as well suppose that technological knowledge is included in this aggregate.

Frankel (1962) observed that because of this similarity between knowledge[19] and capital, an AK structure does not require the fixed coefficients and ever-increasing unemployment of the Harrod-Domar model. Frankel assumed instead that each firm j has a production function of the form

$$Y_j = \overline{A} K_j^\alpha L_j^{1-\alpha},$$

where K_j and L_j are the firm's own employment of capital and labor. If all firms face the same technology and the same factor prices, they will hire factors in the same proportions, so that aggregate output can be written in the same form:

$$Y = \overline{A} K^\alpha L^{1-\alpha}.$$

He then assumed that the common scale factor $\overline{A}$ is a function of the overall capital/labor ratio:

$$\overline{A} = A \, (K/L)^\beta$$

because in many respects the stock of knowledge depends on the amount of capital per person in the economy. He supposed that although $\overline{A}$ was endogenous to the economy, it was taken as given by each firm, because the firm would only internalize a negligeable amount of the effect that its own investment decisions have on the aggregate stock of capital.

Frankel drew attention to the special case where $\alpha + \beta = 1$, and noted that in this case the two equations above imply $Y = AK$. In other words, as capital increases, output increases in proportion, even though there is continual full employment of labor and even though there is substitutability in the aggregate production function, because knowledge automatically increases in proportion. The rest of the model is like the Harrod-Domar model, except that now an increase in the saving propensity s will increase the growth rate permanently even in the case where output per person is growing at a positive rate to begin with.

---

19. He called it "development" rather than "knowledge."

Frankel's contribution seems to have gone unnoticed by the profession for thirty-five years. However, the basic idea of his AK model was rediscovered by Romer (1986),[20] who cast his analysis in terms of the Ramsey model of intertemporal utility maximization by a representative individual, taking into account that individuals do not internalize the externalities associated with the growth of knowledge. Romer's contribution, which was popularized by the influential article of Lucas (1988), became a benchmark for the modern literature on endogenous growth.

Romer assumed a production function with externalities of the same sort as considered by Frankel, and focused on the case in which the labor supply per firm was equal to unity and the rate of depreciation was zero. Saving was determined by the owner of the representative one-worker firm, whose dynamic optimization problem was to

$$\max \int_0^\infty u(c_t)e^{-\rho t}\,dt$$

s.t. $\dot{K} = \overline{A}K^\alpha - c$ and $\dot{K} \geq 0,$

taking the time path of $\overline{A}$ as exogenously given.

Assuming a constant intertemporal elasticity of substitution as we did before, namely $u(c) = \frac{c^{1-\varepsilon}-1}{1-\varepsilon}$, one obtains the Euler condition[21]

$$-\varepsilon\frac{\dot{c}}{c} = \rho - \alpha\overline{A}K^{\alpha-1}. \tag{1.14}$$

Having rational expectations, individuals correctly anticipate the same level of capital to be chosen at each time by all firms (given that these firms are all identical), hence $\overline{A} = AK^\beta$. The above Euler condition can then be written as

$$-\varepsilon\frac{\dot{c}}{c} = \rho - \alpha A K^{\alpha+\beta-1}. \tag{1.15}$$

If $\alpha + \beta = 1$— in other words, if there are *constant* social returns to capital (as in the case that Frankel drew attention to)—then the economy will sustain a strictly positive but finite growth rate g, in which diminishing private returns to capital are just offset by the external improvements in technology $\overline{A}$ that they bring about. More precisely, in this case (1.15) implies

---

20. Romer actually laid out more than an AK model, in as much as his approach allowed for a general utility function and assumed that there were strictly *increasing* social returns to capital. What we present here is the limiting special case that many followers have extracted from Romer's analysis, in which there are constant social returns to capital and an isoelastic utility function.

21. Condition (1.14) follows from (1.12), because in this case the net private marginal product of capital is: $F_1(K, A) - \delta = \alpha\overline{A}K^{\alpha-1} - 0.$

$$g = \frac{\alpha A - \rho}{\varepsilon}. \tag{1.16}$$

In particular, we see that the higher the discount rate ρ (that is the lower the propensity to save), or the lower the intertemporal elasticity of substitution measured by $1/\varepsilon$, or the more diminishing the private return to capital K (i.e., the lower α), the lower will be the steady-state growth rate g.

Furthermore, had we taken the technology parameter A to be equal to the *total* (rather than average) stock of accumulated capital, we would have had $\overline{A} = A (NK)^{\beta}$ in equilibrium, with a corresponding steady-state growth rate equal to

$$g = \frac{N^{1-\alpha} A\alpha - \rho}{\varepsilon}. \tag{1.17}$$

Thus the larger the number of firms N, the more externalities there will be in generating new technological knowledge in the economy and therefore the faster the economy will grow. In other words, the growth rate should be positively correlated with the scale of the economy, measured here by the number of firms N. This *scale effect* turns out to be a common feature of most endogenous growth models, and we will have more to say about it later.

An immediate implication of the positive correlation between size and growth is that *trade liberalization* may be *growth-enhancing*. Although free trade had already been advocated on purely static grounds (from Ricardo's theory of comparative advantage up to the more recent explanations based on product diversification by Dixit and Norman, among others), no coherent dynamic story could be told until the first endogenous growth models. In particular the earlier neoclassical growth models surveyed in the previous sections were bound to remain mute on the relationship between trade and growth.[22]

Romer actually assumed $\alpha + \beta > 1$; that is, *increasing* social returns to capital. In this case, he showed that growth will accelerate indefinitely. In the case of *decreasing* returns, $\alpha + \beta < 1$, growth will vanish asymptotically as in the Solow (or Ramsey) model without technological progress.

To summarize the main results obtained in this first endogenous growth model: First, when there are constant social returns to capital, then characteristics of the economy such as the discount rate (i.e., the saving behavior of individual consumers) or the size of the economy (i.e., the number of firms) will affect long-run growth. Second, precisely because individuals and individual firms do not internalize the effect of individual capital accumulation

---

22. We deal with trade and growth issues in greater details in Chapter 11.

on knowledge $\overline{A}$ when optimizing on c and K, the equilibrium growth rate $g = \frac{\alpha A - \rho}{\varepsilon}$ is less than the socially optimal rate of growth.[23]

Third, although growth has been endogenized, it relies entirely on *external* (and therefore unremunerated) accumulation of knowledge. Introducing rewards to technological progress adds a new dimension of complexity, because it moves us away from a world of perfect competition into a world with large individual firms. Incorporating imperfect competition into a general-equilibrium growth model is one of the major achievements of the second Romer model (1987, 1990a) presented in the next section.

Fourth, in the case where $\alpha + \beta = 1$, cross-country variations in parameters such as α and ρ will result in permanent differences in rates of economic growth. Thus, the simple AK approach does *not* predict conditional convergence in income per capita; the cross-section distribution of income should instead exhibit both absolute and conditional divergence.

Fifth, and last, the presence of an AK technology has important implications for the welfare effects of fiscal policy. In the neoclassical model it could be the case that an economy "overaccumulates" capital. When the capital stock is very large, and hence its marginal product is very small, the cost in terms of foregone consumption of replacing the machines that depreciate becomes higher than the marginal product of these machines. There is a "dynamic inefficiency," and consumption in all periods can be increased by a *reduction* of the capital stock. However, when the technology is AK, the marginal product is constant; hence there will be no dynamic inefficiency no matter how large the capital stock is.[24]

1.5 The Solow-Swan Model versus the AK Approach: The Empirical Evidence

At this point in the theoretical debate, the Solow-Swan and AK models stand as two competing explanations of the growth process. In this section, we discuss

---

23. More formally, the social planner would solve the dynamic program

$$\max \int_0^\infty e^{-\rho t} u(c_t) dt$$

s.t. $\dot{K} = AK^{\alpha+\beta} - c$

(this program internalizes the fact that $\overline{A} = AK^\beta$). When $u(c) = \frac{c^{1-\varepsilon}-1}{1-\varepsilon}$, we obtain the Euler equation (see equations (1.8) and (1.9) of section 1.2) $-\varepsilon\frac{\dot{c}}{c} = \rho - (\alpha+\beta)AK^{\alpha+\beta-1}$. With constant social returns to capital ($\alpha + \beta = 1$), this yields the socially optimal rate of growth

$$g^* = \frac{(\alpha+\beta)\,A - \rho}{\varepsilon} > g = \frac{\alpha A - \rho}{\varepsilon}.$$

24. See problems 6 and 7.

existing empirical evidence in order to compare the explanatory power of each model and, if possible, to discriminate between them.

At first it appears that determining the most appropriate framework should be easy, given the sharp differences in their respective predictions. There are two main issues: the nature of returns to capital and the determinants of long-run growth rates. As underlined earlier, the neoclassical growth model assumes diminishing returns to capital, whereas the AK model exhibits constant returns necessary to generate sustained but nonexplosive accumulation. In the simplest versions of the models, this difference has consequences for convergence in per capita incomes.

A related point is that the models disagree on the determinants of the long-run growth rate. According to the Solow-Swan model, this is entirely determined by exogenous factors such as population growth and technological change. It is therefore independent of the structural characteristics of the economy, such as its scale or the rate of time preference, which determine only the steady-state level of income per capita. In contrast, the AK model displays a strong influence of these characteristics on long-run growth.

In this section, we shall only briefly discuss the evidence drawn from cross-country growth regressions and then turn to the empirical debate on convergence and diminishing returns to capital. Much of our discussion in this section is based on Barro and Sala-i-Martín (1995).

1.5.1 Growth Regressions

A first body of empirical evidence resulting from cross-country analysis, concerns the existence of significant correlations between the long-run average growth rate of real per capita GDP and a number of structural and policy variables.

More specifically, based on a cross-country regression covering 90 countries over the period 1965–1985, Barro and Sala-i-Martín (1995) show that the average growth rate of GDP per capita is positively correlated with the level of educational attainment,[25] with life expectancy, with the investment to GDP ratio, and with terms of trade, and is negatively correlated with the ratio of government spending to GDP. It might seem that these standard cross-country growth regressions support the AK framework, in as much as they suggest a strong influence of structural variables on the long-run rate of growth. However this is not quite correct, not least because such regressions may rather reflect a reverse impact (or causation) of growth on these other economic variables. For example, a larger fraction of GDP is likely to be invested in physical capital and education as the economy becomes more developed.

---

25. Especially with educational attainment in secondary schools.

Subsequent cross-country growth regressions include King and Levine (1992), who points at a positive impact of financial sector development (e.g., measured by the ratio of bank debt to GDP) on growth;[26] Alesina and Rodrik (1994), who provide evidence that political instability (e.g., measured by the frequency of government changes or strikes) is detrimental to growth;[27] and Benhabib and Spiegel (1994), who stress the importance of human capital (e.g. measured by school attainment) especially when combined with technological progress.[28] Although they tend to favor the endogenous growth approach, these empirical studies do not provide particular support to the AK model and especially to its extreme predictions regarding convergence and the dynamic returns to capital accumulation.

1.5.2   Returns to Capital and Conditional Convergence

A second piece of empirical evidence based on cross-section data deals with convergence in the levels of income per capita and the nature of returns to capital.[29] Two main types of convergence appear in the discussions about growth across regions or countries, which we have already defined in the previous sections. *Absolute convergence* takes place when poorer areas grow faster than richer ones whatever their respective characteristics, whereas there is *conditional convergence* when a country (or a region) grows faster the farther it is below its own steady state. The latter form of convergence is definitely the weaker. Under certain conditions, conditional convergence even allows for rich countries to grow faster than poorer ones.

If there are diminishing returns to capital, the level of income per capita should converge toward its steady-state value, with the speed of convergence increasing in the distance to the steady state. In other words, lower initial values of income per capita generate higher transitional growth rates, once the determinants of the steady state are controlled for. In contrast, assuming constant returns usually means that one would not expect to find conditional convergence.

A wide empirical literature has developed on this issue, testing the influence of initial income per capita on subsequent growth rates. For regions within countries, such as the American states or Japanese prefectures, there is good evidence that initially poor areas grow more quickly. Turning to the evidence on convergence of countries, researchers have to be more careful to control for the determinants of the steady state, given the wide disparities in steady state

---

26. See Chapter 2.
27. See Chapter 9.
28. See Chapter 10.
29. The standard reference on convergence is again Barro and Sala-i-Martín (1995).

per capita income that are likely to hold. When this is done, the evidence is again clear: countries are converging to their steady states. The mean reversion found in per capita income in cross-section studies provides some indication that the Solow-Swan model, with its emphasis on diminishing returns to capital and transitional dynamics, is closer to the truth than the *AK* model. Against this must be set the findings of studies using single time series, which often indicate that per capita income may not revert to a trend. A second concern with the evidence is that convergence may be driven by technology transfer rather than differences in initial capital (see Chapter 2).

Moreover, several authors have questioned the assumption that constant returns to physical capital are incompatible with convergence. Transitional dynamics can be included in *AK* models. Another argument starts from the observation that growth is likely to be stochastic. Kelly (1992), Kocherlakota and Yi (1995), and Leung and Quah (1996) all show how certain kinds of technology disturbances can generate convergence even when returns to capital are constant. It could be argued, however, that the required form for the disturbances is often unrealistic.

Where conditional convergence is taking place, its speed can be used to estimate the importance of capital in the aggregate production function. Unfortunately, the evidence on convergence rates is not unproblematic. Measurement error in initial income or the presence of omitted variables (including country fixed effects, such as initial efficiency) is likely to bias the estimates of convergence rates. Imposing homogeneous rates of technological progress is also likely to lead to substantial biases (Lee, Pesaran, and Smith 1996). In the panel data studies, which typically average growth over short time periods, business-cycle effects may play a role.

A second line of empirical research has more directly addressed the issue of returns to capital by estimating the elasticity of output with respect to physical capital. Early empirical work on endogenous-growth models centered on this question. In particular, Romer (1987) carries out the following test. Suppose first that the consumption good is produced according to a Cobb-Douglas production function as in the simplest version of the Solow model. We have

$$Y = K^\alpha (AL)^{1-\alpha}, \quad 0 < \alpha < 1. \tag{1.18}$$

Under perfect competition in the market for final goods, and given the assumption of constant returns to scale implicit in (1.18), the coefficients α and $(1 - \alpha)$ should be equal to the shares of capital and labor in national income respectively, that is approximately 1/3 and 2/3 in the U.S. case. However, using both time series and cross-section data, Romer estimated the true elasticity of final goods output with respect to physical capital to be higher than the value 1/3 predicted by the Solow model, and perhaps lying in the range between 0.7 and 1.0. This result in turn appeared to be consistent with the existence of externalities to capital accumulation, as captured by the formalization $A \approx K^\eta$ analyzed in Romer (1986) and surveyed earlier. Such externalities imply that the elasticity of final output with respect to physical capital will be larger than the share of capital income in value added.

However, there are several problems in estimating the elasticities of output with respect to the inputs of capital and labor. The simplest and best known is the simultaneity bias present in estimating a production function. Any shock to output, such as an improvement in technology, is likely to be met with accumulation of inputs. This means that the regressors are correlated with the error term, and the estimated input elasticities will be biased.

The biases present in estimating elasticities in growth accounting equations have been studied by Benhabib and Jovanovic (1991) and Benhabib and Spiegel (1994). Benhabib and Jovanovic examine the case where technology follows the same underlying stochastic process across countries, but realizations differ. Benhabib and Spiegel study the simpler case in which technology grows at the same rate across countries. Both analyzes suggest that the estimated output-capital elasticity is likely to be biased upward. When technology grows at different rates across countries and this effect is not controlled for, it seems likely that this upward bias will be reinforced. It is problems like these that led Romer (1990b) to revise his earlier views and acknowledge that there seem to be decreasing returns to capital.

More recent studies, such as King and Levine (1994), have also concluded in favor of decreasing returns. Overall, there seems to be little empirical support for constant returns to physical capital: long-run growth is not driven simply by replicating existing machines; technological progress must play a role. Aware of this, many theorists have called for a broader definition of capital when using AK models. This "broad capital" should include not only privately held machines but also other accumulable factors: human capital, public infrastructure, and possibly knowledge.

There does seem to be a need to widen our conception of accumulable factors because, in the words of Mankiw, Romer, and Weil (1992), "all is not right for the Solow model." They find that the rate at which countries converge to their steady states is slower than that predicted by a Solow model with a capital share of one-third. The empirically observed speed of convergence suggests a share of broad capital in output of around 0.7–0.8. This leads them to augment the Solow model to include a role for human capital. They specify the following production function:

$$Y = K^{\alpha} H^{\beta} (AL)^{1-\alpha-\beta}. \tag{1.19}$$

Using a simple proxy for the rate of investment in human capital, they argue that this technology is consistent with the cross-country data. Their cross-section regressions indicate that both α and β are about 1/3, suggesting that the AK model is wrong in assuming constant returns to broad capital.

Interestingly, the elasticity of output with respect to the investment ratio becomes equal to $\frac{\alpha}{1-\alpha-\beta}$ in the augmented model, instead of $\frac{\alpha}{1-\alpha}$. In other words, the presence of human capital accumulation increases the impact of physical investment on the steady state level of output. Moreover, the Solow model augmented with human capital can account for a very low rate of convergence to steady states. It is also consistent with evidence on international capital flows; see Barro, Mankiw, and Sala-i-Martín (1995) and Manzocchi and Martin (1996). Yet, the constant-returns specification in (1.19) delivers the same long-run growth predictions as the basic Solow model, namely that long-run growth is exogenous, equal to $(n + g)$, where n is the rate of population growth and g is the rate of exogenous technological progress ($n = \frac{\dot{L}}{L}$ and $g = \frac{\dot{A}}{A}$).

Overall, empirical evidence regarding returns to capital tends to discriminate in favor of decreasing returns, and hence in favor of the neoclassical growth model. Mankiw, Romer, and Weil (1992) claim that the neoclassical growth model is correct not only in assuming diminishing returns, but also in suggesting that efficiency grows at the same rate across countries. We now turn to subsequent empirical assessments of their work.

1.5.3   Testing the Augmented Solow Model

Many of the cross-country growth regressions in the literature build on the work of Mankiw, Romer, and Weil (1992) on the augmented Solow model. However, the framework has not been without its critics. One of the main objections is that Mankiw, Romer and Weil assume that a country's initial level of technical efficiency is uncorrelated with the regressors. In practice, this seems unlikely to be the case. Because the initial level of technical efficiency is not observable and has to be omitted from the regressions, the coefficient estimates will be biased. This casts doubt on several of the results in the empirical literature.

One solution is to use panel data methods, differencing the regression equation to eliminate the unobserved "fixed effects." Islam (1995) and Caselli, Esquivel, and Lefort (1996) have followed this course, among others. The panel data estimates tend to be rather different from the cross-section ones, particularly in the estimates of the rate of convergence. This suggests that the fixed effects problem is an important one. However, panel data methods are not without their own difficulties. Results when controlling for fixed effects are often disappointingly imprecise, because the standard transformations remove much of the identifying variance in the regressors.

From our point of view, the important point is that the panel data estimates suggest systematic variations in technical efficiency across countries, albeit imprecisely estimated (Islam 1995). Given variation in efficiency levels, it is natural to assume that rates of technological progress must also differ, as some countries catch up while others lag behind. This is what development economists have always argued, and there is increasing evidence that their position is the right one.

The work of Mankiw, Romer, and Weil was soon followed by Benhabib and Spiegel (1994). They pointed out that the countries that accumulated human capital most quickly between 1965 and 1985 have not grown accordingly. Instead, growth appears to be related to the initial level of human capital. This casts doubt on the augmented Solow model. It suggests that, at least when explaining the historical experience of developing countries, one should turn to models in which technology differs across countries, and human capital promotes catching up.

The augmented Solow model has not been short of other critics. Lee, Pesaran, and Smith (1996) argue that time-series estimates indicate that rates of technological progress vary across countries. Cho and Graham (1996) have pointed out that for the model to fit the data, one corollary is that many countries (especially poor ones) have been converging to their steady states from *above*. Counterintuitively, many poor countries are thus found to have been running down their capital-labor ratios over 1960–85.

Overall, the augmented Solow model is almost certainly better at explaining growth than simple AK formulations. However, it has several problems of its own. The empirical evidence suggests that it is not the last word on growth. Moreover, from a theoretical point of view, a clear shortcoming of the model is that it leaves the rate of technological change exogenous and hence unexplained. More generally, both the orthodox and the AK models provide accounts of growth using a high level of aggregation. As Romer recently stressed, a deeper understanding of the growth process requires that we "explore a theoretical framework that forces us to think more carefully about the economics of technology and knowledge."

The next section will take the first step in this direction by addressing the issue of rewards to innovation. The subsequent chapters will examine the mechanisms underlying the production and diffusion of technological change. In these subsequent chapters we argue that the framework is likely to give insights into the growth process going well beyond those of the neoclassical model, at least for the advanced industrial countries.

1.6 Monopoly Rents as a Reward of Technological Progress

At the AEA meeting of December 1986, Paul Romer presented a six-page paper entitled "Growth Based on Increasing Returns Due to Specialization." Casual readers of that paper might have seen it at the time as little more than an "elaboration" of his previous model, with the growth of knowledge A now being the result, not of learning externalities among individual firms, but of the continuous increase in the variety of inputs. This second model of Romer formalizes an old idea that goes back to A. Young (1928), namely that growth is sustained by the increased specialization of labor across an increasing variety of activities: As the economy grows, the larger market makes it worth paying the fixed cost of producing a large number of intermediate inputs, which in turn raises the productivity of labor and capital, thereby maintaining growth. In this model as in the earlier Romer model, the growth in A is directly attributable to the growth in K, but those who accumulate the capital are not rewarded for having caused A to grow.

The model employs the product variety theory of Dixit and Stiglitz. There is a continuum of intermediate goods, measured on the interval [0,A]. Each good is produced by a local monopolist. Final output is produced using labor and the intermediate goods according to the production function.

$$Y = L^{1-\alpha} \int_0^A x_i^\alpha di, \quad 0 < \alpha < 1, \tag{1.20}$$

where x_i is the input of the ith intermediate good. In a symmetric equilibrium, $x_i = \overline{x}$ for all i. The value of $\overline{x}$ is determined by the condition that marginal cost equal marginal revenue for each monopolistic competitor. Marginal revenue comes from taking the marginal product of each intermediate good as its demand function. Marginal cost comes from a technology according to which each intermediate good is produced using only capital. The equilibrium value of A is determined by the zero-profit condition of free entry in the intermediate-good industry. Romer shows that this equilibrium value of A is $[(2 - \alpha)/2h]K$, where h is the fixed cost in each intermediate sector and K the stock of capital. This results in the aggregate production function.

$$Y = bL^{1-\alpha} A^{1-\alpha} K^\alpha, \tag{1.21}$$

where b is a positive coefficient. The function exhibits increasing returns to scale in L and K once A is replaced by its equilibrium value expressed above. However, the above equation is formally identical to the production function in the earlier Romer model analyzed in the previous section, in the special case of constant returns to K and A.

It would be quite wrong, however, to see in this second model nothing but a variant or a slight extension of the first Romer model. A key feature of the second model is its introduction of imperfect competition (monopoly rents) in the intermediate good sector, which not only allows the problem of increasing returns to be handled in a (balanced) growth model,[30] but also allows firms to be represented as engaging in deliberate research activities aimed at creating

30. The problem of increasing returns can be handled in a model with imperfect competition because in such a model the factors K and L will generally be paid *less* than their marginal product by the imperfectly competitive users of these factors.

new knowledge, and thereby being compensated with monopoly rents for a successful innovation.

Thus, for example, Romer (1990a) extended the model by assuming that in order to enter a new intermediate sector firms must pay a sunk cost of product development, whose outlay is compensated with monopoly rents.

Where do monopoly rents come from? From the existence of *fixed* production costs, that is, of increasing returns in the intermediate-good sector. Due to the presence of these costs, the intermediate-good sector can at best be *monopolistically* competitive (not *perfectly* competitive). What makes the intermediate-good sectors monopolistically competitive in both Romer (1987) and Romer (1990a) rather than, say, oligopolistic, is a *free-entry assumption,* which, as in the literature on product differentiation,[31] determines the equilibrium number of intermediate inputs A at each date. We shall henceforth concentrate on Romer (1990a).

Final output is again produced using labor and intermediate goods, but now labor can be used either in manufacturing the final good (L_1) or alternatively in research (L_2). (We denote by $\overline{L} = L_1 + L_2$ the total flow of labor supply.) Research in turn generates designs (or licenses) for new intermediate inputs, and A now refers indifferently to the current number of designs or the current number of intermediate inputs.

So, as before,

$$Y = L_1^{1-\alpha} \cdot \int_0^A x_i^\alpha di,$$

but now there is also a sunk cost of producing x units of a given intermediate input, namely the price P_A for the corresponding design or license. The speed at which new designs are being generated depends on both the aggregate amount of research and the existing number of designs, according to

$$\frac{\dot{A}}{A} = \delta L_2. \tag{R}$$

This equation reflects the existence of *spillovers* in research activities: all researchers can make use of the accumulated knowledge A embodied in the existing designs, in other words technological knowledge is a *nonrival* good. But knowledge is also *excludable* in the sense that intermediate firms must pay for the *exclusive* use of *new* designs. Note that there are *two* major sources of increasing returns in this Romer (1990a) model: specialization or product differentiation as in Romer (1987) *and* research spillovers.

Now the analysis becomes pretty straightforward. We can first determine P_A by an arbitrage condition between research and manufacturing labor. Workers

---

31. See Tirole (1988).

are free to choose between either of these two activities. One unit flow of labor spent in research generates a revenue equal to $P_A \cdot \delta A$ (from equation (R)). The same unit of labor, when used in manufacturing, generates a wage equal to the marginal product of manufacturing labor, namely $(1 - \alpha)L_1^{-\alpha} \cdot \int_0^A x_i^\alpha di = (1 - \alpha)(\overline{L} - L_2)^{-\alpha}Ax^\alpha$, in a symmetric equilibrium where all firms produce the same amount x of intermediate input. Hence

$$P_A = \frac{1 - \alpha}{\delta}(\overline{L} - L_2)^{-\alpha}x^a \tag{1.22}$$

in an equilibrium where workers are indifferent between research and manufacturing, which they must be if both activities are being undertaken.

Second, the value of x is determined by the conditions of profit maximization by each local intermediate monopolist. Assuming that one unit of capital can produce one unit of an intermediate good, marginal cost is the rate of interest r. The inverse demand function $p(x)$ is the marginal product of the corresponding input in manufacturing the final good,[32] that is,

$$p(x) = L_1^{1-\alpha} \cdot \alpha x^{\alpha-1}.$$

The corresponding intermediate firm's revenue $R(x)$ is

$$R(x) = p(x)x = (\overline{L} - L_2)^{1-\alpha}\alpha x^\alpha.$$

Equating marginal revenue $R'(x)$ with marginal cost r yields

$$r = \alpha^2 \left(\frac{x}{\overline{L} - L_2}\right)^{\alpha-1} \tag{1.23}$$

It follows that the monopolist's flow of profit will be $\pi = \frac{1-\alpha}{\alpha}rx$, and hence the value of each product design will be the present value of this flow, discounted over an infinite horizon at the rate of interest r:

$$P_A = \frac{1 - \alpha}{\alpha}x \tag{1.24}$$

In a steady state the growth rate of output is equal to the growth rate of A, which in turn satisfies the above equation (R). Hence

$$g = \delta L_2. \tag{1.25}$$

Equations (1.22)–(1.25) together with the familiar steady-state Euler equation

$$g = \frac{r - \rho}{\varepsilon}$$

---

32. The final-good sector is assumed to be competitive, an assumption we shall make repeatedly throughout these chapters.

can be solved for the steady-state growth rate:

$$g = \frac{\alpha \delta \overline{L} - \rho}{\alpha + \varepsilon}. \tag{1.26}$$

We immediately see that growth increases with the productivity of research activities δ and with the size of the economy as measured by total labor supply $\overline{L}$, and decreases with the rate of time preference ρ. Furthermore, both because intermediate firms do not internalize their contribution to the division of labor (i.e., to product diversity) and because researchers do not internalize research spillovers, the above equilibrium growth rate is always *less* than the social optimum.[33]

An important limitation of this approach to innovations and growth based on product variety, however, is that it assumes away obsolescence of old intermediate inputs, which, as was stressed by Schumpeter in his work on creative destruction, is a critical component of technological progress and growth. Indeed, if old intermediate inputs were to become "obsolete" over time, the division of labor summarized in the aggregate factor A would cease to increase systematically over time, and hence would cease to ward off the growth-destroying forces of diminishing returns. In any case, in order to formalize the notion of (technical or product) obsolescence, one needs to move away from *horizontal* models of product development à la Dixit and Stiglitz (1977) into *vertical* models of quality improvements. This brings us to the second chapter in which we present our basic model of growth "through creative destruction."

Appendix: Dynamic Optimization in Continuous Time

The problem of optimal growth is a special case of the problems analyzed by "optimal control" theory, a branch of mathematics developed by the Russian mathematician Pontryagin in the 1950s. This appendix attempts to provide an intuitive account of the theory as it is typically used in macroeconomics, without pretending to be rigorous.

In the typical optimal control problem, an agent chooses a time path $\{c_t\}_{t=0}^{t=\infty} \equiv \{c_{1t} \ldots c_{nt}\}_{t=0}^{t=\infty}$ of n "control variables," and a time path $\{k_t\}_{t=0}^{t=\infty} \equiv \{k_{1t} \ldots k_{mt}\}_{t=0}^{t=\infty}$ of m "state variables." A state variable is one whose value at any date is historically predetermined, like the stock of capital. A control variable, by contrast, is one whose value can be chosen at any date, like the current flow of consumption; there may be some constraints limiting the choice of control variables, but the choice is not entirely determined by history.

---

33. Benassy (1996) shows, however, that with a slightly more general form of the Dixit-Stiglitz product-variety model, the equilibrium growth rate could exceed the optimal rate.

Technically, control variables are only required to follow a piecewise continuous path; that is, they can "jump" discontinuously from time to time. However, state variables must be continuous; they cannot jump. Instead, nature or some other outside force imposes "laws of motion" that govern their evolution over time. These laws of motion take the form of ordinary differential equations:

$$\dot{k}_{it} = g_i\left(k_t, c_t, t\right), \text{ for all } i = 1 \ldots m \text{ and for all } t \geq 0, \tag{1.27}$$

where the "investment" functions g_i are continuous. Equation (1.7) is an example.

The agent seeks to maximize a discounted sum of future payoffs $\int_0^\infty e^{-\rho t} v\left(k_t, c_t\right) dt$, where $\rho > 0$ is the subjective rate of discount, and where the instantaneous payoff function v is continuous in the current state and control variables. The optimized value of this integral will depend on the historically given initial conditions, as determined by the given initial values k_0 of the state variables, and also on the initial date (because time enters as an argument in the investment functions), according to the "value function" $V\left(k_0, 0\right)$, defined as:

$$V(k_0, 0) = \max_{\{k_t, c_t\}} \int_0^\infty e^{-\rho t} v\left(k_t, c_t\right) dt$$

s.t.: $\begin{cases} \dot{k}_{it} = g_i(k_t, c_t, t) & \text{for all } i = 1 \ldots m \text{ and all } t \geq 0, \\ k_{it} \geq 0 & \text{for all } i = 1 \ldots m \text{ and all } t \geq 0, \text{ and} \\ k_0 \text{ given.} \end{cases}$ (1.28)

This is a difficult problem because it involves choosing not just a finite number of variables but an uncountably infinite number: m state variables and n control variables for every real number $t > 0$. Optimal control theory shows how the problem can be solved by reducing it to a large number of simpler problems, in much the same way as an idealized Walrasian economy solves a complex resource-allocation problem by decentralizing the decision making. In both cases, individual choices are coordinated by prices that reflect social costs.

More specifically, at each date t the choice of the current vector of control variables c_t affects not only the current payoff $v(k_t, c_t)$ but also future payoffs, because it affects the future evolution of the state variables that will condition future choices. Nevertheless, the choice of each c_t can be made almost independently of these future considerations; all the agent needs to know about the future is summarized in a vector of prices attached to the different state variables. These prices are generally referred to as "costate variables," and are denoted by $\lambda_t = (\lambda_{1t} \ldots \lambda_{mt})$.

Thus the appropriate objective for the choice of c_t is given by the "Hamiltonian" function

$$H\ (k_t, c_t, \lambda_t, t) = v(k_t, c_t) + \lambda_{1t} g_1(k_t, c_t, t) + \cdots + \lambda_{mt} g_m(k_t, c_t, t). \quad (1.29)$$

The first term is the immediate payoff from the choice of c_t, and the others are the value (price times quantity) of the "investments" that are affected by c_t. According to the "maximum principle" of optimal control theory, the control variables must be chosen so as to maximize the Hamiltonian at each date, given the current values of the state and costate variables. If we assume continuous differentiability of the Hamiltonian, this implies that

$$\frac{\partial}{\partial c_{it}} H\ (k_t, c_t, \lambda_t, t) = 0 \text{ for all } i = 1 \ldots n \text{ and all } t \geq 0. \quad (1.30)$$

As we have indicated, the nice thing about this maximum principle is that it allows the agent to choose the current set of controls at any date without worrying directly about any future or past variables; every variable entering the Hamiltonian at date t has a time subscript equal to t. Of course, this does not eliminate the difficulties of intertemporal choice, for it leaves the agent with the problem of assigning appropriate values to the costate variables λ_t in (1.30).

In principle, each λ_{it} is the marginal value $\frac{\partial}{\partial k_{it}} V\ (k_t, t)$ of the state variable. Unfortunately it is usually impossible to evaluate the marginal value directly. Instead, optimal control theory provides us with a set of necessary conditions that the costate variables must satisfy. The first set consists of the Euler equations

$$\dot{\lambda}_{it} = \rho \lambda_{it} - \frac{\partial}{\partial k_{it}} H\ (k_t, c_t, \lambda_t, t) \text{ for all } i = 1 \ldots m \text{ and all } t \geq 0, \quad (1.31)$$

and the second consists of the transversality conditions

$$\lim_{t \to \infty} e^{-\rho t} \lambda_{it} k_{it} = 0 \text{ for all } i = 1 \ldots m. \quad (1.32)$$

To understand the Euler equations, consider the following conceptual experiment. Suppose the agent is on an optimal path to begin with, and at date t some unexpected miracle raises state variable i by a small amount dk_i over and above what history would otherwise have determined. The marginal value of this exogenous change is clearly λ_{it}.

The agent will now revise the original plan, but the marginal value of this windfall change will be the same no matter what revisions are made, because condition (1.30) ensures that the controls have no marginal effect on the objective function.[34] So to evaluate the marginal value we are free to suppose whatever revisions we find convenient. Suppose accordingly that the agent chooses to make the increase in state variable i permanent, and

---

34. This is just another example of the famous envelope theorem of micro theory.

to insulate all the other state variables from the change. That is, the control variables are revised in such a way as to keep all the investment levels g_j unchanged.[35]

Given any future date $t + dt$, the marginal value can be decomposed into

$$\lambda_{it} = dV_1 + dV_2, \tag{1.33}$$

where dV_1 is the effect of the change on the discounted sum of payoffs between t and $t + dt$, and dV_2 is the effect from $t + dt$ on. Because the increment in k_i is permanent and the other k_j's have not been affected, the effect from $t + dt$ on is just the value of a marginal increment in k_i at $t + dt$, discounted back to t: $dV_2 = e^{-\rho dt} \lambda_{i,t+dt}$.

For small values of dt we can approximate this effect by

$$dV_2 = (1 - \rho dt)\, \lambda_{i,t+dt}, \tag{1.34}$$

and we can approximate the first component by

$$dV_1 = dv_t dt, \tag{1.35}$$

where dv_t is the effect on the payoff flow at date t.

Because all the investment flows $\frac{dk_{jt}}{dt} = g_j$ are assumed to remain unchanged, the effect on the payoff at t will equal the effect on the Hamiltonian:

$$dH\,(k_t, c_t, \lambda_t, t) = dv_t + \sum_j \lambda_{jt} dg_{jt} = dv_t. \tag{1.36}$$

Moreover, by (1.30) the effect on the Hamiltonian is just the partial effect of k_{it}. Together with (1.35) and (1.36), this implies

$$dV_1 = \frac{\partial}{\partial k_{it}} H\,(k_t, c_t, \lambda_t, t)\, dt \tag{1.37}$$

So, from (1.33), (1.34) and (1.37):

$$\frac{\lambda_{i,t+dt} - \lambda_{it}}{dt} = \rho \lambda_{it} - \frac{\partial}{\partial k_{it}} H\,(k_t, c_t, \lambda_t, t) \tag{1.38}$$

Because equation (1.38) is built up from approximations that hold for small values of dt, it must hold exactly when we take the limit of both sides as $t \to 0$. But taking this limit yields exactly the Euler equation (1.31) for state variable i.

---

35. More specifically, for all $j = 1 \ldots m$ and all $\tau \geq t$:

$$\sum_{h=1}^{n} dc_{h\tau} \frac{\partial}{\partial c_{h\tau}} g_j\,(k_\tau, c_\tau, \tau) + dk_i \frac{\partial}{\partial k_{i\tau}} g_j\,(k_\tau, c_\tau, \tau) = 0,$$

where $dc_{h\tau}$ is the change in control h at date τ.

An alternative interpretation of the Euler equations is as equilibrium conditions for asset prices. That is, each state variable can be thought of as an asset in the agent's portfolio, and each costate variable is the corresponding price at which the agent is content to hold the asset given rational expectations about the future flows of "dividends" (what we have been calling payoffs) and capital gains. Because the agent discounts future dividends at the rate ρ, each asset must yield a marginal rate of return equal to ρ. That is, the marginal flow of income must equal ρ times the price λ_{it}. Because, as we have seen, the marginal dividend flow is $\frac{\partial}{\partial k_{it}} H (k_t, c_t, \lambda_t, t)$, and because the flow of capital gain on a marginal unit is $\dot{\lambda}_{it}$, this implies

$$\rho\lambda_{it} = \frac{\partial}{\partial k_{it}} H (k_t, c_t, \lambda_t, t) + \dot{\lambda}_{it},$$

which is just the Euler equation (1.31) for state variable i.

In case you forget the exact form of the Euler equations, here is an easy way to remember, one that involves just the usual theory of constrained maximization and integration by parts. Think of each λ_{it} as the undiscounted value of the Lagrange multiplier on the constraint determining $\dot{k}_{it}$. (That is, suppose the multiplier is $e^{-\rho t}\lambda_{it}$.) The continuous-time analog to the Lagrangian expression for the problem (1.28) is

$$\int_0^\infty e^{-\rho t} v (k_t, c_t) \, dt + \int_0^\infty \sum_{i=1}^m e^{-\rho t}\lambda_{it} \left(g_i (k_t, c_t, t) - \dot{k}_{it} \right) dt.$$

Integrating by parts to get rid of the $\dot{k}_{it}$'s, and making use of the transversality conditions, we can rewrite this "Lagrangian" as

$$\int_0^\infty e^{-\rho t} \left\{ v (k_t, c_t) + \sum_{i=1}^m \left[\lambda_{it} g_i (k_t, c_t, t) \right. \right.$$

$$\left. \left. + \left(\dot{\lambda}_{it} - \rho\lambda_{it} \right) k_{it} \right] \right\} dt - \sum_{i=1}^m \lambda_{i0} k_{i0}.$$

Now proceed as in the usual case of constrained maximization; for each date t differentiate the integrand with respect to the date t choice variables and set the resulting derivatives equal to zero. Doing this with the control variables c_{it} yields the equations of the maximum condition (1.30), and doing it with the state variables k_{it} yields the Euler equations.

To understand the transversality conditions, consider the case where the agent has a finite horizon T rather than an infinite horizon. If you care nothing about what happens beyond T, then clearly it is optimal to exhaust all your assets by date T, except in the limiting case where an asset is not worth anything. For example, a rational person with no children and no other bequest motive who was certain to die at date T would liquidate and spend all assets by T, unless infirmity, transactions costs, or some other impediment made the agent incapable of deriving any more utility from them. In other words, the agent would obey the conditions

$$e^{-\rho T}\lambda_{iT}k_{iT} = 0 \text{ for all } i = 1 \ldots m,$$

which say that either the holding of each asset i will be exhausted by date T $(k_{iT} = 0)$, or its marginal value at T must be zero $\left(e^{-\rho T}\lambda_{iT} = 0\right)$. The transversality conditions (1.32) are just limiting versions of these finite-horizon terminal conditions.

We can be more formal about all this by asserting the proposition that a necessary condition for a time path $\{k_t, c_t\}_{t=0}^{t=\infty}$ satisfying the constraints of the optimal control problem (1.28) to solve that problem is that there exists a time path for the costate variables $\{\lambda_t\}_{t=0}^{t=\infty}$ such that the maximum principle (1.30), the Euler equations (1.31), and the transversality conditions (1.32) are satisfied. Moreover, if the payoff function v and all the investment functions g_j are concave, these conditions are sufficient as well as necessary to solve the problem. For more details on these and other related propositions, see Arrow and Kurz (1970) or Kamien and Schwartz (1981).

Problems

Difficulty of Problems:

No star: normal

One star: difficult

Two stars: very difficult

1. Utility functions

In this chapter and in subsequent ones, we use a utility function with constant intertemporal elasticity of substitution, CES, (also called constant relative risk aversion, or CRRA) to represent the preferences of consumers. The aim of this problem is simply to show that such utility function is needed in order to have steady-state growth paths with positive growth rates.

Consider the intertemporal utility maximization problem in continuous time. Show that the utility function must exhibit constant intertemporal elasticity of substitution (have a constant relative risk aversion) for a non-zero balanced growth path to exist.

⋆ **2. Convergence in the neoclassical model and the "augmented Solow model" (based on Mankiw, Romer, and Weil 1992, and the mathematical appendix in Barro and Sala-i-Martín 1995)**

This problem examines in more detail the derivation of the convergence equation obtained in section 1.1.3 in the text. We also examine the "augmented Solow model" and its implications for the long-run growth rate and for the convergence hypothesis.

Consider the neoclassical model of section 1.1 where output is given by $Y_t = (A_t L_t)^\alpha K_t^{1-\alpha}$. The technology grows at rate x, the population at rate n, and the stock of capital depreciates at rate δ. There is a constant saving rate, s.

a. Derive the convergence equation, that is, find an expression for the rate of growth of income toward the steady state that depends on initial income. What is the rate of convergence?

(Hint: log-linearize your expression for the rate of growth of output.)

b. Some authors have talked about "conditional convergence." Given your preceding equation, what is convergence conditional on?

c. Consider the augmented Solow model of Mankiw, Romer, and Weil, where output is a function of human capital, H, as well as of labor and physical capital,

$$Y_t = K_t^\alpha H_t^\beta (A_t L_t)^{1-\alpha-\beta} \quad \text{where } 0 < \alpha + \beta < 1$$

The gross investment rates in the two types of capital are a fraction s_k and s_h of output, respectively. Both depreciate at the same rate. Show that, as in the neoclassical model, the long-run growth rate of output per capita is the rate of technical change. Derive the convergence equation. Is it likely that there is absolute convergence?

3. The AK model with an exogenous saving rate (based on Barro and Sala-i-Martín 1995)

Here we want to illustrate the crucial role played by the assumption of constant returns in the results obtained by the new growth theories. To do so, we use the simplest growth model: a neoclassical model in which the savings rate is constant.

Consider the Romer (1986) production function for firm j

$$y_{jt} = k_{jt}^\alpha A_t^\eta \quad \text{where } 0 < \alpha < 1 \text{ and } A_t = A_0 \sum_j k_{jt}/N,$$

where y and k are output and capital per worker, and N is the number of firms. Suppose that s is the constant saving rate, n is the constant population growth rate, and δ the rate of depreciation of physical capital.

a. Find the differential equation for k when all firms are identical.

b. Represent graphically the solutions to the model for the cases where the production function exhibits (i) diminishing returns to scale, $\alpha + \eta < 1$, (ii) constant returns, $\alpha + \eta = 1$, (iii) increasing returns, $\alpha + \eta > 1$. What is meant by the "knife-edge property" of the AK model? (See the critique by Baldwin (1989)).

c. Examine the effect on the long-run growth rate of a change in the saving rate for each of the three cases.

d. Consider the effect of a once-off shock. Suppose an earthquake destroys half of the capital stock of the economy. Examine what happens in each of the three cases to: the growth rate immediately after the shock, the long-run growth rate, and the level of income once the new steady state has been reached compared to the level of income that would have been reached if there had been no shock. Do shocks have temporary or permanent effects?

4. Justification for the AK model: human capital

Consider a simple model of human capital in which production is given by $Y_t = K_t^{1-\alpha} (A_t L_t)^{\alpha}$, and A is a measure of the efficiency of labor, such that the productive capacity of the stock of labor, or level of human capital, is $H = AL$. Then $Y_t = K_t^{1-\alpha} H_t^{\alpha}$. A proportion s_k of income is invested in physical capital, and a proportion s_h in human capital. The depreciation rates are respectively δ_k and δ_h. The population does not grow.

a. Find the equilibrium physical capital to human capital ratio, using the condition that both investments must yield the same return.

b. Show that the production function can be written as an AK function and find the growth rate. Why are the results different from those in the augmented Solow model of Problem 2?

5. Justification for the AK model: government expenditure (based on Barro 1990)

This problem has two purposes. First, it provides a justification for the presence of constant returns in the aggregate production function. Second, it introduces a major mechanism through which the government can affect the output level and its rate of growth. The crucial assumption is that government expenditures, γ, affect the productivity of privately owned factors. A possible interpretation of this production function is that γ represents the infrastructure provided by the government. The better the roads are, the more efficient capital and labor will be.

The saving rate is endogenously determined as in Ramsey-Cass-Koopmans with a CES utility function. Output per capita depends on public expenditure on a public good, γ , as well as on capital. That is,

$y_t = A k_t^{1-\alpha} \gamma_t^{\alpha}$ where $0 < \alpha < 1$

Public expenditure is financed by a proportional tax on income, τ. The government cannot borrow; hence it must always have a balanced budget.

a. Find the dynamic equation for consumption in a competitive economy. What does it depend on?

b. Show that, in equilibrium, output is given by an AK production function. That is, that it can be expressed as being proportional to the stock of capital.

c. How can the government maximize growth in a competitive economy? What happens when there are no taxes? What happens when $\tau = 1$?

d. Is the competitive equilibrium socially optimal? Why?

6. The Cass-Koopmans-Ramsey model: the golden rule and dynamic inefficiency

Consider the model presented in section 1.2. Agents face the following problem:

$$\max_{c_t} \int_0^\infty \frac{c_t^{1-\varepsilon} - 1}{1 - \varepsilon} L_t \, e^{-\rho t} \, dt \tag{1.39}$$

subject to

$$\dot{k}_t = f(k_t) - c_t - \delta k_t, \qquad k_0 = \bar{k}$$

where k_t denotes the capital stock per worker, c_t per capita consumption and L_t the population, which grows at a rate n. Suppose there is no technical progress. We assume that $(\rho - n) > 0$, as otherwise the expression under the integral sign in (1.39) would not be bounded as t tends to infinity. The production function is $F(K_t, L_t) = K_t^\alpha L_t^{1-\alpha}$, and output per worker is $f(k_t) = k_t^\alpha$.

a. Obtain the steady state stock of capital per worker in a competitive economy.

b. Find the "golden rule of capital accumulation." That is, from the dynamic budget constraint, find the level of capital that would maximize consumption, when both consumption and the capital stock are constant over time.

c. We say that there is dynamic inefficiency if the steady-state stock of capital is greater than that implied by the golden rule. If this were the case, the economy could increase its steady state level of consumption by *reducing* its capital stock today. Because this implies more consumption today and more consumption in all future periods (as steady-state consumption is greater), it is a Pareto improvement. On the other hand, if the stock of capital is below the golden rule, steady-state consumption can only be increased by increasing the stock of capital today (i.e., reducing consumption). Because such a change would not be a Pareto improvement, we say that the economy is dynamically efficient. Could the economy above be dynamically inefficient?

★★ **7. Dynamic inefficiency and fiscal policy in the neoclassical versus the AK models (based on Blanchard 1985, Saint-Paul 1992, and Barro and Sala-i-Martín 1995)**

This problem has two purposes. On one hand, it examines which of the assumptions of problem 6 need to be relaxed in order to introduce the possibility that the competitive equilibrium in the neoclassical model is dynamically inefficient. We will see that it is required that agents be finitely lived and that their labor income fall as they grow older, so that they save when young in order to consume when old. In this context, a social security-system or government debt can be used to solve the inefficiency. On the other hand, it shows an important difference between the neoclassical and the AK models, as in the latter dynamic inefficiency can never occur, and hence fiscal policy or government debt will never be Pareto improving.

Consider the following version of the Cass-Koopmans-Ramsey model. At each date there is a continuum of generations indexed by their date of birth, s. Agents have an infinite horizon but die with a constant probability per unit of time, p. The number of agents born each period is large, although we normalize it to 1 so that the population is $1/p$ at all times. At time t there are $e^{-p(t-s)}$ people of generation s. Expected utility is assumed to be

$$E \int_s^\infty \log c(t, s) e^{-\rho(t-s)} \, dt,$$

where expectations are taken over the random length of life, and $c(t, s)$ denotes the consumption at time t of an individual born at time s. We can then express expected utility as

$$U_{ts} = \int_s^\infty \log c(t, s) e^{-(p+\rho)(t-s)} \, dt. \tag{1.40}$$

In the absence of insurance, uncertainty about the length of life would imply undesired bequests. We therefore assume that there is insurance that, given the large size of each cohort, can be provided risklessly. The life-insurance contract consists in the agent's receiving a predetermined amount each period if she does not die, and paying her entire wealth if she dies. Each individual has a labor endowment each period. It is $(\beta + p)$ when she is born, where the first term corresponds to remuneration to work and the second term captures the amount paid by the life-insurance company. We assume that the labor endowment declines at a rate β. That is, young individuals work more (or harder) than older ones. Labor income at time t of an individual born at s is then $l(t, s) = (\beta + p)\omega(t)e^{-\beta(t-s)}$, where $\omega(t)$ is the wage rate at time t. The aggregate labor endowment is one and the aggregate wage bill is equal to $\omega(t)$.

Let r be the interest rate which will be constant in steady state. Capital markets are perfect, so agents behave as if they were infinitely lived and the market interest rate were equal to $(r + p)$. The budget constraint at period t is then

$$\dot{w}(t, s) = (r + p)w(t, s) + l(t, s) - c(t, s), \tag{1.41}$$

where $w(t, s)$ denotes financial wealth at time t of an individual born at s.

a. Find the rate of growth of consumption given that individuals maximize (1.40) subject to (1.41). What is the transversality condition? Write down the individual's lifetime budget constraint, which equates lifetime consumption to lifetime income. Using the dynamic equation for consumption and the lifetime budget constraint, obtain an expression for consumption as a function of current wealth.

b. Integrate across individuals to express aggregate consumption, $C(t)$, as a function of the aggregate levels of human and financial wealth, $H(t)$ and $W(t)$ respectively. Show that the rate of growth of aggregate consumption is given by

$$\frac{\dot{C}(t)}{C(t)} = (r + \beta - \rho) - (p + \beta)(p + \rho)\frac{W(t)}{C(t)}.$$

c. Suppose the economy produces according to a constant returns production function $Y_t = BK_t^\alpha L_t^{1-\alpha}$. Let $B \equiv p^{1-\alpha}A$, hence $F(K_t) = AK_t^\alpha$, because the population has been normalized to $1/p$. Let A be a constant. The stock of capital depreciates at a constant rate δ.

i. What are the dynamic equations for aggregate consumption and aggregate wealth? Find the steady state capital stock and interest rate.

ii. Find the golden rule stock of capital.

iii. Show, by contradiction, that the equilibrium interest rate is less than $(p + \rho)$, and that the marginal product of capital lies in the interval $[\delta + \rho - \beta, \delta + \rho + p]$. Saint-Paul (1992) shows that in continuous-time models a necessary and sufficient condition for an allocation to be dynamically efficient is that the net marginal product of capital be strictly greater than the growth rate, $\partial F(K, L)/\partial K - \delta > g$. Can the economy be dynamically inefficient?

iv. Consider a social-security system that transfers resources across generations, so as to reallocate income towards the older age. There are transfers such that the labor endowment declines at a rate $\bar{\beta} < \beta$ instead of at rate β, and there is a tax $\tau < 1$ such that the net wage rate is $(1 - \tau)\omega(t)$. The government holds a balanced budget, which requires that the tax rate be $(1 - \tau) = (p + \bar{\beta}) / (p + \beta)$. Is it more or less likely that the equilibrium is dynamically efficient than before the system was introduced? Consider what would happen in the limit case in which the labor endowment is constant over time, $\bar{\beta} = 0$.

v. Suppose that the government spends a constant amount G in a public good that does not affect private productivity. Suppose that it initially finances this expenditure through a proportional tax on labor income, τ. At time t the government decides to issue public debt, denoted $D(t)$, and to no longer hold a balanced budget. A higher tax rate is levied in order to meet interest payments. Consider the new steady state, with the same level of expenditure G as initially but positive debt and a higher tax rate (all of which are constant). Write the new dynamic equations for consumption, capital stock, and debt. How does the new steady state compare to the initial one? If the economy was initially dynamically inefficient, can this be solved by issuing debt?

d. Suppose the private production function is $F(K_t) = A_t K_t^\alpha$. Let A_t be a measure of the level of technology such that $A_t = A K_t^{1-\alpha}$, where A is a constant. That is, the social production function is AK. The stock of capital depreciates at a constant rate δ.

i. Write the dynamic equations for aggregate consumption and aggregate wealth, and find the steady state growth rate and interest rate.

ii. Can the economy be dynamically inefficient?

iii. Consider the same unfunded social security system as in (c)(iv) above. What is its effect on the growth rate? Can it be Pareto improving?

iv. Consider the introduction of government debt as in (c)(v) above. Show that it has a negative effect on the growth rate. Suppose now that the economy is initially in a steady state in which there is a positive and constant debt to output ratio. Can a reduction in the debt ratio be Pareto improving?

⋆ **8. Welfare analysis when there is product diversity (based on Romer 1990a)**

Consider the Romer (1990a) model presented in section 1.6. Show that the competitive equilibrium is not socially optimal. Identify the various aspects in which the behavior of competitive agents departs from what the planner would choose.

⋆ **9. The role of the linear R&D function (based on Jones 1995)**

Jones has criticized the implication of the Romer model (and, as will be seen in subsequent chapters, several others) that there are scale effects associated to the research process. The data shows that the doubling of the number of workers employed in research has never doubled growth rates, or been close to it. This indicates that there may be a misspecification of research production functions. Consider Jones's version of the Romer model presented in section 1.6. All functions are identical except for the R&D function. There are constant returns to the level of employment in the sector, L_2. Suppose, however, that the externality due to past innovations exhibits diminishing returns, that is, only A^ϕ of past designs can be used in the generation of new ideas, where $0 \leq \phi \leq 1$. Assume also that because there are several firms doing research, some of them duplicate the research that others do. Hence, labor productivity is given by $A^\phi L_2^{\lambda-1}$, where $0 < \lambda \leq 1$. The aggregate R&D equation is thus

$$\dot{A} = \delta(A^\phi L_2^{\lambda-1})L_2.$$

The term in parentheses represents the total productivity of the L_2 workers employed in the sector, which depends on A (spillover) and the level of employment (duplication). The population grows at a constant rate n.

a. Solve the model with the above R&D equation.

b. Discuss the main features of the growth rate in this model.

c. Find the level of R&D employment chosen by a social planner, and the corresponding growth rate. How do they differ from the competitive outcome?

2 The Schumpeterian Approach

The earliest attempt at providing a Schumpeterian approach to endogenous growth theory was that of Segerstrom, Anant, and Dinopoulos (1990), who modeled sustained growth as arising from a succession of product improvements in a fixed number of sectors, but with no uncertainty in the innovation process.

In this chapter we will sketch a simple model (see Aghion and Howitt 1988, 1992a) where growth is generated by a random sequence of quality improving (or "vertical") innovations that themselves result from (uncertain) research activities.

This model of growth with vertical innovations has the natural property that new inventions make old technologies or products *obsolete*. This obsolescence (or "creative destruction") feature in turn has both *positive* and *normative* consequences. On the *positive* side, it implies a negative relationship between current and future research, which results in the existence of a unique steady-state (or balanced growth) equilibrium and also in the possibility of cyclical growth patterns. On the *normative* side, although current innovations have positive externalities for future research and development, they also exert a negative externality on incumbent producers. This *business-stealing effect* in turn introduces the possibility that growth be *excessive* under laissez-faire, a possibility that did not arise in the endogenous growth models surveyed in the previous chapter.

2.1 A Basic Setup

The basic model abstracts from capital accumulation completely.[1] The economy is populated by a continuous mass L of individuals with linear intertemporal preferences: $u(y) = \int_0^\infty y_\tau e^{-r\tau} d\tau$, where r is the rate of time preference, also equal to the interest rate. Each individual is endowed with one unit flow of labor, so L is also equal to the aggregate flow of labor supply. Output of the consumption good depends on the input of an intermediate good, x, according to[2]

$$y = Ax^\alpha, \tag{2.1}$$

---

1. The implications of introducing human and physical capital accumulation are explored in the next chapter.

2. Throughout much of this book we restrict attention to the simple Cobb-Douglas form (2.1), because it is simple and involves handy formulas that the reader will quickly get used to. However, almost all of the analysis could be conducted under the more general hypothesis

$$y = AF(x),$$

where the production function F has a positive and diminishing marginal product, and where monopolist's marginal revenue schedule: $A\left(F'(x) + xF''(x)\right)$ is decreasing in x.

where $0 < \alpha < 1$. Innovations consist of the invention of a new variety of intermediate good that replaces the old one, and whose use raises the technology parameter, A, by the constant factor, $\gamma > 1$.

Society's fixed stock of labor has two competing uses. It can produce intermediate goods, one for one, and it can be used in research. That is:

$$L = x + n, \tag{L}$$

where x is the amount of labor used in manufacturing and n is the amount of labor used in research.

When the amount n is used in research, innovations arrive randomly with a Poisson arrival rate λn, where $\lambda > 0$ is a parameter indicating the productivity of the research technology. The firm that succeeds in innovating can monopolize the intermediate sector until replaced by the next innovator. As in the basic Romer model, there are positive spillovers from the activities that generate growth in A, in two senses. The monopoly rents that the innovator can capture are generally less than the consumer surplus created by the intermediate good, and, more important, the invention makes it possible for other researchers to begin working on the next innovation. However, there is a negative spillover in the form of a "business-stealing effect," whereby the successful monopolist destroys the surplus attributable to the previous generation of intermediate good by making it obsolete.

The research sector is portrayed as in the patent-race literature that has been surveyed by Tirole (1988) and Reinganum (1989). The amount of labor devoted to research is determined by the arbitrage condition

$$w_t = \lambda V_{t+1}, \tag{A}$$

where t is not time but the number of innovations that have occurred so far, w_t the wage, and V_{t+1} the discounted expected payoff to the $(t + 1)^{th}$ innovation. The left-hand side is the value of an hour in manufacturing, whereas the right-hand side is the expected value of an hour in research—the flow probability λ of an innovation times the value V_{t+1}.

This arbitrage equation governs the dynamics of the economy over its successive innovations. Together with the labor market equation (L), it constitutes the backbone of the basic Schumpeterian model.

The value V_{t+1} is determined by the following asset equation:

$$r V_{t+1} = \pi_{t+1} - \lambda n_{t+1} V_{t+1},$$

which says that the expected income generated by a license on the $(t + 1)^{th}$ innovation during a unit time interval, namely $r V_{t+1}$, is equal to the profit flow π_{t+1} attainable by the $(t + 1)$ intermediate good monopolist minus the expected "capital loss" that will occur when the $(t + 1)^{th}$ innovator is replaced

Box 2.1
Poisson Processes

Throughout these chapters we will often assume that some random event X is governed by a "Poisson process," with a certain "arrival rate" μ. What this means mathematically is that the time T you will have to wait for X to occur is a random variable whose distribution is exponential with parameter μ:

$$F(T) \equiv \text{Prob } \{\text{Event occurs before } T\} = 1 - e^{-\mu T}.$$

So the probability density of T is

$$f(T) = F'(T) = \mu e^{-\mu T}.$$

That is, the probability that the event will occur sometime within the short interval between T and $T + dt$ is approximately $\mu e^{-\mu T} dt$. In particular, the probability that it will occur within dt from *now* (when $T = 0$) is approximately μdt. In this sense μ is the probability per unit of time that the event will occur now, or the "flow probability" of the event.

For example, in the present chapter the event that an individual researcher discovers innovation number $t + 1$ is governed by a Poisson process with the arrival rate λ. The expression λV_{t+1} on the right-hand side of the arbitrage equation (A) represents the expected income of an individual researcher, because over a short interval of length dt the researcher will make an innovation worth V_{t+1} with probability λdt.

If X_1 and X_2 are two distinct events governed by independent Poisson processes with respective arrival rates μ_1 and μ_2, then the flow probability that at least one of the events will occur is just the sum of the two independent flow probabilities $\mu_1 + \mu_2$, because the probability that both events will occur at once is negligible. In this sense, independent Poisson processes are "additive." This is why, in the present chapter, when n_t independent researchers each innovate with a Poisson arrival rate λ, the Poisson arrival rate of innovations to the economy as a whole is the sum λn_t of the individual arrival rates.

If a sequence of independent events takes place, each governed by the same independent process with the constant arrival rate μ, then the expected number of arrivals per unit of time is obviously the arrival rate μ. For example, in the present chapter the expected number of innovations per year in a balanced growth equilibrium is the arrival rate λn.

Moreover, the number of events x that will take place over any interval of length Δ is distributed according to the "Poisson distribution" that you will find described in most statistics textbooks:

$$g(x) = \text{prob } \{x \text{ events occur}\} = \frac{(\mu \Delta)^x e^{\mu \Delta}}{x!},$$

whose expected value is the arrival rate times the length of the interval $\mu \Delta$. This distribution is used in section 2.3 to express the expected present value of future output in a balanced growth equilibrium.

by a new innovator and therefore loses V_{t+1}. The flow probability of this loss is the arrival rate λn_{t+1}. Put in slightly different terms, the value V_{t+1} of the $(t + 1)^{th}$ innovation is the net present value of an asset that yields π_{t+1} until it disappears, which it does at the expected rate λn_{t+1}.[3]

---

3. n_{t+1} is the amount of labor devoted to R&D after the $(t + 1)^{th}$ innovation.

Note that this equation presupposes that the incumbent innovator does not perform R&D, so that λn_{t+1} is indeed the probability of that innovator losing his or her monopoly rents. In fact, there is a simple reason why the incumbent innovator chooses to do no research; all the other researchers have immediate access to the incumbent technology A_t as a benchmark for their own research, and the value to the incumbent innovator of making the next innovation is $V_{t+1} - V_t$, which is strictly less than the value V_{t+1} to an outside researcher. This is an example of the "Arrow effect," or "replacement effect."

We thus have

$$V_{t+1} = \pi_{t+1}/(r + \lambda n_{t+1}). \tag{2.2}$$

The denominator of (2.2), which can be interpreted as the obsolescence-adjusted interest rate, shows the effects of creative destruction. The more research is expected to occur following the next innovation, the shorter the likely duration of the monopoly profits that will be enjoyed by the creator of the next innovation, and hence the smaller the payoff to innovating.

The model is now almost entirely specified, except for the profit flow π_t and also the flow demand for manufacturing labor x_t. Both are determined by the same profit-maximization problem solved by the intermediate producer that uses the tth innovation. This producer could either be thought of as being the tth innovator (who then sets up a new intermediate firm), or as an existing intermediate firm that purchases (at price V_t) the patent for the innovation from the tth innovator. In either case, the tth innovator is able to extract the whole expected NPV of (monopoly) profits generated by that innovation during the lifetime of this innovation, namely V_t.

The tth incumbent innovator will determine π_t and x_t by solving

$$\pi_t = \max_x [p_t(x)x - w_t x],$$

where w_t is the wage and $p_t(x)$ the price at which the tth innovator (or intermediate firm) can sell the flow x of intermediate input to the final good sector. We assume the final good sector to be competitive, so that $p_t(x)$ must equal the marginal product of the intermediate input x in producing the final (or consumption) good. Thus, from equation (2.1), $p_t(x) = A_t \alpha x^{\alpha-1}$ is the inverse demand curve facing the tth innovator.

The first-order condition to the above maximization program yields immediately the following expressions for x_t and π_t:

$$x_t = \arg \max_x \{A_t \alpha x^\alpha - w_t x\}$$

$$= \left(\frac{\alpha^2}{w_t/A_t} \right)^{1/(1-\alpha)}$$

and

$$\pi_t = \{A_t \alpha x_t^\alpha - w_t x_t\}$$

$$= \left(\frac{1}{\alpha} - 1\right) w_t x_t = A_t \widetilde{\pi} \left(\frac{w_t}{A_t}\right)$$

Before proceeding, note that x_t and π_t are both decreasing functions of the productivity-adjusted wage rate $\omega_t = \frac{w_t}{A_t}$. That π_t decreases with respect to ω_t in turn introduces an additional reason, besides creative destruction, for the negative dependency of current research on the amount of expected future research: specifically, a higher demand for future research labor will push future wage ω_{t+1} up, thereby decreasing the flow of profits π_{t+1} to be appropriated by the next innovator. This, in turn, will tend to discourage current research, that is, to drive n_t down.

The model is now fully characterized by both:

• the *arbitrage equation* (A), which reflects the fact that labor can be freely allocated between manufacturing and research, and which can now be reexpressed (after substituting for V_{t+1} and π_{t+1} and dividing both sides of equation (A) by A_t) as

$$\omega_t = \lambda \frac{\gamma \widetilde{\pi}(\omega_{t+1})}{r + \lambda n_{t+1}}. \tag{A}$$

• the *labor market clearing equation* (L), which reflects the frictionless nature of the labor market and determines the growth-adjusted wage rate ω_t as a function of the residual supply of manufacturing labor $L - n_t$:

$$L = n_t + \widetilde{x}(\omega_t), \tag{L}$$

where the demand for manufacturing labor $x_t = \widetilde{x}(\omega_t)$ is a decreasing function of the growth-adjusted wage rate ω_t.

2.2   Steady-State Growth

2.2.1   Comparative Statics on the Steady-State Level of Research

A steady-state (or balanced growth) equilibrium is simply defined as a stationary solution to system (A) and (L), with $\omega_t \equiv \omega$ and $n_t \equiv n$. In other words, both the allocation of labor between research and manufacturing and the productivity-adjusted wage rate remain constant over time, so that wages, profit, and final output are all scaled up by the same $\gamma > 1$ each time a new innovation occurs.

In a steady state the *arbitrage* and *labor market clearing* equations simply become

$$\omega = \lambda \frac{\gamma \tilde{\pi}(\omega)}{r + \lambda n} \qquad\qquad (\widehat{A})$$

$$n + \tilde{x}(\omega) = L. \qquad\qquad (\widehat{L})$$

Because the two curves corresponding to $(\widehat{A})$ and $(\widehat{L})$ in the (n, ω) space are respectively downward and upward sloping, the steady-state equilibrium $(\widehat{n}, \widehat{\omega})$ is unique. Using figure 2.1, we easily see that the equilibrium level of research $\widehat{n}$ will be raised by a lower interest rate r, a higher size of the labor market L, a higher productivity of R&D λ, and a higher size of innovation γ. These comparative-statics results are all intuitive: (a) A decrease in the rate of interest increases the marginal benefit to research, by raising the present value of monopoly profits. (b) An increase in the size of each innovation also increases the marginal benefit to research, by raising the size of the next interval's monopoly profits relative to this interval's productivity. (c) An increase in the endowment of skilled labor both increases the marginal benefit and reduces the marginal cost of research, by reducing the wage of skilled labor. (d) An increase in the arrival parameter decreases both the marginal cost and the marginal benefit of research, because on one hand it results in more "effective" units of research for any given level of employment, but on the other hand it also increases the rate of creative destruction during the next interval. The former effect turns out to dominate.

Also, using the fact that in a steady state the productivity-adjusted profit flow $\tilde{\pi}$ is equal (from above) to

$$\tilde{\pi} = \frac{1 - \alpha}{\alpha} \omega x = \frac{1 - \alpha}{\alpha} \omega(L - n),$$

we see that $(\widehat{A})$ and $(\widehat{L})$ can be combined as

$$1 = \lambda \frac{\gamma \frac{1-\alpha}{\alpha}(L - n)}{r + \lambda n}, \qquad\qquad (2.3)$$

according to which the steady-state level of research $\widehat{n}$ is a *decreasing* function of α; that is, a decreasing function of the elasticity of the demand curve faced by the intermediate monopolist.

In other words, *product market competition is unambiguously bad for growth*: the more competition, the lower the size of monopoly rents that will be appropriated by successful innovators, and therefore the smaller the incentives to innovate. This unambiguous—but also somewhat simplistic—prediction of the basic Schumpeterian model will be discussed in detail in Chapter 7.

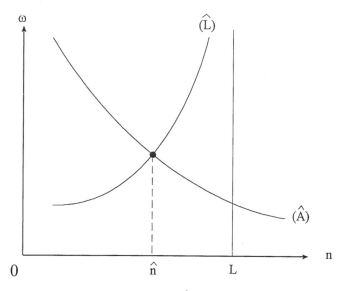

Figure 2.1

2.2.2   Comparative Statics on the Steady-State Rate of Growth

In a steady state the flow of consumption good (or final output) produced during the time-interval between the tth and the $(t + 1)^{th}$ innovation is

$$y_t = A_t \widehat{x}^\alpha = A_t (L - \widehat{n})^\alpha$$

which implies that

$$y_{t+1} = \gamma y_t \tag{2.4}$$

Now, the reader should remember that the variable "t" does not refer to real time, but rather to the sequence of innovations $t = 1, 2, 3$, and so on. What happens to the evolution of final output in real time, that is, as a function of τ?

From equation (2.4) we know that the log of final output $\ln y(\tau)$ increases by an amount equal to $\ln \gamma$ each time a new innovation occurs. However, the real time interval between two successive innovations is random. Therefore, as shown in figure 2.2, the time path of the log of final output $\ln y(\tau)$ will itself be a random step function, with the size of each step being equal to $\ln \gamma > 0$ and with the time interval between each step being exponentially distributed with parameter $\lambda \widehat{n}$. Taking a unit-time interval between τ and $\tau + 1$, we have: $\ln y(\tau + 1) = \ln y(\tau) + (\ln \gamma)\varepsilon(\tau)$, where $\varepsilon(\tau)$ is the number of innovations between τ and $\tau + 1$. Given that $\varepsilon(\tau)$ is distributed Poisson with parameter $\lambda \widehat{n}$, we have: $E(\ln y(\tau + 1) - \ln y(\tau)) = \lambda \widehat{n} \ln \gamma$, where the LHS is nothing but the average growth rate.

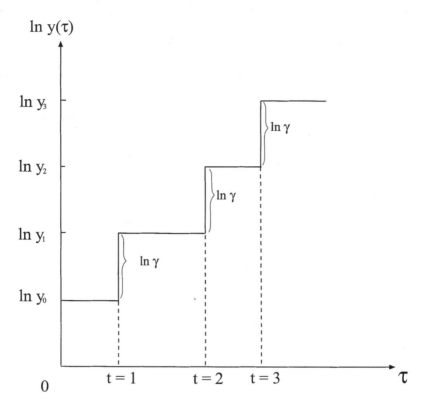

Figure 2.2

We thus end up with a very simple expression for the average growth rate in a steady state:

$$g = \lambda \widehat{n} \ln \gamma. \tag{G}$$

Combining this equation with the previous comparative-statics analysis on the steady-state level of research $\widehat{n}$, we are now able to sign the impact of parameter changes on the average growth rate. Increases in the size of the labor market L or a reduction of the interest rate r and in the degree of market competition α will increase $\widehat{n}$ and thereby also g. Increases in the size of innovation γ and/or in the productivity of R&D λ will also foster growth, directly (by increasing the factor $\lambda \ln \gamma$) and also indirectly through increasing $\widehat{n}$.

Although the relationship between trade and growth is not our primary focus in this chapter,[4] these comparative-statics results suggest the following

---

4. See Chapter 11.

ambiguous effect of trade liberalization on long-run growth: on one hand, by increasing the size of the overall labor market pool, trade liberalization appears to be growth-enhancing; on the other hand, to the extent that it may also increase product market competition (or the possibility of imitating current innovations), trade liberalization may reduce the reward to new innovations and thereby discourage research and growth.

2.3   Welfare Analysis

This section compares the laissez-faire average growth rate derived earlier with the average growth rate that would be chosen by a social planner whose objective was to maximize the expected present value of consumption $y(\tau)$. Because every innovation raises $y(\tau)$ by the same factor γ, the optimal policy consists of a fixed level of research. Expected welfare is

$$U = \int_0^\infty e^{-r\tau} y(\tau) d\tau = \int_0^\infty e^{-r\tau} \left(\sum_{t=0}^\infty \Pi(t, \tau) A_t x^\alpha \right) d\tau, \tag{2.5}$$

where $\Pi(t, \tau)$ equals the probability that there will be exactly t innovations up to time τ. Given that the innovation process is Poisson with parameter λn, we have

$$\Pi(t, \tau) = \frac{(\lambda n \tau)^t}{t!} e^{-\lambda n \tau}$$

The social planner will then choose (x, n) to maximize U subject to the labor resource constraint $L = x + n$. Using the fact that $A_t = A_0 \gamma^t$, we can reexpress the expected welfare U as

$$U(n) = \frac{A_0 (L - n)^\alpha}{r - \lambda n(\gamma - 1)}.$$

Then, the socially optimal level of research n^* will satisfy the first-order condition $U'(n^*) = 0$, which can be equivalently expressed as

$$1 = \frac{\lambda(\gamma - 1)\left(\frac{1}{\alpha}\right)(L - n^*)}{r - \lambda n^*(\gamma - 1)}. \tag{2.6}$$

This level of research would produce an average growth rate equal to

$$g^* = \lambda n^* \ln \gamma.$$

Whether the laissez-faire economy's average growth rate $g = \lambda \widehat{n} \ln \gamma$ is more or less than the optimal rate g^* will depend upon whether the steady-state equilibrium level of research $\widehat{n}$ determined earlier is greater or smaller than the socially optimal level n^*.

Now, in order to simplify the comparison between n^* and $\widehat{n}$, we can use equation (2.3), that is

$$1 = \frac{\lambda\gamma\left(\frac{1-\alpha}{\alpha}\right)(L - \widehat{n})}{r + \lambda\widehat{n}} \tag{2.7}$$

which determines $\widehat{n}$ just as (2.6) determines n^*. There are three differences between (2.6) and (2.7). The first is that the social discount rate $r - \lambda n(\gamma - 1)$ appears in (2.6) instead of the "private discount rate" $r + \lambda n$. The social rate is less than the rate of interest, whereas the private rate is greater. This difference corresponds to the *intertemporal spillover effect* discussed earlier. The social planner takes into account that the benefit to the next innovation will continue forever, whereas the private research firm attaches no weight to the benefits that accrue beyond the succeeding innovation.[5] This effect tends to generate insufficient research under laissez-faire.

The second difference is the factor $(1 - \alpha)$, which appears on the right-hand side of (2.7) but not in (2.6). This is an *appropriability effect* that reflects the private monopolists' inability to appropriate the whole output flow (he or she can appropriate only a fraction $(1 - \alpha)$ of that output). This effect also tends to generate too little research under laissez faire.

The third difference is that the factor $(\gamma - 1)$ in the numerator (2.6) replaces γ in the RHS of the arbitrage equation. This corresponds to a *"business-stealing" effect*. The private research firm does not internalize the loss to the previous monopolist caused by an innovation. In contrast, the social planner takes into account that an innovation destroys the social return from the previous innovation.[6] This effect will tend to generate *too much* research under laissez-faire.

Thus, both the intertemporal-spillover and appropriability effects tend to make the average growth rate less than optimal, whereas the business-stealing effect tends to make it greater. Because these effects conflict with each other, the laissez-faire average growth rate may be more or less than optimal.

---

5. Two additional spillovers could easily be included. First, researchers could benefit from the flow of others' research, so that an individual firm's arrival rate would be a constant-returns function of its own and others research. Second, there could be an exogenous Poisson arrival rate μ of imitations that costlessly circumvent the patent laws and clone the existing intermediate good. Both would have the effect of lowering the average growth rate relative to its optimal value.

6. Under more general production technologies than Cobb-Douglas, there is a further "monopoly distortion effect" that arises from the fact that private firms choose x to maximize profits, not final consumption (whereas the former is always equal to $(1 - \alpha)$ times the latter in the Cobb-Douglas case).

The appropriability and intertemporal-spillover effects dominate when the size of innovations γ is large, in which case $\widehat{n} < n^*$. However, when there is much monopoly power (α close to zero) *and* innovations are not too large, the business-stealing effect dominates, in which case $\widehat{n} > n^*$. In that case, and unlike in the models analyzed in the previous chapter, *laissez-faire growth will be excessive*!

This new possibility is the main welfare implication of introducing obsolescence (or creative destruction) in the process of economic growth. The idea that laissez-faire growth can be "excessive" because of the negative externality that new innovators exert upon incumbent firms will come up again in the following chapters, in particular Chapter 4 on growth and unemployment.

2.4   Uneven Growth

Going back to the basic model of section 2.1, we have already hinted at a negative correlation between current and future research in equilibrium: a higher level of research n_{t+1} tomorrow will both imply more creative destruction ($r + \lambda n_{t+1} \uparrow$) and less profit ($\pi_{t+1} = A_{t+1}\widetilde{\pi}(\omega_{t+1}) \downarrow$) after the next innovation ($t + 1$) occurs. This in turn will unambiguously discourage current research, that is, n_t will decrease.

In other words, the two basic equations (A) and (L) boil down to a single negative relationship between n_t and n_{t+1}[7]

$$n_t = \psi(n_{t+1}), \quad \psi' < 0. \tag{2.8}$$

A perfect foresight equilibrium (PFE) is defined as a sequence $(n_t)_0^\infty$ satisfying (2.8) for all $t \geq 0$. In figure 2.3, the sequence $\{n_0, n_1, \ldots\}$ constructed from the clockwise spiral starting at n_0 constitutes a PFE. The steady-state $\widehat{n}$ analyzed in the previous sections is defined as the fixed point of the mapping ψ, or equivalently as the intersection between the ψ-curve and the 45°-line. Other equilibria may also exist. A two-cycle is a pair (n^0, n^1) such that $n^0 = \psi(n^1)$ and $n^1 = \psi(n^0)$. It defines a PFE of period two. If both n^0 and n^1 are positive, the PFE is a "real" two-cycle. If either n^0 or n^1 is zero, it is a "no-growth trap." In a real two-cycle, the prospect of high research in odd

---

7. Dividing both sides of equation (A) by A_t, and using the fact that $n_{t+1} = L - \widetilde{x}(\omega_{t+1})$ (equation (L)), we obtain

$$\omega_t = \frac{\lambda\gamma\widetilde{\pi}(\omega_{t+1})}{r + \lambda(L - \widetilde{x}(\omega_{t+1}))} = \theta(\omega_{t+1}),$$

where $\theta' < 0$. Using again the fact that $n_t = L - \widetilde{x}(\omega_t)$ and therefore is increasing in ω_t for all t, we indeed get $n_t = \psi(n_{t+1})$ with $\psi' < 0$.   □

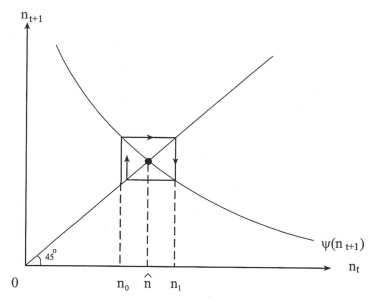

Figure 2.3

intervals discourages research in even intervals, and the prospect of low research in even intervals stimulates research in odd intervals. On such a PFE,
growth will be cyclical. Although the analysis in this section does not claim to
explain the relationship between growth and cycles (see rather Chapter 8), it
nevertheless points at the possibility of deriving causal interactions between
fluctuation and growth. As we will argue in Chapter 8, the two phenomena have traditionally been analyzed separately prior to endogenous growth
theory.

Finally, one can show the existence of a no-growth trap equilibrium under
suitable parameter conditions. A no-growth trap is the extreme case in which
the prospect of high research in odd intervals shuts down research completely
in even intervals.[8] Although the no-growth trap defines an infinite sequence
$\{n_t\}_0^\infty$, the oscillation will cease after one innovation. From then on no growth
will occur because the innovation process has stopped. Thus whether or not
the economy grows at all can depend on the psychology of innovators. The
expectation that the economy will grow at the steady-state rate $\lambda \widehat{n} \ln \gamma > 0$
will be self-fulfilling, but so might the expectation that the economy will not
grow at all!

---

8. It is straightforward to show (Aghion and Howitt 1992a) that a no-growth trap and a steady
state with positive growth will both exist for small enough rates of interest, given all the other
parameters of the model.

2.5   Discussion

The basic Schumpeterian model outlined in this chapter shares a number of limitations with previous endogenous growth models. A first limitation is its reliance on steady-state constructions. Both the Romer (1987, 1990a) model of horizontal innovations and the vertical (or quality ladders) model presented in this section make assumptions that ensure the existence of a steady state with balanced growth. These assumptions are quite severe and have nothing to recommend them except for tractability. We have already pointed out that in the Solow-Swan model with technological change one needs to assume Harrod-neutral (purely labor-augmenting) technical change at a constant exponential rate. In the Cass-Koopmans-Ramsey model one needs in addition a utility function in the one-parameter iso-elastic class. Analogous assumptions are needed even when technology is endogenized, and there is no good reason for thinking that they apply, even roughly.[9]

These strong assumptions rule out important phenomena, and answer important questions, by mere assertion. For example, they miss the stages of development in which resources are gradually reallocated from agriculture to manufacturing and then to services, all with different factor requirements and with different technological dynamics. The economy is always a scaled-up version of what it was years ago, and no matter how far it has developed already the prospects for future development are always a scaled-up version of what they were years ago. It seems just as likely that economies go through long phases of rises and decline or through periodic fluctuations, when introducing and/or diffusing new technological paradigms. (See Chapter 8, which discusses some first attempts at explaining aggregate output [and employment] fluctuations on the transition path between two technological paradigms.)

A second limitation lies in the description of *knowledge* as a parameter A, which fits into the aggregate production function much like any other factor of production. In reality, the growth of technological knowledge takes the form of new ideas or, in Schumpeter's terms, new combinations known to

---

9. More specifically, suppose that society's production possibilities at each date are given by the function

$$c = G(L, K, A; dk/dt, dA/dt), \tag{2.9}$$

which indicates how much consumption can be produced by the resources L, K, and A, when some of those resources must also be devoted to making K and A grow at the specified rates. Then in order for a balanced growth path to exist, with capital, output, consumption, and the productivity parameter A all rising at the same constant exponential rate, the production function G must obviously be homogeneous of degree one in all arguments exept L, at all points on the balanced path. Furthermore, if this homogeneity property holds everywhere in a neighbourhood of the balanced path, then the path can be optimal only if the utility function is isoelastic. All models of balanced endogenous growth assume this homogeneity property and isoelastic utility.

produce useful output. Assuming that labor and capital can be aggregated, as in all the literature we have cited, strains credibility, but it is hard to know even what is meant by assuming that ideas can be aggregated. A more natural way to think about the growth of knowledge would be to use either the adaptive models of learning found in the macroeconomic literature on convergence (or nonconvergence) to rational-expectations equilibrium (for example, Frydman and Phelps 1983), or Bayesian models of learning by experimentation. Such models assume that people do not know the "true" parameter or function describing technology. Instead they must learn about them through some combination of experience, experimentation, intuitive guessing, and creative extrapolation. There is no guarantee in general that the corresponding learning processes converge quickly, or at all, to the truth, especially when the possibilities for controlled experimentation are severely limited, and when the behavior of the variables that people are trying to forecast is affected by the forecasts themselves. (See Chapters 6 and 8 for first attempts at introducing *learning* and *experimentation* as important components of the growth process.)

A third main limitation is the lack of attention to *institutions and transaction costs*. Evidence that the Solow residual accounts for most of long-run growth in per capita income is not compelling evidence of the primary importance of technological knowledge in the same growth. The Solow residual is just, as Abramowitz once put it, "a measure of our ignorance," and evidence that it "explains" a lot is just evidence that our ignorance is very large. Douglas North (1989) has argued forcibly that the growth of productivity that has occurred since the rise of the West is as much attributable to the development of institutions that have allowed us to reduce transaction costs, and thereby to exploit more fully the potential gains from exchange, as it is to our increased control over nature. Yet with few exceptions the endogenous-growth literature has focused on our increased ability to understand and master nature as the ultimate mainspring of growth.

A related shortcoming of all endogenous growth models is their representation of firms and R&D activities. Most of the existing literature models R&D as being performed by the same individual (or by indeterminate collections of individuals). In practice, however, research and development are not performed by the same individuals. Typically R&D takes place within firms where employee-inventors are subject to assignment contracts with their employers, the employer providing the financing and physical capital, and the employee providing skills and ideas. Contractual provisions on how to share property rights on inventions, on how to structure the monetary and nonmonetary compensations to the inventor, are far more complex than the simple representation in terms of individual patents. Going farther into understanding the *financial and institutional aspects* of R&D in situations where individual researchers are cash or credit-constrained should undoubtedly enrich the Schumpeterian approach to growth. (See Chapters 7, 13, and 14 for preliminary attempts in that direction.)

Moving away from the representative agent assumption would also allow these models to incorporate the *political dimension* of "creative destruction." The old paradigm makes economic growth appear as an unmixed blessing that raises everyone's welfare, thereby ignoring obsolescence and other resource-allocation aspects of growth that explain why there is always a vested interest opposed to the introduction of new technologies and new institutions. Until this distributional tussle is incorporated into the heart of endogenous growth theory (and again, the Schumpeterian model of creative destruction appears to be the most natural framework to use) it is hard to see how proponents of such models can claim any deep understanding of why some societies acquire and adopt new technologies and institutions more rapidly than others, or how they will ever understand the phenomenon that Olson (1982) calls the rise and decline of nations. Preliminary attempts at introducing distributional and political considerations into an endogenous growth framework will be analyzed and discussed in Chapters 9 and 10.

Although the following chapters will explore several important dimensions in which the Schumpeterian paradigm can be fruitfully applied or developed, the most immediate extensions of the basic model will now be addressed in the next and last section of this chapter.

2.6   Some Immediate Extensions of the Basic Schumpeterian Model

2.6.1   Technology Transfers and Cross-Country Convergence

The earlier model suggests that two independent economies should always *diverge* in log of GDP terms; indeed, to the extent that the log of GDP in each country follows a *random walk with drift*, the fact that country C has innovated more than country D (and therefore $A(C) > A(D)$), does not imply that the latter country is more likely to make the next innovation(s). Having a tendency to diverge even with the same parameters (λ, γ), two independent economies will a fortiori exhibit divergent development paths if $(\lambda_C, \gamma_C) \neq (\lambda_D, \gamma_D)$.

Although the basic Schumpeterian model appears to be strongly biased toward nonconvergence, a straightforward extension of that model can nevertheless account for β-convergence, that is, for the evidence that conditional on a given steady-state path, those countries that are currently farther below that path tend to grow faster. The following extension emphasizes knowledge spillovers (or technology transfers) across countries instead of decreasing returns to capital accumulation as the main source of β-convergence.

Consider an open economy, and suppose that the rest of the world grows at an average rate g. Thus, at any date τ, the average worldwide knowledge parameter is proportional to $A_\tau^* = e^{g\tau}$. Now, if A_t denotes the economy's current productivity parameter at date τ and if the next innovation occurs in the short time-interval between date τ and date $(\tau + d\tau)$, we assume that

$$A_{t+1} = F(A_t, e^{g\tau}), \tag{2.10}$$

where:

a. F is an increasing function of its two arguments. (That F is increasing in its second argument reflects the existence of positive knowledge spillovers across countries; that F is increasing its first argument reflects the existence of intertemporal domestic knowledge spillovers within each economy.)

b. $F(A, A) = \gamma A$, where $\gamma > 1$. (That is, the average economy with current productivity parameter $A = A_\tau^*$ will not benefit from cross-country spillovers, and therefore the actual size of its next innovation [if made at date τ] will be the same γ as under autarky.)

It is easy to see why the above assumption generates conditional convergence: any country with current knowledge A_t *below* the average A_τ^* will achieve innovations of size greater than average, that is,

$$\frac{F(A_t, A_\tau^*)}{A_t} > \gamma,$$

because $F(A_t, A_\tau^*) > F(A_t, A_t) = \gamma A_t$.

Similarly, any country with current knowledge A_t *above* the average steady-state level A_τ^* will make innovations of size less than γ, that is,

$$\frac{F(A_t, A_\tau^*)}{A_t} < \gamma,$$

because $F(A_t, A_\tau^*) < F(A_t, A_t) = \gamma A_t$.

Everything else remaining equal, including the frequency parameter λ,[10] this implies that the farther below its steady-state path A_τ^*, the faster a country will grow, which is nothing but our previous definition of conditional convergence.

Thus the evidence described above on conditional convergence is also consistent with the Schumpeterian paradigm,[11] which in turn implies that a con-

---

10. The β-convergence result would obviously be reinforced if also the *frequency* parameter λ were subject to similar knowledge spillovers as those assumed here regarding the size of innovations.

11. This does not mean that convergence is implied or predicted by the Schumpeterian paradigm. There are indeed potential obstacles to knowledge spillovers between advanced and less advanced countries, which the basic formalization outlined above does not capture. One obstacle has to do with specialization: as argued by Young (1991), as a result of trading with more advanced economies, less developed countries may keep on specializing in traditional production activities that generate little new knowledge. (See Chapter 11.) Another obstacle, pointed out by Quah

vincing test of that paradigm against other models will have to rely on something other than convergence analysis (see Chapter 12 for preliminary thoughts on how to "test" the Schumpeterian approach).

2.6.2   Research Externalities and Threshold Effects

We now depart for one moment from the (constant-return) assumption that the marginal productivity of research measured by the frequency parameter λ is independent of the total number of researchers in the economy. Instead we assume that $\lambda = \lambda(n)$ follows a logistic curve as described in figure 2.4. Then, going through exactly the same steps as in the basic model, one can show that in a steady state the equilibrium research level $\widehat{n}$, whenever positive, must satisfy the following equation:

$$1 = \frac{\lambda(n)\gamma \frac{1-\alpha}{\alpha}(L - n)}{r + \lambda(n)n} = \Psi(n). \tag{2.11}$$

Given the inverted U-shape of the Ψ-curve, we then immediately get a *multiplicity* of *steady-state* growth paths. (See figure 2.5.) Although the no-research trap O and the high research steady-state H are both stable, the intermediate equilibrium M is unstable.

This multiplicity of (stable) steady-state paths captures a *threshold effect* similar to those obtained in other models with human capital externalities, in particular Azariadis-Drazen (1990).[12]

The interplay between education, human-capital accumulation, technical change and growth will be analyzed in greater detail in Chapter 10.

2.6.3   Imperfect Credit Markets

An important aspect, that appears to have been missed by all the endogenous-growth models we have surveyed so far, and in particular the basic Schumpeterian model of this chapter, concerns the relationship between growth and finance.

As it turns out, capital markets can easily be introduced into these models, although with little gain in terms of new economic insights. More specifically, there are two alternative interpretations of the basic model: (a) There exists a frictionless Walrasian credit market in which future expected consumption is

---

(1996) among others and which can also be formalized within the Schumpeterian framework, has to do with the existence of "clubs," that is, of *clusters* of countries which maintain intense research cooperation and exchange of knowledge among themselves but not with the rest of the world. Mainly empirical, this literature on *clubs* has not yet fully uncovered the (micro) economic mechanisms underlying the formation and dynamic evolution of clubs.

12. A main difference with Azariadis and Drazen is that here human-capital externalities are contemporaneous instead of being intergenerational. See Chapter 10.

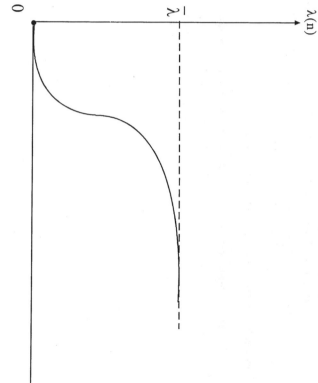

Figure 2.4

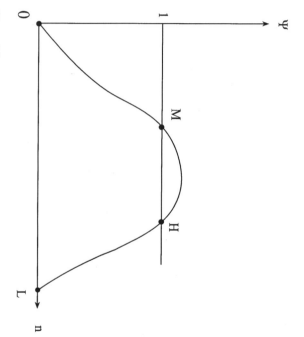

Figure 2.5

discounted at the constant rate r. Credit is costlessly provided to researchers (or research firms) who then reimburse the lenders out of the revenue flows they get from the intermediate manufacturing sector; (b) There is no credit market. According to the latter interpretation, all nonresearch workers consume their wage income at each instant, the owners of the monopoly intermediate firm consume their flow of profits at each instant, and research workers receive no pay unless their firms innovate, at which time they are paid in shares of the next intermediate firm. According to either specification, all research firms could be assumed to be owned by their workers, and $(\lambda.V)$ would represent the expected flow of surplus to be divided among them. The crucial assumption that utility is linear in consumption makes these two different interpretations equivalent, by removing any motive to use capital markets for risk-sharing.

However, the relationship between growth and finance starts gaining substance once agency considerations are introduced as potential sources of capital-market imperfections. Thus, King and Levine (1993b) extend the basic framework by introducing an *agency cost* of figuring out the time capacity of researchers (or the time value of a research project). With ex-ante probability ϕ, a researcher is *capable* (or equivalently his research project is *relevant*) and can then generate an innovation with flow probability λ. With probability $(1 - \phi)$, the researcher generates no value at all. If f denotes the flow cost (in labor units) incurred by a financial intermediary to discover the true type of each researcher (or research project), then the intermediary will require a flow repayment equal to f/ϕ per successful researcher or project in order to break even.

The *arbitrage equation* (A) then becomes

$$w_t(1 + f/\phi) = \lambda V_{t+1}, \tag{A}$$

which in a steady state becomes

$$\omega = \frac{\lambda}{1 + f/\phi} \frac{\gamma \widetilde{\pi}(\omega)}{r + \lambda n}; \tag{A}$$

whereas the *labor market clearing equation* (L) becomes

$$\widetilde{x}(\omega) + (1 + f/\phi)n = L \tag{L}$$

In particular, the larger the agency cost f, the lower the equilibrium level of research $\widehat{n}$ and therefore the lower the growth rate g. However, the more developed the financial system and therefore the lower the intermediation cost f (as a result of scale economies), the faster the rate of economic growth. Evidence on the positive correlation between *financial development* (measured either by the ratio of liquid liabilities of the financial system to GDP or by the

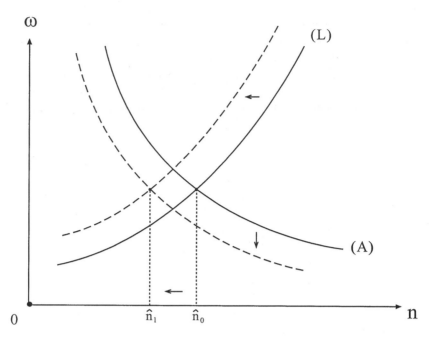

Figure 2.6
Effect of an increase in the agency cost f.

ratio of commercial bank credit to central bank credit) and *growth* is provided by King and Levine (1993a, 1993b).

Using the same model, King and Levine can conclude at once that raising taxes on the financial sector will discourage research and growth by increasing the break-even cost of financial intermediation (which is now equal to $f/\phi(1-\tau)$, where τ denotes the tax rate on financial revenues).

The King-Levine argument concentrates on *monitoring costs.* (Indeed, the role of financial intermediaries in reducing individual monitoring costs has already been stressed by the existing corporate finance literature, e.g., by Diamond 1984. But, the monitoring of entrepreneurs and/or research projects might be equally well performed by the stock market; see Holmstrom-Tirole 1993.)

There is, however, one important feature of debt that could have important implications for innovations and growth in a more explicit agency context than the one considered by King and Levine: namely, debt as a *hard claim* in the sense that the nonrepayment of debt obligations can lead to creditors' either shutting down or taking over the firm, with corresponding loss of control benefits by the firm's manager.[13] Now, suppose we extend the basic framework by

---

13. This in turn presupposes that enforcement institutions or mechanisms are put in place, which in turn is another key measure of financial development.

assuming that the adoption of new technologies by intermediate firms is costly for managers[14] and *cannot* be *directly* monitored by outside financiers; then debt financing, by reducing (ex-post) the amount of free cash available to intermediate firms' managers, will also reduce the managerial slack in adopting new technologies: indeed, by delaying too much the adoption of more productive technologies, intermediate firms will end up unable to meet their debt-repayment obligations (especially when facing additional fixed costs, which increase over time as more productive firms continuously enter the market). In order to avoid bankruptcy and the resulting loss of private benefits of control, intermediate firms managers will then *speed up* the adoption of new technologies, thereby contributing to *faster growth*. (We refer the reader to Aghion, Dewatripont, and Rey 1997a and Chapter 7 for a formalization of this more "Jensenien" view of the relationship between finance and growth; see also Chapter 13 for a microanalysis of the interplay between finance and the organization of R&D.)

One last remark concludes this subsection. In the preceding analysis, we have taken monitoring costs per project to remain constant over time. However, if there are increasing returns in monitoring, the higher the number of projects in the economy, the lower the monitoring costs per project should be. Now, if we follow Acemoglu and Zilibotti (1997) in postulating a minimum size requirement (or minimum sunk cost) for high-yield projects, the total number of projects that can be undertaken at any point in time will depend on the total amount of accumulated resources (or savings) available at that time. This in turn implies that the risk involved in investing in high-yield, risky projects will be better diversified when the economy has reached an advanced stage in its development process. But then, precisely because diversification opportunities have improved, individuals will be more inclined to invest in high-yield, risky projects rather than restrict themselves to safe but low-yield investments. The rate of return on investments will thus increase at later stages of development, and therefore so will the average savings rate. Hence, while growth will generally be slow and risky at early stages of development (with few individuals investing in high-yield projects, and only in a small number of them, so that aggregate risk remains high), growth will accelerate while also becoming less volatile at later stages of development when a large number of risky projects can be simultaneously undertaken and monitored by the financial sector. The Acemoglu-Zilibotti model is consistent with existing evidence on the existence of a positive correlation between growth and financial depth (King and Levine 1993a) and on the existence of a negative correlation between development (measured by GDP per capita) and the

---

14. As an example, because it forces managers to reorganize the firm or to retrain before the adoption of the new technologies.

variability of growth[15] (measured by the average deviation from the mean growth path).

Finally, the idea that aggregate performance is more volatile at early stages of development, is also consistent with historical evidence, as shown by Braudel (1962) and North (1990).

2.6.4   Nondrastic Innovations

Until this point the analysis has assumed that innovations are drastic: that the intermediate monopolist is not constrained by potential competition from owners of previous patents. The present section shows that the analysis of stationary equilibria in the previous sections can be generalized to the case where innovations are nondrastic.

Innovations are nondrastic if and only if the previous incumbent could make a positive profit when the current one is charging the monopolistic price $p_t(x_t) = \alpha A_t x_t^{\alpha-1} = \frac{1}{\alpha} w_t$ which yields an unconstrained maximum to the current incumbent's profit. If innovations are nondrastic, then the current incumbent sets the maximum price that gives the previous incumbent non-positive profits and satisfies all the demand at that price, leaving none to the previous incumbent.

The previous incumbent could make a positive profit if and only if a competitive producer of consumption goods could produce at a smaller cost using the previous incumbent's intermediate good, buying the latter at a price equal to its average cost of production w_t. The cost of producing y units of consumption would be

$$C_{t-1}(w_t, y) = w_t x \quad \text{where} \quad y = A_{t-1} x^\alpha,$$

that is,

$$C_{t-1}(w_t, y) = w_t \left(\frac{y}{A_{t-1}}\right)^{1/\alpha}.$$

The cost of producing y units of consumption good using the new intermediate input priced at the unconstrained monopolistic maximum $p_t = \frac{1}{\alpha} w_t$ is

$$C_t(p_t, y) = p_t x \quad \text{where} \quad y = A_t x^\alpha,$$

that is,

$$C_t(p_t, y) = \frac{1}{\alpha} w_t \left(\frac{y}{A_t}\right)^{1/\alpha}.$$

---

15. That the variability of growth tends to decrease with the degree of development had already been formally shown by Greenwood and Jovanovic (1990).

It follows that innovations are *drastic* if and only if $C_t(p_t, y) \le C_{t-1}(w_t, y)$ for all y, which, given that $A_t = \gamma A_{t-1}$, is equivalent to

$$\gamma \ge \alpha^{-\alpha}.$$

However, innovations are *nondrastic* whenever

$$\gamma < \alpha^{-\alpha}.$$

In that case, the maximum price that can be charged by the current incumbent to the consumption good sector is $\widehat{p}_t$ such that

$$C_t(\widehat{p}, y) = C_{t-1}(w_t, y),$$

that is,

$$\widehat{p} = \gamma^{1/\alpha} w_t.$$

The corresponding profit flow $\widehat{\pi}_t$ and labor demand $\widehat{x}_t$ are respectively given by

$$\widehat{\pi}_t = (\gamma^{1/\alpha} - 1) w_t \widehat{x}_t$$

and

$$\widehat{x}_t = (\gamma^{1/\alpha} \omega_t / \alpha)^{\frac{1}{\alpha-1}},$$

where $\omega_t = \frac{w_t}{A_t}$ is the productivity-adjusted wage rate.

These expressions are almost identical to those in the drastic case, except that the markup $\gamma^{1/\alpha}$ replaces the markup $1/\alpha$ in the drastic case. The equation defining the stationary (or steady-state) equilibrium level of research in the nondrastic case will thus be

$$1 = \frac{\lambda \gamma (\gamma^{1/\alpha} - 1)(N - \widehat{n})}{r + \lambda \widehat{n}}. \tag{2.12}$$

It is straightforward to check that all the comparative statics results derived for the case of drastic innovations are valid also when innovations are nondrastic. Furthermore, the comparison between (2.12) and (2.3) shows that the same welfare effects analyzed in section 2.3 operate in the case where innovations are nondrastic, again with the result that research and growth under laissez-faire may be more or less than optimal.

As is customary in the patent-race literature, this analysis has ruled out the possibility that the current and previous incumbent might contract to share the higher monopoly profits that could be earned if the previous incumbent agreed never to compete. For example, the previous incumbent might sell its patent to the current one; in the extreme case where the previous incumbent always had no bargaining power in negotiation with the current one, competition from previous vintages of the intermediate good would never constrain the monopolist, and the earlier analysis of drastic innovations would apply no matter how small the innovations were.

2.6.5   Endogenous Size of Innovations

This section generalizes the preceding analysis of stationary equilibria by allowing research firms to choose not only the frequency but also the size of innovations. It shows that under laissez-faire, innovations will be too small if they are drastic. In the nondrastic case, the tendency to make innovations too small is at least partly mitigated by the incentive for innovators to move away from their competitive fringe, which they can do by increasing the size of innovations.

Assume that the arrival rate of innovations to a firm employing z units of research labor and aiming for innovations of size γ is $\lambda z v(\gamma)$, where $v'(\gamma) < 0$: that is the bigger the innovation, the harder it is to discover. Assume $v''(\gamma) < 0$: that is, the marginal cost (in terms of lower arrival rate) of aiming for larger innovations increases with the size of innovations. Then the product $\gamma v(\gamma)$ is a concave function of γ.

The analysis focuses again on stationary equilibria with positive growth. Consider first the case of drastic innovations. By the same logic as before, the payoff to the $t + 1st$ innovator is

$$V_{t+1} = \frac{A_{t+1}\widetilde{\pi}(\widehat{\omega})}{r + \lambda \widehat{n} v(\widehat{\gamma})} = \frac{A_{t+1}(1/\alpha - 1)\widehat{\omega}\widehat{x}}{r + \lambda \widehat{n} v(\widehat{\gamma})}, \tag{2.13}$$

where $\widehat{\gamma}$ is the stationary-equilibrium value of γ. If the $t + 1st$ innovation has size γ, not necessarily equal to $\widehat{\gamma}$, then $A_{t+1} = \gamma A_t$ and $V_{t+1} = \gamma V_t$. Therefore the expected flow of profits to the research firm in interval t is

$$\lambda z v(\gamma)\gamma V_t - w_t z. \tag{2.14}$$

The firm takes V_t as given. Thus its profit-maximizing choice of γ also maximizes the product $v(\gamma)\gamma$. Because this product is a concave function of γ, $\widehat{\gamma}$ is defined by the condition[16]

$$v(\widehat{\gamma}) + \widehat{\gamma} v'(\widehat{\gamma}) = 0. \tag{2.15}$$

The first-order condition for profit maximization with respect to research labor z together with (2.14) produces the new arbitrage equation

$$w_t = \lambda \gamma v(\gamma) V_t. \tag{A}$$

---

16. Note that it is always possible to choose the function v so that the solution to (2.15) satisfies the condition for innovations to be drastic $\gamma \geq \alpha^{-\alpha}$.

Dividing both sides of (A) by A_t, and using (2.13) and the labor market clearing equation $L = \hat{n} + \hat{x}$, we obtain the following equation for the equilibrium steady-state level of research $\hat{n}$:

$$1 = \lambda v(\hat{\gamma}) \frac{\hat{\gamma}(1/\alpha - 1)(L - \hat{n})}{r + \lambda v(\hat{\gamma})\hat{n}}. \tag{2.16}$$

The comparative-statics analysis of the previous chapter carries through unchanged, because $\hat{\gamma}$ is determined by (2.15) independently of all parameters that do not enter the function v, with the obvious exception that it is no longer permissible to investigate the effects of a change in γ.

More interesting are the *welfare implications* of endogenizing the size of innovations. As in section 2.3, the expected present value of consumption equals

$$U = \frac{A_0(N - n)^\alpha}{r - \lambda n v(\gamma)(\gamma - 1)}, \tag{2.17}$$

where the denominator is the social discount rate. Therefore, independently of the choice of n, the social planner will choose γ so as to maximize the expression $v(\gamma)(\gamma - 1)$. The socially optimal value γ^* is then defined by

$$v(\gamma^*) + \gamma^* v'(\gamma^*) - v'(\gamma^*) = 0. \tag{2.18}$$

By concavity of $\gamma v(\gamma)$,[17] $\hat{\gamma} < \gamma^*$. Innovations are too small under laissez-faire. This result is another manifestation of the business-stealing effect. The social planner chooses γ so as to maximize the arrival rate multiplied by the net size $(\gamma - 1)$ of innovations, whereas the private research firm, which does not internalize the loss of the existing vintage of intermediate good, maximizes the arrival rate times the gross size γ. The socially optimal level of research n^*, determined by maximizing the social utility U with respect to n (with $\gamma = \gamma^*$), satisfies the new social arbitrage condition

$$1 = \frac{v(\gamma^*)(\gamma^* - 1)(N - n^*)}{r - \lambda n^* v(\gamma^*)(\gamma^* - 1)}. \tag{2.19}$$

Comparison between (2.16) and (2.19) reveals the same welfare effects as in the analysis of section 2.3. In addition, the fact that $\hat{\gamma} < \gamma^*$ in itself makes $\hat{n} < n^*$. This is because, as we have seen, $v(\hat{\gamma})(\hat{\gamma} - 1) < v(\gamma^*)(\gamma^* - 1)$. So if the other four effects were absent, and both $\hat{n}$ and n^* were determined by (2.19), the effect on research employment would be the same as if the laissez-faire economy had a smaller arrival parameter λ, which would reduce $\hat{n}$ below n^*.

---

17. As illustrated in figure 2.7, because $v' < 0$, equation (2.18) implies that γ^* lies on the decreasing part of the $\gamma v(\gamma)$ curve, that is to the right of $\hat{\gamma}$ by concavity of $\gamma v(\gamma)$.

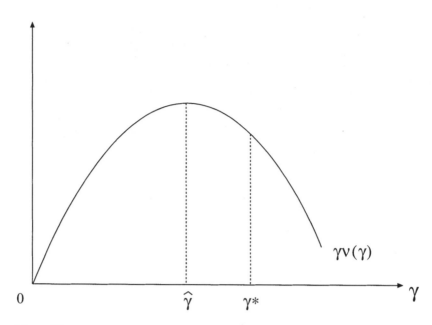

Figure 2.7

The economy's average growth rate (AGR) $\lambda \widehat{n} v(\widehat{\gamma}) \ln \widehat{\gamma}$ is affected by the fact that innovations are too small under laissez-faire, although the direction of the overall effect is ambiguous. The direct effect on $\ln \widehat{\gamma}$ is to decrease AGR. The direct effect on the arrival rate working through $v(\widehat{\gamma})$ is to increase AGR. The indirect effect on the arrival rate working through $\lambda \widehat{n}$ is to decrease AGR.

In the nondrastic case, the above business-stealing effect whereby innovations are too small under laissez-faire is mitigated by an additional effect, namely that private innovators tend to increase the size of innovations in order to increase their profit margins. This margin is independent of the size γ in the drastic case, but it increases with γ in the nondrastic case. (Remember that the profit margin is $\alpha^{-1} - 1$ if the innovation is drastic and $\gamma^{1/\alpha} - 1$ if nondrastic.) However, this additional "profit-margin" effect does not necessarily overturn our earlier result to the effect that innovations are too small under laissez-faire. (See Aghion and Howitt 1992a).

2.7   Summary

This chapter has presented a simple model of growth through creative destruction. Output of the economy depends on how much intermediate input is employed and on the quality of that intermediate input. Succeeding vintages of intermediate goods embody quality improvements, which render their predecessors obsolete. These quality improvements also produce economic growth. They result from "research" activities by firms that generate a random sequence of product innovations. The uncertainty of the research process implies that growth will be stochastic.

Society has two uses for its fixed labor force: the manufacture of the latest generation of intermediate goods, and research aimed at discovering the next generation. Firms are motivated to hire labor for research by the prospect of monopoly rents. That is, if the research results in an innovation, the firm will get to monopolize the intermediate-goods industry until someone else comes along with a better product to replace it.

The model possesses a unique steady-state equilibrium in which society's division of labor between research and manufacturing remains unchanged over time, so that growth is stochastic but balanced. The average growth rate in steady-state equilibrium is an increasing function of the propensity to save, the productivity of the research technology that relates R&D employment to the expected arrival rate of innovations, and the degree of market power enjoyed by a successful innovator, all of which encourage more labor to be transferred from manufacturing to research.

The average growth rate may be either too low or too high to maximize welfare, because there are both positive and negative externalities in research, and it is not clear which will predominate. The positive externalities are the *intertemporal spillover* whereby the knowledge embedded in each innovation can be used by all future researchers, and the *appropriability effect* whereby the monopoly rents that motivate research firms constitute only part of the immediate social gain from an innovation, the rest being consumer surplus. The main negative externality is the *business-stealing effect* whereby a research firm does not internalize the loss to society from the obsolescence created by its innovation.

This chapter focuses mainly on steady-state balanced growth. However, there may also exist unbalanced equilibrium growth paths, in which the level of research switches with each innovation, between a high level and low level. When firms expect low research after the next innovation they are encouraged to do much research because the next successful innovator will retain its monopoly position for a long time. When they expect high research after the next innovation, however, they are discouraged by the prospect of rapid obsolescence. Not only does this make oscillatory equilibrium possible, it also creates the possibility of a *no-growth trap*; a situation in which people expect so much research to take place after the next innovation that no research at all is done, and the economy stagnates at the current level of output.

This chapter also shows how to incorporate "technology transfer" in the basic model. If two economies were completely unconnected, there would be no possibility of convergence; each would grow at a rate determined by its own research effort. But in reality, research in one country benefits from knowledge created in others; this provides a simple mechanism by which a laggard country would tend to catch up.

One can also allow contemporaneous technology spillovers in research, whereby the productivity of any one research firm depends on the economy-wide level of research. This implies that there can be more than one equilibrium growth rate. In a low-growth equilibrium, firms are discouraged from doing research because they cannot benefit from the work of many others; conversely, in a high-growth equilibrium they are encouraged to do a lot of research by the ease with which they can learn from each others' efforts.

Imperfections in capital markets can also be incorporated. Agency costs in discovering which research projects are more promising than others have the expected effect of reducing the steady-state level of research and rate of growth. This and the related idea of increasing returns to scale in the financial system both shed light on why the level of financial development is important in the growth process.

Most of this chapter assumes that innovations are "drastic," that each new generation of intermediate good is so much better than its predecessors that the latest innovator is not threatened by competition from previous innovators. It also shows, however, that all the comparative-statics results of the analysis go through in the nondrastic case. Finally, it allows research firms to choose not only the frequency but also the size of innovations. This generalization shows that under laissez-faire, innovations will be too small if they are drastic. In the nondrastic case, the tendency to make innovations too small is at least partly mitigated by the incentive for innovators to move away from their competitive fringe, which they can do by increasing the size of innovations.

Problems

Difficulty of Problems:

No star: normal

One star: difficult

Two stars: very difficult

1. Innovation by the leader (based on Barro and Sala-i-Martín 1995)

In the text we saw that the incumbent monopolist never does research. The evidence, however, tells us that a large proportion of improvements in the quality of existing products is done by the monopolist who is already manufacturing them. This can be due to the fact that the monopolist has a lower cost of research or a better knowledge of the product that implies a higher probability of success. Consider first an extension of the Schumpeterian model in which only the monopolist can undertake research.

a. Find the equation that determines the level of R&D employment.

b. Now suppose that both the incumbent monopolist and outsiders can do research, but the former has a higher probability of success, given by $\lambda_I z$, with $\lambda_I > \lambda$, and where z is the number of researchers employed by the firm. All other firms innovate with probability λz. Under which parameter values will the incumbent invest in R&D?

2. Welfare and patent auctions (based on Kremer 1996)

Despite the results of the quality ladder models, most empirical research has found that the rate of innovation is below the social optimum. Patents have the problem that the monopolist cannot appropriate the full social return, and hence too little is spent on research. They also lead to inefficient research targeted at inventing "around" the patent. The first-best solution are subsidies to R&D, but in practice they often result in more slack rather than more research, and they do not solve the problem of inventing around the patent. Government funded research might not be targeted at the most profitable innovations and is often burdened by bureaucracy. Kremer has proposed an auction mechanism that combines the advantages of direct funding of research with those of the patent system.

Assume that the economy behaves like the one-sector model of quality ladders presented in the text. Now consider the following system to purchase patents. The patent is auctioned and the (market) value of the patent is determined by the bidding. The government then offers to buy out patents at this private value times a fixed markup that covers the difference between the social and private values of the innovation. Inventors can decide whether or not to sell their patent. If sold, the patent is then placed in the public domain. However, there is a small proportion of the auctioned patents that are sold to the highest bidder, who then becomes a monopolist. This ensures truthful revelation, in as much as bidders are prevented from making offers at prices they would not be willing to pay.

Suppose that there is a standard patent system in the economy, and then the mechanism just described is introduced. Agents know that the mechanism will be used in all subsequent periods.

a. Find the social value of an innovation. What should the markup be?

b. Would this mechanism ensure static allocative efficiency? Would it ensure dynamic efficiency, that is, the socially optimal level of R&D?

c. Could this mechanism be implemented if the competitive economy generated excessive growth?

⋆ **3. Financial intermediation and growth (based on Berthelemy and Varoudakis 1996)**

An alternative reason why financial markets may affect growth is that financial intermediation, that is, turning savings into loanable funds, is costly. We are going to look at a model in which a labor input is necessary for this. We will see that financial markets do not affect growth directly (by making R&D investment relatively more costly just as we saw in King and Levine 1993a), but only indirectly through the impact of the financial sector on the availability of labor.

Consider a Schumpeterian economy like that in this chapter, but with a financial sector. The real interest rate on savings is r. There is an endogenously determined cost of intermediation, i, such that the borrowing rate is $R = (1+i)r$. There is monopolistic competition among the B symmetric banks, where the number of banks is endogenously determined. Intermediation requires employing workers, so that a bank that employs v_j workers and has S_j deposits can lend a fraction $f(v_j)S_j$ of these deposits, where $f(.)$ is increasing. Assume that this function exhibits a constant elasticity, $f(v) = v^\varepsilon$, where $0 < \varepsilon < 1$. There is free entry in the sector. Firms that do research or produce intermediate goods have to borrow in order to finance the wages of their employees. The discounted cost of one unit of labor is then $w_t(1+i)$.

a. Assume that consumers maximize intertemporal utility and that the instantaneous utility function is given by $\frac{c_t^{1-\sigma}-1}{1-\sigma}$. Obtain the dynamic equation for consumption and from it the elasticity of saving with respect to the lending interest rate.

b. What is the arbitrage condition? Obtain the profits of the firm producing the intermediate good and the value of an innovation.

c. Each bank takes the actions of other banks as given. Therefore it takes the lending rate R as fixed, as no firm will borrow from it if it charges a higher interest rate. However, it knows that its behavior will affect the amount of savings it can attract, and thus the market clearing rate r, which in turn affects $(1+i)$. Set up the optimization problem of a bank and obtain the two first order conditions. Use the first-order conditions and the free-entry condition to show that the intermediation cost is a function of v (the level of employment of a representative bank), of the form $1+i = 1/(1-\varepsilon)f(v)$. Show that the number of banks is $B = \sigma/\varepsilon$.

d. What is the market clearing condition in the lending market?

e. In equilibrium the wages in the financial and the research sector have to be the same. Obtain the equilibrium conditions that determine the level of employment in research (and thus the growth rate) in the economy.

4. Multidimensional quality ladder model (based on Li 1996b)

The basic quality ladder model assumes that there is only one direction along which quality can be improved. Here we extend the model by introducing the possibility that quality has two-dimensional attributes. Since quality enhancement in one attribute requires its own research, we now allow for heterogeneous R&D.

Consider the quality-ladder model with the two-dimensional quality index

$$y(\tau) = A(\tau) x(\tau)^{\alpha}, \quad 1 > \alpha > 0$$

where

$$A(\tau) = \gamma_1^{i(\tau)} \gamma_2^{j(\tau)}, \quad \gamma_1, \gamma_2 > 1, \quad i, j = 0, 1, 2, \ldots$$

Entrepreneurs can freely choose to target at γ_1^i and γ_2^j for improvement at any point of time. There are two types of workers: H skilled workers are employed in R&D and L unskilled laborers in manufacturing. Innovations occur with Poisson arrival rates of

$$\lambda_k H_k(\tau), \quad \lambda_k > 0, \quad k = 1, 2,$$

where H_k, $k = 1, 2$ is the number of skilled workers employed in aggregate R&D aimed at improving γ_1^i and γ_2^j respectively. When γ_2^j is improved, an innovator produces the state of the art. But she still needs a blueprint for the highest γ_1^i. She is assumed to pay a fraction $1 > \kappa > 0$ of her profits as royalty to its patent holder. Similarly, when γ_1^i is enhanced, an innovator pays $1 - \kappa$ of her profits to the patent holder of the highest γ_2^j.

a. Find profits of each type of innovation.

b. Find the value of innovations of each type in a stochastic steady state.

c. What conditions are required for a stochastic steady-state equilibrium? Show that there exists a unique equilibrium. (Hint: entrepreneurs must be indifferent between the two types of R&D.)

d. Find the expected growth rate. What does an isogrowth contour look like?

e. What patent laws should the government implement in order to ensure that the growth rate is maximized?

3 Innovation and Capital Accumulation[1]

The two preceding chapters presented quite different approaches to the study of economic growth, representing two alternative visions of the growth process. One vision puts capital accumulation at the heart of the process, the other innovation. Much has been written on the relative merits of these two approaches. In our view[2] capital accumulation and innovation should be regarded not as distinct causal factors but as two aspects of the same process. For new technologies are almost always embodied in new forms of human and physical capital that must be accumulated if the technology is to be used.

Thus, the purpose of this third chapter is to show how the two approaches can be integrated into a single framework. We develop a model that can be seen as either a Schumpeterian model with capital or a Solow-Swan model with endogenous technological progress. With this integrated model we can study the separate long-run effects on economic growth of policies that directly affect the investment rate on the one hand, and the incentive to perform R&D on the other.

Our strategy will be to take the basic Schumpeterian model of the previous chapter and introduce capital accumulation into it. But in order to make the model comparable with the Solow-Swan model, and to give it a plausible macroeconomic structure, we must first address another shortcoming of that basic model, namely the fact that there is only one intermediate good used throughout the economy, whose monopoly producer captures all the economy's rents.

3.1 Multisectors

In reality, final output is produced not with a single intermediate good but with a large variety of different intermediate goods. Cars, for example, are made out of tires, steel, windows, light bulbs, transistors, upholstery, crankshafts, batteries, and so forth. For the purpose of illustrating clearly the role of innovation in the growth process it was useful to ignore the diversity of intermediate goods. But to understand the detailed dynamics of growth we need to take diversity into account.

In particular, new technologies do not get implemented instantaneously throughout the economy. Instead, they diffuse gradually, through a process in which one sector gets ideas from the research and experience of others. This process has been described by such writers as Rosenberg (1963) who told of the diffusion of American machine-tool technology. Lessons learned in one sector were often instrumental to progress in another. It has also been measured by many writers on "technology spillover,"[3] who have found that R&D often has

---

1. See Howitt (1997).

2. In this we have been influenced by the writings of Maurice Scott (1989).

3. See, for example, the survey by Griliches (1992).

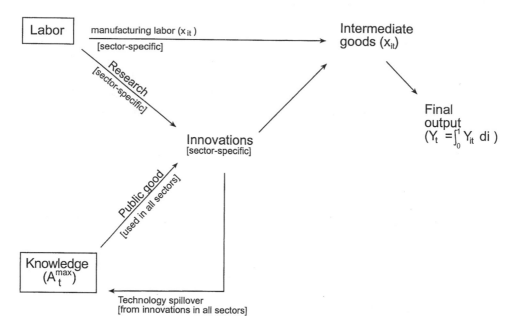

Figure 3.1
A schematic representation of economic activities in the multisector model.

an even bigger effect on productivity in other sectors than in the sector doing the R&D.

These intersectoral spillovers are similar in many respects to the intertemporal spillover effect found in our basic Schumpeterian model. However, the dynamics are quite different. If ideas filter only gradually through the economy going from one sector to another, then the growth process will not be as irregular as in the basic one-sector model. The discontinuous jumps in aggregate output that follow each major innovation will be replaced by smoother responses.

3.1.1 Extending the Basic Model

Consider the following multisectoral extension, which has been inspired by the work of Caballero and Jaffé (1993). (Figure 3.1 may help you keep track of the overall conceptual scheme.) There is still just one final good, which can only be consumed, but the final good is now produced by a continuum of intermediate goods, indexed on the unit interval. Each intermediate good is produced from labor using the same one-for-one technology as in the basic model. And each can be used to produce the final good independently of the other intermediate goods, with no complementaries between them.

More specifically, the flow of final good that can be produced using intermediate good i at date t depends only on the flow x_{it} of intermediate good i

that is put into the production process, according to the same production function

$$Y_{it} = A_{it} F(x_{it}) = A_{it} x_{it}^{\alpha}$$

that applied to the single intermediate good of the basic model. The parameter A_{it} represents the productivity of the latest generation of intermediate good i. (Note that t here denotes calendar time, not generation of intermediate good.) Aggregate output of the final good is the sum

$$Y_t = \int_0^1 Y_{it} di.$$

Each intermediate sector is monopolized, as before, by the holder of a patent to the latest generation of that good. The local monopolist sells output to the competitive final-good sector, in which its marginal product, and thus its price measured in consumption goods, is given by the same formula as in the basic model:[4] $p_{it} = A_{it} F'(x_{it}) = A_{it}\alpha x_{it}^{\alpha-1}$. Thus the monopolist's output and demand for labor will again be

$$x_{it} = \widetilde{x}\left(\frac{w_t}{A_{it}}\right) = \left(\frac{w_t}{\alpha^2 A_{it}}\right)^{\frac{1}{\alpha-1}} \tag{3.1}$$

where w_t is the wage rate (measured in consumption goods), and its equilibrium profit will again equal the fraction $1 - \alpha$ of its revenue, with the remaining fraction α going to its workers:

$$\pi_{it} = A_{it}\widetilde{\pi}\left(\frac{w_t}{A_{it}}\right) = A_{it}\frac{1-\alpha}{\alpha}\frac{w_t}{A_{it}}\widetilde{x}\left(\frac{w_t}{A_{it}}\right). \tag{3.2}$$

3.1.2 Technology Spillover

Instead of one research sector that tries to monopolize all the rents in the economy, we assume in this chapter that there is a different research sector for each intermediate good, with the firms in each research sector competing to discover the next generation of that particular good. The Poisson arrival rate of innovations in each sector i is λn_{it}, where n_{it} is the amount of labor devoted to research in that sector.

Although the arrival rates in different sectors are independent of each other, the innovations themselves all draw on the same pool of shared technological

---

4. We assume that once a previous incumbent has left it is not able to reenter. Hence even if the productivity parameter of the latest generation of intermediate good in a sector is only slightly higher than that of the previous generation, the holder of the latest patent will drive out the previous incumbent, and from then on will be unconstrained by potential competition from previous technologies. In this way we are able to simplify the analysis by treating all innovations as being "drastic."

knowledge. The state of this knowledge is represented by a "leading-edge" technology, whose productivity parameter at date t is $A_t^{\max}$. Each innovation at date t in any sector i permits the innovator to start producing in sector i using the leading edge technology. The previous incumbent in sector i, whose technology is no longer on the leading edge, will be displaced. When this happens the technology parameter A_{it} in that sector will jump discontinuously[5] to $A_t^{\max}$.

The leading edge parameter $A_t^{\max}$ grows gradually, at a rate that depends on the aggregate flow of innovations. Because the prospective payoff to research is the same in all sectors, the same equilibrium flow of research labor n_t will be applied in each sector. Thus in the economy as a whole there will be a continuous flow of λn_t innovations per unit of time. We suppose that the rate of growth of the leading edge parameter is proportional to this aggregate flow of innovations, with a factor of proportionality equal to $\ln \gamma$:

$$\dot{A}_t^{\max} / A_t^{\max} = \lambda n_t \ln \gamma, \quad \gamma > 1. \tag{S}$$

Equation (S) is the law of motion governing the evolution of social knowledge. It is the multisector version of the spillover assumption made in Chapter 2 for the one-sector case, where each innovation brought the leading edge from A_{t-1} to $A_t = \gamma A_{t-1}$, thereby raising the log of the leading-edge parameter by $\ln \gamma$. In that case the expected flow rate of innovations was λn_t, so the expected proportional growth rate of the leading-edge parameter was $\lambda n_t \ln \gamma$. In the multisector case, the actual flow rate of innovations is λn_t, so the actual proportional growth rate of the leading-edge parameter is $\lambda n_t \ln \gamma$. Each discovery is implementable only in the innovator's chosen sector, but its discovery allows the next innovator to discover a marginally better technique in another sector, by adding to the general knowledge used by that innovator.

At any point in time there will be a distribution of productivity parameters A_{it} across the sectors of the economy, with values ranging from 0 to $A_t^{\max}$. Over time the distribution will be displaced rightward as innovating sectors move up to $A_t^{\max}$ and as technological progress raises $A_t^{\max}$ itself.

Fortunately, the shape of the distribution does not have to change, even if the names of the sectors occupying the different places in the distribution are continually changing. More specifically, in the long run the cross-sectoral distribution of the relative productivity parameters $a_{it} \equiv \frac{A_{it}}{A_t^{\max}}$ will be given by the distribution function:

---

5. If we supposed instead that each innovation raises the productivity parameter in that particular sector by a fixed multiple γ, this would not capture the phenomenon of intersectoral spillover, for a sector would achieve the same improvement with each innovation no matter how much knowledge had accumulated in the rest of the economy since the last one. (See problems 3.2 and 3.3.)

$$H(a) \equiv a^{\frac{1}{\ln \gamma}}, 0 \leq a \leq 1 \tag{3.3}$$

no matter what is happening to the aggregate rate of innovation over time.[6] To simplify matters we suppose that a is distributed according to $H(\ )$ right from the beginning at date 0.

Thus technological progress will produce a uniform proportional shift in the whole distribution of absolute productivity parameters A_{it}, at the rate indicated by the spillover equation (S). This will also turn out to be the growth rate of aggregate output.

3.1.3   Intersectoral Allocation and Aggregate Output

Because innovations are continually arriving somewhere in the economy, wages will continually rise. This in turn implies that there will be a continual reallocation between sectors. For according to equations (3.1) and (3.2), both employment and profits in any sector that is not innovating will decrease as the wage rate rises. This phenomenon of gradual decline in non-innovating sectors, which we will encounter again, is a second, more gradual form of creative destruction, which we call "crowding out." Of course the more drastic form of creative destruction that we met in the previous chapter is also present here, because whenever a sector innovates, the incumbent monopolist disappears altogether.

Because the distribution of relative productivities is unchanging, we will find it convenient when aggregating to classify sectors not by their index i but by their relative productivity a. Define the productivity-adjusted wage rate as $\omega_t \equiv w_t / A_t^{\max}$. Then we can rewrite the labor-demand function (3.1) for a sector with relative productivity a at date t as

$$\widetilde{x}(\omega_t/a) \equiv \left(\frac{\omega_t/a}{\alpha^2} \right)^{\frac{1}{\alpha-1}}$$

and the aggregate demand for labor can be found by multiplying this demand by the density of such sectors: $h(a) \equiv H'(a)$, and summing over a.

Accordingly, the labor-market clearing condition that determines the productivity-adjusted wage ω_t in terms of the mass n_t of research workers is

$$n_t + \int_0^1 \widetilde{x}(\omega_t/a)h(a)da = L. \tag{L'}$$

This labor-market condition holds whether or not the economy is in a steady state equilibrium, as long as the distribution of relative productivities is constant. As in the basic model, it corresponds to an upward-sloping locus in (n, ω)

---

6. See Appendix 1 to this chapter.

space. That is, as more labor goes into research, its increased scarcity in manufacturing drives up the wage.

The aggregate flow of output in the economy can be calculated by summing the amount produced by each sector. If we again classify sectors by relative productivities a, then we can sum over a as long as we multiply each sectoral output by the density $h(a)$. Thus aggregate output will be

$$Y_t = \int_0^1 A_{it} F(x_{it}) di = A_t^{\max} \int_0^1 a \tilde{x}(\omega_t/a)^\alpha h(a)\, da.$$

It follows that, as we anticipated in the previous section, the instantaneous growth rate of aggregate output at each date will be the growth rate of the leading edge parameter $A_t^{\max}$ indicated by the spillover equation (S):

$$g_t = \lambda n_t \ln \gamma. \tag{G}$$

The growth equation (G) is identical to that of the one-sector model of the previous chapter. It holds at each point in time, even when the level of research n_t is not constant over time.

3.1.4   Research Arbitrage

For the rest of this section on multisectors we will focus attention exclusively on steady-state equilibria, that is, on situations in which the level of research is constant: $n_t \equiv n$. Then according to (L′) and (G) the productivity-adjusted wage rate and the growth rate will also be constant: $\omega_t \equiv \omega$ and $g_t \equiv g \equiv \lambda n \ln \gamma$.

Consider a firm that innovates at date t. Its productivity parameter will equal $A_t^{\max}$ from then until it is replaced by the next innovator in that sector. In a steady-state equilibrium the wage rate will be rising constantly at the rate g. Thus according to equation (3.2), if the firm is still producing at some future date $t + s$ its flow of profit at that date will be $A_t^{\max} \tilde{\pi}(\omega e^{gs})$. The probability that the firm will still be producing is the probability that it will not yet have been replaced, which is $e^{-\lambda ns}$. Hence the value of innovating at date t is the expected present value of all the profits from date t until infinity, discounted at the rate of time preference r:

$$V_t = A_t^{\max} \int_0^\infty e^{-(r+\lambda n)s} \tilde{\pi}(\omega e^{gs}) ds.$$

The research arbitrage condition determining the level of research in a steady-state equilibrium is that the wage w_t equal the expected marginal value product of research λV_t. If we divide both sides of this equation by $A_t^{\max}$ we arrive at

$$\omega = \lambda \int_0^\infty e^{-(r+\lambda n)s} \tilde{\pi}(\omega e^{\lambda n \ln \gamma \cdot s}) ds. \tag{A′}$$

As before, this arbitrage equation defines a downward-sloping locus in (n, ω) space. That is, as the wage in manufacturing rises, fewer people will go into research.

3.1.5 Steady-State Equilibrium

As in the basic model, the steady-state equilibrium values of the productivity-adjusted wage rate ω and the level of research n are determined by a downward-sloping research-arbitrage curve (A′) and an upward-sloping labor-market curve (L′). So again there exists a unique steady-state equilibrium, on which we can perform the same comparative-statics experiments as in the previous chapter.

It turns out that the comparative statics of the model are almost identical to those of the basic one-sector model, but with some new effects introduced by the "crowding out" that takes place in a multisectoral context. To see the connection with the basic model more clearly, it helps to rewrite the two equations[7] (A′) and (L′) as

$$1 = \lambda \frac{\frac{1-\alpha}{\alpha} \tilde{x}(\omega)}{r + \lambda n + \frac{\alpha}{1-\alpha} \lambda n \ln \gamma} \tag{A″}$$

and

$$\tilde{x}(\omega) = \left(1 + \frac{\ln \gamma}{1 - \alpha}\right)(L - n). \tag{L″}$$

Equation (A″) is similar to the research-arbitrage equation (2.3) of the previous chapter, the main difference being the addition of the third term in the denominator on the right-hand side. This is the crowding-out effect referred to earlier. It acts to reduce the value of an innovation, thus reinforcing the creative destruction effect. The other difference is that the numerator of the right-hand side of (A″) includes not average manufacturing labor $L - n$ but the amount $\tilde{x}(\omega)$ employed in a sector with the most advanced technology. Equation (L″) shows exactly by how much this will exceed the average.

Consider the effect of an increase in the R&D productivity parameter λ. As in the basic model, this increase directly encourages research and growth while at the same time indirectly discouraging it by increasing the rate of creative destruction λn. But now, in addition, a higher λ will increase the rate at which a producer's profits fall over time as a result of competing for manufacturing labor with the leading edge. That is, it will also have a crowding-out effect.

---

7. Appendix 2 provides a detailed derivation of (A″) and (L″).

Because λ does not enter the labor-market condition, we can study its effects by seeing which way it shifts the rewritten research-arbitrage condition (A″). This equation shows that in spite of the crowding-out effect's reinforcing the creative destruction effect, the overall effect of an increase in λ on research and growth remains positive. It also shows that the importance of the new crowding-out effect will depend on the degree of substitutability between intermediate goods. If α is small, goods will be poor substitutes, so the improvement of goods in other sectors will have little effect, but if α is large then the crowding-out effect will also be large.

Consider next the effect of an increase in the "size of innovation," that is in the spillover coefficient $\ln \gamma$. As in the basic model, an increase in size will encourage research. It does so by raising productivity at the leading edge, where research takes place, relative to the average sector. More specifically, by using (L″) to substitute for $\tilde{x}(\omega)$ in (A″) we see that an increase in $\ln \gamma$ will raise growth. But (A″) also shows that this direct effect will now be offset to some extent by a crowding-out effect. That is, given any fixed level of research n, the increased size of innovations will result in a faster rate of growth, and hence a faster rate of crowding out, which will discourage research. However, the offset from crowding out will be only partial; the overall effect of an increase in size will still be to increase research and growth.

3.1.6 Using Intermediate Goods in Research

When we introduce capital accumulation, we will want to take into account the fact that high-tech intermediate goods are inputs into research as well as into producing the consumption good. In order to build bridges we first show how the phenomenon can be incorporated into a variation of the above intersectoral model without capital.

Suppose that the production function for innovations is the same as for the consumption good. Then the sum of consumption-good output C_t and research N_t is constrained by the production function

$$Y_t = C_t + N_t = \int_0^1 A_{it} x_{it}^\alpha di,$$

where each x_{it} is now the total input into the two activities of producing consumption goods and research.

As technology advances, it also becomes more complex. Thus it is reasonable to assume that an ever-increasing research input is needed to keep innovating at the same rate. (We could not assume this when labor was the sole variable input to research, because there is a finite limit to the economy's labor supply.) Accordingly, assume that in each sector where the amount N_t of research is done, the Poisson arrival rate of innovations is λn_t, where $n_t \equiv N_t / A_t^{\max}$ is the "productivity-adjusted" level of research.

The growth rate of social knowledge is governed by the same spillover equation as before:

$$\dot{A}_t^{\max}/A_t^{\max} = \lambda n_t \ln \gamma. \tag{S}$$

In a steady state, both C_t and N_t grow at the same rate as $A_t^{\max}$, so the *productivity-adjusted* level of research will be a constant n, and according to (S) the steady-state growth rate will again be $g = \lambda n \ln \gamma$.

Because all labor is now used in manufacturing, the labor market-clearing condition will be

$$\int_0^1 \tilde{x}(\omega_t/a)h(a)da = L$$

which is the same as (L') above with $n = 0$.

To derive the new research-arbitrage equation, note that the marginal benefit of raising n_t in any sector will again be λV_t, but the cost will now be $A_t^{\max}$ instead of w_t, because to raise the research intensity n_t by one unit, N_t must be raised by $A_t^{\max}$ units, which costs $A_t^{\max}$ units of the consumption good. Thus:

$$1 = \lambda \int_0^\infty e^{-(r+\lambda n)s}\tilde{\pi}(\omega e^{\lambda n \ln \gamma \cdot s})ds,$$

which is the same as (A') except that the LHS now is 1 instead of ω.

Because the labor-market clearing and arbitrage conditions are almost the same as before, comparative-statics results are the same. Thus it makes no essential difference whether technological progress at a steady rate requires a constant amount of labor to be used in research, as in the previous sections, or whether it requires an ever-increasing amount (N_t) of the services of high-tech intermediate goods, as in this section.[8]

3.2 Introducing Capital

We have until now ignored the fact that technological innovations are typically embodied in a durable good, either physical or human capital. There is, however, much evidence suggesting that the way technological change affects productivity is by improving the quality of machinery and equipment. For example, DeLong and Summers (1991) have argued that countries with the highest growth rates tend to be those in which equipment investment has been the highest, and in which the relative price of equipment has fallen the fastest.

---

8. Once we introduce capital, however, we shall see that assuming labor to be the only input to research is a very special assumption that makes long-run growth independent of the incentive to accumulate capital.

It is also apparent that the research sector of an economy is highly capital-intensive. Not only does it use a lot of physical capital, like computers, precision instruments, and other kinds of lab equipment, but it also requires the input of personnel who have accumulated a lot of human capital, especially scientists and engineers. Jones (1995) has shown that the number of scientists and engineers engaged in R&D in the U.S. economy has grown much faster than the overall labor force since 1950.

It is important to extend our analysis to include capital, not just on the grounds of realism, but, more important, to confront a variety of empirical challenges that have been posed to innovation-based Schumpeterian growth models. These challenges have tried to argue that the main source of economic growth, even in the long run, is not research, as in the models we have developed so far, but capital accumulation.

Thus, for example, Mankiw (1995) has argued that cross-country variations in growth rates can be accounted for by the Solow model with exogenous technological progress, even assuming that all countries share identical technologies independently of their individual R&D efforts. What matters, according to Mankiw, is cross-country variations in the rate of capital accumulation. Young (1995b) has argued that the rapid growth of newly industrialized countries in Asia can be accounted for on the basis of factor accumulation and intersectoral resource reallocation. Jorgenson (1995) has likewise argued that capital accumulation is the predominant factor underlying growth in the U.S. economy and the main factor accounting for differences in growth rates among industrialized countries. Jones (1995) has argued that the fact that more and more scientists and engineers are doing R&D without any tendency for growth to accelerate constitutes a prima facie rejection of the Schumpeterian approach.

In order to confront these challenges, we will extend the multisectoral model we have just developed so as to include the embodiment of new technologies in new capital goods, and the use of capital in research. The extended model will present what we regard as a more balanced approach than that taken by either side so far in the accumulation/innovation debate. For it will imply that even in the long run the rate of growth will be affected by both the incentives to perform R&D and the incentives to accumulate capital.

3.2.1 The Multisector Model with Capital

Suppose there is a stock of capital K_t, embodied in durable machines. We measure capital not as the total number of machines (because new machines are different from old ones) but as the total cost of those machines, measured in foregone consumption. Let I_t denote gross investment, that is, the rate of production of new capital. Capital is produced, along with consumption and research, by labor and intermediate goods, according to the production function

$$Y_t = C_t + I_t + N_t = L^{1-\alpha} \int_0^1 A_{it} x_{it}^\alpha di, \tag{F}$$

where L is the total amount of labor, and each x_{it} the total amount of intermediate good i, employed in the three uses.

The only input into the production of intermediate goods is capital.[9] For the monopolist in sector i to produce at the rate x_{it} requires the use of $A_{it} x_{it}$ units of capital. Thus newer technologies (larger A_{it}) are more capital intensive.[10]

Assume that each monopolist rents its capital from households[11] in a perfectly competitive market, where the rental rate at each date t is ζ_t. Then its average cost will be $A_{it} \zeta_t$. The equilibrium price of intermediate good i will again be its marginal product in the production function (F), which is now $L^{1-\alpha} A_{it} \alpha x_{it}^{\alpha-1}$, instead of $A_{it} \alpha x_{it}^{\alpha-1}$. Thus the monopolist's profit-maximizing supply will be

$$x_t = \left(\zeta_t / \alpha^2 \right)^{\frac{1}{\alpha-1}} L, \tag{X}$$

and its flow of profit will equal the fraction $1 - \alpha$ of its revenue:

$$\pi_{it} = (1 - \alpha)\, L^{1-\alpha} A_{it} \alpha x_t^\alpha. \tag{Π}$$

Let A_t denote the average productivity parameter across all sectors at date t: $A_t \equiv \int_0^1 A_{it} di$. Because each sector i uses $A_{it} x_{it}$, units of capital and there is a total capital stock of K_t, capital-market equilibrium requires $K_t = \int_0^1 A_{it} x_{it} di$. According to (X), all sectors produce the same amount at any given time: $x_{it} = x_t$ for all i. The last three statements together imply that

$$x_t = k_t \equiv K_t / A_t.$$

That is, the equilibrium flow of intermediate output from each sector at date t must equal the "capital intensity" k_t. This and equation (X) imply

$$\zeta_t = \alpha^2 \left(k_t / L \right)^{\alpha-1}. \tag{E}$$

According to (E), an increase in the historically predetermined capital intensity will reduce the equilibrium rental rate that a monopolist must pay for capital.

---

9. It is straightforward to generalize the analysis to include both capital and labor in the production functions for intermediate goods. We do this in Chapter 12, in the section on the observational implications of Schumpeterian theory.

10. This assumption simplifies our analysis, but under the Cobb-Douglas conditions we have specified it has no substantive implications. For it is equivalent to assuming that machines are all of the same constant size but that the productivity parameter of each sector is $A_{it}^{1-\alpha}$ instead of A_{it}.

11. With our assumption of perfect markets it makes no difference whether the monopolists rent or buy their capital. We just find the rental alternative easier to describe.

This can be interpreted as a consequence of decreasing returns to the accumulation of capital.

3.2.2 Steady-State Growth

Substituting the equilibrium values $x_{it} = k_t \equiv K_t/A_t$ into the production function (F) yields the familiar Cobb-Douglas aggregate production function:

$$Y_t = C_t + I_t + N_t = K_t^\alpha (A_t L)^{1-\alpha}. \tag{CD}$$

What we have just described is a two-sector growth model. That is, the level of output is determined by two stocks, the stock of capital K_t and the stock of knowledge, which is proportional to A_t. Because the production function (CD) exhibits constant returns to scale, in A_t and K_t, the accumulation of both stocks together at the same rate will prevent the marginal product of either stock from falling over time. Because of this, growth can be sustained indefinitely. To determine the equilibrium rate of growth we must examine the factors determining investment, which causes K_t to grow, and innovation, which causes A_t to grow.

We focus attention on steady-state equilibria[12], that is, on situations in which output, consumption, capital and the input N_t to research all grow at the same constant rate g. According to (CD), g must also be the rate at which the average productivity parameter A_t is growing. As before, the distribution of relative productivity parameters is given by the unchanging function (3.3), so the growth rate of A_t is also the growth rate of the leading-edge parameter $A_t^{\max}$. Thus the same argument as in section 3.1.6 implies that this growth rate will again be

$$g = \lambda n \ln \gamma, \tag{G}$$

where $n \equiv N_t/A_t^{\max}$ is the productivity-adjusted level of research, which is constant in a steady state.

Because $x_t = k_t$ and $k_t \equiv K_t/A_t$ is constant in a steady state, therefore, the flow of profit accruing to someone who innovated at time t will be the constant[13] $(1-\alpha) \alpha A_t^{\max} L^{1-\alpha} k^\alpha$, where k is the steady-state capital intensity. The value of an innovation at time t in a steady-state equilibrium will be the expected present value of this flow until the next innovation:

$$V_t = \frac{(1-\alpha) \alpha A_t^{\max} L^{1-\alpha} k^\alpha}{r + \lambda n}. \tag{V}$$

---

12. See Howitt (1997) for an analysis of nonsteady-state dynamics.

13. This follows from (Π) and the fact that a firm that innovates at t will have a productivity parameter $A_{it} = A_t^{\max}$ for all $\tau > t$ until the firm is replaced.

Thus the value of an innovation is an increasing function of the capital intensity k. This is because innovations need capital for their implementation. The more capital there is relative to the state of technological knowledge, the lower will be its equilibrium rental rate, and hence the higher the flow of profit that will accrue to the monopolist who rents it. This positive effect of capital intensity on the value of an innovation is the channel through which capital accumulation stimulates innovation.

As before, the marginal cost of raising the research intensity n by one unit is $A_t^{\max}$. The benefit is λV_t. Equating these two and dividing both sides by $A_t^{\max}$ yields the research-arbitrage equation:

$$1 = \lambda \frac{(1 - \alpha)\, \alpha L^{1-\alpha} k^\alpha}{r + \lambda n}. \tag{R}$$

This equation determines the steady-state research intensity n as a function of the capital intensity k. The "research curve" representing it in figure 3.2 is upward sloping because, as we have seen, an increase in capital intensity encourages innovation by raising the equilibrium flow of rents.

An equation determining the steady-state capital intensity can be derived by looking at the conditions governing the long-run supply of capital. From the point of view of an owner of capital, the rental rate ζ must be enough to compensate for three separate costs: interest, depreciation and taxes. Our assumption of linear intertemporal preferences implies that the steady-state rate of interest will be the rate of time preference r.

As for depreciation, suppose for simplicity that there is no capital obsolescence.[14] That is, machines can be dismantled at no cost. Then the rate of creative destruction will not influence the depreciation cost of capital, for when a monopolist is replaced, the capital that was rented to the monopolist can be reconstituted and rented to another local monopolist. (In the language of neoclassical growth theory, this is a putty-putty model.) Capital does, however wear out through radioactive decay, at a constant exponential depreciation rate δ. Thus the rental rate that would just compensate the owner for interest and depreciation costs would be $r + \delta$.

Suppose that in addition to these two costs an owner of capital must pay a tax, at the proportional rate τ per unit of time per unit of capital. We include this tax just to have a parameter that impinges directly on the incentive to accumulate capital, as distinct from the incentive to perform research, and thus to address the question of how a change in the incentive to accumulate affects the economy's growth rate. For simplicity, suppose that the revenue from the tax is returned to households in the form of a lump-sum transfer.

---

14. Capital obsolescence will be dealt with briefly in section 3.2.4.

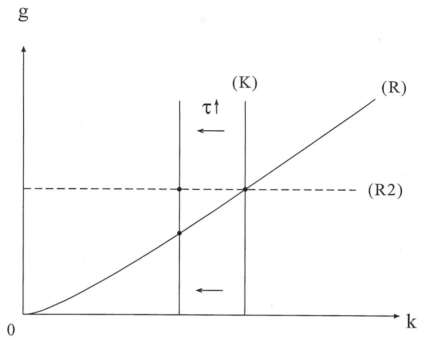

Figure 3.2
The determination of capital intensity k and growth rate g in equilibrium. An increase in the tax rate on capital shifts the vertical capital locus (K) to the left. In the general case of an upward-sloping research curve (R) the effect is to reduce the steady-state growth rate. However, in the special case where labor is the only input into the research technology, the research locus (R2) is horizontal, so an increase in the tax rate on capital leaves the growth rate unaffected.

Then the equilibrium rental rate will be $\zeta = r + \delta + \tau$. This and the above equilibrium condition (E) together imply

$$r + \delta + \tau = \alpha^2 \, (k/L)^{\alpha-1} \,. \tag{K}$$

Equation (K) determines the steady-state capital intensity k as a function of the parameters of the model. It is represented by the "capital curve" in figure 3.2. This curve is a vertical line, because the cost of capital is not directly affected by the research intensity under our assumption of linear intertemporal preferences.[15]

A steady-state equilibrium occurs where the two curves (K) and (R) intersect. As can be seen from the two corresponding equations, the comparative statics of this steady-state equilibrium are much the same as in the basic model without capital. In particular, an increase in the arrival parameter λ of innova-

---

15. As we will see in section 3.2.5, the more general assumption of a finite intertemporal elasticity of substitution, or of a fixed saving rate, would imply a downward-sloping capital curve.

tions will raise the growth rate by shifting the research curve up. An increase in the "size of innovation" γ will not shift either curve, but it will raise the growth rate directly through the growth equation (G). A reduction in thrift, represented by an increase in the rate of time preference r, will lower the growth rate by shifting the research curve down and by shifting the capital curve to the left.

Our introduction of a tax on capital produces a new comparative-static effect not seen before. Specifically, an increase in the tax rate τ will reduce the steady-state growth rate.[16] It does this by raising the cost of capital, which leads in the long run to a lower capital intensity. A lower capital intensity reduces the equilibrium-research intensity by reducing the flow of profit that a successful innovator can anticipate. In terms of figure 3.2, this comparative-static effect works by shifting the capital curve to the left and thus moving the equilibrium point down the upward-sloping research curve.

3.2.3   Capital Accumulation and Innovation as Complements

The effect on growth of the tax rate τ levied on capital illustrates the general proposition that capital accumulation and innovation are complementary processes. More capital accumulation stimulates innovation by raising the equilibrium flow of profits, just as more innovation stimulates capital accumulation by raising the rate of productivity growth. Neither process could take place in the long run without the other. For without innovation, diminishing returns would choke off net investment, and without net investment the rising cost of capital would choke off innovation.

This complementarity proposition runs counter to the conventional belief that the long-run rate of growth is not affected by capital accumulation, a belief that is supported by the neoclassical growth model of Solow and Swan, in which technical progress drives long-run growth independently of capital accumulation. The same conventional belief is supported also by the endogenous growth models of Romer (1990a) and Grossman and Helpman (1991a, chap. 5), in which the incentives to perform R&D determine long-run growth independently of the stock of capital.

The key difference between the model we have just presented and these other endogenous growth models is that we have assumed that research uses the same mix of inputs as does the production of capital and consumption goods, whereas these other models assume that labor[17] is the only input to research. To see how this works, suppose that we modified our model to make labor the only input to research. In a steady state, the flow of aggregate output would be

---

16. See problem 3.4 and section 3.2.5 for setups in which this outcome does not necessarily hold.

17. The unique input to the research technology is called "human capital" by Romer (1990a), but the fact that its supply is fixed, independently of its rate of remuneration makes it just like the labor of this chapter.

the same as (F) except that the labor input to manufacturing would be $L - n$ instead of L, because n units of labor would be used in research. Following exactly the same reasoning as before, we see that the steady-state research-arbitrage equation would be $w_t = \lambda V_t$, or

$$\omega = \lambda \frac{(1 - \alpha)\, \alpha\, (L - n)^{1-\alpha}\, k^{\alpha}}{r + \lambda n}, \tag{R_w}$$

where $\omega = w_t / A_t^{\max}$. This is the same as the research-arbitrage equation (R) except that the flow of profits in the numerator involves $L - n$ instead of L, and the cost of research on the left-hand side is now the productivity-adjusted wage instead of unity, because labor is the only input to research.

In equilibrium, the aggregate production function would again take the Cobb-Douglas form (CD) above, except with $L - n$ replacing L. Because w_t is the marginal product of labor in manufacturing, it follows directly from this aggregate production function that

$$\omega = (1 - \alpha)\, \psi\, (L - n)^{-\alpha}\, k^{\alpha}, \tag{ω}$$

where ψ is the constant ratio $A_t / A_t^{\max}$. Equations (R_w) and (ω) together yield the new research-arbitrage equation

$$\psi = \frac{\alpha\, (L - n)}{\rho + \lambda n}.$$

This equation would determine the level of research n, *independently* of the capital intensity k.

In other words, if labor were the only input to research, the research curve of figure 3.2 would be horizontal, so that shifts in the capital curve would leave the equilibrium rates of innovation and research unaffected. In simple terms, when the capital intensity rises, the rise in the payoff to research rises for the same reason as before, but now the cost of research would also rise, because the increase in k raises labor's marginal product in manufacturing, which would raise the opportunity cost of research. According to equations (R_w) and (ω), both the increase in the payoff and the increase in the cost would be proportional to k^{α}, so the two effects would cancel each other out, leaving the equilibrium level of research unaffected.

However, labor is not the only input to research. On the contrary, research in fact uses a great deal of physical capital, in the form of laboratories, offices, plant and equipment needed for constructing and testing pilot models and prototypes, computers and other scientific instruments, particle accelerators, observatories, space vehicles, and so forth. Thus when the capital stock rises, the cost of research will rise less than in proportion to the wage rate, and hence less than in proportion to the payoff from research. The overall effect of reducing the rate of capital taxation should therefore be a net stimulus to research and hence a rise in the steady-state growth rate.[18]

Moreover, even if labor *were* the only factor of production used in research, a reduced rate of capital taxation would still raise the long-run growth rate if there were a positive elasticity to the supply of labor, because the rise in the wage rate would induce an increased supply available to both manufacturing and research. In fact this seems quite likely, for although there may not be a significant long-run elasticity to the supply of hours of work, a rise in the skilled wage rate would probably induce an increase in supply of the skills used intensively in R&D. People would remain longer in school, demand a higher quality of education, and engage in more training and other skill-acquisition activities. The resulting increase in the supply of skills would dampen the rise in the cost of research without dampening the rise in the payoff to a successful innovator.

To be more precise, if skilled and unskilled wages were to rise by equal proportions when the capital stock rose, as they would if both skilled and unskilled labor worked with capital in a Cobb-Douglas aggregate production function, the rate of return to investing in skills would increase with the capital stock unless labor were the only factor of production used in acquiring skills. In fact, labor is not the only input to skill-acquisition. Higher education uses a lot of physical capital in the form of buildings, computers and other facilities. In addition, the experience of working with modern capital equipment is one of the most important inputs to acquiring skills through learning by doing.

In other words, research uses not only physical capital but human capital, and if these two types of capital are complementary in manufacturing, as they almost certainly are, then a reduced tax rate on either kind of capital accumulation should stimulate an increase in both. The resulting rise in output will raise profits, which are the reward to innovation, and the increase in supplies of the two kinds of capital will keep the cost of research from rising in proportion. In

---

18. Suppose, for example, that research used capital and labor according to a standard constant-returns production function: $n = G^r \left(K^r / A^{\max}, L^r \right)$. Then the research arbitrage equation would have the form:

$$c^r \left(\zeta, \omega \right) = \lambda \frac{\pi \left(\tilde{k} \right) \left[L - n a_L^r \left(\omega / \zeta \right) \right]}{r + \lambda n}$$

where c^r is the average cost of research relative to the leading edge parameter $A_t^{\max}$, a_L^r is the per unit demand for research labor and $\pi \left(\tilde{k} \right)$ is profit per effective worker in manufacturing expressed as a function of the capital labor ratio in manufacturing $\tilde{k}$. The productivity-adjusted wage ω is proportional to $\tilde{k}$, but if research uses any labor at all, then the elasticity of c^r with respect to ω is less than unity. Thus the research curve is upward sloping. In addition, a decrease in the cost of capital ζ will shift the research curve up by reducing the cost of capital used in research.

the rest of this chapter we shall interpret K broadly as a composite of human and physical capital, which are used in the same proportions in producing research as in producing final output. This stark assumption may not be exactly right if, as seems reasonable, R&D and human capital formation are both relatively human-capital intensive. But the preceding discussion suggests that the aggregation of the two types of capital is not crucial.

In summary, there are many reasons[19] for thinking that policies that favor capital accumulation will generally also stimulate innovation and therefore raise the long-run growth rate. This is why we subscribe to the balanced view that both innovation and accumulation are important factors in sustaining long-run growth. Neither can be said to play a dominant role to the exclusion of the other. Even though the growth equation makes innovation the *proximate* determinant of the growth rate, the forces determining the equilibrium rate of innovation and the equilibrium capital intensity cannot be dichotomized.

3.2.4   Obsolescence

Until now we have supposed that the cost of capital is not affected by obsolescence. In reality, however, when a firm's technology becomes obsolete, as it does in our model whenever a firm in the same sector innovates, the scrap value of its equipment is typically just a fraction of the replacement cost. The resulting loss due to obsolescence should be taken into account in the cost of capital.

To do so, we now go to the opposite extreme and assume that machines cannot be recycled at any cost. (That is, we now assume putty clay.) The flow probability that any individual piece of machinery will be destroyed by obsolescence is then the Poisson arrival rate of innovations λn, and this expected loss rate must be added to the other cost components underlying the rental rate of capital. Thus we can write the equation of the new capital curve as

$$r + \delta + \tau + \lambda n = \alpha^2 \, (k/L)^{\alpha-1} \tag{K_o}$$

The research curve is still given by equation (R) of section 3.2.2.

The only difference this makes to steady-state results is that the capital curve (K_o) is now downward-sloping. That is, a rise in the rate of innovation will raise the cost of capital by raising the rate of obsolescence. This increase in cost will reduce the demand for capital and thereby reduce the steady-state capital intensity. However, the fact that the capital curve is now downward sloping does not affect any qualitative comparative-statics effects on the steady-state growth rate.

---

19. Another reason, which does not however fit easily into the present framework, is that capital goods embody new technologies.

Although capital obsolescence has no important effect on the comparative statics of steady-state growth, it does have important consequences for the dynamic adjustment to major technological change. For suppose that a major technological innovation had the effect of opening up new windows of opportunities for further research, thus raising the arrival rate λ. Research would immediately increase, as would the rate of growth of the aggregate productivity measure A_t. But the net growth rate of the economy's stock of capital could be reduced at first, because the rate of capital obsolescence would have gone up. A numerical calibration exercise[20] shows that the overall effect could easily be to reduce the rate of growth of GDP for a long period of time, before eventually putting the economy on a faster long-run growth path. We will return to this aspect of capital obsolescence briefly in Chapter 8.

3.2.5 Alternative Savings Assumptions

Until this point we have dealt only with the special case in which saving is determined by a representative Ramsey household with linear preferences. Although this has been a useful simplifying assumption, it is not very realistic, for it implies that the economy as a whole acts like a household with an infinite elasticity of intertemporal substitution in consumption. Such a household has no desire to smooth consumption over time. If the rate of interest were to rise above the rate of time preference, even by the slightest amount, the household would save all its income and consume nothing at all.

As long as we confine attention to steady states, this unrealistic consumption behavior does not manifest itself, for the rate of interest in a steady state must equal the rate of time preference. But outside of a steady state the rate of interest will generally be determined by the historically predetermined stock of capital (relative to the stock of knowledge). That is, the argument by which we derived the form of the cost of capital in section 3.2.2 implies that the rental rate on capital will be $\zeta_t = r_t + \delta + \tau$, where r_t is the (endogenous) instantaneous real rate of interest. This and the equilibrium condition (E) imply that the rate of interest will be given by the equation

$$r_t + \delta + \tau = \alpha^2 \, (k/L)^{\alpha-1} . \tag{r}$$

So when the capital intensity k is below the steady-state value determined by the capital curve (K), the rate of interest will exceed the rate of time preference and consumption will be zero.

Without entering further into the dynamics of adjustment, this section briefly considers how our steady-state analysis would be affected by relaxing this extreme assumption. There are two commonly used alternatives. One is to

---

20. See Howitt (1998).

follow the AK model described in Chapter 1, and suppose that the elasticity of intertemporal substitution of the representative Ramsey household is the constant $\sigma < \infty$. Let ρ denote the rate of time preference. Then as in the AK model, the steady-state rate of interest would be $\rho + \sigma g$ instead of ρ.

Under this alternative, the same research and capital equations (R) and (K) as in section 3.2.2 would define the research and capital intensities, except that the terms involving ρ would have to be replaced by the new steady-state rate of interest $\rho + \sigma \lambda n \ln \gamma$. Thus we would have

$$1 = \lambda \frac{(1 - \alpha)\, \alpha L^{1-\alpha} k^\alpha}{\rho + \sigma \lambda n \ln \gamma + \lambda n} \tag{R$'$}$$

$$\rho + \sigma \lambda n \ln \gamma + \delta + \tau = \alpha^2 \, (k/L)^{\alpha-1} . \tag{K$'$}$$

The research curve (R$'$) would still be upward sloping, for the same reason as before. But the capital curve (K$'$) would now be downward sloping, because in a steady state with more research and faster growth the representative household's consumption would be growing faster, which would require a higher market rate of interest. (Otherwise everyone would want to borrow against future income growth, and there would be an excess demand for currently produced output.) The rise in the rate of interest would raise the cost of capital, thus leading to a smaller steady-state capital intensity.

The fact that the capital curve is now downward sloping would not alter any of the comparative-statics effects on growth in a qualitative way, although it would affect the size of the effects. In particular, a rise in the tax rate on capital would still reduce growth by shifting the capital curve to the left. But the effect would be dampened by the accompanying fall in the rate of interest. A rise in the size of innovation γ would also now unambiguously reduce the steady-state research intensity; however, because the effect would be less than in proportion to $\ln \gamma$, the overall effect on g in the growth equation (G) would still be positive.

The other alternative is to make the same saving assumption as Solow and Swan: namely, that people save a fixed fraction s of their aggregate output Y_t at each point in time. Under this assumption, the proportional rate of increase in the capital stock would be

$$\frac{\dot{K_t}}{K_t} = \frac{1}{K_t} \, (sY_t - \delta K_t) = s \, (k/L)_t^{\alpha-1} - \delta.$$

In a steady state this would have to equal the growth rate $g = \lambda n \ln \gamma$. Thus the steady-state capital intensity would be determined by the capital curve

$$s \, (k/L)^{\alpha-1} - \delta = \lambda n \ln \gamma \tag{K$''$}$$

The steady-state rate of interest would now be determined not by time preference but by the equilibrium condition (r). Substituting this rate of interest for r in the research arbitrage-equation (R) yields the modified research-arbitrage equation

$$1 = \lambda \frac{(1 - \alpha) \, \alpha L^{1-\alpha} k^{\alpha}}{\alpha^2 \, (k/L)^{\alpha-1} - \delta - \tau + \lambda n}. \tag{R''}$$

Again, the steady-state values of k and n will be determined by the intersection of an upward-sloping research curve with a downward-sloping capital curve. Again, this makes little difference to our main results, except that the effect on growth of the tax on capital is now reversed. The reason is that the tax increase does not directly deter capital accumulation, which now depends only on income, not on the after-tax rate of return. Instead, all that happens is that the lower rate of return lowers the rate of discount applied to the profits from innovation, thus encouraging innovation.

Notice, however, that although the effect of capital taxation on growth has been reversed, a decrease in the saving rate s would reduce growth through the same mechanism as in section 3.2.2. That is, it would shift the capital curve (K'') to the left, moving the equilibrium down the upward-sloping research curve (R''). Thus in a more general analysis in which saving depended on both income and the after-tax rate of return, the effect of capital taxation could go either way. In any case, the conventional dichotomy between capital accumulation and technological progress would still be invalid.

3.2.6 Population Growth

Now that we have dealt with some of the other complications of growth with capital accumulation, we are in a position to consider population growth. In the neoclassical theory of Solow and Swan, population growth was simple to deal with because the assumption of constant returns to scale implied that the size of the population was irrelevant. Twice as many people with twice as much capital would produce twice as much output and save twice as much. Thus the model could be worked out on a per capita basis. In a Schumpeterian model, however, population growth is not so easy to introduce because we no longer have constant returns in all the factors that are growing: capital, knowledge, and now labor.

Indeed, our theory seems to imply that with a growing population the growth rate of output should be growing, because the reward to innovation is increasing in the size of the population.[21] This is the scale effect of an increased value of L that was found in the basic model of the previous chapter, and the fact that

---

21. See, for example, equation (V).

growth does not seem to accelerate as population grows is the basis of Jones's (1995) critique of R&D-based growth theory.[22]

Some might argue that in fact there should be a scale effect of sorts, because of agglomeration economies. Up to a point, at least, a higher density of population within a given geographical region should allow researchers to realize various economies of scale of the sort that Jane Jacobs (1969) describes in her analysis of city life. However, there must be a limit to scale effects or the world would have experienced explosive growth since the industrial revolution.

One possible limit to scale effects might come through the increasing scarcity of natural resources. This is the factor that writers from Malthus to the Club of Rome have emphasized as imposing an ultimate limit to growth and prosperity. Although issues of natural resources are of great importance, it would take us too far afield to deal with them at this point.[23] Instead, we deal with another factor that has recently been elaborated by Young (1995a).

Young's analysis is based on the idea that there are two kinds of innovation, vertical and horizontal. Vertical (quality-improving) innovations work as in the analysis we have laid out here and in the preceding chapter. Horizontal innovations, on the other hand, open up new intermediate products that will then be subject to vertical innovations. As the economy grows, horizontal innovations neutralize the scale effect on the incentive to innovate by adding to the number of independent sectors over which research must be spread, and over which manufacturing labor must also be spread.

A simple model incorporating this idea can be constructed by taking our basic model with capital and labor, and allowing the labor force at each date t to be $L_t = e^{\eta t}$, where the population growth rate η is an exogenous constant. Suppose that there are now two sorts of innovation—the quality-improving innovations that we have already in the model, and imitations, which we now add to the model.

Imitation adds to the variety of intermediate goods in the economy without adding to overall productivity. An imitator simply finds a way to replicate what is done in a randomly chosen intermediate sector that already exists. Suppose we generalize the production function (F) of the previous sections to[24]

---

22. Jones's critique was examined in problem 7, Chapter 1.

23. Chapter 5 is devoted to the effects of limited natural resources and of environmental pollution on endogenous growth.

24. As Benassy (1997) points out, other endogenous growth models that employ the Ethier-Dixit-Stiglitz product variety specification assume arbitrarily that the social return to product variety is determined by the same parameters α as the elasticity of substitution. In (F1) we have set the social return to product variety equal to zero. What matters for the result of this section is that the marginal product of capital depend on the amount of labor input per good. Another way to accomplish this without setting the return to product variety equal to zero is to assume that capital and labor are both used in the production of intermediate goods, as we do in section 12.5. See Howitt (1997) for the details of how this would work with an endogenous number of products.

$$Y_t = C_t + I_t + N_t = L_t^{1-\alpha} Q_t^{\alpha-1} \int_0^{Q_t} A_{it} x_{it}^\alpha di, \tag{F1}$$

where Q_t is the number of intermediate goods that have been created.

As in the basic model, each sector will supply the same flow of intermediate good, which by the capital-market clearing condition must be the capital intensity per sector[25] $\widehat{k}_t \equiv K_t/A_tQ_t$. This and (F1) imply exactly the same aggregate Cobb-Douglas production function as before:

$$Y_t = K_t^\alpha (A_t L_t)^{1-\alpha}, \tag{CD1}$$

in which the number of intermediate sectors Q_t has no effect.

Assume that imitation is an exogenous, serendipitous process. No one spends resources attempting to imitate; imitation just happens. Suppose that each individual in the economy is equally likely to imitate, and that the Poisson arrival rate of imitation to each individual is a constant λ_0. Because imitation is the root of new sectors, this implies that the number of sectors Q_t will grow at the same rate as the number of people L_t, that is, that the number of workers per sector L_t/Q_t will be a constant[26] θ. This is precisely what is needed in order for the scale effect in the reward to innovation to be diluted by the growth in sectors.[27]

The growth of knowledge depends only on the flow of vertical innovations. As before, the aggregate flow of vertical innovations is assumed to be λn_t where $n_t = N_t/A_t$ is the productivity-adjusted level of research. As the number of sectors grows, each sector becomes more specialized, and thus each vertical innovation represents a smaller proportional contribution to the overall stock of knowledge. Accordingly, we assume that the spillover coefficient per innovation is inversely proportional to the number of sectors: $\frac{1}{Q_t} \ln \gamma$, instead of $\ln \gamma$ as before. Thus the steady-state growth rate of productivity will be

$$g = \lambda n \left(\frac{1}{Q_t} \ln \gamma \right) = \lambda \widehat{n} \ln \gamma, \tag{G1}$$

where $\widehat{n} \equiv N_t/A_t^{\max} Q_t$.

As before, we confine attention to steady states, that is, to equilibria in which output Y_t and capital K_t grow at the same constant rate. According to the aggregate production function (CD1), this common growth rate will be

---

25. The average productivity parameter A_t is now defined as $Q_t^{-1} \int_0^{Q_t} A_{it} di$.

26. Mathematically, $\dot{Q}_t = \lambda_0 L_t$ and $\dot{L}_t = \eta L_t$. It follows that the differential equation driving the ratio $\theta_t \equiv L_t/Q_t$ is: $\dot{\theta}_t = \eta \theta_t - \lambda_0 \theta_t^2$, which converges asymptotically to the constant value: $\theta \equiv \eta/\lambda_0$.

27. In section 12.3.2 we show how a similar analysis can be performed under the assumption that horizontal and vertical innovations are motivated by exactly the same considerations and use the same research technology.

the sum of the population and productivity growth rates: $\eta + g$. Because the number of sectors grows at the same rate as does population, this implies that the capital intensity per sector $\widehat{k} \equiv K_t/A_t Q_t$ will be constant in a steady state. The growth equation (G1) implies that the research intensity per sector $\widehat{n}$ will also be constant.

The position of a monopolist producer will be the same as in the basic model with capital and labor, except that the labor force per sector θ will enter its demand function where the aggregate labor force L used to. Thus by the same reasoning that led to (K) in section 3.2.2, the equation determining the capital intensity in each sector will be

$$r + \delta + \tau = \alpha^2 \left(\widehat{k}/\theta\right)^{\alpha-1}, \tag{K1}$$

and by the same reasoning that led to (R), the research-arbitrage condition can be written as

$$1 = \lambda \frac{(1-\alpha)\,\alpha\theta^{1-\alpha}\widehat{k}^\alpha}{r + \lambda\widehat{n}}. \tag{R1}$$

The equations (R1) and (K1) determining the steady-state research and capital intensities per sector are almost identical to those of section 3.2.2. In particular, the comparative-statics effects on the growth rate are identical, except that now there is an additional effect arising from the new parameter θ. Thus an exogenous increase in the steady-state number of workers per line, arising, say, from an increase in the population growth rate η or a decrease in the imitation rate λ_0, will increase the steady-state growth rate by shifting the research curve up and the capital curve to the right.

This new effect shows that what used to be thought of as an embarrassing scale effect in Schumpeterian growth theory can be seen, in the light of this analysis, as a novel prediction that distinguishes it from the neoclassical theory of Solow and Swan. For instead of saying that growth goes up with the *level* of population, it goes up with the *growth rate* of population.

Moreover, the steady state of the model is characterized by exactly the phenomena that Jones claimed constituted a prima facie refutation of R&D-based growth theory. That is, (a) population is growing, (b) the amount of research per person, measured by the input cost of research per person,[28] is also growing, and yet (c) the growth rate g of output per person is constant. These observations are sufficient to reject the elementary Schumpeterian model of the previous chapter, but they are entirely consistent with the generalized Schumpeterian model of this section that takes into account both capital accumulation and population growth. The reason is that in the generalized model, when *techno-*

---

28. That is, $N_t/L_t = (N_t/Q_t)(Q_t/L_t) = A_t^{\max}\widehat{n}/\theta$.

logical progress causes the size of the economy to grow it also becomes more complex, requiring an ever-increasing research input to maintain the same flow rate of innovation as before, whereas when *population growth* makes the economy larger it also increases the number of imitators in the economy and thus increases the number of distinct lines over which research must be spread.

3.2.7 The Full Dynamic Model*

For simplicity we have limited ourselves so far to steady-state analysis. However, if, as several writers have contended, an economy spends most of its time a long way from a steady state, then it is important also to analyze nonsteady-state behavior. That is the purpose of the present section. As we shall see, most of the comparative-statics results of steady-state growth have valid nonsteady-state counterparts. But there are also some aspects of dynamic behavior that one might not have guessed from the steady-state analysis.

In particular, when the economy is out of the steady state, the growth rate of output may be negatively correlated with the intensity of R&D, the rate of innovation, and the level of productivity growth. Thus one could easily get the impression that research, innovation, and productivity growth have no positive effect on the rate of economic growth, even though we know from our previous steady-state analysis that without innovation the economy could not grow at all in the long run.

Consider the model with population growth from section 3.2.6. To simplify notation, normalize the number of sectors per person θ to equal unity. As discussed in section 3.2.5, the rate of interest at each date will be determined by the condition that the supply and demand for capital be equal:

$$r_t + \delta + \tau = \alpha^2 \widehat{k}_t^{\alpha-1}, \tag{r'}$$

where $\widehat{k}_t$ is the capital intensity per sector.

As before, $\widehat{k}_t$ is the equilibrium level of intermediate output in each sector. The equilibrium flow of profit of a monopolist that innovated at date t and is still producing at date $s > t$ will be the fraction $1 - \alpha$ of its revenues: $(1 - \alpha)\, A_t^{\max} \alpha \widehat{k}_t^{\alpha}$. Therefore the value of an innovation at date t is

$$V_t = \int_t^{\infty} e^{-\int_t^s r_u du} e^{-\int_t^s \widehat{\lambda n}_u du} (1 - \alpha)\, A_t^{\max} \alpha \widehat{k}_s^{\alpha} ds, \tag{V2}$$

where the two exponential factors represent respectively the present value of a unit of consumption at date s and the probability that the monopolist will not have been replaced by date s.

Define the "productivity-adjusted" value of an innovation as $v_t \equiv V_t / A_t^{\max}$. Dividing both sides of (V2) by $A_t^{\max}$ and differentiating with respect to t yields a Bellman-like differential form of the research-arbitrage equation

$$\dot{v}_t = -(1-\alpha)\,\alpha\widehat{k}_t^{\alpha} + (r_t + \lambda\widehat{n}_t)\,v_t. \tag{B}$$

By the same reasoning as before, the research-arbitrage condition is that $\lambda V_t = A_t^{\max}$, so v_t is constant even out of the steady state: $v_t \equiv 1/\lambda$. From this, (r') and (B), we get the research-arbitrage equation

$$1 = \lambda\frac{(1-\alpha)\,\alpha\widehat{k}_t^{\alpha}}{\alpha^2\widehat{k}_t^{\alpha-1} - \delta - \tau + \lambda\widehat{n}_t}, \tag{R2}$$

which must always hold whether or not the economy is in a steady state. This equation is the same as the steady-state research-arbitrage equation (R″) of section 3.2.5, in the special case where $L = 1$. At each date t it determines the equilibrium research intensity $\hat{n}_t$ as an increasing function of the historically predetermined capital intensity $\hat{k}_t$, as shown in the top diagram of figure 3.3.

Outside the steady state we must be careful to distinguish between the rate of growth of output per person G_t and the rate of growth of the average (and leading-edge) productivity parameter g_t. The latter will be given by the same spillover equation as before:

$$\dot{A}_t/A_t \equiv g_t = \lambda\widehat{n}_t \ln\gamma. \tag{S2}$$

As already indicated in section 3.2.5, for dynamic analysis we must relax the assumption of an infinite intertemporal elasticity of substitution in consumption. Suppose, accordingly, that there is a fixed saving rate s. Then capital intensity per sector will be governed by almost the same law of motion as in the Solow-Swan model:[29]

$$\frac{d\widehat{k}_t}{dt} = s\widehat{k}_t^{\alpha} - (\delta + g_t + \eta)\,\widehat{k}_t. \tag{3.4}$$

Thus, given any historically predetermined capital intensity per sector, the research-intensity will be given by (R2), the rate of productivity growth will

---

29. Mathematically, the rate of growth of the capital-intensity per sector $\widehat{k}_t \equiv K_t/A_t Q_t$ can be expressed as

$$\frac{1}{\widehat{k}_t}\frac{d\widehat{k}_t}{dt} \equiv \frac{1}{K_t}\frac{dK_t}{dt} - \frac{1}{A_t}\frac{dA_t}{dt} - \frac{1}{Q_t}\frac{dQ_t}{dt}.$$

Given a fixed saving rate

$$\frac{1}{K_t}\frac{dK_t}{dt} = \frac{1}{K_t}\,(sY_t - \delta K_t) = s\widehat{k}_t^{\alpha-1} - \delta,$$

where the last equality follows from the production function (CD1) above and the normalization that makes $L_t = Q_t$. Thus

$$\frac{1}{\widehat{k}_t}\frac{d\widehat{k}_t}{dt} = s\widehat{k}_t^{\alpha-1} - \delta - g_t - \eta.$$

be given by (S2), and the capital intensity will change according to the differential equation (3.4), as shown in the bottom diagram of figure 3.3. As capital intensity approaches its steady-state value $\widehat{k}^*$, the "depreciation line" is rotated counterclockwise by the speedup in productivity growth caused by more research. Outside the steady state, the rate of growth G_t of output per person will be a weighted average of the growth rate of capital per person and the growth rate of productivity:[30]

$$G_t = \alpha \left(s\widehat{k}_t^{\alpha-1} - \delta - \eta \right) + (1 - \alpha) \, \lambda \widehat{n}_t \ln \gamma. \tag{G2}$$

It follows from the research-arbitrage equation (R2) and the growth equation (G2) that, given the historically predetermined capital intensity per sector, the growth rate of output per person is increasing in the saving rate s, the arrival rate parameter λ of innovations, and the spillover coefficient γ. The parameters λ and γ work by raising the rate of productivity growth through the research-arbitrage equation and the spillover equation, as in the steady-state analysis. The parameter s works by raising the rate of change of capital per person.

An increase in the depreciation rate δ will have an ambiguous short-run effect on growth because on one hand it directly reduces the rate of change of capital per person but on the other hand it stimulates productivity growth by reducing the rate of interest used to discount the profits from research. Likewise, an increase in the population growth rate η will have an ambiguous short-run effect because although it reduces the rate of change of capital per person, it also stimulates research, as we saw in section 3.2.6, by increasing the number of workers per sector θ.

As we mentioned in section 3.2.4, if we take capital obsolescence into account, then an increase in the arrival parameter λ could have the short-run effect of reducing the growth rate of output per person by raising the overall rate of depreciation $\delta + \lambda \widehat{n}_t$. Thus the short-run relationship between the flow of innovations and the rate of economic growth could easily appear to be a negative one.

Innovation and economic growth could also appear to be negatively related in the medium term, even with no parameter changes, because as the economy

---

30. From the production function (CD1), and the normalization $L_t = Q_t$, output per person is

$$\frac{Y_t}{L_t} = \widehat{k}_t^{\alpha} A_t.$$

Thus the growth rate of output per person is

$$G_t = \alpha \frac{1}{\widehat{k}_t} \frac{d\widehat{k}_t}{dt} + \frac{1}{A_t} \frac{dA_t}{dt}.$$

Equation (G2) follows from this, (3.4) and (S2).

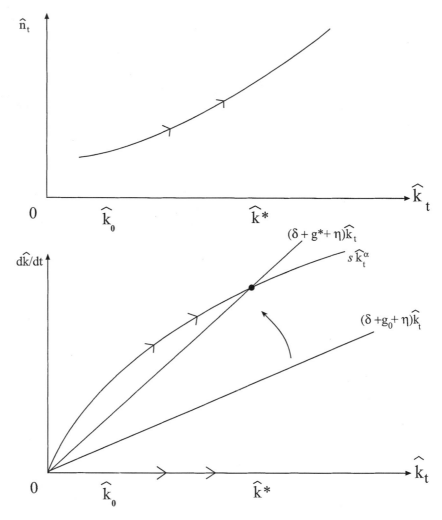

Figure 3.3
Convergence in an endogenous growth model. As the captial stock per efficiency unit of labor rises, the resulting fall in the cost of capital stimulates research in each sector, as shown in the top diagram. This causes, the "depreciation line" in the bottom diagram to rotate counterclockwise, by raising the rate of "dilution" of capital, thus hastening the convergence to the steady state k^*.

approaches its steady state the rate of economic growth could be slowing down as the rate of innovation speeds up. Specifically, suppose the capital intensity per sector is below its steady-state value in figure 3.3. Then as it rises, the flow of innovations $\lambda \widehat{n}_t$ will be increasing over time through the research arbitrage equation (R2). But at the same time the rate of economic growth could be falling through the growth equation (G2). That is, while the rise in innovations will be increasing the rate of productivity growth (the second term in G2), the

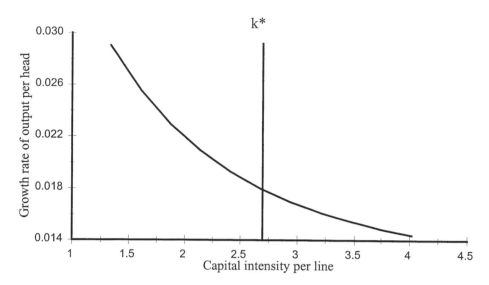

Figure 3.4

rise in capital intensity will be decreasing the rate of increase in capital per person (the first term in G2).

Now, the result that growth slows down as you approach a steady state is simply the conditional-convergence result of the Solow-Swan model. And the mechanism that can produce the result in this endogenous growth model is the same as the one at work in the Solow-Swan model—diminishing returns. That is, as the capital stock rises, investment rises less than in proportion because diminishing returns makes output rise less than in proportion and there is a fixed saving rate.

Although conditional convergence is not strictly implied by the assumptions we have made so far, numerical simulation shows that it is likely for realistic parameter values. For example, figure 3.4 shows that it will occur in the particular case where $\delta = .08$, $\alpha = 2/3$, $s = .15$, $\eta = .01$, $\lambda = 1$, and $\gamma = 1.1$. Conditional convergence, together with the fact that innovation is stimulated by a rise in capital intensity, means that in the intermediate run economic growth and innovation will typically move in opposite directions, even though in the long run we know they will be positively correlated.

3.3   Summary

This chapter extends the basic model of creative destruction to include capital accumulation. Because the main purpose of the extension is to use the theory to interpret evidence drawn from a world of many sectors, the chapter first generalizes the basic model so as to include more than one intermediate sector.

The chapter first assumes that there is a continuum of different intermediate sectors, each just like the single intermediate sector of the basic model of Chapter 2. Research is targeted at specific sectors and is again motivated by the prospect of (local) monopoly rents. Although innovations arrive only sporadically within a sector, there is now a continuous flow of innovations in the whole economy. Each innovation has only an incremental effect on the growth of knowledge in the economy, through a technology spillover.

The generalization leaves the basic structure and results of the Schumpeterian growth model unaffected, except that the law of large numbers prevents the uncertainty of the innovation process within each sector from showing up at the macroeconomic level. Thus in a steady state growth is constant at each point in time rather than being stochastic.

The chapter grafts capital accumulation onto this multisectoral model by assuming that intermediate goods are produced not by labor but by capital and that final output can be used for more than consumption; specifically, it can also be used as an input to research and to produce capital goods. This model can be described in aggregate terms by a familiar Cobb-Douglas aggregate production function in capital and "efficiency units" of labor, where the efficiency parameter represents the state of technological knowledge to which all innovations contribute. The steady-state growth rate is described by almost the same equations as before, with comparative statics results the same as before.

The main result of this chapter is that capital accumulation and innovation are both essential inputs to long-run growth. More innovation stimulates capital accumulation by raising the marginal product of capital. More capital accumulation stimulates innovation by raising the profits accruing to a successful innovator. This result runs counter to the conventional belief to the effect that innovation alone determines the long-run growth *rate* while capital accumulation determines only the *level* of the long-run growth path. The chapter shows that the problem with this conventional view is that it ignores the role of capital as an input to research. If only labor were used in research, then more capital accumulation would raise the opportunity cost of research, by raising the equilibrium wage of labor in manufacturing, exactly offsetting the effect of higher profits on the incentive to do research. But as long as capital plays some role as an input to research, the offset is less than one hundred percent.

The chapter shows how to generalize the analysis to allow for endogenous capital obsolescence created by the innovation process, and to allow for alternative assumptions concerning the determination of saving behavior. It also shows how the model can be used to address the empirical critique of Jones

(1995) by showing that as the economy gets larger and an ever increasing input is applied to research, the economy's growth rate can indeed remain constant. The reason is that (a) when *technological progress* causes the size of the economy to grow, technology becomes more complex, requiring an ever-increasing research input to maintain the same flow rate of innovation as before, whereas (b) when *population growth* makes the economy larger it also increases the number of imitators in the economy and thus increases the number of distinct lines over which research must be spread.

Appendix 1: The Invariant Cross-Sectoral Distribution of Relative Productivities

This appendix shows that equation (3.3) of section 3.1 does indeed characterize the long-run distribution of relative productivity parameters, independently of the behavior of the aggregate flow of innovation.

Let $F(\cdot, t)$ denote the cumulative distribution of the absolute productivity parameters A across sectors at any arbitrarily given date t. Pick any $A > 0$ that was the "leading edge" parameter at some date $t_0 \geq 0$, and define $\Phi(t) \equiv F(A, t)$. Then

$$\Phi(t_0) = 1, \quad \text{and} \tag{3.5}$$

$$\frac{d\Phi(t)}{dt} = -\Phi(t)\lambda n_t \quad \text{for all} \quad t \geq t_0. \tag{3.6}$$

Equation (3.5) holds because no sector can have a productivity parameter larger than that of the leading edge at date t_0, which by construction is A. To understand equation (3.6), note that after t_0 the rate at which the mass of sectors behind A falls is the overall flow of innovations occurring in sectors currently behind A. There are $\Phi(t)$ such sectors, each innovating with a Poisson arrival rate of λn_t.

Equations (3.5) and (3.6) above define a simple differential equation that $\Phi(t)$ must obey. This equation has the unique solution

$$\Phi(t) = e^{-\lambda \int_{t_0}^{t} n_s ds} \quad \text{for all } t \geq t_0. \tag{3.7}$$

Also, because $\frac{dA_t^{\max}}{dt} \equiv A_t^{\max} \lambda n_t \ln \gamma$, and $A \equiv A_{t_0}^{\max}$:

$$A_t^{\max} = A e^{\lambda \ln \gamma \int_{t_0}^{t} n_s ds} \quad \text{for all } t \geq t_0. \tag{3.8}$$

From equations (3.7) and (3.8):

$$\Phi(t) = \left(A/A_t^{\max}\right)^{1/\ln \gamma} \tag{3.9}$$

Define a to be the relative productivity $A/A_t^{\max}$. By construction, $\Phi(t)$ is the fraction of sectors in which the productivity parameter is less than $aA_t^{\max}$. Hence equation (3.9) establishes that this fraction is indeed given by equation (3.3) at date t if a is the relative productivity at t of a sector that innovated on or after date 0. When t is large, this will include almost all values of $a \in [0, 1]$.

Appendix 2: Research Arbitrage and Labor Market Equilibrium in the Multisector Economy

The task of this appendix is to provide a detailed derivation of the basic equations (A″) and (L″) of section 3.1.5. Because $\tilde{x}(\omega) = \left(\frac{\omega}{\alpha^2}\right)^{\frac{1}{\alpha-1}}$, therefore $\tilde{x}(\omega/a) = \tilde{x}(\omega) a^{\frac{1}{1-\alpha}}$. Using this, and using formula (3.3) to express the density h, rewrite equation (L′) as

$$n + \int_0^1 \tilde{x}(\omega) a^{\frac{1}{1-\alpha}} \frac{a^{\frac{1}{\ln \gamma}-1}}{\ln \gamma} da = L.$$

Evaluating the integral yields (L″).

Because $\tilde{\pi}(\omega) = \frac{1-\alpha}{\alpha} \omega \tilde{x}(\omega)$, and $\tilde{x}(\omega)$ is proportional to $\omega^{\frac{1}{\alpha-1}}$, therefore $\tilde{\pi}(\omega)$ is proportional to $\omega^{\frac{\alpha}{\alpha-1}}$. Hence: $\tilde{\pi}(\omega e^{gs}) = \tilde{\pi}(\omega) e^{-\frac{\alpha}{1-\alpha}gs} = \frac{1-\alpha}{\alpha} \omega \tilde{x}(\omega) e^{-\frac{\alpha}{1-\alpha}gs}$. Use this to rewrite (A′) as

$$\omega = \lambda \int_0^\infty e^{-(r+\lambda n)s} \frac{1-\alpha}{\alpha} \omega \tilde{x}(\omega) e^{-\frac{\alpha}{1-\alpha}\lambda n \ln \gamma \cdot s} ds.$$

Dividing both sides by ω and evaluating the integral yields (A″).

Problems

Difficulty of Problems:

No star: normal

One star: difficult

Two stars: very difficult

1. Intermediate goods in research in a one-sector model

To check that you have understood the implications of section 3.1.6, this problem asks you to consider the implications of using capital goods in research in the basic model of Chapter 2. There is only one sector, which at time t employs an amount N_t of capital goods in research. If N_t units of capital are employed in research, the Poisson arrival rate of innovations is $\lambda N_t/A_t$. In all other aspects the production sector of the economy is like the one in Chapter 2. When a new quality is discovered, intermediate goods are produced one-to-one by labor, and they are in turn used to manufacture the unique final good, according to a Cobb-Douglas technology, $A_t x_t^\alpha$. This final good is then used both for consumption and as research input. Firms discount their profits by the interest rate r. Consumers maximize intertemporal utility, and their instantaneous utility function is CES with coefficient $\sigma < \infty$.

a. Find the arbitrage and labor-market equilibrium conditions, and obtain the steady state level of expenditure in research.

b. What is the growth rate of the level of technology?

c. Use the goods-market equilibrium condition to show that in steady state the rate of growth of consumption must be equal to the rate of growth of the level of technology.

d. Use the fact that $\dot{C}/C = (r - \rho)/\sigma$ to obtain the steady state level of research employment and the growth rate in terms of model parameters only. Why does a higher γ have both a positive and a negative effect on the steady state level of research expenditure?

e. Suppose there is a central planner that wants to maximize the present value of consumption (from zero to infinity). Show that the equation that determines the level of steady state R&D expenditure is

$$1 - \frac{\lambda(\gamma - 1)}{r}n = \lambda \frac{(\gamma - 1)L^\alpha}{r - \lambda(\gamma - 1)n}. \tag{3.10}$$

⋆ **2. The multisector economy with a nonconstant Poisson arrival rate (based on Barro and Sala-i-Martín 1995, chap. 7; see also Grossman and Helpman 1991a, chap. 4)**

Consider the simplest version of a multisector economy without spillovers across sectors. There is a given number of sectors, I (where I is large), each producing a different type of intermediate good, indexed i. The aggregate production function for the unique consumption good is then

$$Y = A \sum_{i=1}^{I} \left(\gamma^{t_i} x_i\right)^\alpha.$$

A is a constant and $\gamma^{t_i} x_i$ is the *quality-adjusted* amount of intermediate input of type i used (that is, the number of units multiplied by its quality or productivity). t_i is the highest quality that has been reached in sector i at time t. For simplicity denote γ^{t_i} as q_{it}.

Firms in each sector engage in research for a higher quality of the intermediate good, using as the only input units of the final good. When an amount N_{it} of final good is invested, innovations occur randomly with a Poisson arrival rate $\lambda(t_i)N_{it}$. The term $\lambda(t_i)$ is decreasing in t_i, and it represents the fact that the higher the quality that is being produced, the harder it is to go one step farther up the quality ladder. When a new quality of a particular type of intermediate good is discovered, the new good is produced, by the firm that first found it, at a constant unit cost, which for simplicity we take to be one unit of the final good. The price of final output is normalized to unity.

a. Examine the pricing decisions of intermediate goods firms, assuming that only one firm can produce the latest vintage, and that firms within a sector engage in price competition. Show that if $\alpha\gamma \geq 1$, the price charged by the producer of the latest quality is $1/\alpha$, and if $\alpha\gamma < 1$, then the price is γ. Are lower quality intermediate goods ever produced?

b. Find the expected present value of an innovation in sector i, V_{it}, and then obtain the equation that determines the equilibrium level of R&D expenditure in the sector.

c. Given your results in (b), discuss how the probability of innovating in a sector depends on the level of technology already attained in that sector. Suppose that the Poisson parameter is given by the following expression

$$\lambda(t_i) = q_{it+1}^{-\frac{\alpha}{1-\alpha}}.$$

Show that in this case, the probability of a discovery is the same in all sectors.

d. Under the assumption that

$$\lambda(t_i) = q_{it+1}^{-\frac{\alpha}{1-\alpha}}$$

find the rate of growth of the aggregate quality index, defined as

$$Q \equiv \sum_{i=1}^{I} q_{it}^{\frac{\alpha}{1-\alpha}},$$

which in turn determines the rate of output growth. Assume that the utility function is logarithmic and that agents discount rate is ρ. Obtain the steady-state growth rate.

⋆ **3. Welfare analysis in the multisector economy (based on Barro and Sala-i-Martín 1995, section 7.5)**

Consider the multisector model of the previous problem. Assume that the utility function is logarithmic and that $\lambda(t_i) = q_{it+1}^{-\frac{\alpha}{1-\alpha}}$.

a. Calculate the social value of an innovation.

b. Obtain the dynamic equation for the quality index as a function of the levels of R&D expenditure, N_{it}.

c. Construct the Hamiltonian for the problem faced by the central planner, and find the steady state rate of growth of output and consumption of the economy.

4. Capital income taxation and growth (based on Uhlig and Yanagawa 1996)

Conventional economic wisdom has it that higher capital income taxes lead to lower growth (as we will see in Chapter 8). The purpose of this problem is to make you rethink this conventional wisdom. Consider a two-period overlapping-generations model. The utility function is given by

$$U(c_{y,t}, c_{o,t+1}) = \log(c_{y,t}) + \log(c_{o,t+1}),$$

where $c_{y,t}$ is consumption of generation t when young, and $c_{o,t+1}$ is their consumption when old. The young are endowed with one unit of time, which they supply inelastically as labor. For that, they receive a fraction $(1 - \theta)$ of output y_t as wages. Wages can be either consumed or saved. The only asset is physical capital, thus the savings of the young at date $t - 1$ equal capital at date t. In period t, the old possess all the capital k_t used in production for that period and receive a fraction θ of output y_t as capital share, or $\theta y_t / k_t$ per unit of capital. After production, the capital depreciates at rate δ and is then sold to the young. Capital at date $t + 1$ is then given by

$$k_{t+1} = (1 - \delta)k_t + x_t,$$

where x_t is gross investment. Output is produced using capital and labor by an AK technology, $y_t = Ak_t$, where A is a positive constant.

The government levies a proportional tax τ_K on total capital income, that is, $\theta y_t + (1 - \delta)k_t$, and a proportional tax τ_L on labor income. Initially suppose that the revenue is spent outside the domestic economy.

a. Define formally the equilibrium of this economy taking into account:

i. consumer equilibrium

ii. market clearing in the savings and goods markets, and

iii. the determination of the wage and rate of return. Calculate the growth rate of the economy, which is equal to the rate of growth of the stock of capital.

b. Suppose the government consumes a constant fraction γ of output every period, $h_t = \gamma y_t$, which is financed through either the proportional tax on capital income, τ_K, or on labor income, τ_L, so as to keep the government budget balanced each period. Given the capital income tax rate τ_K, calculate the labor income tax rate τ_L that balances the government budget.

c. Calculate the growth rate of the economy, under the assumptions in (b). What happens to the growth rate as the capital income tax is increased if a balanced government budget is maintained through adjustment of the labor income tax?

d. Reexamine the last result by changing the preferences to allow for elasticities of substitution different from unity. Let the utility function of the agents be CES,

$$u(c_{y,t}, c_{o,t+1}) = \frac{c_{y,t}^{1-\sigma} - 1}{1 - \sigma} + \beta \frac{c_{o,t+1}^{1-\sigma} - 1}{1 - \sigma},$$

where $\sigma > 0$ is the intertemporal elasticity of substitution and β is the discount factor. Examine how the rate of growth varies as the capital income tax rate is changed.

e. Interpret your results and reevaluate the "conventional wisdom."

⋆ **5. Physical capital obsolescence and the lock-in effect (based on Redding 1996c)**

This problem examines a situation in which physical capital is used to produce the intermediate good. If physical capital depreciates when a new quality of intermediaries is introduced, the profitability of the innovation is reduced. The effect of this depreciation can be so large that the new technology is not introduced. It might then be the case that an "early starter," that is, an economy that has accumulated a lot of physical capital, will not introduce a technology that an economy with a smaller capital stock would adopt. Other sources of lock-in will be examined in Chapter 6.

Consider a discrete time economy in which a homogeneous final good is produced according to the technology

$$Y_t = A_t x_t^\alpha \qquad 0 < \alpha < 1. \tag{3.11}$$

A_t is the level of technology or quality index, where $A_t = \gamma^m$, and x_t^α the amount of intermediate input used. This intermediate input is in turn produced by physical capital, K, and by unskilled labor, L, according to the Cobb-Douglas technology

$$x_t = K_t^\beta L_t^{1-\beta} \qquad 0 < \beta < 1. \tag{3.12}$$

What we have in fact are two types of capital: one which is not subject to technological improvements, K, and another whose quality can be increased over time, x. The former is used in the production of the latter. Physical capital in turn is obtained from foregone consumption. That is, it is produced with the same technology as the final good. Assume that agents save a constant fraction s of output, which is invested in physical capital. The stock of unskilled labor is given and constant over time.

There is a given stock of skilled labor, or human capital, in the economy, H. Skilled workers are all employed in research. In any given period of time t there are two subperiods, 1 and 2. In subperiod 1, there is a level of technology

$A_{m,t,1} = \gamma^m$, which is available to all firms. In this period skilled workers engage in research for the next quality, γ^{m+1}, and with probability λH one of them discovers it. If so, she sells it to one producer which then becomes a monopolist during subperiod 2. At the start of period $t+1$, the patent expires and the technology is available to all producers. At this instant, researchers start searching for the next quality level (that is, no research is done in subperiod 2). If quality γ^{m+1} is not discovered or the patent not bought, all firms keep producing with technology $A_{m,t+1,1} = A_{m,t,2} = A_{m,t,1} = \gamma^m$. Physical capital accumulates according to

$$
\begin{aligned}
K_{m,t,2} - K_{m,t,1} &= sY_{t,1} & &\text{if there is no innovation,} \\
K_{m+1,t,2} - K_{m,t,1} &= sY_{t,1} - \theta K_{m,t,1} & &\text{if there is an innovation,}
\end{aligned}
\tag{3.13}
$$

where $0 < \theta < 1$. That is, whenever an innovation occurs a fraction θ of the capital stock depreciates, as the innovation for a higher quality of x renders obsolete some of the machines that were being used to produce the previous quality of x.

a. Obtain the inverse demand for intermediate goods. Given that the existing technology is common knowledge, find the wage and interest rate paid to physical capital in subperiod 1.

b. What are the wage and the rate of interest in subperiod 2 if no innovation is implemented (i.e., if the same level of technology is used)?

c. If an innovation occurs and is adopted, the monopolist in subperiod 2 has to pay labor and capital their external options. Find the profits of the monopolist. Comment on when the innovation would be introduced.

4 Growth and Unemployment

Does technical progress create or destroy jobs? More generally, is productivity growth positively or negatively correlated with unemployment in the long run? Popular views on this question are mixed. On one hand, there is the view that technical progress destroys jobs because it is primarily labor-saving.[1] On the other hand, to the extent that it enriches society as a whole, productivity growth should stimulate demand and therefore the creation of new jobs. Indeed, as shown by Pissarides (1990), an increase in productivity growth that affected all sectors and firms *uniformly* would necessarily raise aggregate employment, because firms would be induced to intensify their recruiting efforts in order to capitalize on more rapidly growing productivity.

History shows, however that technical progress does not raise productivity equally rapidly in all jobs and sectors. Instead it destroys old jobs at the same time as it creates new ones. To the extent that industrial innovations raise the job-destruction rate through automation, skill-obsolescence, and the bankruptcies associated with the process of creative destruction, there will be a *positive* long-run tradeoff between growth and unemployment.[2] Such a possibility appears to be consistent with the empirical results of Davis and Haltiwanger (1992) which show that periods of high unemployment tend to be periods of high job turnover. Productivity growth is thus essentially *re-allocative,* and the question is whether faster technical progress speeds up the destruction of old jobs by more or less than it fosters the creation of new jobs. This question will be the main focus of the present chapter, which investigates some implications of creative destruction for the relationship between growth and unemployment, first treating the growth rate as an exogenous variable when analyzing the creation and destruction of jobs by individual firms, and then endogenizing the growth rate by linking it to the innovation process.

Focusing on the determinants of the so-called natural rate of unemployment, our analysis in this chapter will deliberately ignore other, more cyclical aspects of the relationship between growth and unemployment, and those implied by the *skill-biased* nature of technical progress. These additional aspects will be taken up in Chapters 8 and 9.

4.1 Two Opposite Effects of Growth on Unemployment

As in the basic model of Chapter 2, the economy comprises a continuum of infinitely lived individuals, whom we index from 0 to 1. Each individual is

---

1. As a matter of fact, industrial history abounds with episodes (such as the "Canuts de Lyon" in the late nineteenth century) where the introduction of new technologies has resulted in protests and even revolts by incumbent employees and workers.

2. The existence of a positive long-run relationship between average rates of growth and unemployment across major industrial countries has been identified by Saint-Paul (1991), Caballero (1993), and Aghion and Howitt (1992b).

endowed with a flow of one unit of labor services and a stock of X units of a fixed production factor, say, land.

All individuals share the same linear preferences over lifetime consumption:

$$U(c) = E_0 \int_0^\infty c_t e^{-rt} dt,$$

where $r > 0$ is the subjective rate of time preference (equal to the interest rate) and c_t is the individual's current consumption flow at time t.

Production of the final good at any point in time takes place within a continuum of "production units," where each production unit consists of:

a. a plant embodying a technology of vintage t, where t is the birthdate of the plant.

b. a worker, appropriately matched with the plant.

c. a (variable) amount of land x.

We denote by C_t the output cost of constructing the plant that embodies the new technology at date[3] t.

The output flow of a production unit of vintage t at any time $s \geq t$ is given by

$$y_s = A_t \psi (x_s - a),$$

where $a > 0$ is the minimum land input representing overhead costs; ψ is a regular production function with $\psi(z) = 0$ for all $z \leq 0$ (the plant closes if it cannot cover the overhead cost a), $\psi' > 0$, $\psi'' < 0$, $\psi'(0) = +\infty$, $\psi'(+\infty) = 0$; and $A_t = A_0 e^{gt}$ is the unit's productivity parameter. While the leading-edge A_τ grows at the exogenous[4] rate g over time τ, the technology parameter A_t within a plant of vintage t remains fixed forever; that is, the plant is unable to update its technology. (Later, we shall introduce the possibility that plants can update technology.)

Along a steady-state growth path where all values, including the price of land, grow at the same rate g, production units with fixed vintages A_t will eventually become unable to cover their overhead cost in land. At this point the units will shut down, forcing their workers into unemployment. How do we determine the *finite* lifetime S of a production unit?

Let $t_0 = t + \varepsilon$ be the date at which a plant of vintage t finds an adequate worker to operate its technology. At any date $s \geq t_0$, the surplus flow generated by this plant (i.e., output minus land cost) is

$$\max_{x \geq a} \{A_t \psi(x - a) - p_s x\} = A_t \pi \left(\frac{p_s}{A_t}\right).$$

---

3. Where $C_t = C_0 e^{gt}$ in steady state.

4. In section 4.3 we endogenize g along the lines of Chapter 2.

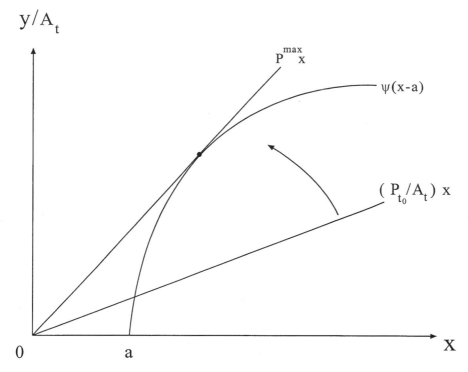

Figure 4.1

Because A_t remains constant while the price of land p_s grows at the steady-state rate g ($p_s = p_0 e^{gs}$), the unit will produce less and less as p_s grows (figure 4.1) until it becomes unprofitable at date $t_0 + S$ where the cost line $\frac{P_{t_0+S}}{A_t} x$ becomes tangent to the productivity adjusted production-function ψ. Let $P^{\max}$ denote the slope of that tangent.[5] We have:

$$P_{t_0+S}/A_t = p_0 \frac{e^{gt_0} e^{gS}}{A_0 e^{gt}} = P^{\max}.$$

Hence

$$S = \frac{\Gamma}{g},$$

---

5. Note that P^{max} depends on the production function ψ and the fixed cost a, but not on the economy's growth rate. Indeed P^{max} satisfies the zero-profit condition

$$A\psi(x - a) = A P^{\max} x, \qquad (1^*)$$

where the input x satisfies the first-order condition:

$$A\psi'(x - a) = A P^{\max} \qquad (2^*)$$

It is easy to see that P^{max} defined by (1*) and (2*) is a decreasing function of the overhead cost a, and is independent of the growth rate g.

where $\Gamma = \ln P^{\max} - \ln \frac{p_\varepsilon}{A_0}$. We may interpret Γ as the economic lifetime of a plant, measured in "technological" time, that is, the amount by which $\ln A_t$ must change before the plant yields no further surplus. In what follows we treat it as an exogenous constant.[6]

Intuitively, the faster the steady-state growth rate g, the faster the price of land grows and therefore the sooner will a production unit's surplus reach zero. Hence the inverse relationship between the growth rate and the duration of a plant S. Job destructions, however, are not sufficient to generate equilibrium unemployment. A laid-off worker could always find a new job in a newly created plant instantaneously if there were no *frictions* in the labor market. To model these frictions we follow Pissarides (1990), and assume a time-consuming matching process with a finite rate of matching $m(1, v)$ between workers and production units, where 1 is the whole labor force involved in the matching process and v denotes the mass of vacancies in the economy. The total matching rate m is an increasing function of v, but the average matching rate m/v decreases with v.

In steady-state the mass v of vacancies remains constant over time, and the equilibrium rate of unemployment is determined as follows:

a. At each date the flow of workers *into* unemployment is the frequency of production units' obsolescence ($= 1/S$) times the number of units currently producing, that is $(1 - u)$ where u is the unemployment rate or equivalently the total mass of unemployed workers (because the labor force is equal to 1).

b. At each date the flow of workers *out of* unemployment is the rate at which workers are matched with plants (i.e., the job-finding rate)[7] that is: $p(v) = \frac{m(1,v)}{1} = m(1, v)$.

Therefore, in equilibrium

$$(1 - u)1/S = p(v),$$

or equivalently, using the above expression for the lifetime of plants S,

$$u = 1 - p(v)\frac{\Gamma}{g}. \tag{U}$$

---

6. An alternative approach would be to endogenize Γ by supposing that the initial productivity-adjusted price p_ε/A_0 adjusts so as to equate the steady-state aggregate demand for land $\frac{1-u}{\Gamma}\int_0^\Gamma \widetilde{x}$ $(P^{\max}e^{\sigma-\Gamma})d\sigma$ to a fixed supply X. In Aghion and Howitt (1994) we show that this alternative approach yields exactly the same qualitative effects of g on u, as does the simpler approach followed here.

7. Although all workers are searching, only the unemployed find jobs. Implicitly we are assuming the matching process is deterministic: As soon as one job is found, a worker starts looking for a new one, but the time required to find it ($1/p(v)$) is longer than the duration of the current job (S). In section 4.5 we consider stochastic matching.

This *unemployment equation* implies a *direct creative destruction effect of growth on unemployment*: holding the mass of vacancies v constant, an increased growth rate directly raises the job-destruction rate g / Γ, thereby increasing the unemployment rate.

In addition to the direct effect that works through the job-destruction rate, there is an indirect affect working through the job-creation rate $p(v)$. In order to analyze this indirect effect we introduce a free-entry condition to determine the equilibrium mass of vacancies v; that is, we assume that the cost and benefit of creating a new production unit are equal.

Let β denote the constant fraction of surplus that the plant's owner can bargain for, and let $1/q(v) = \frac{v}{m(1,v)}$ denote the amount of time a new plant must spend before finding an adequate worker. We have, after dividing both the cost and benefit sides by the productivity parameter A_t,[8]

$$C_0 = \beta e^{-r/q(v)} \int_0^{\Gamma/g} e^{-rs} \pi_s ds, \quad \text{where } \pi_s = \pi(P^{\max} e^{gs-\Gamma}), \tag{FE}$$

(we use the fact that $p_{t_0+s}/A_t = P^{\max} e^{gs-\Gamma}$ for all $s \leq \frac{\Gamma}{g} = S$).

An increase in growth reduces the lifetime of a production unit and also induces a faster decline of profits during this lifetime, because the price of land also grows at a faster rate. According to (FE), the implied reduction in the benefit to creating a production unit causes vacancies to fall until the free entry condition is restored, through a reduction in the waiting time $1/q(v)$. This *indirect creative destruction effect* reinforces the direct creative destruction effect pointed out above by reducing the job-creation rate $p(v)$.

So far we have an unambiguously positive overall effect of growth on unemployment. Pissarides (1990), however, found a *negative* effect, namely a *capitalization effect*, whereby an increase in growth raises the rate at which the returns from creating a plant (or a firm) will grow and hence increases the capitalized value of those returns, thereby encouraging more entry by new plants and therefore more job creation. In short, the creation of new jobs should be fostered by productivity growth because "with higher productivity, the demand for labor at given wages will be higher" (Mortensen and Pissarides 1995). Now, why did we not get any capitalization effect in our analysis above?

The explanation is simple: it lies in the assumption that jobs are created by production units that cannot adapt to technological progress and thus cannot take advantage of productivity growth. However, if we introduce the possibility that plants can *upgrade* their technology with positive probability, the *capitalization effect* will reappear. Suppose, for example, that before

---

8. The term $e^{-\frac{r}{q(v)}}$ reflects the fact that it takes the amount of time $\frac{1}{q(v)}$, discounted at rate r, before the new plant finds an adequate worker to start operating.

becoming obsolete (say, when reaching age $\delta < S$), production units can costlessly adapt to the newest technology with probability $\overline{p} \in (0, 1)$. The above free-entry condition will then become:

$$C_0 = \beta e^{-r/q(v)} \left[\int_0^\delta Y(s)ds + (1 - \overline{p}) \int_\delta^S Y(s)ds \right.$$

$$+ \overline{p} \cdot e^{-(r-g)\delta} \left(\int_0^\delta Y(s)ds + (1 - \overline{p}) \int_\delta^S Y(S)ds \right)$$

$$+ \overline{p}^2 \cdot e^{-2(r-g)\delta} \left(\int_0^\delta Y(s)ds + (1 - \overline{p}) \int_\delta^S Y(S)ds \right)$$

$$\left. + \cdots \right]$$

where $Y(s) = e^{-rs} \cdot \pi_s$, or equivalently:

$$C_0 = \frac{\beta e^{-r/q(v)} \left[\int_0^\delta Y(s)ds + (1 - \overline{p}) \int_\delta^{\Gamma/g} Y(s)ds \right]}{1 - \overline{p}e^{-(r-g)\delta}} \tag{4.1}$$

Although an increase in growth reduces the numerator of (4.1), which again reflects the *indirect creative destruction* effect of growth on unemployment, the same increase in growth also reduces the denominator of (4.1), which in turn acts positively on the equilibrium rate of vacancy creation; that is, by reducing the net discount rate $(r - g)$ at which production units capitalize the expected income from future upgradings, an increase in growth encourages the entry of new units and therefore the creation of new jobs. This *capitalization effect* thus works in the direction of increasing the equilibrium level of vacancies v and hence decreasing unemployment.

Whether the capitalization or the creative destruction effects dominate will depend on the parameters of the model. In particular one can show[9] that $\frac{du}{dg}$ remains strictly positive when $p'(v)$ is small (the direct creative destruction effect dominates the indirect effects working through v) but $\frac{du}{dg}$ becomes strictly negative for $p'(v)$ large, g sufficiently close to r, and $\overline{p}$ sufficiently close to 1 (the capitalization effect dominates in this case).

The capitalization effect allows for the possibility that growth be negatively correlated with unemployment, but it does not capture the popular view stated at the beginning of this chapter, namely the idea that productivity growth can *stimulate* the creation of new jobs *through stimulating demand*. One simple

9. See Aghion and Howitt (1992b) for a similar analysis.

way to "account" for demand effects in the above model is by introducing "complementarities" across firms or sectors.

More specifically, we shall see in the next section that low substitutability across sectors may result in reversing the indirect creative destruction effect and thereby introducing the possibility of a *negative* correlation between growth and unemployment *even in the absence of a capitalization effect.*

4.2   The Effect of Intersector Complementarities*

Implicit in the previous section was the assumption that the goods produced by the various sectors of the economy were *perfect substitutes*, so that the price of each good would equal unity.[10] In this section, we briefly investigate the implications for the equilibrium rate of unemployment of reducing the degree of substitutability between goods of different vintages.

We extend the previous model by assuming that final output (or consumption) is produced from a continuum of distinct (and imperfectly substitutable) intermediate inputs of different vintages.

Thus, final output at date t is given by the production function

$$y_t = \left(\int_0^1 (A_{jt} Q_{jt})^\alpha d_j \right)^{1/\alpha}, \quad 0 < \alpha < 1, \tag{4.2}$$

where Qjt is the flow output of intermediate good j and A_{jt} the productivity parameter that measures the quality of intermediate good j. (For convenience, we label intermediate goods in increasing order of age.[11]) The parameter α is a measure of the degree of substitutability; the previous section assumed implicitly that $\alpha = 1$.

In a steady state the age of intermediate inputs is uniformly distributed over the internal $[\varepsilon, \varepsilon + S]$, where $\varepsilon \equiv 1/q(v)$. We can thus rewrite equation (4.2) as

$$y_t = \left[\int_\varepsilon^{\varepsilon+S} \left(A_{t-s} Q_{t-s} \right)^\alpha \frac{1}{S} ds \right]^{1/\alpha}, \tag{4.3}$$

where $A_{t-s} = e^{g(t-s)}$, $\frac{1}{S}$ is the uniform density of goods across ages in steady-state, and Q_{t-s} is the flow output of any intermediate good of age s at date[12] t.

---

10. The reason why older plants could still coexist with new plants is the assumed capacity constraint of plants, which prevents each of them from hiring more than one worker.

11. This means that the label attached to any good will rise continuously over time, from 0 to 1. The change of labels will not alter the form of the production function, because the correspondence between A's and Q's remains unchanged and the function is symmetrical.

12. We assume that all the plants producing the same good are constructed at the same time, so that the age of a good is the age of the technology used by all plants producing that good.

The modification of the demand structure introduced by having less than perfect substitutability among intermediate goods will clearly *not* affect the unemployment equation (U) and therefore the direct creative destruction effect. It will, however, affect the free-entry equation (FE) and therefore the indirect effect of growth on unemployment, because now growth will generate a continual increase in demand for each existing firm's output as well as a continual increase in the cost of operating a plant. Thus with enough complementarity, as we shall see, the indirect effect of growth on unemployment can become negative.

The free-entry condition can be written as

$$C_0 = \beta \int_\varepsilon^{\varepsilon+S} e^{-rs} \pi_s ds, \qquad (FE1)$$

where C_0 is the (productivity-adjusted) cost of creating a vacancy, and π_s is the productivity-adjusted surplus of an intermediate plant of age s. That is, with final output as the numeraire:

$$\pi_s = \frac{1}{A_{t-s}}(R_{t,s} - p_t a), \qquad (4.4)$$

where $R_{t,s}$ is the flow-revenue of an intermediate plant of age s at time t and $p_t \cdot a = p_\varepsilon e^{g(t-\varepsilon)}a$ is the overhead flow cost in land, also expressed in units of final output. Now for simplicity, let the technology of a plant be defined by:

$$\psi(x - a) = \begin{cases} 0 & \text{if } x < a \\ 1 & \text{if } x \geq a \end{cases} \qquad (4.5)$$

Then, $R_{t,s}$ will simply be equal to the price of intermediate good of age s at date t, $P_{t,s}$,[13] where $P_{t,s}$ is itself equal to the marginal product of the corresponding intermediate input in producing final output. (As always, we assume that the final output sector is competitive.) Therefore, from (4.2):

$$P_{t,s} = \frac{\partial y_t}{\partial Q_{jt}} = A_{t-s}^\alpha \left(\frac{Q_{t-s}}{y_t}\right)^{\alpha-1} ; s = t - jS - \varepsilon. \qquad (4.6)$$

In the perfect substitutability case analyzed in the previous section, we had: $\alpha = 1$, so that $P_{t-s} = A_{t-s}$ and therefore: $\pi_s = 1 - p_0 a e^{gs}$. The fact that in this case the surplus π_s decreases more rapidly with age s as the growth rate increases is simply due to the fact that growth raises the overhead cost in land without raising the demand for intermediate input s (indeed, when $\alpha = 1$, this intermediate input is perfectly substituted for by new inputs). This, together

---

13. That is, $R_{t,s} = P_{t,s} \times 1 = P_{t,s}$.

with the fact that the life-time of plants $S = \frac{\Gamma}{g}$ was also a decreasing function of the growth rate g, would in turn generate an unambiguously negative correlation between growth and vacancy creation (the term $\int_{\varepsilon}^{\varepsilon+S} e^{-rs}\pi_s ds$ in the RHS of (FE1) is unambiguously decreasing in g in the perfect substitutability case). This negative correlation was referred to above as the *indirect creative destruction effect*.

Now, what happens when intermediate inputs are less than perfect substitutes, in other words, when $\alpha < 1$? First, note that in steady state there are $(1 - u)$ plants producing any of the intermediate goods, where u is the unemployment rate.[14] Thus:

$$Q_{t-s} \equiv 1 - u \quad \text{for all } s.$$

Substituting for Q_{t-s} in equation (4.3), and using the fact that $A_{t-s} = e^{g(t-s)}$, we obtain the following simple expression for aggregate final output:[15]

$$y_t = e^{g(t-\varepsilon)}(1 - u)\underbrace{\left(\frac{1 - e^{-\alpha\Gamma}}{\alpha\Gamma}\right)^{\frac{1}{\alpha}}}_{\text{constant}}.$$

Substituting in turn for y_t in equation (4.6) yields

$$P_{t,s} = e^{g(t-\alpha s-(1-\alpha)\varepsilon)}\left(\frac{1 - e^{-\alpha\Gamma}}{\alpha\Gamma}\right)^{\frac{1-\alpha}{\alpha}}.$$

It follows that the revenue flow of a plant, which in the perfect substitutability case was constant equal to 1 (in productivity-adjusted terms), now *increases* over time at a rate proportional to the growth rate g when $\alpha < 1$, that is:

$$\frac{P_{t,s}}{A_{t-s}} = e^{g(1-\alpha)(s-\varepsilon)}\left(\frac{1 - e^{-\alpha\Gamma}}{\alpha\Gamma}\right)^{\frac{1-\alpha}{\alpha}}.$$

The intuition is straightforward: due to the *imperfect* substitutability between intermediate inputs, growth in the rest of the economy raises the output price of any intermediate plant.

---

14. Indeed, we know that each active intermediate plant employs *one worker* and produces *one unit* of productivity-adjusted (intermediate) output. Furthermore, each of the plants producing the same intermediate good was created at the same time, so they all have the same productivity parameter.

15. To derive this equation, substitute for $Q_{t-s} = 1 - u$ in equation (4.3) and then calculate the integral in (4.3), taking into account that $\Gamma = gS$.

Substituting for $P_{t,s}$ in equation (4.4), we finally obtain the following expression for the productivity-adjusted surplus of an intermediate plant of age s:

$$
\pi_s = \frac{P_{t,s}}{A_{t-s}} - e^{g(s-\varepsilon)} a p_\varepsilon
$$

$$
= e^{g(1-\alpha)(s-\varepsilon)} \left(\frac{1 - e^{-\alpha\Gamma}}{\alpha\Gamma} \right)^{\frac{1-\alpha}{\alpha}} - e^{g(s-\varepsilon)} a p_\varepsilon.
$$

(4.7)

As indicated above, both cost *and revenue* (in productivity-adjusted terms) will rise as an intermediate plant ages, because when intermediate inputs are imperfect substitutes, growth in the rest of the economy will raise an intermediate plant's (productivity-adjusted) output price.

As a result, the overall effect of an increase in g on the capitalized value of a plant (that is, on the value of creating a new vacancy), will cease to be automatically negative, in contrast to the perfect substitutability case. Let

$$
F(g, \alpha) = \int_0^{\Gamma/g} e^{-rs} \pi_{\varepsilon+s} ds
$$

denote the capitalized value of a plant.

Because growth raises both cost and *revenue*, the capitalized value of a plant $F(g, \alpha)$ (and therefore the RHS of the free-entry condition (FE1) for any given v) may *increase* with g if there is enough intersectoral complementarity (if α is small enough). This is illustrated by the numerical example in figure 4.2, where[16] we fixed $p_\varepsilon a = \frac{1}{8}$, and $r = .05$. When α is equal to .6 or greater, the value $F(g, \alpha)$ decreases monotonically with growth, and therefore higher growth, discourages the creation of new vacancies as in the perfect substitutability case $\alpha = 1$. When α becomes smaller there is a range of initial growth rates over which the value $F(g, \alpha)$ increases with growth. When α has fallen to .01 that range extends up to an interval $[0, \overline{g}]$ where $\overline{g}$ is almost equal to the rate of interest.

Thus, when intermediate inputs become sufficiently "complementary" or "imperfectly substitutable," the indirect effect of growth will always be to *increase* the rate of job creation, that is to encourage vacancy creation. If $p'(v)$ is large enough this indirect effect will dominate the direct creative

---

16. The technological lifetime $\Gamma = gS$ is simply derived from the fact that $\pi_{\varepsilon+S} = 0$, where π_s is given by equation (4.7). That is,

$$
e^{-\alpha\Gamma} \left(\frac{1 - e^{-\alpha\Gamma}}{\alpha\Gamma} \right)^{\frac{1-\alpha}{\alpha}} = p_\varepsilon a,
$$

the solution to which can be expressed as $\Gamma(\alpha)$, but is independent of g.

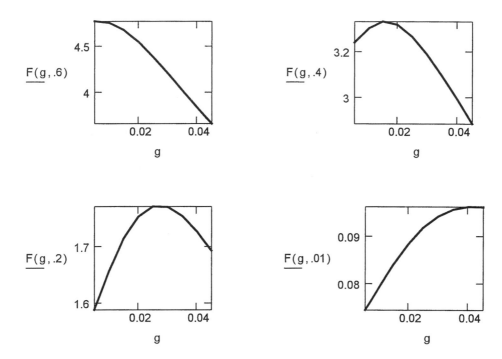

Figure 4.2
$F(g, \alpha)$ is the capitalized value of a plant. When $\alpha = .6$ the value decreases monotonically with growth. When α is smaller there is a range over which the value increases with growth. When α has fallen to .01 that range extends up to a growth rate almost equal to the rate of interest.

destruction effect, so that the overall effect of increased growth will be to reduce unemployment, even in the absence of any capitalization effect!

4.3   Innovation-Driven Growth

In this section we come closer to the basic model of Chapter 2 by assuming that growth is the result of innovations. There is a continuum of *research facilities* in the economy, whose total mass will be endogenously determined in steady-state equilibrium. Like individuals, these research facilities are infinitely lived. We denote by D_t the sunk cost of setting up a research facility at date t.[17] Once this research cost has been sunk, each research facility generates a stream of *innovations* or new technological vintages, according to a Poisson process with parameter λ.[18] Each technological vintage is then sold by the research facility

17. We assume that D_t and other fixed costs all grow at the economy-wide growth rate in order to guarantee the existence of a steady-state equilibrium: that is, $D_t = d\, e^{gt}$, where g is the growth rate of the economy.

18. The innovation technology is thus similar to that postulated in Aghion and Howitt (1992a), except for the fact that there the R&D cost is a flow cost, not a sunk cost.

to a production unit, which implements the innovation at a zero cost. The price the production unit pays for the innovation is equal to the net present value of profits from that innovation, namely the RHS of (FE).

Thus, although the unemployment equation remains the same as in section 4.1, the free-entry condition (FE) for production units has to be replaced by a free-entry condition for research, which plays a similar role to the arbitrage equation (A) in the previous chapters (whereas the unemployment equation (U) replaces the labor-market clearing equation (L)).

Consider the entry decision of a research facility at any date t. The fixed cost of entry at that date can be written as $D_t = dA_t$. The expected net benefit of entry, which also grows at the steady rate g, can be expressed as

$$W_t = WA_t = E_{\theta \geq 0}\left[\left(V_{t+\theta} + W_{t+\theta}\right) e^{-r\theta}\right] \tag{4.8}$$

where $t + \theta$ is the arrival date of the first innovation experienced by the firm that enters at date t and $V_{t+\theta} = V.A_{t+\theta}$ is the present value (as of time $t + \theta$) of the profit stream accruing from that innovation. We then have, after eliminating A_t from both sides of (4.8),

$$W = (V + W)E_{\theta \geq 0}(e^{-(r-g)\theta})$$

$$= (V + W) \int_0^\infty e^{-(r-g)\theta} \lambda e^{-\lambda \theta} d\theta$$

$$= \frac{\lambda}{\lambda + r - g}(V + W).$$

That is,

$$W = \frac{\lambda V}{r - g}.$$

The expected benefit takes this form because a firm's innovations occur at the Poisson rate λ and because in a steady state V_t grows at the economy-wide growth rate g. Hence $\lambda.V_t$ is the instantaneous expected income from having created a research facility, and $r - g$ is the net discount rate used in capitalizing that expected income. So, we have the free-entry condition

$$d = \lambda V/(r - g), \tag{4.9}$$

where

$$V = \text{RHS of (FE)}$$

$$= \beta e^{-r/q(v)} \int_0^{\Gamma/g} e^{-rs} \pi_s ds = \beta e^{-r/q(v)} \int_0^{\Gamma/g} e^{-rs} \pi (P^{\max} e^{gs-\Gamma}) \, ds$$

is the (normalized) value of an innovation, that is of the stream of profits this innovation generates until the corresponding production unit becomes obsolete. (We again assume that an individual production unit cannot adapt to new technologies.) Hence the free-entry condition becomes

$$d = \frac{\lambda}{r - g} e^{-r/q(v)} \left\{ \beta \int_0^{\Gamma/g} e^{-rs} \pi (P^{\max} e^{gs - \Gamma}) ds \right\}. \qquad \text{(FE}')$$

Note that even though individual production units have been assumed *not* to be adaptable to further technological progress, the mere fact that research units are *forward-looking* (that is, evaluate the whole stream of innovations they can potentially generate when deciding whether or not to enter) is enough to reintroduce a *capitalization effect;* an increase in growth will reduce the net discount rate $(r - g)$ at which research facilities capitalize their expected income, thereby encouraging the entry of research facilities. More research facilities means more future production units to create jobs. From the unemployment and above free-entry equations, we could (again) show that the capitalization effect of an exogenous increase in g dominates when g is close to r and that the creative destruction effects dominate when d or $p'(v)$ are sufficiently small (see Aghion and Howitt 1992b).

However, growth is now endogenous and if λ denotes the arrival rate of innovations in each research facility, γ is the size of technological improvements, and f is the total number of research facilities firms in the economy, we then have, as in the spillovers equation (S) in Chapter 3:

$$g = \lambda f \ln \gamma. \qquad (4.10)$$

In steady-state equilibrium, the flow of new plants must equal the flow of old plants that become obsolete. The former is λf; the latter is the same as the flow of workers into unemployment, because each plant employs one worker only, namely $(1 - u)g/\Gamma$. We thus have

$$\lambda f = (1 - u)g/\Gamma. \qquad (4.11)$$

Now, using the unemployment equation (U) we get from (4.10) and (4.11)

$$g = p(v) \ln \gamma. \qquad (4.12)$$

We can use the above "growth" equation (4.12) and the free-entry condition (FE') in order to solve for v and g as shown in figure 4.3. Note that, as Figure 4.3 shows, there may exist multiple equilibria, one where a low rate of vacancy creation corresponds to a small number of research facilities operating and therefore to a low rate of productivity growth,[19] and one where a high rate

---

19. Figure 4.3 suggests, however, that the high growth/high vacancy equilibrium will be unstable.

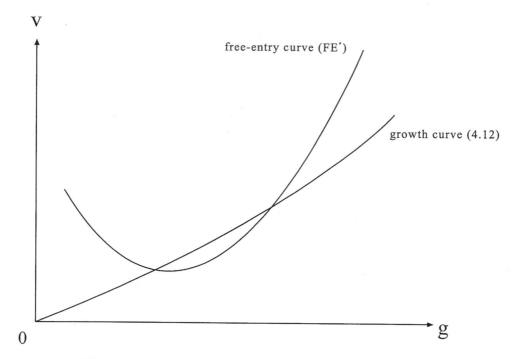

Figure 4.3

of vacancy creation will similarly correspond to a higher rate of productivity growth.

How is unemployment affected by the two sources of growth, namely the frequency and size of innovations? It turns out that in spite of the possible multiplicity of equilibria in the (g, v) space, the effects of these two components of growth on unemployment is unambiguous. Consider first the effect of an increase in the *frequency* parameter λ. In the absence of any other source of growth than innovations, the effect of such increase on unemployment will be totally neutral.[20] Indeed, using (4.10) and (4.11), we have

$$1 = (1 - u)\frac{\ln \gamma}{\Gamma}. \tag{4.13}$$

Hence $\frac{du}{d\lambda} = 0$. However, an increase in the size of innovation will (again from equation (4.13)) increase unemployment.

To summarize, when the only source of growth is the innovation process generated by firms economy-wide, and the corresponding innovation technol-

---

20. If growth depended partly on innovations but partly also on an exogenous invention process, that is, $g = g_0 + \lambda f \ln \gamma$, then this neutrality result clearly would no longer hold.

ogy exhibits constant returns to scale, increasing the frequency of innovations has no effect on unemployment because it increases *both* the flow of new plants and the flow of old plants which become obsolete *in the same proportions.* Conversely, an increase in the size of innovations speeds up the obsolescence process without affecting the job creation rate directly. We then have another case where creative destruction dominates.

4.4   Learning by Doing*

Keeping the same framework as in section 4.3, we now introduce learning-by-doing as a primary source of growth. Learning by doing, that is, the steady improvement of productivity engendered by the experience of producing, will end up introducing a feedback from unemployment to growth. To see this, assume for simplicity that the effects of learning by doing are completely external to each firm. Specifically, assume that the productivity of each unit grows at the rate $b(1 - u)$, and that the "leading technology parameter" A_t grows at a rate that depends on this learning by doing:

$$g = g_0 + b(1 - u), \quad \text{where } g_0, b, b' > 0.$$

The main difference introduced in the model by this feedback of unemployment on growth is through the free-entry condition, which becomes[21]

$$d = \frac{\lambda e^{-r/q(v)}}{r - g_0 - b(1 - u)} \left\{ \int_0^{\Gamma/g_0} e^{-rs + b(1-u)s} \cdot \beta\pi \left[P^{\max} e^{g_0 s - \Gamma} \right] ds \right\} \quad \text{(FE'')}$$

---

21. To derive (FE'') let A_{t, t_0+s} denote the productivity parameter of a production unit of age s that was formed at date t_0 (using a machine of vintage t). The flow of surplus to the match is

$$A_{t, t_0+s} \pi(p_{t_0+s}/A_{t, t_0+s}). \tag{3*}$$

Because the unit's productivity parameter starts off as the leading technology as of the date of innovation and grows from t_0 to $t_0 + S$ at the constant proportional rate $b(1 - u)$, we have

$$A_{t, t_0+s} = A_t e^{b(1-u)s}; s \in [0, S]. \tag{4*}$$

Because, in addition, the price of land grows at the constant proportional rate $g = g_0 + b(1 - u)$, we have

$$p_{t_0+s}/A_{t, t_0+s} = (p_{t_0}/A_t)e^{g_0 s}; s \in [0, S]. \tag{5*}$$

As before, the match dissolves when this productivity-adjusted price reaches the shut-down value $P^{\max}$. From (3*)–(5*) and the definition of Γ, the net present value of an innovation at t becomes

$$e^{-r/q(v)} \left\{ \int_0^{\Gamma/g_0} A_t e^{b(1-u)s} e^{-rs} \beta\pi \left[P^{\max} e^{g_0 s - \Gamma} \right] ds \right\} \tag{6*}$$

Equation (FE'') follows from (6*) by the same argument as the one surrounding (FE').

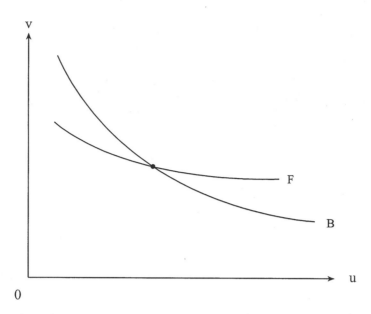

Figure 4.4

where, as before, $\Gamma = \ln P^{\max} - \ln(P\varepsilon/A_0)$, with $\varepsilon = 1/q(v)$. The replacement of g by g_0 in the integrand of (FE″) comes from the fact that a production unit's productivity-adjusted price for land now grows at rate g_0 not g. The new factor $e^{b(1-u)s}$ in the integrand appears because learning by doing causes the productivity of each match to rise at the rate $b(1-u)$, thereby enhancing the value of each innovation. (We assume that learning by doing does not enhance the productivity of an innovation until a worker is found to implement it.) The unemployment equation becomes

$$u = 1 - \Gamma p(v)/g_0, \tag{U'}$$

because the length of each match is now Γ/g_0 instead of Γ/g.

The curve labeled F in figure 4.4 corresponds to the new free-entry equation (FE″). It is downward-sloping because an increase in u will directly reduce the solution v by reducing learning by doing during each match and also by raising the net discount rate used to capitalize the returns to creating a research facility. The curve B pictures the new unemployment equation (U′) and it is also downward-sloping.

The introduction of learning by doing leads to three main conclusions. First, because learning by doing is experienced by all productive units, and hence does not by itself involve creative destruction, an increase in the growth rate that results from an exogenous change in the pace of learning by doing (i.e., a shift in the b function) will unambiguously reduce the rate of unemployment. Second, because the feedback of unemployment onto growth creates a macroeconomic complementarity of the sort that Cooper and John (1988) have analyzed, it creates a multiplier effect; thus increases in the exogenous part g_0 of growth will have the same qualitative effects (creative destruction and capitalization) as when learning by doing was absent, *but the overall effect will be quantitatively larger*. Thus, for example, if the capitalization effect dominates so that an increase in g_0 reduces unemployment, this will result in more learning by doing and therefore an even stronger capitalization effect. Third, as in the Cooper and John analysis, the macroeconomic complementarity may lead to multiple equilibria.

We now proceed to a more formal analysis of these three conclusions. First, an exogenous increase in the rate of learning by doing (a shift in the b function) will shift the modified free-entry curve F up by increasing the value of each match, and also by reducing the net discount rate, but it will not shift the modified unemployment curve B because the rate of learning by doing does not enter the unemployment curve. Thus, as figure 4.4 makes clear, unemployment will fall as long as the free entry curve is shallower than the unemployment curve.[22]

Next, an increase in the exogenous component g_0 of growth has the same ambiguous effect on unemployment as before because, unlike an exogenous increase in learning by doing, it has creative destruction effects, both direct (U') and indirect (FE''). Indeed, when creative destruction dominates, and therefore unemployment increases, then, provided again that F is shallower than B, learning by doing will amplify the increase in unemployment. Intuitively, the rise in unemployment reduces learning by doing, which feeds back through the free-entry condition to amplify the fall (or moderate the rise) in vacancies, thereby causing an even greater rise in unemployment.

Finally, it is easy to see that there can be multiple equilibria, with F intersecting B more than once. In a low-level equilibrium, high unemployment inhibits growth by slowing down learning by doing, and the slow learning keeps unemployment high by making it unprofitable to create a lot of vacancies. In the high-level equilibrium, low unemployment stimulates growth through learning by doing, and the prospect of fast learning provides the incentive for firms to create enough vacancies to keep unemployment low.

---

22. An equilibrium with the relative slopes reversed would appear unstable, because a small rise in u would reduce vacancies (on the free-entry curve) by more than it would take to keep unemployment at its now higher level (according to the unemployment curve), which suggests that the feedback to unemployment would drive it even further away from the initial equilibrium.

4.5   Stochastic Matching

In deriving the unemployment equation (U) and the free-entry equation (FE) we assumed that the matching process was deterministic, not just in the aggregate but also at the individual level. That is, *every* spell of job search lasted $1/p(v)$, not just the average spell. Likewise, *every* vacancy took $1/q(v)$ to fill, not just the average vacancy. These assumptions rendered the analysis as simple as possible. But it is important to note that they can be replaced by an assumption of stochastic matching, which is not only more familiar and more intuitively plausible but also avoids an unnecessary parameter restriction in the preceding analysis.

To be more specific, the unemployment equation as it stands makes no sense unless we add restrictions, until now implicit, guaranteeing that the deterministic length of a spell of job search $1/p(v)$ is no less than the economic lifetime of a plant S. Otherwise the equation would solve for a negative unemployment rate. In simple economic terms, if the restriction were violated then each worker, who begins a new search as soon as a new job begins, would find a job at a newer plant, which would pay more and would have a longer remaining duration, before obsolescence destroyed the current job. It would make sense for the worker to accept this alternative job—to move directly from the current job without passing through unemployment. Thus there would be idle plants in the economy, but no unemployment.

It would be more realistic to assume, however, that even if the average spell of job search were less than the economic lifetime of a plant, some workers will not be lucky enough to find a job before their current plants become obsolete. It turns out that we can take this possibility into account at the cost of a bit of additional complexity, without changing the analysis in any essential way. This section indicates how to do this by modeling search as a Poisson process at the level of individual plants and workers, as in the modern job-search literature synthesized by Pissarides (1990).[23] We depart from this literature in one important way, however, by retaining our previous assumption that all workers search, not just the unemployed. That is, no one in our analysis is forced to enter unemployment in order to find a better job.

Consider thus the following matching process. All workers experience contacts with plants at discrete points in continuous time, at a Poisson arrival rate equal to αf, where α is a parameter indicating the efficiency of the search process, and f the mass of plants. Because there is a mass 1 of workers, αf is also the aggregate flow of contacts. Not all contacts will result in a new spell of

---

23. See Mortensen and Pissarides (1995) for a similar theory of growth and unemployment based on the usual assumption that on the job search is impossible.

employment, only those whereby a plant that does not currently have a worker is contacted by a worker who is not already working at a newer plant. In such cases the worker will leave unemployment, or quit his or her current job, to start working at the newly contacted plant.

The age of plant in each contact is randomly drawn from the steady-state age distribution, which is uniform on the interval $[0, S]$. Let $C(s)$ denote the category of all workers who are employed at plants no older than s, and let $N(s)$ denote the mass of such workers. The flow into $C(s)$ is the flow of workers from outside who contact a vacant plant younger than s. The fraction of all contacts that involve such workers is $1 - N(s)$, which is the mass of workers outside $C(s)$. The fraction that involve such plants is $(sf/S - N(s))/f$, because sf/S is the mass of plants younger than s, of which $N(s)$ already have a worker. The flow into $C(s)$ is the aggregate rate of contacting multiplied by these two fractions: $\alpha(1 - N(s))(sf/S - N(S))$. The flow out is $N'(s)$—the density of employment at plants that have just reached age s. In a steady state these two flows must be equal.

Therefore $N(s)$ solves the differential equation

$$N'(s) = \alpha(1 - N(s))(\phi s - N(s)) \tag{4.14}$$

where ϕ is the density of plants within each age category: $\phi = f/S = fg/\Gamma$. The unique solution to this differential equation with the initial condition $N(0) = 0$ is

$$N(s, \phi) = 1 - \frac{e^{-\alpha\phi(s-1/\phi)^2/2}}{\alpha \int_0^s e^{-\alpha\phi(\tau-1/\phi)^2/2}d\tau + e^{-\alpha/2\phi}}. \tag{4.15}$$

Because no one works at a plant older than $S = \Gamma/g$, the unemployment equation is

$$u = 1 - N(\Gamma/g, \phi). \tag{4.16}$$

The direct creative destruction effect of growth on unemployment is the effect working through the length Γ/g of a plant's economic lifetime in equation (4.16). The effect is positive as before, because the function $N(s, \phi)$ represents employment at plants younger than s and hence is increasing in s.

The indirect effect of growth on unemployment now works through ϕ, the density of plants. This variable plays the same role as vacancies did in the preceding analysis. Specifically, when the density of plants increases, there are more contacts with plants of each age, and hence employment in each age category of plant will be higher; that is, the function N is increasing[24] in ϕ.

---

24. See the appendix to this chapter.

Thus the indirect effect will also be positive if an increase in growth results in a decrease in ϕ.

To analyze the effect of growth on density of plants, we need to specify a free-entry condition. The condition is the same as (FE) except that instead of premultiplying the present value of profits by a discount factor indicating the presence of a deterministic hiring lag, profits at age s must now be multiplied by the probability that a plant of age s will have a worker. The probability is $(\partial N(s, \phi)/\partial s)/\phi$—the density of employment at plants of age s divided by the density of plants of age s. Accordingly, we have

$$C_0 = \beta \int_0^{\Gamma/g} e^{-rs} \frac{\partial N(s, \phi)/\partial s}{\phi} \pi(P^{\max}e^{gs-\Gamma})ds. \tag{4.17}$$

An increase in growth will reduce the value of a plant, as defined by the right-hand side of (4.17). This is the usual indirect creative destruction effect that arises from a faster increase in the price of the factor needed to work with labor. If the value of a plant is decreasing in the density of plants, then this indirect effect will be in the direction of raising unemployment. For in that case (4.17) will imply that $d\phi/dg < 0$, whereas (4.16) implies that $du/d\phi < 0$. The value of a plant can be rewritten, using integration by parts, as

$$\beta \int_0^{\Gamma/g} e^{-rs} \frac{N(s, \phi)}{\phi} \left\{ r\pi(\,) - g P^{\max}e^{gs-\Gamma}\pi'(\,) \right\} ds. \tag{4.18}$$

Thus we need only show that the ratio $\frac{N(s,\phi)}{\phi}$ is decreasing in ϕ; that is, that the usual congestion effect of having a higher density of plants results in less employment per plant within each age category. This is established in the appendix to this chapter.

4.6   Summary

This chapter analyzes the relationship between growth and unemployment, first assuming that growth is exogenous and then endogenizing growth. New technology is embodied in plants which are costly to build. Unemployment is caused by workers having to move from a plant embodying old technology to one embodying new technology. Because it takes time for workers to move from one job to another, they will need to spend time between jobs. The unemployment rate is the fraction of workers who are between jobs. The rate at which workers leave unemployment is determined by an aggregate matching function, which depends positively on the number of job vacancies created by firms with a plant embodying a new technology.

If the rate of technological progress in plants is very fast, then plants will have a short lifetime and hence the proportion of workers released every period will be high. The rapid flow of workers into unemployment will cause the steady-state unemployment rate to be high, ceteris paribus. This effect is called *direct creative destruction.*

This, however, is not the only effect of faster productivity growth. The faster rate of plant obsolescence also reduces the payout period to a firm's investment in plants. By discouraging the creation of the new plants that are the source of new job openings, it thus tends to reduce the job-finding rate in the economy, leading to a higher steady-state unemployment rate. We call this effect *indirect creative destruction.*

Thus if existing plants could never take advantage of technological growth, an increase in the growth rate would unambiguously raise the unemployment rate. Suppose, however, that some technological advances are of a form that can be utilized by existing plants. Then investors will be encouraged to create new plants and vacancies by the possibility of benefiting from future technological advances. This *capitalization effect* could more than offset the two creative destruction effects, resulting in an overall decrease in unemployment when growth rises.

A similar effect obtains when there is more than one intermediate input. If steel and glass are complements, then the value of a plant producing glass will increase when there is an improvement in productivity in the steel sector, because the demand for glass will increase. Thus, when goods are strongly complementary, an increase in productivity growth (in all sectors) can reduce the rate of unemployment even in the absence of a capitalization effect.

The second part of the chapter assumes that unemployment feeds back onto the equilibrium growth rate by influencing the rate of innovation. First it sets up a model like that of Chapter 2, but in which the cost of research is a pure sunk cost rather than being paid at each point of time. As in Chapter 2, an improvement in the research technology (size or frequency) will induce a higher level of research. Increasing the frequency has no effect on unemployment because it increases *both* the flow of new job openings and the rate of obsolescence of old plants *in the same proportions.* On the other hand, an increase in the size of innovations speeds up the obsolescence process without affecting the job creation rate directly, resulting in a net increase in unemployment.

The chapter also studies the interaction between unemployment and the rate of learning by doing by manufacturing workers. Because learning by doing is experienced by all productive units, and hence does not by itself involve creative destruction, an increase in the growth rate that results from an exogenous change in the pace of learning by doing will unambiguously reduce unemployment. The feedback of unemployment onto growth creates a macroeconomic complementarity of the sort that Cooper and John (1988) have analyzed; thus it creates a multiplier effect, and also the possibility of multiple equilibria.

Finally, the chapter shows how the analysis can be generalized to allow for a matching technology that is stochastic at the individual level, as is usually assumed in search theory, but without the usual assumption that workers can not search on the job.

Appendix: Some Details of Stochastic Matching

This appendix shows that the function $N(s, \phi)$ defined in the last section above is increasing in ϕ, and that $N(s, \phi)/\phi$ is decreasing in ϕ. We invoke the following elementary proposition:

Proposition A1   Suppose the differential equation: $\dot{y} = f(y, s)$ has a solution $Y(s)$ such that $Y(0) = 0$ and $Y(s) > 0$ for all $s > 0$ in a neighborhood of 0. Suppose that f is continuous and $f(0, s) > 0$ for all $s > 0$. Then $Y(s) > 0$ for all $s > 0$.

Consider the function $Y(s) \equiv N_2(s, \phi)$ (where the subscript 2 denotes the partial derivative with respect to the 2nd argument). Differentiation of (4.14) with respect to ϕ shows that $Y(s)$ solves

$$\dot{y} = f(y, s) \equiv \alpha \left\{ (1 - N(s, \phi))s - y(1 + s\phi - 2N(s, \phi)) \right\}. \tag{4.19}$$

Because $N(0, .) \equiv 0$, therefore $Y(0) \equiv N_2(0, \phi) = 0$. From this and (4.19), $\dot{Y}(0) = 0$ and $\ddot{Y}(0) = \alpha > 0$. Also, $f(0, s) = \alpha[1 - N(s, \phi)]s > 0$ for all $s > 0$, by inspection of (4.15). Thus Y and f satisfy the premises of Proposition A1. Accordingly $N_2(s, \phi) \equiv Y(s) > 0$ for all $s > 0$, which establishes our first desired result.

Next redefine $Y(s)$ as $\phi s - N(s, \phi)$. According to (4.14), Y solves

$$\dot{y} = f(y, s) \equiv \phi - \alpha(1 - N(s, \phi))y.$$

Because this combination of Y and f also satisfy the premises of Proposition A1,

$$\phi s - N(s, \phi) > 0 \quad \text{for all } s > 0. \tag{4.20}$$

From this, (4.14) and the fact, already noted, that $1 - N(s, \phi) > 0$ for all $s > 0$, we have

$$N(s, \phi) > 0 \quad \text{for all } s > 0. \tag{4.21}$$

Define $x(s, \phi) \equiv N(s, \phi)/\phi$. Dividing (4.14) by ϕ yields

$$x_1(s, \phi) = \alpha(1 - \phi x(s, \phi))(s - x(s, \phi)). \tag{4.22}$$

Differentiation of (4.22) with respect to ϕ yields

$$x_{12}(s, \phi) = -\alpha \left\{ x(s, \phi) \left[s - x(s, \phi) \right] + x_2(s, \phi) \left[1 + s\phi - 2\phi x(s, \phi) \right] \right\}.$$

Because $x(0, \phi) = 0$, we have $x_1(0, \phi) = 0$, $x_2(0, \phi) = 0$ and $x_{12}(0, \phi) = 0$. Repeated differentiation with respect to s yields: $x_{112}(0, \phi) = 0$, $x_{1112}(0, \phi) = 0$ and $x_{11112}(0, \phi) = -3\alpha x_{11}(0, \phi) = -3\alpha^2 < 0$. Therefore $x_{12}(s, \phi) < 0$ and $x_2(s, \phi) < 0$, for all $s > 0$ in a neighborhood of 0.

It follows that the function $Y(s) \equiv -x_2(s, \phi)$ solves

$$\dot{y} = f(y, s) \equiv \alpha \left\{ x(s, \phi) \left[s - x(s, \phi) \right] - y \left[1 + s\phi - 2\phi x(s, \phi) \right] \right\},$$

with $Y(0) = 0$ and $Y(s) > 0$ for all $s > 0$ in a neighborhood of 0. Also, $f(0, s) = \alpha x(s, \phi)[s - x(s, \phi)] > 0$ for all $s > 0$, by (4.20), (4.21) and the definition of $x(\ )$. Thus Y and f as defined in this paragraph satisfy the premises of Proposition A1. Hence the conclusion of Proposition A1 establishes that $x(s, \phi)$ is decreasing in ϕ for all $s > 0$.

Problems

Difficulty of Problems:

No star: normal

One star: difficult

Two stars: very difficult

1. First elementary look (based on Blanchard et al. 1996)

This problem takes a first elementary look at the relationship between growth and unemployment. Consider the following identity:

$$\text{employment} = \frac{\text{output}}{\text{productivity}}, \tag{4.23}$$

which holds both at the firm-wide and the economy-wide level.

a. Discuss under which conditions a rise in productivity reduces employment.

b. Consider identity (4.23) at the firm level. Assume a monopolist faces an inverse demand function $p(x) = x^{-(1-\alpha)}$ with $0 < \alpha < 1$, where x is the firm's output level. Further this monopolist's constant marginal labor cost of production equals δ. Find the firm's profit maximizing employment level as a function of δ. What is the effect on employment of a labor saving innovation (in the sense that δ is reduced)? What is the intuition for this result?

c. Does this result hold at the economy-wide level as well?

d. In the light of this, which features of the model in the text cause a negative relation between growth and employment?

2. Search and matching with high implementation costs (based on Mortensen and Pissarides 1995)

Problems 2 and 3 compare the different relations between growth and unemployment if existing firms can and cannot implement a new technology. The model here is a simplified version of the one used in the text. This problem shows that for industries where firms cannot update their technology, there is a positive correlation between growth and unemployment. However, if firms can update their technology continuously, there is a negative correlation between growth and unemployment, as shown in the next problem. The conclusion is that because implementation costs vary from industry to industry, there is no reason to expect a clear-cut relation in aggregate data.

A newly created firm posts a vacancy. Once the vacancy is matched with a worker, the firm can produce x units of output. If the match occurs at time τ, the firm's technology is such that consumers are willing to pay $p(\tau)$ for its output, with $p(0) = 1$.

Assume that at time t each worker who has a job earns the same wage in this economy: $w(t) = w_0 p(t)$. Hence profits at time t of a firm that started to produce at time τ equal $p(\tau)x - w_0 p(t)$. Further, the cost of posting a vacancy at time t equals $p(t)c$ and the cost of creating a new job at time t equals $p(t)K$.

The labor market is characterized by a search and matching process. Let u denote the number of unemployed workers, and normalize total inelastic labor supply at 1. The number of vacancies is denoted by v. The flow rate of matches formed equals $m(v, u)$, where $m(., .)$ is homogenous of degree 1 in its two arguments, is continuous, bounded and differentiable with $m(v, u)/v$ decreasing in v and $m(v, u)/u$ decreasing in u. Finally, let $\theta = v/u$ denote the tightness of the labor market.

a. Assume that all unemployed workers and unfilled vacancies are symmetric with respect to the matching process. Show that the Poisson arrival rate of a job for someone who is unemployed equals $m(\theta, 1)$. And show that the arrival rate for a vacancy to be matched with a worker equals $m(\theta, 1)/\theta$.

b. Let $V(t)$ denote the value of a job vacancy at time t, $J(t)$ the value of a job created at time t, and r the discount rate. Explain why $V(t)$ satisfies the following Bellman equation:

$$rV(t) = \frac{m(\theta, 1)}{\theta}(J(t) - V(t) - p(t)K) - p(t)c + \dot{V}(t).$$

Further, assume that there is free entry into the job creation business. Show that the above Bellman equation implies

$$\theta c/m(\theta, 1) + K = J(t)/p(t). \tag{4.24}$$

c. Assume that existing firms cannot implement a new technology Let d denote the exogenous Poisson arrival rate of bankruptcy. Show that $J(t)$ satisfies

$$J(t) = \max_{T \geq 0} \int_0^T (p(t)x - w(t+s))e^{-(r+\delta)s}ds. \tag{4.25}$$

d. Assume the exogenous growth rate equals $\dot{p}(t)/p(t) = g$ with $g < r + \delta$. Show that (4.24) and (4.25) can now be written as

$$\theta c/m(\theta, 1) + K = J, \tag{4.26}$$

$$J(t) = Je^{gt}, \tag{4.27}$$

with

$$J = \frac{x}{r+\delta}\left(1 - e^{-(r+\delta)T^*}\right) - \frac{w_0}{r+\delta-g}\left(1 - e^{-(r+\delta-g)T^*}\right)$$

and

$$T^* = [\ln(x/w_0)]/g.$$

Draw equations (4.26) and (4.27) in (J, θ) space and show graphically the point of intersection (J^*, θ^*).

e. Show that as the growth rate g rises, θ^*, T^*, and J^* fall. What is the intuition for this?

f. Explain why job creation (JC) and job destruction (JD) satisfy the following two equations:

$$JC = m(\theta, 1)u,$$

$$JD = \delta(1 - u) + JC \cdot e^{-\delta T^*}.$$

Using the fact that in steady state $JC = JD$, derive the expression for the steady-state unemployment rate u.

g. Show that a rise in g leads unambiguously to an increase in the steady-state unemployment rate. How does the expression for steady-state unemployment show the direct and indirect creative destruction effects of growth?

3. Search and matching with zero implementation costs (based on Mortensen and Pissarides 1995)

This problem has the same framework as the previous one. However, now firms can continuously update their equipment with the latest technology at zero implementation cost.

a. Show that equation (4.26) above is unchanged: $\theta c/m(\theta, 1) + K = J$.

b. Show that equation (4.27) now becomes $J = (x - w_0)/(r + \delta - g)$.

c. Draw (4.26) and (4.27) in (J, θ) space and show graphically the point of intersection (J^*, θ^*). Show that J^* and θ^* increase with g.

d. Explain why job creation (JC) and job destruction (JD) satisfy $JC = m(\theta, 1)u$ and $JD = \delta(1 - u)$. Derive the steady state unemployment rate and how it is affected by the growth rate g. What is the intuition for this result?

⋆ 4. Form of technological progress and unemployment (based on Boone 1996a)

The idea in the next two problems is to analyze whether the market can choose a *form* of technological progress that leads to higher unemployment and lower welfare. Problem 4 analyzes the market outcome. Problem 5 compares the market outcome with the social optimum.

Consider the following two-period economy. In period 1 a firm denoted by a invests a fixed amount of resources (for example human capital) to create its product and production technology for period 2. The firm can invest to increase the quality of its product $\gamma \geq 1$ or to reduce the fixed labor cost f of production for next period. Assume the firm produces with constant marginal labor costs equal to 1. Denote the innovation possibility set by I, where $I \subseteq [1, \gamma^*] \times [0, f^*]$ is convex and compact. Then the firm chooses $(\gamma, f) \in I$ to maximize profits in period 2. The social planner would choose $(\gamma, f) \in I$ to maximize welfare in period 2.

In period 2 the demand for goods follows from the optimization problem of a representative consumer with utility function $u(x_a, x_r) = (\gamma x_a^\alpha + R x_r^\alpha)^{1/\alpha}$ with $0 < \alpha < 1$ and budget constraint $p_a x_a + p_r x_r \leq 1$ where (second period) income is normalized at 1. Good a is produced by the monopolist a described above. Good r denotes the rest of the economy, the output of which is aggregated into x_r and the size of the rest of the economy is R. For simplicity, the rest of the economy produces without fixed costs and with a constant marginal cost equal to 1. Assume industry a is small relative to the rest of the economy in the sense that $\gamma^* < R$.

From this utility function the following demand functions can be derived: $p_a(x_a) = \gamma A x_a^{-(1-\alpha)}$ and $p_r(x_r) = R A x_r^{-(1-\alpha)}$, where

$$A = \frac{1}{\left(\gamma^{\frac{1}{1-\alpha}} p_a^{\frac{-\alpha}{1-\alpha}} + R^{\frac{1}{1-\alpha}} p_r^{\frac{-\alpha}{1-\alpha}} \right)^{1-\alpha}}.$$

Assume that both sectors $(i = a, r)$ behave as if they choose x_i to solve $max_{x \geq 0}\{p_i(x)x - wx\}$, taking A as given.

a. Show that the profit maximizing outcomes for the sectors are $p_a = w/\alpha$, $x_a = (\alpha \gamma A/w)^{1/(1-\alpha)}$, $p_r = w/\alpha$ and $x_r = (\alpha R A/w)^{1/(1-a)}$. Derive the price/cost margin for firm a and explain why α can be interpreted as a measure of competition.

Define a's share in the economy as $s_a \equiv x_a/(x_a + x_r)$ and show that

$$s_a = \frac{\gamma^{1/(1-\alpha)}}{\gamma^{1/(1-\alpha)} + R^{1/(1-\alpha)}}.$$

b. Write firm a's profits as $\pi(\gamma, f) = w(1-\alpha)/\alpha(\alpha \gamma A/w)^{1/(1-a)} - wf$, and show that the marginal rate of substitution in (γ, f) space for firm a equals $mrs^P \equiv -(d\pi/df)/(d\pi/d\gamma) = \gamma w/s_a$, where mrs^P denotes the marginal rate of substitution in the laissez-faire economy. Explain the effect of a low equilibrium wage in period 2 on firm a's choice of technology $(\gamma, f) \in I$ in period 1.

The labor market in period 2 is characterized by labor union bargaining, which is modeled as $w = \theta b(1 - \lambda^d)$ with the scalar $\theta > 0$ and the function $b(\cdot) > 0$ and $b'(\cdot) < 0$. With total labor demand $\lambda^d = x_a + x_r + f$ and inelastic labor supply normalized at 1, unemployment equals $1 - \lambda^d$.

c. Why is the wage decreasing in unemployment? What is the interpretation of θ? Show that the equilibrium wage in period 2 satisfies $w = \theta b(1 - \alpha/w - f)$.

d. Show that the equilibrium unemployment rate u in period 2 satisfies $\partial u/\partial \alpha < 0$, and interpret this result using α as a measure of competition. Further show $\partial u/\partial f < 0$ and explain how firm a's choice of technological progress affects unemployment in period 2. Discuss the effects on unemployment of a labor-saving innovation that reduces f and a labor-saving innovation that reduces marginal labor costs as in problem 1 (b).

e. How does α affect firm a's choice of $(\gamma, f) \in I$ in period 1? What is the intuition for this result? What is the overall effect of monopoly power $(1 - \alpha)$ on unemployment? How does θ affect a's choice of technology $(\gamma, f) \in 1$? What is the interpretation of this result?

★ **5. Form of technological progress and unemployment: welfare analysis (based on Boone 1996a)**

The social planner takes firms' output choices and the imperfection in the labor market at time 2 as given. The social planner evaluates a choice $(\gamma, f) \in 1$ using the representative agent's utility function. Define the social-welfare function as $W = ln[u(x_a, x_r)]$, with the utility function $u(., .)$ given earlier.

a. Substituting the output levels derived in problem 4 into $u(., .)$ show that

$$W(\gamma, f) = ln(\alpha) - ln(w) + (1-\alpha)/\alpha ln(\gamma^{1/(1-\alpha)} + R^{1/(1-\alpha)}),$$

where the wage rate w satisfies $w = \theta b(1 - \alpha/w - f)$.

b. Show that the social planner's marginal rate of substitution equals $mrs^s \equiv -(dW(\gamma, f)/df)/(dW(\gamma, f)/d\gamma) = [\gamma\alpha(dw/df)/w]/s_a$.

c. To see how mrs^s and mrs^p are related, first consider the benchmark case where the labor market clears in period 2. That is, w solves $\alpha/w + f = 1$. Find mrs^s/mrs^p and give the intuition for this result.

d. Show that in the labor union bargaining case

$$\frac{dw}{df} = \frac{-b'(\cdot)}{1 + [-b'(\cdot)]\frac{\alpha}{w^2}}$$

and use this to prove that $mrs^s/mrs^p < 1$.

What does this say about the social planner's choice of (γ, f) as compared with the laissez-faire outcome? Comment on the claim that the market can choose a form of technological progress that leads to higher unemployment and lower welfare.

5 Endogenous Growth and Sustainable Development

In the 1970s, economists reacted to the challenge of OPEC and the doomsday predictions of the Club of Rome by introducing energy, natural resources, and environmental pollution into the neoclassical theory of growth. In the 1990s, they reacted to global climate change and the report of the Brundtland Commission (World Commission on Environment and Development 1987) by introducing these same considerations into the theory of endogenous growth. Although endogenous growth theory is still quite young in comparison to the mature state of neoclassical growth theory in the mid-1970s, it is also inherently more suitable for addressing the problems of sustainable development than is the neoclassical theory, because whether or not growth can be sustained is the central question to which endogenous growth theory is addressed.

The purpose of this chapter is to try to clarify some of the issues raised by sustainable development by casting them in terms of endogenous growth theory. Sections 5.1 and 5.2 show how energy, natural resources, and environmental pollution can be introduced into the theory, and how the concept of sustainable development can thereby be given greater precision. Section 5.3 then shows how different models of endogenous growth, namely the AK model of Chapter 1 and the Schumpeterian model of Chapter 2, answer the question of whether or not, or more precisely under what conditions, economic development can indeed be sustained.

Although it would be presumptuous, indeed wrong, to lay claim to a definitive analysis of sustainable development, nevertheless the chapter suggests one conclusion that is roughly consistent with historical experience in industrialized countries, namely that the chances of achieving sustainable growth depend critically on maintaining a steady flow of technological innovations. If it had not been for resource-saving innovations it is unlikely that our finite planet could have supported the expansion in material welfare that has taken place since the industrial revolution.[1] Furthermore, although serious environmental concerns remain, especially concerning the global rise in emissions of greenhouse gases and the depletion of the ozone layer, nevertheless the introduction of more environmentally friendly technologies has helped reverse the decline in air and water quality in many countries.[2] Although there is nothing in endogenous growth theory implying that these trends will necessarily sustain development into the indefinite future, nevertheless the theory does imply that with enough innovations, and the right direction of innovations, such an outcome is at least within the realm of possibility.

---

1. Barnett and Morse (1963) provide evidence that natural-resource prices have had a secular tendency to fall since the mid-nineteenth century, a trend that, as Romer and Sasaki (1986) show, could not have existed without resource-saving technological progress.

2. See, for example, the analysis of the World Bank (1992).

This extension of endogenous growth theory shows the advantage of the Schumpeterian approach and its explicit treatment of innovation as a distinct economic activity, over the more aggregated AK approach. Because the AK approach does not distinguish between innovation and capital accumulation, it cannot capture the critical role of innovation in making growth sustainable. More specifically, it turns out to be crucial for sustainability in the face of natural-resource constraints that the technology for producing knowledge is generally cleaner than that for producing physical capital.

One rather surprising result in the following is that in order for growth to be sustainable in the face of environmental pollution, the elasticity of intertemporal substitution in consumption must be less than unity. This restriction on preferences is necessary to ensure that people with rational expectations will never choose to flirt with a threshold level of environmental quality below which the environment would be subject to a catastrophic deterioration. Another surprising result is that the problem of finite, nonrenewable natural resources, which was the primary focus of the earlier neoclassical literature on growth on a finite planet, appears to be less of an obstacle to sustainable development than is the problem of environmental pollution. For in the Schumpeterian model with nonrenewable resources, growth is sustainable even without this restriction on preferences.

5.1   Optimal Growth in the AK and Schumpeterian Frameworks

We consider an economy populated by a continuum of infinitely lived individuals with lifetime utility function

$$W = \int_0^\infty e^{-\rho t} u(c) dt,$$

where $c(t)$ is the time path of consumption per head, $u(c) = \frac{c^{1-\varepsilon}-1}{1-\varepsilon}$ is the (isoelastic) instantaneous utility function with $\varepsilon > 0$, and ρ is a positive rate of time preference.

The optimal growth path is one that maximizes W subject to the constraint that consumption plus investment must equal net national product (or aggregate output)

$$\dot{K} = Y - C.$$

Aggregate production is expressed differently depending on whether we are considering an AK model, where knowledge is just another kind of capital good, or a Schumpeterian model, which specifically distinguishes technological knowledge from more tangible and conventional forms of capital.

5.1.1   The AK Model

Consider the following aggregate production technology, where K is an aggregate of different sorts of capital good and also reflects the current state of technological knowledge in the economy, and A is a positive constant:

$$Y = AK. \tag{5.1}$$

When analyzing the problem of maximizing W subject to (5.1), only two cases need be considered:

If $A < \rho$ then it will never be optimal to accumulate more capital, as the marginal product always falls short of the rate of time preference. In the long run it is optimal not only to cease growing but also to exhaust all capital. Rather than study this degenerate case, therefore, we assume from now on that $A > \rho$. Then it will be optimal to accumulate more capital indefinitely, because the marginal product will always exceed the rate of time preference. From our analysis in Chapter 1, we know that there exists a steady-state optimal growth path in which consumption, capital, and output all grow at the same rate, namely,

$$g^* = (1/\varepsilon)\,(A - \rho)\,. \tag{5.2}$$

This steady state will indeed constitute an optimal growth path provided that g^* satisfies the modified transversality condition:

$$\rho + (\varepsilon - 1)g^* > 0 \tag{5.3}$$

5.1.2   The Schumpeterian Approach

Coming back to the Schumpeterian framework developed in Chapters 2 and 3, suppose that final output is produced using labor and a continuum of different intermediate goods, according to the production function: $Y = L^{1-\alpha} \int_0^1 B(i)x(i)^\alpha di$, where each $B(i)$ is a quality parameter indicating the productivity of intermediate good i. Each intermediate good is produced according to the constant-returns production function $x(i) = K(i)/B(i)$, where $K(i)$ is the amount of capital used to produce good i. The negative effect of $B(i)$ reflects the fact that succeeding vintages of goods are increasingly capital intensive.

It is optimal to produce the same quantity of each intermediate good[3] $x(i) = x = K/B$, where the parameter B indicates the average quality $B \equiv \int_0^1 B(i)di$.

---

3. Maximizing Y subject to $\int_0^1 B(i)x(i)di = K$ yields the optimality conditions for each $x(i)$:

$\alpha B(i)L^{1-\alpha}x(i)^{\alpha-1} = \psi B(i),$

where ψ is a Lagrange multiplier. Hence $x(i) = (\psi/\alpha)^{\frac{1}{\alpha-1}} L = x$, and $x \int_0^1 B(i)di = K$.

Hence the production function can be written as[4]

$$Y = F(K, BL) \equiv K^\alpha (BL)^{1-\alpha} \tag{5.4}$$

As in Chapter 3, let B^{max} denote the maximum of all existing $B(i)$'s, which we called the leading edge technology. Each time an innovation occurs in a sector i it creates a new generation of intermediate good i with a quality parameter equal to the current value of B^{max}.

Suppose that the economy-wide frequency of innovations is proportional to the amount of R&D: ηn, where η is a positive parameter of the research technology indicating the Poisson arrival rate of innovations to a single research worker. The leading-edge technology grows over time as a result of the gradual accumulation of knowledge from innovations. Specifically, the exponential rate at which B^{max} grows is proportional to the frequency of innovations: $\frac{dB^{max}}{dt} = \sigma \eta n B^{max}$, where σ is a parameter representing the size of each innovation; that is, σ indicates the rate at which the flow of innovations pushes out the economy's technological frontier.

Under the assumption that each innovation is equally likely to occur in any sector regardless of the preexisting quality of the intermediate good in that sector, it can be shown[5] that the leading-edge parameter in the long run will be exactly proportional to the average parameter: $B^{max} = (1 + \sigma)B$. It follows that

$$\dot{B} = \sigma \eta n B \tag{5.5}$$

Now, the problem of optimal growth is that of choosing the rates of consumption and R&D at each date so as to maximize W subject to (5.4) and (5.5), and the labor constraint $L + n = 1$. The Hamiltonian is

$$u(c) + \lambda[F(K, B(1 - n)) - c] + \mu \sigma \eta B n. \tag{5.6}$$

Proceeding as in Chapter 1, one can then show the existence of an optimal steady state in which the common growth rate of consumption, tangible capital K, and intellectual capital B is

$$g^* = (1/\varepsilon)(\sigma \eta - \rho). \tag{5.7}$$

Once again, unlimited growth is sustainable, because the common rate of return $\sigma \eta$ to the two kinds of capital does not diminish as more and more capital is accumulated.

---

4. Because $\int_0^1 B(i)x(i)^\alpha di = x^\alpha \int_0^1 B(i)di = x^\alpha B = (K/B)^\alpha B$.

5. That is, by construction B/B^{max} is the mean of the distribution of relative productivities $B(i)/B^{max}$. That distribution is given by equation (3.3) of Chapter 3, with $\ln \gamma = \sigma$. The mean of this distribution is easily calculated to be $\frac{1}{1+\sigma}$.

5.2   The Notion of Sustainable Development

The Brundtland Commission defined the term *sustainable development* as "development that meets the needs of present generations without compromising the ability of future generations to meet their needs." As a general statement of intent, this definition is not without meaning. It calls for attention to intergenerational justice with respect to the use of the world's limited resources. But it is clearly too vague to use as a working definition, and leaves itself open to widely differing interpretations.

Writers like Solow (1993) have pointed out that it would make no sense to interpret sustainable development as requiring us to leave each and every resource stock in its initial situation. Americans, for example, would be much worse off if early settlers had left the forests in their aboriginal state rather than clearing the land. What this illustrates is that there are ways of substituting one kind of resource for another—in this case, of substituting cleared arable land for natural forest land.

Other writers have argued that although some substitution is possible, nevertheless each generation should leave intact the overall stock of "natural capital,"[6] for which other kinds of capital cannot be a substitute. But even this limited form of nonsubstitutability seems far from compelling when we recall that the main sorts of capital that succeeding generations have inherited from their predecessors, and that have allowed them almost invariably to enjoy a more abundant level of material welfare than their predecessors, are physical and intellectual capital. The average citizen of industrial countries at the end of the twentieth century is far richer than his or her counterpart at the end of the nineteenth century, not because we have more natural resources or because our environment is cleaner. (The first is certainly not true and the second at least debatable.) Instead, it is because we know how to produce goods and to perform services that were unthinkable a hundred years ago, and we have the equipment with which to do so. This is why life expectancy is longer, infant mortality lower, career opportunities for women more abundant, leisure time more available, travel more affordable, communication cheaper, and so forth.

Thus, although it is true that the degree of substitutability between various kinds of capital—physical, natural, intellectual—is often low and even more often hard to estimate with precision, nevertheless any realistic assessment of the demands placed on us by intergenerational equity must define those demands not in terms of moral obligations to preserve this and that but in terms of an obligation to leave an adequate capacity for material development, where that capacity is to be represented by a comprehensive measure of capital.

---

6. For example, Pearce, Barbier, and Markandya (1990).

Along the same lines, critics of neoclassical economics have also argued that environmental and ecological concerns should be taken into account in addition to the concern for economic welfare. But, as Dasgupta (1994) has argued forcefully, this dichotomy between ecology and economy is unhelpful and often misleading. For just as one kind of capital can be substituted for another, so there is a tradeoff that can be exploited between the material enjoyment of, say, manufactured commodities and the preservation of raw materials. Not to allow any fossil fuel at all to be used would be to deprive humanity of much of the material benefits that technological progress has made possible over the generations. To allow it to be used at no cost at all in order to maximize the current flow of produced goods would also be preposterous. Some tradeoff must be sought, and to analyze this tradeoff we must define welfare in a comprehensive way that recognizes some substitutability between manufactured goods and ecological or environmental concerns.

Thus "sustainable development" is development that takes into account not only the welfare of current generations but also that of future generations, where welfare is defined comprehensively, where all of the possibilities for technological substitution between different sorts of capital goods are taken into account, and where all of the constraints imposed by the finiteness of resources and by the environmental costs of production and consumption are taken into account.

As Dasgupta points out, sustainable development thus defined is almost exactly what has been analyzed for decades now in the literature on optimal growth theory—the theory that we used in the previous section. For we may reinterpret the representative infinitely lived individual as the representative "dynasty," and reinterpret consumption at each date as consumption of each generation. All that needs to be added to that framework in order to address the issue of sustainable development as defined here is some consideration of the role of exhaustible resources and the costs of environmental pollution. Indeed this is already happening with recent developments in the theory of endogenous growth.[7] The rest of this section describes in general terms the modifications that these developments have made to endogenous growth theory.

First, consider the objective function. We should take into account that people's welfare depends not only on the current flow of material consumption goods but also on the quality of the environment. Although in principle there are many dimensions to the environment, in the spirit of the present macroeconomic analysis the endogenous-growth literature represents environmental quality in terms of an aggregate indicator E. Thus the instantaneous utility

---

7. See the other surveys by Smulders (1994a), Beltratti (1995), and Gastaldo and Ragot (1996).

function that defines welfare at each date is now given by the function $u(c, E)$ of consumption and environmental quality.

We can regard E as a capital good, that is depleted over time by pollution, but that also has its own regenerative capabilities. The flow of pollution P is an increasing function $P(Y, z)$ of the level of output and the "intensity of pollution" z.

Suppose there is finite upper limit to environmental quality, a limit that would only be reached if all production were to cease indefinitely. We measure E as the difference between the actual quality and this upper limit. Thus E is constrained always to be negative. The differential equation governing the evolution of environmental quality over time takes the form

$$\dot{E} = -P(Y, z) - \theta E \tag{5.8}$$

where the parameter $\theta > 0$ represents the maximal potential rate of regeneration.

We can recognize a critical ecological threshold[8] by supposing that there is a finite lower limit below which environmental quality cannot fall without starting in motion an irreversible and cumulative deterioration entailing a prohibitive cost. This, together with the nonpositivity of E, implies that the optimal growth path must obey a constraint of the form

$$E^{\min} \leq E(t) \leq 0 \text{ for all } t. \tag{5.9}$$

If we are to address the question of sustainable development, we must also take into account the stock S of nonrenewable natural resources. The stock must remain nonnegative, and its rate of change is the negative of the flow R of resource extraction.

The flow of newly extracted resources can be used as an input to production. Likewise, the intensity of pollution can also be regarded as a factor of production, because the relaxation of environmental standards allows dirtier but more productive techniques to be used. Thus we can write the aggregate production function as[9]

$$Y = F(K, B, R, z).$$

The optimal growth path maximizes $\int_0^\infty e^{-\rho t} u(c, E) dt$ subject to the initial values of tangible and intellectual capital, environmental quality and natural

---

8. For an analysis of such thresholds, see Common and Perrings (1992).

9. Some writers (for example, Smulders 1994b and Bovenberg and Smulders 1995) allow E to enter F as an independent factor of production, as well as entering the utility function. We lose nothing essential to the analysis of optimal growth by supposing that all of the beneficial effects of E are captured in u. The distinction between utility-enhancement and productivity-enhancement matters mainly for issues of public finance, because output is considerably easier to tax than is utility.

resources, the laws of motion governing the rates of change of these state variables, the constraints that K, B and S must remain nonnegative, and the ecological threshold constraint (5.9).

The Hamiltonian of this maximization problem will have the form

$$H = u(c, E) + \lambda \dot{K} + \mu \dot{B} + \zeta \dot{E} + \xi \dot{S} \qquad (5.10)$$

and the control variables will be consumption, research, pollution intensity, and resource extraction. Along an optimal path, these controls will be set at each date so as to maximize the current Hamiltonian.

As before, the Hamiltonian is just a nonlinear utility-based version of net national product (NNP), except that this time it is a "green" NNP that takes into account the flow of environmental amenities (the interpretation of E in the utility function), and the depreciation of the environment and of the stock of natural resources. Thus the optimal growth path constantly arbitrates between the welfare of current and future generations by attaching prices to the costs and benefits associated with the environment, pollution, and natural-resource extraction. The question of whether or not growth is sustainable can be interpreted as a question of whether or not there exists an optimal growth path along which NNP grows without bound.

5.3   The Analysis of Sustainable Development

5.3.1   Environmental Pollution

Most of the papers in the recent literature deal with environmental pollution, rather than with nonrenewable natural resources. Stokey (1996), for example, analyzes pollution in terms of an AK model. Because her analysis contains what seems to us to be the most sensible specification of pollution intensity, we now proceed to describe a slightly modified version of her analysis. Later in this section we will translate this analysis into the Schumpeterian framework outlined earlier. To summarize in advance, it turns out that growth is not sustainable according to the AK approach, but that it can be in the Schumpeterian framework, even with constant returns in both types of capital taken together.

The reason for the difference of results is that the Schumpeterian approach, by making the distinction between the two kinds of capital, recognizes that the technology of innovation is relatively clean compared to the technology of producing tangible capital goods. That is, in both approaches, whenever production increases, the optimal intensity of pollution decreases, and the cost of reducing the intensity of pollution implies a reduction in the social marginal product of capital. Eventually the marginal product would fall below the rate of time preference if growth were unbounded. However, this tendency for the marginal product to fall can be offset by accumulating intellectual capital at a faster rate than tangible capital. Because intellectual capital is produced by a clean technology, pollution does not cause its marginal social product to diminish, and the fact that it is rising faster than tangible capital can exert a positive influence on the marginal product of tangible capital that just compensates for the extra pollution-control costs of having more tangible capital.

The AK Approach to Pollution

Stokey assumes that final output can be produced by a variety of known techniques, which differ in cleanliness. Let $z \in [0, 1]$ be a measure of the "dirtiness" of the existing technique. Then the flow of pollution is $P = Yz^\gamma$, where $\gamma > 0$. That is, if a technique of given cleanliness is used, then pollution is proportional to the level of production, but the use of increasingly clean techniques can reduce the pollution/output ratio. The aggregate production function is $Y = AKz$. That is, the cost of using a cleaner technique is that less output can be obtained per unit of input.

Constraints (5.8) and (5.9) together imply that the rate of pollution $AKz^{\gamma+1}$ cannot rise above the rate $-\theta E^{\min}$ indefinitely without engendering an environmental catastrophe. This implies that if capital is to grow without bound then the pollution intensity z must fall asymptotically to 0 in the long run.

The Hamiltonian of the optimal growth path is

$$H = u(c, E) + \lambda[AKz - c] - \zeta[AKz^{\gamma+1} + \theta E]$$

First-order conditions for maximizing H with respect to the two control variables c and z are

$$\partial u(c, E)/\partial c = \lambda \quad \text{and} \quad \lambda = (\gamma + 1)z^\gamma \zeta$$

The Euler equations are

$$\rho\lambda = \lambda Az - \zeta Az^{\gamma+1} + \dot{\lambda} \quad \text{and} \quad \rho\zeta = \partial u(c, E)/\partial E - \zeta\theta + \dot{\zeta}$$

Therefore

$$\frac{\dot{\lambda}}{\lambda} = \rho - \frac{\gamma}{1 + \gamma}Az \tag{5.11}$$

For simplicity, consider the special case in which the utility function u is additively separable[10] and where the utility of consumption is again given by

---

10. Michel and Rotillon (1996) discuss how sustainability depends on the nature of the utility function u. In their analysis the optimal growth path can exhibit unbounded growth if (and only if) c and E are substitutes, in the sense that the marginal utility function $\frac{\partial}{\partial c}u(c, E)$ is decreasing in E holding c fixed. In this case the continuous degradation of the environment prevents marginal utility from falling as consumption rises. Thus it is possible to have both unbounded growth in consumption and a vanishing social marginal product of capital without ever violating the Euler equation (5.11). This requires, however, that we ignore the threshold constraint (5.9), for it involves unbounded environmental decay in the long run.

a function in the isoelastic class: $\partial u(c, E)/\partial c = c^{-\varepsilon}$. It follows from this and (5.11) that consumption must grow according to

$$\frac{\dot{c}}{c} = (1/\varepsilon)\left(\frac{\gamma}{\gamma + 1}Az - \rho\right),\tag{5.12}$$

where the term $\frac{\gamma}{1+\gamma}Az$ can be interpreted as the social marginal product of capital; that is, the marginal product net of the associated pollution cost.

The growth rate cannot be positive in the long run, because as we have seen this would require z to fall asymptotically to zero, which, according to equation (5.12), would require the growth rate of consumption to fall to $-\rho/\varepsilon < 0$. That is, the cost of the increasingly clean techniques needed to avoid environmental catastrophe would eventually reduce the social marginal product of capital below the value needed to sustain growth.[11]

The Schumpeterian Approach to Pollution

Now consider what this problem looks like in a Schumpeterian framework that distinguishes between tangible and intellectual capital. Adapting the production function (5.4) to the Stokey model yields the revised production function: $Y = K^{\alpha}(BL)^{1-\alpha}z$. The evolution of intellectual capital continues to be governed by the fundamental innovation equation (5.5), so that the Hamiltonian to be maximized is

$$H = u(c, E) + \lambda[K^{\alpha}(B(1 - n))^{1-\alpha}z - c]$$
$$+ \mu\eta\sigma Bn - \zeta[K^{\alpha}(B(1 - n))^{1-\alpha}z^{\gamma+1} + \theta E].$$

First-order conditions with respect to the three control variables c, z, n can be written as

$$\partial u(c, E)/\partial c = \lambda, \quad \lambda = (\gamma + 1)z^{\gamma}\zeta \quad \text{and} \quad \eta\sigma B\mu = (1 - \alpha)\frac{\gamma}{1 + \gamma}\frac{\lambda Y}{1 - n}.$$

$$\tag{5.13}$$

The first Euler equation is

$$\frac{\dot{\lambda}}{\lambda} = \rho - \alpha\frac{Y}{K}\left[1 - \frac{\zeta}{\lambda}z^{\gamma}\right].$$

---

11. Musu (1994) and others have found that growth is sustainable in the long run in a modified AK model, but only by assuming that it is always possible to double the rate of production by doubling the stock of capital, without creating any increase in pollution, a possibility which this framework rules out.

Assume that the utility function has an additive isoelastic form.[12] Using the first-order conditions, this Euler equation can be written as

$$\frac{\dot{c}}{c} = (1/\varepsilon)\left[\alpha\frac{\gamma}{1+\gamma}\frac{Y}{K} - \rho\right] \tag{5.14}$$

The important thing to notice about equation (5.14) is that it allows K and Y to grow at the same rate in the long run without a diminishing rate of return to capital. This is because the ratio $\frac{Y}{K}$ is no longer equal to Az, which declines to zero with z, but is now equal to $(BL/K)^{1-\alpha}z$, which can remain unchanged indefinitely as long as intellectual capital B grows faster than tangible capital K, and by enough to offset the fall in z.

This is not to say that in fact sustainable growth is always guaranteed by the above assumptions, just that it is possible. Specifically, Appendix 1 shows that if conditions (5.15) through (5.17) below hold, then given any initial level of environmental quality E_0 there exists a pair of hypothetical initial values of the two capital stocks K_0, B_0 such that a balanced optimal growth path—that is, an optimal growth path with constant rates of growth in the stocks E, K, B and in the controls c, z, n—can be reached immediately from this initial position, and that consumption grows without bound along this path. The critical conditions are

$$\varepsilon - 1 > 0 \tag{5.15}$$

$$\eta\sigma - \rho > 0 \tag{5.16}$$

$$(\varepsilon - 1)(\eta\sigma - \rho) < \theta\left[\varepsilon(1 + \omega) + \frac{\varepsilon + \omega}{(1 - \alpha)\gamma}\right] \tag{5.17}$$

Condition (5.15) was found by Stokey to be necessary, in a model with exogenous technological progress, for there to exist an optimal balanced growth path with environmental quality bounded below. Otherwise, if it were not for the catastrophe threshold assumed in (5.9) (which Stokey does not assume), then it would be optimal to reduce z over time but not fast enough to avoid unlimited environmental deterioration. In effect, the marginal utility of consumption must be declining fast enough for people to choose, even in this optimal growth setting with no regard for political and free-rider constraints, to make the sacrifices in consumption needed to sustain growth indefinitely.[13]

---

12. That is, for all $c > 0$, $E < 0$: $\frac{\partial}{\partial c}u(c, E) = c^{-\varepsilon}$ and $\frac{\partial}{\partial E}u(c, E) = (-E)^\omega$ for parameters ε, $\omega > 0$.

13. Note that (5.15) guarantees that the transversality condition will be satisfied.

Condition (5.16) is a familiar condition in Schumpeterian growth models that makes the research technology productive enough to avoid a corner solution with no research, no innovations, and no growth. Condition (5.17) is needed to avoid such strong growth relative to the regenerative capacity of the environment that environmental quality falls below the catastrophe threshold.

Thus it appears that unlimited growth can indeed be sustained, but it is not guaranteed by the usual sorts of assumptions that are made in endogenous growth theory. The assumption that the elasticity of marginal utility of consumption be greater than unity seems particularly strong, in as much as it is known to imply odd behavior in the context of various macroeconomic models.[14]

5.3.2   Nonrenewable Natural Resources

The environment can be considered a renewable natural resource because of its regenerative capacity. We could thus reinterpret the earlier analysis as dealing with the optimal management of such resources as forests or fisheries. Many resources, however, are clearly not renewable, such as fossil fuels and metals. Although the ecologically motivated endogenous growth theory of the 1990s has been concerned almost exclusively with the environment, the same techniques as those deployed above can be used to treat the issue of nonrenewable resources that was the primary concern of the ecologically motivated exogenous growth theory of the 1970s.

The following analysis shows that qualitatively similar results hold for the two cases; that is, the one-sector AK model implies that unlimited growth is never sustainable with nonrenewable resources, whereas the two-sector Schumpeterian approach with constant returns in overall capital implies that it is sustainable, at least under some circumstances. Again the difference arises from the ability of the Schumpeterian approach to take into account that the accumulation of intellectual capital is "greener" (in this case, less resource-intensive) than the accumulation of tangible capital.

The AK Approach to Nonrenewable Resources

Suppose, by analogy with the AK case of the previous section, that the production function for final output is $Y = AKR^v$, with $0 < v < 1$. Then the Hamiltonian to be maximized is

$$H = u(c) + \lambda[AKR^v - c] - \xi R$$

---

14. Such as, for example, a demand function for money that depends positively on the expected rate of inflation in the standard two-period overlapping generations model of money, or a savings function that depends negatively on the expected rate of return to savings in the same overlapping generations model with or without money.

First-order conditions with respect to the controls c, R are

$$u'(c) = \lambda \tag{5.18}$$

and

$$\nu \lambda AKR^{\nu-1} = \xi. \tag{5.19}$$

The Euler equations are

$$\rho \lambda = AR^{\nu} \lambda + \dot{\lambda} \tag{5.20}$$

and

$$\rho \xi = \dot{\xi}. \tag{5.21}$$

The second Euler equation (5.21) is a utility-based version of Hotelling's rule, which states that the price ξ of the resource in terms of utility must grow exponentially at the (utility-) rate of interest ρ. Thus ξ must go to infinity in the long run.

It is easy to use these equations to show that consumption cannot go to infinity. For again, the Euler equation (5.20) can be written in terms of the growth rate of consumption:

$$\frac{\dot{c}}{c} = (1/\varepsilon)[AR^{\nu} - \rho]. \tag{5.22}$$

Clearly the flow of extraction R must go to zero in the long run no matter how large the initial stock of resources. This and equation (5.22) imply that the growth rate of consumption must approach $-\rho/\varepsilon < 0$, so that unbounded growth in consumption cannot take place. Again this is because ecological concerns eventually reduce the marginal social product of capital below the minimum value ρ needed to sustain growth.

The Schumpeterian Approach to Nonrenewable Resources

Suppose now that we modify the Schumpeterian approach to take finite non-renewable natural resources into account. Suppose the production function for final output is $Y = L^{\beta} \int_0^B x\,(i)^{\alpha}\,di\,R^{\nu} = K^{\alpha} B^{1-\alpha} L^{\beta} R^{\nu}$, where again $x\,(i) = x = K/B$ is the amount produced of each intermediate good, and where the coefficients α, β, ν are all positive with $\alpha + \beta + \nu = 1$. (That is, for a given state of knowledge there are constant returns to scale in the three inputs capital, labor, and natural resources.) Assume that the accumulation of the two capital stocks K and B are governed by the same forces as before. Then the Hamiltonian to be maximized is

$$H = u(c) + \lambda[K^{\alpha} B^{1-\alpha}(1-n)^{\beta} R^{\nu} - c] + \mu \eta \sigma Bn - \xi R.$$

The first-order conditions for maximizing H with respect to the controls c, n, R are

$$u'(c) = \lambda \tag{5.23}$$

$$\beta\lambda\frac{Y}{1-n} = \mu\eta\sigma B \tag{5.24}$$

$$\nu\lambda\frac{Y}{R} = \xi \tag{5.25}$$

and the Euler equation with respect to the shadow value of capital is

$$\rho\lambda = \alpha\lambda\frac{Y}{K} + \dot{\lambda}$$

which can be converted, as usual, into a consumption-growth equation:

$$\frac{\dot{c}}{c} = (1/\varepsilon)[\alpha\frac{Y}{K} - \rho]. \tag{5.26}$$

As in the case of environmental pollution, the marginal social product of capital $\alpha\frac{Y}{K}$ does not decline when output and tangible capital grow at the same rate in a steady state, provided that intellectual capital grows sufficiently faster than tangible capital, fast enough to offset the inevitable decline in the use of the natural resource. Appendix 2 makes this argument more formally by showing that if condition (5.27) holds then, given any initial stocks $S_0, B_0 > 0$ of the natural resource and knowledge capital, there is a hypothetical initial stock K_0 of tangible capital such that an optimal balanced growth path can be reached instantaneously from this initial position, along which consumption grows without bound.

The sufficient condition for such an optimal balanced growth path to exist is that

$$0 < \eta\sigma - \rho < \varepsilon\eta\sigma \tag{5.27}$$

This condition is considerably weaker than the analogous conditions (5.15)–(5.17) above. Indeed, it is implied by but does not imply (5.15)–(5.17).

5.4   Summary

We can summarize our findings briefly by saying that innovation is a necessary but not sufficient ingredient for unlimited growth in consumption to be sustainable, in the normative sense defined by the theory of optimal growth, when account is taken of environmental pollution and nonrenewable resources. Moreover, the Schumpeterian approach to endogenous growth theory appears to be more useful than the simpler AK approach for addressing the question of sustainable development, because it allows one to distinguish innovation from other investment activities that are less "green."

The analysis has uncovered some conditions under which growth can possibly be sustained, but it has not addressed the critical questions of what policies might implement the optimal sustainable growth paths that have been found.[15] Moreover, it has not characterized the optimal paths in cases where growth with unbounded consumption is not sustainable. The fact that the most widely raised ecological problems nowadays are ones involving open-access common-property resources, such as the depletion of the ozone layer and the emission of greenhouse gases, suggests that implementation of a sustainable growth policy will require new institutions of international cooperation, so that we can achieve with the global environment what many advanced industrial countries seem now to be achieving with their local environments. Constructing such institutions is the most challenging problem facing those interested in sustainable development.

Appendix 1: Existence of Steady-State with Environmental Pollution

This appendix shows that a balanced optimal-growth path with a positive growth rate exists in the Schumpeterian model with environmental pollution, given conditions (5.15)–(5.17). We are given $E_0 \in \left(E^{\min}, 0\right)$, and it suffices to construct constant growth paths for $E, K, B, Y, c, n, z, \lambda, \mu, \zeta$ with $g_Y > 0$ that satisfy the initial condition on E; the threshold condition (5.9); the nonnegativity conditions $K_0, B_0 \geq 0$; the first-order conditions (5.13); the Euler equation (5.14); the other two Euler equations

$$\dot{\zeta} = \rho\zeta - (-E)^\omega + \theta\zeta$$

$$\dot{\mu} = \rho\mu - \eta\sigma n\mu - (1-\alpha)(Y/B)\,\lambda\frac{\gamma}{1+\gamma};$$

the production function: $Y = K^\alpha B^{1-\alpha}(1-n)^{1-\alpha}z$; the laws of motion $\dot{K} = Y - c$, $\dot{B} = \eta\sigma nB$ and $\dot{E} = -Yz^\gamma - \theta E$; and the transversality conditions $\lim_{t\to\infty} e^{-\rho t}\lambda K = 0$, $\lim_{t\to\infty} e^{-\rho t}\mu B = 0$, and $\lim_{t\to\infty} e^{-\rho t}\zeta E = 0$.

Such a path can be defined recursively as follows. The growth rates are

$$g_n = 0$$

$$g_K = g_c = g_Y = (\eta\sigma - \rho)\left(\varepsilon + \frac{(\varepsilon+\omega)/(1+\omega)}{\gamma(1-\alpha)}\right)^{-1}$$

---

15. Some progress has been made by writers using the product-variety version of endogenous growth theory. See, for example, Verdier (1993), Hung, Chang, and Blackburn (1993), and Gastaldo and Ragot (1995).

$$g_\lambda = -\varepsilon g_K$$

$$g_E = \frac{1-\varepsilon}{1+\omega} g_K$$

$$g_B = \left(1 + \frac{(\varepsilon+\omega)/(1+\omega)}{\gamma(1-\alpha)}\right) g_K$$

$$g_\mu = (1-\varepsilon) g_K - g_B$$

$$g_\zeta = \omega \frac{1-\varepsilon}{1+\omega} g_K$$

$$g_z = -\frac{1}{\gamma} \frac{\varepsilon+\omega}{1+\omega} g_K$$

The initial values are:

$$\zeta_0 = (-E_0)^\omega / \left(\rho + \theta - g_\zeta\right)$$

$$K_0 = \left(\frac{(\rho+\varepsilon g_K)\left(\frac{1+\gamma}{\alpha\gamma}(\rho+\varepsilon g_K)-g_K\right)^{-\varepsilon}}{\alpha\gamma(-E_0)(\theta+g_E)\zeta_0}\right)^{\frac{1}{\varepsilon-1}}$$

$$c_0 = \left(\frac{1+\gamma}{\alpha\gamma}(\rho+\varepsilon g_K) - g_K\right) K_0$$

$$\lambda_0 = c_0^{-\varepsilon}$$

$$z_0 = (\lambda_0/\zeta_0 (1+\gamma))^{1/\gamma}$$

$$n = g_B/\eta\sigma$$

$$B_0 = \left(\frac{c_0+g_K K_0}{K_0^\alpha z_0}\right)^{\frac{1}{1-\alpha}} / (1-n)$$

$$Y_0 = K_0^\alpha B_0^{1-\alpha}(1-n)^{1-\alpha} z_0$$

$$\mu_0 = \frac{(1-\alpha)\gamma\lambda_o Y_0}{(1+\gamma)(\rho+(\varepsilon-1)g_K)B_0}.$$

It follows immediately from (5.16) that the growth rate g_Y is positive. The threshold condition (5.9) is also satisfied at all times because it holds at time 0 by assumption and because (5.15) ensures that $g_E < 0$. Because $g_K > 0$ and $\varepsilon > 1$, K_0 is positive if $\theta + g_E > 0$, which is ensured by condition (5.17). Condition (5.15) and the definition of g_K imply that $g_B < \eta\sigma - \rho < \eta\sigma$, which together with the definition of n implies that $B_0 > 0$.

It is straightforward to verify that each of the first-order conditions, Euler equations, and laws of motion is satisfied, by first showing that it holds at time 0 and then showing that the right-hand and left-hand sides have identical growth rates:

• First-order condition with respect to c:

$$c^{-\varepsilon} = \lambda.$$

This holds at 0 by the definition of λ_0. Both sides grow at the rate $-\varepsilon g_K$.

- First-order condition with respect to z:

$$\lambda = (1 + \gamma) \zeta z^{\gamma}.$$

This holds at 0 by the definition of z_0. Both sides grow at the rate $-\varepsilon g_K$.

- First-order condition with respect to n:

$$\mu \eta \sigma B = (1 - \alpha) \lambda \frac{Y}{1 - n} \frac{\gamma}{1 + \gamma}.$$

This holds at 0 by the definition of μ_0 if $\eta \sigma (1 - n) = \rho + (\varepsilon - 1) g_K$, which can be shown to hold by the definitions of g_K and g_B. Both sides grow at the rate $(1 - \varepsilon) g_K$.

- Euler equation (5.14):

$$g_c = (1/\varepsilon) \left[\alpha \frac{\gamma}{1 + \gamma} \frac{Y}{K} - \rho \right].$$

At date 0 the RHS equals (by the definition of Y_0)

$$(1/\varepsilon) \left[\alpha \frac{\gamma}{1 + \gamma} K_0^{\alpha - 1} B_0^{1 - \alpha} (1 - n)^{1 - \alpha} z_0 - \rho \right],$$

which equals (by the definition of B_0)

$$(1/\varepsilon) \left[\alpha \frac{\gamma}{1 + \gamma} \left(\frac{c_0}{K_0} + g_K \right) - \rho \right],$$

which equals (by the definition of c_0) $g_K \equiv g_c$. The growth rate of each side is zero.

- The Euler equation for ζ:

$$g_\zeta = \rho + \theta - (-E)^\omega / \zeta.$$

This holds at 0 by the definition of ζ_0. The growth rate of each side is zero.

- The Euler equation for μ:

$$g_\mu = \rho - \eta \sigma n - (1 - \alpha) \frac{\gamma}{1 + \gamma} \frac{\lambda Y}{\mu B}.$$

At 0, the right-hand side equals (by the definition of μ_0)

$$-\eta \sigma n - (\varepsilon - 1) g_K,$$

which equals g_μ by the definition of n. The growth rate of each side is zero.

- The production function:

$$Y = K^\alpha B^{1-\alpha} (1-n)^{1-\alpha} z.$$

This holds at 0 by the definition of Y_0. Both sides grow at the rate g_K.

- The law of motion of K:

$$g_K K = Y - c.$$

This holds at 0 by the definitions of Y_0 and B_0. Both sides grow at the rate g_K.

- The law of motion of E:

$$g_E = -\frac{Y z^\gamma}{E} - \theta.$$

At time 0 the RHS equals (by the definitions of Y_0 and B_0)

$$- (c_0 + g_K K_0) z_0^\gamma / E_0 - \theta,$$

which equals (by the definitions of z_0 and λ_0)

$$- (c_0 + g_K K_0) c_0^{-\varepsilon} / E_0 \zeta_0 (1+\gamma) - \theta,$$

which equals (by the definition of c_o)

$$-\frac{1+\gamma}{\alpha\gamma} (\rho + \varepsilon g_K) \left(\frac{1+\gamma}{\alpha\gamma} (\rho + \varepsilon g_K) - g_K \right)^{-\varepsilon} K_0^{1-\varepsilon} / E_0 \zeta_0 (1+\gamma) - \theta,$$

which equals g_E by the definition of K_0. Both sides grow at the rate 0.

- The law of motion of B:

$$g_B = \eta \sigma n.$$

This holds at 0 by the definition of n. Both sides grow at the rate 0.

- The first transversality condition:

$$\lim_{t \to \infty} e^{-\rho t} \lambda K = 0.$$

This holds because the growth rate of the product λK is $(1 - \varepsilon) g_K$, which, by condition (5.15), is negative.

- The second transversality condition:

$$\lim_{t \to \infty} e^{-\rho t} \mu B = 0.$$

This holds because the growth rate of the product μB is also $(1 - \varepsilon) g_K < 0$.

• The third transversality condition

$$\lim_{t \to \infty} e^{-\rho t} \zeta E = 0$$

holds because the growth rate of the product ζE is also $(1 - \varepsilon) g_K < 0$.

Appendix 2: Existence of Steady-State with Nonrenewable Natural Resources

This appendix shows that a balanced optimal growth path with positive growth exists in the Schumpeterian model with finite nonrenewable natural resources, given condition (5.27). We are given S_0, $B_0 > 0$, and it suffices to construct constant growth paths for S, K, B, Y, c, n, R, λ, μ, ξ with $g_Y > 0$ that satisfy the initial conditions on S and B; the nonnegativity condition $K_0 \geq 0$; the first-order conditions (5.23) to (5.25); the Euler equation (5.26); the other two Euler equations

$$\dot{\xi} = \rho \xi$$

$$\dot{\mu} = \rho \mu - \eta \sigma n \mu - (1 - \alpha) \lambda Y / B;$$

the production function $Y = K^\alpha B^{1-\alpha} (1 - n)^\beta R^v$; the laws of motion $\dot{K} = Y - c$, $\dot{B} = \eta \sigma n B$, and $\dot{S} = -R$; and the transversality conditions $\lim_{t \to \infty} e^{-\rho t} \lambda K = 0$, $\lim_{t \to \infty} e^{-\rho t} \mu B = 0$, and $\lim_{t \to \infty} e^{-\rho t} \xi S = 0$. (The resource constraint $S(t) \geq 0$ will be satisfied for all t because $S_0 > 0$ and g_S is constant.)

Such a path can be defined recursively as follows. The growth rates are:

$$g_n = 0$$
$$g_K = g_c = g_Y = (1/\varepsilon)(\eta \sigma - \rho)$$
$$g_\lambda = \rho - \eta \sigma$$
$$g_S = \frac{1-\varepsilon}{\varepsilon} \eta \sigma - \frac{1}{\varepsilon} \rho$$
$$g_B = g_K - \frac{v}{1-\alpha} \cdot g_S$$
$$g_\mu = (1 - \varepsilon) g_K - g_B$$
$$g_\xi = \rho$$
$$g_R = g_S$$

The initial values are:

$$n = g_B / \eta \sigma$$
$$R_0 = -g_S S_0$$

$$K_0 = B_0 \left[\alpha \, (1-n)^\beta \, R_0^\nu / \eta \sigma \right]^{\frac{1}{1-\alpha}}$$

$$Y_0 = \eta \sigma \, K_0 / \alpha$$

$$c_0 = Y_0 - g_K K_0$$

$$\lambda_0 = c_0^{-\varepsilon}$$

$$\xi_o = \nu \lambda_o Y_0 / R_0$$

$$\mu_0 = \beta \lambda_0 Y_0 / \eta \sigma \, (1-n) \, B_0$$

It follows immediately from (5.27) that the growth rate g_Y is positive. The nonnegativity condition $K_0 \geq 0$ will be satisfied if $n \in (0, 1)$, which is guaranteed by (5.27), the definition of g_B, and the fact that $\frac{\nu}{1-\alpha} = \frac{\nu}{\nu+\beta} < 1$.

Again, we can show that each of the first-order conditions, Euler equations, and laws of motion is satisfied by showing that it holds at time 0 and then showing that the right-hand and left-hand sides have identical growth rates.

• First-order condition with respect to c:

$$c^{-\varepsilon} = \lambda.$$

This holds at 0 by the definition of λ_0. Both sides grow at the rate $-\varepsilon g_K$.

• First-order condition with respect to R:

$$\nu \lambda Y / R = \xi.$$

This holds at 0 by the definition of ξ_0. Both sides grow at the rate ρ.

• First-order condition with respect to n:

$$\beta \lambda Y / (1-n) = \mu \eta \sigma B.$$

This holds at 0 by the definition of μ_0. Both sides grow at the rate $(1-\varepsilon) \, g_K$.

• Euler equation (5.26):

$$g_c = (1/\varepsilon) \, (\alpha Y / K - \rho) \, .$$

This holds at 0 by the definitions of g_c and Y_0. Both sides are constant.

• Euler equation for ξ:

$$g_\xi = \rho.$$

This holds at all times by the definition of g_ξ.

• Euler equation for μ:

$$g_\mu = \rho - \eta \sigma n - (1-\alpha) \, \lambda Y / \mu B.$$

By the definitions of g_μ and n, this can be rewritten as

$$(1 - \varepsilon)\, g_K = \rho - (1 - \alpha)\, \lambda Y / \mu B.$$

By the definition of μ_0, the RHS at 0 equals

$$\rho - \frac{1 - \alpha}{\beta} \eta\sigma\, (1 - n)\,.$$

By the definitions of n, g_B, g_S and g_K, this equals

$$\rho - \frac{1 - \alpha}{\beta} \left(\eta\sigma - \frac{1}{\varepsilon}\, (\eta\sigma - \rho) \right) - \frac{v}{\beta} \left(\frac{1 - \varepsilon}{\varepsilon} \eta\sigma - \frac{1}{\varepsilon} \rho \right).$$

Because $\alpha + \beta + v = 1$, this equals

$$(1 - \varepsilon)\, (1/\varepsilon)\, (\eta\sigma - \rho)\,,$$

which equals the LHS by the definition of g_K. Both sides are constant.

• The production function:

$$Y = K^\alpha B^{1-\alpha}\, (1 - n)^\beta\, R^v$$

holds at 0 by the definitions of K_0 and Y_0. Both sides grow at rate g_Y.

• Law of motion of K:

$$g_K K = Y - c.$$

This holds at 0 by the definition of c_0. Both sides grow at the rate g_K.

• Law of motion of S:

$$g_s = -R/S.$$

This holds at 0 by the definition of R_0. Both sides are constant.

• Law of motion of B:

$$g_B = \eta\sigma n.$$

This holds at all times by the definition of n.

• Transversality conditions. All of the products λK, ξS, and μB grow at the rate $(1 - \varepsilon)\, g_K = (1 - \varepsilon)\, (\eta\sigma - \rho)\, /\varepsilon$ which, by (5.27), is less than ρ.

A common feature of the endogenous growth models surveyed earlier is their representation of R&D activities as homogeneous, performed by only one kind of researcher and generating just one kind of innovation and one kind of knowledge. In fact, there are many kinds of innovative activities, generating many different kinds of knowledge. An aggregate theory that fails to distinguish between these different activities is potentially misleading. Whether growth will be enhanced by a subsidy to innovation, for example, might depend crucially on whether product or process innovations are subsidized, or on whether basic or applied research is encouraged by the subsidy.

The purpose of this chapter is to introduce into Schumpeterian growth theory an important element of heterogeneity in the structure of innovative activity, namely the distinction between fundamental and secondary research. More specifically, any new product, process, or market is created not by one innovation but by a whole sequence of innovations. Some of those innovations are more fundamental than others, in the sense that they open up more windows of opportunity for future development. Some of them are more secondary than others, in that they do more to bring about the realization of possibilities that have been created by previous innovations, and less to open further windows of opportunity.

In reality, every innovation is fundamental to some extent and secondary to some extent. Even Newton claimed to have benefited from standing on the shoulders of giants, and people often find inspiration in the most mundane creations. But the distinction is clearly important, and shows up in many different guises—basic versus applied research, research versus development, invention versus innovation, innovation versus diffusion, innovation versus imitation, innovation versus learning by doing, scientific revolution versus normal science, and so forth. For the sake of analytical clarity we will suppose that a clear distinction can be drawn between just two kinds of innovation, one of which is entirely fundamental and the other entirely secondary. For concreteness we suppose that the fundamental innovative activity is R&D and the secondary activity is learning by doing. We focus on learning by doing partly because it is such an important source of new technological knowledge and partly because it has been such an important topic in the history of growth theory. However, our analysis applies more broadly to the other fundamental/secondary dichotomies listed above; we illustrate this below by reinterpreting the analysis in terms of research and development rather than research and learning by doing.

Fundamental and secondary research are complementary activities; in order to exploit fully the fundamental knowledge generated by R&D, a firm must put that knowledge into practice and resolve the unexpected problems and opportunities that only experience can reveal. However, empirical estimates of learning curves suggest that if there were not a continual flow of fundamental innovations to be exploited, the point would eventually be reached where there was nothing more to learn. We capture this distinction by supposing that each innovation resulting from research consists of a potential new product, and each innovation resulting from learning by doing consists of a way to improve the quality of goods that have already been invented.

Now a case[1] can be made that most of the fundamental discoveries that led to what we now recognize as basic science were not the intended outcome of basic research, but rather the (often serendipitous) outcome of narrowly focused problem-solving activities. This suggests that fundamental knowledge can be generated by learning by doing as well as by research. To accommodate this phenomenon, we need to recognize that there is a kind of knowledge that creates new opportunities and which arises not just from research but also from learning by doing. This knowledge, which we call *general knowledge*, is the common scientific, technological, and cultural heritage potentially available to everyone.

Two relationships will jointly determine the steady-state rate of economic growth and the amount of research relative to learning by doing. The first is a *growth equation*, which governs the evolution of general knowledge over time, and thereby determines the steady-state growth rate as a function of the mix between research and learning by doing. The second is an *arbitrage* equation that results from the attempt by workers to engage in the most profitable type of innovative activity, either research or learning by doing, depending on the growth rate.

Alwyn Young (1992) has argued that an economy that devotes too many resources to research at the expense of learning by doing may actually slow the long-run rate of growth. We argue below that this possibility depends crucially on the nature of technology spillovers. It has commonly been assumed in growth theory that learning by doing is purely external to the firm, that each firm benefits from all others' experience, and that no one internalizes the benefit. We find that if this is the case, more research may indeed slow the steady-state rate of growth.

If, however, we go to the other extreme and suppose that each product's quality improvements depend only on the experience of the firm producing that product, not upon other firms' experience, then research will always have a positive effect on growth on the margin in a steady state, even in the extreme case where general knowledge can be produced only by *secondary* innovations arising from learning by doing. This is because the more forward-looking nature of research (research is aimed at capturing rents from future products, whereas learning by doing is concerned only with present products) and the

---

1. See Rosenberg and Birdzell (1986).

positive net rate of interest[2] implies that even the flow of secondary innovations will be affected more, on the margin, by research than by learning by doing.

We also find that the level of research and the rate of growth can be increased if production workers become more *adaptable*; that is, if the rate at which they are able to switch from producing old products to producing new ones increases. This result supports Lucas's (1993) claim to the effect that the key to success of some newly industrialized countries is their ability to move skilled workers quickly between sectors. In Chapter 7, when we endogenize this adaptability parameter, we will find that the same result implies a *positive effect of competition on growth*. That is, an increase in the substitutability between new and old products, which implies an increase in competitiveness between them, may induce production workers to leave old products more rapidly, with the effect of inducing a higher level of research. Contrary to previous Schumpeterian models, this implies that increased competition may lead to faster growth.

Another striking result is that any parameter change that raises the productivity of the innovation process will shift resources out of learning by doing and into research. This is even true of a parameter change whose only direct effect is to raise the productivity of *learning by doing*. This result also reflects to some extent the more forward-looking nature of research, which means that research capitalizes more of the benefits of increased growth. It also reflects the complementarity between research and learning by doing, and the way rents are shared between the two types of innovators; an increase in the productivity of learning by doing will generate increased rents for both.

As a first step in modeling the rent-sharing arrangements between researchers and developers, we assume that there is perfect competition in the market for production workers, and no problems of enforcing contracts. However, our framework clearly opens the door for studying organizational aspects of R&D in the context of an endogenous growth model. These aspects will be addressed in greater detail in Chapter 13.

6.1   The Basic Model

6.1.1   Basic Assumptions

We consider an infinite-horizon continuous-time model[3] with a constant mass H of skilled workers, each living forever. Each worker can choose whether to engage in research or production. There is a single final good, which can

---

2. Net of the growth rate.

3. This model will be used repeatedly over the following chapters. See Chapter 7 (section 7.5), Chapter 9 (section 9.2.3), and Chapter 10 (section 10.2.4).

be used only for consumption, and a continuum of intermediate goods, which constitute the only inputs into producing the final good. All individuals have intertemporally additive risk-neutral preferences over consumption, with a constant rate of time preference r. There is no disutility of work.

The production (or "input-output") matrix can be described as follows:

1. Final output is produced with a continuum of intermediate goods of different vintages.

2. New intermediate goods of vintage τ are invented by workers who have chosen to do research, making use of general knowledge. Let H^r denote the mass of researchers. The flow of new products is $\lambda^r H^r$, where λ^r is each researcher's Poisson arrival rate of fundamental innovations, an exogenous parameter.

3. Intermediate goods of more recent vintage are (potentially) better, because they embody a higher level of *general knowledge*. More specifically, let A_τ denote the state of general knowledge at date τ, let x_a denote the labor input used in the production of each intermediate good of age a, and let Z_a denote the quality of the good. Each intermediate good is produced by labor alone under constant returns to scale, so by an appropriate normalization x_a also equals the output of each intermediate good of age a. In a steady state there will be $\lambda^r H^r$ different products of each vintage.[4] Thus aggregate final output at date t is

$$Y_t = \int_{-\infty}^{t} \lambda^r H^r A_\tau Z_{t-\tau}(x_{t-\tau})^\alpha d\tau = \int_{-\infty}^{t} Y_{t,\tau} d\tau, \tag{6.1}$$

where the parameter α lies between 0 and 1 and $Y_{t,\tau} = \lambda^r H^r A_\tau Z_{t-\tau}(x_{t-\tau})^\alpha$ denotes all the aggregate final output produced using intermediate goods of vintage τ.

4. The quality of each newly invented good is zero. Quality improvements come at a rate equal to the flow of secondary innovations across the whole economy, which we denote as LBD. Learning by doing takes place in each firm at the rate $\lambda^d (x_a)^{1-\nu}$, where λ^d is a parameter indicating the productivity of learning by doing, and $0 < \nu < 1$. Thus production workers produce two joint products, output and secondary innovations. The firm can appropriate the output but not the innovations. Hence

$$Z_0 = 0, \text{ and } \frac{dZ_a}{da} = LBD = \int_0^\infty \lambda^r H^r \lambda^d (x_s)^{1-\nu} ds; a > 0. \tag{6.2}$$

---

4. We are assuming that old products are never completely replaced by new ones. All obsolescence takes the form of "crowding out" (see section 3.1) rather than "creative destruction," and the number of products of any given vintage remains equal to $\lambda^r H^r$, the number that were originally created.

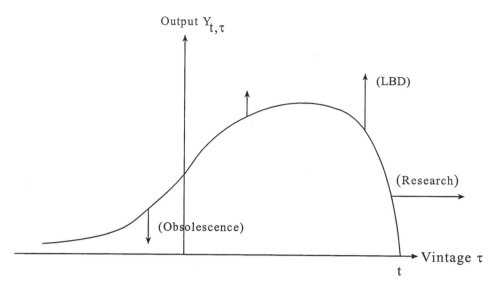

Figure 6.1
The profile of output across lines of different vintages, at date t.

5. Finally, new general knowledge is created by research and learning by doing throughout the entire economy, using the existing stock of general knowledge.[5]

Before filling in all the details of the model, we can use figure 6.1 to give an idea of the structure of output in the economy at any given date t. Because each product starts life with a quality of zero, therefore $Y_{t,\tau} = 0$ for all $\tau \geq t$. Because older products embody less general knowledge, their contribution to output will tend to be low. Hence the profile will tend to have the wave form depicted by figure 6.1. Over time, the profile will shift to the right, as research opens up new product lines. Near the leading edge the profile will be shifting up, as learning by doing improves the quality of new goods. But far back from the leading edge the profile will be shifting down, as workers leave old firms for better paying new ones. As time passes, the growth of general knowledge will be improving the productivity of products of any given age, thus shifting the entire profile upward.

6.1.2   The Research Arbitrage Equation

In order to simplify the analysis we assume that the rate at which workers can move from producing an old product to producing a new product or to doing research is fixed exogenously. That is, a worker who chooses to produce a product cannot do anything else until exogenously upgraded. Upgrading arrives to

---

5. See the subsection 6.1.3 for more details on the dynamics of the general knowledge parameter A_τ.

each worker at the fixed Poisson rate σ, which is our measure of adaptability. When allowed to upgrade we assume the worker always chooses to go either into research or into producing a product of the most recent vintage. (In Chapter 7 we relax this restriction and allow workers to move instantaneously and costlessly between research and production of each product.) Hence the amount of production labor per good will decline at the exponential rate σ with the age of the good:

$$x_a = x_0 e^{-\sigma a}. \tag{6.3}$$

The producer of any intermediate good of vintage τ has a monopoly in that good, and sells to a competitive final output sector at a price equal to the marginal product $\alpha A_\tau Z_{t-\tau}(x_{t-\tau})^{\alpha-1}$. It hires x_0 production workers when the good is first invented, and offers them lifetime employment contracts under the understanding that a worker will quit as soon as an opportunity to relocate is received. Let $V_\tau^d = A_\tau V^d$ be the expected present value of the wages received under each such contract. New firms compete with each other in hiring, each taking V^d as given. They choose x_0 so as to maximize the expected present value of profits: $W_\tau = \int_0^\infty e^{-ra} \alpha A_\tau Z_a(x_a)^\alpha da - x_0 V_\tau^d$. By substituting from (6.2) and (6.3), and performing the integration, we can express the firm's maximand[6] as

$$W_\tau = A_\tau W = A_\tau \left(\Phi (x_0)^\alpha - V^d x_0 \right). \tag{6.4}$$

As in any Cobb-Douglas factor demand system (for example, Chapter 2, pp. 56–7) the maximized value is proportional to the present value of wage payments:

$$W = \frac{1-\alpha}{\alpha} V^d x_0. \tag{6.5}$$

We are now in a position to derive the research arbitrage equation. For research and production to coexist in a steady state, workers who have just been upgraded must be indifferent between research and production. Let $V_t^r = V^r e^{gt}$ denote the expected present value of the income that a researcher will receive until the alternative choice as a production worker is upgraded to a new product. That is, V_t^r is the expected value of a claim to all the researcher's rents from fundamental innovations made over the time period (of stochastic length) during which the worker could have been working on a product of vintage t. Because a newly upgraded skilled worker can freely choose either activity, a steady state with both research and development requires

$$V^r = V^d. \tag{6.6}$$

---

6. $\Phi = \int_0^\infty e^{-ra} \alpha Z_a e^{-\sigma \alpha a} da = \int_0^\infty e^{-ra} \alpha a L B D e^{-\sigma a \alpha} da = \alpha L B D / (r + \sigma \alpha)^2$.

In a steady state the value V_t^r grows at rate g and capitalizes flow payoffs (per unit of time) equal to the flow probability of discovering a new product λ^r times the value to a researcher of a new product W_t. Because upgrading occurs at Poisson rate σ, the Bellman equation defining the steady-state value of V^r is

$$rV^r = \lambda^r W - \sigma V^r + gV^r. \tag{6.7}$$

Equations (6.5)–(6.7) yield the provisional arbitrage equation

$$r + \sigma - g = \frac{\lambda^r W}{V^d} = \frac{1-\alpha}{\alpha}\lambda^r x_0. \tag{6.8}$$

To finish the description of research arbitrage, we now derive the steady-state value of x_0 in terms of the stock of researchers H^r. First, note that the flow of workers into production of new goods in a steady state will be the number of relocated production workers: $h \equiv \sigma(H - H^r)$. From this and the fact that there are $\lambda^r H^r$ goods per vintage we have

$$x_0 = \sigma \frac{(H - H^r)}{\lambda^r H^r}. \tag{6.9}$$

Substituting from (6.9) into (6.8) yields the final research arbitrage equation:

$$r + \sigma - g = \sigma \frac{1-\alpha}{\alpha}\frac{H - H^r}{H^r}. \tag{6.10}$$

According to (6.10) an increase in the growth rate or a decrease in the rate of interest will result in a larger equilibrium level of research. These effects reflect the more forward-looking nature of research as compared with learning by doing.

6.1.3   The Growth Equation

In accordance with the discussion of the previous section, we assume that the growth of general knowledge is a function of the current flow of innovations of both types, and also of the accumulated *stock* of general knowledge, which embodies all previous innovations. Hence

$$\frac{\dot{A}_t}{A_t} = G(\lambda^r H^r, LDD), \tag{6.11}$$

which satisfies:

a. $G = 0$ when $H^r = 0$ and when $LBD = 0$

b. G is strictly increasing and concave in both arguments.

In a steady state the economy's growth rate will equal the growth rate of general knowledge. By combining equations (6.2, 6.3, 6.9, and 6.11) we arrive at the growth equation:

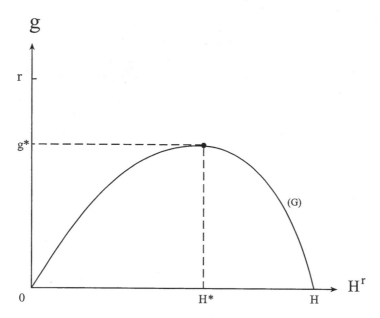

Figure 6.2

$$g = G\left(\lambda^r H^r, \frac{(\lambda^r)^{\nu}\lambda^d}{\sigma^{\nu}(1-\nu)}\left(H^r\right)^{\nu}\left(H - H^r\right)^{1-\nu}\right). \tag{6.12}$$

Thus growth can be expressed as a concave function of the level of research H^r as shown by the growth curve (G) figure 6.2. The growth rate achieves a maximum g^* when research and learning by doing are both strictly positive. In order to rule out bliss, assume that $g^* < r$.

Thus the level of research can conceivably be pushed so far at the expense of production that the steady state rate of growth goes down. This is because in the long run the rate of growth depends upon both fundamental and secondary innovations, and the secondary innovations arise directly out of the experience of production. Having too many fundamental innovations at the expense of secondary innovations can make research sterile by depriving it of feedback from experience. Until g^* is reached, further increases in research will raise the growth rate, but beyond that point it will reduce the growth rate.

6.1.4   Comparative Statics of Steady-State Growth

The steady-state values of g and H^r are jointly determined by the arbitrage equation (6.10) and the growth equation (6.12). The two curves in figure 6.3 depict these two equations.

There might exist multiple steady-state equilibria, with (G) and (A) inter-secting more than once over the range where the growth curve is increasing. We

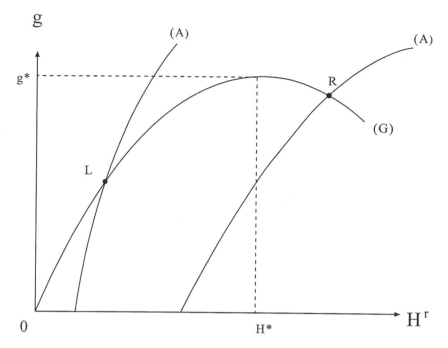

Figure 6.3

will restrict attention, however, to cases in which there is a unique steady-state equilibrium. Then it is clear from examination of figure 6.3 that this must be an equilibrium in which the arbitrage curve cuts the growth curve from below, because the former has a positive horizontal intercept. However, the intersection point may occur to either side of the point of maximal growth g^*. For example, take the case where the G function depends entirely on LBD. Then g^* occurs when LBD is maximized: $H^r = \nu H$, whereas according to the arbitrage equation (6.10) the equilibrium value of H^r is

$$\frac{1}{1 + \frac{\sigma + r - g}{\sigma} \frac{\alpha}{1 - \alpha}} H > \frac{1}{1 + \frac{\sigma + r}{\sigma} \frac{\alpha}{1 - \alpha}} H.$$

Thus for small values of ν the equilibrium will occur to the right of the maximal growth point. In this case, subsidizing research at the expense of production will *reduce* the steady-state rate of growth.

We might call the case in which research goes so far as to reduce the steady-state growth rate the "tale of two cities" case, in reference to the work of Young (1992). Specifically, Young studied the cases of two similarly situated countries, Hong Kong and Singapore. Both countries had the same experience of very rapid output growth (over 6 percent per year) between 1960 and 1985. But the nature of the growth was quite different between the two countries.

In Hong Kong, productivity grew at an average rate of 2.3 percent rate per year. In Singapore, however, productivity hardly grew at all; almost all of its growth was accounted for by capital accumulation. Young attributed Singapore's poor productivity growth to a government policy of relying heavily on foreign investment and encouraging rapid introduction of new sectors. Both of these policies gave little chance for local entrepreneurs to learn from experience. More rapid introduction of new sectors and too little learning also characterize what happens in our model when research goes so far as to reduce growth.

Implications for Education Policy

A slight variation on the preceding analysis has important implications for education policy. Until now we have been assuming implicitly that everyone in the labor force is equally qualified to engage in primary or secondary innovative activity. But in reality one's qualifications for either sort of activity will be affected importantly by one's education. Thus an understanding of how these two activities interact in the growth process should be an important input in society's choice of how much public support to provide to education, and also of the direction of that support—whether to support more primary or higher education, and whether to support more basic scientific education through universities or specialized technical education through vocational institutes and apprenticeship programs.

Suppose, for example, that the level of research H^r depended entirely not on the decisions of individuals through their private arbitrage decisions, but on the government's decision as to what fraction of public support for education to channel towards universities instead of towards primary and vocational education. Suppose, for simplicity, that the cost of training a researcher was the same as the cost of training a production worker. Then if the choice of H^r were entirely motivated by the objective of maximizing the expected present value of GDP, clearly it would make no sense for society to push research beyond the point of maximal growth in figure 6.3. For to do so would take workers out of production, thereby reducing the level of output of each product and slowing down its rate of quality improvement through learning by doing, and would also reduce the rate at which general knowledge was growing. We would in effect be in the situation of overaccumulation of capital[7]—in this case, research capital—in which consumption could be raised at every point in time.

In other words, an economy that found itself beyond the point of maximal growth in figure 6.3 would probably be better off channeling its public support to primary, secondary and vocational education, rather than to higher education. This way it could have a more highly skilled stock of production workers,

---

7. See, for example, Diamond 1965.

better able to learn from experience and to recognize possible solutions to the day-to-day production problems whose resolution is critical to the successful exploitation of new technologies. The alternative would be to generate more basic academic research that will fall on the infertile soil of an underskilled labor force. These and other aspects of the role of education in the growth process will be discussed at greater length in Chapter 10.

6.2 Internalized Learning by Doing

In the preceding section we assumed that the quality-enhancing effect of each firm's learning is not appropriated by that firm but is shared by all firms. In many cases, however, it would be reasonable to assume the opposite—that the quality enhancement effect of learning is fully internalized. Under this opposite assumption, although there may be a technology spillover working through the growth of general knowledge, only the firm that solves practical production problems benefits directly from that experience by being able to raise the quality of its existing intermediate good. The present section reworks the basic model of the previous section accordingly. As we shall see, it turns out that when the quality-enhancement effect of learning by doing is internalized, the equilibrium level of research will never exceed the growth maximizing level shown in figure 6.3; more research will always result in more growth on the margin.

The only change in the technological environment of the model that this reworking entails is in equation (6.2), determining the evolution of a product's quality. This evolution now depends not on the economy-wide rate of learning by doing LBD, but on the rate of learning by doing within the firm producing the good. Accordingly we replace (6.2) with the alternative:

$$Z_0 = 0, \quad LBD = \int_0^\infty \lambda^r H^r \lambda^d (x_s)^{1-v} ds, \quad \text{and} \quad \frac{dZ_a}{da} = \lambda^d (x_a)^{1-v}; a > 0.$$

$$(6.13)$$

This change will leave the growth equation (6.12) unaffected but will alter the research arbitrage equation (6.10) because the production workers will be able to appropriate at least some of the fruits of their learning by doing, in as much as researchers will be forced to compensate them accordingly in a competitive equilibrium.

To see this, note that the value of a new product to the researcher will still be given by $W_t = \int_0^\infty e^{-ra} \alpha A_t Z_a (x_a)^\alpha da - x_0 V_t^d$, but now using (6.3) and (6.13) and performing the integration yields[8]

---

8. $\Psi = \int_0^\infty e^{-ra} \alpha \left(\int_0^a \lambda^d e^{-\sigma s (1-v)} ds \right) e^{-\sigma a \alpha} da = \frac{\alpha \lambda^d}{(r+\sigma \alpha)(r+\sigma(\alpha+1-v))}.$

$$W_t = A_t W = A_t \left(\Psi \, (x_0)^{\alpha+1-\nu} - V^d x_0 \right) \tag{6.14}$$

instead of the former equation (6.4). Thus, instead of production labor getting the fraction α of the present value of an innovation, it gets the fraction $\alpha + 1 - \nu$ corresponding to its exponent in the first term on the right-hand side of (6.14). The extra $1 - \nu$ is the extra compensation that a researcher must make to production workers because the quality-enhancement effects of their learning can now be appropriated.

Accordingly if we redo the analysis that was underlying equations (6.5)–(6.10) we now arrive at the alternative research arbitrage equation

$$r + \sigma - g = \sigma \frac{\nu - \alpha}{1 - \nu + \alpha} \frac{H - H^r}{H^r}, \tag{6.15}$$

which is identical with the previous research arbitrage equation (6.10), except that the previous workers' share α has been replaced by its new value $\alpha + 1 - \nu$.

This new research arbitrage equation will solve for positive values of research and of production workers if and only if the learning parameter $1 - \nu$ is not too large; that is, $1 - \nu < 1 - \alpha$. Otherwise the workers would have to appropriate more than one 100 percent of the surplus of a product in a competitive equilibrium, which would obviously result in a corner solution with no research. We suppose that this restriction is satisfied.

To see that it is now no longer possible for research to be pushed beyond the growth-maximizing level in a steady state, first note that, as we saw above, growth would be maximized at the level $H^r = \nu H$ if the growth function G depended only on learning by doing. Clearly, in the general case where research also had a positive marginal effect on G the growth-maximizing point would occur at a value of H^r even greater than νH. Now suppose that we took into account that raising the steady-state level of research requires a temporary sacrifice of current production by even more than in the new steady state, and that we discounted future learning by doing. That is, consider the artificial planning problem of maximizing the present value of output, taking the evolution of A_t as given.[9] The steady state to this problem would clearly be less than νH; that is, you would stop accumulating "research capital" H^r before you had reached the point of maximal steady-state learning by doing, because by that point the marginal return would have fallen to zero but the marginal cost as measured by the discount rate would always be positive. The

---

9. There are $\lambda^r H_t^r$ new products at t and h_t workers to produce them. The present value of output produced by each new product is proportional to $(h_t/H_t^r)^{1-\nu+\alpha}$. So the problem is to maximize $\lambda^r \int_0^\infty e^{-(r-g)t} H_t^r \, (h_t/H_t^r)^{1-\nu+\alpha} \, dt$ subject to $\dot{H}_t^r = \sigma \left(H - H_t^r \right) - h_t$, given H_0^r.

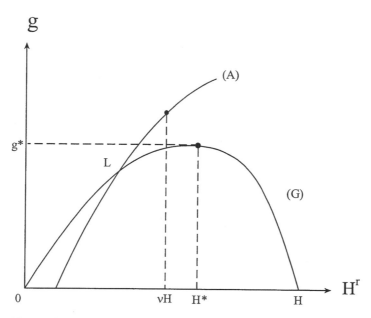

Figure 6.4

problem that the steady-state equilibrium actually solves is just the same as this artificial problem, because the only externalities in the model are the spillovers through which both research and learning by doing affect the growth rate.[10] Thus the equilibrium steady state involves even less research than the amount that would maximize the rate of learning by doing. The amount that would maximize the rate of learning by doing is in turn less than the amount that would maximize the steady-state growth rate. Thus the equilibrium necessarily involves less research than the amount that would maximize the growth rate. That is, when firms can internalize the direct quality-enhancing effects of learning by doing, it is impossible for the economy to accumulate too much research capital.

We restrict attention again to cases in which there is a unique steady-state equilibrium. This and the result of the previous paragraph imply that a steady state will occur on the rising part of the growth curve (G) as shown in figure 6.4. Then we have the following comparative-statics results:

---

10. Recall that the artificial planner problem is equivalent to maximizing the present value: $\int_0^\infty e^{-(r-g)t} H_t^r \left(h_t / H_t^r \right)^{1-v+\alpha} dt$ subject to $\dot{H}_t^r = \sigma \left(H - H_t^r \right) - h_t$, with H_0^r given. The steady state to this problem is $\overline{H}^r = \frac{1}{1+(r-g)(1-v+\alpha)/\sigma} (v - \alpha) H$. Because the net discount rate $r - g$ is positive and (by assumption) $1 - v + \alpha > 0$, therefore $\overline{H}^r$ is less than the value vH that maximizes the rate of learning by doing, which in turn is less than the value H^* that maximizes the steady-state growth rate. According to the research arbitrage equation (6.15), $\overline{H}^r$ is also identical to the steady-state equilibrium level of research.

Proposition 6.1 When learning by doing is internalized, the rate of growth g and the level of research H^r are both:

a. increasing in λ^r, λ^d and H, and decreasing in r; and

b. increasing in σ and ν if the elasticity of the growth function G with respect to learning by doing is sufficiently small.

Proof All of these results can be established graphically, using figure 6.4. Increasing λ^r or λ^d shifts the (G) curve up without affecting (A). Increasing H shifts the (G) curve up and the (A) curve to the right. Increasing r shifts the (A) curve to the left without affecting (G). To establish part (b) note that increasing σ or ν shifts the (A) curve to the right, whereas in the limiting case where the effect of *LBD* vanishes, neither σ nor ν affects (G); thus the results of part (b) hold in this case, and by continuity they hold when the elasticity is small enough.   □

Thus the steady-state growth rate responds to parameters changes much as in conventional Schumpeterian models, even though the overall level of innovative activity, which drives growth in conventional models, has been assumed constant. So, for example, an increase in the rate of discount r will reduce both research and the growth rate, as in conventional models.

A remarkable feature of these results is that, even in the case where general knowledge is assumed to be created only by secondary innovations arising from the *learning by doing* process, the growth rate almost always covaries positively with the level of *research*. The intuitive reason for the positive covariance between growth and research is the more forward-looking nature of research compared with learning by doing (research is aimed at capturing rents from future products, whereas learning by doing is concerned only with present products).

The fact that an increase in λ^d should affect research positively is perhaps surprising. It occurs because λ^d does not impact directly on the arbitrage equation. This property reflects the *complementarity* of research and learning by doing; an increase in λ^d enhances the total present value to be shared by researchers and production workers, without affecting the relative profitability of either kind of activity. Instead, the impact of λ^d is entirely on the growth equation, where it tends to raise the growth rate. Because, as we have seen, research is more forward looking than learning by doing, the prospective increase in growth draws resources out of production and into research.

Also remarkable is the possible positive effect of the upgrading rate σ on research and growth. This effect can be explained as follows. Holding the total supply of skilled workers H constant, an increase in σ implies an increase in the initial flow of workers into newly discovered products, which enhances the profitability of research by reducing the cost of implementing a successful innovation. Although it also increases the rate at which these workers will quit, time-discounting implies that the former effect dominates the latter; that is, a higher σ increases the value of being a researcher relative to that of being a worker. Hence the positive effect of the upgrading rate σ on research through the arbitrage equation. Because the growth curve is upward-sloping at the steady-state point this will raise growth. As long as the growth of fundamental knowledge does not depend too much on the rate of learning by doing, the growth curve will not shift enough to reverse this effect.

This is the *"Lucas effect,"* whereby adaptability increases growth. However, contrary to Lucas (1993), a higher mobility of production workers across products enhances growth not because it increases aggregate learning by doing but rather because it increases the steady-state mass of researchers,[11] and *reduces* learning by doing. As we show in Chapter 7, the same effect translates into a positive effect of competition on growth when we endogenize σ.

6.3   Research and Development

In this section we show how the preceding analysis can be applied to other examples of the fundamental/secondary dichotomy. Specifically, we treat the case of research versus development. Each fundamental innovation resulting from research consists of a potential line of new products, and each innovation resulting from development consists of a workable plan for producing one of those products.

The fundamental "input-output" structure of the economy is changed as follows:

1. In addition to a constant masses H of *skilled workers* there are now L *laborers*. Each skilled worker can choose whether to engage in research or development. The laborers can only work in production, and no longer generate any secondary innovations.

2. The vintage of a good is now determined not by the date at which it was discovered, but by the date of discovery of the line from which the good emanates. Thus all the goods emanating from a single line of vintage τ embody the same amount of general knowledge A_τ. Let S_a denote the number of different intermediate goods that have been invented on lines of age a, and let x_a denote the labor input used in the production of each such good. Then aggregate final output is just

---

11. Indeed, higher mobility of production workers from old to new lines enhances the profitability of research (a successful fundamental innovator benefits from having more workers starting up on a line he or she has just discovered); furthermore, as we have already shown, insofar as learning by doing is not purely external to firms, research has an unambiguously positive effect on growth at the margin in steady state.

$$Y_t = \int_{-\infty}^{t} S_{t-\tau} A_\tau (x_{t-\tau})^\alpha d\tau = \int_{-\infty}^{t} Y_{t,\tau} d\tau, \tag{6.16}$$

where $Y_{t,\tau} = S_{t-\tau} A_\tau (x_{t-\tau})^\alpha$ denotes all the aggregate final output produced using intermediate goods of vintage τ.

3. New intermediate goods (or "plans") of a given vintage are invented by skilled workers who have chosen to develop a product line of that vintage, with the assistance of the researcher who discovered the line. Secondary innovations (plans for new intermediate goods) on any given line of age a arrive at the rate[12] $\lambda^d \cdot (h_a / \lambda^r H^r)^{1-\nu}$ where h_a is the number of developers on all lines of age a and $\lambda^r H^r$ is the number of such lines. Accordingly,

$$S_a = \int_0^a \lambda^d (h_s)^{1-\nu} (\lambda^r H^r)^\nu ds \text{ for } a \geq 0. \tag{6.17}$$

4. Laborers are free to relocate among different firms with no lag, but developers who have chosen to develop a new line must stay on that line until upgraded according to the same Poisson process as before, at which time they can either start developing a new line or go into research. Hence

$$h_a = h_0 e^{-\sigma a} \text{ for } a \geq 0. \tag{6.18}$$

5. Finally, new general knowledge is created by research and development throughout the entire economy, using the existing stock of general knowledge, according to the growth equation:

$$g = \dot{A}_t / A_t = G(\lambda^r H^r, DEV) \tag{6.19}$$

where G has all the same properties assumed above and the economy-wide amount of development DEV is, by analogy to LBD, the integral of all secondary innovations across product lines of all vintages s:

$$DEV = \int_0^\infty \lambda^r H^r \cdot \lambda^d (h_s / \lambda^r H^r)^{1-\nu} ds. \tag{6.20}$$

The steady-state relationship between the stock of research and the flow of upgrading will be exactly the same as before. Hence, by analogy with (6.9)[13] the number of developers on new lines will be:

$$h_0 = \sigma (H - H^r). \tag{6.21}$$

---

12. Thus the rate of secondary innovations on a line depends on the number of developers on that line according to the same function as determined the rate of learning by doing on a product as a function of the number of production workers on that product in the previous section.

13. Recall that h_0 refers to all the secondary innovators across new lines, whereas in (6.9) x_0 referred to the number per product.

From equations (6.18)–(6.21) we arrive at exactly the same growth equation:

$$g = G\left(\lambda^r H^r, \frac{(\lambda^r)^\nu \lambda^d}{\sigma^\nu (1-\nu)} (H^r)^\nu (H - H^r)^{1-\nu}\right) \tag{6.22}$$

as in the previous section.

In order to derive the research arbitrage equation, note first that the producer of any product of age a at time t will choose the amount of production labor x_a that maximizes its flow of profit: $\alpha A_{t-a}(x_a)^\alpha - w_t x_a$. Hence the firm's demand for labor and its flow of profit can both be expressed as functions of its productivity-adjusted wage $\frac{w_t}{A_{t-a}}$:

$$x_a = \bar{x}\left(\frac{w_t}{A_{t-a}}\right) = \left(\frac{w_t}{\alpha^2 A_{t-a}}\right)^{\frac{1}{\alpha-1}} \tag{6.23}$$

$$\pi_{a,t} = A_{t-a}\bar{\pi}\left(\frac{w_t}{A_{t-a}}\right) = A_{t-a}\psi(\alpha)\left(\frac{w_t}{A_{t-a}}\right)^{\frac{\alpha}{\alpha-1}} \tag{6.24}$$

where $\psi(\alpha) = (1-\alpha)\,\alpha^{\frac{1+\alpha}{1-\alpha}}$.

The equilibrium wage must solve the market-clearing condition:

$$L = \int_0^\infty S_a \bar{x}\left(\frac{w_t}{A_{t-a}}\right) da = \int_0^\infty S_a \bar{x}\left(\frac{w_t}{A_t}e^{ga}\right) da \tag{6.25}$$

which implies that in a steady state the wage rate grows like A_t at the rate g: $w_t = \omega e^{gt}$. From this and equation (6.24) the expected present value of the profits accruing to all the goods emanating from a new product line of vintage t will be $A_t \int_0^\infty e^{-ra}\bar{\pi}(\omega e^{ga})\left(\int_0^a \lambda^d \left(\eta e^{-\sigma s}\right)^{1-\nu} ds\right) da = A_t \Lambda \eta^{1-\nu}$, where η is the number of developers hired when the line was first opened up, and $\left(\int_0^a \lambda^d \left(\eta e^{-\sigma s}\right)^{1-\nu} ds\right)$ is the number of products when the line reaches age a.

Let $A_t V^d$ denote the expected present value of the wages that must be offered in a competitive market to each developer of a new line at date t. Then the researcher who opens up a new line will choose η so as to maximize

$$W_t = A_t W = A_t\left(\Lambda \eta^{1-\nu} - V^d \eta\right). \tag{6.26}$$

As before, this means that the share of rents that will be paid to the secondary innovators on a line will be the exponent of η, which in this case is just $1-\nu$. Hence

$$W = \frac{\nu}{1-\nu} V^d \eta. \tag{6.27}$$

Note that the share going to developers in this analysis is smaller than the share going to production workers in the previous section's analysis, because developers produce only secondary innovations, and do not also produce output as the production workers of the previous section did.

In equilibrium, because there are $\lambda^r H^r$ lines,

$$\eta = h_0/\lambda^r H^r. \tag{6.28}$$

From equations (6.27) and (6.28), the arbitrage condition (6.6), the Bellman equation (6.7), and the steady-state condition (6.21), we arrive finally at the research-arbitrage condition

$$r + \sigma - g = \sigma \frac{\nu}{1 - \nu} \frac{H - H^r}{H^r}. \tag{6.29}$$

which is identical to the two previous research arbitrage equations (6.10) and (6.15), except that this time the share going to secondary workers is $1 - \nu$ instead of α as in equation (6.10) or $\alpha + 1 - \nu$ as in equation (6.15).

Thus the steady-state values of g and H^r are determined by the same two curves as before, with this one change of parameter values. Because the direct benefits accruing to development can be and are internalized by firms, we find as in the case of internalized learning by doing that the steady-state amount of research will always fall short of the growth-maximizing amount.[14] Thus if we assume once more that there exists a unique steady-state equilibrium it must occur on the rising portion of the growth curve, and the following variant of Proposition 6.1 above can be demonstrated using exactly parallel reasoning:

Proposition 6.2 In the case of research and development, the rate of growth g and the level of research H^r are both:

a. increasing in λ^r, λ^d and H, and decreasing in r; and

b. increasing in σ and ν if the elasticity of the growth function G with respect to the flow of secondary innovations DEV is sufficiently small.

6.4   Preliminary Thoughts on Growth and the Organization of R&D

Opening the black box of R&D activities, as we have started to do in this chapter by distinguishing between *fundamental* and *secondary* innovations, raises the important issue of the *management of innovation*. In practice, R&D takes

---

14. That is, according to the above research arbitrage equation,

$$H^r = \frac{\nu}{1 + \frac{(r-g)(1-\nu)}{\sigma}} H < \nu H$$

because $r > g$, whereas the growth-maximizing value of H^r exceeds νH.

place either within firms where researchers are subject to complex employment contracts, or through contractual arrangements between independent research labs and the developer or users of their (basic) innovations. In either case, the contractual provisions on how to finance research activities and on how to structure the monetary compensations and the allocation of property rights on innovations are far more complex than the models surveyed earlier would suggest.

To illustrate the importance of organizational considerations, let us slightly modify the above framework and assume that, instead of competing ex-post for one another, researchers and developers are involved in specific contractual relationships whereby a developer's private investment combined with a (non-describable) training effort by the researcher jointly generate new intermediate plans on the line discovered by the researchers. If the applied innovation, that is the intermediate plan corresponding to it, cannot be described and there-fore contracted upon ex-ante, the rents W accruing to the researcher will now depend upon the allocation of *property rights* over intermediate innovations between the researcher and the developer.

More precisely, let $\lambda^d = d^{1-s}.r^s$ be the arrival rate of new intermediate plans, where r and d denote respectively the (noncontractable) training effort by the researcher and the developer's private investment; both are supplied at a linear cost. If property rights are allocated to the developer,[15] the researcher will receive no reward for innovating. The growth process will be driven en-tirely by developments on the initial product line. However, if property rights are allocated to the researcher,[16] because the developer is indispensable for commercializing the innovation, there will be Nash bargaining between the re-searcher and the developer over the innovation rents. Assume for simplicity that the rents X are equally split ex-post between the two parties. Then, the equilibrium levels of r and d will satisfy the first-order conditions

$$\frac{1}{2}(1-s)\cdot\left(\frac{r}{d}\right)^s X = 1 = \frac{1}{2}s\left(\frac{r}{d}\right)^{s-1}\cdot X \qquad (6.30)$$

More generally, as we show in Chapter 13, any share $\kappa \in \left[0, \frac{1}{2}\right]$ [17] for developers can be implemented through allocating ownership rights on new intermediate plans to researchers but with "cofinancing" of the development

---

15. This is called the *integrated* case in Aghion and Tirole (1994b).

16. This is called the *non-integrated* case in Aghion and Tirole (1994b). See also Chapter 13.

17. Obviously, if the intermediate plan was contractable ex-ante, any sharing rule $\kappa \epsilon$ [0, 1] would become implementable without having to specify an allocation of property rights between the researcher and the developer.

investment d by a third party (in exchange for a claim of a fraction $(1 - \alpha)$ of the researcher's rent $\frac{X}{2}$ if $\kappa = 1 - \frac{\alpha}{2}$).

Which ownership structure will emerge in equilibrium will obviously depend (as in Grossman and Hart 1986) on the *marginal efficiency* of the researcher's effort compared with the *marginal efficiency* of the developer's investment, that is on the parameter s. It will also depend on other considerations such as *cash constraints* (in case the developer's investment is monetary).

Providing a more adapted framework to discuss the organization of R&D activities, the above model also suggests a more *targeted* or *qualitative* approach to government intervention in the R&D sector. In particular, compared with existing endogenous growth models, the framework provides a new rationale for the use of patents, in addition to their role in protecting innovators' rents against potential imitators: namely, the fact that patents can help achieve a better coordination between research and development through imposing more efficient rent-sharing κ between researchers and developers.

A natural issue raised by the above discussion is the fact that in practice governments, or any third party in general, cannot easily distinguish between research and development. It often takes years before figuring out the true nature of a discovery, that is, how much of a breakthrough this discovery represents. This, in turn, limits the extent to which the patent legislation can itself discriminate between research and development. In other words, it may be quite inefficient for a government to rely entirely upon patent policy as the instrument for intervention in the R&D sector; the double objectives of inducing an efficient total amount of innovative activity H and efficiently allocating this activity between research and development are unlikely both to be achieved through patent policy alone. A first way around this problem would be to make the patent policy sufficiently flexible (e.g., through being contingent on the breadth of innovations or on the organization of R&D—for example, distinguishing between innovations generated by independent laboratories and innovations generated by integrated research units). A second, somewhat more natural approach is for the government to combine patent policy with direct or indirect subsidies to institutions like universities or research laboratories that are most likely to perform fundamental research activities. To be cost effective, such subsidies might take various forms, including equity participation in the research labs in exchange for the developer also contributing to the increase in investment (See Aghion and Tirole 1994a and Chapter 13), and/or a direct but partial subsidy to developers also conditional upon the developers' contribution.

The organizational aspects of R&D activities and their impact on growth will be addressed in greater detail in Chapter 13.

6.5   Toward More Radical Fundamental Innovations

There is one important aspect of the fundamental/secondary distinction, however, which the preceding analysis does not capture; that is, the radical nature of fundamental innovations. In our analysis there is a steady stream of knowledge of all types coming on line, which pushes out the frontier of knowledge in a gradual and continuous fashion. Thus the model seems to come down on the side of Kuznets, who criticized Schumpeter for his emphasis on large economy-wide innovations, and against the recent Schumpeterian models (including our own basic model from Chapter 2) that emphasize such radical innovations.

The only reason for assuming that innovations coming from research are gradual in our model is simplicity. It allows us to avoid the changes that would take place during the intervals between the discovery of new lines in the incentive to engage in research versus development. The next task will be to analyze this dynamic decision, in the hopes of deriving endogenous Schumpeterian waves.[18] In Chapter 8 we analyze such waves.

6.6   Summary

In the Schumpeterian framework developed in Chapters 2 and 3, workers could freely choose between research and production activities in the intermediate good sector(s); the number of workers in the production sector had no effect on the growth rate, which was entirely determined by research. In practice, however, not all advances arise from research: many pieces of knowledge that are needed for researchers to make a discovery are discovered incidentally or by attempts by other people to solve completely different problems.

This suggests the possibility that the second group of workers, who produce the intermediate good, may also influence the growth rate. During the production of a new intermediate good, such workers inevitably encounter problems which they gradually learn to overcome by trial and error. These problems cannot be anticipated: it is only possible to learn their solutions by the act of production. We called this process "learning by doing."

Thus, although fundamental research opens up new windows of opportunity or new product lines, learning-by-doing or development activities fill up those windows and/or bring incremental improvements to those product lines.

18. See Jovanovic and Rob (1990) and Cheng and Dinopoulos (1992) for earlier attempts to generate Schumpeterian waves, also based on the dichotomy between fundamental and incremental innovations.

Fundamental and secondary innovations (or research and learning by doing) are thus complementary.

In this chapter we analyze a simple model of fundamental versus secondary innovations in which: (i) aggregate output is equal to the sum of output flows generated on all existing lines; (ii) fundamental research leads to the discovery of new, more productive lines, at a rate proportional to the total number of fundamental researchers in the economy; (iii) learning-by-doing or development activities on a line leads *either* to quality improvements for intermediate goods currently used on this line *or* to the discovery of new intermediate goods on the same product line; (iv) productivity on newly invented lines reflects the current level of general knowledge, and it evolves over time according to a *growth equation* that determines the steady-state growth rate of productivity as a function of the mix between research and learning by doing; (v) workers can choose at birth whether to engage in fundamental research or in secondary activities on a particular line, and thereafter they have only limited opportunities to relocate to new lines and/or to shift from secondary into fundamental research in the future.

The main conclusions emerging from our analysis of this model can be summarized as follows.

First, when learning by doing is purely *external* to firms, then in equilibrium too many resources may end up being devoted to research at the expense of learning by doing, which in turn will slow down growth. This possibility, which we refer to as the "tale of two cities effect," was earlier pointed out by Young (1992).

Second, when each product's quality improvements depends on only the *internal* learning by doing of the firm producing that product, then research always has a positive effect on growth at the margin in a steady state; this is due to the more forward-looking nature of research compared with learning by doing. This, together with positive discounting and decreasing returns to learning by doing on existing lines, implies than even the flow of secondary innovations will be affected more, on the margin, by research than by learning by doing.

Third, the steady-state rate of growth may be increased if production workers become more *adaptable*, that is, if the rate at which workers are able to switch to newer lines or into research increases. We refer to this result as the "Lucas effect," in as much as it supports Lucas's (1993) claim that a key to high growth performance lies in the ability to move skilled workers quickly between sectors. However, contrary to Lucas (1993), a higher mobility enhances growth not because it increases the pace of learning by doing but rather because: (i) it enhances the profitability of research (a successful fundamental innovator benefits from having more workers starting up on a line he or she has just discovered) and (ii) as we have argued above, insofar as learning by doing is internalized by firms, research has an unambiguously positive effect on growth at the margin in a steady state.

Problems

Difficulty of Problems:

No star: normal

One star: difficult

Two stars: very difficult

1. Learning by doing has no effect on general knowledge

In the R&D models with learning by doing developed in Chapter 6, the serendipitous learning activities exert two effects; they (i) raise quality of intermediate goods and (ii) expand general knowledge. This problem considers the case where the effect of learning by doing is limited to (i), that is, general knowledge increases solely due to deliberate research activity. Consider the R&D model with unappropriated learning by doing in section 6.1. Assume that the equation for the growth of general knowledge takes the form of

$$\dot{A}_t = \lambda^r H_t^r A_t \tag{6.31}$$

instead of (6.11).

a. Under what conditions does the model exhibit a unique equilibrium?

b. How do H^r and g change if ρ, H, α, σ, λ^r, and λ^d, rise?

2. Welfare analysis when learning by doing has no effect on general knowledge

Consider the R&D model with internalized learning by doing developed in section 6.2. Under the same assumption as in the previous problem, $\dot{A}_t/A_t = \lambda^r H_t^r$, show that the steady-state laissez faire rate of growth is smaller than the one chosen by a social planner.

⋆ 3. Arrow's learning by doing (based on d'Autume and Michel 1993)

It is sometimes said that Arrow (1962) is closest to endogenous growth theory. In what sense? In models which exhibit *constant* endogenous growth, some parameter restrictions are required. In problem 9 in Chapter 1, we saw, following Jones (1995), that if there are diminishing returns to the externality generated by knowledge, then growth is no longer "endogenous" and becomes zero in the absence of exogenous population growth. The same thing is found in Arrow (1962), in which learning by doing leads to knowledge accumulation with diminishing returns. This problem studies how we can change Arrow's learning model to get endogenous growth.

Consider a vintage model in which output of vintage v, $v \leq t$, denoted by $Y(t, v)$, is produced with the Leontief technology

$$Y(t, v) = \min \left\{ aI(v), \frac{aK(v)^{\alpha}}{b} L(t, v) \right\}, \quad a, b, \alpha > 0. \tag{6.32}$$

$I(v)$ denotes investment goods made at v, $L(t, v)$ is employment and $K(v)$ represents the externality generated by past investment, which is equal to cumulative gross investment

$$K(v) = \int_{-\infty}^{v} I(i)\, di. \tag{6.33}$$

The total labor force is constant, L. Let $T(t)$ be the age of the oldest equipment in use and let $M(t) = K(t - T(t))$ denote cumulative gross investment up to this equipment.

a. What condition is required for the efficient use of inputs in (6.32)?

b. Show that the full employment of labor requires

$$L = \begin{cases} \frac{b}{1-\alpha} \left[K(t)^{1-\alpha} - M(t)^{1-\alpha} \right] & \text{if } \alpha \neq 1, \\ b \left[\ln K(t) - \ln M(t) \right] & \text{if } \alpha = 1. \end{cases} \tag{6.34}$$

c. Show that total output in the economy is

$$Y(t) = \begin{cases} a \left[K(t) - \left(K(t)^{1-\alpha} - \frac{1-\alpha}{b}L \right)^{1/(1-\alpha)} \right] & \text{if } \alpha \neq 1, \\ aK(t)\left(1 - e^{-L/b}\right) & \text{if } \alpha = 1. \end{cases} \tag{6.35}$$

d. Assuming a constant saving rate, show that the growth rate of capital

i. tends to zero in the long-run for $1 > \alpha > 0$ (diminishing returns of learning effects; Arrow's case)

ii. is given by $sa(1 - e^{-L/b})$ for $\alpha = 1$ (constant returns of learning effects)

iii. is given by sa for $\alpha > 1$ (increasing returns of learning effects).

e. With the instantaneous utility function $u(C(t)) = C(t)^{1-\sigma}/(1-\sigma)$, show that the equilibrium condition for the social optimum when $\alpha = 1$ is given by

$$g = \frac{A - \rho}{\sigma}, \quad A = a(1 - e^{-L/b}) > \rho. \tag{6.36}$$

f. The long-run equilibrium of the laissez-faire economy when $\alpha = 1$.

i. Consider the profitability of investment made at time t. Show that the future quasi-rent per unit of equipment at $\tau \geq t$ is given by $\pi(\tau, t) = a[1 - e^{g(\tau - T - t)}]$. (Hint: the quasi-rent of $M(t)$ is zero at time t.)

ii. Show that $T = L/(bg)$ holds in the long run.

iii. Confirm that equilibrium conditions consist of

$$1 = \int_t^{t+L/(bg)} e^{-r(\tau-t)} a[1 - e^{g(\tau-t)-L/b}] d\tau, \qquad g = \frac{r - \rho}{\sigma}. \qquad (6.37)$$

iv. How does g change as a, b, ρ, σ, and L increase?

g. Show that the market economy always grow too slowly compared to the social optimum. (Hint: draw a figure.)

⋆ 4. Bounded learning by doing (based on Young 1991, 1993a)

An important empirical regularity concerning learning by doing is that its external effect is bounded. This observation reveals a major shortcoming of learning-by-doing models such as Arrow (1962). If the number of industries is fixed and their learning effects are bounded, growth cannot be sustained in the long run. A solution to this problem is to introduce the possibility that new products are constantly introduced by way of learning externality across industries and/or R&D. This problem studies this idea and is related to the next problem, based on Lucas (1993).

Consider an economy in which there is a continuum of final goods denoted by $s \in (0, +\infty)$. Their blueprints are freely available; hence their markets are perfectly competitive. There are L consumers who supply one unit of labor services. Their instantaneous utility function is given by

$$u(t) = \int_0^\infty \ln [x(s, t) + 1] \, ds \qquad (6.38)$$

where $x(s, t)$ is the quantity of the sth good. As there is no storage technology, a consumer spends all income on consumption at each instant. Consumption goods are produced with the production technology $x(s, t) = L(s, t)/a(s, t)$ where $L(s, t)$ denotes the number of workers used in the production of good s, and $a(s, t)$ is the unit labor requirement. Learning by doing is captured by the fact that $a(s, t)$ falls over time. Let $a(s, t) = e^{s-2S(t)}$ for a good in which there is still scope for learning, where the term $S(t)$ captures the learning by doing effect and is increasing in time, t. Eventually learning by doing is exhausted and $a(s, t) = \bar{a}(s) = e^{-s}$. Assume $\bar{a}(s)$ is reached in finite time. The fact that $\bar{a}(s)$ is decreasing in s reflects the fact that newer products (higher s) are more sophisticated than old ones (lower s). Note that $S(t)$ also defines the threshold good such that all goods $s \leq S(t)$ have reached their lower labor requirement, $\bar{a}(s)$, and all more sophisticated goods exhibit scope for more learning by doing. Then, we can express the learning by doing function as

$$a(s, t) = \begin{cases} e^{-s} & \text{for } s \leq S(t) \\ e^{s-2S(t)} & \text{for } s > S(t) \end{cases} \qquad (6.39)$$

Economy-wide learning by doing occurs according to

$$\dot{S}(t) \equiv \frac{dS(t)}{dt} = \int_{S(t)}^{N(t)} \psi L\,(s,t)\,ds, \quad \psi > 0, \tag{6.40}$$

where $N\,(t)$ denotes the newest (highest s) good actually produced. Equation (6.40) implies that each worker learns at a rate of ψ, no matter which good she is producing.

a. Show that $a(s,t)$ is a U-shaped function of s, symmetric around $S(t)$.

b. Find the prices of consumption goods.

c. Consumers consume only a limited range of goods at any point in time. Why is it so?

d. Static equilibrium:

i. Show that the demand functions of consumption goods are given by

$$x\,(s,t) = \begin{cases} e^{s-M(t)} - 1 & \text{for } M\,(t) \le s \le S\,(t) \\ e^{N(t)-s} - 1 & \text{for } S\,(t) \le s \le N\,(t) \end{cases} \tag{6.41}$$

where $M(t)$ denotes the oldest (lowest s) good actually consumed.

ii. Show that $x(s,t)$ is symmetric and $\bigcap$-shaped around $S(t)$.

iii. Show that the range of goods actually consumed ($N(t) - M(t)$) is implicitly determined by

$$S\,(t) = \ln 2 \left[(\tau\,(t) - 1)\, e^{\tau(t)} - 1 \right]. \tag{6.42}$$

where $\tau(t) = (N(t) - M(t))/2 = (S(t) - M(t))$.

e. Dynamic equilibrium:

i. Show that $S(t)$ increases over time according to

$$\dot{S}\,(t) = \frac{\Psi L}{2}. \tag{6.43}$$

ii. Find the growth rate of this economy, which is equivalent to the average proportional rate of reduction of $a(s,t)$.

f. Assume that the creation of blueprints for every consumption good requires deliberate research. Blueprints for goods $s \in [\infty, A(t)]$ have been invented at t. R&D technology to expand the knowledge frontier is given by $\dot{A}(t) = L_R/a_R$ where $a_R > 0$ and L_R is the number of researchers. Assume that research activities are entirely financed from abroad. If $N(t) \le A(t)$, show that the steady state growth rate is now given by

$$g = \frac{\Psi L}{2 + \Psi a_R}. \tag{6.44}$$

** **5. Learning by doing in a small open economy (based on Lucas 1993)**

Differences in growth rates among economies may depend on how workers are allocated to different sectors, especially if learning possibilities are different and bounded. This is the contention of Lucas, who argues that this is consistent with what he calls the East Asian miracles (Hong Kong, Korea, Singapore, and Taiwan), in that their spectacular growth experiences involve the movement of the workforce from less to more sophisticated products.

Consider a small open economy that produces a subset of a continuum of products that are invented abroad. We use $x(s, t)$, $s \in [0, \lambda t]$, to denote the quantity of the sth good at time t. λ denotes the endogenous speed at which goods are introduced into the economy. The production of the (λt)th good begins at t, and products indexed by $s = \lambda \tau$ were introduced into the economy at time $\tau < t$. The higher s implies more advanced goods, so that their prices are given by $p(s, t) = e^{\mu s}$, $\mu > 0$. $x(s, t)$ is produced with the following technology:

$$x(s, t) = k\varphi(t - \tau) z(s, t)^{\alpha}, \quad k > 0, \quad 1 > \alpha > 0. \tag{6.45}$$

$\varphi(t - \tau) = \sigma e^{-\sigma(t-\tau)}$, $1 > \sigma > 0$, is the number (density) of workers employed, as total working population is normalized to 1. $z(s, t)$ represents a learning-by-doing externality. For products whose production has already started in the economy, $z(s, t)$ increases according to

$$\frac{dz(s, t)}{dt} = \varphi(t - \tau) z(s, t)^{\alpha} \qquad \text{for } s \leq \lambda t. \tag{6.46}$$

In other words, the learning effects arise from cumulative experience on the sth good only. As for goods that are not yet produced, $z(s, t)$ increases due to the economy-wide experience accumulated in producing all goods that were previously introduced (i.e., $s \leq \lambda t$):

$$z(s, t) = \delta \int_0^{\lambda t} e^{-\delta(s-u)} z(u, t) \, du \qquad \text{for } s > \lambda t \tag{6.47}$$

where $\delta > 0$ indicates the decay rate of spillover experience. To put a limit on the number of goods produced in the economy, it is assumed that the production of (λt)th good starts once the right-hand side of (6.47) equals 1.

a. What is the value of the total production of the economy?

b. Solve the differential equation (6.46), integrating from τ to t.

c. Confirm that the economy introduces goods sequentially from less advanced goods over time.

d. Show that λ is determined in the long run by the condition

$$1 = \int_0^{\infty} \delta \lambda e^{-\delta \lambda v} \left[1 + (1 - \alpha) \left(1 - e^{-\sigma v} \right) \right]^{\frac{1}{1-\alpha}} \, dv \tag{6.48}$$

where $1 - e^{-\sigma v}$ is the fraction of people employed in producing goods that were introduced less than v years earlier.

e. How does λ change, if (i) δ increases, and (ii) σ increases, that is, more workers are reallocated to the production of more sophisticated goods?

f. Show that the asymptotic growth rate of the economy is $\mu\lambda$, so that its qualitative change in response to a rise in σ is the same as given in (e).

g. Suppose that there exists another economy that is specialized in one particular product (the sth product for $s < \lambda t$), devoting all workforce to its production, i.e. $\varphi (t - s/\lambda) = 1$. Using (6.45) and (6.46), show that the rate of growth for this economy monotonically declines to zero.

⋆⋆ 6. Technological "lock-in" (based on Jovanovic and Nyarko 1994)

The theory of endogenous growth emerged against the background of the growing concern about the economic slowdown of the industrialized countries in the 1970s and 1980s. It also coincides with the spectacular growth performance of some Asian countries, notably Hong Kong, Korea, Singapore, and Taiwan, that have overtaken some slow-growing economies. Moreover, "catch-up" and "overtaking" have been historically observed; for example, the United States and Germany surpassed the United Kingdom in GDP per capita, and the relative decline of the United States compared with Japan has been much debated. This problem provides one possible rationale for this phenomenon. The idea is that if an economy learns too much from one technology, it may be locked into it, allowing other economies with frequent technological upgrading to overtake it.

A risk-neutral agent produces net output by investing z without any costs at $t = 0, 1, 2, \ldots$, using the following production function

$$y_t = \gamma^m \left[1 - (q_{mt} - z_t)^2 \right], \qquad \gamma > 1, \quad m = 1, 2, 3, \ldots \tag{6.49}$$

The level of technology is given by γ^m, and q_{mt} is a random "target" that fluctuates around a technology-specific parameter θ_m:

$$q_{mt} = \theta_m + w_{mt} \tag{6.50}$$

where $w_{mt} \sim N(0, \sigma_m^2)$. The agent does not know θ_m, but q_{mt} is observed after z is chosen. Having used γ^m at t, he has two choices at $t + 1$: (i) sticks to γ^m and (ii) switches to γ^{m+1}. If (i) is chosen, learning by doing takes place. Before using γ^m at the beginning of t, he forms beliefs about θ_m, which is normally distributed with the prior variance $\text{Var}_t (\theta_m) \equiv x_{mt}$. At the end of t, after using it, the agent learns about θ_m and renews his beliefs about θ_m with the posterior variance h_{mt}

$$h_{mt} = \frac{\sigma_w^2 x_{mt}}{\sigma_w^2 + x_{mt}},$$

through Bayesian updating. Learning by doing takes the form of the reduction of the variance from x_{mt} to h_{mt}. Note that $h_{mt} = x_{mt+1}$. If the agent upgrades his technology to γ^{m+1}, no cost is incurred. But θ_m changes to θ_{m+1} according to

$$\theta_{m+1} = \sqrt{\alpha}\theta_m + \varepsilon_{m+1}, \quad \alpha \geq 0 \tag{6.51}$$

where $\varepsilon_{m+1} \sim N(0, \sigma_\varepsilon^2)$. This implies that what the agent has learned from γ^m may not necessarily carry over to the use of γ^{m+1}.

a. Show that the optimal z that maximizes the expected net output is $z_t = E_t[\theta_m]$, which is the expectation conditional on information available at the beginning of t.

b. Given this optimal decision of z, show that the expected net output at the beginning of t is given by

$$E_t\left[y_t\right] = \gamma^m \left[1 - x_{mt} - \sigma_w^2\right]. \tag{6.52}$$

c. Long-run growth:

i. Does learning by doing alone create unbounded growth?

ii. Does the continual upgrading of technologies in every period lead to unbounded growth for a given x_{mt}?

d. The prior and posterior precision of θ_m, $1/x_{mt}$ and $1/h_{mt}$ can be interpreted as the level of human capital, and equation (6.51) summarizes how such human capital is transferred in the process of upgrading technologies. Given this, interpret the parameters α and σ_ε^2.

e. Consider t when technology γ^m is used. Show that the expected net output at the beginning of $t + 1$ is

$$\pi\left(h_{mt}, m\right) = \gamma^m \left[1 - h_{mt} - \sigma_w^2\right], \tag{6.53}$$

if the agent continues to use the same technology in that period, but it is given by

$$\pi\left(h_{mt}, m + 1\right) = \gamma^{m+1} \left[1 - \alpha h_{mt} - \sigma_\varepsilon^2 - \sigma_w^2\right]. \tag{6.54}$$

if he switches to new technology γ^{m+1} at $t + 1$.

f. The agent decides whether to continue to use old technology γ^m or to switch to the frontier technology γ^{m+1} at $t + 1$. Find the conditions for:

i. Continual switching to higher technologies in every period

ii. Technological lock-in into the initial technology γ from $t = 0$ on.

g. How is the agent's incentive for technology upgrading affected by α, σ_ε^2, σ_w^2, γ and h_{mt}?

⋆ **7. "Penalty" to a pioneer (based on Redding 1996c)**

In problem 6, we considered the model of technology adoption by a single agent and saw that too much learning on one technology reduces his incentive to adopt a superior technology and may prevent him from doing so. Arguably, the model gives one possible rationale for the relative declines of some economies observed in the past. However, its analysis is of a partial-equilibrium nature and it does not consider the creation of new technology. The aim of this problem is to show that the same result can be obtained in a general equilibrium dynamic model in which new technologies are invented through research activity. A modified version of this model was examined in Chapter 3, problem 5.

Assume there is a sequence of nonoverlapping generations indexed by t. Each generation consists of a continuum of consumer-producers of mass L. Time is discrete and indexed by τ. Agents live for one time unit, which we divide into two subperiods, j. Each agent has one unit of labor. At birth she must make the (irreversible) decision of whether to work in the production of intermediate goods or in research. The rate of time preference is ρ, which is equal to the interest rate.

Consider the basic quality ladder model, where R&D improves the productivity of intermediate goods. Suppose that there are two types of innovations: "fundamental," denoted Fm, and "secondary," Sm. Final good production is now

$$Y_{jt} = F_{jt} \cdot S_{jt} \cdot x_{jt}^{\alpha}, \quad 0 < \alpha < 1, \, j = 1, 2. \tag{6.55}$$

There is perfect competition in the sector, and the price of final output is 1.

One unit of labor is required to produce one unit of intermediate good, $x_t = l_t$. Let $l_t = L - n_t$ denote the number of agents from generation t that enter production, whereas n_t is the number that enters research. There are spillovers of fundamental and secondary knowledge across generations. Hence in subperiod 1, all agents have access to the same knowledge, and intermediate good production occurs under conditions of perfect competition. Whether or not there is monopolistic competition in subperiod 2 depends on whether the next fundamental innovation is discovered.

Fundamental knowledge is increased through R&D so that if n_t agents do research, the probability of discovery is $\lambda \cdot n_t$. An innovation raises F by an amount γ, so that $F_{jt} = \gamma^m$. Secondary knowledge grows at a given rate, $\theta > 0$. Assume that when a new fundamental innovation is discovered, part of the secondary knowledge specific to it is lost:

$$S_{2t}(m + 1) = (S_{1t}(m))^{\sigma} \quad 0 \le \sigma < 1 \tag{6.56}$$

a. Intermediate good sector:

i. Find the inverse demand for intermediaries and the wage in subperiod 1, w_{1t}.

ii. Find the wage in the sector in subperiod 2 if no innovation has occurred. What is the inverse demand for intermediaries?

iii. Suppose an innovation occurs in subperiod 2. The innovator (monopolist) can offer workers their outside option, w_{2t}. Given the inverse demand for the previous generation of goods, find the inverse demand for the state-of-the-art technology.

iv. Show that the state-of-the-art technology is used whenever $\gamma \cdot S_{1t}^{\sigma-1} > (1 + \theta)$. Assume this restriction holds.

v. What is the expected discounted value of a lifetime in the production sector B, V_{xt}?

b. Research sector: Find the subperiod 2 profits of a successful researcher. What is the expected discounted value of a lifetime in the research sector, V_{rt}?

c. Obtain the equilibrium level of research given by the indifference condition, $V_{xt} = V_{rt}$. Under which parameter restrictions does an interior solution exist?

d. Show that the expected rate of growth between the births of generations t and $t + 1$ is

$$g_{t,t+1} = (1 - \lambda\widehat{n}_t)\theta + \lambda\widehat{n}_t(\sigma - 1) \ln S_{1t} + \lambda\widehat{n}_t \ln \gamma. \tag{6.57}$$

e. A "pioneer" economy is one that adopted a given fundamental technology at an earlier date than a "latecomer" economy. Explain how their rates of growth differ.

7 Market Structure

7.1 Introduction

Is market competition good or bad for growth? The Schumpeterian answer to this question, as described in Chapters 2 and 3 above, appeared to be one-sided: to the extent that monopoly rent is what induces firms to innovate and thereby makes the economy grow, product market competition can only be detrimental to growth. By the same token, more intense imitation discourages technological innovations and growth. Hence the importance of preserving intellectual property rights through an adequate system of (international) patent protection (see Grossman and Helpman 1991a).

On the other hand, recent empirical work (e.g., by Nickell 1996 or Blundell et al. 1995)[1] points to a *positive* correlation between *product market competition* (as measured either by the number of competitors in the same industry or by the inverse of a market share or profitability index) and *productivity growth* within a firm or industry. This evidence, in turn, appears to be more consistent with the "Darwinian view" (see, for example, M. Porter 1990) that product market competition is good for growth because it *forces* firms to innovate in order to survive.

How can we reconcile the Darwinian view supported by Nickell et al. with the Schumpeterian paradigm developed earlier? Several tentative answers to this question will be explored in this chapter. The first approach, developed in section 7.3, is to introduce *agency considerations* in the decision-making process of innovating firms, and then investigate the idea that by reducing "slack" (i.e., the amount of free cash available to managers), product market competition combined with the threat of liquidation can act as a disciplinary device which fosters technology adoption and thus growth. The second approach, developed in section 7.4, is to replace the assumption made earlier that incumbent innovators are automatically leap-frogged by their rivals, by a more *gradualist* ("*step-by-step*") technological progress assumption. Finally, a third approach, based on Chapter 6, will be to decompose R&D activities into *research* (leading to the discovery of new fundamental paradigms or product lines) and *development* (aimed at exploiting the new paradigms and filling up the new product lines).

Although our main focus in this section is on *product market* competition, we shall first turn our attention to the effect(s) on growth of *competition in the innovation sector*. Unlike product market competition, the latter was explicitly advocated by Schumpeter as unambiguously good for innovation and growth. The following section will show why Schumpeter was right.

---

1. See Chapter 12.

7.2   Barriers to Entry in Research

Schumpeter's notion of creative destruction projects a view of the "competitive struggle" somewhat at odds with the standard textbook version, one in which the main instrument of competition is innovation rather than price. Clearly, "more competition" in this Schumpeterian sense means not a higher price-elasticity of demand faced by a producer, but an increased freedom of entry into the competitive innovation sector by potentially rent-stealing rivals. It is relatively straightforward to show that more competition in this sense will lead to higher growth.

The Arrow Effect

Recall the basic Schumpeterian model of Chapter 2, where the research sector was assumed to be competitive (with any individual being free to engage in research activities). What would happen to the steady-state growth rate if the research sector was instead monopolistic? The main difference between the two cases is that, in the latter, research would be done by the incumbent innovator. More formally, the equation governing the level of research would become

$$w_t = \lambda(V_{t+1} - V_t) \tag{7.1}$$

where

$$rV_t = \pi_t + \lambda n_t(V_{t+1} - V_t) \tag{7.2}$$

The RHS of (7.1) expresses the fact that the incumbent innovator internalizes the business-stealing effect of his or her new innovation: the difference between (7.1) and the analogous arbitrage equation (A) in Chapter 2 reflects the well-known *replacement effect* of Arrow. The RHS of (7.2), in turn, expresses the fact that the incumbent innovator internalizes the positive (intertemporal spillover) externality of current innovation on future research activities. In other words, a monopolist researcher will essentially[2] behave like a benevolent social planner. The comparison between research (and growth) respectively in the benchmark model with competitive research and in the monopolistic research case will thus boil down to a reinterpretation of the welfare analysis of the benchmark model. Whether or not demonopolizing the research sector will create more growth depends on whether the business-stealing (Arrow) effect exceeds the intertemporal spillover effect.

This apparent ambiguity of the effect of demonopolizing research is, however, an artifact of the simplifying assumption that there is only one interme-

---

2. Except for the fact that a monopolist maximizes profits, whereas the social planner would seek to maximize intertemporal consumption.

diate good sector. In the multisector extension of Chapter 3, the ambiguity disappears, because even if each sector is monopolized, no sector is large enough to internalize the intertemporal spillovers, which benefit all the other local monopolists, not just the monopolist generating the spillovers. In this case only the Arrow-effect remains, and competition is unambiguously favorable to growth.

The Case of **U-Shaped** Individual **R&D Cost Functions**

The same result can be demonstrated in the basic (one-sector) model when there exists initially more than one research firm. To show this we must relax the assumption made up to now that there are constant returns to scale in research activities.[3] Instead assume that each individual firm faces a Poisson probability equal to $\lambda\theta(z - \phi)$, where the innovation function θ is increasing and concave, z is the firm's total labor input, and ϕ is an entry fee (expressed in labor units) to be paid by each research firm to the government.

Because any research firm willing to pay this fee is free to enter, the expected profit of each research firm must be zero in a steady state: $\lambda\theta(z - \phi)V_{t+1} = w_t z$. The first-order condition for each research firm is $\lambda\theta'(z - \phi)V_{t+1} = w_t$. Hence the marginal and average product of research will be equal in a steady state:

$$\frac{\theta(z - \phi)}{z} = \theta'(z - \phi) \tag{C}$$

Let N denote the number of research firms in equilibrium. Because the aggregate arrival rate of new innovations is equal to $\lambda N\theta(z - \theta)$, the steady-state *arbitrage equation* becomes

$$\omega = \lambda\theta'(z - \phi)\gamma\frac{\widetilde{\pi}(\omega)}{r + \lambda N\theta(z - \phi)}, \tag{A}$$

where z is defined by (C). The steady-state equilibrium $(\widehat{\omega}, \widehat{z}, \widehat{N})$ is then fully determined by (C), (A) and the *labor market-clearing equation*

$$Nz + \widetilde{x}(\omega) = L \tag{L}$$

How does the steady-state growth rate $g = \lambda\widehat{N}\theta(\widehat{z} - \phi)\ln\gamma$ respond to a reduction in the entry fee ϕ, that is to an increase in competitiveness in the research sector? To answer that question, make the change of variables:

$$\widetilde{\lambda} = \lambda\frac{\theta(z - \phi)}{z} \quad \text{and} \quad \widetilde{n} = Nz.$$

Using (C) to determine $\widetilde{\lambda}$, we can reexpress (A) and (L) respectively as

---

3. That is, we have assumed that individual firms have Poisson innovation rates of the form: λz, where z is the firm's R&D effort.

$$\omega = \widetilde{\lambda}\gamma \frac{\widetilde{\pi}(\omega)}{r + \widetilde{\lambda}\widetilde{n}} \tag{A}$$

and

$$L = \widetilde{n} + \widetilde{x}(\omega), \tag{L}$$

which are identical to (A) and (L) in the basic model of Chapter 2, except that λ and n have been replaced by $\widetilde{\lambda}$ and $\widetilde{n}$ respectively.

A reduction in the entry fee ϕ amounts to increasing $\widetilde{\lambda}$ (the arrival rate of innovations per research worker). Now, we know from our comparative statics analysis of the basic model in Chapter 2 that $\frac{d\widetilde{n}}{d\lambda} > 0$. Therefore the steady-state growth rate, which is equal to $\widetilde{\lambda}\widetilde{n} \ln \gamma$, will also increase as a result of a lower entry fee. This vindicates the Schumpeterian claim that more competition in research is growth-enhancing.

7.3   Introducing Agency Considerations

The next three sections[4] all deal with competition in output markets. First, we relax the assumption that innovating firms maximize profit. Instead, we assume that managers are mainly concerned with preserving their private benefits of control while at the same time minimizing (innovation) costs, an assumption commonly made in the corporate finance literature. (Innovation costs here refer to the *private* managerial costs—training costs or nonmonetary costs of reorganizing the firm—of switching to a new technology.) Intensifying product market competition may then become growth-enhancing by forcing managers to *speed up* the adoption of new technologies in order to avoid bankruptcy and the resulting loss of control rights. This Darwinian argument is consistent with Porter's (1990) view of the role of competition in fostering growth.

More formally, consider the multisector model of Chapter 3, with the final good being produced using a continuum of intermediate inputs of different technological vintages according to the production function

$$y = \int_0^1 A_i x_i^\alpha di,$$

where A_i is the productivity parameter in sector i.

Intermediate firms are now involved in two kinds of decisions:

Production Decisions (for a Given Technology)

As before, an intermediate firm with technological vintage A_τ will choose its current output flow $x = x_{t,\tau}$ so as to

---

4. See Aghion, Dewatripont, and Rey (1997) from which this section is drawn.

$$\max_{x}\{p_\tau(x)x - w_t x\}$$

where

$$p_\tau(x) = A_\tau \alpha x^{\alpha-1}.$$

In a steady state, we have $w_t = A_t \omega$, where $A_t = A_0 e^{gt}$ is the leading-edge and g is the steady-state growth rate. Therefore the output flow of a firm of vintage τ at date t (also the flow demand for labor by that firm) is

$$x_{t,\tau} = \tilde{x}(\omega) e^{-\frac{g(t-\tau)}{1-\alpha}} = \left(\frac{\omega}{\alpha^2}\right)^{1/\alpha-1} e^{-\frac{g(t-\tau)}{1-\alpha}};$$

that is, it decreases exponentially with the age of the firm's technology $(t - \tau)$.

Assume that intermediate firms must incur a fixed operating cost (also in terms of labor) equal to $k_{t,\tau} = w_t k e^{\rho(t-\tau)}$ with $\rho \geq r$. Then the firm's *net* profit flow is given by

$$\pi_{t,\tau} = \left(\pi e^{-\frac{g(t-\tau)}{1-\alpha}} - \omega k e^{\rho(t-\tau)}\right) e^{gt}$$

$$= \psi(\pi, u) e^{gt},$$

where $u = t - \tau$ is the age of the firm's technology and $\pi = \tilde{\pi}(\omega) = \frac{1-\alpha}{\alpha} \omega \tilde{x}(\omega)$ is the productivity-adjusted variable profit of a leading-edge firm.[5]

The productivity-adjusted profit flow, ψ, is thus positive for $u = 0$[6] but decreasing in age and negative for u sufficiently large. This, in turn, will play a key role in the Darwinian argument developed below.

Technological Adoption

We now depart from the previous sections by supposing that each firm's local monopoly is permanent. In a steady state it is never replaced by an outside innovator. We also suppose that new technological vintages result from *once-over* investments made by intermediate firms rather than from a continuous *flow* of research investments. Let f denote the sunk cost (in labor units) of adopting the leading-edge technology.[7] Measured in units of final output, the adoption cost at date τ is $f_\tau = f w_\tau = f \omega e^{g\tau}$. In a steady state each intermediate firm adopts the leading-edge technology every T units of time, and the age distribution of firms remains uniform on $[0, T]$. Thus the aggregate flow of

---

5. Clearly, ψ depends also on ω, independently of the indirect effect working through π. We suppress this extra argument of the ψ function for notational simplicity.

6. At least for ω sufficiently low.

7. We posit a deterministic innovation process at the firm level, which in turn can be interpreted as assuming either that each intermediate firm hires a large number (continuum) of researchers subject to uncorrelated Poisson processes or that it adopts existing new inventions.

new adoptions per unit of time is $1/T$, and the aggregate flow of research labor is $n = f/T$. As in the multisector model of Chapter 3, assume that adoptions lead incrementally to growth in the leading-edge, at the rate $\ln \gamma$ per unit of innovation. Then, as before, the steady-state growth rate is

$$g = \dot{A}/A = \ln \gamma / T \tag{G}$$

Thus, the average growth rate of the economy hinges entirely on the timing of innovations decided by intermediate firms. This in turn will depend on the objective function of intermediate firms' managers.

Departing from the previous chapters, we do not restrict our analysis to the case where firms are pure profit-maximizers, but also consider the case where firms' managers are "conservative" in the sense that they incur a *private cost* from adopting new technologies.[8] There is more than one reason why nonprofit maximizing firms (or managers) can survive in a capitalistic environment. A first reason has to do with the *competitive environment* itself: the less the competition among domestic intermediate producers or between them and the "outside world," the bigger the scope for entrepreneurial slack in (small) firms whose owners are not primarily interested in profit maximization. A second reason is the existence of an *agency problem* between intermediate producers and their outside financiers.

1. Profit-Maximizing Firms

First consider an intermediate firm born at date 0 that does *not* face agency problems. Such a firm will, in steady state, choose to switch to the leading-edge at times T_1, $T_1 + T_2$, ..., $T_1 + \cdots + T_k$, etc, where (T_k) is a solution of the maximization program:

$$\rightarrow \max_{(T_k)} [W - f\omega + \int_0^{T_1} \psi(\pi, u)e^{-(r-g)u}\, du$$

$$+ e^{-(r-g)T_1}[-f\omega + \int_0^{T_2} \psi(\pi, u)e^{-(r-g)u}\, du]$$

$$+ e^{-(r-g)(T_1+T_2)}[-f\omega + \int_0^{T_3} \psi(\pi, u)e^{-(r-g)u}\, du]$$

$$+ \cdots]$$

where W is the firm's initial endowment at date 0.

---

8. Such a cost may refer to the required effort by a manager to train for the next technology or to his or her cost of training workers and/or reorganising the firm. In practice, a manager's objective function is likely to be a convex combination of profit-maximization and conservative management.

One can easily see that the optimal adoption policy is stationary ($T_k \equiv \widehat{T}$ for $k \geq 1$), where

$$\widehat{T} = \arg\max_{T} \frac{[-f\omega + \int_0^T \psi(\pi, u)e^{-(r-g)u}du]}{1 - e^{-(r-g)T}} \tag{A^P}$$

Equation (A^P) is the research-arbitrage equation under profit maximization.

It turns out (see Aghion, Dewatripont, and Rey 1997a) that the equilibrium adoption policy $\widehat{T}$ defined by (A^P) and labor market clearing[9] satisfies:

$$\frac{d\widehat{T}}{d\alpha} > 0$$

This is again the appropriability effect pointed out in the basic Schumpeterian model: more product market competition (i.e., a lower π) will discourage technological adoptions ($\widehat{T} \nearrow$) and thereby reduce growth.

2. Non–profit-Maximizing Firms

A common assumption in the corporate-finance literature is that managers of large companies (especially those with high levels of outside [equity] financing—see Aghion, Dewatripont, and Rey 1997a) are mainly concerned with preserving their private benefits of control over the company while also minimizing "effort." Thus assume the following utility function for intermediate firms' managers:

$$U_0 = \int_0^\infty B_t e^{-\delta t} dt - \sum_{j \geq 1} C e^{-\delta(T_1 + \cdots + T_j)},$$

where C is the *private cost to the manager of adopting* a new vintage (training cost, for example); B_t is the *current private benefit of control* at date t, equal to $B > 0$ if the firm has survived up to t and zero otherwise; and δ is the managers' subjective discount rate.

---

9. The labor market clearing condition that determines the productivity-adjusted wage ω in a steady state can be expressed as

$$\frac{e^{\rho T} - 1}{\rho T} \cdot k + \frac{f}{T} + \widetilde{x}(\omega) \left[\frac{1 - e^{-\ln \gamma/(1-\alpha)}}{\ln \gamma/(1-\alpha)} \right] = L \tag{L^P}$$

where the first term on the LHS of (L^P) is the aggregate operating cost, the second term is the aggregate demand for research labor, and the third term is the aggregate demand for manufacturing labor. Note that this last term includes another "productivity effect," whereby an increase in γ reduces the aggregate demand for labor relative to the leading-edge demand $\widetilde{x}(\omega)$, as in Chapter 3.

For B and δ sufficiently large, one can show that this objective function is observationally equivalent to a lexicographic preference ordering whereby the manager always seeks to delay as much as possible the next innovation subject to keeping the firm afloat, that is with a positive net financial wealth. Consider now an intermediate firm where the manager obeys such a lexicographic preference ordering, and suppose that this firm entered the market with wealth ωf and innovated at date $t = 0$.

If the firm has not innovated thereafter, its accumulated profits at date $t = T$ (discounted back to date 0) will equal

$$\int_0^T \psi(\pi, u) e^{-(r-g)u} du.$$

Given that $\psi(\pi, 0) > 0$, $\psi(\pi, u) < 0$ for u large and $\psi_u < 0$, these cumulative profits will be inverted-U-shaped with respect to T, being initially increasing and positive for T small and then decreasing. Eventually they will be negative for T sufficiently large. This implies that the intermediate firm will necessarily become insolvent (and therefore go bankrupt) if it never again innovates after date 0. More precisely, there exists a maximum date $\widetilde{T}$ at which the firm's cumulative profits just cover the adoption cost $f e^{-(r-g)\widetilde{T}}$ at that date, (evaluated as of date zero), where $\widetilde{T}$ is defined by

$$\omega f e^{-(r-g)T} = \int_0^T \left[\tilde{\pi}(\omega) e^{\frac{-gu}{1-\alpha}} - \omega k e^{\rho u} \right] e^{-(r-g)u} du$$

$$= \int_0^T \psi(\pi, u) e^{-(r-g)u} du \tag{7.3}$$

Now, consider the effect of an increase in product market competition (e.g., due to an increase in the degree of substitutability between intermediate goods, i.e., an increase in α): intuitively, an increase in competition, by reducing the flow of variable profits π, will hasten the day when a firm's wealth (the RHS) is exhausted by the rising overhead costs $\omega k e^{\rho u}$, thus forcing it to adopt sooner, while it still has enough wealth remaining to do so. (See figure 7.1 below, where g and ω are both being taken as given). One can also show that an increase in product market competition, as measured by α, will still have the *overall* effect of speeding up innovations and thereby increasing growth in steady-state, when the wage ω and the growth rate g adjust. To see this more clearly, we use the fact that $\pi = \frac{1-\alpha}{\alpha} \omega x$, the labor-market clearing condition (L^p) of note 9, and the growth equation (G) to derive from (7.3) the reduced-form arbitrage equation:

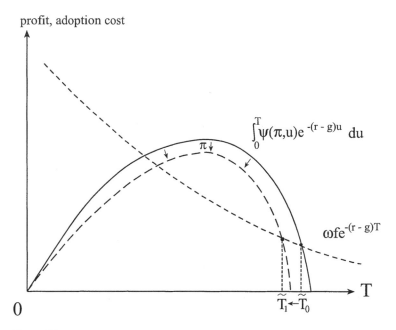

Figure 7.1
Effect of an increase in product market competition, for given ω and g.

$$fe^{-rT+\ln\gamma} = \int_0^T \left\{ \overbrace{\frac{1-\alpha}{\alpha}}^{\text{appropriability}} \overbrace{\left[\frac{\ln\gamma/(1-\alpha)}{1-e^{-\ln\gamma/(1-\alpha)}}\right]}^{\text{productivity}} \left[L - \frac{f}{T} - \frac{e^{\rho T}-1}{\rho T}k \right] \right.$$

$$\left. \overbrace{e^{\frac{-\ln\gamma u}{T(1-\alpha)}}}^{\text{crowding out}} - ke^{\rho u} \right\} e^{-(r-\ln\gamma/T)u}du$$

(A^F)

The two sides of (A^F), adoption cost and wealth, are described in figure 7.2. Wealth is less than cost for $T = 0$ and again as $T \to \infty$. So the equilibrium, which is the *maximal* delay possible, occurs at a point like E where wealth is falling faster than cost. Thus an increase in the competitiveness parameter α will reduce T, and hence raise growth, because it shifts the wealth curve down.

Contrary to the basic Schumpeterian model where a higher productivity of R&D has an ambiguously boosting effect on growth, a lower adoption

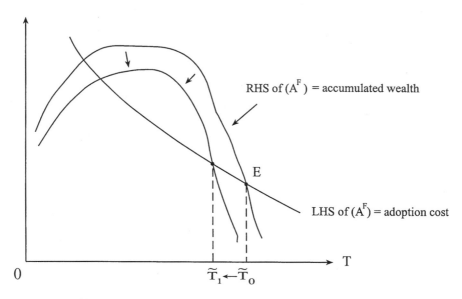

Figure 7.2
Overall effect of an increase in α.

cost f, for example, induced by "industrial policy," may *slow down* adoptions and growth: indeed for given wage ω, a lower f increases the financial slack of intermediate firms, thereby allowing managers to delay the next technological adoption while keeping their firm solvent. This model thus has important policy implications for the current debate on competition and industrial policies. Indeed, both ($\alpha \nearrow$ and/or $f \downarrow$) will have reversed effects on technological change and growth depending on the magnitude of agency problems in intermediate firms. Its conclusions are summarized in table 7.1.

It is thus clear that the correct behavioral model of firms has a profound impact on the preferred recipe for faster technological change, for *both* policy effects are reversed when moving from profit maximizing to "conservative" behavior. In fact, the contrast even extends to the effect of wage costs or taxation: whenever firms earn excessive rents in the conservative case, taking

Table 7.1
Policy impact on the rate of technology adoption

	Profit maximizing firms	Conservative firms
Competition policy	Negative	Positive
Industrial policy	Positive	Negative

them away through wage or tax increases reduces slack and fosters technology adoption. Of course, going "too far," however, becomes very damaging in as much as firms may be unable to survive even after having eliminated all slack! But otherwise, helping firms, even through adoption subsidies, is completely counterproductive in the conservative case: it is worse than offering a subsidy for investments that would have taken place anyway, since it even *retards* investment.

The main lesson of table 7.1 is the contrast between competition policy and industrial policy: whatever the behavioral model of firms, the effect of these two policies goes in opposite directions in terms of technological change. You may disagree as to which behavior better fits reality, but in any case you are faced with a *choice* between competition policy and industrial policy: if you like one policy, you should dislike the other.

Remember that we have so far assumed that firms are fully internally financed. This may be a reasonable first approximation, given the preeminence of retained earnings as a source of finance for investment. In Aghion, Dewatripont, and Rey (1997a), we relax this assumption, however, by introducing competitive debt markets in which managers can borrow provided their firm is able to keep servicing its debt (the threat of liquidation upon default insures that debt repayments are made whenever feasible). In the framework described earlier, debt accumulation serves as a commitment device for the firm to eliminate slack in order to keep servicing its debt and avoid liquidation.[10] While debt accumulation initially serves to delay adoption, it thus accelerates it in steady state, forcing profit maximization behavior, with the policy implications described above.

The effectiveness of financial discipline in eliminating all slack is reduced when uncertainty is introduced, for example in the extent of improvement in quality that a given innovation cost implies. In this case, high debt accumulation becomes dangerous, because it can precipitate the fall of a firm that is unlucky in its innovation attempts. Consequently, debt accumulation is lower, and financial discipline only partly eliminates slack. This leaves a role for competition policy to eliminate it further. However, making product markets more competitive is a mixed blessing: firms will tend to reduce their debt level further as a protection against an environment that has become tougher. This *crowding-out effect* may even dominate the direct positive effect of product market competition on technology adoption that is stressed in table 7.1.

---

10. This approach to the corporate governance problem is in the spirit of the "free cash flow" approach of Jensen (1986).

7.4   From Leap-Frogging to Step-by-Step Technological Progress

An alternative approach[11] for reconciling the Schumpeterian paradigm with recent empirical evidence on productivity growth and product market competition is to replace the *leap-frogging* assumption of the basic Schumpeterian model (with incumbent innovators being systemically overtaken by outside researchers), with a less radical *step-by-step* assumption. That is, a firm that is currently *m* steps behind the technological leader in its industry must catch up with the leader before becoming a leader itself. This step-by-step assumption can be rationalized by supposing that an innovator acquires tacit knowledge that cannot be duplicated by a rival without engaging in its own R&D to catch up. Once it has caught up we suppose that no patent protects the former leader from Bertrand competition.

This change leads to a richer analysis of the interplay between product market competition, innovation, and growth by allowing firms in an industry to be *neck-to-neck*. A higher degree of product market competition, by making life more difficult for neck-to-neck firms, will encourage them to innovate in order to acquire a significant lead over their rivals.

More formally, suppose that final output is produced at any time *t* using input services from a continuum of intermediate sectors, according to the production function

$$\ln y_t = \int_0^1 \ln x_i(t)\,di.$$

As shown in Grossman and Helpman (1991a), this logarithmic technology implies that the same amount $E(t)$ will be spent at any time *t* by the final good sector on *all* intermediate industries. Choosing current aggregate spending as the numeraire, we then have $E(t) \equiv 1$.

Each sector *i* is assumed to be *duopolistic* with respect to both production and research activities, with firms A and B, and

$$x_i = v(x_{Ai}, x_{Bi}),$$

where v is homogenous of degree one and symmetric in its two arguments.[12]

Let *k* denote the technology level of a duopoly firm in a given industry. That is, in order to produce one unit of intermediate good, this firm needs to employ γ^{-k} units of labor, where $\gamma > 1$. An industry is thus fully characterized

---

11. See Aghion, Harris, and Vickers (1995).

12. A particular case is when $x_i = x_A + x_B$, that is, when the two intermediate inputs produced in industry *i* are perfect substitutes.

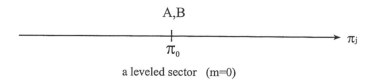

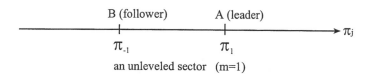

Figure 7.3

by a pair of integers (l, m), where l is the leader's technology and m is the technological gap between the leader and the follower.

Let π_m(resp. π_{-m}) denote the equilibrium profit flow of a firm m steps ahead of (resp. behind) its rival.[13] For expositional simplicity, we assume that knowledge spillovers between leader and follower in an industry are such that the maximum sustainable gap is $m = 1$. That is, if a firm one step ahead innovates, the follower will automatically learn to copy the leader's previous technology and will then remain only one step behind.

At any point in time, there will thus be two kinds of intermediate sectors in the economy: *leveled* sectors where firms are neck-and-neck, that is, with $m = 0$; and *unleveled* sectors where one firm (the *leader*) is one step ahead of its competition (the *follower*) in the same industry (see figure 7.3). We now come to the basic feature of the model, namely the *step-by-step* technological assumption. We denote by $\psi(n) = \frac{1}{2}n^2$ the R&D cost (in units of labor) of a firm moving one technological step ahead with Poisson hazard rate n. Let n_0 denote the R&D intensity put up by each firm in a leveled industry; and let n_{-1} denote the research intensity by the follower firm in an unleveled industry. Note that $n_1 = 0$, because our assumption of automatic catchup means a leader cannot get any further advantage by innovating.

Let V_m denote the steady-state value of being currently a leader (or a follower if $m < 0$) in an industry with technological gap m, and let w denote the steady-state wage. We have the following Bellman equations:[14]

---

13. The above logarithmic final good technology, together with the linear production cost structure $c(x) = x \cdot \gamma^{-k}$, imply that the equilibrium profit flows of the leader and the follower in an industry depend on only the technological gap m between them, not on their absolute technology levels.

14. Where r still denotes the individual rate of time preference. The π's and V's in this and the following equations are expressed in units of the numeraire, which is current total expenditures.

$$rV_1 = \pi_1 + n_{-1}(V_0 - V_1) \tag{7.4}$$

$$rV_0 = \pi_0 + \bar{n}_0(V_{-1} - V_0) + n_0(V_1 - V_0) - wn_0^2/2 \tag{7.5}$$

$$rV_{-1} = \pi_{-1} + n_{-1}(V_0 - V_{-1}) - wn_{-1}^2/2 \tag{7.6}$$

In words, the annuity value of being a technological leader in an industry with technological gap m is equal to the current profit flow π_m, plus the expected capital gain if the leader makes a further innovation and thereby increases the gap from m to $m + 1$, minus the expected capital loss if the follower makes an innovation and thereby reduces the gap from m to $(m - 1)$, minus the R&D cost.

In equations (7.5) and (7.6) respectively, n_0 and n_{-1} are chosen to maximize the RHS. Thus we have the first-order conditions

$$wn_i = V_{i+1} - V_i; \quad i = -1, 0 \tag{7.7}$$

Equations (7.4) $\sim$ (7.7), together with the symmetric-equilibrium condition $n_0 = \bar{n}_0$, yield the reduced-form research equations

$$(w/2)n_0^2 + rwn_0 - (\pi_1 - \pi_0) = 0 \tag{7.8}$$

$$(w/2)n_{-1}^2 + (r + n_0)wn_{-1} - (\pi_0 - \pi_{-1}) - (w/2)n_0^2 = 0 \tag{7.9}$$

Given any wage w, these equations solve for unique positive values of n_0 and n_{-1}, as long as $\pi_{-1} < \pi_0 < \pi_1$, which we assume. The model is then closed by a labor market-clearing equation which determines w as a function of the n's and the π's.[15] We shall ignore that equation and take the wage rate w as given in our analysis below.

We represent an increase in competition as an increase in the elasticity of substitution between the products A and B in each sector in a neighborhood of the 45° line, which translates into a reduction in the profit level π_0 earned by a firm that is neck and neck with its rival.[16] It is then straightforward to show that n_0 will rise while n_{-1} falls. The latter effect is the basic Schumpeterian effect that results from reducing the rents that can be captured by a follower who succeeds in catching up to its rival by innovating. The former is the new effect introduced by tacit knowledge; competition reduces the rents in the neck-and-neck status quo, and thus encourages innovation among firms that are even with their rivals, by raising the incremental value of getting ahead. On average, an increase in product market competition will have an ambiguous effect on growth because it will induce faster productivity growth

---

15. See Aghion, Harris, and Vickers (1995).

16. For simplicity we assume that π_1 and π_{-1} are unaffected by a change in competitiveness, although the analysis goes through essentially unmodified if π_1 is increased and/or π_{-1} is reduced.

in currently leveled sectors and slower growth in currently unleveled sectors. The overall effect on growth will thus depend on the (steady-state) fraction of leveled versus unleveled sectors. The main subtlety of this model lies in the fact that the steady-state fraction of leveled (resp. unleveled) sectors is *endogenous.*

More formally, let μ_1 denote the steady-state fraction of industries with technological gap $m = 1$, and $\mu_0 = 1 - \mu_1$. During time interval dt, in $\mu_1 n_{-1} dt$ sectors the follower catches up with the leader; in $2\mu_0 n_0 dt$ sectors one firm acquires a lead. Because the distribution of sectors (the μ_m's) remains stationary over time, we have

$$\underbrace{\mu_1 n_{-1}}_{\substack{\text{flow of sectors that} \\ \text{become } leveled}} = \underbrace{2\mu_0 n_0}_{\substack{\text{flow of sectors that} \\ \text{become } unleveled}} \tag{7.10}$$

Each industry follows a strict two-stage cycle, alternating between $m = 0$ and $m = 1$. The log of its output rises by $\ln \gamma$ with each completed cycle. The frequency of completed cycles is the fraction μ_1 of time spent in stage 2, times the frequency n_{-1} of innovations in stage 2. Hence the average growth rate of each industry is $\mu_1 n_{-1} \ln \gamma$. From (7.10) it follows that the fraction of industries with a leader is $\mu_1 = \frac{2n_0}{2n_0 + n_{-1}}$. Hence we have the following expression for the average growth rate of final output:

$$g = \mu_1 n_{-1} \ln \gamma = \frac{2n_0 n_{-1}}{2n_0 + n_{-1}} \ln \gamma. \tag{G}$$

From (G) it is clear that increased competition can either raise growth or lower it, depending on which effect is stronger; the rise in n_0, which raises g, or the fall in n_{-1}, which lowers g. The non-Schumpeterian effect n_0 will be dominant when a substantial fraction of sectors are *leveled* in steady state. Somewhat paradoxically, this will be the case whenever leveled firms do not have much incentive to acquire a technological lead over their rivals, that is when product market competition is *not* too intense already! If product market competition is too intense and as a result the flow of sectors becoming unleveled is too high, an overwhelming fraction of sectors will be unleveled at any point in time and we know that the effect of PMC on growth in unleveled sectors is Schumpeterian. To summarize this discussion, we should expect the non-Schumpeterian effect of a decrease in π_0 to dominate when π_0 is not too small already, and the Schumpeterian effect to dominate when π_0 is initially small. This is precisely what we get by simulating the model. Figure 7.4 shows a numerical example in which $r = .04$, $\pi_{-1} = 0$, $\pi_1 = 10$, $w = 1$ and $\gamma = 1.02$. As π_0 rises, growth rises at first, but then falls as π_0 approaches π_1.

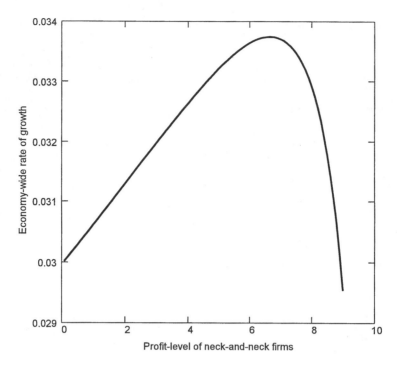

Figure 7.4
As competition decreases, the equilibrium profit level of neck-and-neck firms increases, resulting eventually in a fall in the economy-wide rate of growth.

7.5   Research and Development

In this section, we show that the Lucas effect pointed out in the previous chapter implies a *positive effect of competition on growth* once we endogenize the adaptability parameter σ that measures the rate at which developers switch from old lines to new. More specifically, an increase in the substitutability between new and old product lines, which implies an increase in competitiveness between them, will induce developers to leave old lines more rapidly, with the effect of inducing a higher level of research and growth. Contrary to the basic Schumpeterian model of Chapter 2, this implies that *increased competition may again lead to faster growth.*

From the model of research and development introduced in Chapter 6, we know that the steady-state proportion of skilled workers H^r engaged in fundamental research, is given by the arbitrage equation

$$r + \sigma - g = \frac{\nu}{1 - \nu} \sigma \frac{H - H^r}{H^r}, \tag{A}$$

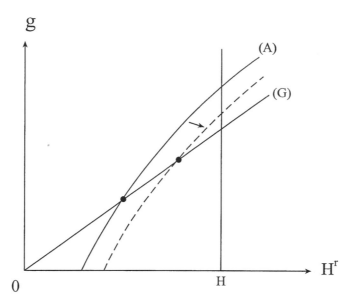

Figure 7.5
Effect of an increase in the relocation rate [$\sigma = g/v(1 - \alpha)$ when developers are free to relocate on any line; thus an increase in α implies an increase in σ].

where r is the interest rate, v is the fraction of monopoly rents accruing to researchers in equilibrium,[17] and H is the total number of skilled workers in the economy.

The steady-state values of g and H^r are jointly determined by the arbitrage equation (A) and the growth equation (G): $g = \lambda^r H^r$, shown in figure 7.5. As we have seen, both are upward-sloping. An increase in the relocation rate σ will increase both the amount of research H^r and the growth rate g, by shifting the (A) curve to the right.

The positive "Lucas effect" of the upgrading rate σ on research and growth was explained as follows: Holding the total supply of skilled workers H constant, an increase in σ implies an increase in the initial flow of developers into newly discovered lines. This tends to encourage research by lowering the cost of developing a fundamental innovation. The increase in σ also increases the speed at which current lines are being depleted of their developers, but time-discounting implies that the former effect dominates the latter; that is, on balance a higher σ increases the value of being a researcher relative to that of being a developer. Hence the positive effect of the upgrading rate σ on research and thus on growth by equation (G).

17. We saw in Chapter 6 that v is also one minus the elasticity of the secondary innovation function with respect to the number of developers.

Suppose now that developers are free at each instant to engage in research or to do development on any line. It turns out that an analogous arbitrage equation holds, because developers will again relocate at a constant rate in the steady-state equilibrium, except that the rate of upgrading is now endogenous. The positive results are identical to those obtained under an exogenous σ, except that the Cobb-Douglas parameter α now matters for positive results, because it affects the endogenous upgrading rate.

Let $W_{t,\tau}$ denote the value at date t of a plan of vintage τ: $\int_t^\infty e^{-r(s-t)} \pi_{s,\tau} ds$, where $\pi_{s,\tau}$ is the flow of profits to the producer of an intermediate good of vintage τ. As we saw in section 6.3, $\pi_{s,\tau} = \delta A_\tau^{1/(1-\alpha)} w_s^{\alpha/(\alpha-1)}$, where δ is a positive constant. Because A_τ grows at the constant rate g in a steady state; therefore,

$$W_{t,\tau} = W_{t,t} e^{-g(t-\tau)/(1-\alpha)}.$$

Because skilled workers are mobile across all innovative activities, they must all earn the same expected income w_t^s at date t. In particular, a researcher who has a line of vintage τ at date t will have to pay w_t^s to each developer employed at that date. Thus the number of developers $\eta_{t,\tau}$ will be chosen so as to maximize the flow of new development royalties:

$$\text{Max}\{\lambda^d \eta_{t,\tau}^{1-\nu} W_{t,t} e^{-g(t-\tau)/(1-\alpha)} - w_t^s \eta_{t,\tau}\}.$$

(Recall that each developer's arrival rate is $\lambda^d \eta_{t,\tau}^{-\nu}$). The solution to this maximization problem is

$$\eta_{t,\tau} = [(1-\nu)\lambda^d W_{t,t} e^{-g(t-\tau)/(1-\alpha)}/w_t^s]^{1/\nu} = \eta_{t,t} e^{-g(t-\tau)/\nu(1-\alpha)}.$$

This shows that the unique candidate for an endogenous steady-state relocation rate is $\sigma = \frac{g}{\nu(1-\alpha)}$. We can derive the same arbitrage equation (A) as before,[18] but with σ replaced by this endogenous value:

$$r + [g/\nu(1-\alpha)] - g = \frac{\nu}{1-\nu}[g/\nu(1-\alpha)]\frac{(H-H^r)}{H^r} \tag{A'}$$

A steady-state equilibrium occurs when the growth equation (G) and the modified arbitrage equation (A') are both satisfied. It is straightforward to verify that the curve representing (A') in figure 7.5 would be upward-sloping and would be affected by parameter changes in exactly the same direction as is the curve representing (A), except that now an increase in the Cobb-Douglas parameter α will shift it to the right because it has a direct effect on the endogenous upgrading rate $[g/\nu(1-\alpha)]$, whereas neither α nor any parameter

---

18. See Aghion and Howitt (1996b) for a detailed derivation.

of the general production function F had an effect when the upgrading rate was exogenous.

Thus the only effect endogenizing the upgrading rate has on the comparative-statics results of the model is to add an effect of α. In particular, because an increase in α has the effect of increasing the upgrading rate, it will work through the "Lucas effect" to shift the modified arbitrage curve to the right, resulting in more research and more growth. That is, the effect on the overall level of development of the fact that innovators will be choosing to remain for a shorter time on old lines outweighs the effect created by more of them going into lines of the most recent vintage, with the result that there will be fewer people in development, and hence more in research, in the new steady state.[19]

We have thus obtained a third explanation for the observed positive correlation between product market competition and productivity growth, which again relies on extending the basic Schumpeterian model of Chapter 2.

7.6   Summary and Conclusions

We began this book by claiming that Schumpeterian models of endogenous growth are shedding new substantive light on structural aspects of growth, because of their specificity concerning the details of the innovation process. In this chapter we illustrate the claim by showing how Schumpeterian models can help to explain the apparent fact that competition and growth are positively correlated, even though the fact contradicts the most elementary Schumpeterian models, which embody only the appropriability effect of competition.

We end the chapter by observing that the various Schumpeterian explanations of this apparent fact provide a number of empirical hypotheses that are worth pursuing, and that suggest a potential empirical test of the Schumpeterian approach. First, the argument of section 7.2 suggests that competition in research, as opposed to product market competition, is almost always likely to be favorable to growth.

As for product market competition (PMC), we have analyzed three potential explanations for the observed positive correlation between competition and growth. The first explanation is based on the idea that PMC may force nonprofit-maximizing firms (e.g., firms subject to agency problems between owners and managers) to *speed up* technological adoptions in order to remain

---

19. Of course, if there were a variable sum of research and development, then we would expect to find both our effect and the traditional Schumpeterian effect at work.

solvent. We refer to this as the *Darwinian effect* of product market competition. The second explanation is based on the existence of tacit knowledge in some industries and the resulting possibility that firms below the frontier may first have to catch up with the technological leader and compete with him or her on an equal basis (or neck-and-neck) before becoming leaders themselves. Then more PMC also means more intense *neck-and-neck* competition, which in turn induces neck-and-neck firms to invest more efforts into R&D in order to acquire a lead over their rivals and thereby avoid being increasingly cramped. The third explanation is based on the learning-by-doing model developed in the previous chapter, but where we endogenize the relocation rate of workers across lines. Namely, as PMC increases, it becomes increasingly unattractive for workers on old lines to remain on those lines, producing goods that are now closer substitutes to high quality goods on new lines. Hence the *mobility* of workers to newer lines, which is now endogenous, will increase, thereby generating higher growth as a result of the Lucas effect.

The various explanations presented earlier suggest that the correlation between competition and growth is more likely to be positive in subgroups of the economy where the various factors introduced in each of the explanations is prevalent to a large enough extent that the positive effects derived from them might outweigh the negative appropriability effect that is always present.

Thus, for example, if industries were classified into two subgroups characterized respectively by strong and weak control of managers by shareholders, one ought to find a stronger positive effect of competition on growth within the latter group than within the former, in that the agency problems at the heart of our *Darwinian* argument of 7.3 are more likely to prevail in the latter group. Likewise, there should be a stronger positive effect of competition on growth between sectors where tacit knowledge is the limiting barrier to imitation relative to the effect between sectors where patent protection is the limiting barrier, because patent protection reduces the scope for the *neck-and-neck competition* shown in section 7.4 to be favorable to growth. By the same token, the positive effect of competition on growth should show up more strongly within a group of sectors or countries where developers are *mobile* across product lines than where heavy technology-specific fixed investments limits their ability to move in response to increased competition, because it is this response that gives rise to the positive effect shown in section 7.5. Our hope is that empirical work aimed at testing these various propositions will allow econometricians not only to confront Schumpeterian growth theory with evidence, but also to sharpen our understanding of how competition affects growth.

Nickell, Nicolitsas, and Dryden (1997) shows that the positive effect of competition on productivity growth tends to be reduced (and even inverted) in firms with a dominant external shareholder, but remains substantial in firms without a dominant shareholder (and therefore more subject to agency problems); the article is a pioneering step in this direction. It is also encouraging evidence for the theory developed in this chapter.

Problems

Difficulty of Problems:

No star: normal

One star: difficult

Two stars: very difficult

1. Example of product market competition

In the section on step-by-step technological progress, the effects of PMC (product market competition) on profits are considered in the cases where firms are leveled and unleveled. In this problem an explicit parametrization of PMC is analyzed.

Consider a CES utility function $u(x_1, x_2) = (x_1^\alpha + x_2^\alpha)^{1/\alpha}$ with $0 < \alpha < 1$, where firm 1 produces good 1 and firm 2 produces good 2.

a. Explain why an increase in α can be interpreted as an increase in competition between firms 1 and 2.

b. Show that the consumer's optimization problem $max_{x_1, x_2} (x_1^\alpha + x_2^\alpha)^{1/\alpha}$ subject to the budget constraint $p_1 x_1 + p_2 x_2 \leq y$ yields a demand function for firm i of the form

$$p_i(x_1, x_2) = \frac{\frac{y}{x_i^{1-\alpha}}}{x_1^\alpha + x_2^\alpha}.$$

Further, show that the Cournot Nash profits and output levels equal

$$\pi_i(c_1, c_2; \alpha) = y \frac{1 + (1 - \alpha) \left(\frac{c_i}{c_j}\right)^\alpha}{\left(1 + \left(\frac{c_i}{c_j}\right)^\alpha\right)^2}$$

and

$$x_i(c_1, c_2; \alpha) = \frac{y}{c_i} \frac{\alpha \left(\frac{c_i}{c_j}\right)^\alpha}{\left(1 + \left(\frac{c_i}{c_j}\right)^\alpha\right)^2},$$

respectively, with $i, j = 1, 2$ and $i \neq j$.

c. Define γ as $\gamma = c_i/c_j$ and rewrite i's profits as $[1 + (1 - \alpha)\gamma^\alpha]/(1 + \gamma^\alpha)^2$. Show that $d\pi(\gamma, \alpha)/d\alpha < 0 <=> (-ln\gamma) < (1 + \gamma^\alpha)/[(1 + \alpha) + 2(1 - \alpha)\gamma^\alpha]$.

Discuss the following claims:

i. In the leveled case ($c_i = c_j$), both firms lose if PMC increases;

ii. the follower ($c_i > c_j$) always loses as PMC increases;

iii. the leader always loses as PMC becomes more intense.

d. This problem analyzes the general equilibrium effects of an increase in PMC. Consider an economy with only one production factor: labor. Labor is used to produce the goods 1 and 2 and invested to do research. If an increase in PMC increases the demand for labor in production, this draws resources away from R&D. This would be a negative general equilibrium effect of PMC on research and growth.

Show that total production employment equals $c_1x_1 + c_2x_2 = 2y\alpha\gamma^\alpha/(1 + \gamma^\alpha)^2$. Analyze the sign of $d(c_1x_1 + c_2x_2)/d\alpha$ as a function of γ.

2. Product market competition and concentration

In the empirical literature on the relation between innovative behavior and market structure, PMC is usually measured by a concentration index. High concentration is then interpreted as saying that the industry is not competitive. This problem shows that with asymmetric firms such an interpretation of concentration is not necessarily correct.

Consider an Hotelling beach of length one. Firm A is located on the extreme left and B on the extreme right of this beach. Consumers are distributed uniformly over the beach with density 1. Each consumer buys one and only one product if the price of the product plus the travel cost does not exceed his valuation v. Throughout this problem, assume that v is high enough that each consumer buys one product. Naturally, a consumer buys from the firm with the lowest effective price, that is the sum of the price charged by the firm and the travel cost incurred by the consumer to reach this firm. Let t denote travel costs, c_i the constant marginal production costs of firm i and p_i the price charged by firm i ($i = A, B$).

a. Explain why a decrease in travel cost t can be interpreted as an increase in PMC.

b. Show that demand for firm i is of the form $q_i(p_i, p_j; t) = 1/2 + (p_j - p_i)/(2t)$. Further, show that the Bertrand-Nash equilibrium solution of $max_{p_i} q_i(p_i, p_j; t)(p_i - c_i)$ equals $p_i = (3t + 2c_i + c_j)/3$ and that the Nash equilibrium output levels equal $q_i = 1/2 + (c_j - c_i)/(6t)$ with $i, j = A, B$ and $i \neq j$.

c. Show that travel costs do not affect concentration if firms are leveled ($c_i = c_j$). Further, show that when firms are unleveled, concentration rises as travel costs decrease. What is the intuition for this relation between PMC and concentration?

⋆ 3. Product market competition and the speed of technological progress (based on Boone 1996b)

This problem shows that as the identity of the innovator may change with intensity of competition, the relation between intensity of competition and the speed of technological progress is nonmonotone.

Consider a model with three production firms, where firm 1 has the lowest constant marginal cost level and firm 3 the highest ($c_1 < c_2 < c_3$). In a separate R&D sector, laboratories race to get a patent on the innovation $c_0 < c_1$. The higher the price a production firm wants to pay for c_0, the higher the prize in the patent race. It is a standard result in the industrial organization literature that a higher prize leads to more investment in the patent race, and hence c_0 is found sooner. The problem is how PMC affects the prize in the research laboratories' patent race and hence the speed of technological progress.

The product market is modeled as a triangular Hotelling beach. Each leg of the triangle is of length one and the three firms are positioned on the three corners. Consumers are uniformly distributed with density one on the three legs of the triangle and travel to a firm over the legs of the triangle (that is, not through its interior). With this setup the profit functions equal $\pi(c_1, c_2, c_3; t) = (5t + \sum_{j \neq i} c_j - 2c_i)^2/(25t)$ where $i = 1, 2, 3$.

Finally, if firm i knows that firm j buys c_0 if i does not, i's valuation of c_0 equals $V_i(t) = \pi_i(c_0, c_j, c_k; t) - \pi_i(c_i, c_0, c_k; t)$ with $i, j, k = 1, 2, 3$ and $i \neq j, i \neq k, j \neq k$.

a. Show that for each firm it is the case that its valuation of c_0 is highest if its opponent with highest marginal costs buys c_0 if it doesn't buy c_0 itself. What is the intuition for this result?

Consider the case where $c_0 = 1$, $c_1 = 2$, $c_2 = 4$, and $c_3 = 8$. Assume for simplicity that a firm values c_0, thinking that its highest-cost opponent buys c_0 if it does not buy c_0 itself. As the R&D laboratory that wins the patent race and finds c_0 sells the patent to the highest bidder, it gets $V(t) = max\{V_1(t), V_2(t), V_3(t)\}$.

b. Show that at $t = 4$, it is the case that $V(t) = V_2(t) = (130t + 39)/(25t)$ and that at $t = 10$ it is the case that $V(t) = V_3(t) = (170t - 153)/(25t)$. Why does firm 3 have the highest valuation of c_0 for high values of t?

c. Show that $dV(t)/dt|_{t=4} < 0$ and $dV(t)/dt|_{t=10} > 0$. What can you say about the relation between PMC and the speed of technological progress?

** **4. Product market competition and the socially optimal allocation of labor (based on Stokey 1995)**

The text analyzes the effects of PMC on the market allocation of resources over production and research. This problem considers the effects of PMC on the social optimum. As in problem 1, PMC is parameterized here as α in a CES utility function. In particular, assume discounted utility is determined in the following three steps.

First, for given technology, the relative utility of the goods is determined by

$$u(x) = \left[\sum_{i \geq 0} (\gamma^{-i} x_i)^{\alpha} \right]^{1/\alpha}$$

with $\gamma > 1$. Let n denote the current best technology. Then x_0 is the quantity of labor used to produce output with the current best technology and x_1 the quantity of labor used to produce with technology $n - 1$. So when technology $n + 1$ is invented, there is some relabeling such that x_0 is the quantity of labor used with technology $n + 1$, and so on. Second, with n as the current best technology, utility equals $U(n, x) = \{[\gamma^n u(x)]^{1-\sigma} - 1\}/(1 - \sigma)$ with $\sigma > 1$. Finally, expected discounted utility equals

$$E \left\{ \sum_{t \geq 0} U(n(t), x(t))/(1 + \rho)^t \right\}$$

where $\rho > 0$ is the discount factor and the expectation is taken with respect to the arrival dates of the innovation.

Let L denote the inelastic supply of labor each period. And let $\Theta(z)$ be the probability of making a discovery in a period, if z is the quantity of labor devoted to R&D. Assume the function $\Theta(.)$ is strictly increasing and concave with $\Theta(0) \geq 0$ and $\Theta(L) \leq 1$.

a. Let $f(\lambda) = \max_x \{u(x) | \Sigma x_i \leq \lambda\}$. Using the property that $u(.)$ is homogenous of degree 1 in output, show that the function $f(.)$ is linear $f(\lambda) = a\lambda$.

b. Explain why the socially optimal amount of labor allocated to research (z) solves the following Bellman equation:

$$W(n) = \max_{z \in [0,L]} \left\{ ([\gamma^n a(L - z)]^{1-\sigma} - 1)/(1 - \sigma) \right.$$

$$\left. + [\Theta(z)W(n + 1) + (1 - \Theta(z))W(n)]/(1 + \rho) \right\}.$$

c. How does a change in PMC, modeled here as a change in α in the function $u(x)$, affect the social allocation of labor over research and production?

5. Market structure and firms' investments in R&D

An earlier literature on the relation between market structure and firms' innovative behavior is in the industrial organization tradition. The next four problems look at this literature. In response to empirical work on how market structure affects firms' incentives to reduce costs, Dasgupta and Stiglitz (1980) show that it is not the case that market structure causes a certain level of investment. Instead, investment to reduce costs and market structure are jointly determined by the underlying parameters of the model.

Dasgupta and Stiglitz use the Herfindahl index $H = \Sigma_j (q_j/Q)^2$ to measure concentration, where q_j is firm j's output level and $Q = \Sigma_j q_j$ is total industry output. They focus on symmetric equilibria and use H as a measure for market structure.

Assume industry demand is of the following form $p(Q) = 1 - Q$. A firm can invest $\psi(c)$ to reduce its cost level from $c = 1$ to $c \geq 0$, where the function $\psi(.)$ satisfies $\psi(1) = 0$, $\psi(.) \geq 0$, $\psi'(.) \leq 0$ and $\psi''(.) > 0$. Finally, there is free entry into the industry.

Firm i chooses q_i that solves $\max_{q_i}\{(1 - Q)q_i - c_i q_i\}$. Let $\pi_i(c_1, \ldots, c_n)$ denote the Cournot-Nash profits of this production stage, where the cost levels $\{c_1, \ldots, c_n\}$ are taken as given.

a. Show that $\pi_i(c_1, \ldots, c_n) = [(1 - nc_i + \Sigma_{j \neq i} c_j)/(n + 1)]^2$.

b. Show that in a symmetric equilibrium, the values of c and n are determined by the following two equations:

$$[(1 - c)/(n + 1)]^2 = \psi(c)$$

and

$$2n(1 - c)/(n + 1)^2 = -\psi'(c).$$

Show that these two equations can be summarized as $H = 2\psi(c)/[-\psi'(c)(1 - c)]$.

c. Consider the following specification of the function $\psi(.)$:

$$\psi(c) = \psi_0(1 - c)^{\psi_1} \text{ with } \psi_0 > 1 \text{ and } \psi_1 > 2.$$

Determine n and c as functions of ψ_0 and ψ_1. Show that $dn/d\psi_1 > 0$, $dc/d\psi_0 > 0$ and interpret these results.

d. Consider the following equation $c_k = \beta_0 + \beta_1 H_k + \varepsilon_k$. Using cross-section data on industries ($k = 1, \ldots, N$), this equation can be estimated. Discuss how meaningful the results of such an estimation will be.

6. A simple patent race

Another part of the industrial organization literature on market structure and R&D has concentrated on the investments in the patent race. Examples are

Loury (1979), Lee and Wilde (1980), and Dixit (1988). The research laboratories race to get a patent. The winner sells this patent to a production firm at price V. Let $p_i(x_1, \ldots, x_n)$ denote the probability that firm i wins the patent race if laboratories $1, \ldots, n$ invest $x_1, \ldots, x_n$ respectively. Assume $p_i(x_1, \ldots, x_n) \geq 0$, $\Sigma_i p_i(x_1, \ldots, x_n) \leq 1$, $\partial p_i(.)/\partial x_i > 0$, $\partial^2 p_i(.)/\partial x_i^2 < 0$ and $\partial p_i(.)/\partial x_j < 0 (j \neq i)$.

a. Lee and Wilde (1980) interpret an increase in x_j as an increase in competition or rivalry for firm i ($j \neq i$). Derive conditions under which such an increase in rivalry leads to more investments by firm i.

b. Let V^s denote the value of the innovation for a social planner. Discuss why V^s may differ from the market valuation V of the innovation.

Assume $p_i(x_1, \ldots, x_n) = (x_i/\Sigma_j x_j)\Theta(\Sigma_j x_j)$ where $\Theta(.)$ is strictly increasing, concave with $\Theta(0) = 0$ and $\Theta(.) \leq 1$. Further, assume that research laboratories are small in the sense that they take $X = \Sigma_j x_j$ as given and suppose that there is free entry and exit into the research sector.

c. Show that in the market equilibrium X^m solves $\Theta(X^m)/X^m = 1/V$.

d. Show that the social planner's optimal investment in research X^s solves $\Theta'(X^s) = 1/V^s$.

e. Under the assumption that $V = V^s$, does X^m fall short of X^s?

★★ 7. The evolution of duopoly

This problem analyzes how step-by-step technological progress affects market structure in the following sense. With two firms in the market, is it the case that the leader increases his dominance and thus eventually monopolizes the market? Or does the follower catch up by bridging the technological gap such that the market is characterized by two firms that are more or less leveled? Unlike the text, here we do not constrain the gap s, but allow $s \in \Re$. The problem is based on Budd, Harris, and Vickers (1993) and demonstrates a technique called asymptotic expansions. This method reveals the effects that affect market structure.

There are two firms A and B. Let $s \in \Re$ denote A's advantage over B. Assume that A's profits in state s equal $\pi(s)$ while B's profits equal $\pi(-s)$, where $\pi'(.) > 0$ and $\pi(\Re)$ is a bounded set.

a. How should s be defined such that the profit function in problem (1) satisfies these conditions?

Because $\pi'(.) > 0$, firm A invests in order to increase the gap s, while B invests to reduce s. Firm A's (Markov) strategy describes A's investment as a function of the state s: denoted by $x(s)$. Similarly, write $y(s)$ for B's (Markov) strategy. Assume that the cost of investing $x, y = z$ equals $z^2/2$. So in state s firm A's payoff equals $\pi(s) - [x(s)]^2/2$ and B's payoff equals $\pi(-s) - [y(s)]^2/2$.

A's normalized discounted payoff starting from state s_0 equals $V(s_0) = r \int_0^\infty \{\pi(s(t)) - [x(s(t))]^2/2\} e^{-rt} dt$, where r is the discount factor. Because in the asymptotic expansions below the focus is on large values for r, the discounted profits need to be normalized by r. Similarly, B's normalized discounted payoffs equal

$W(s_0) = r \int_0^\infty \{\pi(-s(t)) - [y(s(t))]^2/2\} e^{-rt} dt$. Finally, the motion of the gap s is governed by the differential equation $ds = [x(s) - y(s)] dt$.

b. Given B's strategy $y(s)$, show heuristically that A's optimal strategy $x(s)$ solves the following Bellman equation:

$$rV(s) = \max_x \{r(\pi(s) - x^2/2) + V'(s)(x - y(s))\}.$$

c. Show that the optimal strategy $x(s)$ satisfies

$$x(s) = V'(s)/r \tag{7.11}$$

$$V(s) = \pi(s) - [x(s)]^2/2 + x(s)(x(s) - y(s)). \tag{7.12}$$

And show that similarly the optimal $y(s)$ satisfies

$$y(s) = -W'(s)/r \tag{7.13}$$

$$W(s) = \pi(-s) - [y(s)]^2/2 + y(s)(y(s) - x(s)). \tag{7.14}$$

The idea is now to approximate $x(s)$ by a polynomial of the form $x_0(s) + r^{-1}x_1(s) + r^{-2}x_2(s) + \cdots + r^{-n}x_n(s)$, where r is large. Using the preceding equations, it is possible to determine $x_0(s)$ and $x_1(s)$. Similarly, one can find a first-order approximation of $y(s)$ equal to $y_0(s) + r^{-1}y_1(s)$. Using these first-order approximations, we will be able to identify the joint profit effect that determines the sign of $[x(s) - y(s)]$.

d. Write $V(s)$ as $V_0(s) + r^{-1}V_1(s) + \cdots + r^{-n}V_n(s)$, and differentiate term by term to obtain $V'(s)$ as $V_0'(s) + r^{-1}V_1'(s) + \cdots + r^{-n}V_n'(s)$. Substitute this approximation of $V'(s)$ and the approximation of $x(s)$ into equation (7.11) and equate terms of the order 0 in r. What do you find for $x_0(s)$? What is the intuition for this result? (Hint: $x_0(s)$ is only a good approximation of $x(s)$ if r is high.) Similarly, what do you find for $y_0(s)$?

e. Substitute the approximation for $V(s)$, $x(s)$ and $y(s)$ into equation (7.12) and again equate terms of order 0. What do you find for $V_0(s)$, and what is the intuition?

f. Substitute the approximation for $V(s)$ and $x(s)$ into equation (7.12) and equate terms of order 1 in r. Similarly, substitute the approximations for $W(s)$ and $y(s)$ into (7.13). Show that the principal contribution to $x(s) - y(s)$ is of order 1 and that $x_1(s) - y_1(s) = \partial[\pi(s) + \pi(-s)]/\partial s$. Interpret this result and explain why it is called the joint profit effect.

⋆ **8. Product market competition and the identity of the innovator (based on Boone 1996b)**

The previous problem showed that the joint profit effect is one of the factors shaping the evolution of market structure. However, it does not say in which direction the joint profit effect works—that is, whether this effect works in the direction of the leader increasing its dominance or the follower leap-frogging. This is the topic of this problem.

In a duopoly context, let $\pi(c_1, c_2; \theta) \geq 0$ denote profits, where $c_1 \geq 0$ is the firm's own cost level, $c_2 \geq 0$ is the cost level of its opponent and $\theta \geq 0$ is a measure of intensity of product market competition. Let $\theta = 0$ denote intensity of competition so weak that firms are unaffected by each other's actions: $\partial \pi(c_i, c_j; \theta)/c_j|_{\theta=0} = 0$. At the other extreme, let $\theta \to \infty$ describe the case where product market competition is so intense that only the most efficient firm survives. Further, if both firms are equally efficient ($c_i = c_j$), very intense competition dissipates all profits. Thus $\lim_{\theta \to \infty} \pi(c_i, c_j; \theta) > 0$ for $c_i \geq c_j$.

Assume that for each $\theta > 0$ with $\pi(c_i, c_j; \theta) > 0$ and $\pi(c_j, c_i, \theta) > 0$ it is the case that $\partial \pi(c_i, c_j; \theta)/\partial c_i < 0$, $\partial \pi(c_i, c_j; \theta)/\partial c_j|_{\theta>0} > 0$ and $\partial^2 \pi(c_i, c_j; \theta)/\partial c_i \partial c_j|_{\theta>0} < 0$.

a. Use the Hotelling beach example in problem (7.12) to illustrate the conditions $\partial \pi(c_i, c_j; \theta)/\partial c_j|_{\theta=0} = 0$ and $\lim_{\theta \to \infty} \pi(c_i, c_j; \theta) = 0$ for $c_i \geq c_j$.

b. Assume that $c_1 < c_2$ and that there is an innovation $c_0 < c_1$ on offer. Show that the low-cost firm's valuation exceeds the high-cost firm's valuation if and only if

$$\pi(c_0, c_2; \theta) + \pi(c_2, c_0; \theta) \geq \pi(c_1, c_0; \theta) + \pi(c_0, c_1; \theta). \tag{7.15}$$

What is the interpretation of this condition?

c. Check that (7.15) can be rewritten as

$$\{[\pi(c_0, c_2; \theta) - \pi(c_1, c_2; \theta)] - [\pi(c_0, c_1; \theta) - \pi(c_1, c_1; \theta)]\}$$
$$+ \{[\pi(c_1, c_1; \theta) - \pi(c_1, c_0; \theta)] - [\pi(c_2, c_1; \theta) - \pi(c_2, c_0; \theta)]\}$$
$$+ \{[\pi(c_1, c_2; \theta) - \pi(c_1, c_1; \theta)]\}$$
$$\geq \pi(c_1, c_1; \theta) - \pi(c_2, c_1; \theta).$$

Show that the LHS of this inequality is equal to zero at $\theta = 0$. Assuming that $\pi(c_1, c_1; \theta) > 0$, which firm innovates at $\theta = 0$? Further, show that for $\theta \to \infty$, the previous inequality holds strictly. What is the intuition for these results?

d. Now assume that firms produce conventional complements, where each firm's output level is decreasing in its own cost level. That is, $\partial \pi(c_i, c_j; \theta)/\partial c_j \leq 0$. Further, suppose that cost levels interact as strategic complements, $\partial^2 \pi(c_i, c_j; \theta)/\partial c_j \partial c_i \geq 0$. How does this affect inequality (7.15)?

8 Growth and Cycles

8.1 Introduction

To Schumpeter, productivity growth and the business cycle were closely interrelated. Yet, for several decades, the two phenomena have been investigated separately in the economics literature: on one hand, business cycle theorists have analyzed detrended data and considered the trend as exogenous to the cycle; on the other hand, growth theorists have focused on characterizing a long-run deterministic growth path.

However, the emergence in the 1980s of the real business cycle literature, emphasizing productivity shocks as a main driving force behind cyclical fluctuations, called into question the traditional division of macroeconomic theory between trend and cycles and suggested a return to the Schumpeterian view of growth and cycles as a unified phenomenon.

In this chapter, we report on some recent attempts at deriving causal relationships between productivity growth and the structure of economic fluctuations. Whether they emphasize the causal links *from* cycles *to* growth or the *reverse* causality, most of these attempts build (more or less directly) on the Schumpeterian paradigm introduced and discussed in the previous chapters.

The chapter is organized as follows. Section 8.2 briefly reviews the parallel but separate evolutions of growth and cycle theories prior to the endogenous growth literature. Section 8.3 analyzes the long-run growth effects of real business fluctuations: first, in the context of an *AK* model (section 8.3.1); and second, in a more Schumpeterian context where productivity improvements result from deliberate R&D and/or reorganization decisions (section 8.3.2). In particular, it discusses the idea that *small* fluctuations may sometimes favor the occurrence of (aggregate) productivity improvements. Section 8.4 concentrates on the reverse causality from productivity growth to economic fluctuations. In particular, it addresses the intriguing question as to why the adoption of new technological paradigms may sometimes lead to cyclical growth patterns involving the occurrence of (temporary) recessions.[1] Section 8.5 discusses an alternative hypothesis suggested by the Schumpeterian approach, namely that the arrival of a new technological paradigm can create the illusion of a slowdown because of various measurement problems that are exacerbated when the pace of innovation increases.

---

1. An alternative explanation for cyclical patterns in the adoption of new technologies, based on political economy considerations and more precisely on the notion of vested interests, will be developed in the following chapter (section 9.3).

8.2   A Few Historical Benchmarks

One early model of the trade cycle—the so-called multiplier/accelerator model —was developed as an extension of Keynesian income-expenditure analysis where the disequilibrium between demand and supply on the goods market gives rise to quantity adjustments, through investments in new capacity. Assuming that current investment is equal to the difference between the desired level of capital stock this period K_t, and its previous level K_{t-1}, and that the desired level K_t is proportional to consumption C_t, we have $I_t = vC_t - K_{t-1} = v\left(C_t - C_{t-1}\right)$. This would determine the supply response of investment to an increase in consumption demand, that is, the so-called accelerator effect.

Conversely, a current increase in investment would induce a bigger increase in consumption demand next period according to the multiplier effect, because[2] $C_t = cY_{t-1}$, where c is the aggregate marginal propensity to consume, and $Y_t = C_t + I_t$. Putting these equations together yields the difference equation $Y_t = c\left(1 + v\right)Y_{t-1} - cvY_{t-2}$, describing the oscillator of Samuelson.

As already noticed by Kaldor in the mid-1950s, the oscillator model had no trend component in it. "As a pure cyclical model," Kaldor remarks, "it had therefore little resemblance to the cyclical fluctuations in the real world, where successive booms carried production to successively higher levels." The absence of a growth component from the oscillator model might seem somehow paradoxical for those who remember that the first *balanced* growth model[3] by Domar (1947) had also been formulated in terms of the multiplier/accelerator. The main point there was to derive a necessary and sufficient condition under which an increase in capacity subject to the accelerator mechanism would exactly match the increase in demand induced by the multiplier mechanism. However, the model could not produce both growth and cycles.

The same criticism also applies to other versions of the oscillator model (for example, Hicks 1950) that superimpose a linear trend on the original model without altering its basic properties. The trend itself is introduced from the outside, either by assuming a constant percentage growth in population or by introducing an exogenous source of technical progress. In either case the trend is left unexplained.

Goodwin (1967) is probably the first model of cyclical growth where the occurrence of economic fluctuations was modeled as a deterministic consequence of the growth process and more specifically of the variations in income distribution (between wages and profits) this process induces over time.[4]

---

2. Thus, it is assumed that consumption depends on income with a one period lag.

3. See subsection 1.4.1.

4. The business cycle in Goodwin (1967) follows from the following predator-prey relationship betwen unemployment (i.e., wages) and profits: when the economy is in expansion, growth is high

The post-Keynesian models mentioned above were all *non*-market clearing models, where economic fluctuations resulted either from capacity adjustments in accelerator-multiplier models, or from employment adjustments in the labor market in the Goodwin model. More recent growth or business cycle models have gotten rid of non-market clearing assumptions, yet without solving the difficulty of explaining the growth trend and its current relationship with the business cycle. This is true of Solow's (1956) seminal contribution (and its various extensions prior to the endogenous growth literature[5]) where again no long-run trend would obtain in the absence of population growth or of exogenous technical progress. This is also true of business cycle models developed in a market-clearing context, either on the basis of unanticipated monetary shocks and informational rigidities (as in Lucas (1972)), or resulting from strong non-linearities in intertemporal preferences (as in Benhabib and Day 1981 and Grandmont 1985), or arising from the combination between temporary productivity shocks and adjustment lags or inter-sectorial inertia (as in the real business cycle literature pioneered by Kydland and Prescott 1982 and Long and Plosser 1983): none of these models were concerned with explaining the existence of a trend in (causal) relation to the business cycle.

Existing business cycle models based on exogenous productivity or monetary shocks were unsatisfactory in several respects: first, they could not account for the existence of stochastic trends[6] evidenced in empirical studies by Nelson and Plosser (1982) and Campbell and Mankiw (1987); second, aggregate demand shocks could have no lasting consequences on technology and growth; third, money had to remain neutral in the long-run, with monetary shocks being completely dichotomized in the long run from real technological shocks. Endogenizing the growth process through the introduction of human capital investments, as in King and Rebelo (1986), or learning by doing, as in Stadler (1990), removed these restrictive or counterfactual features for the following natural reasons: to the extent that suddenly increasing the quantity of money could stimulate a higher level of real economic activity in the short run,[7] then the same increase in money supply would be likely to result in more rapid

---

and so is investment, with the effect of decreasing unemployment. (The labour market does not clear and the real wage is a decreasing function of the unemployment rate.) As unemployment decreases, real wage increases and the share of profits decreases accordingly. The economy thus enters a "recession" period where the growth in production capacity becomes less than the growth in labour supply. Unemployment then starts increasing again, thereby inducing a decrease in real wages. This in turn inverts the falling movement in profit share and thus announces a forthcoming acceleration of growth.

5. Notable exceptions being Arrow (1962), Kaldor (1957), and Shell (1973).

6. That is, aggregate output seems to have a greater-than-unit root.

7. For example as a result of nominal contractual rigidities à la Fischer (1977) and Taylor (1980) or of informational rigidities à la Lucas (1972).

learning by doing or in more intense research and development, and therefore in a burst of technological growth that would not otherwise have occurred. This brings us to the next section.

8.3   From Cycles to Growth*

8.3.1   The Long-Run Effects of Temporary Shocks

Once technological knowledge is endogeneized in a model of sustained growth, one can show that even such propositions as the neutrality of money cease to be valid. For it is quite uncontroversial that suddenly increasing the quantity of money will stimulate a higher level of real economic activity in the short run. But if so, then this is likely to result in a burst of technological growth that would not otherwise have occurred, either as a result of a more rapid learning by doing or as a result of more rapid research and development to take advantage of temporarily enhanced profit opportunities. Even when prices and expectations have fully adjusted to the monetary shock, the result will be a permanently higher level of real income and a price level that has gone up less than in proportion to the money stock.

More generally, endogenizing the growth process can help remove some restrictive or counterfactual features in the existing business-cycle literature. Based on an exogenous productivity assumption, this literature is unsatisfactory in several respects: *first,* it cannot account for the existence of stochastic trends (evidenced in empirical studies by Nelson and Plosser (1982) and Campbell and Mankiw (1987)); on the other hand, by embedding temporary shocks into the economy's long-run growth path, the endogenous growth approach calls into question the traditional division of macroeconomic theory between trend and cycles; *second* (and relatedly), in the business-cycle literature aggregate demand shocks can have no lasting consequences on technology and growth and, similarly, money is bound to remain neutral in the long run, with monetary shocks being completely dichotomized from real technological shocks in the long run; this again will no longer be the case in an endogenous growth framework.

The remaining part of this section summarizes the contribution by Stadler (1990), even though the conclusions relative to the long-run growth effects of real productivity shocks are equally attributable to King and Rebelo (1986).

The main idea underlying Stadler (1990) can be summarized as follows: a positive productivity shock (or a positive money supply shock *with real temporary effects)* due to nominal contractual rigidities à la Fischer (1977) and Taylor (1980) or to informational rigidities à la Lucas (1972) should induce a

* This section borrows unrestrainedly from Aghion-Saint Paul (1993).

higher level of real economic activity in the short run. Then, either because of learning by doing à la Arrow or Frankel-Romer, or as a result of more intense R&D investments,[8] there will be a burst of technological growth. Real income will end up at a permanently higher level, even after individual expectations have fully adjusted to the initial monetary shock.

More formally, the individual output supply by any individual firm i[9] at time t is given by the following Cobb-Douglas technology:

$$Y_t^i = k(L_t^i)^\alpha (Z_t)^{1-\alpha} F_t, \tag{8.1}$$

where L_t^i is the amount of labor currently employed by firm i, F_t is a positive productivity shock with both a temporary and a permanent component in it, and Z_t is the accumulated aggregate knowledge in the economy. The evolution of this aggregate knowledge variable reflects total learning by doing from past aggregate employment, according to the dynamic equation

$$Z_t = Z_{t-1} \left[\frac{Y_{t-1}}{L_{t-1}} \right]^\lambda (L_{t-1})^Y. \tag{8.2}$$

In words, a greater level of aggregate labor input L_{t-1} and/or a higher productivity of labor due to some efficient reorganization of production will both increase the rate of accumulation of knowledge.

Profit maximization subject to the technological constraint (8.1) defines a log-linear labor-demand schedule:[10]

$$l_t^d = a + b(p_t - w_t) + cf_t.$$

This, together with the labor supply schedule, which is also assumed to be log-linear $[l_t^s = \phi_1 + \phi_2(w_t - p_t^e)]$ and depends on the expected equilibrium price as of time t,[11] determines the equilibrium employment level $l_t = l_t^d = l_t^s$ and thus the following (log-linear) aggregate supply function (after substituting for l_t in (8.1)):

$$y_t^s = a^s + b^s(p_t - p_t^e) + c^s \eta_t + d^s \overline{f}_{t-1} + e^s z_t, \tag{8.3}$$

where $\overline{f}_{t-1}$ is the log of the accumulated shock to productivity up to time $(t-1)$, and η_t is the log of the real productivity shock at date t.

---

8. Implicitly, during economic expansions R&D investments either are more profitable or can be more easily financed through retained earnings by otherwise cash-constrained research firms, as correctly pointed out by Stiglitz (1993).

9. The economy comprises a large number of competitive firms all producing the same good as output.

10. Small letters refer to the logarithms of the corresponding capital letters. All coefficients in the log-linear equations are taken to be positive.

11. Individuals ignore the true market price p_t when entering into one-period, fixed-nominal-wage contracts with firms at the beginning of period t. Thus they supply labour on the basis of the expected real wage $w_t - p_t^e$.

The model is then closed by postulating the following aggregate demand schedule, corresponding to a quantity theory equation with unit velocity

$$Y_t^d = \frac{M_t}{P_t},$$ (8.4)

where the money supply M_t follows a random walk with positive drift:

$$m_t = m_{t-1} + \mu + \varepsilon_t,$$ (8.5)

with $m = \log M$ and ε being a zero-mean, constant-variance error term. The model is now completely specified: (8.4) implies that the price error (in log terms) is equal to the unexpected monetary shock $m_t - m_t^e = \varepsilon_t$ minus the unexpected component of aggregate demand $y_t^d - y_t^{de}$, which, by market clearing, is also equal to[12] $y_t^s - y_t^{se} = b^s(p_t - p_t^e) + c^s \eta_t$. The price error term $p_t - p_t^e$ is then given by:

$$p_t - p_t^e = \frac{1}{1 + b^s}(\varepsilon_t - c^s \eta_t).$$

The equilibrium aggregate output y_t is obtained from equation (8.3) by substituting for the price error term $p_t - p_t^e$:

$$y_t = a^s + \frac{b^s}{1 + b^s}(\varepsilon_t - c^s \eta_t) + c^s \eta_t + d^s \overline{f}_{t-1} + e^s z_t.$$ (8.6)

The sources of *non-stationarity* in aggregate output are first the knowledge term z_t (which depends on past employment levels) and second the accumulated shock to productivity $\overline{f}_{t-1}$. This model thus immediately delivers a stochastic trend component to aggregate output.

A special case of the model occurs when unanticipated shocks are *purely monetary*: then, $\eta_t = 0$ and aggregate output is simply given by

$$y_t = a^s + \frac{b^s}{1 + b^s}\varepsilon_t + e^s z_t,$$ (8.7)

where z_t depends on past values of output and employment levels through the accumulation of knowledge (or learning by doing) equation (8.2).

This implies that an unanticipated increase in money supply today, $\varepsilon_t > 0$, by increasing output and employment today, will also increase the level of knowledge z_{t+1} tomorrow. This in turn will induce a further increase in aggregate output and employment tomorrow, thereby increasing z_{t+1}, and so on. Output will thus grow at an *increasing rate* over time and thus will exhibit greater-than-unit roots in its stochastic evolution. Furthermore, this model generates a strong nonneutrality result: namely, the real impact on aggregate output of a temporary monetary shock *increases* over time as a result of learning by doing.

---

12. $\overline{f}_{t-1}$ and z_t are fully expected at the beginning of date t.

Another special case occurs when shocks are purely technological (i.e., $\varepsilon_t = 0$). Again, as a result of learning by doing, a (transitory) productivity shock will have durable (and even increasing over time) effects on aggregate output.

We conclude this section by mentioning what we believe are limitations of this otherwise successful attempt at explaining the trend in a business-cycle model. First, the model as it stands generates *explosive growth*[13] and thus does not allow for a parametrization of the long-run trend as a function of business-cycle characteristics. Second, productivity growth is assumed to be *procyclical*. As we have already discussed above, such an assumption can be justified as resulting from learning by doing or demand spillovers, or as a consequence of capital market imperfections with constrain R&D investments to vary procyclically with current earnings.[14] Furthermore, it is consistent with the observed procyclical behavior of the Solow residual. On the other hand, a more recent theoretical and empirical literature has emphasized several countercyclical factors in the dynamics of productivity growth over the business cycle. This brings us to the next subsection.

8.3.2   Is There a Virtue to Bad Times?

The Schumpeterian view of business cycles (and particularly recessions) as providing a cleansing mechanism for reducing (or eliminating) organizational inefficiencies and resource misallocations has recently been revived by several authors, including Hall (1991), Gali and Hammour (1991), Caballero and

---

13. Or explosive downturns if the initial shock on real output is negative! Note that this explosive growth result could have been avoided, had the elasticity of current knowledge (z_t) with respect to past knowledge (z_{t-1}) been assumed to be *less than* 1. To see this, it suffices to consider the following simplified version of Stadler's pure monetary model (obtained by setting: $\gamma = \lambda$, $a^s = 0$, $e^s = b^s/1 + b^s$ and $\widetilde{\varepsilon}_t = e^s \cdot \varepsilon_t$, $\widetilde{z}_t = e^s \cdot z_t$ in equations (8.6) and (8.7)):

$$\widetilde{z}_t = \widetilde{z}_{t-1} + \lambda y_{t-1} \tag{a'}$$

$$y_t = \widetilde{\varepsilon}_t + \widetilde{z}_t. \tag{b'}$$

Combining these two equations yields the following reduced-form equation:

$$(1 - (1+\lambda)L)y_t = \varepsilon_t \quad \text{(where } L \cdot y_t = y_{t-1}).$$

As a solution to this equation when $\varepsilon_t > 0$ and $\varepsilon_\tau = 0(\tau \gtreqless t)$, aggregate output y_t follows necessarily an explosive growth path because $1 + \lambda > 1$! Now let us modify equation (8.4) by assuming an elasticity of current knowledge with respect to past knowledge strictly less than 1, equal to $1 - \delta$:

$$\widetilde{z}_t = (1-\delta)\widetilde{z}_{t-1} + \lambda y_{t-1}. \tag{c''}$$

The reduced form equation now becomes:

$$(1 - (1+\delta+\lambda)L)y_t = (1 - (1-\delta)L)\varepsilon_t.$$

One can now see that whenever $\delta < \lambda$, growth remains explosive; for $\delta > \lambda$, growth tapers off; and for $\delta = \lambda$, growth becomes asymptotically balanced at a positive (endogenous) rate.

14. See Stiglitz (1993) for a technical change model with credit rationing.

Hammour (1994), Dellas (1993), and Aghion and Saint-Paul (1991). This view was summarized by Schumpeter himself:[15] "[Recessions] are but temporary. They are the means to reconstruct each time the economic system on a more efficient plan." One can indeed think of several reasons why small recessions could have positive effects on productivity. There is first the "cleaning-up" or "lame duck" effect emphasized by Schumpeter and recently formalized by Caballero and Hammour (1994), whereby less productive firms are eliminated during recessions and average productivity increases accordingly. This effect, however, may be offset by the fact that the rate of entry of new (efficient) firms is also lower during recessions, which in turn limits the extent of the phasing out of old (inefficient) firms. In the limit case where the entry cost is independent of the entry flow, fluctuations are entirely accommodated through entry and job destruction over time: the exit rate of firms does not react to the business cycle. This is what Caballero and Hammour call the *insulation effect*.[16] However, if the entry cost increases with the size of the entry flow, for example due to negative *congestion externalities* between the entering firms at a given point in time, the entry process will tend to be smoothed out over time: namely, firms will avoid entering during peak demand periods where the entry cost is likely to be higher. The insulation effect will then be partly neutralized and job destructions corresponding to the exit of old inefficient firms will tend to fluctuate more than job creations by new entering firms, in line with empirical evidence by Davis and Haltiwanger (1992).

A second reason why recessions might have a positive impact on (long-run) productivity lies in the following "opportunity cost" or intertemporal substi-

---

15. The following quote is drawn from Stiglitz (1993).

16. More formally, let $A(t_0)$ denote the constant flow of output generated by a firm created at date t_0. Let $\bar{a}(t)$ be the maximum age of firms at date t. Assuming that each firm employs only one worker and that labour is the numeraire, the profit flow of a firm of age a at date t is given by

$$\pi(a, t) = P(t) \cdot A(t - a) - 1,$$

where $P(t)$ is the current price of output.
Therefore the obsolescence age $\bar{a}(t)$ is defined by

$$\pi(\bar{a}(t), t) = P(t) \cdot A(t - \bar{a}(t)) - 1 = 0. \tag{8.8}$$

Now suppose that $A(t) = A(0)e^{\gamma t}$. The free-entry condition at time t can then by expressed as

$$\underset{\text{entry cost}}{c(f(0, t))} = \int_0^{\bar{a}^t} \pi(a, t + a)e^{-ra}\, da \tag{8.9}$$

$$\underset{\text{from (1)}}{=} \int_0^{\bar{a}^t} A(\bar{a}^t - a)e^{-ra}\, da,$$

r being the interest rate and $\bar{a}^t$ being the lifetime of a firm entering at date t. When $c'(f(0, t)) = 0$, i.e., $c(f(0, t)) = C$, equation (8.9) defines $\bar{a}^t$ as a constant: that is, the obsolescence rate of firms is independent of demand conditions (fluctuations). These must thus entirely be absorbed by the entry rate $f(0, t)$, in constrast to the case where $c'(f(0, t)) >> 0$. □

tution argument: Productivity-improving activities such as reorganizations or training often take place at the expense of directly productive activities (manufacturing). Because the return to the latter is lower in recessions due to lower demand for the manufactured good, the opportunity cost in terms of forgone profits of "reorganization" activities will be lower in recessions than in expansions.

This idea was first formalized by Hall (1991), who constructed a model where a constant labor force is allocated between production and the creation of organizational capital (in contrast to real business cycles models where the alternative activities are production and leisure). As a result of the opportunity cost argument developed above more accumulation of "organizational capital" goes on during recessions. Hall writes, "Measured output may be low during (recession) periods, but the time spend reorganizing pays off in its contribution to future productivity."

Note that the "opportunity cost" approach applies primarily to investments that yield benefits over a long period of time (such as training, reorganization, or machine replacement[17]). These are more likely to be countercyclical than, for example, advertising investments that yield higher profits over a shorter period of time, namely during a current expansion phase. Cash-intensive investments such as R&D are also more likely to be procyclical (due to credit constraints of the kind emphasized by Stiglitz (1993)) than reorganization or training activities based to a larger extent on a redistribution of *existing* labor resources.

The "opportunity cost" approach appears to be supported by recent empirical work, primarily Bean (1990), Gali and Hammour (1991), and Saint-Paul (1992). All three find evidence of a long-run negative effect of a positive demand shock on productivity,[18] thereby emphasizing reallocation effects as more important than the procyclical learning-by-doing (or demand spillover) effect described in the previous section. Bean (1990) goes on to argue that the opportunity cost approach can explain the procyclical behavior of labor

---

17. See Cooper and Haltiwanger (1993), who construct a dynamic model where retooling activities involve nonconvex costs and therefore tend to be concentrated during economic slowdowns or during periods of low productivity. Evidence of such "opportunity cost" behaviour is provided by interwar and postwar data on the U.S. automobile industry, which show that machine replacements are concentrated during the summer months and sometimes extend to the adjacent months if the economy goes through a downturn.

18. Regressing productivity growth (measured by the Solow residual) on the business cycle (measured by the employment rate or the rate of capacity utilization), using U.S. data over the sample period 1890–1987, Gali and Hammour (1991) find that a positive aggregate demand shock increases employment temporarily (by more than 2 percent) but *lowers productivity growth* (by more than 1.4 percent) *in the long run*. Saint-Paul (1991) also finds a positive cross-country correlation in OECD countries between total factor productivity growth and unemployment over the 1974–90 period.

productivity: if firms allocate a larger share of their labor force to "reorganization" activities during recessions, then the actual input to productive activities
goes down by more than the observed labor input, hence accounting for the
measured decrease in total factor productivity during recessions.[19] Further evidence of an opportunity cost effect is provided by Saint-Paul (1992) who shows
(using the same variant of Blanchard and Quah's VAR estimation methods
as Gali and Hammour) that the effect of demand fluctuations on productivity
growth is stronger when demand fluctuations are more *transitory*.[20]

A third reason for why small recessions should have a positive impact on
productivity is the following "disciplinary" effect: recessions increase the
likelihood of bankruptcy for firms that do not undertake the necessary reorganization investments. Aghion and Saint-Paul (1991) get this type of effect
in the context of an "opportunity cost" model of cylical growth by introducing fixed costs of production.[21] Increases in firms' indebtedness should also
reinforce the disciplinary effect of recessions, as argued in Nickell, Wadhwani,
and Wall (1992).

Finally, the following kind of "externality" effect pointed out by Dellas
(1993) may also reinforce the countercyclical impact of recessions on average productivity: "If the difference in expected performance (between good
and bad firms or workers) widens more than proportionally with the degree
of adversity, then adverse conditions can help improve the selection process
by reducing the probability of an occupational mistake.[22] A potential problem
with this story is that the reverse effect should also obtain during expansions
so that an increase in the frequency or magnitude of demand fluctuations might
have no effect on the average rate of productivity growth. This problem can,
however, be mitigated by assuming that the difference in relative performance
between good and bad workers (or firms) is a nonlinear function of the activity
level: namely, the relative performance of good workers is disproportionately

19. This provides one reason why the opportunity cost approach is not inconsistent with the
observed "procyclicality" of the Solow residual, another reason being that some of the productivity
improving activites (like reorganisation) may not be properly measured in the national accounts,
a point Bean (1990) emphasises. Burnside, Eichenbaum, and Rebelo (1993) analyzes labour
hoarding along the business cycle and concludes that it is a significant source of procyclicality of
the Solow residual. It is fair to say that once these two sources of procyclicality are being removed,
there is no evidence left of a procyclical Solow residual. Indeed, under the identifying assumptions
made in Gali and Hammour and Saint-Paul, the evidence points to a countercyclical residual.

20. Saint-Paul (1992) also finds little evidence of any pro- or countercyclical behaviour of R&D.
The reason might be the cash-intensive nature of R&D which should partly offset the opportunity-
cost effect. Or it may just be due to the poor quality of aggregate R&D data. Finally, the response
of productivity growth to demand fluctuations explains a nonnegligible (10–20 percent) share of
the variance of the Solow residual.

21. The basic framework developed in Aghion and Saint-Paul (1991) is presented in problem 8.2.

22. Such improvements in the selection of good firms during recessions are empirically supported
by Dellas (1993) on the basis of business closures in the United Kingdom between 1947 and 1983,
suggesting that business closures are a *convex* function of the degree of adversity and are therefore
countercyclical.

high during recessions. This convexity assumption plays a similar role to Caballero and Hammour's assumption that the unit cost of entry increases during expansion periods together with the total number of entering firms.

Our discussion so far has emphasized the (potentially) positive effects of business fluctuations on the average level of productivity. *However, these effects should not be overemphasized. In particular, the idea that excessive macroeconomic volatility is an obstacle to growth appears to be largely supported by recent empirical evidence*, for example, Bruno (1993) on inflation and growth, and particularly by recent studies on volatility and growth in Latin America.[23]

Yet little (if any) theoretical work has so far been devoted to trying to understand and rationalize this negative relationship between high volatility and growth. Two potential explanations appear to be worth exploring at this stage. One is based on the idea that *macroeconomic instability increases the option value of delaying irreversible (R&D) investments*[24], the other is that aggregate volatility might *delay the diffusion of new technological knowledge* and in particular it may reduce the speed at which the various sectors of the economy may learn from observing each other's experimentation of a new "general purpose technology." Some preliminary sense of how to formalize this second idea may actually be provided by our discussion in the next sections of this chapter.

8.4   From Growth to Business Cycles: Schumpeterian Waves Revisited

Our focus so far has been on the growth effects of economic fluctuations. What about the reverse causality from growth to fluctuations and cycles? We do not know of any empirical work addressing this latter relationship; however, the recent neo-Schumpeterian literature provides some theoretical benchmarks that might serve as a basis for future tests and analysis. Among various attempts at generating Schumpeterian waves,[25] one that appears to be particularly

---

23. In particular, the 1995 IDB Report on Volatility in Latin America provides strong cross-country evidence on the detrimental effects of volatility on Growth throughout this region. See also Gavin and Hausman (1996).

24. See Dixit and Pindyck (1995) for a primary reference on irreversible investments in a stochastic environment.

25. Precusory contributions include Jovanovic and Rob (1990) and Cheng and Dinopoulos (1992) which try to generate Schumpeterian waves based on the dichotomy between fundamental and secondary innovations, with each fundamental innovation being followed by a sequence of more and more incremental innovations. Of particular interest as a macroeconomic model is Cheng and Dinopoulous (1992), in which Schumpeterian waves obtain as a unique (non steady-state) equilibrium solution, in which the current flow of monopoly profits follows a cyclical evolution: "Because the economy's wealth is equal to the discounted present value of aggregate monopoly profits, fluctuations in profits generate procyclical fluctuations in wealth, the interest factor, consumption [. . .] and aggregate R&D investments."

promising and fruitful is the approach based on the notion of "general purpose technologies" (GPTs). Although each GPT raises output and productivity in the long run, it can also cause cyclical fluctuations while the economy adjusts to it. Examples of GPTs that have affected the entire economic system include the steam engine, the electric dynamo, the laser, and the computer. As David (1990) and Lipsey and Bekar (1995) have argued, such GPTs require costly restructuring and adjustment to take place, and there is no reason to expect this process to proceed smoothly over time. Thus, contrary to the predictions of real business cycle theory, the initial effect of a "positive technology shock" may not be to raise output, productivity and employment but to reduce them. If so, then we have yet another reason for expecting a positive relationship between the long-run growth rate and the magnitude of cycles; namely that cyclical downturns may be the price that society needs to pay in order to implement the GPTs that deliver the long-run growth.[26]

To get a preliminary sense of the potential magnitude of the downturn or slowdown that might initially be caused by the arrival of a new GPT, consider the following variant of the Solow model, where the new GPT induces obsolescence of existing capital:

$$\dot{k} = sBk^{\alpha} - (\delta + n + g + \beta)k.$$

where

a. $k = \frac{K}{Le^{gt}}$ and $y = \frac{Y}{Le^{gt}} = Bk^{\alpha}$ denote respectively the capital stock and aggregate output, both per efficiency unit of labor.

b. s is the savings rate;

c. the parameters δ, n, g, β denote respectively the rate of capital depreciation, the rate of population growth, the rate of (exogenous) technological progress and the rate of capital obsolescence.

We assume that both g and β are proportional to the arrival rate of innovations μ; that is,

$$\beta = \mu(1 - \eta) \tag{8.10}$$

and

$$g = \mu\sigma, \tag{8.11}$$

where η is the scrap value of each unit of obsolete capital and σ denotes the size of innovations[27] ($\sigma = \ln \gamma$).

---

26. The idea that long-run cycles may result from technological change is not new and goes back to Kondratieff. For more recent evidence on long-run "Schumpeterian waves," see Gordon (1993).

27. See subsection 3.2.4 for a similar analysis of capital obsolescence.

The growth rate of output per person is given by:

$$G = \frac{\dot{y}}{y} + g = \alpha \frac{\dot{k}}{k} + g$$

$$= \alpha \left[sBk^{\alpha-1} - \delta - n \right] + \left[(1 - \alpha)\sigma - \alpha(1 - \eta) \right] \mu. \tag{8.12}$$

Now, we consider the following thought experiment: starting from a steady state with $G_0 = g$, we analyze the short- and long-run effects of a marginal increase in the arrival rate of innovations μ (implicitly brought about by the arrival of a new GPT). We have

$$\frac{\partial G}{\partial \mu} = (1 - \alpha)\sigma - \alpha(1 - \eta)$$

$$= \sigma(1 - \alpha - \alpha \frac{\beta}{g}).$$

Taking $\alpha = 2/3$ as in Mankiw, Romer, and Weil (1992), $\beta = .04$ as in Caballero and Jaffe (1993) and $g = .02$ from U.S. data, we thus obtain an elasticity of growth with respect to μ equal to $\left(\frac{\mu}{G} \right) \left(\frac{\partial G}{\partial \mu} \right) = -1$. In other words, an increase in μ that raises long-run growth by 10 percent (from 2 percent to 2.2 percent) will on impact *reduce* growth by 10 percent (from 2 percent to 1.8 percent)! Furthermore, using equation (8.12) with the calibration ($\alpha = 2/3$, $\beta = .04$, $g = .02$, $\delta = .02$, $n = .01$, $s = 0.4$) one can show that it will take about two decades for the growth rate to rise back up to 2 percent and over half a century for aggregate output to catch up with the time-path it would have followed had the new GPT (and the resulting shock on μ) not arrived! This illustrates[28] the potential magnitude of the macroeconomic impact of major technological change for reasonable values of the parameters, in particular of the obsolescence rate β as estimated by Caballero and Jaffe (1993).

An interesting Schumpeterian model of cyclical growth based on GPTs is Helpman and Trajtenberg (1994). The basic idea of this model is that GPTs do not come ready to use off the shelf. Instead, each GPT requires an entirely new set of intermediate goods before it can be implemented. The discovery and development of these intermediate goods is a costly activity, and the economy must wait until some critical mass of intermediate components has been accumulated before it is profitable for firms to switch from the previous GPT. During the period between the discovery of a new GPT and its ultimate implementation, national income will fall as resources are taken out of production and put into R&D activities aimed at the discovery of new intermediate input components.

---

28. For similar results in a Schumpeterian endogenous growth framework, see Howitt (1998).

The rest of this section will be organized as follows. In section 8.4.1 we present a simplified version of the Helpman-Trajtenberg model of GPT, which fits nicely into the basic Schumpeterian framework developed in Chapter 2, and which also permits us to endogenize the long-run growth rate that Helpman and Trajtenberg take as given. We then extend this model in section 8.4.2 to introduce social learning considerations with a view to addressing the objections concerning the *timing* of economic slow-downs predicted by the Helpman and Trajtenberg model. Finally in section 8.4.3 we illustrate how the objection concerning the *size* of slowdowns in Helpman and Trajtenberg might be addressed by introducing three alternative features into the basic social learning model of section 8.4.2, namely skill-difference, job search and capital obsolescence.

8.4.1 A Simplified Presentation of the Helpman-Trajtenberg Model of GPTs

A Brief Reminder of the Basic Schumpeterian Growth Model

First, we recall the main features of the basic Schumpeterian growth model as developed in Chapter 2. Final output is produced according to the flow production function:

$$y = Ax^{\alpha},$$

where x is the flow of intermediate input and A is a productivity parameter measuring the quality of intermediate input x. Each innovation results in a new technology for producing final output and a new intermediate good which embodies the new technology. It augments current productivity by the multiplicative factor $\gamma > 1 : A_{t+1} = \gamma A_t$. Innovations in turn are the (random) outcome of research, and are assumed to arrive discretely with Poisson rate $\lambda.n$, where n is the current flow of research.

In a steady state the allocation of labor between research and manufacturing remains constant over time, and is determined by the arbitrage equation

$$\omega = \lambda \gamma v, \tag{A}$$

where the LHS of (A) is the productivity-adjusted wage rate $\omega = \frac{w}{A}$, which a worker earns by working in the manufacturing sector; and $\lambda \gamma v$ is the expected reward from investing one unit flow of labor in research. The productivity-adjusted value v of an innovation is determined by the Bellman equation

$$rv = \tilde{\pi}(\omega) - \lambda n v,$$

where $\tilde{\pi}(\omega)$ denotes the productivity-adjusted flow of monopoly profits accruing to a successful innovator and where the term $(-\lambda n v)$ corresponds to the capital loss involved in being replaced by a subsequent innovator. The above arbitrage equation, which can be reexpressed as

$$\omega = \lambda\gamma \frac{\tilde{\pi}(\omega)}{r + \lambda n},$$ (A)

together with the labor market-clearing equation

$$\tilde{x}(\omega) + n = L,$$ (L)

where $\tilde{x}(\omega)$ is the manufacturing demand for labor, jointly determine the steady-state amount of research n as a function of the parameters $\lambda, \gamma, L, r, \alpha$.

In a steady state the flow of consumption good (or final output) produced between the tth and the $(t+1)^{th}$ innovation is

$$y_t = A_t(L - n)^{\alpha},$$

where n is the steady-state amount of research; this implies that in real time (when we denote by τ), the log of final output increases by $\ln \gamma$ each time a new innovation occurs. Thus in this *one-sector* economy where each innovation corresponds by definition to a *major* technological change (i.e., to the arrival of a new GPT), growth is *uneven* (see figure 8.1) with the time path of log $y(\tau)$ being a random step function. The average growth rate is equal to the size of each step, $\ln \gamma$, times the average number of innovations per unit of time, λn : i.e., $g = \lambda n \ln \gamma$.

Although it is uneven, the time path of aggregate output as depicted above does not involve any slump. Accounting for the existence of slumps requires an extension of the basic Schumpeterian model, for example of the kind developed by Helpman and Trajtenberg, to which we now turn.

The Helpman-Trajtenberg Model Revisited

As before, there are L workers who can engage either in production of existing intermediate goods or in research aimed at discovering new intermediate goods. Again, each intermediate good is linked to a particular GPT. We follow Helpman and Trajtenberg in supposing that before any of the intermediate goods associated with GPT can be used profitably in the final goods sector, some minimal number of them must be available. We lose nothing essential by supposing that this minimal number is one. Once the good has been invented, its discoverer profits from a patent on its exclusive use in production, exactly as in the basic Schumpeterian model reviewed earlier.

Thus the difference between this model and our basic model is that now the discovery of a new generation of intermediate goods comes in *two* stages. First a new GPT must come, and then the intermediate good must be invented that implements that GPT. Neither can come before the other. You need to see the GPT before knowing what sort of good will implement it, and people need to see the previous GPT in action before anyone can think of a new one. For simplicity we assume that no one directs R&D toward the discovery of a GPT.

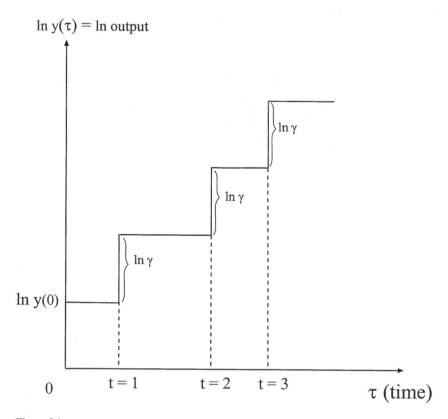

Figure 8.1

Instead, the discovery arrives as a serendipitous by-product of the collective experience of using the previous GPT.

Thus the economy will pass through a sequence of cycles, each having two phases, as indicated in figure 8.2. GPT_i arrives at time T_i. At that time the economy enters phase 1 of the ith cycle. During phase 1, the amount n of labor is devoted to research. Phase 2 begins at time $T_i + \Delta_i$ when this research discovers an intermediate good to implement GPT_i. During phase 2 all labor is allocated to manufacturing until GPT_{i+1} arrives, at which time the next cycle begins. Over the cycle output is equal to $A_{i-1}F(L-n)$ during phase 1 and $A_i F(L)$ during phase 2. Thus the drawing of labor out of manufacturing and into research causes output to fall each time a GPT is discovered, by an amount equal to $A_{i-1}[F(L) - F(L-n)]$.

A steady-state equilibrium is one in which people choose to do the same amount of research each time the economy is in phase 1, that is, where n is constant from one GPT to the next. As before, we can solve for the equilibrium value of n using a research-arbitrage equation and a labor market-equilibrium

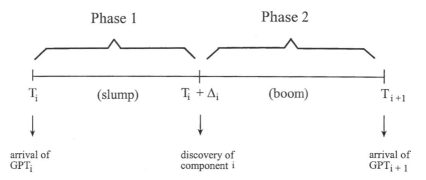

Figure 8.2

curve. Let ω_j be the wage, and v_j the expected present value of the incumbent intermediate monopolist's future profits, when the economy is in phase j, each divided by the productivity parameter A of the GPT currently in use. In a steady state these productivity-adjusted variables will all be independent of which GPT is currently in use.

Because research is conducted in phase 1 but pays off when the economy enters into phase 2 with a productivity parameter raised by the factor γ, the usual arbitrage condition must hold in order for there to be a positive level of research in the economy, namely:

$$\omega_1 = \lambda \gamma v_2. \tag{8.13}$$

Suppose that once we are in phase 2, the new GPT is delivered by a Poisson process with a constant arrival rate equal to μ. Then the value of v_2 is determined by the Bellman equation

$$r v_2 = \tilde{\pi}(\omega_2) + \mu(v_1 - v_2). \tag{8.14}$$

By analogous reasoning, we have

$$r v_1 = \tilde{\pi}(\omega_1) - \lambda n v_1. \tag{8.15}$$

Combining (8.13) – (8.15) yields the research-arbitrage equation

$$\omega_1 = \lambda \gamma \left[\tilde{\pi}(\omega_2) + \frac{\mu \tilde{\pi}(\omega_1)}{r + \lambda n} \right] / [r + \mu]. \tag{8.16}$$

Because no one does research in phase 2, we know that the value of ω_2 is determined independently of research, by the market-clearing condition $L = \tilde{x}(\omega_2)$. Thus we can take this value as given and regard equation (8.16) as determining ω_1 as a function of n. The value of n is determined, as usual, by this equation together with the labor-market equation

$$L - n = \tilde{x}(\omega_1). \tag{8.17}$$

As in the basic model, the level of research n is an increasing function of the productivity of research λ, the size of improvement created by each GPT γ, and the population L; and a decreasing function of the rate of interest r. The arrival rate μ of GPTs has a negative effect on research[29], intuitively, an increase in μ discourages research by reducing the expected duration of the first of the two phases over which the successful researcher can capitalize the rents from an innovation. The size of the slump $\ln(F(L)) - \ln(F(L - n))$ is an increasing function of n, and hence will tend to be positively correlated with the average growth rate.

The average growth rate will be the frequency of innovations times the size $\ln \gamma$, for exactly the same reason as in the basic model. The frequency, however, is determined a little differently than before because the economy must pass through *two* phases. An innovation is implemented each time a full cycle is completed. The frequency with which this happens is the inverse of the expected length of a complete cycle. This in turn is just the expected length of phase 1 plus the expected length of phase 2:

$$1/\lambda n + 1/\mu = \frac{\mu + \lambda n}{\mu \lambda n}.$$

Thus we have the growth equation

$$g = \ln \gamma \frac{\mu \lambda n}{\mu + \lambda n}. \tag{8.18}$$

Thus the expected growth rate will be positively affected by anything that raises research, with the possible exception of a fall in μ. In the limit, when μ falls to zero, growth must also fall to zero as the economy will spend an infinitely long time in phase 2, without growing. Thus for small enough values of μ, g and n will be affected in opposite directions by a change in μ.

One further property of this cycle worth mentioning is that, as Helpman and Trajtenberg point out, the wage rate will rise when the economy goes into a slump. That is, because there is no research in phase 2, the normalized wage must be low enough to provide employment for all L workers in the

---

29. To show this, it suffices to show that an increase in μ shifts the research arbitrage curve to the left. By applying the implicit function theorem to (8.16), we see that the sign of this shift is:

$$sign \frac{dn}{d\mu} = -sign \left(\omega_1 - \frac{\lambda \gamma \tilde{\pi}(\omega_1)}{r + \lambda n} \right).$$

Because no research is done in phase 2, labor market equilibrium requires $\omega_2 < \omega_1$, and hence $\tilde{\pi}(\omega_2) > \tilde{\pi}(\omega_1)$. Applying this to (8.16) yields:

$$\omega_1 > \frac{\lambda \gamma \tilde{\pi}(\omega_1)}{r + \lambda n} \cdot \frac{r + \lambda n + \mu}{r + \mu} > \frac{\lambda \gamma \tilde{\pi}(\omega_1)}{r + \lambda n}.$$

manufacturing sector, whereas with the arrival of the new GPT, the wage must rise to induce manufacturers to release workers into research.

Two aspects of this theory may call its empirical relevance into question. The first is the likely *size of the slump* that it might cause. All of the decline in output is attributable to the transfer of labor out of manufacturing and into R&D. But because the total amount of R&D labor on average is only 2.5 percent of the labor force, it is hard to see how this can account for change in aggregate production of more than a fraction of a percent. (The size of the slump would be even smaller if we assumed, as Helpman and Trajtenberg do, that some national income is imputed to the R&D workers even before their research pays off in a positive stream of profits in the intermediate sector)[30].

The second questionable aspect of this theory has to do with the *timing* of slow-downs: the Helpman and Trajtenberg model implies an *immediate* slump as soon as the GPT arrives. This in turns follows from the assumption that (i) agents need to see the new GPT before investing in research in order to discover the complementary components, and (ii) these research activities are sufficiently profitable that they always divert some labor resources away from manufacturing. In fact, as Paul David (1990) argues, it may take several decades before major technological innovations can have a significant impact on macroeconomic activity (David talks about a preparadigm phase of twenty-five years in the case of the electric dynamo). Then it is hard to believe that labor could be diverted on a large scale into an activity which will pay off only in the very distant future.

The first of these problems is relatively easy to deal with (at least conceptually), as one can think of a number of reasons why the adjustment to a massive and fundamental technological change would cause adjustment and coordination problems resulting in a slump. For example, as Atkeson and Kehoe (1993) analyze, the arrival of a new GPT might induce firms to engage in *risky experimentation* on a large scale with startup firms, not all of which will succeed. The capital sunk into these startup firms will not yield a competitive return right away except by chance; meanwhile national income will drop as a result of that capital not being used in less risky ways using the old GPT. Also, an increase in the pace of innovation aimed at exploiting the new GPT may well result in an increased rate of job turnover, and hence in an increased rate of unemployment (see section 8.4.3(ii)). Greenwood and Yorukoglu (1996) present an analysis in which the costs of learning to use equipment embodying the

---

30. Helpman and Trajtenberg find that a measured slump occurs when the GPT arrives even if the full cost of R&D is as imputed national income. The reason is that the discovery induces workers to leave a sector where their marginal product is higher than the wage (because the intermediate sector is imperfectly competitive and pays according to the marginal revenue product of labour rather than the marginal value product), and to enter a sector—research—where their (imputed) marginal product is just equal to the same wage.

new GPT can account for a prolonged productivity showdown. Howitt (1998) shows how the arrival of a new GPT can cause output growth to slow down because it accelerates the rate of obsolescence of existing physical and human capital.

The second problem is more challenging to deal with. The question is, if the exploitation of a new GPT is spread out over a period of many decades, why should it not result in simply a slow enhancement in aggregate productivity, as one industry after another learns to use the new technology?

Again, several answers come to mind and we actually think of the following three explanations as being complementary. First are the *measurability* problems: as already stressed by David and others, *it may take a while before the new products and services embodying the new GPT can be fully accounted for by conventional statistics.*[31] (This, however, does not explain the possibility of delayed *slumps*.) Second, the existence of *strategic complementarities* in the adoption of new GPTs by the various sectors of the economy may generate temporary lock-in effects, of a kind similar to the *implementation cycles* in Shleifer (1986). It may then take real labor costs or other "exogenous" economic parameters to reach a minimum threshold before a critical number of sectors decide to jump on the bandwagon of the new GPT.

A third explanation, which will be the main focus of our analysis in the next subsection, lies in the phenomenon of *social learning*. That is, the way a firm typically learns to use a new technology is not to discover everything on its own but to learn from the experience of other firms in a similar situation, other firms for whom the problems that must be solved before the technology can successfully be implemented bear enough resemblance to the problems that must be solved in this firm that it is worthwhile trying to use the procedures of those successful firms as a "template."

Thus at first the fact that no one knows how to exploit a new GPT means that almost nothing happens in the aggregate. Only minor improvements in knowledge take place for a long time, because successful implementation in any sector requires firms to make independent discoveries with little guidance from the successful experience of others. But if this activity continues for long enough, a point will eventually be reached when almost everyone can see enough other firms using the new technology to make it worth their while experimenting with it. Thus even though the spread of a new GPT takes place over a long period of time, most of the costly experimentation through which the spread takes place may be concentrated over a relatively short subperiod, during which there will be a cascade or snowball effect resulting sometimes in a (delayed) aggregate slump.

---

31. See section 8.5 and the appendix to Chapter 12 for a discussion of various problems involved in measuring knowledge-based growth.

8.4.2   A Model of Major Technological Change through Social Learning

Basic Setup

We consider the following dynamic model of the spread of technology, which is similar to the sorts of models used by epidemiologists when studying the spread of disease, which also takes place through a process of social interaction between those who have and those who have not yet been exposed to the new phenomenon. The setting of model is like the model we have just described, with a continuum of sectors uniformly distributed on the unit interval, except that now each sector must invent its own intermediate good in order to exploit the GPT. We study here the nature of the cycle caused by the arrival of a single GPT, under the assumption that the arrival rate μ is so small that there is insignificant probability that the next GPT will arrive before almost all sectors have adopted the one that has just arrived. In order to simplify the analysis even further we suppose that the amount of research in each sector is given by a fixed endowment of specialized research labor. Thus all the dynamics will result from the effects of social learning on the payoff rate to experimentation.[32]

Aggregate output at any point in time is produced by labor according to the constant-returns technology

$$Y = \left\{ \int_0^1 A(i)^\alpha x(i)^\alpha di \right\}^{1/\alpha}, \tag{8.19}$$

where $A(i) = 1$ in sectors where the old GPT is still used, and $A(i) = \gamma > 1$ in sectors that have successfully innovated, whereas $x(i)$ is manufacturing labor used to produce the intermediate good in sector i.

Assume that in each sector an innovation requires *three* breakthroughs rather than the two breakthroughs of the previous model. First, the economy wide GPT must be discovered. Second, a firm in that sector must acquire a "template" on which to base experimentation. Third, the firm must use this template to discover how to implement the GPT in its particular sector. (This third stage is equivalent to the component-finding stage in the Helpman and Trajtenberg model, while the second stage is new.) Thus all sectors are in one of three states. In state 0 are those sectors who have not yet acquired a template. In state 1 are those who have a template but have not yet discovered how to implement it. In state 2 are those sectors who have succeeded in making the transition to the new GPT. We let the fraction of sectors in each state be represented by n_0, n_1, n_2, and suppose that initially $n_0 = 1, n_1 = n_2 = 0$.

---

32. This is the phenomenon that we believe to be at the heart of the timing of the delayed cyclical response to GPTs. Endogenizing the allocation of labor between research and manufacturing would just accentuate the effects we find, as it would draw more labor into research, hence augmenting the intensity of experimentation, just when the informational cascade we focus on is already having the same effect.

A sector will move from state 0 to state 1 if a firm in that sector either makes an independent discovery of a template or if it discovers one by "imitation" that is by observing at least k "similarly located" firms that have made a successful transition to the new GPT (firms in state 2). The Poisson arrival rate of independent discoveries to such a sector is $\lambda_0 << 1$. The Poisson arrival rate of opportunities to observe m similarly located firms is assumed to equal unity. The probability that such an observation will pay off (in other words, the probability that at least k among the m similar firms will have successfully experimented the new GPT) is given by the cumulative binomial

$$\varphi(m, k, n_2) = \sum_{j=k}^{m} \binom{m}{j} n_2^j (1 - n_2)^{m-j},$$

because n_2 is the probability that a randomly selected firm will be in state 2. Thus the flow of sectors from state 0 to state 1 will be n_0 times the flow probability of each sector making the transition: $\lambda_0 + \varphi(m, k, n_2)$.

For a sector to move from state 1 to state 2, the firm with the template must employ at least N units of labor per period (the equivalent of n in the Helpman and Trajtenberg model). We can think of this labor as being used in formal R&D, informal R&D, or in an experimental startup firm. In any case it is not producing current output. Instead it is allowing the sector access to a Poisson process that will deliver a workable implementation of the new GPT with an arrival rate of λ_1. Thus the flow of sectors from states 1 to 2 will be the number of sectors in state 1, n_1, times the success rate per sector per unit of time λ_1.

We can summarize the discussion to this point by observing that the evolution over time of the two variables n_1 and n_2 is given by the autonomous system of ordinary differential equations:

$$\dot{n}_1 = \left[\lambda_0 + \varphi(m, k, n_2) \right] (1 - n_1 - n_2) - \lambda_1 n_1$$

$$\dot{n}_2 = \lambda_1 n_1$$

(S)

with initial condition $n_1(0) = 0, n_2(0) = 0$. (The time path of n_0 is then given automatically by the identity $n_0 \equiv 1 - n_1 - n_2$.)

Figure 8.3 depicts the solution to the above system (S). Not surprisingly, the timepath of n_2 follows a logistic curve, accelerating at first and slowing down as n_2 approaches 1, with the maximal growth rate occurring somewhere in the middle. Likewise the path of n_1 must peak somewhere in the middle of the transition, in as much as it starts and ends at zero. If the arrival rate λ_0 of independent discoveries is very small then both n_1 and n_2 will remain near zero for a long time. Figure 8.3 shows the behavior of n_1 and n_2 in the case where $\lambda_0 = .005, \lambda_1 = .3, m = 10$, and $k = 3$. The number of sectors engaging in experimentation peaks sharply in year 20 due to social learning.

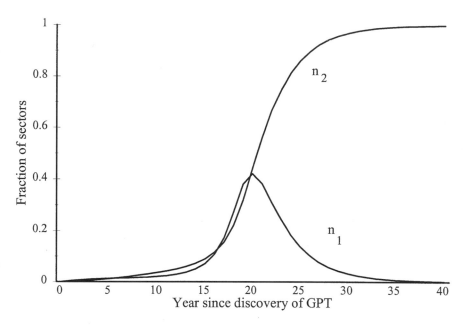

Figure 8.3

The solution to the system (S) can be used together with the aggregate production function (8.19) and the market-clearing condition for labor to determine the time path of aggregate output. Using the symmetry of the production technology (8.19), which implies that all the sectors using the same GPT (either old or new) will demand the same amount of manufacturing labor, we can reexpress the flow of aggregate output as

$$Y = \left\{ \int_0^{1-n_2} x_0(i)^\alpha di + \gamma^\alpha \int_{1-n_2}^1 x_N(i)^\alpha di \right\}^{1/\alpha} \tag{8.20}$$

where x_0 (resp. x_N) denotes the flow of labor demand by a sector using the old (resp. new) GPT.

The local monopolists in sectors in state 0 and 1, who use the old technology, will demand labor according to the demand function.[33]

---

33. This follows from profit-maximization: for any sector i, $x(i) = \arg\max_x \{p_i(x)x - wx\}$, where:

$$p_i(x) = \frac{\partial Y}{\partial x} = \begin{cases} x^{\alpha-1} \cdot Y^{1-\alpha} & \text{if sector } i \text{ uses the } old \text{ technology} \\ \gamma^\alpha x^{\alpha-1} \cdot Y^{1-\alpha} & \text{if sector } i \text{ uses the } new \text{ technology.} \end{cases}$$

The corresponding first-order conditions, respectively for old and new sectors, yield the following demand equations (8.21) and (8.22).

$$x_0 = (w/\alpha)^{\frac{1}{\alpha-1}} Y, \tag{8.21}$$

whereas those in sectors in state 2 will demand according to

$$x_N = (w/\alpha\gamma^\alpha)^{\frac{1}{\alpha-1}} Y, \tag{8.22}$$

where w is the real wage rate.

Using (8.21), (8.22) and the labor market-clearing condition:

$$\underbrace{(1 - n_2)x_0 + n_2 x_N}_{\text{manufacturing labor demand}} \quad \underbrace{+n_1 N = L}_{\text{experimenting labor}} \quad , \tag{L}$$

we can solve for the real wage w as a function of Y, n_1, and n_2. Substituting this solution into the above expressions for x_0 and x_N and then substituting the resulting values of x_0 and x_N into (8.20) yields the following reduced form expression for output:

$$Y = (L - n_1 N)\left(1 - n_2 + n_2 \gamma^{\frac{\alpha}{1-\alpha}}\right)^{\frac{1-\alpha}{\alpha}}. \tag{8.23}$$

Figure 8.4 shows the time path of output that results from the above dynamics in n_1 and n_2, in the benchmark case where $N = 6$, $L = 10$, and $\alpha = .5$. As expected, output is not much affected by the new GPT for the first decade and half, but then it enters a severe recession when the number of sectors engaging in experimentation increases sharply as a result of social learning: output reaches a trough in year 19, after a 10.5 percent drop in output. From there output begins to grow, ultimately attaining a value of $\gamma (= 1.5)$ times its original value.

The delay in the slump caused by the GPT could not have occurred without the impact of social learning.[34] That is, suppose that the function $\varphi(m, k, n_2)$ that embodies the effects of social learning were replaced by the constant $\varphi_0 = \int_0^1 \varphi(m, k, n_2) dn_2$, so the average rate of learning would be the same but learning would not be affected by the process of observing other sectors that have succeeded in implementing the new GPT. Then n_2 would still follow a mild logistic curve, but the intensity of experimentation n_1 would rise immediately following the arrival of GPT and would fall monotonically from then on. Output could go through a slump but the maximal rate of decline would occur immediately at year 0. This benchmark case of no social learning is illustrated in figure 8.5.

Intuitively, the reason why the slump cannot be delayed in this case is as follows. In order for output to be falling there must be a positive flow of sectors into state 1, which is drawing workers out of manufacturing. But without social

---

34. Greenwood and Yorukoglu (1996) assume a private learning process that also produces diffusion according to a mild logistic curve.

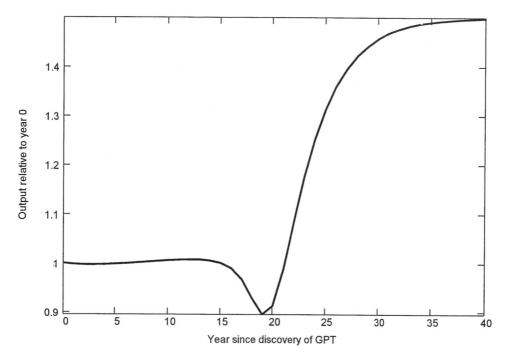

Figure 8.4

learning this flow must be diminishing whenever a slump is underway, in as much as the rise in the level of n_1 (and in n_2) will be reducing the pool $(1 - n_1 - n_2)$ from which new experimenters are drawn, whereas the rise in n_1 increases the flow of successful innovators out of the state of experimentation. (See the above equation for $\dot{n}_1$ in (S)). Thus either the slump starts right away, in which case its intensity will diminish steadily, or it never starts at all.[35]

---

35. To see this more formally, suppose that the output function (8.23) can be approximated by its first-order Taylor expansion around $n_1 = n_2 = 0$:

$$Y \simeq L - N \cdot n_1 + \xi \cdot n_2; \quad \xi \equiv \frac{1 - \alpha}{\alpha} \left(\gamma^{\frac{\alpha}{1-\alpha}} - 1 \right) L > 0.$$

Because $\dot{n}_2$ is always positive, $\dot{n}_1$ must also be positive whenever Y is not rising. Thus, if $\dot{Y} \leq 0$, then

$$\dot{Y} \simeq -N \cdot \dot{n}_1 + \xi \dot{n}_2$$

$$\dot{Y} \simeq -N \left[(\lambda_0 + \varphi_0)(1 - n_1 - n_2) - \lambda_1 n_1 \right] + \xi \lambda_1 n_1$$

$$\ddot{Y} \simeq \left[N(\lambda_0 + \varphi_0 + \lambda_1) + \xi \lambda_1 \right] \dot{n}_1 + N(\lambda_0 + \varphi_0)\dot{n}_2$$

$$\ddot{Y} > 0 \text{ (because } \dot{n}_1 > 0, \dot{n}_2 > 0).$$

Hence a delayed slump, with $\dot{Y}$ turning negative or becoming more negative at some date $t > 0$, is impossible.

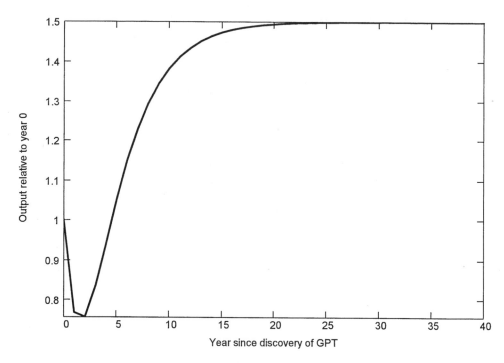

Figure 8.5

What social learning does is to reverse the effect of n_2 on the rate of growth of n_1; that is, as n_2 rises, the resulting increase in the likelihood of imitation counterbalances the fall in the number of possible imitators, thus causing the cascade at the heart of our analysis.

Some Comparative Dynamics

Table 8.1 shows how the time path of aggregate output responds to variations in the basic parameters of the model, namely:

- α, which measures the degree of substitutability across intermediate inputs.
- γ, which measures the size of productivity improvements brought about by the new GPT
- N, the number of workers taken out of manufacturing by each experimenting firm.
- m, the number of sectors potentially "similar" to a given sector.
- k, the required number of observations of successful experimentations in order to acquire a template "by imitation".
- λ_0, the arrival rate of independent ideas for new templates.
- λ_1, the arrival rate of success for experimenting firms.

Table 8.1

Parameter	Value	Slump	Size	Peak date	Trough date
Baseline		yes	11%	12	19
α	0.2	yes	12%	12	19
(0.5)	0.8	yes	8%	15	19
γ	1.1	yes	22%	0	20
(1.5)	3.0	no			
k	1	yes	23%	0	5
(3)	5	yes	4%	37	42
m	3	no			
(10)	30	yes	22%	4	10
N	2	no			
(6)	8	yes	20%	11	19
λ_0	.001	yes	11%	32	40
(.005)	.025	yes	10%	5	10
λ_1	0.1	yes	22%	13	29
(0.3)	1.0	no			

In all cases the simulation produces either a marked slump, as in figure 8.4, or a monotonic increase in output. When there is no slump there is an initial period of relatively slow growth followed by a sharp acceleration coming just after the peak in experimentation. When there is a slump it almost always comes after a period of mild growth, which itself is often preceded by a very mild (less than half a percentage point) recession. The size of slump reported in Table 8.1 is the percentage shortfall from the peak attained at the end of the period of mild growth (or from year 0 if no such period exits) to the trough. From Table 8.1 we can see:

a. the magnitude of slumps increases as α decreases, that is, when intermediate inputs become less substitutable. This is fairly intuitive: as α decreases, the downsizing of old manufacturing sectors, which results from labor being diverted away into experimentation, is less and less substituted for by the new—more productive—intermediate good sectors.

b. the magnitude of slumps decreases as γ increases, and for sufficiently large γ the slump even disappears. Again, this result is intuitive: the bigger productivity of new sectors compensates for the reduction in output in old sectors caused by experimentation (and by the resulting wage increase), thereby reducing the scope for aggregate slumps.

c. If m is too small, output grows steadily: indeed the lower m, the lower the scope for social learning and for the resulting snowball effect on aggregate output.

d. An increase in k leads to bigger delays but smaller slumps: as k increases it will take longer for "imitation" and social learning to become operational. Thus by the time a cascade begins, a higher number of sectors will have already moved into using the new and more productive GPT; hence the smaller the size of aggregate slumps.

e. An increase in N leads to larger slumps. This is straightforward: the bigger N, the more labor will be diverted away from manufacturing into experimentation by firms in state 1, and therefore the bigger the size of slumps when social learning causes the fraction of experimenting sectors to increase sharply.

f. An increase in the arrival rate of independent ideas λ_0 speeds up the macroeconomic response to the new GPT. This is not surprising, for the larger λ_0 the faster the conditions will be created for social learning to operate.

g. An increase in the success rate of experimentation λ_1 reduces the size of slumps: this is again easy to understand, for the larger λ_1 the faster the emergence of sectors using the new GPT that compensate for the downsizing of manufacturing induced by experimentation.

8.4.3 Accounting for the Size of Slowdowns

Skill Differentials

The last five years or so have witnessed an upsurge of empirical papers on skill differentials and wage inequality, and their relationship with technological change (in particular, see Juhn et al. 1993).[36] It turns out that a straightforward extensions of our GPT model can account for an increasing skill and wage differential as a result of the introduction of a new GPT. The same extension can also magnify the slump.[37]

More formally, suppose that the labor force L is now divided into skilled and unskilled workers, and that the implementation of the new GPT requires *skilled* labor whereas old sectors can indifferently use skilled or unskilled workers to manufacture their intermediate inputs. Also, assume that the fraction of skilled workers is increasing over time, for example, as a result of schooling and/or training investments which we do not model here:

---

36. For more on the relationship between technical change and the dynamics of wage inequality, see section 9.2.

37. Our explanation of both the differential and the slowdown is similar in spirit to that of Greenwood and Yorukoglu (1996), who also emphasize the role of skilled labor in implementing new technologies.

$$L_s(t) = L(1 - (1 - \tau)e^{-\lambda_2 t}), \ 0 < \tau < 1,$$

where τ is the initial fraction of skilled workers and λ_2 is a positive number measuring the speed of skill acquisition.

The transition from the old to the new GPT can then be divided into two subperiods. First, in the early phase of transition (i.e., when t is low) the number of sectors using the new GPT is too small to absorb the whole skilled labor force, which in turn implies that a positive fraction of skilled workers will have to be employed by the old sectors at the same wage as their unskilled peers. Thus, during the early phase of transition the labor market will remain "unsegmented," with aggregated output and the real wage being determined exactly as before.[38]

Second, in the later state of transition, where the fraction of new sectors has grown sufficiently large that it can absorb the whole skilled labor force, the labor market will become segmented, with skilled workers being exclusively employed (at a higher wage) by new sectors while the unskilled workers remain in old sectors. Let w_u and w_s denote the real wages respectively paid to unskilled and skilled workers. The demand for manufacturing labor by the old and new sectors are still given by:

$$x_0 = \left(\frac{w_u}{\alpha}\right)^{\frac{1}{\alpha-1}} Y$$

and

$$x_N = \left(\frac{w_s}{\alpha \gamma^\alpha}\right)^{\frac{1}{\alpha-1}} Y,$$

except that we now have: $w_s > w_u$, where the two real wages are determined by two separate labor market clearing conditions, respectively

$$L_s = n_1 N + n_2 x_N \tag{8.24}$$

and

$$L_u = L - L_s = (1 - n_2)x_0. \tag{8.25}$$

These equations yield

---

38. That is, by equations (L) and (8.21)–(8.23), which together yield

$$Y = (L - n_1 N)(1 - n_2 + n_2 \gamma^{\frac{1-\alpha}{\alpha}})^{\frac{1-\alpha}{\alpha}}$$

and

$$w = \alpha \left[1 - n_2 + n_2 \gamma^{\frac{\alpha}{1-\alpha}}\right]^{\frac{1-\alpha}{\alpha}}.$$

$$w_s = \gamma^\alpha \alpha \left(\frac{n_2 Y}{L_s - n_1 N} \right)^{1-\alpha}$$

and

$$w_u = \alpha \left(\frac{(1 - n_2) Y}{L - L_s} \right)^{1-\alpha} .$$

Substituting for x_0 and x_N from (8.24) and (8.25) into (8.20) yields the following expression for aggregate output during the segmented phase of transition:

$$Y = \left[(1 - n_2)^{1-\alpha} (L - L_s)^\alpha + n_2^{1-\alpha} \gamma^\alpha (L_s - n_1 N)^\alpha \right]^{\frac{1}{\alpha}} .$$

(The cut-off date t_0 between the unsegmented and segmented phases of transition to the new GPT is determined by $w_s(t_0) = w_u(t_0)$.)

Figure 8.6a depicts the time-path of real wages and figure 8.6b the time-path of aggregate output in the benchmark case of the previous section with $\lambda_2 = .05$ and $\tau = .0.25$. Two interesting conclusions emerge from this simulation:

a. The skill premium (w_s/w_u) starts increasing sharply in a year $(t = 21)$ when social learning is accelerating the flow of new sectors in the economy, and then the premium keeps on increasing although more slowly during the remaining part of the transition process.[39] Because everyone ends up earning the same (skilled) wage, standard measures of wage inequality first rise and then fall. This yields a simple alternative explanation of the Kuznets curve (rising and then falling inequality) in terms of transition to a new technological paradigm instead of Kuznets's transition to an urban economy. We discuss this in more detail in Chapter 9.

b. Compared to the benchmark case *without* skill differentials and labor market segmentation, the magnitude of the slump is the same (11 percent) but the recovery is slower: the reason is that high productivity sectors are constrained by the short supply of skilled labor; in simulations with other parameter values we see that the slump is exacerbated by the skill shortage if the market becomes segmented earlier.

Job Search

We now extend the basic setup in another direction, namely by introducing costly job search, which, together with the destruction of jobs by new sectors,

---

39. The acceleration in the premium, with w_s increasing and w_u decreasing sharply at the beginning of the segmented phase, has to do with the high demand for skilled experimentation labor during this time interval where social learning peaks. The skilled real wage w_s starts tapering off thereafter where most sectors are already in phase 2 and the supply of skilled labor keeps on increasing over time.

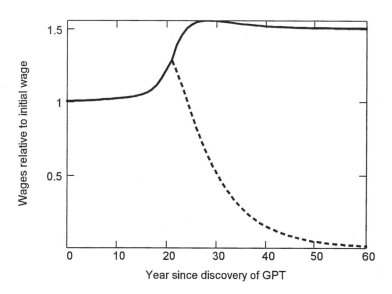

Figure 8.6a
The solid line indicates the skilled wage, and the dashed line the unskilled wage.

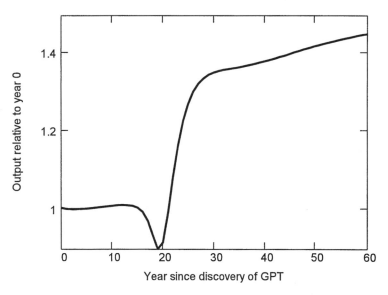

Figure 8.6b

generates unemployment on the transition path. Unemployment in turn diverts a higher fraction of the labor force out of manufacturing thereby *increasing* the size of slumps relative to the benchmark case simulated in section 8.4.2. Indeed, slumps can now occur even if the labor N needed to perform experiments is negligible, as we argued in section 8.4.1.

More formally, suppose that the fraction β of workers in each sector that adopts the GPT (and moves in to n_2) go into temporary unemployment, because they are unable to adapt to the new GPT in the sector where they were formally unemployed. Suppose also that the fraction λ_3 of the unemployed per period succeed in finding a new job. Then the evolution of U, the number of unemployed, is governed by

$$\dot{U} = \underbrace{\beta x_0(w)\lambda_1 n_1}_{\text{job destruction}} - \underbrace{\lambda_3 U}_{\text{job creation}} \quad .$$

Output and the real wage are determined exactly as in the basic model of section 8.4.2 except with the "effective labor force" $L - U$ instead of L.[40] Putting this real wage into the demand function (8.21) and substituting for Y using (8.23) yields the equilibrium quantity

$$x_0(w) = \frac{L - U - n_1 N}{1 - n_2 + n_2 \gamma^{\frac{\alpha}{1-\alpha}}}.$$

Figure 8.7 depicts the time paths of unemployment and aggregate output with the benchmark parameter set from section 8.4.2 together with $\beta = 0.5$ and $\lambda_3 = 2$. The unemployment rate reaches a sharp peak in year 20, just after experimentation reaches its peak, with the predictable effect of increasing the size of the slump (from 11 percent to 13 percent).

Obsolescence

Our analysis in the previous section has already discussed various mechanisms that may potentially account for the significant size of macroeconomic fluctuations caused by the arrival of a new GPT: in particular, the existence of labor market segmentations, or the occurrence of errors in the experimentation process, which, together with labor market frictions, will generate unemployment fluctuations on the transition path to the new GPT. There is however, another and perhaps more straightforward explanation for the slowdowns or slumps induced by major technological changes, one that should immediately

---

40. For simplicity, we identify flows into unemployment with flows out of the labor force. This allows us to bypass the technical complications involved in modeling explicitly the bargaining game between new sectors and workers. Taking the latter, more traditional modeling route would needlessly complicate the algebra.

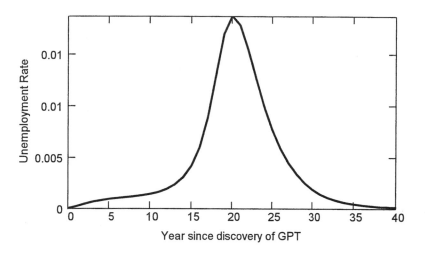

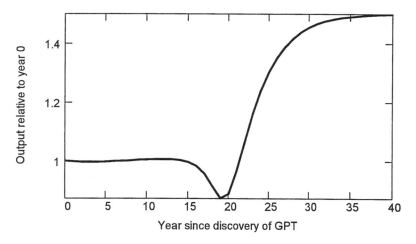

Figure 8.7

occur to anyone familiar with Schumpeter's ideas: namely, the (capital) obsolescence caused by the new wave of (secondary) innovations initiated by a new GPT.

To capture this idea, we first reinterpret the model of section 8.3 by supposing that the factor used in both production and research is not labor but capital, either physical or human. Each time an innovation arrives implementing the GPT in a sector it destroys a fraction δ of the capital that had previously been employed in that sector, because all capital must be tailor-made to use a specific technology in a specific sector, and some of the capital is lost when it is converted to use in another sector or with another technology.[41] For simplicity, suppose that people are target savers, that is, they save a constant fraction s per period of the gap between the desired capital stock L and the actual stock K. Then the rate of net accumulation of capital is

$$\dot{K} = \underbrace{s(L - K)}_{\text{gross saving}} - \underbrace{\delta x_0(w)\lambda_1 n_1}_{\text{obsolescence}} .$$

Output and the real wage (that is, the real rate of return to capital) are determined as in the basic model of section 8.4.2, but with L replaced by K. The initial stationary state with $n_1 = 0$ has $K = L$.

It is easy to see that this modification of the basic model of section 8.4.2 is formally equivalent to that of the previous section, with the gap $L-K$ replacing the number unemployed U, the saving rate s replacing the job-finding rate λ_3, and the obsolescence fraction δ replacing the job-destruction fraction β. Thus, for the same reasons as in the previous section, the capital shortfall will peak sharply around the same time as the peak in experimentation, and the slump will be larger than if there were no obsolescence.

8.5   Measurement Problems

The analysis of the previous section provided several theoretical mechanisms by which the introduction of a major new technological paradigm might lead to a slump in economic activity before finally paying off in higher aggregate output. But it should be emphasized that the empirical evidence on GPT-induced downturns is scanty at best. The fact that there have been so few examples of economy-wide technological innovations of such significance that the adjustment to them might cause major macroeconomic problems makes it difficult to provide convincing evidence in support of the theory. Moreover, the fact that, as we have seen, there are likely to be long and variable lags between the original innovation and the subsequent slump means that identifying a causal relationship might be impossible even if we had a large number of observations.

Measurement problems might also cause the very opposite problem. That is, when a new GPT is being introduced, various measurement problems may combine so as to create the illusion that there is an aggregate slump when in fact the economy is growing at a healthy pace. The rest of this section addresses this possibility.[42] The Schumpeterian approach that we are putting forth in this

---

41. This is the assumption made in Howitt (1998).

42. We explore it in more detail in the appendix to Chapter 12.

book is well suited to address it, for the measurement problems in question arise from the very distinction at the heart of the Schumpeterian approach, namely the distinction between knowledge, which is created by innovations, and other forms of capital, which grow from the activity of investment.

The main measurement problem that we wish to emphasize here is the problem of measuring the output from innovative activity. (This is what we call the "knowledge-investment problem" in the appendix to Chapter 12). That is, knowledge, like physical capital, is produced at an opportunity cost of current consumption, and like physical capital it will allow society to produce more in the future than otherwise, given the same inputs of all other factors of production. So when resources are diverted from producing consumption goods into producing knowledge, there is no more reason to think that the overall level of output or income has fallen than when they are diverted to producing physical capital. Nevertheless, under standard national income accounting procedures, measured GDP will fall in the first case and not in the second.

The reason for this asymmetry is that physical capital can be measured a lot more easily than can knowledge. Knowledge is typically not traded on open markets in which prices and quantities are recorded. Instead, it is usually either created by the same agent that uses it, or it is acquired from others through a spillover process without being purchased in the market. In neither case does its acquisition contribute to measured GDP. The firm doing R&D on its own account does not capitalize this expenditure. If it ends the year with a better idea of what to produce, or of how to produce it, or of how to sell it, this may raise its future sales or profits, but it will add nothing to the firm's books that the national income accountant will consider part of society's current output of goods and services, as it would if instead of accumulating ideas the firm had been accumulating capital.

So, when the introduction of a new GPT creates a wave of new innovations centering on the new technological paradigm, these innovations will typically contribute nothing to measured GDP. If resources are diverted away from producing measured output by the new opportunities for R&D, the overall effect will be to reduce measured GDP, even though there has been no real decrease in the overall level of activity or output, just a redirection. Moreover, because a GPT acts like the fundamental innovations discussed in Chapter 6 above—that is, it opens up new windows of opportunity for secondary innovations—there will be an unmeasured real increase in aggregate output because the innovation sector will now be more productive than it was before.

In short, if we abstract from the adjustment costs caused by such factors as learning, unemployment, skill bottlenecks, and obsolescence, which were discussed in the previous section, the fact that a new GPT is likely to redirect resources from the measured sector, in which there is no immediate change in productivity, into the nonmeasured sector, where there *has* been an increase in productivity, is likely to imply an increase in the actual growth rate, but a decrease in the measured growth rate.

Eventually, as more sectors of the economy learn to use the new GPT, productivity in the measured sector should increase also, and measured growth should pick up. However, as Griliches (1994) and others have emphasized, much of the productivity enhancement effect arising from computers (the latest GPT) is probably taking place in service industries where output is measured so imperfectly that the productivity gains are likely not to be recorded. For example, we measure the output of hospital services by the number of patient-days spent in the hospital. If new computer-assisted surgical procedures cure people in fewer days it will appear that the output of hospital services has gone down as a result of the new technology!

In addition, as several authors have pointed out (e.g., David 1991, Griliches 1994) the fact that the new goods created by the wave of innovations will take time to be included, means that the benefit that people typically get from falling prices of new high-tech goods in their first year or so of introduction will tend to be missed in official statistics.

Whether or not these measurement problems are so severe as to cause a measured slump, they are likely at least to result in a slowdown of measured aggregate productivity when we combine them with another measurement problem, which we call in the appendix to Chapter 12 the "knowledge input" problem. That is, many of the activities that should be thought of as contributing to knowledge are actually classified as inputs to the production of goods and services. For example, most of the time that people spend learning on the job how to master computer technology is considered an input to the production of goods and services. This time is really being spent producing knowledge, not goods. If we were to exclude its contribution to input at the same time as we exclude its contribution to output, this would not affect the measurement of productivity. But because we actually consider it as input to the production of goods and services, the fact that it contributes nothing means that measured productivity will go down when people are induced by the arrival of a new GPT to do more of this kind of knowledge investment.

In the end, we are left with a lot of possibilities. New GPTs may cause actual slumps that are hard to detect, or illusory slumps when in fact things are booming. Sorting out which of these possibilities is closer to the truth, or whether the third alternative is true, is a difficult task. All we can do at this stage is to develop models in which the different alternatives can be expressed and in which the various mechanisms that produce them can be elucidated. For these tasks we believe that our Schumpeterian approach will continue to be invaluable.

8.6 Summary

For a long time economics treated cycles and trend growth separately. For example, the multiplier/accelerator model could generate cyclical behavior due to investment alternating between high and low levels, leading to corresponding changes in aggregate demand and output, but could not also explain trend growth. Extensions of the model included an exogenous growth trend, but this trend had no effect on the duration or size of the cycle. On the other hand, the neoclassical model of (exogenous) growth totally ignored the business cycle.

This dichotomy was also associated with a difference in assumptions: neoclassical growth theory assumed that markets worked perfectly, whereas the cycles literature assumed that they did not. This meant that there was little to be said about monetary influences on growth (because such money is typically assumed neutral in neoclassical models). Within an endogenous growth model the neutrality of money, a cornerstone of much neoclassical economics, ceases to be true.

To provide a framework for discussion, we analyzed the relationship between trend and cycle from two directions: the effect that the cycle may have on the trend, and the effect that the trend has on the cycle. As an example of the former, a temporary boom caused by monetary expansion will also temporarily increase output, research and the aggregate amount of learning by doing in the economy. This, in turn, will put the economy on a higher trend path, with permanently higher output, R&D, and therefore growth under AK or Schumpeterian assumptions.

Notice that we have assumed that research rises in the boom. Several theories, however, suggest that the slump is more important for research. Inefficient firms are bankrupted, freeing resources for employment by new, more efficient firms. During times of low demand more resources are available for research. When times are bad, firms are forced to become more efficient to survive, whereas booms and easily earned high profits provide little incentive to be more efficient. Finally, during recessions, the relative performance of good firms might rise, allowing investors to discriminate more carefully between good and bad firms.

Despite these arguments, we must be cautious about extolling the benefits of slumps, especially because evidence in support of their growth-enhancing effect is thin. Large swings in output increase uncertainty, which may be a major factor in delaying or stopping investment and R&D.

Having looked at the effect of the cycle on the trend growth rate, we turned to the possible effects of the trend growth rate on the cycle. Often, growth has been characterized by relatively lumpy advances, which sometimes took a long time to have their full effect on the economy. The steam engine is an example:

although the steam engine continued to develop after its first introduction, its arrival and diffusion provided a large shock to the economy. Such technologies are called "general purpose technologies" (GPTs): they make a major advance, and initiate a wave of further innovations.

However, as argued by David (1990), it may take several decades before new GPTs can have a significant impact on macroeconomic activity. (It also takes a while before the contribution made by a new GPT in terms of new and/or higher-quality goods can be fully taken into account by the statistics.) A puzzle for economic theorists is then to understand why, in spite of being diffused over long time intervals, the implementation of new GPTs seems to generate an uneven transition path for *aggregate* output, where prolonged periods of relative stagnation (including the possibility of aggregate slumps) are followed by an acceleration in the pace of technological diffusion. One explanation, which we explore in some details in the last part of the chapter, is based on *social learning*; firms do not learn about new technologies in a vacuum but from observing other firms. This means that the speed at which firms learn about new technologies depends partly on how easy it is to observe other firms. This strategic complementarity between firms in their experimentation of new GPTs in turn generates the possibility of delayed adoption patterns, with most of the costly experimentation of new GPTs being concentrated over relatively short periods of time during which they will be a cascade or snowball effect resulting sometimes in a (delayed) aggregate slump. This is one among several possible mechanisms whereby growth generates (long-run) aggregate fluctuations.

We also explore the role that unemployment, skill differentials, and capital obsolescence can play in exacerbating the slump caused by a new GPT. Finally, we discuss the alternative hypothesis to the effect that various measurement problems associated with the growth of knowledge can be exacerbated by the wave of innovations triggered by a new GPT, creating the illusion of a slump but not the reality.

Problems

Difficulty of Problems:

No star: normal

One star: difficult

Two stars: very difficult

1. Obsolescence and GPT in neoclassical models (based on Howitt 1998)

Chaper 8 showed that the introduction of GPT brings about the acceleration of technological innovations. But at the same time it can cause significant economic slowdown. A faster pace of technological change will cause both physical and human capital to become obsolete more rapidly, and therefore the growth rate of GDP may fall. This problem examines this argument by further exploring the neoclassical growth model.

Consider a constant-returns-to-scale production function

$$Y_t = K_t^\alpha \left(e^{gt} L_t\right)^{1-\alpha}, \quad 1 > \alpha > 0 \tag{8.26}$$

where e^{gt} is exogenous Harrod-neutral technological progress, the working population grows at a constant rate n, and K_t denotes the aggregate capital stock. The capital stock depreciates at a rate of $\delta > 0$. Moreover, capital becomes obsolete because of technological progress at a rate given by $\beta(g)$, $\beta' > 0$. A constant fraction s of income is saved and invested in capital.

a. Find the differential equation which governs changes of capital per efficiency unit of labor, $k_t \equiv K_t/(e^{gt} L_t)$.

b. Find the steady state level of k and the long-run growth rate of per capita output $y_t \equiv Y_t/L_t$.

c. Show that the growth rate of y_t off steady state is given by

$$\frac{\dot{y}_t}{y_t} = g + \alpha \left[s k_t^{-(1-\alpha)} - (\delta + n + g + \beta(g))\right]. \tag{8.27}$$

How does it change as the economy accumulates more capital per efficiency unit of labor?

d. Suppose the introduction of a new GPT raises g. How does the long-run growth rate respond to it? What about the short-run growth rate (for a given k_t)?

e. Suppose now that consumers maximize the intertemporal utility function

$$U = \int_0^\infty e^{-\rho t} L_t \frac{(C_t/L_t)^{1-\sigma} - 1}{1 - \sigma} dt, \quad \sigma \geq 0. \tag{8.28}$$

i. Find the rate of growth of consumption.

ii. How does y_t change in the long-run when g varies? Assuming the economy is initially in a steady state, how does it respond in the short run (i.e., when k_t is held constant)?

⋆ **2. The effects of fluctuations on growth (based on Aghion and Saint-Paul 1991)**

Chapter 8 reviewed several possible reasons why business cycles or recessions may exert positive effects on economic growth. One of them is that the opportunity cost of investing in technological progress or managerial reorganization is lower in recessions. This problem formalizes this idea.

Consider an infinitely lived representative firm. It employs a fixed number of workers at each point in time, and if all of them are employed in manufacturing, the firm earns a flow of profits

$$\pi = e^x y,$$

where e^x measures labor productivity and y is a profitability parameter reflecting the demand for the firm's product. The firm can reallocate workers to R&D to improve x. Let $v = dx/dt$ denote the speed of its technological progress. If the firm engages in R&D to achieve v, its profits are reduced to $h(v)\pi$, where $h(v) = 1 - v^2$, $v \in (0, 1)$.

To introduce fluctuations, y exogenously fluctuates between y_E (expansion) and y_R (recession), $y_E > y_R$. Transitions from one state to another follow a Poisson process whereby an economy drops from y_E to y_R with flow probability γ and the reverse occurs with flow probability ε. The net present value of the firm when its current productivity is x is denoted by $V_i(x)$, $i = R, E$. The firm endogenously determines v through the trade-off between current profits (net of R&D costs) and the valuation of the firm.

a. Write down and explain the Bellman equations that V_E and V_R must satisfy.

b. Show that the first-order conditions for the optimal speed of technological progress are given by

$$v_i = \frac{V_i^0}{2y_i}, \quad i = E, R, \tag{8.29}$$

where $V_i(x) = V_i^0 e^x$, V_i^0 being the initial net present value of the firm.

c. Equilibrium:

i. Reexpress the Bellman equations obtained in (a) by letting $dt \to 0$.

ii. Using the result in (i), equation (8.29) and assuming $r > v_i, i = E, R$, where r is the rate of discount, show that there is a unique equilibrium.

iii. Using the result in (i), verify that the rate of productivity growth is higher in recessions than in expansions. (Hint: the initial net present value of the firm is lower in recession than in expansion, i.e., $V_R^0 < V_E^0$.)

iv. Give an intuitive explanation for the result in (iii).

v. Show that the expected growth rate of the firm's productivity is given by

$$g = \frac{\gamma}{\gamma + \varepsilon} v_R + \frac{\varepsilon}{\gamma + \varepsilon} v_E. \tag{8.30}$$

⋆⋆ **3. Obsolescence and GPT in R&D-based model (based on Howitt 1998)**

In Chapter 8 and problem 1, we saw how the introduction of GPT can generate economic slowdown before it accelerates growth. But because we used neoclassical growth models, technological progress was taken as exogenous. Does the result still hold for endogenous technological progress? In order to answer this problem, we formally introduce an R&D sector, thereby generalizing the results.

The production function of final output (a numeraire), which can be used for consumption, capital or R&D, is given by

$$y_t = \int_0^1 \gamma^{m_{it}} x_{it}^\alpha di, \quad 1 > \alpha > 0, \quad \gamma > 0, \quad m_{it} = 0, 1, 2, \ldots \tag{8.31}$$

where x_{it} is an intermediate product with quality $\gamma^{m_{it}}$. Because the number of workers is normalized to one, y_t represents per capita output. Successive vintages of x_{it} are produced by increasingly capital intensive techniques

$$x_{it} = \frac{K_{it}}{\gamma^{m_{it}}} \tag{8.32}$$

where K_{it} is capital used. Higher-quality goods are invented through R&D, and the Poisson arrival rate of innovations for a research project using capital R_{it} is given by

$$\phi_{it} = \lambda \frac{R_{it}}{\gamma^{m_{it}}}, \quad \lambda > 0, \tag{8.33}$$

which implies the increasing difficulty in inventing higher quality products. Each time the state-of-the-art good is invented, the production of lower-quality ones ceases and capital is resold as final output. If this happens, each unit of capital, which is bought at a price of unity relative to consumption, is only worth $1 > \eta > 0$. A smaller η means greater capital obsolescence. Aggregate savings are given by a fixed fraction $1 > s > 0$ of output.

a. Equilibrium in the R&D sector:

i. Find the equilibrium quantities and profits of the ith new intermediate good.

ii. Find the value of innovation V_{it} and the free-entry condition.

iii. Show that $\phi_{it} = \phi_t$ for all i.

iv. Show that

$$x_t = k_t \tag{8.34}$$

where $k_t = K_t / A_t$, $K_t = \int_0^1 K_{it} di$ is aggregate capital stock, and $A_t = \int_0^1 \gamma^{m_{it}} di$ is the technological level of this economy.

v. Find the following equilibrium condition

$$\phi_t = \frac{\alpha k_t^\alpha}{\eta} \left[\lambda (1 - \alpha) - \frac{\alpha}{k_t} \right]. \tag{8.35}$$

(Hint: the cost of capital is given by $\omega_t = r_t + (1 - \eta)\phi_t$ where r_t and $(1 - \eta)\phi_t$ are rates of interest and obsolescence of capital respectively.)

b. Equilibrium in the production sector:

i. Write the income identity for this economy.

ii. Show that

$$y_t = A_t k_t^\alpha, \tag{8.36}$$

iii. Find the growth rate of A_t.

iv. Derive the following differential equation for k_t from the income identity:

$$\dot{k}_t = s k_t^\alpha - (\gamma - \eta)\,\phi_t k_t. \tag{8.37}$$

c. Using (8.35) and (8.37), show that this economy has a stable unique equilibrium.

d. Find growth rates for this economy in the long run and short run (that is, off steady state).

e. Suppose a new GPT is introduced, raising the R&D productivity parameter λ.

i. How does the growth rate of per capita output change in the long run?

ii. How does the rate of technological progress $\dot{A}_t/A_t$ respond in the short run (i.e., k_t held constant)?

iii. Suppose $1 > (1 - \alpha)\gamma$. Show that the growth rate of per capita output $\dot{y}_t/y_t$ is more likely to fall in the short run (i.e., for a given k_t) the higher the rate of capital obsolescence.

⋆ **4. Unequal technological opportunities (based on Cheng and Dinopoulos 1992)**

The basic Schumpeterian model of Chapter 2 exhibits two-period cycles in research intensity off steady state. But in a steady state, the economy grows without such fluctuations. This problem will show that the same model can be easily extended to generate cycles in R&D intensity even in a steady state if we introduce uneven technological opportunities: *breakthroughs* and *improvements* that differ in the size of quality improvement of existing products. The model exhibits a recurrent reallocation of workers between manufacturing and R&D, which in turn can cause booms and slumps in a growth process.

Consider the quality-ladder model with risk-neutral consumers who supply a total amount of labor N. The aggregate production function is given by

$$y = Ax, \quad A = \gamma_B^i \gamma_I^j, \quad \gamma_B > \gamma_I > 1, \quad i, j = 0, 1, 2, \ldots \tag{8.38}$$

Technological breakthroughs increase γ_B^i and improvements raise γ_I^j through deliberate R&D. Denoting research workers as $n_k, k = I, B$, innovations occur with Poisson arrival rates of $\lambda_k n_k$, $k = I, B$, respectively. One cycle consists of two phases I and B. Phase I starts when improvement innovation occurs, and final output which embodies the latest improvement is produced and entrepreneurs target at breakthroughs during this state. Phase B begins following breakthrough innovation, and final output producers use the newest breakthrough technology and R&D is directed toward improvement of intermediate goods during this phase. The production of one unit of intermediate good requires one worker.

a. Find the profits and the values of breakthrough and improvement innovations in a stochastic steady state.

b. Find the free-entry conditions for the two types of R&D.

c. Find the labor full-employment conditions in phases I and B.

d. Show that equilibrium research workers for each phase are given by

$$n_I = \frac{\lambda_B (\gamma_B - 1) \gamma_I N - r}{\lambda_I + \lambda_B (\gamma_B - 1) \gamma_I}, \quad n_B = \frac{\lambda_I (\gamma_I - 1) \gamma_B N - r}{\lambda_B + \lambda_I (\gamma_I - 1) \gamma_B}. \tag{8.39}$$

e. Cyclical growth for $\lambda_B = \lambda_I = \lambda$.

i. Show that cycles of $n_I > n_B$ and $x_I > x_B$ occur.

ii. Show that for $\gamma_B^2 - \gamma_B - 1 < 0$, y in phase B is lower than that in phase I (i.e., the slump occurs in phase B)

f. Show that the average growth rate for this economy is given by

$$g = \frac{\lambda_B n_B \lambda_I n_I}{\lambda_B n_B + \lambda_I n_I} \cdot \ln \gamma_B \gamma_I. \tag{8.40}$$

★ 5. Technology specific machines (based on Felli and Ortalo-Magné 1997)

This problem presents a framework where the discovery of a more productive technology is initially followed by an output slump. Output does not rise until a few periods after the discovery, following the delayed implementation of the new technology. The key features of the economic environment presented here (which distinguishes it from the environment described in Chapter 8) are that (1) technology is embedded in the intermediate inputs (machines) and that (2) following the discovery of more productive machines, their market price progressively declines.

Consider an open economy with a measure one of infinitely lived agents and three commodities: output c with fixed price of 1, machines of type 1, k_1, machines of type 2, k_2, with prices q_1 and q_2, respectively. The agents have linear preferences; they maximize $\sum_{t=0}^{\infty} \frac{1}{(1+r)^t} c_t$, $r \geq 0$. Every period, they can either work for a fixed given wage, θ_0, or become entrepreneurs. An entrepreneur who owns k_i machines of type i obtains $\theta_i k_i^\alpha$ units of output where $i \in \{1, 2\}$, and $\theta_2 > \theta_1 > 0$. Entrepreneurs cannot use both types of machine at once. Machines are produced outside the economy. In particular, we assume that machines of type 1 are supplied according to the following supply function:

$$\kappa_1(q_1) = \begin{cases} 0 & \text{if } 0 \leq q_1 \leq q_1^{\min} \\ \mu_1(q_1 - q_1^{\min}) & \text{if } q_1 \geq q_1^{\min} > 0 \end{cases} \tag{8.41}$$

where $q_1^{\min}$ denotes the minimum price at which positive quantities of machines of type 1 are supplied, and $\mu_1 > 0$ (for example, the technology is characterized by a fixed cost). Furthermore, we assume that machines of type 1 have a scrap-value $0 < q_1^s < q_1^{\min}$ corresponding to the market value of the raw material embedded in the machines. Machines of type 2 are discovered at some unknown time period t_d. This is a surprise discovery; nobody expects it until it happens. When the discovery occurs, a sequence of prices for machines of type 2, $\{q_{2,t}\}_{t=t_d}^{\infty}$ is announced. This sequence has the following properties: for every $t \geq t_d$, $q_{2,t} \geq q_{2,t+1}$, and for every $t > t_s > t_d$, $q_{2,t} = q_{2,t_s}$, t_s given and known at t_d. For example, it could be that this type of machine is produced with a linear technology abroad and the new technology is subject to exogenous growth for a few periods. Both types of machines depreciate at the given rate $0 < \delta < 1$. Agents may freely borrow and lend at the rate r. The timing of the model is such that markets for machines open at the beginning of each period, then production takes place and finally the output market opens.

a. Characterize the behavior of an agent in this economy.

b. Define and characterize the *unique* steady state equilibrium for the economy before the discovery has occurred. What condition must θ_0 satisfy for this equilibrium to be such that all agents are entrepreneurs?

c. Characterize the *set* of steady state equilibria for the economy in which machines of type 2 are available at price q_{2,t_s}. Assume, once again, that θ_0 is such that all agents are entrepreneurs.

d. Prove that following the discovery, there exists a value of q_{2,t_d} such that the economy's output decreases before rising after the *delayed* adoption of the machines of type 2. Characterize the *unique* sequence of prices for type 1 machines along the transition to a new steady state equilibrium.

★ **6. Creative destruction versus the cycle (based on Canton and Uhlig 1996)**

Problem 2 examines the possible relationship between growth and cycles, focusing on the behavior of a single firm. This problem examines the same issue within the framework of the quality-ladder model in Chapter 2.

Output y at t is produced by a competitive sector according to

$$y = \gamma^m x^\alpha, \quad m = 0, 1, 2, \ldots \quad 1 > \alpha > 0,$$

where x is an intermediate input. In the time interval $[t, t + dt]$, a new innovation arrives with probability $\lambda n dt$ where $\lambda > 0$ and n is the amount of skilled labor employed in the R&D sector at t. The production function of the intermediate good x is linear in skilled labor,

$$x = BL.$$

The productivity parameter B can take on two values, $B \in \{1; \delta\}$, where $B = 1$ corresponds to a "recession" or weak customer relationships of the leading firm, whereas $B = \delta > 1$ corresponds to a boom or strong and well-functioning customer relationships of the leading firm. A firm that has just created a new fundamental innovation always starts at $B = 1$. In the time interval $[t, t + dt]$, the parameter B will switch its value (i.e., from $B = 1$ to $B = \delta$ or from $B = \delta$ to $B = 1$) with probability μdt and remain the same otherwise. The total supply of skilled labor is given by N, which thus has to equal the total demand for skilled labor in equilibrium, $n + L = N$. Output can only be used for consumption. Utility is expected instantaneous consumption, discounted at a constant rate.

a. Formally state the steady-state equilibrium in this economy, in which the leading monopolist always maximizes expected, discounted profits, taking as given the wage for skilled labor.

b. Compute the possible steady-state equilibria. How does the equilibrium depend on whether L_b is greater or smaller than N?

c. Calculate the level of employment in R&D. Show that new fundamental innovations are more likely in recessions.

d. Find parameters for which R&D completely ceases in a boom, that is, in which the leading monopolist is completely entrenched, when its customer relationships are strong.

e. Are recessions good for growth?

⋆ 7. Endogenous GPT (based on Li 1997)

The models of GPT in Chapter 8 assume that new GPT's arrive exogenously, although intermediate goods which implement them are endogenously created. The exogenous GPT assumption may miss some interesting interactions between intermediate and GPT research activities, for example, whether one type of R&D raises or reduces the incentive for the other research activity, which in turn is related to the issue of multiplicity of equilibria.

Consider the quality-ladder model, where consumers have a time-separable logarithmic utility function in final output. The production of final output is given by

$$y = \gamma^m x, \quad \gamma > 1, \quad m = 0, 1, 2, \ldots \tag{8.42}$$

where x denotes the amount of intermediate goods of quality γ^m. One unit of labor is needed to produce one unit of intermediate good. The labor force is constant and given by L; m is raised by one if a new GPT is invented first and then followed by the introduction of a new intermediate product which implements it. Hence there are two phases in one cycle: profit-seekers conduct R&D aimed at new GPT and intermediate goods in phases labeled G and I, respectively. Profits are shared by GPT and intermediate innovators: a fraction $0 < \kappa < 1$ goes to the former, while the latter earns $1 - \kappa$. If ξ_G workers are employed in R&D in phase G, a new GPT arrives with Poisson probability ξ_G. If ξ_I workers are employed in R&D in phase I, intermediate innovations occur with Poisson arrival rate ξ_I.

a. Consider a stochastic steady state where w_k (wages) and ξ_k, $k = G, I$, are constant in each state. Show that profits of GPT and intermediate goods innovators are given by

$$\pi_G = \kappa \left(1 - 1/\gamma\right) \quad \text{and} \quad \pi_I = (1 - \kappa)\left(1 - 1/\gamma\right), \tag{8.43}$$

assuming that consumer expenditure is normalized to one.

b. Find the labor market-clearing conditions in phases G and I.

c. Show that the value of intermediate innovation is given by

$$V_I = \frac{(r + \xi_G + \xi_I)\,\pi_I}{(r + \xi_G)\,(r + \xi_I)}. \tag{8.44}$$

d. Show that the value of GPT innovation is given by

$$V_G = \frac{\xi_I\,(r + \xi_G + \xi_I)\,\pi_G}{(r + \xi_G)\,(r + \xi_I)^2}. \tag{8.45}$$

e. Characterize an equilibrium. Are multiple equilibria possible?

f. What is the expected growth rate of this economy? Deduce the time profile of $\ln y_t$.

9 Distribution and Political Economy

In this chapter, we relax the assumption that agents have identical endowments or preferences (i.e., the representative-agent assumption). Introducing such heterogeneity into the theory of endogenous growth raises interesting and important questions.

The first concerns the effects of income and wealth inequality on growth. According to the conventional wisdom, income inequality is fundamentally good for incentives and therefore should be viewed as being unambiguously growth-enhancing (see Rebelo 1991 for a first coherent formalization of this idea).[1] And indeed, if one takes for example the basic Schumpeterian framework of Chapter 2, redistributing part of the innovation rent V away from successful innovators, will have obvious negative effects on research incentives and therefore on the steady-state growth rate.[2] Yet, in the first part of this chapter (section 9.1) we question this wisdom and point to several important reasons why excessive inequality may actually *reduce* investment opportunities and incentives and thereby discourage growth.

In the second part of the chapter, we touch on the reverse causation from growth to inequality, and question the Kuznets hypothesis, according to which development and growth should eventually reduce inequality. Kuznets's theory[3] viewed economic development as a transition process from a traditional/rural economy toward an industrial/urban economy, so it seemed plausible that: (a) in the early stage of development, the distribution of income should widen because only a few individuals have the ability or the required (human) capital to move to the new industrial sector; and (b) in a later stage of development, the distribution of income should narrow down as more people

---

1. The idea that incentive considerations may generate a tradeoff between equity and efficiency goes back to Mirrlees (1971).

2. For example, in the Cobb-Douglas case, if τ denotes the tax rate on innovations, then the research arbitrage equation (A) becomes:

$$w_t = \lambda(1 - \tau)V_{t+1}, \tag{A}$$

so that the equilibrium level of research $\widehat{n}$ in steady state will satisfy the modified equation:

$$1 = \frac{\lambda\gamma(1 - \tau)\frac{1-\alpha}{\alpha}(L - \widehat{n})}{r + \lambda\widehat{n}}. \tag{x'}$$

Not surprisingly, an increase in the redistribution rate τ will negatively affect $\widehat{n}$ and therefore and also $\widehat{g} = \lambda\widehat{n}\ln\gamma$.

3. See Galor and Tsiddon (1994) and Aghion and Bolton (1997) for alternative rationalizations of the Kuznets hypothesis respectively based on human capital accumulation and capital market imperfections. In particular, Aghion and Bolton (1997) argue that as more wealth is being accumulated over time, there are more funds available in the economy to finance individual projects. This in turn should gradually shift lending terms in favor of borrowers (that is, of the less wealthy) so that the wealth of borrowers should eventually catch up with that of rich lenders. This result depends heavily on a decreasing-returns assumption, which in turn implies that the rich end up always lending to the rest of the economy rather than investing their whole inherited wealth into their own individual projects. Similarly, the Kuznets result in Galor and Tsiddon (1994) follows from assuming decreasing returns to family-specific externalities in human capital accumulation. □

are absorbed by the industrial sector and, at the same time, because of the increasing scarcity of agricultural workers, wages in the rural sector are catching up with wages in the industrial sector.[4]

The recent empirical evidence pointing at a sharp increase in wage inequality — both *across* and *within* educational cohorts — in developed countries during the past twenty years, has revived the debate about the relevance of the Kuznets hypothesis, and more generally about the effects of technical change and growth on the dynamics of wage inequality. We reflect on that debate in section 9.2.

Finally, in the third and last part of this chapter (section 9.3) we incorporate the political dimension of "creative destructions." Introducing the notion of vested interests into the Schumpeterian framework indeed provides a natural explanation for why some societies adopt new technologies more rapidly than others and it also sheds some new light into the cyclical growth pattern referred to by Olson (1982) as "the rise and decline of nations."

9.1   The Effects of Inequality on Growth

Until recently, a common wisdom among economists was that inequality should, if at all, have a *stimulating* effect on accumulation and growth; the same line of thought would in turn emphasize a fundamental *tradeoff* between productive efficiency (and/or growth) and social justice, the former requiring more income/wealth inequality across individuals whereas the latter would call for redistribution.

Two main considerations appear to underlie the presupposition that inequality should be growth-enhancing. The first argument has to do with *investment indivisibilities*: the implementation of new fundamental innovations, and in particular the setting up of new industries, have often involved large sunk costs; in the absence of a broad and well-functioning market for shares, wealth obviously needs to be sufficiently concentrated in order for an individual (or family) to be able to cover such large sunk costs and thereby initiate a new industrial activity.

The second argument, based on *incentives* considerations, was first formalized by Mirrlees (1971): namely, in a moral hazard context where output realization depends on an *unobservable* effort borne by agents (or "employees"), rewarding the employees with a constant wage independent from (the observable) output performance, will obviously discourage them from investing any

---

4. Note that in Chapter 8 we formalized a similar dynamic wage pattern in the context of a transition process between two general purpose technologies.

effort. On the other hand, making the reward too sensitive to output performance may also be inefficient from an *insurance* point of view when output realizations are highly uncertain and the employees are *risk averse*. (This insurance argument is nothing but a natural way to formalize the social justice or "equity" motive for reducing inequality.)

There is actually a third consideration pointing at a positive relationship between wealth concentration and growth, one that has been recently emphasized by policy advisers to transition economies in Central and Eastern Europe: namely, *corporate governance* and, more specifically, the need for *concentrated asset ownership* and *controlling majorities* in firms. Besides the fact that a multiplicity of owners tends to complicate the decision-making process within the firm (due to potential conflicts of interest among shareholders), having many (dispersed) shareholders raises the scope for *free-riding* on the necessary monitoring of the performance and effort of the firm's manager and employees. However, as the privatization process currently taking place in Central Europe illustrates, the emergence of controlling majorities can (partly) be achieved without excessive wealth concentration, namely through the creation of new financial intermediaries (typically investment funds) that concentrate the control rights initially carried by individual shareholders, and to which individual shareholders *delegate* their control rights.

Leaving control considerations aside and concentrating on the incentives (and indivisibility) arguments mentioned above, we will now show by means of a simple AK model that these arguments tend to be seriously mitigated, if not *reversed*, once additional aspects are introduced into the picture, in particular the existence of *capital market imperfections*.[5] Subsection 9.1.1 borrows from Benabou (1996a) and Subsection 9.1.2 from Aghion-Bolton (1997).

9.1.1   Credit Market Imperfections and the Growth-Enhancing Effect of Redistribution

Consider the following discrete-time version of the AK model analyzed in Chapter 1. There is only one good in the economy that serves both as *capital* and *consumption* good. There is a continuum of overlapping generations families, indexed by $i \in [0, 1]$. Each individual lives for two periods, and the intertemporal utility of an individual i born at date t is given by

$$U_t^i = \ln c_t^i + \rho \cdot \ln d_t^i,$$

where c_t^i and d_t^i denote current and future consumption respectively.

5. Pioneering work on capital market imperfections, inequality, and economic development includes Galor-Zeira 1993. See also Benabou 1996a for further references on the subject.

Production of future consumption good (i.e., of good available at date $(t+1)$) takes place at date t according to the AK technology

$$y_t^i = (k_t^i)^\alpha (A_t)^{1-\alpha}, \tag{9.1}$$

where k_t^i denotes the amount of investment by individual i at date t, and A_t is the average level of human capital or knowledge available in period t.

In keeping with the AK formulation introduced in Chapter 1, but adapted to a discrete time framework, we assume

$$A_t = \int_0^1 y_{t-1}^i di = y_{t-1}. \tag{9.2}$$

That is, the accumulation of knowledge results from past production activities.

The interesting action in this chapter will result from the introduction of heterogeneity (or *inequality*) among individuals of the same generation, and more specifically from the interplay between *capital market imperfections* and the effect of *redistribution policies*.

To get a first sense of what we have in mind here, note that aggregate output is simply expressed as

$$y_t = A_t^{1-\alpha} E_t(k^\alpha), \tag{9.3}$$

where $E_t(k^\alpha)$ is the mathematical expectation over individual investment levels k at date t.[6]

Because of decreasing returns with respect to individual capital investments k^i (in other words, the fact that $\alpha < 1$ and therefore the function $k \to k^\alpha$ is concave) greater inequality between individual investments for a given aggregate capital stock will reduce aggregate output.[7] Therefore anything that reduces investment inequality will foster aggregate production each period and therefore growth under the preceding AK assumption.

Our analysis in this section will concentrate on establishing the following two results:

---

6. That is:

$$E_t(k^\alpha) = \int_0^\infty k^\alpha \cdot f_t(k) dk,$$

where $f_t(k)$ is the density function over individual investments at date t.

7. This, in turn, follows from the following standard theorem in expected utility theory:
Theorem 1:   Let u be a concave function on the nonnegative reals. Let X and Y be two random variables, such that the expectations $Eu(X)$ and $Eu(Y)$ exist and are finite, and such that Y is obtained from X through a sequence of mean-preserving spreads. Then $Eu(Y) \leq Eu(X)$. Because a convex function is the negative of a concave function, the opposite inequality holds for a convex function.

a. In the absence of capital market imperfections all individuals end up investing the same amount of capital goods $k^i \equiv k$, no matter what the initial distribution of human capital (or "wealth") across individuals. This implies that aggregate output and growth cannot be positively affected by wealth distribution policies.

b. Conversely, when capital markets are highly imperfect and therefore credit is scarce and costly, equilibrium investments under laissez-faire will remain unequal across individuals with heterogenous human-capital endowments; there is now a role for suitably designed redistribution policies in enhancing aggregate productive efficiency and growth.

To prove formally those claims, we first complete the AK model with the following specification of inequality, capital-market imperfections, and wealth redistribution policy.

Inequality

Individuals differ in their initial endowments in human capital. For example, the endowment of individual i upon birth at date t is given by

$$w_t^i = \varepsilon_t^i \cdot A_t,$$

where ε_t^i is an i.i.d. (identically and independently distributed) random shock that measures individual i's access to general knowledge (we normalize the mean of ε_t^i at one, so that $\int_0^1 w_t^i di = A_t$).

Individual i can either "consume" his human capital endowment[8] (possibly augmented with some borrowings) at once, or invest it into the production of future consumption good, according to the AK technology specified in (9.1).

Capital Market Imperfections

A simple way to introduce credit constraints is to assume that an individual with initial endowments w^i cannot invest more than $\overline{k}^i = \nu \cdot w^i$, where $\nu > 0$.[9] When $\nu = +\infty$, capital markets are perfect and individuals face no borrowing constraint, whereas in the opposite case, where $\nu = 0$, credit simply becomes unavailable. We will concentrate on these two extreme cases, leaving it to courageous readers to work out the generalization to any $\nu > 0$.

---

8. That is, individual i can use the efficiency units of labor he is endowed with in order to produce *current* consumption good, according to a linear "one-for-one" technology. Thus

$$c_t^i = w_t^i + \underbrace{b_t^i}_{\text{borrowings}} - \underbrace{k_t^i}_{\substack{\text{investment into} \\ \text{future production}}}.$$

9. See Aghion, Banerjee, and Piketty (1996) for a microeconomic rationalisation of this particular form of credit-constraint, based on (ex-post) moral hazard.

Redistribution

We willl analyze the effects of an ex-ante redistribution of human-capital endowments. Such a (lump-sum) transfer policy will simply consist in taxing highly endowed individuals directly on their endowments,[10] and then using the revenues from this tax in order to subsidize human-capital improvements by the less endowed. Thus, let the post-tax endowment of individual i be simply defined by

$$\widehat{w}^i = w^i + \beta(A - w^i), \quad 0 < \beta < 1, \tag{9.4}$$

where for notational simplicity we omit the subscript t.

Let us first consider what happens in the absence of credit restrictions, that is, when $\nu = +\infty$. Given the redistribution rate β (which we take as given[11]), individual i with initial endowment w^i will choose how much to invest (and therefore how much to borrow), by solving the following maximization program:

$$\max_{b^i, k^i} \left\{ \ln(w^i + \beta(A - w^i) + b^i - k^i) + \rho \ln(y^i - \underbrace{rb^i}_{\text{debt repayment}}) \right\},$$

where b^i is the amount of net borrowing (or lending if $b^i < 0$) by individual i and r is the market interest rate endogenously determined by the loan market-clearing condition $\int_0^1 b^i \cdot di = 0$.

The first-order conditions with respect to k^i and b^i are respectively given by[12]

$$\frac{1}{w^i + \beta(A + w^i) + b^i - k^i} = \frac{\rho \alpha \frac{y^i}{k^i}}{y^i - rb^i}; \tag{9.5}$$

and

$$\frac{1}{w^i + \beta(A + w^i) + b^i - k^i} = \frac{\rho r}{y^i - rb^i}. \tag{9.6}$$

Put together, these two conditions imply that the ratios $\frac{y^i}{k^i}$, and therefore the investments k^i, are the same across all individuals: $k^i \equiv k$. In other words, when credit markets are perfect individual investments and (future) output are inde-

---

10. Or equivalently, to tax the highly endowed on their *current* production activity which we assumed implicitly to be performed according to a linear "one-for-one" technology, that is: one unit of human capital invested in current production yields one unit of current consumption good.

11. See Benabou (1996a) and section 9.2.4 for an endogenization of β based on a simple median-voter approach.

12. Remember that $y^i = (k^i)^\alpha A^{1-\alpha}$, so that $\frac{dy^i}{dk} = \alpha \frac{y^i}{k}$.

pendent from the distribution of human-capital endowments across individuals. Then, one should naturally expect that inequality and/or redistribution should have no impact on growth.

This is indeed what we get through solving the preceding equations. More specifically, let us simply reexpress conditions (9.5) and (9.6) as

$$A^{1-\alpha}(k^i)^\alpha - rb^i = \rho r(w^i + \beta(A - w^i) + b^i - k^i) \tag{9.7}$$

and

$$r = \alpha \left(\frac{A}{k^i}\right)^{1-\alpha}. \tag{9.8}$$

Integrating the two sides of (9.7) with respect to i, then using the loan market clearing condition $\int_0^1 b^i di = 0$, and finally substituting for r, we obtain

$$k = \frac{\rho\alpha}{1 + \rho\alpha}A = s \cdot A. \tag{9'}$$

The steady-state growth rate is now simply expressed as

$$g = \ln\left(\frac{y_t}{y_{t-1}}\right) = \ln\left(\frac{k^\alpha A^{1-\alpha}}{A}\right) = \alpha \ln s.$$

Thus, as we conjectured, distribution and redistribution have no impact on long-run growth when credit is fully available to less endowed individuals.

Consider now the other extreme case where credit is totally unavailable to the poorly endowed (that is, $b^i \equiv 0$ for all i). Individual i will now choose his optimal investment k^i so as to

$$\max_{k^i} \left\{\ln(w^i + \beta(A - w^i) - k^i) + \rho \cdot \ln y^i\right\}.$$

The corresponding first-order condition is given by

$$\frac{1}{w^i + \beta(A - w^i) - k^i} = \frac{\rho\alpha \frac{y^i}{k^i}}{y^i} = \frac{\rho\alpha}{k^i},$$

which yields immediately

$$k^i = \frac{\rho\alpha}{1 + \rho\alpha}((1 - \beta)w^i + \beta A) = s \cdot ((1 - \beta)w^i + \beta A). \tag{9.9}$$

Thus, in contrast to the perfect capital-market case, when credit is unavailable equilibrium investments will differ across individuals (being an increasing function of their initial endowments in human capital), and in a way that depends on the extent of redistribution. As β increases and the distribution of disposable endowments therefore becomes more equal across individuals, investments by the poorly endowed will increase while investments by the rich will decrease. However, as we already argued, because the production technology specified in (9.1) exhibits *decreasing* returns with respect to individual capital investments, we should expect redistribution to have an overall *positive* effect on aggregate output and growth.

This is indeed what the preceding analysis yields: more precisely, from (9.9) we have

$$y = \int_0^1 y^i \, di = \int_0^1 A^{1-\alpha} s^\alpha ((1-\beta)w^i + \beta A)^\alpha \, di.$$

Hence

$$g = \ln\left(\frac{y}{A}\right) = \alpha[\ln s - \ln A + \frac{1}{\alpha} \ln \int_0^1 ((1-\beta)w^i + \beta A)^\alpha \, di]. \qquad (9.10)$$

Now consider the term under the integral sign. As β increases, the heterogeneity among individual investment levels (which are equiproportional to $[(1-\beta)w^i + \beta A]$) decreases, and therefore so does the aggregate efficiency loss due to the unequal distribution of w^i. In the limiting case where $\beta = 1$, the term under the integral sign is constant across individuals i, and therefore the highest possible growth rate is achieved. Hence $\frac{dg}{d\beta} > 0$.

Thus, when credit is unavailable, redistribution to the poorly endowed, that is, to those individuals who exhibit the higher marginal returns to investment, will be growth-enhancing. Correspondingly, *more inequality is bad for growth when capital markets are highly imperfect*.

9.1.2   Questioning the Traditional Incentive Argument

Our modeling of capital-market imperfections in the previous subsection was somewhat extreme, as we were simply assuming away all possibilities of borrowing and lending. Using such a reduced form representation of credit-market imperfections, we were able to show that redistributing wealth from the rich (whose marginal productivity of investment is relatively low, due to decreasing returns to individual capital investments) to the poor (whose marginal productivity of investment is relatively high, but who cannot invest more than their limited endowments w_i), would enhance aggregate productivity and therefore growth in the preceding AK model. In other words, *redistribution creates investment opportunities* in the absence of well-functioning capital markets, which in turn increases aggregate productivity and growth. Note that this "opportunity creation effect" of redistribution does not fundamentally rely on incentive considerations: even in one could force the poor to invest *all* their initial endowments rather than maximize intertemporal utility as in the above analysis, redistributing wealth from the richest to the poorest individuals would still have an overall positive effect on aggregate productivity and growth, again because of decreasing returns to individual investments.

In this subsection we want to push the analysis one step further and introduce incentives as the microeconomic source of capital market imperfections. This will enable us to challenge the view that the incentive effect of redistribution should always be negative. In fact, as we will now illustrate, *redistribution may sometimes be growth-enhancing as a result of incentive effects only*!

The following example introduces moral-hazard considerations as the explicit source of credit-market imperfections, following Aghion and Bolton (1997), into the AK with overlapping generations framework developed above.

Specifically, we again assume the existence of a continuum of nonaltruistic, overlapping-generations families, indexed by $i \in [0, 1]$. The utility of individual i in generation t is

$$U_t^i = d_t^i - c(e_t^i), \tag{9.11}$$

where d_t^i denotes individual i's second-period consumption (for simplicity we assume that individuals consume only when old), and $c(e^i) = A \frac{(e^i)^2}{2}$ denotes the nonmonetary effort cost incurred by individual i when young. (The parameter A still measures productivity on the current technology.)

As before, the human-capital endowment of individual i is taken to be an idiosyncratic proportion of average knowledge at date t, that is,

$$w_t^i = \varepsilon_t^i \cdot A_t, \tag{9.12}$$

where the random variables ε_t^i are again i.i.d. with unit mean values.

The production technology involves an extreme form of U-shaped average cost curve with respect to capital investments,[13] namely:

a. the production activity requires a *fixed* and indivisible capital outlay equal to $k_t^i = \varphi \cdot A_t$;

b. conditional upon the required investment $\varphi \cdot A_t$ being made at date t, the output from investment in this technology is uncertain and given by

$$y_t^i = \begin{cases} \sigma \cdot A_t & \text{with probability } e_t^i \\ 0 & \text{with probability } 1 - e_t^i, \end{cases}$$

where e_t^i is individual i's effort at date t. We assume that second-period outcomes y_t^i are independently identically distributed across individuals of the same generation.

Given this technology, individuals with initial endowments $w_t^i < \varphi A_t$ will borrow (whenever they can) the amount $b_t^i = \varphi A_t - w_t^i$ from wealthy individuals with $w_t^i > A_t$, in order to meet the sunk investment requirement.

---

13. The analysis in this section carries over to the case of more general U-shaped technologies, as argued in Aghion and Bolton (1997).

The source of capital market imperfection will be moral hazard with limited wealth constraints (or limited liability), that is, the following Assumption A1:

a. efforts e^i are not observable;

b. a borrower's repayment to his/her lenders cannot exceed his/her second period output y_t^i.

If either (a) or (b) were violated, then the first-best effort $e^* = \arg\max_e\{e(\sigma A) - c(e)\} = \sigma$ would automatically be elicited from *all* individuals no matter what their differing human-capital endowments. The growth rate would then be unaffected by redistribution and always equal to

$$g = \ln\left(\frac{\sigma \cdot A \cdot \int_0^1 \sigma\, di}{A}\right) = \ln \sigma^2.$$

This corresponds to nothing but the case of *perfect* capital markets, that is of capital markets that do *not* suffer from incentive problems (and therefore can never generate credit-rationing in equilibrium).

Now, coming back to the imperfect capital-market case (defined by A1), an optimal investment contract between a borrower with initial endowment $w^i < A$ and his lender(s) will specify a repayment schedule $R(w^i)$ such that

$$R(w^i) = \begin{cases} (\varphi A - w^i)\rho(w^i) & \text{if the project succeeds,} \\ 0 & \text{if the project fails.} \end{cases}$$

(The latter equation is a direct consequence of the limited-liability assumption made in A1(b)); $\varphi A - w^i = b^i$ is the amount borrowed, and $\rho(w^i)$ is the unit repayment rate owed by individual w^i.)

Given this contract, a borrower with initial wealth w^i will choose his or her effort e^i to maximize the expected second-period revenue net of both repayment to the lender(s) and effort cost, namely

$$e^i = \arg\max_e \left\{ e(\sigma A - \rho(\varphi \cdot A - w^i)) - A\frac{e^2}{2} \right\}$$

$$\tag{9.13}$$

$$= \sigma - \rho\varphi + \rho \cdot \frac{w^i}{A} = e(\rho, w^i).$$

We then see that, for given ρ, the lower a borrower's initial wealth, the *less* effort he or she will devote to increasing the probability of success of his or her project. As we will see, effort will remain an increasing function of initial wealth when we endogenize the repayment rate ρ and take into account the fact it should vary with w.

Thus, the more an individual needs to borrow in order to get production started, the less incentives he has to supply effort, in that he must share a larger fraction of the marginal returns from his effort with lenders. An immediate consequence of this result is that redistributing wealth toward borrowers will have a *positive* effect on their effort *incentives*. Whenever this positive incentive effect more than compensates the potentially negative incentive effect on lenders' efforts, then such a redistribution will indeed be growth-enhancing based on incentive considerations only. In the remaining part of this subsection we shall construct a redistribution scheme that generates an *overall positive incentive effect* on growth.

Before turning to the analysis of redistribution, let us make two important remarks. First, individuals with initial wealth $w^i > \varphi A$ (in other words the lenders), will systematically supply the first-best level of effort because they remain residual claimants on all returns from such effort:

$$w^i > \varphi A \Rightarrow e^i = \arg\max \left\{ e \cdot \sigma A - A \frac{e^2}{2} \right\}$$

$$= \sigma = e^*.$$

Second, when analyzing the relationship between initial wealth and effort, we have treated the repayment schedule ρ as given. However, because the risk of default on a loan increases with the size of the loan (the probability of success $e(\rho, w)$ decreases when w decreases), the unit repayment rate ρ must vary with w to reflect the change in default risk. In fact, in equilibrium, all loans must yield the same expected return so that the following "no-arbitrage" condition must hold:

$$e^i(\rho, w^i) \cdot \rho = r, \tag{9.14}$$

where r is the equilibrium cost of capital, which for simplicity we shall assume here to be exogenous[14] and also sufficiently low that *all* individuals no matter their initial wealth w^i can have access to credit.[15]

---

14. See Aghion and Bolton (1997) for a complete analysis of the capital market and the determination of the equilibrium cost of capital. Here, for simplicity, we take the cost of capital to be exogenously fixed by world market conditions.

15. By removing the potential "opportunity creation" effects of redistribution, this assumption enables us to concentrate on the incentive effects of redistribution. A sufficient condition for this assumption to hold is that the maximum expected repayment from the poorest individual with zero initial wealth $w = 0$, be greater than r. That is:

$$\max_{\rho} \rho e(\rho, 0) > r.$$

Or equivalently

$$\frac{\sigma^2}{4\varphi} > r.$$

The above inequality will be automatically satisfied when the productivity-adjusted return σ on a successful production activity is sufficienty high. □

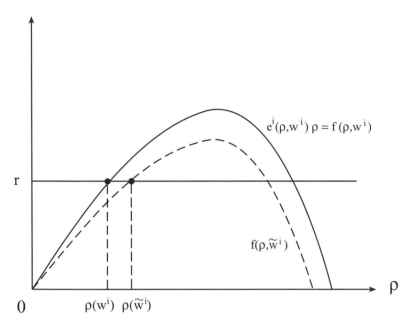

Figure 9.1
The unit repayment, ρ, varies inversely with initial wealth ($\tilde{w}^i < w^i$).

One can easily show that the unit repayment rate $\rho(w^i)$ implicitly defined by equation (9.14) is a *decreasing* function of initial wealth w^i (see figure 9.1):[16] the poorer a borrower, the higher his repayment schedule in order to compensate for his lower probability of success $e(\rho, w)$ for any given ρ. It then follows that the equilibrium effort $e^i = e(\rho(w^i), w^i)$ will indeed remain an increasing function of initial wealth once ρ has been replaced by $\rho(w^i)$.

We now have all the elements we need to analyze the incentive effects of redistribution. Because individuals with initial wealth $w^i > \varphi A$ supply the first-best effort $e^* = \sigma$, raising a lump-sum tax $t^i < w^i - \varphi A$ on the endowment of each such individual and then distributing the total proceeds $\int_{w_i > A} t_i di$ among borrowers

a. will not affect the effort e^* supplied by the wealthy, whose *after-tax* endowments remain strictly above the required fixed cost φA; that is, $w^i - t^i > \varphi A$.

b. will increase the effort supplied by any subsidized borrower (we have just shown that the equilibrium effort of a borrower is monotonically increasing with his or her disposable wealth).

---

16. To see this, let $f(\rho, w) = e(\rho, w)\rho = (\sigma - \rho(\varphi - \frac{w}{A}))\rho$. As a function of ρ, $f(\rho, w)$ is an inverted-U-shaped parabola whose left-hand intersection with the horizontal line r defines the solution $\rho(w)$ to equation (9.14). As the initial endowment w decreases, the $f(\rho, w)$ curve shifts downwards, thereby moving the left-hand intersection with the horizontal line r to the right. □

The above redistribution scheme will then have an unambiguously positive *incentive* effect on growth; the growth rate is indeed given by

$$g = \ln\left(\frac{\int e^i \cdot \sigma A}{A}\right) = \ln\left(\sigma \cdot \int_0^1 e^i di\right),$$

with efforts e^i either increasing or remaining constant as a result of redistribution.

Some readers may legitimately object to the fact that we are putting too much emphasis on tax/subsidy schemes that only affect first-period wealth w^i. Benabou (1996) writes, "since w^i is here exogenously determined for each generation, this is equivalent to an unanticipated capital levy."[17]

More satisfactory in this respect, and also because it yields a more balanced view of the positive *and negative* incentive effects of redistribution, would be, for example, to analyze a redistribution scheme that

a. taxes linearly the output y_t^i of the *old*;

b. uses the proceeds from such a tax to subsidize the wealth endowments of *young borrowers* (with wealth $w^i < \varphi A$).

One can actually show that the disincentive effects such a scheme is bound to have on the wealthy, will be more than compensated by its positive incentive effects on borrowers whenever the return σ is smaller than the repayment rate.

9.1.3   Inequality versus Cooperation

Although inequality may have a disincentive effect on borrowers in the context of an imperfect credit market with moral hazard (see section 9.2.2), for quite similar reasons inequality will tend to discourage cooperation between uneven equity holders engaged in a same venture or partnership. This lack of cooperation may typically take the form of *free-riding* by the poor on the rich's effort, but it may also degenerate into some kind of a social conflict, with the poor actually engaging into *expropriation* activities instead of contributing to aggregate production.[18] In either case, the effect on (long-run) growth will obviously be negative.

Inequality and Free-Riding

Suppose that the economy gives birth to only two individuals each period, and that these two individuals (who both live for two periods) need to join forces

---

17. See Benabou (1996a).

18. Legros and Newman (1994) have also emphasized the idea that a high degree of inequality between the rich and the poor may induce the rich to choose inefficient organizational structures in order to better take advantage of their bargaining power vis-à-vis poor partners within the same firms.

(that is, to pool their initial resources) in order to produce. Let $\overline{w}_t = \overline{w}A_t$ and $\underline{w} = \underline{w}A_t$ denote the initial endowment of the richer and the poorer of these two individuals. As in the previous section, we denote by $\varphi \cdot A_t$ the fixed cost of the project initiated at date t, and we assume that

$$\overline{w} + \underline{w} \geq \varphi > \overline{w}(> \underline{w}).$$

In other words, the project requires the financial participation of both individuals in order to be at all implemented.

Letting $\overline{e} \in \{0, 1\}$ and $\underline{e} \in \{0, 1\}$ denote the productive effort invested ex-ante by the rich and poor respectively, we formalize the "moral hazard in team" problem between the two individuals in a very simple way: once the fixed cost φA_t has been sunk, the project yields $\sigma \cdot A_t$ with probability $\frac{e+e'}{2}$ and zero with probability $(1 - \frac{e+e'}{2})$.

Let $c \cdot A > 0$ denote the (nonmonetary) effort cost (that is, the cost of investing one unit of effort) for any of the two individuals, and let us assume, as in the previous section, that individuals only care for expected second-period output net of their effort cost. Then, for both individuals to invest in effort in (a Nash) equilibrium, the following incentive constraints (respectively for the rich and poor) must simultaneously hold:

$$\overline{\alpha} \cdot \sigma A - cA > \overline{\alpha}\sigma A \cdot \frac{1}{2}$$

and

$$\underline{\alpha} \cdot \sigma A - cA > \underline{\alpha}\sigma A \cdot \frac{1}{2},$$

where $\overline{\alpha} = \frac{\overline{w}}{\overline{w}+\underline{w}}$ and $\underline{\alpha} = \frac{\underline{w}}{\overline{w}+\underline{w}}$ denote the rich and poor individuals' shares in the joint venture.

In particular, when the discrepancy between the rich and the poor is sufficiently large that

$$\frac{\underline{\alpha}\sigma}{2} < c < \frac{\overline{\alpha}\sigma}{2},$$

full cooperation between the two individuals (i.e., $\overline{e} = \underline{e} = 1$) will not be sustainable in equilibrium. Rather, the poor individual will free-ride on the rich, as part of the (unique) equilibrium $\overline{e} = 1, \underline{e} = 0$.

Now, whenever $\frac{\sigma}{4} > c$, moving torward a more egalitarian distribution of wealth (i.e., toward $\overline{\alpha} = \underline{\alpha} = \frac{1}{2}$) between the two individuals, will favor their cooperation and thereby increase the growth rate from $\sigma/2$ to σ.

Inequality and Expropriation

Benabou (1996a) surveys recent work that examines various aspects of the relationship between inequality, expropriation, and growth. That a high degree of inequality between rich and poor individuals may encourage the poor to expropriate the rich at the expense of aggregate investment and growth can easily be illustrated using the toy model introduced above.

More precisely, suppose that the poor can expropriate the rich by a positive fraction $\beta > 0$ of her endowment $\overline{w}A$, thereby reducing the rate of return on the project from $\frac{\sigma}{\varphi}$ to $\frac{\sigma'}{\varphi} < \frac{\sigma}{\varphi}$. Letting $p = \frac{\overline{e}+\underline{e}}{2}$ denote the probability of project success, the poor will always choose to expropriate the rich whenever

$$\underline{\alpha} p \sigma' A + \beta \overline{w} A > \underline{\alpha} p \sigma A, \tag{9.15}$$

which in turn is automatically satisfied whenever $\underline{\alpha}$ is sufficiently small and/or $\overline{w}$ is sufficiently large, in other words, when the inequality between the rich and poor is sufficiently marked.

Starting from a highly unequal distribution of wealth that satisfies (9.15), redistributing wealth from the rich to the poor will eliminate the incentives for expropriation and thereby increase the growth rate from σ' to $\sigma > \sigma'$.

Table 9.1, drawn from Benabou (1996a), summarizes the main findings from the recent literature on inequality, social conflicts, and growth. Column (9) shows that income inequality is positively correlated with "instability,"[19] whereas column (10) shows that instability is negatively correlated with growth.

9.1.4 Political Economy[*]

Social conflicts do not take only the direct form of noncooperative or predatory behavior by individuals within a same firm or neighborhood. They also surface through the political process, especially when the society as a whole must decide about redistribution or public-good investments such as education or health. By affecting the outcome of the political game, inequality will directly influence the extent of redistribution and thereby the rate of growth. Interestingly, the *direction* in which inequality affects growth through the political process turns out to depend heavily on the importance of credit constraints, as we will now illustrate, following Benabou (1996a) quite closely.[20]

Consider the AK with overlapping generations model of section 9.1.1, but with the tax rate now being endogenously determined through majority voting. Following Benabou (1996a), we consider the following log-linear investment tax scheme,[21] whereby an individual with pre-tax investment k^i

---

19. *Political* instability is typically measured by the frequency of strikes, government changes, and so on; *institutional* instability is measured by indicators such as the expropriation risk, the degree of enforceability of contracts, and the like.

20. Benabou himself draws heavily on Alesina and Rodrik (1994) and Persson and Tabellini (1994).

21. Note that we are switching from a linear to a log-linear distribution scheme. The latter specification works better when analyzing the effect of inequality changes on the median voter's decision.

Table 9.1

| | 1 | 2 | 3 | 4 INEQ on REDIST | | 5 REDIST on GR, INV | | 6 | 7 | 8 | 9 | 10 |
	INEQ on GR, INV	DEM on GR, INV	DEM*INEQ on GR, INV	TRAN, TAX	EDEXP	TRAN, TAX	EDEXP	HUMCAP on GR, INV	CRED on GR, INV	CRED*INEQ on GR, INV	INEQ on INSTAB	INSTAB on GR, INV
1 Alesina Rodrik (94)	--	0	0					++				
2 Alesina Perotti (96)								++			++	-
3 Alesina et al (96)		0						++			++	--
4 Barro (96)		^					+	M++, F--				--
5 Benhabib-Spiegel (96)	(-)							++				(-)
6 Bourguignon (94)	--							++				
7 Brandolini-Rossi (95)	0											
8 Clarke (92)	--		0					++				
9 Deininger-Squire (95)	(-)	±	+					+				
10 Devarajan et al (93)						+	(-)					
11 Easterly-Rebelo (93)					+	(-)		++				+-
12 Keefer-Knack (95)	--	(-)	±	(-)				++			++	--
13 Levine-Renelt (92)												-
14 Lindert (96)				--	(-)	±	++	++				
15 McCallum-Biais (87)						++						
16 Perotti (92)	--			(-)	±	+		+	--	-	++	--
17 Perotti (94)	--			(-)		(+)		0				
18 Perotti (96)	--	0	(-)	(+)	(+)	++	++	M ++, F --			++	--
19 Persson-Tabellini (94)	--		--			(-)		++				
20 Persson-Tabellini (96)	--	-	--	(+)		(-)		++				
21 Sala-i-Martín (92)						++						
22 Svensson (93)								++			+	--
23 Venieris-Gupta (86)	--											--

Effects of inequality on growth or investment and some of their derminants

Symbols: $++, --$ consistent sign and generally significant;
         $+, -$ consistent sign, sometimes significant;
         $(+), (-)$ consistent sign but generally not significant;
         $(\pm)$ inconsistent sign with significant coefficients;
         0   inconsistent sign or close to zero, and not significant;
         ^   inverse u-shaped and signficant

INEQ
Measures of inequality: [1] uses income and land Ginis; [5], [16] and [23] use $-Q3$; [6] uses Q1, Q1+Q2 and $-Q5$; [7], [9] use income Ginis; [8] and [11] use income Gini, Theil, coefficient of variation and Q5/(Q1+Q2); [12] uses Gini, land Gini and $-Q3$; [14] uses $\ln(Q5/Q3)+\ln(Q3/Q1)$; [17] uses $-Q3$ and Q1+Q2; [18] uses $-(Q3+Q4)$; [19] uses $-Q3$ and land Ginis; [20] uses Q5 and $-Q3$; [22] uses $-(Q1+Q2)/Q5$.

DEM
Measures of political rights and degree of democracy; see each study.

REDIST
Measures of redistribution: EDEXP is the share of education expenditures in GDP; TRAN and TAX are various transfers and tax rates, as detailed below. [10] uses current govt. expenditure/GDP $(++)$, health and education $(\pm)$; [11] uses 12 difference average and marginal tax rates; only one has a significant effect; [12] uses shares in GDP of: social security, welfare, government transfers, tax revenues, government expenditures and government consumption, as well as the share of employment in the state sector; [14] uses the shares in GDP of payments for: social security, welfare, unemployment, health (as well as the sum of these four transfers), and education; [16], [17] and [20] use total transfers/GDP; [18] uses GDP shares of: social security, health plus housing, and education; also the labor tax rate, average and marginal income tax rates; [15], [21] use GDP share of social security.

CRED
Credit market imperfections measured in [16] by (minus) the loan-to-value ratio for mortgages.

HUMCAP
[4], [5], [9] and [15] use initial stock of human capital (primary and/or secondary education); M=males, F=females; all others proxy for the stock with enrollment ratios.

INSTAB
[1], [2], [3], [5], [13], [16] and [18] focus on socio-political instability, measured by various combinations of protests, strikes, government turnover, political violence, coups, revolutions, etc., [4], [12] and [22] focus on the security of property rights, measured by indicators of country risk (default, expropriation, nationalization), contract enforceability, corruption, etc.

ends up with the post-tax investment

$$k^i(\tau) = (k^i)^{1-\tau} \cdot (\tilde{k})^\tau,$$

with the average investment $\tilde{k}$ being determined by the balanced-budget condition

$$\int_0^1 k^i(\tau) di = \int_0^1 k^i di = \tilde{k}.$$

Consider first what happens in the absence of credit constraints. Expecting the investment tax rate τ, individual i will choose its investment k^i and its borrowings b^i to maximize

$$\max_{b^i, k^i} \left\{ \ln(w^i + b^i - k^i) + \rho \ln \underbrace{((k^i(\tau))^\alpha w^{1-\alpha} - rb^i)}_{=y^i} \right\}.$$

The first-order condition for this maximization, together with the loan market-clearing condition $\int_0^1 b^i di = 0$, yields the investment and net borrowing decisions:

$$k^i = \frac{\rho\alpha(1-\tau)}{1+\rho\alpha(1-\tau)} w = s(\tau).w \quad \text{and} \quad b^i = \frac{\rho}{1+\rho}(w - w^i), \qquad (9.16)$$

with the resulting intertemporal utility for individual i

$$U^i(\tau) = V(\tau) + (1+\rho) \ln[1 + (\frac{w^i}{w} - 1)(1 + \rho\alpha(1-\tau))/1 + \rho],$$

where $V(\tau)$ is the intertemporal utility of the individual with wealth equal to the average w,[22] who in this case is also the individual with average investment $\tilde{k}$. Not surprisingly, $V(\tau)$ is decreasing with τ as a result of the negative *incentive* effect of redistribution. (By definition, this redistribution scheme leaves the individual with average investment $\tilde{k}$ otherwise unaffected.) Individuals with initial wealth $w^i < w$ will prefer a positive tax rate τ^i, defined by the first-order condition $U'^i(\tau) = 0$; or equivalently, using the explicit expression for $V(\tau)$,

---

22. Namely:

$$V(\tau) = \ln(w - k) + \rho \ln(k^\alpha w^{1-\alpha})$$
$$= (1 + \rho) \ln w + \ln(1 - s(\tau)) + \rho\alpha \ln(s(\tau)),$$

where

$$s(\tau) = \frac{\rho\alpha(1-\tau)}{1+\rho\alpha(1-\tau)}.$$

$$\frac{\tau(1 + \rho)}{(1 + \rho(1 - \tau))(1 + \rho\alpha(1 - \tau))} = 1 - \frac{w^i}{w}. \tag{9.17}$$

Not surprisingly, the poorer individuals will prefer a higher redistribution rate τ^i.

Given that the intertemporal utilities $U^i(\tau)$ are single-peaked for $w^i < w$, the equilibrium tax rate τ will be that chosen by the median voter. The higher the degree of wealth inequality, the lower the median wealth w^i compared to the average wealth w, and therefore the higher the redistribution rate τ. Now, remember from section 9.1.2 that in the absence of capital-market imperfections, redistribution did not have any positive-incentive effect on investment and growth. Hence *more inequality* (in the sense of a lower ratio of median to average wealth) *will lead to more redistribution but not to higher growth in the absence of credit market imperfections.*

Consider now the same problem, but without credit markets. Expecting the investment tax rate τ, but with no access to borrowing or lending, individual i will now choose his or her investment k^i to maximize

$$\max_{k^i}\{\ln(w^i - k^i) + \rho \ln((k^i(\tau))^\alpha w^{1-\alpha})\}.$$

Assuming that wealth endowments are log-normally distributed, with mean m and variance Δ^2, the intertemporal utility of individual i can be shown to be equal to

$$U^i(\tau) = V(\tau) - (1 + \rho\alpha(1 - \tau)^2)\frac{\Delta^2}{2} + (1 + \rho\alpha(1 - \tau))(\ln w^i - m). \tag{9.18}$$

The second (negative) term in this expression reflects the aggregate loss from investment inequality, which arises in the no-credit market case. As already argued in 9.1.1 above, this loss is itself a consequence of the assumption of decreasing returns to individual capital investments; to the extent that it affects aggregate knowledge w at any point in time, this cost of inequality is to be borne by *all* individuals, the poor *and* the rich, in the economy. In particular, the individual with average wealth w will now vote for a positive tax rate because

$$U'(\tau) = V'(\tau) + (1 - \tau)\rho\alpha\Delta^2 - \rho\alpha\frac{\Delta^2}{2}$$

$$= \rho\alpha\frac{\Delta^2}{2} > 0 \text{ at } \tau = 0.$$

One can guess from equation (9.18) that the larger the degree of inequality (measured by Δ), the more the median voter (whose wealth is less than w by a distance which increases with Δ) will favor redistribution. Thus it seems that to a larger extent than in the perfect credit market case, an increase in inequality should lead to more redistribution. But now there is again an *opportunity creation* effect of redistribution. More specifically, one can show that the growth rate g, which in the perfect credit-market case can be shown to be unambiguously decreasing in τ ($g = \alpha \ln s(\tau) = \alpha \ln \frac{\rho\alpha(1-\tau)}{1+\rho\alpha(1-\tau)}$), becomes a nonmonotonic function of τ in the absence of borrowing and lending. Namely[23]

$$g = \alpha \ln s(\tau) - \alpha(1-\alpha)(1-\tau)^2 \frac{\Delta^2}{2}.$$

In this case, the increase in redistribution induced by higher inequality may result in a *higher* rate of growth.

So far we have restricted the analysis to the case where the pivotal individual is the median-voter, that is the voter with wealth $\overline{w}$ such that $pr(w_i \leq \overline{w}) = \frac{1}{2}$. More generally, one might consider the possibility of *biased* voting rules whereby the pivotal voter's wealth would satisfy

$$pr(w_i \leq \overline{w}) = p, \quad \text{with } p \lessgtr \frac{1}{2}.$$

For example, an elitist (or wealth-biased) system would involve having $p >> \frac{1}{2}$. In the log-normal case where $\ln w^i \sim N(m, \Delta^2)$, this would correspond to having the pivotal wealth lie *above* the average wealth, by an amount proportional to the degree of inequality Δ:

$$\overline{w} = m + \lambda\Delta, \quad \lambda > 0.$$

In this case, an increase in inequality might actually result into less redistribution and therefore into *more* growth (resp. *less* growth) whenever the negative effect of redistribution on $s(\tau)$ dominates (resp. is dominated by) the opportunity creation effect.

9.2   Technological Change as a Source of Inequality

General interest into questions of how technical change and growth affect inequality has been recently revived by new empirical evidence questioning the relevance of the so-called Kuznets hypothesis. Based on a cross-section regression of GNP per head and income distribution across a large number of countries, Kuznets (1955) had found an inverted U-shaped relation between income inequality and GNP per head. That is, the lowest and highest levels of GNP per head were associated with low inequality but middle levels were

---

23. A similar point is made by Saint-Paul and Verdier (1993), who analyze the voting process over public education spending aimed at circumventing wealth constraints in private investments. See also Galor and Zeira (1993) and Perotti (1993).

associated with higher inequality. This, in turn, would suggest that in the long run growth is bound to bring about a durable reduction in inequality.

However, recent empirical studies (e.g., Juhn, Murphy, and Pierce 1993 and Bourguignon and Morrison 1992) have pointed to a substantial increase in wage and income inequality in OECD countries during the past twenty years.[24]

Various explanations have been offered for this observed upsurge of inequality in developed countries; the evidence, however, on both the importance of the *wage component*[25] in the measured increase in income inequality *and* the *episodic nature* of inequality changes during the past fifty years, leads us to believe that *technological change* is an important part of the story.

Now, if technological change is to generate an increase in wage inequality, it must be because technological change is *biased* toward certain skills or specializations, in the sense that it reveals and enhances new differences in abilities among workers across or within educational cohorts.[26] And indeed, writes Atkinson, "there appears to be widespread agreement on the fact that there has been a shift in demand away from unskilled labor in favor of skilled workers,"[27] and that this provides a straightforward explanation of rising earning dispersion.

That technological change can induce episodic increases in wage differentials between skilled and unskilled workers has already been hinted at in the previous chapter when we analyzed the effects of major technological change (i.e., of the arrival of new general purpose technologies) on wage dispersion and unemployment. In a nutshell, although technological change can exert an upward pressure on the demand for skilled workers and thereby increase their wage premium over unskilled workers, education should eventually lead to an expanded supply of skilled labor and thereby to a fall of the wage differential.[28]

Our analysis in this section will be organized as follows: subsection 9.2.1 will formally introduce *skill-biased technical progress* into the basic Schumpeterian model of Chapter 2. Subsection 9.2.2 will then discuss another important channel whereby technical change may affect wage inequality, namely *organizational change*. Finally, subsection 9.2.3 introduces learning-by-doing and intersectoral-mobility considerations using the framework developed in Chapter 6 to provide another explanation for the observed increase in wage inequality *within* education groups during the past twenty five years.

---

24. See Atkinson (1996) and Piketty (1996) for surveys of the relevant empirical and theoretical literature on the determinants of income and wage inequality.

25. See Atkinson (1996), pages 4 and 12 and figure 1.

26. See Juhn et al. (1993) and Piketty (1996).

27. See Atkinson (1996).

28. See Chapter 8; see also Galor and Tsiddon (1994).

9.2.1   Skill-Biased Technical Progress

Consider the following extension of the basic Schumpeterian model of Chapter 2: final output is now produced with both intermediate good *and unskilled labor*, that is,

$$y_t = \ln(z + A_t \cdot x_t), \tag{9.19}$$

where (a) z is unskilled labor and (b) x_t denotes the quantity of intermediate good currently used in final production. One can think of "*robots*" whose productivity A_t increases by a factor $\gamma > 1$ each time a new innovation occurs. Then, what equation (9.19) says is that unskilled labor must compete with increasingly productive robots in the production of final output.[29]

Apart from the introduction of unskilled labor in equation (9.19), the model is identical to that in Chapter 2: robots are produced with skilled labor according to a linear one-for-one technology; innovations occur at Poisson rate λn_t, where n_t is the "number" of skilled workers currently employed in research. Therefore, we still have

$$L = x_t + n_t, \tag{L}$$

where L measures the total population of skilled workers and x_t denotes the fraction of that population currently employed in the manufacturing of new robots by the intermediate sector.

The research-arbitrage equation (A), which reflects the skilled workers' indifference between research and manufacturing, is still given by

$$w_t = \lambda \cdot \frac{\pi_{t+1}}{r + \lambda n_{t+1}} = \lambda \cdot V_{t+1}, \tag{A}$$

where w_t is the wage rate currently earned by skilled workers employed in manufacturing, and

$$V_{t+1} = \frac{\pi_{t+1}}{r + \lambda n_{t+1}}$$

is the value of the next innovation (assuming that t innovations have already occurred and therefore the current productivity parameter is A_t).

Now, when expressing the profit flow π_{t+1}, we have to be a bit careful and beware that innovations may be nondrastic (see section 2.6.4). This turns out to be the case under the logarithmic final-good technology specified in (9.19), provided the productivity parameter A is sufficiently large.[30] In that case, the

---

29. This model is based on Samuelson (1988).

30. When A is large, the demand for intermediate good is indeed almost unit-elastic. Then, we know from Grossman and Helpman (1991) or problem 3.1 that innovations are necessarily nondrastic, with profit flows being given by equation (9.20).

profit flow π_{t+1} is simply given by

$$\pi_{t+1} = (\gamma - 1) \underbrace{w_{t+1} \cdot x_{t+1}}_{\text{wage bill}} . \tag{9.20}$$

Finally, the equilibrium wage of *skilled* workers, namely w_t if t innovations have already occurred, must be equal to the marginal value product of robots, that is,

$$w_t = \frac{1}{\gamma} \cdot \frac{A_t}{z + A_t x_t}. \tag{9.21}$$

Similarly, the equilibrium unskilled wage w_t^u must be equal to the marginal productivity of unskilled labor, namely,

$$w_t^u = \frac{1}{z + A_t x_t}. \tag{9.22}$$

Using (L), (9.21) and (9.22), and letting $v_t = z + A_t x_t$, we can reexpress the arbitrage equation (A) as

$$\frac{A_t}{v_t} = \lambda \frac{(\gamma - 1) \cdot \frac{v_{t+1}-z}{v_{t+1}}}{r + \lambda (L - \frac{v_{t+1}-z}{A_{t+1}})},$$

or equivalently, after dividing both hand sides by A_t,

$$v_t = \frac{v_{t+1}}{v_{t+1} - z} \cdot \left[r A_{t+1} + \lambda (z + A_{t+1} L - v_{t+1}) \right] \frac{1}{\lambda (\gamma - 1)} \cdot \frac{1}{\gamma}, \tag{9.23}$$

where

$$z \leq v_t \leq z + A_t \cdot L.$$

This difference equation, together with the dynamic equation for productivity, namely $A_{t+1} = \gamma A_t$, will fully characterize the evolution of skilled and unskilled wages over time.

Dealing with a two-dimensional dynamic system, the most natural thing to do is to analyze its asymptotic behavior near the long-run steady state, with the hope of getting a nice phase diagram.

Letting

$$\phi_t = \frac{z + A_t x_t}{A_t} = \frac{v_t}{A_t} \text{ and } h_t = \frac{z}{A_t},$$

we have:

$$h_{t+1} = \frac{1}{\gamma} h_t \tag{D_1}$$

and, from (9.23):

$$\phi_t = \frac{\phi_{t+1}}{\phi_{t+1} - h_{t+1}} \left[r + \lambda(L + h_{t+1} - \phi_{t+1}) \right] \frac{1}{\lambda(\gamma - 1)}. \tag{D$_2$}$$

The corresponding steady state is simply given by: $\widehat{h} = 0, \widehat{\phi} = \frac{r + \lambda L}{\lambda \gamma}$.[31]

Linearizing the system (D_1)–(D_2) around its steady state, we obtain the linear system[32]

$$\begin{pmatrix} \phi_{t+1} - \hat{\phi} \\ h_{t+1} \end{pmatrix} \simeq \begin{pmatrix} 1 - \gamma, & \frac{1}{\gamma} \\ 0, & \frac{1}{\gamma} \end{pmatrix} \begin{pmatrix} \phi_t - \hat{\phi} \\ h_t \end{pmatrix}.$$

For a saddle path to exist we need the negative eigenvalue $1 - \gamma$ to be greater than 1 in absolute value. For this we need $\gamma > 2$. Under this restriction the behavior of the system in the neighborhood of the steady state $(0, \widehat{\phi})$ will be as described in figure 9.2.

Thus, we see that the skilled wage $w_t = \frac{1}{\phi_t}$ increases on its (saddle-path) way toward the long-run steady state. However, the unskilled wage

$$w_t^u = \frac{1}{z + A_t x_t} = \frac{1}{A_t \phi_t}$$

---

31. We assume r sufficiently small, namely $r < (\gamma - 1)\lambda L$, in order to guarantee the existence of a solution (h_t, ϕ_t) to the dynamic system (D_1)-(D_2), at least in a neighborhood of the steady state $(\widehat{h} = 0, \widehat{\phi})$. Indeed, one can easily check that when $r < (\gamma - 1)\lambda L$, $v_t = A_t \phi_t < z + A_t L$ for t sufficiently large. $\square$

32. To see this, rewrite equation (D$_2$) as

$$\phi_t - RHS \text{ of } (D_2) = \varphi(\phi_t, \phi_{t+1}, h_{t+1} = \frac{h_t}{\gamma}) = 0.$$

By the implicit function theorem, at $(h, \phi) = (0, \hat{\phi})$, we have:

$$\frac{\partial \phi_{t+1}}{\partial \phi_t} = -\frac{\varphi_{\phi_t}}{\varphi_{\phi_{t+1}}} = +\frac{1}{\frac{\phi_t}{\phi_{t+1}} - \frac{\phi_t}{\phi_{t+1}} - \frac{\lambda \phi_t}{r + \lambda L - \lambda \phi_{t+1}}}$$

$$= +\frac{1}{1 - 1 - \frac{\lambda \widehat{\phi}}{\lambda \gamma \widehat{\phi} - \lambda \widehat{\phi}}} = 1 - \gamma.$$

Similarly,

$$\frac{\partial \phi_{t+1}}{\partial h_t} = -\frac{\varphi_{h_t}}{\varphi_{\phi_{t+1}}}$$

$$= -\frac{\frac{\lambda}{\gamma} \cdot \frac{1}{\lambda(\gamma - 1)}}{\frac{\lambda \widehat{\phi}}{\lambda \gamma \widehat{\phi} - \lambda \widehat{\phi}}}$$

$$= \frac{1}{\gamma}. \quad \square$$

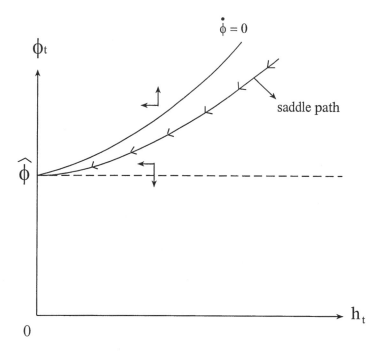

Figure 9.2

is (eventually) going down to zero (because $\phi_t \to \widehat{\phi} > 0$ and $A_t \to +\infty$). In particular, the wage premium $w_t - w_t^u$ increases over time as more and more productive robots come to compete with unskilled labor.

Perhaps more surprising is the fact that the skilled wage w_t reaches a horizontal asymptote when t goes to infinity: $w_t \to \frac{1}{\phi} < +\infty$. In other words, although the unskilled wage reduction benefits the skilled labor force initially (i.e., for low t), when there are already many (or very powerful) computers in the economy, skilled labor as such stops eventually gaining from further technical progress. The gains from technical progress will then accrue to the rest of the economy, namely to consumers who obviously benefit from the production of final goods becoming continuously more efficient as $A_t \to \infty$.[33]

Three quick but important remarks conclude our analysis in this section. First, a natural next step is to introduce *education*, that is, the possibility for

---

33. We could have arrived at somewhat different results concerning the skilled and unskilled wage rates by assuming a different pattern of substitutability/complementarity in the aggregate production function (9.19). For example, if we had assumed $y_t = (z + A_t^{\frac{1}{\alpha}} x_t)^{\alpha}$, then again $w_t^u \to 0$, but in this case w_t grows without bound, at the same asymptotic rate as A_t. Alternatively, if $y_t = z_t + A_t x_t^{\alpha}$, then w_t^u is constant while x_t grows asymptotically at the same rate as A_t. A variant of this last model will be examined in Chapter 10.

unskilled workers to become skilled. How the dynamics of the equilibrium wage premium $(w_t - w_t^u)$ will be affected by the cost of education is indeed an interesting question, which we shall briefly take up in the next chapter (see section 10.3). Second, we have assumed away the existence of a *reservation wage* below which employment would simply become unattractive (or illegal). Introducing a positive reservation wage $\underline{w} > 0$ in the preceding analysis yields the immediate result that skilled-biased technical progress can generate an increasing amount of unemployment among unskilled workers. This, rather than the intersectoral-job reallocations emphasized in Chapter 4, might explain a substantial fraction of the unemployment rise experienced in the past fifteen years by several OECD countries.[34] Third, in this subsection we have concentrated on the dynamics of wage inequality *across* different education cohorts (i.e., between skilled and unskilled workers). The effects of technical change and growth on the evolution of wage inequality *within* educational cohorts turns out to be somewhat more subtle, as we argue in the next two subsections.

9.2.2   Organizational Change and Wage Inequality

The preceding analysis of skill-biased technical progress and wage inequality may appear too simplistic in its representation of firms as "production functions" in which educational skills *and* current wages are both being taken as given. The reality is indeed more complex: (a) skills are only partly acquired at school, and to a substantial extent they end up being firm-specific, that is, specific to the particular type of production activity and also to the *organizational* form chosen by enterprise; (b) accordingly, wages are not entirely market determined, but instead result from complicated bargaining processes that are also affected by the organizational structure of firms.[35]

In this subsection we would like to touch briefly on what strikes us as an important issue for further research, namely *organizational change* as a source of increased wage inequality.

Recent history about U.S. companies points to the following trends:

a. a move toward decentralization of decision making within firms, with the creation of independent profit centers, greater flexibility, and authority being allocated to units' managers;[36]

---

34. Various empirical studies, including Murphy and Topel (1987), have shown that most of the unemployment rise of the (early) 1980's in the United States had taken place within the lower-skilled fraction of the population, and without being accompanied by a corresponding increase in the amount of intersectoral job reallocations. See Piketty (1996) for a good discussion of the relevant literature.   □

35. See Stole and Zwiebel (1996).

36. See Chandler (1962).

b. a move toward "flatter" organizations involving a smaller number of hierarchical layers but a bigger *span of control* at each layer. (By *span of control* we mean the number of downstream agents or units that are being supervised or monitored by a given layer).[37]

c. a shift away from hierarchical into more "organic" structures, with both the replacement of vertical communication channels by *horizontal* (cross-department) *channels* and a reduction in specialization (i.e., of the extent to which a particular agent can be identified with any particular task).[38]

d. an increase in *intra-industry* wage inequality.

e. an increase in *educational* wage differentials, that is, in wage inequality across different educational cohorts.[39]

f. an increase in *occupational* wage differentials, including *within* a same educational cohort, that cannot be entirely accounted for by differences in "skills."[40]

These above stylized facts raise a number of interesting questions. For example, how can the organizational evolutions mentioned in (a)–(c) be mapped up to technical progress in particular areas? Also, is there a clear causal relationship between these evolutions and the evidence on increased wage differentials in (d)–(f)? Analyzing only those two questions in detail would bring us much beyond the scope of these chapters, not least because of our poor understanding of organizations and of their interplay with markets and technologies. However, let us have a go and suggest some preliminary "explanations" for these above pieces of evidence.

First, the move toward flatter organizations might simply result from technical progress in monitoring, which in turn makes it *possible* for a principal to monitor *directly*[41] more agents without becoming overloaded. Whether the principal (e.g., a top manager) will have the incentive to engage in extra supervisory activities will in turn partly depend on his monetary incentives (Qian

---

37. See Scott, O'Shaughnessy, and Cappelli (1996).

38. See Piore (1988).

39. See Cappelli and Daniel (1995).

40. Scott et al. (1996) try to measure the skill requirement of jobs in the insurance industry. They construct an aggregate index of skill (which is meant to reflect such dimensions as know-how, problem-solving, accountability, or autonomy in decision making) and which they try to map onto occupations and wages. They find that during the period between 1986 and 1992 top managers in the insurance industry have received a 28 percent increase in income compensation, although nonsupervisory layers have barely benefited from the organizational change. Meanwhile, none of the hierarchical layers, including the top management, seems to have experienced increases in skill that were significant.

41. Directly, that is without resorting to intermediate supervisory layers.

1994). One can thus potentially account for the observed increase in *occupational* wage differential in relation to the observed increase in the span of control.

Second, the move toward less hierarchical firms can also be partly attributed to technical progress, namely to a reduction in communication costs. A major comparative advantage of a nonhierarchical (organic) structure (e.g., think of an assembly line) over a hierarchical one lies in the former's ability to process new information more quickly and thereby to respond faster to changes in demand.[42] This comparative advantage is enhanced when communication costs are reduced. For example, suppose there are two ways in which individuals can acquire information about a project. They can either acquire the information directly, which takes $r > 0$ units of time per "item," or they can get the information secondhand by communicating with other agents. However, communication is also time consuming: namely, it takes $r(\lambda + am)$ units of time to communicate m informational terms.

Now, consider a project comprising n items. If the whole information processing is performed by a single individual, the total processing time will be $r \cdot n$, whereas if the processing activity is split between say two individuals, with individual 1 processing $\frac{n}{2}$ items directly and learning about the remaining $\frac{n}{2}$ items though communication with individual 2, the total processing time will be $r\frac{n}{2} + r(\lambda + a\frac{n}{2})$. Delay will thus be reduced by having *parallel processing* whenever n is sufficiently large and/or there are enough economies of scale in communication (i.e., if a is sufficiently small). The lower is a, the better a nonhierarchical firm will perform in comparison to a hierarchical firm.

Now, to the extent that nonhierarchical firms rely to a larger extent on *polyvalent* agents, which can both perform a given task *and* learn from other agents activities through horizontal communication, such firms are likely to give a higher premium to educated workers (assuming that education provides the kind of general knowledge that is required for a worker to be truly polyvalent). This in turn may explain why the move toward less hierarchical firms (induced by the reduction in communication costs) has often been accompanied by an increase in the *educational* wage differential between educated and less educated employees. More generally, any technological change that enhances the positive externalities among educated workers is likely to result in an increased in wage inequality across educational cohorts of the kind mentioned in (e).[43] Furthermore, as shown by Kremer and Maskin (1994), such externalities may also result in intra-industry segregation between firms that

---

42. This, in turn, enables nonhierarchical organizations to reduce the volume of "in-process" inventories and to move closer towards "just-in-time" manufacturing. See Bolton and Dewatripont (1995).

43. See Caroli et al. (1997).

choose to rely more heavily on educated workers (typically more polyvalent and also better remunerated) and firms that rely on a large number of less educated workers (typically specialized in one task and low-paid). This segregation between "lean" and "mass" production firms may in turn account to some extent for the observed increase in *intra-industry* wage inequality mentioned in (d).

Third, and last, the greater availability of well-educated workers who can (individually or collectively) process information about new projects at a lower cost[44] makes it profitable for firm owners and/or top managers to delegate some decision rights (or "authority") to lower layers of the hierarchy.[45] Now, in order to avoid moral hazard in team (or free-riding) problems, it may be optimal to concentrate the delegated-decision rights on a small number of "team leaders." This unevenness in authority allocation may in turn result in an increased wage differential between the team leader and its team members,[46] all of whom are likely to be drawn from the same educational cohort.[47] Finally, the evolution toward more decentralized organizations is often accompanied by a removal of (some) intermediate supervisory layers. Part of the supervisory authority is being transferred to lower layers of the hierarchy, while the remaining part is being transferred upstream. Whether the wage differential between top managers (or top supervisors) and the downstream teams should increase or decrease will depend to a large extent on the nature of tasks or decision rights that are being transferred upstream and downstream. If only the simpler tasks are being transferred downstream, although top managers have to deal with increasingly more complicated tasks (including the task of supervising a self-managed team), then the move toward decentralization is likely to translate into a bigger revenue gap between the top management and the downstream units, in accordance with the evidence in Scott et al. (1996).

Although the preceding rationalizations are largely tentative and speculative, they provide some benchmarks on how to use (and possibly develop) the existing theories of organizations in order to establish some kind of a mapping between technical progress, the direction of organization change (e.g., (a), (b), or (c)), and the particular form of increased wage differential (e.g., (d), (e), or (f)).

---

44. For example, as a result of a reduction in communication costs, as argued above.

45. That lower costs of processing information about new projects may encourage the delegation of authority to downstream units, is shown in Aghion-Tirole (1997). See the Appendix to Chapter 13, for a brief presentation of the Aghion-Tirole model of authority and delegation. □

46. This is most likely to be the case whenever: (a) employees are highly responsive to monetary incentives and do not only value the private benefits of control (see Aghion-Tirole (1997)); (b) there is *little* job rotation between current team leaders and other team members. □

47. See Hernandez (1996). □

9.2.3   Growth and Wage Inequality within Educational Cohorts

In a very interesting paper, Violante (1997) develops a new explanation for the increasing wage dispersion *within* educational groups during the past twenty-five years in the United States. This explanation is based on the notion of vintage-specific skills primarily acquired by workers through learning by doing. More specifically, suppose that technological knowledge is embodied in equipments (or "lines," using our terminology in Chapter 6) of different vintages. Workers are ex-ante identical (they share the same educational background), but then are randomly matched with machines of different vintages and become increasingly heterogenous as their specific labor-market histories unfold, involving different patterns of accumulation or transfer of skills on the job and between jobs. Indeed, workers can either remain on the same job and improve their skills on the current machine through learning by doing or move to newer machines. New machines are more productive than old machines, but leaving an old machine involves a (partial) loss of skills for the worker.[48]

By means of calibrations, Violante finds that the higher the rate of technological change, the higher the (steady-state) variance of wages. The basic intuition for this finding can be summarized as follows. As technological progress speeds up, the cross-sectional variance of productivity across vintages increases. This implies, first, that high-skilled workers are more likely to turn down old vintages and instead keep searching for jobs in newer vintages (or "lines"), and, second, that due to decreasing returns to learning by doing on any particular vintage, the high-skilled workers (who work on newer vintages than low-skilled workers) will improve their productivity faster than the low-skilled. At the same time, being increasingly remote from the leading edge, less skilled workers will be less able to transfer their previous skills to newer vintages, and therefore less willing to move from old to new vintages. This, in turn, will generate an increased variance in productivity, and thus in wages, among workers with different matching and vintage histories.

Although this intuition is reasonably transparent, solving Violante's model analytically turns out to be prohibitively difficult. In the remaining part of this subsection we shall propose an alternative formalization, based on our own learning-by-doing framework introduced in Chapter 6 which appears to be more tractable while delivering the same basic conclusions.

Thus, consider the model of Chapter 6 (section 6.1), but where the arrival rate of new vintages (i.e., of new fundamental discoveries) is exogenous equal to $g > 0$. Final output is still produced with a continuum of intermediate goods (machines) of different vintages, where more recent vintages are better than

---

48. Violante assumes that the transferability of skills (accumulated on a particular vintage through learning by doing) is inversely proportional to the technological distance between the old and the new vintages.

older ones because they embody a higher level of general knowledge (assumed to grow at rate g). Let $A_\tau = e^{g\tau}$ denote the state of general knowledge at date τ; let Z_a denote the "quality" of a worker on a line of age a: that is, labor input x_a on a line of age a produces $Z_a(x_a)^\alpha$ units of intermediate good of the corresponding vintage.[49] Thus aggregate final output at date τ is simply

$$Y_t = \int_{-\infty}^t A_\tau \cdot Z_{t-\tau}(x_{t-\tau})^\alpha d\tau = \int_{-\infty}^t Y_{t,\tau} d\tau,$$

where the parameter α lies between 0 and 1.

The quality of workers on a newly invented vintage is $q_0 > 0$, and quality improvements come at a rate equal to the amount of learning by doing in the economy, which we normalize at one: $\frac{dZ_a}{da} = 1$. Thus, the quality of workers on a line of age a is

$$Z_a = q_0 + a.$$

The wage of someone working on a product line of vintage τ when that vintage is a years old is the marginal value product

$$w(a, \tau) = e^{g t} \alpha (q_0 + a) x_a^{\alpha-1},$$

where the number of workers on the product line is $x_a = x_0 e^{-\sigma a}$, and σ is the rate at which workers can move to the leading edge.

The expected value of future wages until the next move[50] to a worker now on the frontier line at date t is

$$v_1 = e^{g t} \cdot \int_0^\infty e^{-(\rho+\sigma)a}(\alpha(q_0 + a)(x_0 \cdot e^{-\sigma a})^{\alpha-1})da.$$

(ρ still denotes the individual rate of time preference.)

The expected value of future wages until the next move to a worker now on a product line of age Δ at date t is

$$v_1(\Delta) = e^{g(t-\Delta)} \cdot \int_\Delta^\infty e^{-(\rho+\sigma)(a-\Delta)}(\alpha(q_0 + a)(x_0 \cdot e^{-\sigma a})^{\alpha-1})da.$$

The ratio of these two expected present values is the relative value of staying on the old technology

$$v(\Delta) = \frac{v_1(\Delta)}{v_1} = \frac{(q_0 + \Delta)(\rho + \sigma\alpha) + 1}{q_0(\rho + \sigma\alpha) + 1} e^{-\Delta(g-\sigma(1-\alpha))}.$$

Using this formula, we can divide the parameter space into three regions, corresponding to three different cases.

---

49. The initial allocation of workers to lines is assumed to be purely random.

50. That is until the worker has the opportunity of moving to the leading edge.

Case 1

$$g > \sigma(1 - \alpha) + \frac{\rho + \sigma\alpha}{q_0(\rho + \sigma\alpha) + 1}.$$

In that case, $v(\Delta)$ is monotonically decreasing with Δ, which means that lifetime earnings will also decrease monotonically with age. Furthermore, *the higher the growth rate, the more unequal the lifetime earnings of workers across different lines:* indeed the ratio $v(\Delta)$ decreases faster with Δ as g increases. Violante's conjecture is thus automatically validated in that case.

However, the relationship between growth and (lifetime earnings) inequality becomes somewhat more involved when

$$g < \sigma(1 - \alpha) + \frac{\rho + \sigma\alpha}{q_0(\rho + \sigma\alpha) + 1}.$$

Case 2

$$g < \sigma(1 - \alpha).$$

In this case the relative value $v(\Delta)$ of staying on a line of age Δ, conditional on *all* upgraded workers systematically relocating to newer vintages, will become monotonically *increasing* in Δ, which in turn is a contradiction: indeed, why would upgraded workers decide to move to newer vintages if doing so leads to a lower expected value of future wages? (We implicitly assume that upgraded workers always have the right *not* to relocate to newer vintages.) As it turns out, the equilibrium will involve having only a fraction of upgraded workers relocate to newer lines, in such a way that workers will end up being indifferent between relocating to *any* line: this in turn will result in *complete equality of lifetime earnings across different lines.*

To see this in slightly greater detail, let us reason by contradiction and suppose that there is some line X to which nobody wishes to relocate (because the lifetime wage on that line is lower than on other lines). Then, the fact that some workers are constantly relocating to the newest lines (this must be true because the marginal productivity of labor on new lines goes to infinity when $x_0 \to 0$) means that the relative value of staying on line X is constantly increasing relative to the value of relocating to the newest lines (because $g < \sigma^*(1 - \alpha)$ and therefore $v(\Delta)$ increases with Δ). This in turn implies that it cannot be an equilibrium for all workers to avoid line X.

Therefore, when $g < \sigma(1 - \alpha)$ an increase in the rate of growth g will have no effect on earnings inequality because inequality stays equal to zero in that case.

Case 3

$$\sigma(1 - \alpha) < g < \sigma(1 - \alpha) + \frac{\rho + \sigma\alpha}{q_0(\rho + \sigma\alpha) + 1}.$$

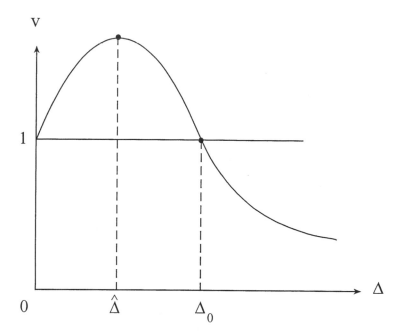

Figure 9.3

In this case, the relative value $v(\Delta)$ of staying on a line of age Δ, conditional on *all* upgraded workers relocating to newer vintages, becomes nonmonotonic, as shown in figure 9.3. (where $\widehat{\Delta}$ satisfies: $g = \sigma(1-\alpha) + \frac{\rho+\sigma\alpha}{(q_0+\widehat{\Delta})(\rho+\sigma\alpha)+1}$).

This again implies that it cannot be an equilibrium for *all* upgraded workers and in particular for those currently working on lines of age $\Delta < \widehat{\Delta}$ to systematically relocate to the leading edge. Instead, *one can show the existence of a non-empty interval of recent vintages* $[0, \overline{\Delta}]$ to which workers relocate (randomly), but no one will voluntarily relocate to an older vintage. The expected present value of earnings on a line of age Δ in equilibrium, EPV(Δ), will then vary with age according to figure 9.4. Indeed, all sufficiently new lines will continue to attract new relocating workers until the expected present value of earnings for workers on those lines has been bid down to equality with newer lines. However, beyond some $\overline{\Delta} \geq \widehat{\Delta}$ nobody will voluntarily relocate to a line of age $\Delta > \overline{\Delta}$ because doing so would depress the relative value of staying on that line even further below the value $v(\Delta)$ indicated in figure 9.3.

Now an increase in the rate of growth g will shift the curve EPV(Δ)$/V_{\max}$ to the left (as shown in figure 9.5). So fewer lines will share in the high earnings $V_{\max}$; furthermore, the expected present value of earnings EPV(Δ) will decrease more rapidly with age Δ for $\Delta > \widehat{\Delta}$. *Overall, an increased growth rate will have the unambiguous effect of increasing earnings inequality.*

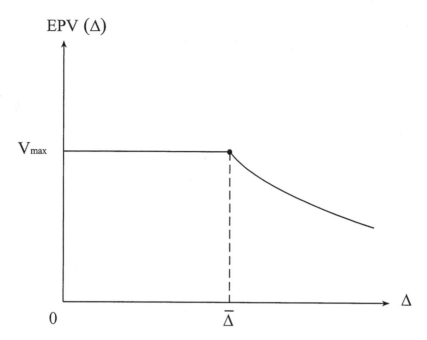

Figure 9.4

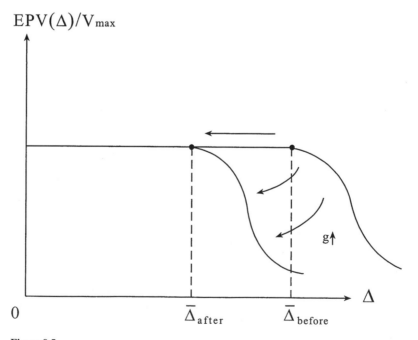

Figure 9.5

9.3   The Political Economy of Technological Change: Vested Interests as a Source of Stagnation

In his celebrated book *The Rise and Decline of Nations*, Olson (1982) addresses the important question of why some societies acquire and adopt new technologies and institutions more rapidly than others. A major source of slowdown in technical progress appears to lie in the existence of *vested interests* among individuals (firm owners, managers, workers, researchers and so on) specialized in the old technologies and who may therefore be tempted to collude and exert political pressure in order to delay or even prevent the arrival of new innovations that might destroy their rents.

Economic historians such as Mokyr (1990, 1992)[51] have indeed argued that the same forces that produced the first industrial revolution in Britain in the mid-nineteenth century came successfully to oppose further technological progress later on, thereby contributing to the industrial slowdown in the late nineteenth century. One can find more examples in past and recent history, where technological change (and therefore economic development) has been stalled or delayed by the introduction of administrative procedures, taxes, trade barriers, and regulations imposed by governments under the political pressure of lobbying groups with vested interests.[52]

The opposition between innovative forces and the vested interests of those working with the old technologies will typically result in cycles with prolonged periods of stagnation followed by innovative phases. The duration of slowdowns will partly depend on the design of political institutions (which may indirectly favor one or the other group) and also on the "balance of power" between innovators and incumbents, measured, for example, by the relative proportions of winners and losers from new innovations and/or by the relative lobbying powers of the two groups. But it will also depend on technological characteristics such as the returns to learning by doing on a technology that is being maintained during several periods in a row, or the knowledge externalities that might exist between two successive innovations.

More formally, consider the following toy model of innovations and vested interests, which is inspired from Krusell and Ríos-Rull (1996) and Jovanovic and Nyarko (1994).

The economy consists of overlapping generations of individuals, each of whom lives for two periods. At any point in time, all individuals, whether old or young, work on the same production technology. For simplicity we assume that

---

51. See Krusell and Ríos-Rull (1996) for more detailed references.

52. See Laffont and Tirole (1993) for a formal analysis of innovations in a regulatory context.

they equally share the returns on that technology.[53] Finally, the intertemporal utility of an individual born at date t is given by

$$u_t = c_t^y + \delta c_{t+1}^0,$$

where c_t^y (resp. c_{t+1}^0) denotes his or her consumption when young (resp. when old), and $\delta \leq 1$ is the discount factor. Thus, at date $(t+1)$, the present utility of the same individual will simply be equal to c_{t+1}^0.

The production side of the economy can be described as follows: there is a countably infinite set of technologies indexed by $v = 1, 2, \cdots$. A technology of vintage v produces an output flow equal to

$$(1 - \widetilde{\alpha}) \cdot \gamma^v \quad \text{upon being introduced,}$$

$$\gamma^v \quad \text{after one period of implementation,}$$

where $0 < \widetilde{\alpha} < 1$ and $\gamma > 1$.

We thus assume the existence of *learning by doing* on any given technology. Finally, to capture the possibility of a positive spillover between learning by doing on a previous technology and learning by doing on the current technology,[54] we assume that

$$\widetilde{\alpha} = \begin{cases} \alpha' & \text{if learning by doing took place on the previous technology,} \\ \alpha & \text{otherwise,} \end{cases}$$

where $\alpha' < \alpha$. That is, less learning by doing is required on the current technology if more experience has been accumulated on the previous technology. We shall henceforth assume that

$$(1 - \alpha)\gamma < 1 < (1 - \alpha')\gamma. \tag{A1}$$

A *strategy* for each individual will consist of a mapping from history (summarized by whether or not an innovation occurred last period) into the decision whether or not to vote in favor of innovating *this* period. A strategy can thus be represented by a pair $\binom{a}{b}$, where $a \in \{0, 1\}$ denotes the individual's decision this

---

53. One interpretation is that the output is a public good, which therefore is equally accessible to the old and the young: $y_t = A_t = c_t^y = c_t^0$, where c_t^y (resp c_t^0) denotes the consumption of a young (resp. old) individual at date t. An alternative interpretation is that the old and the young provide different labor inputs into a symmetric Cobb-Douglas technology. We leave it as an exercise to the reader to extend the analysis in this section to the case of more general Cobb-Douglas technologies of the form

$$y_t = A_t (\ell_t^y)^\alpha (\ell_t^0)^{1-\alpha},$$

where ℓ_t^y and ℓ_t^0 denote the (inelastic) labor supplies by the young and the old at date t, and A_t is the productivity parameter corresponding to the current technology.   □

54. See Jovanovic and Nyarko (1994).

period if *no* innovation has occurred last period, and $b \in \{0, 1\}$ is the agent's decision this period if an innovation *did* occur last period; a or b being equal to 0 corresponds to a vote *against* innovating this period, and a or b being equal to 1 corresponds to a vote *in favor* of innovating this period.

The final decision whether or not to innovate this period will be determined by *majority voting* and therefore will depend on the relative proportions of old and young individuals in the population. (To the extent that the only source of heterogeneity in this model is age, there is no loss of insight in restricting attention to symmetric strategy profiles where all young [resp. old] agents choose the same strategy $\binom{a^y}{b^y}$ [resp. $\binom{a^0}{b^0}$]).

Concentrating on *stationary* subgame-perfect (or rational-expectations) equilibria where $\binom{a^y}{b^y}$ and $\binom{a^0}{b^0}$ are *time-invariant*, one can compare the equilibrium outcomes $\binom{A^y}{B^y}$ and $\binom{A^0}{B^0}$ when the young and the old respectively win the majority vote. Given that new innovations require some time (namely, one period) before becoming fully operational, one can reasonably expect that technological stagnation is more likely to occur when the political process is controlled by the old, that is, when the old command a majority of votes.

More formally, suppose first that, because of a *negative* rate of population growth, the old outnumber the young and therefore determine the final technological outcome $\binom{A}{B}$. Then, one can easily show that $\binom{A=1}{B=0}$ is the unique equilibrium outcome.

To see this, suppose that the incumbent technology is currently of vintage v and consider the voting decision of an old individual when *no* innovation has occurred last period. His or her utility, which is nothing but his or her current consumption c_t^0, will be equal to $\gamma^{v+1}(1 - \alpha')$ if a new innovation is to be adopted this period and to γ^v otherwise. The corresponding utilities will be $\gamma^{v+1}(1 - \alpha)$ and γ^v when an innovation *did* occur last period.

Now the assumption A1 immediately implies that the old will oppose a new innovation in the current period whenever the previous innovation occurred last period, whereas they will vote for a new innovation if the previous innovation occurred before last period and therefore will exert positive learning externalities on the new technology. This, in turn, establishes our claim that the cycle $\binom{A=1}{B=0}$, which involves periods of stagnation being followed by periods of technological change, is the unique equilibrium outcome when the old control the political process.

Let us now analyze what happens when, because of a *positive* rate of population growth, the young are in control of the political process. Under suitable conditions on the parameters $(\gamma, \alpha, \alpha')$, permanent innovation $\binom{A=1}{B=1}$ can be shown to be the unique equilibrium outcome in that case. More precisely, one can prove:

Proposition 9.1 If assumption A1 holds but with α remaining sufficiently small, then $\binom{1}{1}$ is the unique equilibrium outcome when the young decide, whereas $\binom{1}{0}$ is the unique equilibrium outcome when the old decide. In particular, although stagnation phases occur periodically in the former case, they can never occur in the latter case.

This proposition, which is proved in the appendix, vindicates Olson's view that the periodic occurrence of technological slowdowns and economic stagnation may entirely result from the political opposition between vested interests and those who benefit from new innovations.

We leave it to the reader to analyze the case where there are *no* learning externalities across successive innovations (that is, where $\alpha' = \alpha$).[55] In that case, insofar as $\gamma(1 - \alpha) < 1$, the economy will end up being locked into permanent stagnation $\binom{0}{0}$ when the old control the political process.

Conversely, this will never happen when the young are in control and the following condition is satisfied:[56]

$$\underbrace{(1 - \alpha)\gamma - 1}_{\substack{\text{short-term loss due to}\\\text{foregone learning by doing}}} + \underbrace{\delta(\gamma - 1)}_{\substack{\text{long-term gain from}\\\text{technological innovation}}} > 0 \tag{9.24}$$

This simple framework can easily be extended in several interesting directions. One of them would consist in adding other dimensions of heterogeneity between the old and the young: for example, by assuming that the old have accumulated specific human capital that allows them to appropriate a larger fraction of the returns on old technologies; or by assuming that the young have a comparative advantage in learning about new technologies (i.e., $\alpha^0 > \alpha^y$). Any of these two assumptions would naturally reinforce the result that stagnation periods are more likely to occur when the old are in control of the political process. Another extension, suggested to us by N. Crafts, would be to introduce uncertainty and risk into the analysis, and then link technological stagnation to the notion of "status-quo bias."

9.4   Summary

In this chapter we analyzed the relationship between distribution and growth from two directions: the effect of inequality on growth and *vice versa*. In the

---

55. See Chapter 9, problem 6.

56. To see this, let us reason by contradiction and suppose that $\binom{0}{0}$ is an equilibrium outcome when the young are pivotal. Then, correctly anticipating that no innovation will occur next period, the young must decide between innovating this period, which yields an intertemporal utility equal to $(1 - \alpha)\gamma^{v+1} + \delta\gamma^{v+1}$; and not innovating this period, which yields an intertemporal utility equal to $\gamma^v + \delta\gamma^v$. The young will then vote in favor of innovating this period whenever condition (9.24) is satisfied. $\square$

first case we were particularly interested to see if government redistribution is harmful for the growth rate.

It is usually assumed that government policies to redistribute income or wealth from the rich to the poor will lead to inefficiency, because incentives to earn money will be reduced if it is known that some of it is to be taken away in tax. In traditional models, inefficiency would reduce the level of output, but not necessarily the growth rate. But where the growth rate is endogenous, inefficiency will also tend to reduce the growth rate, either because less effort will be devoted to research or because lower levels of output depress learning by doing.

However, this conclusion turns out to depend heavily on the implicit assumption that capital markets are perfect. Indeed, the problem faced by the poor is that they have very little capital. This means that the marginal return to capital for poor workers will be high, so it would be optimal for the rich to lend some capital to the poor, in as much as the marginal return of capital to poor workers is higher than for rich workers. In practice, however, the poor will be unable to borrow due to credit rationing and a lack of collateral. If the government redistributes capital, output will rise because it would be effecting the same transfer of capital that would obtain in a perfectly operating credit market. Note that redistribution here increases efficiency as well as equity. If there were learning-by-doing effects, raising the level of output would improve the growth rate as well. We call this effect "opportunity creation."

Now, what about the incentive effects of redistribution: are they systematically negative, as is commonly argued in the existing literature?

We have already considered the possibility that market failure will make it hard for the poor to borrow. But even if they can borrow, the terms of their loan will mean that many of the results of their hard work will accrue to the lender (through interest and the like). So lending to the poor reduces their incentives; if we gave resources instead of lending them, then poor workers would get more of the benefits from working hard, which would encourage them to work harder. Thus the reduced incentives to the rich must be weighed against increased incentives to the poor, and it often happens that a properly designed redistribution policy toward borrowers will enhance *aggregate* incentives.

So far we have assumed that the poor and rich work in isolation, but, in fact, production is an essentially cooperative process: workers almost invariably work in firms or other social organizations. This is because such organizations raise each individual worker's productivity. But working in organizations also encourages shirking, because workers will tend to free-ride on others' efforts. Although this problem can be overcome in several ways (monitoring, and the like), distributional considerations should also come into play. Under a highly unequal distribution poor workers may have visibly very little capital to contribute, and so their payoff will be low, regardless of their effort. Redistribution so that the payoffs are more equally shared will increase the incentives of the poor and raise output.

Having investigated how the distribution of wealth affects the growth rate, we then asked how the growth rate may affect the distribution of income. A pioneering contribution in this field was by Kuznets, who found that inequality at first grew and then declined again as output increased. More recent studies, however, have shown a further increase in inequality, suggesting that inequality may change in a cyclical fashion. One reason for this is increases in the wages of skilled workers relative to unskilled workers. The relative wage will depend on what the two sorts of workers are needed for.

One possibility is that skilled workers are needed to develop new intermediate goods after a general purpose technology has been invented (as already discussed in Chapter 8). Immediately after the arrival of a GPT, the demand for skilled workers will be high, and they will command a high premium over unskilled workers: inequality will increase. As the scope for development declines, demand for skilled workers and hence the wage premium will fall, reducing inequality. This leads to a cyclical pattern in inequality, as the evidence suggests.

However, this explanation does not exhaust the range of effects that we observe on the wage premium. One concern is that the invention of better machinery (e.g., robots) means that there is an inherent tendency for unskilled workers to be replaced over time. Skilled workers cannot be replaced (yet!) because they are needed to make the innovations that lead to the better machinery. We call this phenomenon "skill bias." With the demand for skilled workers constant and the demand for unskilled workers falling, the wage premium could potentially increase for ever (as the wages for unskilled workers would fall to zero). The reason that this does not occur is that the choice to be skilled or unskilled is itself partly endogenous, so the number of skilled workers will clearly react to any wage premium for such workers.

A further reason for rising inequality could be due to changes in organizational structure. At the moment we observe a simplification in the hierarchies of many firms, with increasing decentralization. This may arise from the greater ease of communication between workers due to technical change in computers and the like. The workers most able to take advantage of these new structures will be skilled workers, because they are more adaptable and able to learn new techniques. Thus skilled workers will command a higher wage premium than hitherto, because they are better fitted to the new style of workplace organization.

We have just described a plausible mechanism whereby technical change increases the wage differential between skilled and unskilled workers. Now, one should recall that workers differ in skills not only because of differences in school qualifications, but also because of differences in work experience. Workers have considerable experience (due to learning by doing) in production techniques that are relatively inefficient. It may not be worthwhile for these workers to move to newer jobs because they would have to learn a new trade from scratch. Even if you can teach an old dog new tricks, it is not necessarily worth the time and effort to do so! Thus, if innovation increases, workers locked into older techniques will lag farther behind workers in more modern techniques and will be paid relatively less accordingly. Of course, if inequality became too great, workers on old lines would bestir themselves to move to new jobs, but this effect could only partially offset the increased inequality, in as much as there must be a net increase in inequality to ensure greater mobility.

These two mechanisms, respectively based on skill-biased technical change and on vintage effects, find support in the recent empirical literature on the evolution of wage inequality *across* and *within* educational cohorts.

Because a natural consequence of growth arising from creative destruction is that not everyone gains from the arrival of innovations, many people will have an incentive to use what ever means they have, perhaps political, to resist change. We refer to such groups as "vested interests". Vested interests will tend to cause stagnation as they stifle innovation. Olson suggested that external shocks, such as wars, could periodically break the power of vested interests. However, it is *not* necessary to have external shocks for vested interests to be undermined. As the possibility of learning by doing is exhausted in existing technologies, the potential gain from an innovation is increased. So long as some of the benefits from such an innovation would be felt by some of the vested interests, the latter's determination to resist change will be eroded, and eventually they will countenance a new innovation. The frequency of innovation will thus vary inversely with the scope for learning by doing on existing technologies as well as the relative power of the vested interests vis-à-vis innovators.

Appendix: Proof of Proposition 9.1

We want to show that permanent innovation $\binom{1}{1}$ is the unique equilibrium outcome where (i) α is sufficiently small while still satisfying assumption A1 and (ii) the young control the political process.

So, let us assume that $\gamma(1 - \alpha) = 1$, and then prove proposition 9.1 in three steps, namely,

Step 1: $\binom{1}{1} = \binom{a^y}{b^y}$ is an equilibrium.

Step 2: $\binom{0}{0} = \binom{a^y}{b^y}$ is not an equilibrium.

Step 3: $\binom{1}{0} = \binom{a^y}{b^y}$ is not an equilibrium.

Let us now establish these three steps in turn:

Step 1 $\binom{1}{1}$ is an equilibrium.

Proof   Take any period t and suppose first that no innovation did occur in the previous period. Then, correctly anticipating a new innovation next period, the young will vote in favor of innovating this period (that is, will choose $a^y = 1$) if and only if[57]

$$(1 - \alpha')\gamma^{v+1} + \delta(1 - \alpha)\gamma^{v+2} \geq \gamma^v + \delta(1 - \alpha')\gamma^{v+1}$$

or equivalently

$$(1 - \alpha')\gamma - 1 + \delta((1 - \alpha)\gamma^2 - (1 - \alpha')\gamma) \geq 0,$$

which is indeed the case when $(1 - \alpha')\gamma > 1 = (1 - \alpha)\gamma$, because $\delta < 1$.

Now suppose that an innovation did occur last period. Then, again correctly anticipating a new innovation next period, the young will choose $b^y = 1$ if and only if

$$(1 - \alpha)\gamma^{v+1} + \delta(1 - \alpha)\gamma^{v+2} \geq \gamma^v + \delta(1 - \alpha')\gamma^{v+1},$$

or equivalently

$$(1 - \alpha)\gamma - 1 + \delta[(1 - \alpha)\gamma^2 - (1 - \alpha')\gamma] \geq 0$$

which is indeed satisfied when $(1 - \alpha)\gamma = 1$. This establishes Step 1.   □

Step 2 $\binom{0}{0}$ is not an equilibrium

Proof   By contradiction, suppose that $\binom{0}{0}$ is an equilibrium. Then take any period t and suppose that no innovation has occurred last period. Then, correctly anticipating that no new innovation will occur next period, the young would indeed choose not to innovate this period (i.e., $a^y = 0$) if and only if

$$\gamma^v + \delta\gamma^v \geq (1 - \alpha')\gamma^{v+1} + \delta\gamma^{v+1},$$

or equivalently

$$1 - (1 - \alpha')\gamma + \delta(1 - \gamma) \geq 0,$$

which is obviously *not* the case when $(1 - \alpha')\gamma > 1$. This establishes Step 2.   □

Step 3 $\binom{1}{0}$ is not an equilibrium

Proof   Again, by contradiction, suppose that $\binom{1}{0}$ is an equilibrium. If an innovation *did* occur last period, then, correctly anticipating that a new innovation

---

57. The LHS (resp. RHS) of the following inequality is the intertemporal utility of the young if an innovation (resp. no innovation) occurs this period, given the expectation that a new innovation will be implemented anyway in the next period.

will occur next period *if and only if* no innovation occurs this period, the young will choose not to innovate this period if and only if:

$$(1 - \alpha)\gamma^{v+1} + \delta\gamma^{v+1} \leq \gamma^v + \delta(1 - \alpha')\gamma^{v+1},$$

or equivalently

$$(1 - \alpha)\gamma - 1 + \delta\gamma[1 - (1 - \alpha')] \leq 0,$$

which is obviously *not* the case when

$$(1 - \alpha')\gamma > 1 = (1 - \alpha)\gamma.$$

That is, the young will choose to innovate this period even when an innovation did occur last period. This, in turn, establishes Step 3. □

To complete the proof of proposition 9.1, it now suffices to show that $\binom{0}{1}$ cannot be an equilibrium either, but this last step is trivial: because of learning by doing spillovers ($\alpha' < \alpha$), it cannot be the case that the young will choose *both* to innovate this period whenever an innovation already occurred last period, *and* not to innovate this period whenever no innovation occurred last period. The former is indeed equivalent to

$$\gamma^v + \delta\gamma^v \leq (1 - \alpha)\gamma^{v+1} + \delta(1 - \alpha)\gamma^{v+2},$$

whereas the latter is equivalent to

$$\gamma^v + \delta\gamma^v \geq (1 - \alpha')\gamma^{v+1} + \delta(1 - \alpha)\gamma^{v+2}.$$

These two inequalities are obviously incompatible because $\alpha' < \alpha$.

This completes the proof of proposition 9.1. □

Problems

Difficulty of Problems:

No star: normal

One star: difficult

Two stars: very difficult

1. The incentive effect and intergenerational redistribution

Consider the model in section 9.1.2. Suppose that the redistribution scheme takes the following form: the output of the old (i.e., second-period output) is taxed at a proportional rate τ, and the revenue is used to subsidize the young that have an initial endowment less than φA_t. They all receive the same subsidy, $s A_t$.

a. Set up the individual's maximization problem and find the optimal effort for agents with initial endowment smaller than φA_t. What is the optimal effort for those with endowment greater than φA_t?

b. Write the government's intergenerational budget constraint and obtain the subsidy rate, s, for any given tax rate, τ.

c. For which values of the tax rate is the effort of those with endowment less than φA_t increased?

d. Under which circumstances will the introduction of a subsidy increase the aggregate effort level?

2. Complementarities in production and skill-biased technical change (based on Krusell, Ohanian, Ríos-Rull, and Violante 1996)

In the chapter we saw that technical change can be skill-biased. Here we examine an alternative reason why this may occur. It is assumed that the degree of complementarity between equipment and skilled labor is different from that between equipment and unskilled labor. As a result, changes in the quantity or quality of equipment affect the demand for the two types of labor differently. We abstract from the underlying research sector, which could be modeled in the same way as in Chapter 2, and focus only on how changes in the quantity/quality of intermediate goods can affect relative wages.

Consider an economy with two production sectors: one produces consumption goods, and the other produces producers' equipment or capital goods. Output is given by

$$c_t = A_t f(q_t k_t^c, u_t^c, s_t^c), \tag{9.25}$$

$$x_t = B A_t f(q_t k_t^x, u_t^x, s_t^x). \tag{9.26}$$

c_t is the consumption good, x_t is equipment, k_t denotes the capital input, u_t is unskilled labor, s_t is skilled labor, and the superscripts indicate the sector in which these factors are employed. The production function, $f(.)$, is common to both sectors. There is a common technology factor, A_t, and a capital-specific one, q_t. The latter can be understood as a measure of the quality of this input. Total output, measured in consumption units, is then

$$c_t + \frac{x_t}{B} = A_t f(q_t k_t, u_t, s_t). \tag{9.27}$$

The production function takes the following form:

$$f(q_t k_t, u_t, s_t) = \left[\mu u_t^\sigma + (1 - \mu)\left(\lambda(q_t k_t)^\rho + (1 - \lambda)s_t^\rho\right)^{\sigma/\rho}\right]^{1/\sigma}, \tag{9.28}$$

where $\sigma, \rho \in (-\infty, 1)$. This is a "nested CES" production technology, which allows for a different degree of complementarity between the two types of labor and equipment.

a. Discuss the complementarities between the different factors in this production function. What happens when $\sigma = \rho = 0$? And when $\sigma > \rho$?

b. Obtain the skill premium, that is, the ratio of skilled to unskilled wages, for given amounts of all inputs. How does it depend on the quality and quantity of equipment capital?

c. Take logarithms of your expression for the skill premium and find its rate of growth as a function of the growth rates of all inputs. Is technical change skill-biased?

⋆ **3. The factor distribution of income and economic growth (based on Alesina and Rodrik 1994)**

This problem presents a model inspired in Kaldor (1956). The main idea is that the saving behavior of capitalists and workers is different, and hence the pattern of ownership of the means of production can affect economic growth.

Consider an economy with two types of individuals, workers and capitalists. Workers supply inelastically one unit of labor, do not save, and consume all their income. The capitalists own all the stock of capital, do not work, consume and save. Output depends on public expenditure on a public good, γ, as well as on labor and capital (see Barro 1990 and Chapter 1, problem 5). That is,

$$y = Ak^\alpha \gamma^{1-\alpha} l^{1-\alpha} \quad \text{where } 0 < \alpha < 1. \tag{9.29}$$

The labor endowment is constant and normalized to unity.

Public expenditure is financed by a tax on the return to capital, τ. The government cannot borrow, hence it must always have a balanced budget. Tax revenues can be spent on transfers to workers as well as on the provision of γ. Let $\lambda \in [0, 1]$ be the share of government revenue which is transferred to workers. Transfers are then $\lambda \tau k$, and the budget constraint implies

$$\gamma = (1 - \lambda)\tau k. \tag{9.30}$$

The representative capitalist faces the following problem:

$$\max U^k = \int_0^\infty \log c^k e^{-\rho t}\, dt \tag{9.31}$$

s.t. $\dot{k} = (r - \tau)k - c^k,$

where c^k is the capitalist's consumption level. Similarly, denote a worker's consumption by c^l. Her consumption decision problem is then given by

$$\max U^l = \int_0^\infty \log c^l e^{-\rho t} \, dt \tag{9.32}$$

$$\text{s.t.} \quad c^l = w + \lambda \tau k,$$

where w is the wage, which is equal to the marginal product of labor.

The government chooses λ and τ at each point in time to maximize the weighted average of the welfare of the two groups. Let $\beta \in [0, 1]$ be the weight given to workers' welfare, and $(1 - \beta)$ that of capitalists' welfare.

a. Find the dynamic equation for the capitalists' consumption. What are the steady-state rates of growth of capital and of workers' consumption? Express the steady-state rate of growth of the economy in terms of model parameters and the policy instruments only.

b. How does the steady-state rate of growth depend on λ and τ? Find the values of these two policy instruments that maximize the steady-state growth rate.

c. Suppose the government maximizes the welfare of the capitalists (i.e., $\beta = 0$). Which values of λ and τ will it choose?

d. Suppose the government cares also about the welfare of the workers (i.e., $\beta > 0$). Obtain the first-order conditions for welfare maximization. Examine them to see that whenever workers' welfare enters the welfare function, the growth rate is not maximized. Show that if $\beta \geq [(1 - \alpha)A]^{1/\alpha}/\rho$, then the optimal transfers value is $\lambda^{**} = 1 - [(1 - \alpha)A]^{1/\alpha}/\beta\rho$, and the optimal tax rate is $\tau^{**} = \beta\rho$. What are the optimal values of λ and τ if the above restriction is not satisfied?

★ **4. Majority voting, the distribution of factor endowments and economic growth (based on Alesina and Rodrik 1994)**

Consider the same economy as in the previous problem, except that now all individuals own some labor and some capital, although in different proportions. Let l^i and k^i denote the amount of labor and of capital owned by agent i. Let k denote the aggregate stock of capital. Then, her relative factor endowment is given by

$$\sigma^i = \frac{l^i}{k^i/k} \qquad \sigma^i \in [0, \infty).$$

The tax system is the same as in problem 3, except that there are no transfers ($\lambda = 0$). The instantaneous-utility function is logarithmic for all agents. All agents save and borrow at the risk-free interest rate.

a. Show that the rate of growth of individual consumption is the same for all agents.

b. Which is the tax rate that maximizes the growth rate?

c. Which is the tax rate preferred by individual i?

d. If the tax rate is chosen by majority voting, is there a relationship between inequality and growth?

⋆ **5. R&D and the distribution of firm sizes (based on García-Peñalosa 1996a)**

This problem examines the effect of market concentration, measured by the Herfindahl index, on the expected rate of technical change. Although it is concerned with the relationship between market concentration and growth, examined in Chapter 6, concentration depends on the distribution of firm sizes in the market, and hence it uses the techniques that have been presented in this chapter.

Consider an economy where the source of growth are intentional R & D investments done by firms to increase the number of "designs" for capital goods, denoted D_t. Let N be the given number of firms in an industry. The firm is an integrated unit: it does research, produces capital goods, and produces the single final good. At any time, it is producing using all its existing designs. The discounted value of an innovation is constant and equal to P. Heterogenous firms are indexed by i. In period t, firm i has size D_{it}. Hence its discounted value is $P D_{it}$, and its total profits at time t are $\pi_{it} = P D_{it}/r$.

Firm size is distributed in the interval $[0,\infty)$, with mean D_t. Define δ_{it} as the ratio of a firm's designs to the average number of designs in its industry, D_{it}/D_t. This firm-size variable is distributed in $[0,N]$, with mean 1 and density $\phi_t(\delta_{it})$. Firms also differ in the quality of the project that they undertake at time t, q_{it}. Quality is independent of the firm's size. Assume that q is uniformly distributed in $[0,1]$. All firms have the same probability of success of their project, λ. The change in the number of designs exhibits diminishing returns in the number of researchers that the firm employs, h_{it}. It is given by

$$D_{it} - D_{it-1} = \log(q_{it}h_{it})D_{t-1} \qquad \forall q_{it}h_{it} \geq 1.$$

When the project fails or the quality is so low that $q_{it}h_{it} < 1$, the change in the number of designs is zero. There is a perfectly elastic supply of educated workers, that command a given wage w_t. Firms are risk-neutral. They can lend funds (their profits) at the given risk-free interest rate, r. When they borrow to finance a risky research project they are charged a higher rate, R. Assume that $\lambda (1 + R) > (1 + r)$.

a. Show that the number of researchers employed by a firm that does not need to borrow is independent of the firm's quality and is the same for all firms. Show that any firm of size $\delta_i \geq \delta_1 \equiv \lambda r/(1 + r)$ will not borrow. What is the level of employment for the firms that borrow?

b. Firms invest only if their quality is high enough to ensure a nonnegative expected return. Find the constant minimum quality, q_0, that a firm larger than δ_1 needs in order to invest. Show that the minimum quality required by a firm $\delta_i > \delta_1$ to invest is given by

$$q_m(\delta_i) = q_0 \lambda \frac{1+R}{1+r} Exp\left[-\left(\lambda \frac{1+R}{1+r} - 1\right)\frac{\delta_i}{\delta_1}\right].$$

c. What is the shape of the minimum quality function? Is it continuous?

d. The Herfindahl index is defined as the sum of the squares of the market share of each firm, that is, $H = \sum_{i=1}^{N} s_i^2 di = N \int_0^N s(\delta)^2 d\Phi(\delta)$. Show that, in this model, a mean-preserving spread (MPS) of the distribution of firm sizes increases the Herfindahl index.

e. Integrate over q and δ to find the (expected) average quality of research. How is it affected by a mean-preserving spread of the distribution of firm sizes? Find the expected rate of growth of the stock of knowledge (use the fact that $\int \log x\, dx = x(\log x - 1)$), and show that an MPS will reduce it. Is there a relationship between market concentration and technical change?

6. Vested interests with no learning externalities

Consider the model presented in section 9.3, with the difference that now there are no learning externalities across successive innovations. That is, $\alpha = \alpha'$. Show that there are two possible equilibria, $\binom{0}{0}$ and $\binom{1}{1}$. How does the outcome depend on parameter values?

10 Education

In his pioneering contribution to the endogenous-growth literature, Lucas (1988) emphasizes human capital accumulation as an alternative[1] source of sustained growth. More specifically, Lucas distinguishes between two main sources of human capital accumulation (or skill acquisition), namely *education* and *learning by doing*. We have already discussed learning by doing in Chapter 6, and thus, even though the ideas and conceptual framework developed in that chapter will prove to be quite useful when analyzing the relationship between education, learning by doing, and wage inequality, our primary focus in this chapter will be on education policy and its relations to growth.

Although there is always a danger in trying to map a very broad literature into a small set of "categories" or "classes," we find it quite useful to distinguish between two basic frameworks in which to model and analyze the relationship between education and growth. The first approach, initiated by Lucas (1988) and inspired by Becker's (1964) theory of human capital, is based on the idea that growth is primarily driven by the *accumulation* of human capital, so that differences in growth rates across countries are mainly attributable to differences in the *rates* at which those countries accumulate human capital over time. The second approach, which goes back to the seminal contribution by Nelson and Phelps (1966) and which has been recently revived by the Schumpeterian growth literature, describes growth as being driven by the *stock* of human capital, which in turn affects a country's ability to innovate or catch up with more advanced countries. Differences in growth rates across countries are then primarily due to differences in human-capital stocks and thereby in those countries' abilities to generate technical progress.

As we will argue in the next two sections, both the "Lucas approach," where growth is primarily driven by the *accumulation* of human capital (section 10.1), and the "Nelson-Phelps approach," where growth is primarily driven by the *stock* of human capital (section 10.2), appear to deliver interesting insights as to the growth effects of various educational policies. Thus, whereas such questions as (i) should education be funded locally (privately) or nationally and (ii) can education policies promote economic development, can be addressed using a suitable variant of the Lucas model, other questions such as (i)′ should governments emphasize primary/secondary or higher education, (ii)′ should governments subsidize formal education versus on-the-job-training and apprenticeship, (iii)′ should educational policy be elitist or broadly based, (iv)′ how does education affect the relationship between growth and inequality, these last questions gain substance when addressed in the context of a model with endogenous technical change, following a Nelson-Phelps approach.

Most interesting among the existing empirical studies of the education/ growth relationship, are, we believe: the growth regressions in Barro and

---

1. Alternative to technological change.

Sala-i-Martín (1995), and the empirical criticism of Mankiw, Romer, and Weil (1992) by Benhabib and Spiegel (1994). Let us briefly summarize these two contributions, each of which opens up new research avenues for theoretical and further empirical work on education and growth.

The growth regression results are clearly spelled out in Barro and Sala-i-Martín (1995, chap. 13). Based on a large sample of countries during the time period 1965–1985, the authors have regressed the average growth rate on several macroeconomic variables, including educational attainment, and public spending on education as a fraction of GDP. Their main findings are: (i) that educational attainment (measured by average years of schooling) is significantly correlated with subsequent growth (with a correlation coefficient at around 0.05), although if we decompose the aggregate measure of educational attainment the impact of primary education remains largely insignificant; (ii) that public spending on education also has a significantly positive effect on growth: a 1.5 percent increase of the ratio of public education spending to GDP during the period 1965–1975 would have raised the average growth rate during the same period by .3 percent per year.

More recently, Benhabib and Spiegel (1994) have tried to "decompose" the contribution of human capital and education to growth. Whereas past educational attainment (as a measure of the current stock of human capital) remains essentially *uncorrelated* with growth if one uses an augmented Solow model à la Mankiw, Romer, and Weil (1992) where human capital is nothing but an ordinary input in the aggregate production function, the effect of (past) educational attainment levels on current growth rates becomes *significant* if one follows Nelson and Phelps (1966) in assuming: (i) that growth is positively affected by the rate of technological innovations and also by the rate of diffusion or adoption of existing innovations; (ii) that the *stock* of human capital affects both of these rates. Indeed, although the correlation coefficient is essentially zero (or even negative) in the former case, it becomes positively significant (at around .12) in the latter case.

The Benhabib-Spiegel analysis is interesting, not only because it provides additional support to the endogenous-growth approach (and in particular to the innovation-based models developed in the previous chapters), but also because it suggests that the divergence in growth rates across countries could be due not so much to differences in the *rates of accumulation* of human capital, as suggested by Lucas (1988), as to differences in the *stocks* of human capital, which in turn will affect the various countries' ability to innovate and/or catch up with more advanced countries' technologies.

The chapter is organized as follows. Section 10.1 develops the Lucas approach, which includes the analysis of threshold effects and development traps following Azariadis and Drazen (1990), and of the relationship between the financing of education, social stratification, and short versus long-term growth following Benabou (1996b). Section 10.2 reformulates the Nelson-Phelps approach in terms of the Schumpeterian models of Chapters 2 and 6. The emphasis is first, on the strategic complementarity between human capital and R&D investments and the resulting scope for multiple equilibria and low development traps; and second on the contrasted effects of various educational policies on steady-state growth and also on the evolution of wage inequality across and within educational cohorts. Section 10.3 concludes this chapter with a brief reference to recent empirical and theoretical contributions on the microeconomics of education.

10.1   The Lucas Approach

10.1.1   Basic Equations

Inspired by Becker's (1964) theory of human capital, Lucas (1988) considers an economy populated by (infinitely lived) individuals who choose at each date how to allocate their time between current production and skill acquisition (or schooling), where skill acquisition increases productivity in future periods. Thus, if h denotes the current *human capital* stock of the representative agent, and u denotes the fraction of his or her time currently allocated to production, the two basic equations of the Lucas model are

$$y = k^\beta (uh)^{1-\beta}, \tag{10.1}$$

which describes the way human capital affects current production (k denotes the physical capital stock, which evolves over time according to the same differential equation as in the Solow or Ramsey models, namely $\dot{k} = y - c$, where c is current consumption), and

$$\dot{h} = \delta h (1 - u), \quad \delta > 0, \tag{10.2}$$

which spells out how current schooling time $(1 - u)$ affects the accumulation of human capital.[2] The reader will have certainly noticed the similarity between equation (10.2) and the differential equation that describes the growth of the leading-edge technology parameter A in Chapter 3 (and/or the equation that describes the accumulation of horizontal innovations in the product variety model of Romer 1990a presented in Chapter 1, section 1.8). However, in contrast to the nonrival technological knowledge embodied in innovations, human

---

2. If learning by doing rather than education were the primary source of human capital accumulation, equation (10.2) should be replaced by something like

$$\dot{h} = \delta h u. \tag{10.3}$$

That is, the growth of human capital increases with *production*.

capital acquisition does not necessarily involve externalities (or "spillovers") across individuals of a same generation.[3] Yet, the assumption that human capital accumulation involves constant returns to the existing stock of human capital produces a positive growth rate in steady state equal to

$$g = \delta(1 - u^*),$$

where u^* is the optimal allocation of individuals' time between production and education.[4] Education effort $(1 - u^*)$ can in turn be shown to depend negatively on the rate of time preference ρ and the coefficient of relative risk-aversion σ and positively on the productivity of schooling measured by δ, therefore displaying similar comparative statics properties as the steady-state research investment $\widehat{n}$ derived in Chapter 2.

This paradigmatic model has been extended in various directions. For example, Rebelo (1991) introduces physical capital into the human capital accumulation equation (10.2) while maintaining constant returns of $\dot{h}$ with respect to *human* and *physical* capital stocks. This allows him to analyze the effects of taxation policies on steady-state growth. In particular, whereas an increase in the rate of income tax has no effect on the steady-state growth rate in the Lucas model, it does when physical capital is introduced as an input into human capital accumulation (see Rebelo 1991 and problem set 10.2).

The Lucas model is elegant and simple, but as always this comes at the expense of some realism. For example, equation (10.2) means that an individual's returns to education remains constant over his or her whole lifetime, an assumption that is at odds both with the empirical evidence on education and with Becker's theory of human capital. Becker (1964) indeed suggests that returns to education tend to *decrease* over the lifetime of an individual. One easy way to deal with this objection is to reformulate the Lucas model in the context of an overlapping generations framework where individuals inherit the

---

3. To be precise, Lucas (1988) generalizes (10.1) by allowing for some degree of *contemporaneous* spillovers among workers of the form

$$y = k^\beta (uh)^{1-\beta} (h_a)^\gamma, \tag{10.4}$$

where $h_a = \frac{1}{n} \sum_{i=1}^{n} h_i$ denotes the average human capital stock across individuals. Although assuming $\gamma > 0$ introduces the possibility that laissez-faire growth be socially suboptimal (individuals do not fully internalize human and physical capital spillovers when allocating their time between current production and skill acquisition, and therefore tend to underinvest in the latter), it is not necessary in order to obtain sustained growth (in contrast to the AK model introduced in Chapter 1). What produces sustained growth here is rather the assumption, implicit in equation (10.2), of constant returns to the accumulation of human and physical capital. This production function is examined in problem 10.1.

4. That is, u^* maximizes the representative consumer's intertemporal utility

$$\int_0^\infty \frac{c_t^{1-\sigma}}{1-\sigma} e^{-\rho t} dt$$

subject to: (10.1), (10.2) and $\dot{k} = y - c$. See problem 10.1 for details.

human capital accumulated by their parents.[5] A particularly successful attempt in this direction is the influential contribution by Azariadis and Drazen (1990), which points to the existence of low-development traps in the context of an OLG model with human capital accumulation, and to which we now turn.

10.1.2   Threshold Effects and Low-Development Traps

Consider the following extremely simple OLG model with human accumulation: there is a continuum of overlapping generations families, in which each individual lives for two periods. All individuals born at date t inherit the aggregate human capital accumulated by the previous generation of individuals born at date $t - 1$, that is

$$h^i_{1,t} \equiv h_{1,t} = H_{2,t-1}, \tag{10.5}$$

where

$$H_{2,t-1} = \int h^i_{2,t-1} di.$$

[Subscript "1" (resp. "2") refers to a young (resp. an old) individual]. Thus, if for simplicity we assume that individuals of a same generation are identical and of total mass equal to one (so that total population remains constant equal to two), we have

$$h_{1,t} = h_{2,t-1},$$

where $h_{2,t-1}$ is the human capital accumulated when old by an individual born at date $t - 1$.

Next, we must specify how human capital accumulates during the lifetime of an individual. We shall assume, for all t,

$$h_{2,t} = (1 + \gamma(v_{t-1}) \cdot v^\theta) h_{1,t} \tag{10.6}$$

where v is the fraction of time allocated to education by a young individual born at date t; $\gamma(v_{t-1})$ is a positive number that is nondecreasing in the amount of time v_{t-1} devoted to education by the previous generation, and $\theta < 1$.[6]

The complementary time $1 - v$ is allocated to production activities, and to simplify the argument to the extreme, we will assume that an individual with current human-capital endowment h contributes a marginal product equal to h and therefore earns a wage also equal to h.[7] Therefore, an individual born

5. See d'Autume and Michel (1994) for a systematic analysis of the overlapping generations version of the Lucas model.

6. See Section 10.2.2 for an alternative model with multiple development paths, but that does not rely on intertemporal threshold externalities, that is, in which, $\gamma(v) \equiv \gamma = $ constant.

7. Equivalently, we could assume that all individuals are self-employed, and that the self-employment technology is linear, with s working-time units producing $h \cdot s$ units of output, where h denotes the individual's current human capital endowment.

at date t (with initial skills $h_{1,t}$) will choose how much time v to spend in education so as to maximize his or her intertemporal utility of consumption. Assuming linear preferences, and letting ρ denote the discount factor, the optimal education time v^* solves the maximization program

$$\max_v (1-v)h_{1,t} + \rho h_{2,t}$$

s.t. $h_{2,t} = (1+\gamma v^\theta)h_{1,t}.$ (10.7)

A special case is when γ is a constant. Then, we obtain the unique solution

$$v^* = (\rho\theta\gamma)^{\frac{1}{1-\theta}},$$

which in turn corresponds to a unique steady-state growth path, at rate

$$g^* = \frac{h_{2,t}}{h_{2,t-1}} = 1 + v^{*\theta} = 1 + \gamma(\delta\theta\gamma)^{\frac{\theta}{1-\theta}}.$$

As in the Lucas model, we see that g^* is an increasing function of the productivity of education measured by γ, and a decreasing function of the rate of time preference r (where $\rho = \frac{1}{1+r}$).

However, the more interesting case considered by Azariadis and Drazen (1990) is when the education technology in (10.7) displays positive *threshold externalities*. In particular, suppose that

$$\gamma(v_{t-1}) = \begin{cases} \underline{\gamma} & \text{if } v_{t-1} \leq 0 \\ \overline{\gamma} & \text{if } v_{t-1} > v_0, \end{cases}$$

where $0 < v_0 < 1$ and $\underline{\gamma} << \overline{\gamma}$. Then, if the previous generation has insufficiently invested in education, and therefore $\gamma(v_{t-1}) = \underline{\gamma}$, investing in education tends to become unattractive for the current generation as well, hence the possibility of a low-growth path where all successive generations invest too little in education. This low-growth path or "low-development trap," can naturally coexist with a high-growth path where all generations invest at least v_0 in education and therefore $\gamma(v_{t-1}) \equiv \overline{\gamma}$ for all t.

More precisely, a low-growth steady-state equilibrium will involve the stationary educational attainment level $\underline{v}$, where

$$\underline{v} = \arg\max_v (1-v)h_{1,t} + \rho(1+\underline{\gamma}v^\theta)h_{1,t},$$

that is: $\underline{v} = (\rho\theta\underline{\gamma})^{\frac{1}{1-\theta}}$, with corresponding growth rate

$$\underline{g} = 1 + \underline{\gamma} \cdot \underline{v}^\theta = 1 + \underline{\gamma}(\rho\theta\underline{\gamma})^{\frac{\theta}{1-\theta}}.$$

Similarly, the high-growth equilibrium will involve the educational attainment level $\overline{v}$, where

$$\overline{v} = \arg \max_{v}(1 - v)h_{1,t} + \rho(1 + \overline{\gamma} \cdot v^\theta)h_{1,t},$$

that is: $\overline{v} = (\rho\theta\overline{\gamma})^{\frac{1}{1-\theta}}$, with correspondingly high growth rate

$$\overline{g} = 1 + \overline{\gamma} \cdot \overline{v}^\theta = 1 + \overline{\gamma}(\rho\theta\overline{\gamma})^{\frac{\theta}{1-\theta}}.$$

For these two equilibria to actually coexist, it is necessary and sufficient that $\underline{v} < v_0 < \overline{v}$, which in turn imposes restrictions on the parameters $v_0, \rho, \theta, \underline{\gamma}, \overline{\gamma}$.

In short, the existence of threshold externalities in the education technology can naturally lead to a multiplicity of steady-state growth paths, including a low-development trap where insufficient investment in education in the past discourages further skill acquisition and thereby future growth. Thus Azariadis and Drazen provide a perhaps more natural story than Lucas (1988) for why countries with unequal initial human-capital endowments may keep growing at different rates forever. But they also suggest a role for government intervention in the education sector, namely to avoid low-development traps and thereby promote high sustained growth.[8] Although the main policy prescription that emerges from their model does not go far beyond recommending education subsidies (during at least one period t in order to induce $v_t \geq v_0$), we will see in the next subsection that new interesting insights on the growth effects of education finance and organization come about once we move away from the representative agent assumption and take a more disaggregated view of the process of human-capital accumulation.

10.1.3   Inequality, School Finance, and Growth*

A few recent papers have analyzed how the heterogeneous (or "stratified") access to human capital across individuals of a same generation can affect the dynamics of inequality and growth, depending on the particular system (or organization) of education. A pioneering contribution to this literature is the paper by Glomm and Ravikumar (1992). The main distinguishing features of their model are (1) that human-capital endowments are *unevenly* distributed across individuals born at a same date; (2) that human capital accumulation is governed by a dynamic equation of the form

$$h_{t+1}^i = \theta(1 - u_t)^\beta e_t^\gamma (h_t^i)^\delta, \tag{10.8}$$

---

8. Becker, Murphy, and Tamura (1990) develop a similar model but in which individuals decide also about "fertility," that is, about how many children they wish to have. Assuming that the returns to human capital investments increase with the human capital stock, the authors show the existence of multiple equilibria. One equilibrium corresponds to a "development trap," with a high rate of population growth but low levels and low growth rates of individual human capital. The other equilibrium instead corresponds to a low rate of population growth but also to high levels and rapid growth of human capital per head. The contrast with the Solow-Swan model is interesting: here, the rate of population growth is negatively correlated with the rate of productivity growth.

where h_t^i denotes the human capital accumulated by parents in family i, e_t is a spillover variable that reflects the "quality" of the schooling system, and $(1 - u_t)$ is the amount of time devoted to education upon birth at date t (we were implicitly assuming $\beta = \delta = 1$ and $\gamma = 0$ in the Lucas model considered above earlier); and (3) that the externality factor e_t depends on the way education is being financed.

Thus, for example, if aggregate output is produced from human capital according to a linear one-to-one technology, and if education is public and entirely financed through taxes, then

$$e_t = \tau \cdot \overline{y}_t = \tau \cdot \overline{h}_t,$$

where $\overline{y}_t$ and $\overline{h}_t$ denote respectively the average revenue and average human-capital endowments at date t, and τ denotes the tax rate. In that case, the less endowed individuals will be indirectly subsidized by the more endowed and as a result the heterogeneity in human-capital endowments across families will tend to disappear over time. In particular, when $\gamma + \delta = 1$, equation (10.8) becomes:

$$\frac{h_{t+1}^i}{h_t^i} = \theta \left(\frac{\overline{h}_t}{h_t^i} \right),$$

which makes it clear that the less endowed individuals will experience a higher rate of growth in their human capital.

On the other hand, when education is private and therefore directly financed by the individual's parents, then

$$e_t = y_t^i = h_t^i.$$

In that case, not surprisingly, the initial heterogeneity in human-capital endowments will persist over time.

Now what about the growth paths respectively generated by a public and a private education system? Already considered by Glomm and Ravikumar (1992), this question has been analyzed in greater detail by Benabou (1996b).

Benabou considers an overlapping generations model where, within any given family i, human capital accumulates across generations according to the difference equation

$$h_{t+1}^i = \theta \cdot \epsilon_t^i \underbrace{\left(h_t^i \right)^\alpha}_{\text{parents}} \cdot \underbrace{\left(L_t^i \right)^\beta}_{\substack{\text{community(e.g.} \\ \text{schooling) spillovers}}} \cdot \underbrace{\left(H_t \right)^\gamma}_{\substack{\text{economy-wide} \\ \text{spillover}}} \tag{10.9}$$

with $\alpha + \beta + \gamma = 1$, and where (1) L_t^i and H_t respectively refer to local and global linkages, and are both "CES" outcomes of individual human-capital contributions, namely,

$$L_t^i = \left(\int_0^\infty h^{\frac{\chi-1}{\chi}} d\mu_t^i(h) \right)^{\frac{\chi}{\chi-1}}$$

and

$$H_t = \left(\int_0^\infty h^{\frac{\sigma-1}{\sigma}} d\mu(h) \right)^{\frac{\sigma}{\sigma-1}},$$

where μ_t^i and μ_t denote the distributions of human-capital endowments, respectively within the local community to which family i belongs[9] and economy-wide; and χ and σ are elasticity-of-substitution parameters that measure respectively the cost of heterogeneity within the local community and economy-wide. (2) ε_t^i is a noise (or "ability") parameter that embodies the possibility of *social mobility* from one generation to the next. This random variable is assumed to be log-normally distributed with mean $-\frac{s^2}{2}$ and variance s^2. (3) Initial human-capital endowments across families at date 0 are also assumed to be log-normally distributed with mean m and variance Δ^2.

One extreme case is perfect segregation, with $L_t^i = h_t^i$; the other extreme case is perfect integration, with $L_t^i = L_t$ being the same for all individuals i in the economy. Although segregation will naturally result from an education system that emphasizes local funding, ability tracking, and segregated housing policies, integration will be favored by systems that rely on national or federal funding and promote the development of mixed-income neighborhoods through appropriate housing and taxation policies. Before looking more explicitly at education policies and in particular at the issue of "local" versus "global" funding of education, a preliminary step will be to compare between segregated and integrated human-capital "technologies" from the point of view of their respective growth performances.

Consider first the case of *perfect segregation*, where $L_t^i = h_t^i$ and therefore

$$h_{t+i}^i = \theta \varepsilon_t^i (h_t^i)^{\alpha+\beta} (H_t)^\gamma. \tag{10.10}$$

Because h_0^i and ε_t^i are both log-normally distributed, h_t^i will be also; now, if $\ln h_t^i \sim N(m_t, \Delta_t^2)$, one can show immediately that

a. $\ln H_t = m_t + \Delta_t^2 \frac{\sigma-1}{2\sigma}$;

b. Taking logarithms on both sides of equation (10.10) in order to derive the mean and variance of $\ln h_{t-1}^i$,

---

9. Community composition is taken to be exogenous in this model, although in practice better educated parents will tend to segregate away from the less endowed families, e.g., through spending on real estate or through voting in favor of high entry fees into the neighborhood.

$$(S) \begin{cases} m_{t+1} &=& f - \frac{s^2}{2} + m_t + \gamma \left(\frac{\sigma-1}{\sigma}\right) \frac{\Delta_t^2}{2} \\ \Delta_{t+1}^2 &=& (\alpha+\beta)^2 \Delta_t^2 + s^2, \end{cases}$$

where $f = \ln \theta$.

Using (a) and (b), one can finally compute the rate of productivity growth in the case of perfect segregation. Indeed, let $A_t = \int h \, d\mu_t(h)$ denote the average endowment in human capital at date t. Taking expectations with respect to i on both sides of equation (10.10), we have[10]

$$A_{t+1} = \theta \left(\int_0^\infty h^{\alpha+\beta} d\mu_t(h) \right) H_t^\gamma. \tag{10.11}$$

This, together with (S) and the identity: $m_t = \ln A_t - \frac{\Delta_t^2}{2}$, yields the following expression for the current rate of productivity growth under perfect segregation

$$\ln \frac{A_{t+1}}{A_t} / \text{seg} = f - \mathcal{L}^s \frac{\Delta_t^2}{2}, \tag{G_s}$$

where $\mathcal{L}^s = (\alpha+\beta)(1-\alpha-\beta) + \frac{\gamma}{\sigma}$ is the efficiency loss per unit of heterogeneity in the *segregated* case.

Similarly, in the *integrated* case, where

$$L_t^i = L_t = \left(\int h^{\frac{\chi-1}{\chi}} d\mu_t(h) \right)^{\chi/\chi-1}$$

and

$$h_{t+i}^i = \theta \varepsilon_t^i (h_t^i)^\alpha \cdot L_t^\beta \cdot H_t^\gamma, \tag{10.12}$$

if $\ln h_t^i \sim N(m_t, \Delta_t^2)$, then

a'. $\ln L_t = m_t + \Delta_t^2 \cdot \frac{\chi-1}{2\chi}$

b'. Taking logarithms on both sides of equation (10.12) in order to derive the mean and variance of $\ln h_{t+1}$,

$$(I) \begin{cases} m_{t+1} &=& f - \frac{s^2}{2} + m_t + \left(\gamma \frac{\sigma-1}{\sigma} + \beta \frac{\chi-1}{\chi}\right) \frac{\Delta_t^2}{2} \\ \Delta_{t+1}^2 &=& \alpha^2 \Delta_t^2 + s^2, \end{cases}$$

where again $f = \ln \theta$.

From (a)' and (b)', one can compute the rate of productivity growth in the integrated case. Indeed, taking expectations with respect to i on both sides of equation (10.12) and then using (I) together with the identity $m_t = \ln A_t - \frac{s_t^2}{2}$, we obtain

---

10. The assumption that $\ln \varepsilon_t^i \sim N(-\frac{s^2}{2}, s^2)$ implies that $E(\varepsilon_t^i) \equiv 1$.

$$\ln \frac{A_{t+1}}{A_t} \Big/_{Int} = f - \mathcal{L}^I \cdot \frac{\Delta_t^2}{2}, \tag{G_I}$$

where $\mathcal{L}^I = \alpha(1 - \alpha) + \frac{\beta}{\chi} + \frac{\gamma}{\sigma}$ is the efficiency loss per unit of heterogeneity in the integrated case.

Now, to compare between the growth outcomes under segregation and integration, we just need to sit back and look carefully at equations (G_s) and (G_I), keeping in mind that the dynamics of heterogeneity Δ_t^2 is governed by different equations in the two cases (namely, by (S) in the segregated case and by (I) in the integrated case). This, in turn, will imply that when comparing the growth performances under the two regimes, one ought to distinguish between the short run (where Δ_t^2 is taken as given) and the long run (where the evolution of Δ_t^2 over time must be taken into account).

In particular, suppose that $\mathcal{L}^s < \mathcal{L}^I$ (that is: $(\alpha + \beta)(1 - \alpha - \beta) + \frac{\gamma}{\sigma} < \alpha(1 - \alpha) + \frac{\beta}{\chi} + \frac{\gamma}{\sigma}$), which will hold for example when parental background matters a lot (α large) and/or when the heterogeneity cost of *mixed* communities $\left(\frac{1}{\chi}\right)$ is large. In that case, *for given* Δ_t^2, the current growth rate will be higher under segregation than under integration. The intuition goes as follows: poorly educated individuals will drag down the quality of a community the more heterogenous the community is. True, the less educated will also benefit more from a more heterogenous community that comprises highly educated individuals. However, when $\frac{1}{\chi}$ is positive and large, the former effect outweighs the latter, that is, poorly educated individuals "will drag down the quality of a mixed community more than the well-educated will pull this quality up."[11] In that case, segregation will be growth-enhancing in the short run.

However, the picture becomes quite different in the long run. Comparing between the dynamic systems (S) and (I), we can show that integration accelerates convergence toward a more "homogeneous economy," that is, an economy with a lower amount of heterogeneity Δ_∞^2. Indeed, taking limits in (S) and (I) when $t \to \infty$, one can immediately see that in the limit the degree of heterogeneity in the segregated case, namely

$$\Delta_\infty^2 = \frac{s^2}{1 - (\alpha + \beta)^2},$$

is strictly greater than that in the integrated case, where $\Delta_\infty^2 = \frac{s^2}{1 - \alpha^2}$. Because for given $\mathcal{L}$ the current rate of productivity growth has been shown to be a decreasing function of heterogeneity Δ_t^2 (equations (G_s) and (G_I)), it follows that the positive growth differential that *might*[12] have arisen in the short run between segregation and integration will tend to be reduced in the long run,

11. Benabou (1996a).

12. Indeed, whenever $\mathcal{L}^s > \mathcal{L}^I$, the integrated economy will perform better *also* in the short-run.

with the possibility of becoming negative. In short, although segregation tends to reduce the negative consequences of heterogeneity for a given amount of *heterogeneity*, it also prevents the economy from eventually converging toward more equality and therefore toward more aggregate efficiency and growth in the long run.

This comparison between segregated and integrated regimes has interesting implications for education policy, for example, when comparing between national and local funding of education. Indeed, if L_t^i now refers explicitly to *education quality* and is measured by the level of per-capita expenditures on schooling within the community (as in Glomm and Ravikumar 1992), and if those expenditures are financed through a uniform tax rate across community members, then it is easy to see that national (resp. local) funding will lead to a more integrated (resp. segregated) regime of human capital accumulation. Indeed, if we assume that taxable income is produced from human capital according to a linear one-for-one technology, then in the national funding case, we have $L_t^i = \tau_0 Y_t = \tau_0 \cdot H_t$, where Y_t denotes the average economy-wide revenue; whereas in the local funding case, we have: $L_t^i = \tau_0 \cdot y_t^i = \tau_0 \cdot h_t^i$. Hence, from this analysis, we can conclude that centralized funding of education will always favor human-capital accumulation and therefore growth in the long run, even though local funding may sometimes be growth-enhancing in the short run.

10.2   The Nelson-Phelps Approach

A problematic feature shared by the standard neoclassical approach (see Mankiw, Romer, and Weil 1992) *and* of the Lucas approach, is the implicit assumption that education affects individuals' productivity equally on all jobs, no matter whether these jobs are already routinized or innovative. In other words, human capital remains an ordinary input in the production function and the marginal productivity of education (i.e., of additional units of human capital) can remain positive forever even if the technology and/or set of products remains stationary.

Departing from this standard view of human capital as "simply another factor in growth accounting,"[13] Nelson and Phelps (1966) provided a first attempt at modeling the idea that a major role for education is to increase the individual's capacity, first, to *innovate* (i.e., to create new activities, new products, new technologies) and, second, to *adapt* to new technologies, thereby speeding up technological *diffusion* throughout the economy.

---

13. Benhabib and Spiegel (1994).

10.2.1   Some Distinctive Predictions of the Nelson-Phelps Approach

This alternative approach to education as being closely intertwined with the process of technological change turns out to deliver a number of new interesting results and insights.

A first testable prediction of the Nelson-Phelps approach is that productivity growth and the rate of innovations should increase with the *level* of education attainment, and particularly with the enrolment in secondary and higher education that best reflects the number of potential researchers/developers in an economy. (Note that this prediction is fully consistent with the Schumpeterian model in which the equilibrium amount of R&D, $\widehat{n}$, and therefore the steady-state growth rate $\widehat{g} = \lambda \widehat{n} \ln \gamma$, were shown to be increasing functions of the number of *potential* researchers N.[14] In contrast, the Lucas model would emphasize the relationship between productivity growth and the *rate* of human-capital accumulation.) As it turns out, the growth regressions performed so far (in particular by Barro and Sala-i-Martín (1994) and Benhabib and Spiegel 1994) point seriously toward a significant impact of the *level* of secondary and higher education attainment on the rate of productivity growth.

A second testable result is that the marginal productivity of education attainment is an increasing function of the rate of technological progress (which itself reflects both the innovation rate and the speed at which individuals and firms adapt to new technologies). Again, both the neoclassical and Lucas models would yield quite different predictions, because in those models it is the *accumulation* of human capital that determines the marginal productivity of education and maintains it at a positive level. This second prediction of the Nelson-Phelps approach has also found empirical support: first with Benhabib and Spiegel (1994), who saw no significant contribution of education to productivity growth unless education is being explicitly linked to the rate of innovations and the speed of technological catch-up; second, through other— more microeconomic—studies like Bartel and Lichtenberg (1987), who found that "the relative demand for educated workers declines as the capital stock ages."

The complementarity between educational attainment and R&D activities that such findings imply, has in turn interesting policy implications. First, it suggests that "macroeconomic policies which affect rates of innovation and investment will affect the relative demand for workers classified by education, and hence the aggregate skill distribution of employment and earnings."[15] In other words, governments will increase the average level of education not only directly through education policy but also indirectly by actively supporting

---

14. And it is equally consistent with the Romer (1990a) model developed in section 1.8, where the steady-state growth rate is also an increasing function of the number of (skilled) workers.

15. Bartel and Lichtenberg (1987).

R&D activities.[16] Conversely, government subsidies to education will increase the profitability of research and development activities, and thereby speed up technological progress.[17]

A third testable prediction of the Nelson-Phelps approach, which follows directly from our analysis of cross-country convergence in Chapter 2, is that education should allow those countries with currently less advanced technologies (i.e., with productivity parameters A_i below the average) to learn more from advanced countries and thereby achieve a higher degree of productivity improvement (i.e., a higher $\widehat{\gamma_i} = \frac{F(A_i,\overline{A})}{\overline{A}}$) when innovating. This conjecture is again confirmed by the empirical analysis in Benhabib and Spiegel (1994), which finds that the effect of past educational attainment levels on current growth rates is more pronounced in the case of countries with current aggregate productivity below the average, where growth is to be primarily driven by technological catch-up and less by innovations at the technological frontier. The comparison between the growth performances of Latin America and the so-called East Asian tigers may be quite enlightening at this point, not only to illustrate the importance of education in general as a contributing factor to technological progress and growth, but also with regard to the optimal organization of education in technologically less advanced countries. In particular, the excessive emphasis on higher education and basic research at the expense of primary/secondary education in Latin American countries such as Mexico or Brazil may partly explain why these countries have underperformed in growth terms compared to the East Asian tigers, where education has remained somewhat less elitist.

In our discussion so far, we have treated education as a policy parameter to be exclusively influenced by centralized government policy. Formalizing the demand side of education, that is endogenizing the individuals' incentives to invest in human capital, turns out to considerably enrich the analysis.

10.2.2   Low-Development Traps Caused by the Complementarity between R&D and Education Investments

The following model, inspired by Acemoglu (1994, 1997) and developed by Redding (1996a), delivers multiple development paths as in the Azariadis-Drazen model developed in Section 10.1.2, although under more natural assumptions about human-capital accumulation. In particular, the following story does not rely on intertemporal threshold externalities in human-capital accumulation.

---

16. See Chapter 14.

17. Scherer and Huh (1992) provides evidence, based on a panel data surveying R&D expenditures and the educational backgroung of top managers from 221 U.S. research-intensive companies during the period 1970–1985, of a positive and significant correlation between the technical education level of firm managers and firms' R&D spending.

There is again a continuum of overlapping generations of individual workers each of whom lives for two periods and has preferences

$$u(c_1, c_2) = c_1 + \delta c_2,$$

where δ is the discount factor. All individuals are born with one unit of human capital ($h_{1,t} \equiv 1$ for all t) and, by investing the fraction v of their working time to education when young, individuals can end up with $h_{2,t} = 1 + \gamma \cdot v^{\theta}$ units of human capital, where γ is now constant and $0 < \theta < 1$.

There is also a continuum of overlapping generations of entrepreneurs, who can produce only when old according to the linear technology

$$y^i_{j,t+1} = A^i_{t+1} \cdot h_{j,t+1}, \tag{10.13}$$

where (i) A^i_{t+1} denotes entrepreneur i's productivity at date $t + 1$ (which itself depends on whether or not the entrepreneur has innovated upon the existing leading-edge technology $A_t = \max_i A^i_t$ available to him or her upon birth at date t; (ii) $h_{j,t+1}$ is the human capital of *the* j—worker employed by the entrepreneur at date $t + 1$.

The time-path of productivity parameters A^i_t is then governed by the following innovation technology: by investing a nonmonetary cost equal to $\alpha \mu A$, entrepreneurs can increase productivity from A (the current leading edge) to λA with probability μ, where $\lambda > 1$ and $0 < \mu < 1$.

Now assume that individual workers remain self-employed when young, producing output $(1 - v)A$ where $(1 - v)$ is production time and A denotes the current leading-edge technology,[18] and when old are randomly matched with firms from which they earn the fraction β of output surplus.[19] Then the optimal allocation of working time between current production and education will solve the following maximization program:

$$\max_{v}\{(1 - v)A + \beta \rho [\mu \lambda + 1 - \mu](1 + \gamma v^{\theta})A\}.$$

This yields the optimal education time

$$v^* = \min(1, [\beta \rho \theta \gamma (\mu \lambda + 1 - \mu)]^{\frac{1}{1-\theta}}),$$

which is an increasing function of the probability of innovation μ.

The entrepreneurs, in turn, will choose R&D effort (i.e., μ) to

$$\max_{\mu} V(\mu) = \{-\mu \alpha A + \rho (1 - \beta)(\mu \lambda + 1 - \mu) \cdot (1 + \gamma v^{\theta})A\}.$$

---

18. The analysis would remain essentially unchanged if A were instead taken to be the average technology.

19. As in Chapter 4, we assume a one-to-one matching process between firms and workers, based on the implicit assumption that firms are capacity constrained and can employ at most one worker.

Hence

$$\mu^* = \begin{cases} 1 & \text{if } \alpha < \rho(\lambda - 1)(1 + \gamma v^\theta)(1 - \beta) \\ 0 & \text{otherwise,} \end{cases}$$

thus the more workers invest in education (i.e., the higher v) the more will entrepreneurs invest in R&D.

This strategic complementarity between workers' education decisions and firms' R&D decisions will not surprisingly open the possibility for multiple steady-state growth paths, including a low-development trap. Such a trap will involve $\mu^* = 0$ and therefore $v^* = \underline{v} = (\beta\rho\theta\gamma)^{\frac{1}{1-\theta}}$. For it to exist we then simply need

$$\alpha > \delta(1 - \beta)(\lambda - 1)(1 + \gamma(\beta\rho\theta\gamma)^{\frac{1}{1-\theta}}). \tag{10.14}$$

Conversely, a high-growth equilibrium will involve $\mu^* = 1$ and therefore $v^* = \overline{v} = (\lambda\beta\rho\theta\gamma)^{\frac{1}{1-\theta}}$. In order for a high-growth steady-state path to exist, we need

$$\alpha < \delta(1 - \beta)(\lambda - 1)(1 + \gamma(\lambda\beta\rho\theta\gamma)^{\frac{1}{1-\theta}}). \tag{10.15}$$

The corresponding growth rates will be $g = \overline{g} = \ln \lambda$ in the high-growth equilibrium and $g = \underline{g} = 0$ in the low-development trap.[20]

Two quick remarks conclude our analysis in this section. First, because of the strategic complementarity between R&D and education, we did not have to introduce threshold externalities in the accumulation of human capital in order to generate multiple equilibria and low-development traps. Second, targeted education policies and R&D subsidies appear as substitutable instruments for moving the economy away from a low-development trap. In practice, however, education subsidies may be easier to monitor than R&D subsidies to industries (the scope for diversion and manipulation being presumably larger in the latter case).[21]

10.2.3 Education and Skill-Biased Technical Progress

Consider a variant of the basic Schumpeterian model of Chapter 2, in which final output is produced not just by intermediate goods but also by unskilled labor, according to the aggregate production function

$$Y_t = z_t + A_t x_t^\alpha,$$

---

20. Had we introduced an intertemporal human capital externality, of the kind assumed in section 10.1.2, namely $y_{1t} = (1 - d)H_{t-1}$, where $H_{t-1} = \int_i h_{2,t-1}^i di$, the analysis would remain identical except that $\overline{g} = \ln \lambda + \ln(1 - d)(1 + \gamma \cdot \overline{v}^\theta)$ and $\underline{g} = \ln(1 - d)(1 + \gamma \cdot \underline{v}^\theta) \neq 0$. Interestingly, in that case the growth differential $\overline{g} - \underline{g}$ is magnified by the fact that the high-growth equilibrium also displays a higher rate of human capital accumulation. See Redding (1996a).

21. See our discussion in Chapter 14.

where z_t is the stock of unskilled labor after t innovations, $A_t = \gamma^t$ is the productivity parameter of the tth innovation, and x_t the flow of intermediate goods of vintage t during the interval between innovations t and $t + 1$.

Assume the same research technology as before, so that innovations arrive at the Poisson rate λn_t when n_t is the amount of skilled labor allocated to research. Suppose the total labor force is constant and equal to N. Then

$$L_t + z_t = N,$$

where L_t is the stock of skilled labor. As before, skilled labor is allocated between manufacturing and research. With a one-to-one technology in the intermediate sector this implies the usual labor-market clearing condition

$$L_t = n_t + x_t.$$

As a benchmark, suppose that the division between skilled and unskilled workers is fixed for all time

$$L_t \equiv L, \qquad z_t \equiv z.$$

Then the model is almost identical to that of Chapter 2. That is, all we have done to that model is add an extra "sector" that produces output one-for-one using unskilled labor. But this new unskilled sector does not interact in any way with the "skilled sector," which therefore continues to be described by the basic model of Chapter 2.

So, in particular, the wage of skilled workers w_t will behave exactly as described in the model of Chapter 2, growing at the average rate $g = \lambda \widehat{n} \ln \gamma$, where $\widehat{n}$ is the steady-state equilibrium research level. The unskilled wage w_t^u will be just the marginal product of unskilled labor[22]

$$w_t^u = 1.$$

Thus there will be an ever-increasing skill differential, and an ever-increasing wage inequality between skilled and unskilled workers, if nothing is done to alter the skill composition of the work force. (See Chapter 9.)

Now, suppose we allow people to alter this composition through education. A worker who chooses to be educated will be skilled. Others will be unskilled. To simplify the analysis, suppose that with each innovation people must become reeducated in order to qualify as skilled workers with the new generation of technology. Let e_t denote the fraction who choose to be educated after the tth innovation. Then

$$L_t = e_t \cdot N.$$

---

22. By symmetry with the skilled sector we assume perfect competition in the sector that produces final output with unskilled labor.

We may interpret the benchmark model of Chapter 2 as the special case in which e_t is constant.

We now move beyond this benchmark model by assuming that each individual decides whether or not to become educated by making a cost-benefit analysis of education. To simplify the analysis we suppose that the cost of becoming educated, in units of final good, vary with a person's native ability. Specifically, the fraction of people to whom the cost is less than or equal to any amount c of the final good is given by the distribution function $F(c)$. The private benefit to becoming educated is the expected present value of the corresponding gain in earnings until the next innovation. Thus, the fraction of workers who choose to become educated will be the fraction for whom the education cost is less than or equal to this benefit:

$$e_t = F\left(\frac{w_t - 1}{\rho + \lambda \cdot n_t}\right).$$

Because the demand for skilled manufacturing labor will be given by the same function $\widetilde{x}(w_t/A_t) = \widetilde{x}(\omega_t)$ as in Chapter 2, the stock of skilled workers after the tth innovation will be governed by the condition

$$L_t = F\left(\frac{w_t - 1}{\rho + \lambda[L_t - \widetilde{x}(\omega_t)]}\right) \cdot N.$$

The solution to this equation can be expressed as

$$L_t = L(w_t, \omega_t). \tag{L}$$
$${\scriptstyle(+)}\ \ {\scriptstyle(+)}$$

Thus the supply of skilled workers depends positively on the absolute real wage, which directly governs the wage-differential that a skilled worker can enjoy, and negatively on the productivity-adjusted wage, which encourages research and thus shortens the expected duration of the payoff to education through creative destruction.

Each time an innovation occurs, the (productivity-adjusted) skilled wage will be determined by the usual research-arbitrage equation

$$\omega_t = \frac{\lambda \cdot \gamma \cdot \frac{1-\alpha}{\alpha} \widetilde{\pi}(\omega_{t+1})}{\rho + \lambda[L_t - \widetilde{x}(\omega_{t+1})]} \tag{A}$$

where L_t is determined by (L).

Suppose that there is a finite upper limit to the cost of education—that is, there exists $\overline{c} > 0$ such that $F(\overline{c}) = 1$. Then, as long as research always takes place, eventually the gain to becoming educated will exceed $\overline{c}$. From then on every person will supply skilled labor, with $z_t = 0$ and $L_t = N$. Specifically, let $\widehat{\omega}$ denote the steady-state, productivity—adjusted skilled wage in the basic model when $L = N$; that is, $\widehat{\omega}$ is the fixed point of (A) when $L_t \equiv N$. Let $\widehat{t}$ be the number of innovations such that

$$\frac{\widehat{\omega} \cdot A_{\widehat{t}} - 1}{\rho + \lambda[N - \widetilde{x}(\widehat{\omega})]} < \bar{c} \leq \frac{\widehat{\omega} A_{\widehat{t}+1} - 1}{\rho + \lambda[N - \widetilde{x}(\widehat{\omega})]}.$$

Then after $\widehat{t}$ innovations the productivity adjusted wage will equal $\widehat{\omega}$, so that it will become optimal for everyone to acquire skills through education.

Thus in this model education will eventually eliminate the inequality in wages across the population, because eventually everyone working at date t will receive the same skilled wage w_t. However, it will not eliminate the skill differential $w_t - 1$.

If we had modified the model a little so as to make the aggregate production function

$$Y_t = z_t^\alpha + A_t x_t^\alpha,$$

then as the number of unskilled workers z_t falls down to zero the wage of unskilled workers would rise to infinity, because the scarcity of unskilled labor would benefit those who continue to remain unskilled. But whether or not this increasing scarcity would exert a stronger force on the unskilled wage than would the "automation" effect of the nonlinear robot model of Chapter 9 (section 9.2.1), which acts in the opposite direction, cannot be determined a priori. In any event the only way for increasing scarcity to continue to pull up the unskilled wage is for the skill differential to continue to grow. Otherwise the fraction of educated workers e_t would stabilize at a value less than unity and unskilled labor would cease to benefit from increased scarcity. Thus although education may eliminate wage inequality, it will not eliminate the skill differential.

Notice also that private education will not eliminate lifetime wealth inequality. For even if everyone ends up earning the skilled wage, some will have sacrificed more lifetime consumption to pay for the cost of their education. Only publicly subsidized education can thus eliminate lifetime wealth inequality attributable to differences in native ability. Moreover, if innate ability affects not just the cost of education but also a person's productivity while employed, even public education will not go all the way to eliminating wealth inequality.

10.2.4   Vintage Effects and the Relationship between Education, Growth, and Earnings Inequality

Although education has the unambiguous effect of fostering growth and reducing wage inequality between skilled and unskilled workers in the absence of vintage effects (see the previous subsection), the relationship between education and growth and between education and inequality becomes more subtle and, we believe, also more interesting in the case where technical progress is embodied in particular product lines (or "vintages") and mobility of developers between those lines is limited.

More precisely, we are interested in the effects of education policy on growth and wages in the context of the vintage model introduced in Chapter 6 and already used in the previous chapter (section 9.2.3). Remember that there are only skilled individuals in this model, and that H denotes the constant mass of skilled workers. Each worker can choose whether to engage in research or production, and production activities take place within a continuum of intermediate-good industries. Aggregate final output at date t is expressed as

$$Y_t = \int_{-\infty}^{t} \lambda^r H^r A_\tau Z_{t-\tau}(x_{t-\tau})^\alpha d\tau = \int_{-\infty}^{t} Y_{t,\tau} d\tau,$$

where $Y_{t,\tau}$ denotes the aggregate *final* output produced using intermediate goods of vintage τ.[23] A_τ is the productivity parameter that reflects the level of general knowledge at the time a product line of vintage τ was being introduced. $Z_{t-\tau}$ denotes the quality of workers on a line of age $t - \tau$, it is assumed to increase over time at a rate that equals to the flow of secondary innovations (or learning by doing, which we denote as LBD) across the whole economy:

$$Z_0 = 0 \quad \text{and} \quad \frac{dZ_a}{da} = LBD = \int_{0}^{\infty} \lambda^r H^r \lambda^d (x_s)^{1-\nu} ds,$$

where $\lambda^d (x_s)^{1-\nu}$ is the arrival rate of quality improvements on a line of age s.

As we saw in section 6.1, the steady-state growth rate g and the steady-state number of researchers H^r are jointly determined by a research-arbitrage equation (R) and a growth equation (G). The former expresses the fact that, in order for research and production to coexist in a steady state, workers who have just been upgraded (i.e., allowed to choose between research and producing on the most recent product line) is indifferent between research and production. The latter expresses the growth of general knowledge A_t as a function of the current flow of both fundamental discoveries (whose arrival rate is $\lambda^r H^r$) and secondary innovations (whose flow is equal to LBD).

More formally, we have

$$\rho + \sigma - g = \sigma \cdot \frac{1 - \alpha}{\alpha} \cdot \frac{H - H^r}{H^r}, \tag{R}$$

where σ denotes the upgrading rate, and

$$g = G(\lambda^r H^r, LBD). \tag{G}$$

---

23. λ^r is the productivity parameter for research; H^r is the number of researchers who work on discovering new product lines. $H - H^r$ is the number of developers in the whole economy.

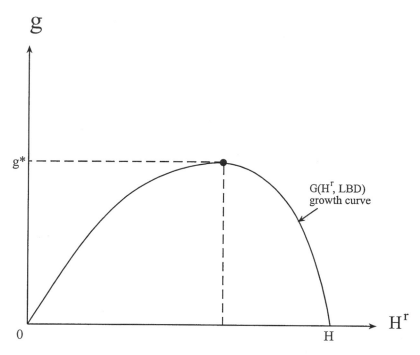

Figure 10.1

Education and Growth

Consider first the case where G is concave (inverted U-shaped) and equal to zero when either H^r or LBD are zero (see figure 10.1). Education policy will typically affect research and/or LBD productivity, research incentives, and the mobility of workers across lines. For example, a policy that puts all the emphasis on increasing research *productivity* λ^r will have an unambiguously positive effect on growth (as it shifts the G-curve upward). On the other hand, as already mentioned in Chapter 6, if the government decides to encourage research at the expense of production (i.e., to increase H^r) by channeling public resources toward universities instead of toward primary/secondary and vocational education, growth will be increased only if initially $g_0 < g^*$ and it will be decreased otherwise! Finally, an education policy that emphasizes polyvalence and enhances the mobility of workers across lines (i.e., increases σ)[24] will be growth-enhancing, at least when the elasticity of G with respect to learning by doing is sufficiently small. One could go on trying to provide a more detailed interpretation of alternative educational policies in the context

---

24. Such a policy should typically avoid excessive specialization in product-specific skills and knowledge.

of this model of primary versus secondary innovations, although our main point in this discussion was to show that public support to education needs to be adequately designed and channeled in order to be unambiguously growth-enhancing.

Education and Inequality

In the previous chapter (section 9.2.3), we argued that an exogenous increase in the rate of growth g should result into a higher degree of earnings inequality across (skilled) workers on different product lines. What about the effects of increasing education spending?

The answer to this question will again depend on the particular kind or design of public support to education. More concretely, any policy that increases the growth rate g without changing the cut-off values $\sigma(1 - \alpha)$ and $\sigma(1 - \alpha) + \frac{\rho + \sigma\alpha}{q_0(\rho + \sigma\alpha) + 1}$ derived in section 9.2.3, will automatically *increase* earnings inequality. Thus, any policy that induces an increase in either of the parameters λ^r, λ^d, H (and v as long the elasticity of G with respect to LBD is sufficiently small) will *increase* inequality.

More interesting are the effects of education policies aimed at increasing the adaptability of workers to new lines, in other words which result into increasing the value of the mobility parameter σ. There does not seem to be any major loss of economic insight in restricting the analysis to the case where:

a. $G(\lambda^r H^r, LBD) \equiv \lambda^r H,$

so that only fundamental research contributes directly to the growth in general knowledge, and

b. $g_0 > \sigma(1 - \alpha) + \frac{\rho + \sigma\alpha}{q_0(\rho + \sigma\alpha) + 1} = E(\sigma),$

so that in equilibrium the ratio between the expected present values of earnings (until the next upgrading opportunity) for a worker currently on a product line of age Δ and for a worker currently at the leading edge, is given by

$$v(\Delta) = \frac{(q_0 + \Delta)(\rho + \sigma\alpha) + 1}{q_0(\rho + \sigma\alpha) + 1} \cdot e^{-\Delta(g - \sigma(1 - \alpha))},$$

which decreases with Δ when $g > E(\sigma)$, as depicted in figure 10.2.

We see that, for given g, $v(\Delta)$ decreases less rapidly with Δ the higher σ,[25] in other words, increasing worker mobility *reduces* earnings inequality. Intuitively, as mobility increases and therefore more workers leave their current line to relocate at the leading edge, the productivity of non-upgraded workers

---

25. Indeed, $v(\Delta)$ is the product of two terms, the first of which increases more rapidly with Δ the higher σ, and the second (the exponential term) of which decreases less rapidly with Δ as σ increases.

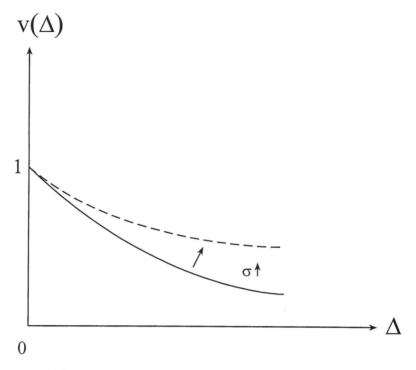

Figure 10.2

on old lines increases more rapidly (remember that the production of any intermediate good involves decreasing returns with respect to labor, i.e., $\alpha <$ 1); this in turn will have a boosting effect on future wages of the non-upgraded workers compared to those of workers at the leading edge. Let us thus refer to this effect as a *decreasing returns effect.*

However, an increase in the mobility rate σ will also affect the steady-state growth rate g. Specifically, if we solve for g using (R) and (G) with $G(\lambda^r H^r, LBD) \equiv \lambda^r H^r$, we find

$$g = \frac{1}{2}\left(\rho + \frac{\sigma}{\alpha}\right)\left[1 + \sqrt{1 + \frac{4\lambda^r \sigma(1-\alpha)H}{\alpha(\rho + \frac{\sigma}{\alpha})^2}}\right].$$

In particular, $\frac{dg}{d\sigma} > \frac{1}{2\alpha} > 0$. This, in turn, induces a counteracting *growth effect* of mobility on earnings inequality: to the extent that it enhances growth and therefore speeds up the emergence of new—more productive—lines, mobility-enhancing education will increase the technological gap, and therefore the earnings gap, between those workers that who have the opportunity of relocating (early) to newer lines and the other workers in the economy.

Whether the *decreasing return effect* or the *growth effect* dominates will obviously depend on the parameters of the model. In particular, the growth effect will dominate when λ^r or H are sufficiently large and the decreasing return effects will dominate when λ^r and H are small and α is bounded away from zero.

To summarize our analysis in this section: (a) educational policy will not systematically be growth-enhancing, although it can always be made so through adequate design and targeting; (b) in contrast to our analysis in the previous section, educational policy—even when aimed at increasing adaptability and mobility of workers across lines—may sometimes result in a higher degree of inequality across workers employed on different vintages. Yet, although more elitist (e.g., research-oriented) education policies will unambiguously increase inequality, the overall impact of mobility-enhancing policies will be more ambiguous as it results from two counteracting effects, namely a decreasing returns effect whereby mobility reduces earnings inequality and a growth effect whereby mobility enhances inequality.

10.3   Microfoundations of Education Policy: An Informal Look at Some Preliminary Contributions

A main conclusion that emerges from our analysis in this chapter, is that the way in which education policy should affect growth and also the structure of earnings in an economy hinges heavily on several dimensions or aspects in the *design* of such policy. In particular, the *organization of funding* (e.g., local versus decentralized) and also the *targeting of public resources* (e.g., to primary/secondary versus higher education, or to schooling versus training programs, and so on) appear to be of paramount importance when assessing the short and/or long-term growth impact of government intervention in the education sector. This in turn suggests that more careful attention should be devoted to the *microeconomic* aspects of education. Although we are unable to talk about the microfoundations of education policy with the same level of detail as we do for research and development in the last two chapters of this book (if only because there is not much in the existing theoretical literature on the organization of education) we would like nevertheless to mention a few empirical and theoretical contributions to what promises to become a fascinating research area.

First, there is a whole empirical literature, partly surveyed by Hanushek (1986)[26], that attempts to evaluate the effects of school expenditures, teachers pay, pupil/teacher ratio, private versus public schools, and so forth on

---

26. See also Card and Krueger (1992).

student performance (e.g., measured by future earnings and/or by test scores). Although Hanushek (1986) had found no significant relationship between school expenditures and student performance measured by test scores, Card and Krueger (1992) point to a significant correlation between school quality (also measured by teacher pay, student-teacher ratio, teacher education, and so on) and student performance, this time measured by (future) earnings.[27]

The evidence both of a high variance in the quality of education across schools and teachers and of the important impact of school quality or type on student's performance may partly explain the renewed interest for education policy among economic theorists. At the same time, recent developments in incentives theory and the theory of contracts have produced new analytical tools for studying the organizational aspects of education. Finally, at a time where privatizations are being strongly advocated in all sectors of developed market economies (including public infrastructure and utilities), microtheorists interested by the issue of ownership and control allocation within or across firms, and/or by applications of mechanism design, are naturally turning their attention to sectors and activities for which the privatization debate remains controversial, in particular education and public health.

A pioneering contribution in this respect is Bolton and Xu (1997). Based on the observation that in sectors where there is strong competition, like the universities sector in the United States,[28] the particular form of ownership (e.g., state-owned versus privately owned) does not seem to matter much, Bolton and Xu develop a simple incomplete contracting[29] model to analyze the interplay between competition and ownership in the education sector. That the incomplete contract approach should be relevant when analyzing incentive problems in schools follows quite naturally from the difficulties in measuring (verifying)

---

27. More recent contributions to this empirical literature include, papers in the 1996 Review of Economics and Statistics Symposium on "School Quality and Educational Outcomes." (In particular, we refer to Muffih's introduction to the Symposium, and to the papers by Betts and by Heckman, Layne-Farrar, and Todd.) The main conclusions that emerge from these papers are, first that school-quality effects appear to be quite dependent on the level of aggregation at which the analysis is conducted; second, that family background is of paramount importance when analyzing the impact of various measures of school quality; third, that family background, neighborhood effects, and cohort effects seem to increasingly prevail over traditional school input measures. Finally, in ongoing work, based on UK data, Dearden, Ferri, and Meghir (1997) find that the traditional measures of school quality have no systematic influence on educational and/or labor market outcomes once one controls for family background and school type (private, selective, comprehensive, and so on). □

28. Bolton and Xu give the example of Harvard University versus Berkeley, which appear to be roughly equivalent in terms of their overall performances in education and research, although Harvard is privately owned whereas Berkeley is state-owned. This may indeed by attributed to the high degree of competition among universities (both private and public), but it maybe also be due to the fact that "real authority" or "effective control" is exerted in either case by tenured faculties.

29. The methodology and formalization of incomplete contract theory will be introduced in Chapter 13 when addressing the issue of the optimal organization of R&D.

educational inputs by teachers and by school administrations (see Hanushek 1986). More precisely, to the extent that contracts between teachers, students, and school owners cannot be made contingent upon the amount of knowledge that teachers can transmit to students, teachers are facing a "hold-up" problem: that is, they have no guarantee of being properly compensated by the school for their sunk educational investments (contracting is assumed to take place *after* the teachers have acquired knowledge through research and/or further reading and trained themselves into conveying this knowledge to students). Anticipating this hold-up problem, teachers will typically underinvest in educational quality. One way around this problem is to allocate ownership (or control) of schools to teachers. However, Bolton and Xu argue that teacher-ownership may become unnecessary and even counterproductive if there is strong competition among teachers for attracting students.[30]

Although a properly designed education policy must provide adequate incentives for teachers and/or schools to invest in quality and educational equipments, it must also generate an efficient matching between individuals with heterogenous ability levels and schools with heterogeneous quality standards. Following a mechanism design approach, Fernandez and Gali (1996) compare the *market mechanism* (in which there is a price for each school, which is a priori independent of student's quality) with alternative mechanisms such as *tournaments* (where individuals are ranked according to an idiosyncratic signal that reflects quality but also requires cash spending on the student's part) as methods to allocate students to schools. Students' abilities and schools' qualities are taken to be exogenous in this model, and the two are strategic complements: that is, the higher a school's quality, the more an individual's future income (performance) will increase with ability, and vice versa. Fernandez and Gali consider two polar cases. On one hand, when capital markets are fully efficient and higher-ability individuals can costlessly borrow up to their net present value of earnings, the market mechanism will allocate individuals to schools efficiently, because higher-ability individuals will be able to pay a higher price to enroll into better schools. Tournaments will generate the same efficient allocation of individuals to schools, but with a waste of resources in trying to improve the quality of signals. On the other hand, when individuals are credit-constrained, tournaments will tend to outperform the market mechanism: by spending a given amount of money, higher-ability individuals can generate a better signal than the less able who spend the same amount of money, and therefore the former will gain access to better schools than the latter as a result of tournaments, but the market mechanism that is fully anonymous will

---

30. That the nature of competition should affect the outside options of the different contracting parties and therefore the optimal ownership structure, is an idea that we shall encounter again in Chapter 13 when analyzing the relationship between *ownership* and the *size* of innovations.

not be able to discriminate between two individuals with different abilities but who spend the same amount of money on schooling. In other words, tournaments provide a positive bias in favor of higher ability individuals. This bias, in turn, enhances allocative efficiency in situations where credit constraints prevent more capable individuals to borrow up to the net present value of their future revenues.

These are only two among many (potential) contributions that microeconomic theory could make to improve our understanding of how to design education policy. However, our purpose in this section was by no means to provide an exhaustive account of a literature that is still embryonic and fairly sporadic, but rather to stimulate research interests on the microfoundations of education policies and the process of human-capital accumulation.

Incidentally, we should mention an interesting paper by Acemoglu (1996), which provides microeconomic foundations for the observed evidence of increasing returns in human capital accumulation. (Remember from section 10.1 that the existence of such increasing returns was a key assumption in what we called the "Lucas approach.") But rather than being based on purely technological externalities, increasing returns in Acemoglu's model are "social," based on a "moral hazard in teams" story similar to the one considered in Bolton and Xu (1997). More precisely, suppose—which is quite realistic—that individuals need to sink a large fraction of their human-capital investments (e.g., schooling, acquisition of general knowledge, and so on) *before* they know which firm they are going to work for and thus before contracting with such a firm. Then such individuals will again face a hold-up problem and underinvest in human capital accumulation. Now, here comes the most interesting part of Acemoglu's argument. Suppose that matching process between firms and workers is imperfect (as in Chapter 5) and random. Then, if a positive fraction of individuals decided to (jointly) increase investments in education, firms would respond with correspondingly higher investments in labor market search, equipment, and training programs so as to (a) attract those better educated individuals and (b) better take advantage of the average improvement in human capital induced by this joint education investment. This positive feedback from firms would in turn increase the expected return to human-capital investments of those individuals who did not participate to the initial educational effort—hence a "social" increasing return to human capital accumulation. An interesting next step in the analysis would be to investigate the extent to which, by improving individuals' information about firms, an adequately designed education/training policy might be able to mitigate the hold-up problem at a low cost in terms of distortionary tax/subsidies. For example, the preceding story may provide some justification for the education system in Germany, in which schools and enterprises appear to be more intensely interconnected than in other developed economies.

10.4 Summary

The educational achievement of a society, usually referred to as the "human capital stock" plays an important role in economic growth, but the precise mechanism is unclear. In particular, we must distinguish the effects of the level of human capital and the accumulation of human capital (i.e., how much the level of education is increasing over time).

There are two strands of thought, that we may associate with Lucas and Nelson and Phelps respectively. According to Lucasian models, the level of output depends on the level of human capital, because human capital is an input, just like any other input. It follows that the growth rate of output depends on the *growth rate* of human capital, in that it is only possible to get more output if we also have more input. In the Nelson-Phelps approach, however, human capital is not an input just like any other: human capital is the primary source of innovations. Thus the growth rate of output will depend on the rate of innovation and hence the *level,* rather than the growth rate, of human capital.

These two views have very different implications for the extent and type of subsidy for education: what is at stake is whether raising the level of human capital will have either a once-and-for-all effect on output or increase its growth rate effect forever. But it is also plausible that the Lucas and Nelson-Phelps stories could both be true, because they need not be talking about the same thing when they refer to human capital. We can distinguish raising the human-capital stock by improving the basic level of education for all workers (for many countries this would mean improving literacy) from raising the human-capital stock by training a few workers to higher education levels (secondary education, university degrees, doctorates, and so on). The former sort of human capital would appear to be a normal input, whereas the latter is more probably the relevant variable for innovation.

We now turn to a more detailed discussion of the two approaches.

How is human capital created? Lucas's original model assumed that workers either spent their time producing output or being educated, so faster rates of human capital accumulation meant lower levels of output at any moment in time. Education is a form of investment, so, if agents are more impatient, they will tend to have less education and higher current consumption. But if learning by doing is an important part of education, then time spent producing output will also raise the level of human capital accumulation, so the trade-off will not be so stark. Note that we have not recognized the fact that human capital actually consists of individuals who have different characteristics. In particular, the benefits of education for older workers might be low (because they face impending retirement), so the return to education will depend on the age structure of the workforce.

So far we have said that human capital is produced by education without making clear what education is. In fact, education requires human capital as an input as well as producing it as an output. This has important implications, in as much as it may be difficult for an economy to increase its human capital quickly. It is quite possible for economies to get trapped into either vicious circles or virtuous spirals: economies with little human capital to start with do not really have the ability to produce more and are stuck with a low human capital stock forever (or a very long time), whereas economies with high human capital stocks can easily produce more and can thus sustain a high growth rate.

A final concern about education is the effect of externalities between individuals. We often observe that children of poor people, who have low human capital, live in the same area and attend the same schools, and are segregated from the children of richer people with high human capital. Where schools are funded locally, there will be the additional effect that schools for children whose parents have low human capital will be less well resourced. However, the degree of segregation varies and can be influenced by government policy. What degree of segregation is optimal?

In a mixed school, the children of low human-capital parents will tend to hold back the children of high human-capital parents, but the richer children will tend to pull the poorer children up. The effect on the average level of schooling is prima facie ambiguous but, under plausible assumptions, the overall effect will be negative and the average quality of education will suffer. This might suggest that it is better to segregate children on efficiency grounds (although not on equity grounds). This argument, however, fails to take account of the effect of the education system on the distribution of human capital.

If schools are mixed, the levels of human capital between poor and rich will tend to converge and the greater equality will lead to positive benefits in that all children will benefit from being educated with each other. Segregation would prevent this convergence from ever occurring, so the children of the currently rich will never benefit from learning alongside other children, who could have had high levels of human capital but were denied that opportunity. The fundamental trade-off here is a short-run cost to be borne by the rich against a long-run benefit that would be felt by everybody, rich included. Segregation means that the long-run benefits are never felt, which is both inefficient and inequitable.

We now turn to the implications for the Nelson-Phelps approach, where human capital is necessary for innovations. We have already said that human

capital in this context is probably referring to the highly skilled. The decision
to gain a high level of skills is at least partly a choice of agents other than
the government: individuals go to university if they expect a sufficiently high
return.

The forward-looking nature of this decision can lead to both high and low
growth equilibria. If individuals anticipate a high demand for researchers,
then many will choose higher education and the growth rate will be high.
Conversely, if they anticipate a low demand for research, few will choose such
education and the growth rate will be low. Both of these possibilities are due
to expectations that are self-fulfilling. Thus there is a role for government,
which can provide sufficient incentives to research to influence individuals'
expectations.

Now, what is the optimal level of higher education? In previous chapters we
have seen that basic research must be augmented by development. Elitist education policies, that train a few workers to very high standards but ignore the
rest may be inefficient because the poorly trained (perhaps illiterate?) workers
are unable to fully develop, or even utilize, new innovations. This may slow
down the growth rate, in as much as the return to innovators is reduced. Thus
the design of education policy needs to take account of the complementary nature of different forms of human capital and not concentrate too heavily on one
form alone.

Finally, we can return to the relationship between human capital and inequality. Our discussion in Chapter 9 showed that economic development often leads
to workers using different technologies at the same time; the workers using obsolescent technologies will be paid less than those using new technologies, but
have to rest content with their lower wages because they have limited opportunities to change jobs. Elitist education policies that encourage innovation will
certainly increase inequality, because there will be a larger range of technologies in use at any one time and thus a larger gap between the state-of-the-art
technology and the obsolete technology. Education policies that increase workers' mobility should reduce inequality: because the returns to learning by doing
are decreasing, moving a worker from an old to a new technology will increase the productivity of workers remaining on old technologies, narrowing
the difference in the wages between workers on old and new lines. We call
this the "decreasing returns effect." But there will be a second, counteracting
effect: because new technologies will find it easier to employ workers, innovation will be faster, which will increase inequality, as shown in the previous
chapter. We refer to this as the "growth effect." Thus we cannot say unambiguously whether inequality will eventually rise or fall. Mobility, however, is
observable, at least in principle, so we should be able to test its overall effect on
inequality.

Problems

Difficulty of Problems:

No star: normal

One star: difficult

Two stars: very difficult

★ **1. Growth driven by the accumulation of human capital (based on Uzawa 1965 and Lucas 1988)**

Here we solve the Lucas (1988) model discussed in the chapter. Agents are infinitely lived and maximize lifetime utility. The instantaneous utility function is given by $(c_t^{1-\sigma} - 1)/(1 - \sigma)$, and the discount rate is ρ. Consider the following version of the Lucas production function discussed in the chapter:

$$y = Ak^\beta (uh)^{1-\beta} h_a^\gamma,$$

where $u \in [0, 1]$. The last term captures a production externality stemming from the average stock of human capital (that agents take as given). Let A be constant, in order to abstract from technical change. The population grows at rate n. There is no depreciation. Human capital is accumulated according to the function described in the chapter, $\dot{h} = \delta h(1 - u)$.

a. Set up the Hamiltonian of the optimization problem faced by a producer-consumer agent, noting that there are now two dynamic constraints (one for the accumulation of human capital and one for the accumulation of physical capital) and two decision variables, c and u. Find the first-order conditions.

b. From the first-order conditions, obtain the rate of growth of consumption as a function of h and k. In steady state, u is constant and all other variables grow at a constant rate. From the dynamic equations for consumption and physical capital, show that these two variables grow at the same rate. How does the rate of growth of human capital relate to the rate of growth of physical capital/consumption?

c. From the first-order conditions governing the behavior of the shadow prices of human and physical capital, show that the steady-state rate of growth of the stock of human capital is

$$g_h^* = \frac{1 - \beta}{\sigma(1 - \beta + \gamma) - \gamma}(\delta - \rho).$$

d. Obtain the rate of growth of per capita output and the proportion of time spent in production.

e. Would a social planner choose the same level of u as the competitive economy? How does this depend on γ ? Are there any other externalities in the model? Under what circumstances could they cause a divergence between the social optimum and the competitive equilibrium?

f. Consider again the competitive economy. Suppose the government imposes a proportional tax on all income, τ. Show that although the first-order conditions of the consumer maximization problem have changed, the steady-state growth rate is not affected by the tax. Why?

2. The Lucas model with physical capital in the accumulation of human capital (based on Rebelo 1991)

In the Lucas (1988) model, sustained growth stems from an intertemporal externality (or spillover effect) in the generation of human capital. Rebelo modifies the model and shows how an economy can sustain long-run growth even in the absence of this spillover. Instead of using Lucas's function for the accumulation of human capital, Rebelo assumes that h is obtained from existing human and physical capital through a Cobb-Douglas function with no externalities. That is,

$$\dot{h} = A_2((1 - \phi)k)^\gamma ((1 - u)h)^{1-\gamma}, \tag{10.16}$$

where $(1 - \phi)$ and $(1 - u)$ are respectively the fraction of the stocks of physical and of human capital employed in the production of human capital, and $\phi, u \in [0, 1]$. The population is constant and normalized to one.

Output is produced with a Cobb-Douglas function of the two types of capital,

$$Y = A_1(\phi k)^\beta (uh)^{1-\beta} . \tag{10.17}$$

The final good is used both in consumption and as physical capital, so that $Y = I + C$, where I denotes investment and C consumption. The accumulation of physical capital is governed by

$$\dot{k} = I. \tag{10.18}$$

In steady state k, h, and c all grow at the same rate. Agents have to decide, on one hand, how much to consume, and, on the other hand, what proportion of the two types of capital to devote to the production of human capital and final output. Suppose consumers directly operate the economy's technology. They are infinitely lived and maximize their lifetime utility. The instantaneous utility function is given by $(c^{1-\sigma} - 1)/(1 - \sigma)$, and the discount rate is ρ.

a. Obtain the static optimality condition that governs the allocation of the existing stocks of physical and human capital across the two sectors. In doing so, denote by q the relative value of human capital in terms of physical capital. (Do *not* use the Hamiltonian.)

b. Obtain the dynamic optimality condition for investment in the two types of capital (that is, equality between the net rates of return), taking into account that the relative value of human capital in terms of physical capital, q, changes over time. Show that in steady state, there will be no capital gains. What does the dynamic optimality condition look like in the steady state?

c. Using the two optimality conditions derived in (a) and (b), show that in the steady state the "capital-labor intensity" in the final-good sector is constant and given by

$$\frac{\phi k}{uh} = \left(\frac{A_1}{A_2}\frac{\beta}{1-\gamma}\right)^{v/\gamma}\left(\frac{1-\gamma}{\gamma}\frac{\beta}{1-\beta}\right)^{v},$$ (10.19)

where

$$v \equiv \frac{\gamma}{1+\gamma-\beta}.$$

Similarly, obtain the capital-labor intensity in the human capital sector. What is the steady-state interest rate?

d. Find the dynamic equation for consumption and substitute in it the rate of interest to get the steady-state rate of growth of the economy. Why is it non-zero if all cumulable factors exhibit diminishing returns?

e. Suppose the government imposes a proportional tax on all income, τ. Show that the steady-state growth rate is affected by the tax. Compare to the result obtained in the previous problem.

3. Growth and the level of human capital (based on Romer 1990a)

In the Lucas model and in the preceding version of it by Rebelo, sustainable growth is possible due to the accumulation of human capital. However, it is likely that the *level* of human capital also has an impact on the rate of growth. R&D in the Romer (1990a) and Aghion and Howitt (1992a) models, as examined in Chapters 1 and 2, was done by labor. As a result, there were scale effects: the total stock of labor appears in the growth equation as one of the determinants of long-run growth. In practice, the R&D sector employs mainly educated workers, and hence the amount of human capital in the economy determines the input available to generate technological improvements. In this problem we examine Romer's (1990a) original formulation of the model to show that scale effects are associated with the stock of human capital, and that, therefore, its level is a major determinant of the growth rate.

Consider the Romer model presented in Chapter 1. There are two types of workers: unskilled workers or labor, denoted L, and skilled workers or human capital, denoted H. The stock of both is fixed. Both types of workers are employed in production, but only human capital is employed in R&D. Thus

$$Y = H_1^\alpha L^\beta \int_0^A x_i^{1-\alpha-\beta} di \qquad (10.20)$$

and

$$\dot{A} = \delta H_2 A. \qquad (10.21)$$

All other economic relations are just as in Chapter 1. Derive the rate of output growth as we did in Chapter 1. Show that only the stock of human capital, and not that of labor, affects the growth rate.

4. Income distribution, education, and growth (based on Galor and Zeira 1993)

This problem relates to the models in section 10.1.3, considering how the initial distribution of wealth affects the long-run level of income. It is a much simpler model, in as much as there are no spillovers between generations and hence no accumulation of human capital over time (and no growth). Agents with two-period lives decide whether or not to invest in human capital, and all who invest acquire the same level of knowledge. What is interesting is that the investment in human capital is indivisible (quite a realistic assumption), which in turn implies that in the long run there will be a polarization of wealth between high-income/educated individuals and low-income/uneducated ones. Long-run income will depend on both the initial income level and on its distribution. The indivisibility assumed relates the paper to the models studied in section 9.1.

Consider an OLG economy where agents live for two periods. Each agent has one child, hence the population, L, is constant. There is a single good that can be produced with two constant-returns technologies; one uses unskilled labor and the other skilled labor. The wages of skilled and unskilled workers are respectively w_u and w_s. Agents can either work as unskilled for both periods, or invest in human capital when young and work as skilled workers when old. One unit of labor is supplied in each period. The investment in human capital is indivisible; that is, either one invests $h > 0$ or does not invest. Members of a dynasty are linked through the bequests, b, left to their children. Agents consume, c, only in their second period of life. Assume the utility function takes the following form:

$$U = \alpha \log c + (1 - \alpha) \log b, \quad \text{where } 0 < \alpha < 1. \qquad (10.22)$$

The only difference between newborn agents is the amount that they have inherited from their parent. Let x_{jt} denote the inheritance received by the agent from dynasty j born at time t, which is equal to the amount bequeathed by her parent, $x_{jt} = b_{jt-1}$. Individuals who borrow in order to invest in human capital face a rate of interest, i, greater than the risk-free rate, r. This is due to the cost of monitoring investment in an intangible asset.

a. There are three types of agents: those who do not invest in human capital, those who invest and lend ($x \geq h$), and those who invest and borrow. Find the utility levels and bequests of these three groups. Assume that

$$w_s - h(1+r) \geq w_u(2+r). \tag{10.23}$$

How much do individuals need to inherit to invest in h?

b. Let D_t be the distribution of inheritances received by individuals born in period t. Show that it determines the number of skilled workers and hence the level of income.

c. Obtain the relation between inheritances in period t and $t + 1$ for the three types of workers. Find the level to which inheritances converge (steady state) for both those individuals who do not invest in education and for those that invest and do not need to borrow, denoted $\bar{x}_u$ and $\bar{x}_s$ respectively. Will their descendants ever do anything different from what they did? Show that in the case of individuals that invest in education and need to borrow to do so, all dynasties with initial inheritance greater than

$$z = \frac{(1 - \alpha)\left[h(1 + i) - w_s\right]}{(1 + i)(1 - \alpha) - 1} \tag{10.24}$$

converge to $\bar{x}_s$, and those with inheritance below z will eventually stop investing in education and converge to $\bar{x}_u$. Assume $(1 + r)(1 - \alpha) < 1$, in order to ensure the existence of an equilibrium.

d. In the long run, the level of income is determined by how the population is divided between dynasties that have converged to $\bar{x}_u$ or $\bar{x}_s$. Show how the number of skilled workers, and hence income, depends on the initial distribution of bequests. Obtain the long-run level of average wealth as a function of the initial distribution. Discuss what are the growth prospects of countries that are poor-and-equal, rich-and-unequal and rich-and-equal.

5. Education and unemployment (based on Acemoglu 1996)

This problem shows how a coordination failure among workers can lead to slower growth and higher unemployment, as was discussed in section 10.3.

Assume a two-period economy. In the first period a worker $i \in [0, 1]$ can decide to acquire skills at a cost $c > 0$. Simultaneously and independently, firms decide whether to enter or not and post a vacancy at cost γ if they do enter. In the second period a worker is matched with a firm with probability $m(\theta, 1)$ where $\theta = v/u$ measures the tightness of the labor market, as v denotes the number of vacancies and u the number of unemployed workers. Similarly, a firm is matched with a worker with probability $m(\theta, 1)/\theta$. These probabilities are independent of workers' skills. The matching function $m(.,.)$ satisfies the same properties as in Chapter 5, problem 2; in particular, $m(\theta, 1)$ is increasing in θ and $m(\theta, 1)/\theta$ is decreasing in θ. If the firm is matched with a skilled worker, its surplus equals $y + a$ with $y, a > 0$. If the firm is matched with an unskilled worker, its surplus equals y. Assume the firm's surplus is split equally between the firm and the worker. Denote the proportion of workers who acquire skills in period 1 by p (of course, this proportion is endogenously determined in equilibrium).

a. Show that free entry by firms in the first stage implies $m(\theta, 1)/\theta[p(y + a) + (1 - p)y] = 2\gamma$.

b. Show that workers' willingness to acquire skills depends on the sign of $\{m(\theta, 1)a - 2c\}$.

c. Show that a pair (p, θ) is a Nash-equilibrium outcome of this game if it satisfies one of the following cases:

i. (p_1, θ_1) is such that $p_1 = 0$, $m(\theta_1, 1)/\theta_1 = 2\gamma/y$ and $m(\theta_1, 1)a < 2c$;

ii. (p_2, θ_2) is such that $0 < p_2 < 1$, $m(\theta_2, 1)/\theta_2 = 2\gamma/(y + p_2 a)$ and $m(\theta_2, 1)a < 2c$;

iii. (p_3, θ_3) is such that $p_3 = 1$, $m(\theta_3, 1)/\theta_3 = 2\gamma/(y + a)$ and $m(\theta_3, 1)a > 2c$.

d. Suppose for a certain matching function and parameter values, each of these three equilibria exists. What happens to unemployment and total surplus moving from one equilibrium to the next? What stops the economy from always attaining the efficient outcome? Can government intervention help to achieve the efficient outcome?

e. Suppose technological progress is modeled by a, the difference between the surplus with a skilled and an unskilled worker. How does a rise in technological progress (that is an increase in a) affect unemployment?

★ **6. School ownership, competition, and efficiency (based on Bolton and Xu 1997)**

This problem addresses the question of who should own educational institutions (schools). The central idea is that teachers have to invest in knowledge, and that the value of education to students depends on this investment (the level of skill hereby acquired then affects productivity and growth). The problem explores how, under incomplete contracts, ownership affects teachers' investments and hence the level of skills of the labor force. Similar ideas will be applied to ownership of knowledge in the final chapters of the book. (See also Grossman and Hart 1986).

Consider an economy with four agents: a teacher, a body of students, one outsider, and the government. There is one school. Agents are risk-neutral and seek to maximize their income. There is no discounting. The government maximizes the welfare (income) of a body of students of mass one. There are two stages of decisions. In the first stage, teachers make a sunk, unverifiable investment in knowledge, k, at a constant unit cost equal to one. In the second stage, the teacher transmits knowledge to the students for a fee. It can be transmitted outside the school, and in this case its value would be $v(k)$, where $v > 0$, $v' \geq 0$, $v'' \leq 0$. If it is transmitted within the school, its value is $V(k) = f(v(k))$, where $V(k) > v(k)$, $f' \geq 0$, $f'' \leq 0$. f measures the complementaries between the teacher's knowledge and the school's facilities.

The contract to exchange education can only be signed ex-post (after the teacher has invested in k). Prices are determined through bargaining. When there are two players the Nash solution is implemented, that is, the total payoff is divided equally among the two. When there are three players, the Shapley value determines the payoffs: each player gets her outside option plus a third of the prize over which they are bargaining. The government has no more bargaining power than any other player. The fee paid by the students is the total value obtained from education (either $v(k)$ or $V(k)$) minus the share they get in the bargaining process.

a. Suppose there is no school, and the teacher and the government bargain over the cost of education. Find the net payoff to each and the teacher's investment. Compare it to the first-best level.

b. Suppose there is a school. Calculate the payoffs and the teacher's investment when the outsider owns the school. Under what conditions is the level of investment in knowledge greater than in the absence of a school?

c. Suppose that the teacher or the government own the school. Find the level of investment in knowledge. When is it higher than under the ownership of the outsider?

⋆ **7. Competition among teachers within one school (based on Bolton and Xu 1997)**

Suppose in the economy there is one school, with two teachers competing for a teaching position in the school. As before, there is a body of students, and the government represents the students. We denote by V^i the value of education in the school with teacher $i = 1, 2$, and by V the value of education when both teachers are present in the school. Also, we denote by k_i the investment in knowledge of teacher $i = 1, 2$.

Also suppose,

$$V^i(k_i) = \lambda \log(1 + k_i) \text{ and } V^j(k_j) = \log(1 + k_j) \quad \text{with probability } 1/2$$

$$V^i(k_i) = \log(1 + k_i) \text{ and } V^j(k_j) = \lambda \log(1 + k_j) \quad \text{with probability } 1/2$$

with $\lambda > 2$. That is, ex-ante teachers are equally able, but ex-post their acquired knowledge will not have the same value. Thus, when $k_1 = k_2 = k$, each teacher has an equal chance of becoming the better teacher. With probability 1/2 teacher 1 is the "good" teacher and contributes a total value of $V^1 = \lambda \log(1 + k)$, and teacher 2 is the "bad" teacher with a total value of $V^2 = \log(1 + k)$ and vice versa. Moreover, $V(k_1, k_2) = \max\{V^1(k_1), V^2(k_2)\}$.

Last, for the outside-school education value we have $v^i(k_i) = \alpha V^i(k_i)$ with $1 > \alpha > 2/\lambda$.

a. Suppose teachers' investment is observable and verifiable, thus contractible ex-ante. Find the optimal investment level chosen by a social planner who maximizes the expected payoff of education (first best). Consider only the symmetric Nash equilibrium solution.

b. Denote by $\bar{V}$ the value generated by the high-ability teacher and by $\underline{V}$ the value generated by the low-ability teacher. Suppose that the government owns the school and that the outside option of students is binding (i.e., $\underline{V} > \bar{V}/2$). Calculate the payoffs of the different parties. Obtain the teachers' (symmetric) equilibrium investment level, and compare it with the first best.

c. Suppose the school is owned by outside investors. Calculate the payoff and teachers' equilibrium investment.

d. Suppose the school is jointly owned by the two teachers. Under what condition will equilibrium investments be more than under outsider ownership? Discuss this condition.

e. Suppose the school is owned by one of the teachers, say teacher T_1. Find the equilibrium investments. Discuss the impact of different ownership structures on teachers' competition.

11 Growth in Open Economies[1]

11.1 Introduction

So far, our analysis of economic growth has been confined to a closed economy. This is often a convenient assumption, but it is clearly important to consider how our findings will be modified for open economies. In this chapter, we examine the consequences for growth of interaction between countries. We concentrate on international trade in goods, but as we shall see, when we introduce trade in goods, the nature of international flows in knowledge also becomes very important to the results.

There is a large empirical literature on the relation between growth and trade "openness" or "outward orientation," which until recently has proceeded largely independently of formal theory. We will set out some formal models and then discuss relevant empirical work. Space precludes a full treatment of the issues, of the kind provided to good effect by Grossman and Helpman (1991a, 1996) and Obstfeld and Rogoff (1996). Instead, the principal aim of this chapter is to consider the implications of "opening up" our earlier models to international trade and knowledge spillovers.

In the next section, we provide a brief overview of trade and growth, discussing the relevance of open-economy considerations to the analysis in the previous chapters. We then consider three sets of issues in more detail. Section 11.3 examines the effects of international trade in intermediate inputs and international flows of ideas, building on the product-variety model presented in Chapter 1. Then, in section 11.4, we introduce a model with more than one final-goods sector. This allows us to discuss ideas of "dynamic" comparative advantage. Conventionally, trade theorists have taken the state of technology as given. In the Schumpeterian models considered in this section, the rate of technical progress and the pattern of international trade are jointly and endogenously determined. A key implication of these models is that it is no longer possible to draw conclusions a priori about the benefits or costs of free trade. As we discuss in section 11.5, equally ambiguous effects of trade liberalization obtain in models of learning by doing. The ambiguity in the theoretical conclusions reinforces the importance of empirical work, and we review a selection of such work in section 11.6.

11.2 Openness and Growth: An Overview

Sometimes modifying our analysis for open economies is likely to make little difference to the results, and so for some issues the closed economy assumption

---

1. This chapter was written jointly with Stephen Redding and Jonathan Temple.

is a useful simplification. In other areas the assumption is less defensible, as in much existing work on convergence. It is clear that flows of goods, ideas, and capital are likely to have profound implications for the nature and speed of convergence, and we consider some of these issues first.

Chapter 1 began with the neoclassical growth model of Ramsey (1928), Solow (1956), and Swan (1956). The usual conclusion has been that opening up the neoclassical model has straightforward, and to some extent rather un-interesting, implications. More recently, Ventura (1997) has shown that recog-nizing interdependence should change the analysis in more fundamental ways. We first consider the standard points, and then turn to Ventura's ideas.

Within the neoclassical framework, the sole determinant of long-run growth in income per capita is the rate at which exogenous technological break-throughs occur. This suggests that interaction with other countries can have no effect on an economy's long-run rate of growth. However, there may be some interesting effects of openness on the long-run level of welfare, and in the transition to the steady state.

Two points are of particular note. First, in the open-economy version of the neoclassical model, international flows of capital raise the rate of convergence to the steady state. For a small open economy facing an exogenously given world interest rate, one obtains the counterintuitive result that the rate of con-vergence to steady state is instantaneous.[2] More plausible predictions for the rate of convergence may be obtained by introducing capital-market imperfec-tions: for example, Barro, Mankiw and Sala-i-Martín (1995) analyze the speed of convergence when human capital cannot be used as collateral on foreign loans.

Secondly, Ben-David (1993) and Slaughter (1997) have noted that the recent literature on income convergence has proceeded somewhat independently of an earlier international trade literature that discussed "equalizing exchange," and, in particular, *factor price equalization*. For example, under the assumptions of Heckscher-Ohlin theory and assuming that economies remain incompletely specialized, international trade in goods and the attendant equalization in goods prices is sufficient to ensure international equalization of factor prices (see, for example, Samuelson 1949). In itself, factor price equalization will tend to induce income convergence, although whether or not incomes actually do converge will also depend on what is happening to factor quantities.[3]

As we noted above, these standard points give too simple a picture of how the analysis should be modified for open economies. In a very important paper, Ventura (1997) has emphasized the implications of combining a weak form of

---

2. For further discussion, see Barro and Sala-i-Martín (1995), Chapter 3.

3. For further details on this point, see Slaughter (1997).

the factor price-equalization theorem with the Ramsey model. Ventura points out that if some form of factor price equalization holds, interdependence becomes crucial to explaining the growth experience of different countries. The reason is that for trading economies, given factor price equalization, the law of diminishing returns applies only to world averages.

Let us discuss the argument in more detail. Under autarky, accumulating capital leads to a fall in its marginal product, as capital is used more intensively. In a small open economy, the marginal product of capital is determined by the world's capital stock because goods can be exported at prices given by world conditions. As a country accumulates capital, it can shift into more capital-intensive export sectors, and this means that in effect a small open economy can evade diminishing returns, even when its technology would not support sustained growth under autarky. Ventura uses this idea to explain the rapid growth of East Asia. In particular, it explains why East Asia has been able to grow through accumulating large amounts of capital, seemingly without facing a large fall in capital's marginal product.

Ventura's analysis has some other striking implications, notably for conditional convergence. The standard story, discussed in Chapter 1, is that returns to capital are higher in countries with low capital stocks. When economies trade and some form of factor price equalization holds, investment will be equally productive across countries. Differences in growth rates are then due to differences in investment rates, not differences in rates of return. As Ventura points out, investment rates may rise or fall with the stock of capital, and hence diminishing returns does not have to be associated with conditional convergence. Thus Ventura reinforces a point we tried to make in Chapter 1, namely that conditional convergence does not necessarily provide evidence against endogenous growth models in which long-run growth is driven by capital accumulation.

Now turning to the Frankel-Romer model of endogenous growth in which technological knowledge is equal to the total stock of accumulated capital, we noted that this model is characterized by a scale effect, whereby the larger the number of firms in the economy, the larger the amount of knowledge externalities and therefore the higher the growth rate. Insofar as international trade increases market size and raises the equilibrium number of firms, it will be responsible for a rise in the economy's rate of growth.

Emphasizing increasing returns, both the Romer model of increasing product variety developed in Chapter 1 (section 1.8) and the basic Schumpeterian model of Chapter 2, have the implication that free trade is beneficial for growth to the extent that it increases the total size of the market, and hence the monopoly rents that can be appropriated by successful innovators. International knowledge spillovers will obviously reinforce this positive effect of opening up economies: the fact that researchers in each economy can benefit from discoveries made elsewhere will increase the incentive for individuals to engage in research rather than production activities, thereby enhancing growth.

Considerations like these have encouraged a number of economists and decision makers to adopt a very optimistic attitude to the effects of trade liberalization on growth. First, free trade increases the size of the market and therefore the size of rewards to successful innovators; second, it enlarges the scope for knowledge spillovers, both of which are conducive to faster technological change. However, this optimistic view overlooks a number of potentially counteracting effects.

For example, as shown by Grossman and Helpman (1990; 1991a, chap. 6), free trade may sometimes shift labor from research into production. This "allocation effect" will obviously slow down technical change. Trade liberalization will also typically increase the degree of product market competition, which was shown in Chapter 2 to be detrimental to growth [although we saw in Chapter 7 that this "competition effect" becomes ambiguous in suitable extensions of the basic Schumpeterian model].[4]

This "competition effect" relates closely to the issue of imitation: how are the incentives to engage in *innovation* in a developed economy (the North) affected by its trading with a less developed economy (the South) that may invest in *imitating* products already discovered in its developed counterpart. The idea that products are first produced in the North, after which their production is relocated to the South, was the basis for Vernon's (1966) product-cycle theory of international trade. This was first formalized by Krugman (1979) in a model in which the rates of innovation in the North and imitation in the South are exogenous, and then subsequently extended in a Schumpeterian context by Grossman and Helpman (1991a, chaps. 11 and 12) and by Segerstrom (1991).

When there is more than one final-good sector, international trade (in the form of interindustry trade) may have an additional effect on an economy's rate of growth, through the changes in the allocation of resources across sectors induced by comparative advantage. Technology differences are one important source for comparative advantage. In traditional trade models, technology is taken to be exogenous. In contrast, in Schumpeterian models of growth it is endogenously determined within the model and hence, depending on the degree to which knowledge spillovers are national or international in scope, the pattern of comparative advantage may itself become endogenous. The interaction between endogenous technical change and comparative advantage has led a number of authors to speak of "dynamic comparative advantage."

The effect of the reallocations of resources induced by comparative advantage on growth is ambiguous, and depends very much on whether or not in-

---

4. The potentially negative "competition effect" of free trade on growth is also mitigated by the fact that international trade in intermediate inputs will eliminate duplication in research activities. See Grossman-Helpman (1991a).

ternational trade in goods is associated with international spillovers of ideas. If knowledge spillovers are essentially national in scope, then considerations such as those formalized by Young (1991) become relevant. In particular, the well-understood static welfare gains from trade (in terms of an increased variety in consumption patterns) may be offset by dynamic growth and welfare effects resulting from changes in specialization patterns, for example with the less-developed countries specializing in basic production activities in which there is little scope for accumulating new knowledge.

Having briefly discussed some potential implications of trade liberalization in the context of the basic endogenous-growth models (AK, Romer, and the Schumpeterian model) in Chapters 1 and 2, we now consider the effects of trade on growth in some of the extensions analyzed in subsequent chapters.

In particular, in Chapter 6, we drew the important distinction between fundamental and secondary innovations. The effects of international trade on growth within this framework remain a largely open area for further theoretical analysis. Without anticipating too much about the outcome of such research, it seems natural to assume that in an open-economy extension of the learning-by-doing model of Chapter 6, growth of general knowledge in a particular country should depend on the flow of fundamental research and learning by doing in both that country and the rest of the world. Furthermore, the extent to which the elasticity of the G-function[5] with respect to domestic learning by doing should be small or large relative to the elasticity of the G-function with respect to the flow of domestic fundamental research should itself depend on the distance between the domestic leading-edge and the international leading edge technologies. More precisely, recent economic history seems to suggest that for countries that lie significantly below the international leading-edge, it is development (i.e., the flow of domestic secondary innovations and/or domestic learning by doing) rather than the current domestic flow of domestic fundamental research, that drives productivity growth and the accumulation of general knowledge. For example, a number of authors have argued that the rapid growth enjoyed in particular by Japan during much of the postwar period was associated with an ability to adapt, modify, and improve on technologies initially developed in other industrialized economies. In terms of the analysis of Chapter 6, Japan's rapid growth was associated with investments in development and learning by doing rather than research. As a country nears the technological frontier, increased investments in research become necessary in order to sustain growth, as in Van Elkan (1996).

However, as argued by Young (1991), whose model we describe in section 11.5, trade liberalization between developed and less developed countries

5. That is, of the function which determines the rate of growth of general knowledge as a function of the flow of learning by doing (LBD) and the flow of new fundamental innovations ($\lambda^r H^r$). See Chapter 6, equation (G).

(LDCs) may sometimes inhibit learning by doing and therefore growth of general knowledge in LDCs. Trade liberalization could induce LDCs to specialize in product lines in which the potential for learning has been largely exhausted.

Chapter 7 was concerned with market structure and, in particular, the relationship between competition and growth. One of the ways in which international trade may affect rates of innovation and growth is through increasing the extent of product market competition. Within the context of the Schumpeterian model of Chapter 2, this unambiguously reduces the incentive to engage in research. However, as we saw in Chapter 7, modifications to standard Schumpeterian models (which, for example, encompass agency effects, patent-race effects, or cross-sector mobility effects) deliver a positive relationship between product market competition and growth. Other things being equal, international trade will increase rates of growth through the rise in the extent of competition it brings about. A number of authors have argued, typically informally, that this "pro-competitive" effect of international trade is one reason why trade liberalization may raise rates of productivity growth. (Tybout 1992 provides further discussion.) It is worth remembering, though, that the effect of competition on innovation and growth is theoretically ambiguous.

In Chapter 8 we addressed the relationship between growth and cycles. Here the key question is likely to be the extent to which business cycles are synchronized across countries. Other things being equal, output may be more or less volatile in a relatively open economy, and the analysis of Chapter 8 suggests that openness and the degree of volatility may have important implications for growth.

Chapter 9 relaxed the representative agent assumption and considered issues of income distribution and political economy, and in particular the relationship between wage inequality and skill-biased technical change. In the United States, the 1970s and 1980s saw a large rise in the relative wage of skilled workers, while in a number of other OECD countries unskilled unemployment rates rose relative to skilled (see, for instance, Nickell and Bell 1995). Two competing explanations have been proposed for this structural change: skill-biased technological change (which we already analyzed in Chapter 9), and international trade.[6]

The argument that trade is responsible stems largely from Heckscher-Ohlin theory (see in particular Krugman 1995). Rapid growth in East Asia has been associated with an increase in exports of goods intensive in unskilled labor, and (to some degree, although this is partly a point of debate) a fall in the price of those exports. If wages are flexible, then by the Stolper-Samuelson theorem the fall in the price of imports into industrialized countries will be associated

---

6. For discussion, see Katz and Murphy (1992) and Murphy and Welch (1992) on the wage structure, and Wood (1994) on the effect of trade.

with a fall in the price of the factor used intensively in the import-competing sector: unskilled labor. Alternatively, if the wage of unskilled labor is rigid to some extent, the fall in the relative demand for unskilled labor will manifest itself in a rise in unskilled unemployment.

A growing empirical literature has tried to sort out how much of the observed rise in skilled-wage differentials can be explained by skill-biased technical change versus trade with newly industrializing countries. Krugman (1995) summarizes this research as indicating that the effect of East Asian imports on industrialized country labor markets has been small, or at least elusive. For instance Borjas, Freeman, and Katz (1992) find that a maximum of 15 percent of the growth of the college-noncollege wage differential is due to imports. Lawrence and Slaughter (1993) found little evidence that the relative prices of less skill-intensive goods have fallen in the United States, as the trade arguments would require (see also Sachs and Shatz 1994). Bound and Johnson (1992) suggest that recent increases in wage differentials have been driven by skill-biased technical change and unmeasured changes in labor quality, rather than by a decline in manufacturing employment.

More generally, if trade had been the main source of rising skilled-wage differentials, then those sectors *not* threatened by the competition of low-wage countries would presumably have taken advantage of the low relative price of unskilled labor by substituting it for skilled labor. That has not happened. Instead, the empirical observations are what one would expect if there had been an economy-wide increase in the productivity of skilled relative to unskilled labor. Overall, researchers tend to concur that trade has not had a substantial impact on wage inequality, and Lawrence and Slaughter even argue that, if anything, trade has "nudged relative wages toward greater equality."

In the existing literature, international trade and skill-biased technological change have been presented as competing explanations for increased wage inequality and the rise in unskilled unemployment. However, the Schumpeterian approach to growth suggests that the two may be closely intertwined. For example suppose that technological progress is skill-biased (as considered in Chapters 9 and 10) and that research is more intensive in skilled labor than manufacturing production. In this case, changes in the relative wage of the skilled brought about by international trade will affect the quantity of skilled labor devoted to research, and hence the equilibrium rate of (skill-biased) technological change.[7] Conversely, technical progress that reduces transportation and information costs is likely to magnify the effects of trade liberalization on wage inequality.

---

7. García-Peñalosa (1996b) relates the two explanations, technology and trade, in a model with increasing product variety.

In Chapter 5 we addressed the issue of sustainable development. Here, again there seem a number of interesting ways in which international trade may affect the analysis. Copeland and Taylor (1994) consider the relationship between national income, pollution, and international trade within a static model of North-South trade. In equilibrium, the higher income country chooses stronger environmental protection and specializes in relatively clean goods. In Schumpeterian models of endogenous growth, these choices of environmental protection and patterns of international specialization will have implications for the incentives to engage in innovation and hence for the economy's rate of growth.

Finally, looking forward to the last chapter of this book on public aid to innovation, several of the issues addressed here remain of particular interest once one moves from a closed to an open economy. One issue that has already been addressed in the literature is the international enforcement of intellectual property rights. For instance, Helpman (1993) considers the circumstances under which increased property-right protection in developing countries (the South) is beneficial for the North, the South, or both. Problem 2 will consider this analysis in more detail.

Having hinted at some of the ways in which international openness may affect our main conclusions in previous chapters, we now turn to consider some of these effects in greater detail. We begin by introducing international flows of goods and ideas into the Romer (1990a) model discussed in Chapter 1.

11.3   Opening Up the Romer Model

Suppose that the world is populated by two economies, home and foreign, where all foreign variables are denoted by an asterisk. Each economy is exactly as specified in the analysis of the Romer model in Chapter 1. There is a single final-goods sector, so as yet we abstract from considerations of comparative advantage and instead concentrate on the "scale effects" of international trade. Final goods are produced with skilled labor and intermediate inputs according to the same technology as in Chapter 1. Thus, for home,

$$Y = L_1^{1-\alpha} \int_0^A x(i)^\alpha di, \qquad 0 < \alpha < 1, \tag{11.1}$$

The two economies are identical except that the ranges of intermediate inputs produced in each economy are entirely different (there is no duplication in research). New designs for intermediate inputs are produced by the research sector, at a rate given by

$$\dot{A} = \delta L_2 A, \tag{11.2}$$

Suppose that each economy produces entirely in isolation under conditions of autarky. General equilibrium is determined exactly as before, using the requirement that the wage in the manufacturing sector equals the return to entering research,

$$w_1 = w_2,$$

or, in symmetric equilibrium,

$$(1 - \alpha)L_1^{-\alpha}Ax^\alpha = \delta P_A, \qquad (11.3)$$

where P_A denotes the price or value of each design. Solving for the equilibrium allocation of skilled labor and the growth rate as in Chapter 1, we obtain

$$L_2 = \bar{L} - \frac{r}{\alpha\delta}, \qquad g = \frac{\alpha\delta.\bar{L} - \rho}{\alpha + \varepsilon}, \qquad (11.4)$$

where r is the interest rate paid on capital goods, ε is the inverse of the intertemporal elasticity of substitution, and ρ is the subjective rate of time discounting.

The two economies are now allowed to engage in intra-industry trade in differentiated intermediate inputs, assuming that there are no international flows of ideas. On one hand, the increase in the number of available intermediate inputs raises labor's marginal product in the final-goods sector. As a result, the wage in this sector rises from $w_1 = (1 - \alpha).L_1^{-\alpha}.A.x^\alpha$ to $w_1 = (1 - \alpha).L_1^{-\alpha}.(A + A^*).x^\alpha$. On the other hand, trade in intermediate inputs means that the market for any newly designed good is now twice as large as it was before, so that the return to entering research doubles from $w_2 = \delta.P_A$ to $w_2 = 2.\delta.P_A$.[8]

Because the return to labor from entering each sector doubles (remember that the number of varieties in each economy prior to trade is the same), international trade has no effect on the incentive to engage in research, and hence no effect on the economy's rate of growth. Although trade in intermediate inputs has no effect on growth, it does have important *level* effects. The marginal product of labor in (11.1) is increasing in the number of varieties of intermediate inputs, so that international trade raises the level of both final-goods output and economic welfare.

Suppose now that international flows of ideas between the two economies are also allowed. If each economy has discovered a completely different set of intermediate inputs prior to trade, the stock of ideas that can be used in research is now double its previous level. The productivity of labor in research doubles and, from equation (11.2),

---

8. In general, the increase in the number of intermediate inputs brought about through trade may also increase the extent of competition faced by an individual producer (see Grossman and Helpman 1991a). The model considered here is a special case: the competition effect does not arise because the final-goods production technology (11.1) is additively separable in intermediate inputs.

$$\dot{A} = \delta.L_2.2A, \tag{11.5}$$

This has two effects on the economy's equilibrium rate of growth. On one hand, the increase in productivity has a direct positive effect on the rate of growth of the domestic knowledge stock A (for any given value of L_2). On the other hand, because productivity in research has risen while that in the final goods sector has remained unchanged, equilibrium employment in research L_2 will rise. Hence there is an additional indirect positive effect on the economy's rate of growth through increased research employment,

$$L_2 = \bar{L} - \frac{r}{2\alpha\delta}, \qquad g = \frac{2\alpha\delta\bar{L} - \rho}{\alpha + \varepsilon}, \tag{11.6}$$

The result that international flows of ideas raise the economy's rate of growth is very much dependent on the form of the research technology. In equation (11.2), we assume that ideas enter directly into the research technology: each discovery raises the productivity of subsequent research, so that each generation of researchers "stands on the shoulders" of previous researchers. Following Rivera-Batiz and Romer (1991), we term this the "knowledge-driven" specification of research.

Rivera-Batiz and Romer (1991) also consider an alternative specification (the "lab equipment" model) where the research technology is the same as that in the final-goods sector. In this case intermediate inputs enter directly into research (note here the similarity with the analysis in Chapter 3),

$$\dot{A} = \psi.L_2^{1-\alpha} \int_0^A x_2(i)^\alpha di, \qquad 0 < \alpha < 1. \tag{11.7}$$

The fact that ideas in themselves do not affect the productivity of research (and only influence the latter through the production of new varieties of intermediate inputs that they make possible) means that international flows of ideas alone have no effect on an economy's rate of growth. In contrast, international trade in intermediate inputs expands the variety of inputs that may be used in research and increases the marginal product of labor in research. Again, there are two effects on the economy's equilibrium rate of growth: a direct positive effect from the increase in the productivity of research and an indirect positive effect, acting through the incentive to engage in research.

Therefore, the effect of international flows of ideas varies with the nature of the research technology. Even if ideas do enter directly into research, there remain a number of unresolved questions. First, there is the issue concerning the process by which ideas disseminate across countries. A number of authors, including, for example, Grossman and Helpman (1991b), have argued that international trade in goods may itself be central to the spillover of ideas. For example, developing economies may be able to reverse-engineer the capital goods they import.

Secondly, there is a question as to why in the preceding analysis there was no duplication in research prior to international trade. Grossman and Helpman (1991a) argue that international trade in intermediate inputs may have a positive effect on growth insofar as it eliminates duplication in research: researchers in one economy will no longer be able to achieve positive profits from duplicating the designs for intermediate inputs already discovered in a second economy.

Finally, we should note that the conclusion above (idea flows matter, trade flows do not when the research technology is "knowledge-driven") is very much a special case. Devereux and Lapham (1994) consider the effects of international trade in goods between *dissimilar* economies in the "knowledge-driven" specification of Rivera-Batiz and Romer (1991). The finding that international trade in goods has no effect on the economy's growth rate is found to be fragile: it holds only in the knife-edge case where the pre-liberalization stocks of knowledge are exactly equal across countries.

If this condition does not hold, then whichever economy has the higher stock of knowledge will increase its share of human capital engaged in research, while the other economy systematically reduces its share. Ultimately all R&D is undertaken in the economy with the initially larger stock of knowledge. International trade in goods is found to increase the world rate of growth. One economy will experience a decrease in its rate of growth, but not necessarily in its welfare.

Feenstra (1996) derives some similar results: in the absence of international spillovers, free trade may lead to a decline in the growth rates of smaller countries (where size is measured by the labor force in R&D efficiency units). The possibility that openness can lead to a decrease in growth is an intriguing one. In the next section, we shall see that this result may also occur via the introduction of inter-industry trade and considerations of comparative advantage.

11.4 Dynamic Comparative Advantage

This section[9] integrates the Schumpeterian model of endogenous growth into the framework of conventional trade theory. In the latter, the state of technology at any one point in time is taken as given, and the patterns of comparative advantage and international trade are then derived. In contrast, Schumpeterian theories of international trade and economic growth explicitly model the determinants of technical progress. If international knowledge spillovers are imperfect, comparative advantage itself becomes endogenous.

---

9. This section is largely based on Grossman and Helpman (1991a, chap. 7).

The idea that the evolution of comparative advantage and the rate of techno-logical change are jointly and endogenously determined was first formalized by Krugman (1987). Krugman considers the determinants of patterns of inter-national trade within a Ricardian model in which an economy's productivity in a given sector depends on a stock of sector-specific cumulative produc-tion experience. The latter is accumulated through a process of learning by doing, and, although spillovers of learning by doing across economies are al-lowed, they are assumed to be incomplete. Initial conditions (the initial stocks of cumulative production experience) in the two economies determine the ini-tial pattern of comparative advantage and international specialization, which becomes increasingly "locked-in" over time as each economy accumulates pro-duction experience more rapidly in the sectors in which it specializes than in the sectors in which it does not.

The idea that patterns of comparative advantage and rates of technologi-cal change interact with one another is, however, much more general. In this section, we consider the Grossman and Helpman (1991a, chap. 7) model of dy-namic comparative advantage, in which an essentially Heckscher-Ohlin theory of international trade is combined with a Schumpeterian model of endoge-nous growth through profit-seeking R&D. There are two important differences from the analysis of the previous section. First, following Chapter 2, we con-sider a model of growth through rising product quality (rather than increasing specialization). Second, we admit more than one final-goods industry so that considerations of inter-industry trade and comparative advantage become im-portant.

We consider the effects of international trade between two economies A and B. Each economy comprises three sectors (final-goods production, intermediate-input manufacture, and research) and is endowed with two pri-mary factors of production (skilled and unskilled labor). Within the final-goods sector, two final outputs are produced: a low-technology good z and a high-technology good y. Skilled and unskilled labor are used directly to produce the low-technology good, whose production occurs under conditions of perfect competition. The high-technology good is produced with a range of intermedi-ate inputs. The number of these inputs is fixed and endogenous growth occurs as a result of improvements in the *quality* of intermediate inputs. The latter are produced under conditions of imperfect competition, and it is the resulting flow of monopoly profits that provides the incentive to engage in research. Skilled and unskilled labor are employed in both intermediate-input production and research.

Initially, we will be concerned with equilibria in which each economy is incompletely specialized in the four activities of low-technology production, high-technology production, intermediate-input manufacture, and research. The effects of international trade depend crucially on whether or not knowledge spillovers are international in scope, and we begin by assuming that they are. Throughout the analysis, we assume that intermediate inputs must be produced in the same economy in which the associated technological blueprint was discovered in research, so that we abstract from the existence of multinationals and technology licensing.

Consumer preferences in the two economies are assumed to be identical and intertemporally additive-separable with intertemporal elasticities of substitution equal to one. The representative consumer's optimization problem may thus be solved in two stages: the determination of the optimal allocation of instantaneous consumer expenditure between the two final goods, and the characterization of the optimal time profile of consumer expenditure. Instantaneous utility is chosen such that each consumer allocates a constant proportion σ and $1 - \sigma$ of expenditure to the consumption of the high- and low-technology goods respectively. Given the specification for preferences, intertemporal utility maximization by the representative consumer implies that the time profile of aggregate expenditure in economy i obeys the familiar Ramsey condition,

$$\frac{\dot{E}^i}{E^i} = r^i - \rho, \tag{11.8}$$

where r^i denotes the riskless interest rate on consumption in economy i and ρ is the subjective rate of time preference. Perfect capital mobility implies $r_A = r_B = r$, and world aggregate expenditure $E = E^A + E^B$ is chosen as the numeraire so that $E(t) = 1$ for all t. E^i thus denotes the share of world expenditure undertaken by residents in economy i and, in a steady-state equilibrium in which each economy undertakes a constant share of world expenditure, equation (11.8) implies $r_A = r_B = r = \rho$.

The low-technology good is produced from skilled and unskilled labor under conditions of perfect competition. In contrast, the high-technology good is produced from a range of intermediate inputs with a production technology which is a particular multisector version of the model introduced in Chapter 2,

$$\log Y = \int_0^1 \log \left[\sum_m \gamma^m(j).x_m(j) \right] dj, \qquad \gamma > 1, \tag{11.9}$$

where, as before, γ denotes the size of innovations and $x_m(j)$ denotes the quantity of intermediate input j of quality m currently produced using high technology. Production again occurs under conditions of perfect competition. Because high production technology is logarithmically additive and separable in the (quality-adjusted) quantity of each intermediate input employed, in equilibrium high-technology producers allocate their expenditure evenly over intermediate-input sectors.

Intermediate inputs are produced with skilled labor L and unskilled labor H, and the technology in equation (11.9) implies that all innovations are non-drastic. Intermediate-input production occurs under conditions of imperfect competition and the owner of the patent to the state-of-the-art quality of intermediate inputs in each sector charges a limit price γ times that of the next-best quality.[10] Because the lowest price that may be charged by the producer of the latter is the unit cost of intermediate-input production $c_x(w_L, w_H)$, the price p^{ij} charged by a state of the art producer located in economy i when the next best quality is located in economy j is

$$p^{ij} = \gamma . c_x(w_L^j, w_H^j), \tag{11.10}$$

where w_L and w_H are the wages of skilled and unskilled labor respectively.

Intermediate input sectors are symmetric, and hence equation (11.10) holds for all sectors. In an equilibrium in which economies are incompletely specialized in all four activities, we require that the unit costs of production in low-technology, high-technology, and intermediate-input production are the same in both economies. In this case, Grossman and Helpman show that the flow of profits received by the monopoly producer of the state-of-the-art intermediate input is in fact independent of the economy in which both she and the next-best quality producer are located,

$$\pi^{ij} = \pi \equiv (1 - 1/\gamma) . \sigma. \tag{11.11}$$

The quality of intermediate inputs rises over time as innovations are made in the research sector. Researchers in each economy i may target their research at either producers of the state-of-the-art quality of intermediate inputs in economy i or those located in economy j. The research technology is directly analogous to that introduced in Chapter 2: skilled and unskilled labor are employed in research according to a constant returns to scale technology. We assume that the unit cost to a firm located in economy i, $i = A, B$, of achieving a unit Poisson arrival rate of innovation, equals $c_\gamma(w_L^i, w_H^i)$. This technology is the same for all intermediate input sectors and for both economies. Furthermore, each innovation is assumed to spill over perfectly to researchers in both economies.

In a steady-state equilibrium in which both economies are active in research, a free-entry condition in each economy equates the marginal benefit and marginal cost of research,

$$c_\gamma(w_L^i, w_H^i) = v^i, \qquad i = A, B, \tag{11.12}$$

where v^i denotes the growth-adjusted value of an innovation, which, in

---

10. For further discussion, see the analysis of nondrastic innovations in Chapter 2 or Grossman and Helpman (1991a, chap. 4).

equilibrium, is the same in all intermediate input sectors. At each point in time, a no-arbitrage condition requires that the returns to research equal those in a riskless consumption loans market. The steady-state value of an innovation is determined by an asset equation directly analogous to that in Chapter 2,

$$r^i v^i = \pi - \iota^i v^i, \tag{11.13}$$

where $\iota^i \equiv \iota^{Ai} + \iota^{Bi}$ denotes the world intensity of research directed at producers of state-of-the-art intermediate inputs in economy i. Substituting for π in (11.13) from the above and noting that in steady state $r^i = r = \rho$ $(i = A, B)$, then substituting for v^i in (11.12), we obtain the no-arbitrage condition:

$$\frac{\sigma(1 - 1/\gamma)}{c_\gamma(w_L^i, w_H^i)} = \rho + \iota^i, \qquad i = A, B, \tag{A}$$

In order to solve for general equilibrium, we combine this no-arbitrage condition with a labor market-clearing requirement that is directly analogous to equation (L) in Chapter 2. Labor market clearing requires that the demands for skilled and unskilled labor in research, intermediate-input production and low-technology production equal the corresponding endowments of these factors,

$$a_\gamma(w_L^i, w_H^i)(\iota^{iA} n^A + \iota^{iB} n^B) + a_x(w_L^i, w_H^i)X^i$$

$$+ a_Z(w_L^i, w_H^i).Z^i = \begin{bmatrix} L^i \\ H^i \end{bmatrix}, \qquad i = A, B, \tag{11.14}$$

where $a_\gamma(\cdot, \cdot)$, $a_x(\cdot, \cdot)$ and $a_Z(\cdot, \cdot)$ are the vectors of unit labor requirements in research, intermediate-input production, and low technology-goods production respectively; n^i denotes the number of state-of-the-art intermediate input producers located in economy i; ι^{iA} denotes the intensity of research in economy i, directed at intermediate inputs produced in economy A; and x^i and Z^i are the aggregate productions of intermediate inputs and low-technology good in country i.

In steady-state equilibrium, each economy produces state-of-the-art qualities in a constant share of intermediate-input sectors and makes investments in research that are compatible with its maintaining technological leadership in these sectors, whereas aggregate expenditure in each economy constitutes a constant share of world expenditure. It follows that in steady-state equilibrium the number of sectors in which economy A innovates and gains technological leadership must equal the number of sectors in which it loses technological leadership to economy B,

$$\iota^{AB}.n^B = \iota^{BA}.n^A. \tag{11.15}$$

This in turn implies that the aggregate amount of research undertaken in each economy equals the aggregate amount of research targeted at that economy's state-of-the-art products. That is, $\iota^{iA}.n^A + \iota^{iB}.n^B = \iota^i.n^i$ in equation (11.14), so that:

$$a_Y(w_L^i, w_H^i).\iota^i n^i + a_x(w_L^i, w_H^i)X^i$$

$$+ a_Z(w_L^i, w_H^i).Z^i = \begin{bmatrix} L^i \\ H^i \end{bmatrix}, \qquad i = A, B, \tag{L}$$

General equilibrium is fully characterized by the no-arbitrage condition (A) and the labor market-clearing requirement (L). In an equilibrium in which both economies are active in all four activities, it was already noted that we require the unit costs of production in the low-technology and intermediate-input sectors to be the same. Because there are only two factors of production and these are employed in both sectors, it follows (except in the special case where both these sectors have the same production technology) that such an equilibrium must be characterized by *factor price equalization*. Because factor prices are equalized and the research technology is the same in both economies, so are the costs of research. From the no-arbitrage condition (A), it follows immediately that $\iota^A = \iota^B$. That is, in steady-state equilibrium, state-of-the-art producers in each economy face the same probability of replacement, and each economy experiences the same rate of innovation.

Following Grossman and Helpman, we may solve for a factor price equalization (FPE) equilibrium diagrammatically using the techniques of traditional trade theory (as expounded by Dixit and Norman 1980). In order to establish the existence of a FPE equilibrium, we proceed in the following steps. First, we identify the long-run equilibrium that would occur in a hypothetical integrated world economy (in which goods, factors of production, and knowledge are perfectly mobile across economies). Second, we construct allocations of resources that lie within each economy's endowment set and utilize the same techniques of production in each economy as in the hypothetical integrated equilibrium. Third, we see whether these allocations result in the same aggregate output of goods and knowledge as in the integrated equilibrium. Fourth, we require the resulting allocation of resources to satisfy the no-arbitrage conditions in each economy, and to be such that the number of sectors in which each economy produces state-of-the-art intermediate inputs is consistent with the economy's investments in research. Hence each economy produces state-of-the-art products in a constant fraction of sectors. An equilibrium satisfying all four conditions constitutes a FPE equilibrium.

Such an equilibrium is shown diagrammatically in figure 11.1, where the rectangle $O^A Q^A O^B Q^B$ defines world endowments of the two primary factors of production (with unskilled labor measured along the horizontal axis and skilled labor along the vertical). The vectors $O^A M^A$, $M^A N^A$, and $N^A O^B$ represent the vectors of resources devoted to research, intermediate-input production, and traditional-goods manufacture respectively in the steady-state

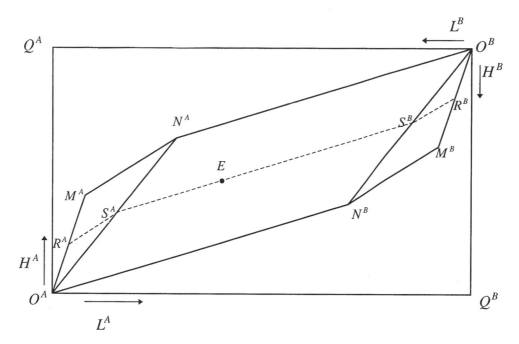

Figure 11.1
Factor price equalization equilibrium. Source: Grossman and Helpman (1991a), p. 184.

equilibrium of the hypothetical integrated economy (these may be found by summing the two economies' endowments and solving for the steady-state equilibrium of the resulting closed economy). As drawn in figure 11.1, these vectors embody the plausible assumption that research is the most human capital-intensive activity and traditional-goods production the least.

The individual endowments of the two countries are shown by the point E in figure 11.1, and, because E lies above the diagonal, country A is assumed to have a relative abundance of human capital. In order for an FPE equilibrium to exist, we require that the two countries' endowments be sufficiently similar: specifically, that the endowment point lie within the parallelogram $O^A N^A O^B N^B$. An FPE equilibrium satisfying all four conditions above is when economy A devotes the vectors of resources $O^A R^A$, $R^A S^A$, and $S^A E$ to research, intermediate-input production, and final-goods production respectively (and economy B the vectors of resources $O^B R^B$, $R^B S^B$, and $S^B E$).[11] In static-trade models with three activities and two primary factors of production, the equilibrium pattern of international specialization is typically non-unique.

---

11. These vectors correspond to the two economies' equilibrium allocations of skilled and un-skilled labor to research, intermediate input production, and low-technology production in equations (A) and (L) above. That is, in terms of equation (L), $a_y(w_L^i, w_H^i).i^i n^i$, $a_x(w_L^i, w_H^i).X^i$, and $a_Z(w_L^i, w_H^i).Z^i$ respectively. For further details, see Grossman and Helpman (1991a: 183–192 and 195–196).

However, in the present dynamic model, the additional requirement that the number of sectors in which each economy produces state of the art products be consistent with the economy's investments in research means that the equilibrium allocation of skilled/unskilled labor over each manufacturing activity and research is unique.[12]

There are two key points to note about the resulting equilibrium. First, *with international knowledge spillovers*, comparative advantage and the equilibrium allocation of resources between research, intermediate-input production, and low technology-goods production is uniquely determined by factor endowments. Therefore, in the presence of international knowledge spillovers, this standard Heckscher-Ohlin result carries over into a dynamic Schumpeterian model where technology is endogenous. As shown in figure 11.1, the economy with a relative abundance of human capital will undertake *relatively* more research in equilibrium than the other economy compared to its relative output of the traditional good ($\iota^A n^A / Z^A > \iota^B n^B / Z^B$). As a result, it will gain technological leadership in a relatively larger number of intermediate input sectors ($n^A / Z^A > n^B / Z^B$) and produce a relatively larger amount of the high-technology good.

Second, because high-technology goods comprise a larger share of output in the economy with a relative abundance of human capital (and the equilibrium rate of innovation $\iota^A = \iota^B = \iota$ is the same in both economies), it follows that the former will enjoy a faster rate of growth of (quality-adjusted) manufacturing output than its trade partner. Nonetheless, although the two economies experience permanently different rates of growth of output, they enjoy the same rate of growth of real consumption and welfare. This follows from factor price equalization at each point in time, and the fact that trade ensures that each economy has access to the same qualities of intermediate inputs.

In order to compare rates of economic growth with their pre-trade levels, we must ascertain first whether the common rate of innovation $\iota^A = \iota^B = \iota$ in the free-trade equilibrium is higher or lower than that in each economy prior to trade. Secondly, we must determine how trade affects the composition of output between high-technology and low-technology sectors. We begin with the second of these tasks. Considerations of comparative advantage imply that the human capital-abundant economy will reallocate resources toward the production of the high-technology good, whereas the converse will be true in the other economy. In itself, this will tend to increase the rate of growth in the human capital-abundant economy and decrease it in the human capital-scarce economy.

---

12. Again, see Grossman and Helpman (1991a) for further discussion of this point. What is not unique is the extent to which entrepreneurs in each economy direct their research at state-of-the-art producers in their own economy versus those in the other economy. A continuum of values of $\iota^{AA}, \iota^{AB}, \iota^{BA}$ and ι^{BB} is consistent with (11.15) and $\iota^{AA} + \iota^{BA} = \iota = \iota^{AB} + \iota^{BB}$.

However, if we return to what happens to the rate of innovation, note that the world economy is relatively better endowed with unskilled labor than the human capital-abundant economy. As a result, the world economy will devote relatively more resources to unskilled labor-intensive activities, and the common rate of innovation may actually be less than in the human capital-abundant economy prior to trade. In itself, this will tend to decrease the rate of growth in the human capital-abundant economy and (by a directly analogous argument) increase it in the human capital-scarce economy.[13]

Therefore the human capital-rich country reallocates resources toward the high-technology sector but may experience a fall in the rate of innovation, while the human capital-scarce economy reallocates resources away from high-technology production but experiences a rise in the rate of innovation. The net effect on each economy's growth rate is ambiguous. The fall in the rate of innovation in the high-technology country means that although it enjoys static welfare gains from trade—from the exploitation of comparative advantage and intra-industry trade in intermediate inputs—these come at the expense of *dynamic* welfare losses.

Within this framework, it is also possible to consider the case where the economies' resource endowments are sufficiently dissimilar that factor prices are not equalized. The interested reader is referred to Grossman and Helpman (1991a, chap. 7). Perhaps a more substantive question is how the relationship between trade and growth is affected when knowledge spillovers are confined to the national level. We address this question within the framework of the Young (1991) model of endogenous growth through bounded learning by doing.[14] The exposition extends that in Chapter 6, problem 5.

11.5   Learning by Doing and Comparative Advantage

The Young (1991) model of bounded learning by doing is an essentially Ricardian model of international trade, in which trade is driven by differences in technology rather than those in factor endowments. It allows a particularly clear analysis of the effects of international trade on economic growth and welfare, and also ties in with our discussion of fundamental and secondary research in Chapter 6.

Because knowledge stocks, and hence technologies, differ across economies, factor price equalization need no longer occur. Hence it becomes

---

13. Effectively, international trade is akin to factor accumulation and, as shown by Grossman and Helpman (1991a, chap. 5), the accumulation of a factor used least intensively in research may, under certain circumstances, reduce an economy's rate of growth.

14. Grossman and Helpman (1991a, chap. 8) address the same question within a model of growth through increasing specialisation following Romer (1990a).

possible to examine the conditions under which income per capita in a less developed economy not only catches up with but also overtakes the level in a more developed counterpart.[15]

Young (1991) considers the effect of international trade between two economies (A and B), each of which is endowed with a single primary factor of production (skilled labor). Both economies may produce any one of an infinite number of goods $s \in [0, \infty)$,[16] where goods are indexed in terms of increasing technological sophistication s. All goods are produced with a constant returns to scale technology under conditions of perfect competition. However, technologies differ in terms of unit labor requirements. More sophisticated goods (produced on more recent product lines) are assumed to be characterized by lower *potential* unit labor requirements, but higher *actual* unit labor requirements when first introduced. Actual unit labor requirements fall over time as learning by doing occurs in the same way as in the LBD model of Chapter 6. However, Young (1991) assumes that there is a lower bound to the potential unit labor requirements for each good. Specifically, we follow Young in considering the special case where potential unit labor requirements $\bar{a}(s)$ are exponentially decreasing in the degree of technological sophistication s,[17]

$$\bar{a}(s) = \bar{a}.e^{-s}. \tag{11.16}$$

For all goods for which the potential for learning by doing has not yet been exhausted, *actual* unit labor requirements $a(s, t)$ are assumed to be increasing in s. Specifically, we again follow Young in considering the special case,

$$a(s, t) = \begin{cases} \bar{a}.e^{-s} & \text{for all } s \leq S(t) \\ \bar{a}.e^{-S(t)}.e^{s - S(t)} & \text{for all } s > S(t), \end{cases} \tag{11.17}$$

where $S(t)$ denotes the most sophisticated good for which all potential for learning by doing has been exhausted and characterizes the stock of technological knowledge.

For those goods for which potential unit labor requirements have not yet been attained, actual unit labor requirements will fall as a result of learning by doing. We assume externalities in learning-by-doing across goods, so that $S(t)$ rises at a rate depending on the economy-wide flow of skilled labor devoted to the production of goods where potential for learning by doing still exists,

---

15. This question has also been considered by Brezis, Krugman, and Tsiddon (1993).

16. Implicitly, we assume that the technological blueprints for an infinite number of goods are available from the beginning of time. Young (1993a) extends the analysis to include a research sector, which is the source of new technological blueprints, as we do in Chapter 6 when formalizing fundamental research and innovations.

17. See Young (1991) for a consideration of more general technologies.

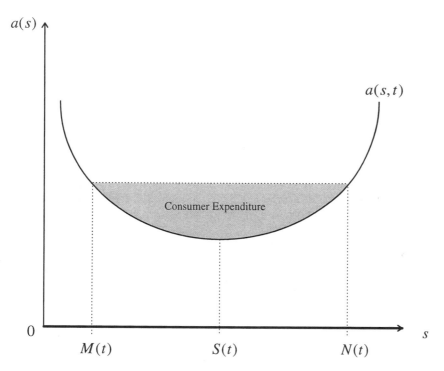

Figure 11.2
Static equilibrium in Young model. Source: Young (1991), p. 383.

$$\frac{dS(t)}{dt} = \int_{S(t)}^{\infty} L(s,t)ds, \tag{11.18}$$

Consumer preferences are assumed to be intertemporally additive-separable, with instantaneous utility logarithmically additive separable in the consumption of each good,

$$u_t = \int_t^{\infty} e^{-\rho(\tau-t)} \cdot \int_0^{\infty} \log\left[c(s,\tau) + 1\right] ds d\tau, \tag{11.19}$$

where ρ denotes the subjective rate of time preference.

This specification for instantaneous utility implies that, in equilibrium, agents consume a variety of final goods. We begin by considering equilibrium in the *absence* of both international trade and international spillovers of ideas. Under perfect competition, the price of each good is simply $p(s,t) = a(s,t).w(t)$, where $w(t)$ denotes the wage rate at time t. Static equilibrium under autarky is illustrated diagrammatically in figure 11.2, where agents consume the range of goods $s \in (M(t), N(t))$. Because actual unit labor requirements are symmetric around $S(t)$, so are prices and the range of goods consumed. The economy's autarkic growth rate depends on the rate of learning by doing on those goods for which potential unit labor requirements have not yet been attained.[18] Because the range of goods consumed in equilibrium is symmetric around $S(t)$, only half of the labor force is devoted to the production of such goods, and it may be shown that the economy's growth rate under autarky is simply

$$g(t) = \frac{\bar{L}}{2},$$ (11.20)

where $\bar{L}$ denotes the size of the economy's labor force.

Now consider the effects of international trade (*without* international spillovers of ideas). The two economies are assumed to be identical except for the size of their labor forces $\bar{L}$ and the stock of technological knowledge $S(t)$. We assume $S^A(t) > S^B(t)$, so that economy A is interpreted as being a developed country (DC) and economy B a less developed country (LDC). The assumption $S^A(t) > S^B(t)$ implies that relative unit labor requirements in the DC $a^A(s, t)/a^B(s, t)$ will be lowest in more sophisticated goods where it has greater opportunity to benefit from learning by doing, whereas those in the LDC $a^B(s, t)/a^A(s, t)$ will be lowest in less sophisticated goods. Hence, under free trade, considerations of comparative advantage imply that the DC will reallocate resources toward more sophisticated goods where learning by doing may still occur, whereas while the LDC reallocates resources toward the least sophisticated goods where no potential for learning by doing exists.

Young (1991) shows that as many as five different types of free trade equilibria exist.[19] The equilibria differ in terms of, for example, whether the LDC specializes exclusively in the production of goods for which all potential for learning by doing has been exhausted and in terms of the range of goods consumed in the LDC. However, a number of general results emerge. First, the DC always produces a more sophisticated set of goods than the LDC. Second, agents in the DC enjoy higher levels of personal income than their counterparts in the LDC and are therefore able to consume more of each good. Third, the reallocation of resources toward goods with greater potential for learning by doing in the DC means that the free-trade growth rate is always as great or greater than that under autarky. Fourth, the reallocation of resources toward goods with less potential for learning by doing in the LDC means that the free-trade growth rate is never greater than that under autarky and may be lower.

---

18. In other words, Young considers the special case of our setup in Chapter 6 where growth of general knowledge in the domestic economy is entirely driven by learning by doing in that economy.

19. Two of these possible equilibria are examined in problem 5.

Within this framework, it is also possible to consider what happens to the "technological gap" or difference in stocks of technological knowledge between the two economies $(X(t) \equiv S^A(t) - S^B(t))$ and what happens to relative levels of per capita income. Here the analysis clearly relates to the cross-country literature on income convergence, and the question of whether poor countries will ever catch up with the rich.

From equation (11.18), the rate of learning by doing in each economy depends on the flow of skilled labor devoted to the production of goods for which actual unit labor requirements exceed potential. As a result, the model is characterized by a scale effect. The larger an economy's supply of skilled labor, then ceteris paribus the greater the rate at which learning by doing occurs and the faster $S(t)$ rises over time. As a result, if the initial "technological gap" $X(t)$ between the two economies is small enough and the LDC's labor force sufficiently large relative to the DC's, the technological gap between the two economies will fall over time and income per capita in the LDC will rise relative to that in the DC until, ultimately, the roles of LDC and DC are reversed.[20]

There are several points to note about the equilibrium when knowledge spillovers are national rather than international in scope. Firstly, in contrast to the model in section 11.4, the equilibrium pattern of international trade is no longer uniquely determined by factor endowments or by exogenously given productivity levels. Comparative advantage itself is now endogenously determined by country-specific stocks of technological knowledge. The past history of technological change dictates current patterns of comparative advantage and international specialization, giving an important role to initial conditions. However, at the same time current patterns of comparative advantage play an important role in determining the rate of technological change. Whether an LDC becomes able to produce more sophisticated goods over time depends on whether it specializes in goods where the potential for learning by doing still exists in the free-trade equilibrium.

Secondly, as in the model of section 11.4 where knowledge spillovers are international, one economy (here the LDC) may experience a reduction in its rate of growth of output as a result of international trade. Considerations of comparative advantage mean that international trade has an *ambiguous* effect on economic growth. However, even if an economy's growth rate falls, this does not necessarily mean that international trade is welfare reducing. A full welfare analysis would require consideration of changes in real consumption, and hence in the terms of trade (see Young 1991).

---

20. Brezis, Krugman, and Tsiddon (1993) argue that relative levels of per capita income are characterised by persistent "leapfrogging" or "cycles of technological leadership." The source for these cycles is technology-specific learning by doing, and their analysis may be interpreted in terms of the distinction between fundamental and secondary knowledge introduced in Chapter 6.

In the equilibrium considered above, both economies experience conventional static gains from trade as a result of the exploitation of current patterns of comparative advantage. In the DC, growth is unchanged or higher under free trade, so there is the possibility of dynamic gains. It follows that the discounted flow of utility in the DC is higher under international trade than under autarky. However, there is an interesting caveat. If the LDC is able to close the technological gap and ultimately attain the status of technological leader, then the economy that starts out as the DC may eventually experience a reduction in its rate of growth.

The LDC may experience a decrease in its rate of growth of output, although not necessarily in its rate of growth of consumption (insofar as it consumes a more sophisticated good produced in the DC, it will experience a terms-of-trade gain). Nonetheless, the rate of growth of consumption may still fall, in which case the LDC undergoes dynamic losses from trade. Free trade will be welfare-reducing if these dynamic losses exceed the static gains.[21]

Suppose that international trade does result in a lower level of economic welfare in the LDC. The role of the current pattern of international specialization in determining rates of productivity growth gives a potential rationale for policy intervention. For instance, trade and industrial policies may be used to induce an LDC to specialize in goods with greater potential for further learning by doing (see Grossman and Helpman 1991a, chap. 8, Lucas 1993, and Redding 1996b). It is often argued that a number of the fast-growing East Asian economies have implemented such policies, and endogenous-growth models with national knowledge spillovers seem to provide a theoretical justification.

However, it is important to realize that trade-based policies are often dominated by domestic policy instruments (e.g., R&D subsidies). Furthermore, as a practical guide for policy-makers, there are some important qualifications. As Krugman (1987) notes, theoretical results are sensitive to assumptions, in particular those concerning the extent of knowledge spillovers and the nature of externalities. More generally, the information requirements of adopting such policies are high because the policy-maker is required to have information about the potential time profile of productivity in a large number of industries. In general, trade restrictions bring some well-known problems in their wake, including rent-seeking. Clearly, empirical evidence on openness and the effectiveness of policy interventions is extremely important, and we briefly survey the recent literature in the next section.

The possibility that income per capita in a DC may be overtaken by that in a LDC is connected with fears about a loss of "international competitiveness."

---

21. Other models of international trade with national-knowledge stocks in which free trade may be welfare reducing include Grossman and Helpman (1991a chap. 8), Redding (1996b), and Stokey (1991).

These fears are often misplaced. Under free trade, the DC still enjoys a higher rate of growth in the transition period while the LDC catches up. Furthermore, even if it is overtaken by the LDC, it may still enjoy a terms-of-trade gain from productivity growth there. As argued forcibly by Krugman (1996), trade between nations is fundamentally different from competition between firms. Even within classical models of international trade, productivity growth in one economy may either increase or decrease welfare in another, depending on whether that productivity growth is export- or import-biased (i.e., depending on what happens to the terms of trade). Indeed, it is unclear how informative the popular concept of "international competitiveness" really is for long-run welfare considerations.

Finally, we note that the Young (1991) model has interesting predictions about the countries with which an economy would most like to trade. In particular, it implies that developed countries would most like to trade with their less developed counterparts, whereas less developed countries would most like to trade between themselves. It would be interesting to see how far these predictions might be taken in explaining observed patterns of trade and protectionist policies.

11.6   Empirical Evidence

Overall, our theoretical discussion indicates that it is difficult to identify a priori the effect of trade policy on long-run income per capita and growth. Although the presumption must be that free trade has a beneficial effect on growth and welfare, counterexamples can also be found. Hence empirical work assumes great importance. On balance, much of the empirical work supports the idea that openness is growth-promoting, but it is controversial and subject to a wide variety of criticisms. In this section, we review some of the evidence from cross-country work. We also examine empirical studies of knowledge spillovers. As we have seen, the extent and scope of these spillovers are central to the policy implications of recent work on the evolution of comparative advantage, and to an assessment of openness more generally.

11.6.1   Openness and Growth

It is frequently suggested that comparative case studies, such as Little, Scitovsky, and Scott (1970), provide the most reliable evidence on openness and growth. Work of this kind has been much discussed, and because space precludes a full survey, in this section we concentrate on the more recent cross-country regressions.[22] These regressions can be seen as a potentially useful

---

22. For more thorough coverage, see Edwards (1993).

complement to case studies. Historical work in the latter tradition permits a readier grasp of complexities, but at the expense of the ability to test generalizations and control rigorously for other factors, so cross-country regressions may have something to contribute.

Unfortunately, researchers in the field immediately have to confront some difficult conceptual and measurement problems. Although it is often convenient to classify countries as either "open" or "closed," in practice this conceals a wide variety and extent of interventions. This is not just academic pedantry: Pritchett (1996) shows that some of the measures of openness widely used in the literature are only weakly correlated with each other. If there is some underlying latent variable representing openness or "outward orientation," at best we have only one measure that captures it, and even then its identity remains uncertain.

Given findings of this kind, perhaps the most convincing evidence is that which makes use of a variety of policy indicators, and shows that the results are robust to the choice of indicator and conditioning variables. One of the first attempts in this vein was the cross-section work of Levine and Renelt (1992), who found that the significance of several proxies for openness was fragile, tending to vary with the omission or inclusion of other variables. More recently Harrison (1996) has found that the estimated effects of openness are stronger when panel data is used: changes in some of the openness measures help explain subsequent changes in growth rates within countries. This is not true for all of the openness measures, but it is interesting to note that whenever an association is found, it is positive.

One of the most interesting studies is that of Frankel et al. (1996). They note that the openness measures used in the literature are often thought to be endogenous. To solve this problem, they use the trade shares predicted by a simple "gravity model" of trade as instruments for actual trade shares. Perhaps surprisingly, this tends to raise the estimated importance of trade.

A related strand of research has investigated the consequences of trade regimes for convergence. The literature on convergence that we discussed in Chapter 1 was based on closed-economy models, in which per capita incomes are seen as drawing closer together if and only if capital-labor ratios converge. As we discussed earlier, Ben-David (1993, 1996) has pointed out that the presence of international trade should lead one to think about additional mechanisms, particularly factor price equalization. Ben-David (1993) shows that the dispersion of per capita incomes has fallen among European countries instituting trade liberalization. He is able to show that the convergence marks neither a continuation of a long-run trend, nor a return to the prewar extent of dispersion.

Equally striking results have emerged from the work of Sachs and Warner (1995). They classify countries as closed or open based on an assessment of their trade regimes against a set of criteria. They go on to show that there is strong evidence of per capita income convergence within the group of open economies, but not within the closed group. Although their work can be criticized on a number of grounds, not least the rather subjective nature of the openness classification, taken as a whole it provides good evidence that openness assists convergence in per capita incomes.

However, the mechanisms remain unclear. Convergence could be taking place through capital accumulation, factor price equalization, knowledge spillovers, or trade-mediated technology transfer.[23] Combinations of all four, even those in which one or two work against convergence, are clearly possible. Further work discriminating between the explanations would be helpful.

Overall, there are many opportunities for interesting further research. For instance, much of the recent empirical work has tended to assume that openness must have the same effect across countries, regardless of circumstances. In practice, in the long run, the effect of openness for a country specializing in natural-resource exports may be less beneficial than for a country specializing in manufactures. In this respect, it is interesting to note that the East Asian countries were already specializing in manufactures by the early 1960s. It has sometimes been argued that East Asia pursued policies of import substitution and then moved away from them at the right time, a conclusion that tends to weaken general arguments against interventionist trade policy. As yet, the cross-country empirical literature is silent on this kind of issue.

These arguments are connected to ideas of dynamic comparative advantage, and, as we have seen in preceding sections, the presence and scope of research spillovers is central to the relevance of such theories. We now turn to the evidence on spillovers.

11.6.2   Research Spillovers

The first point to make is that there is reasonably strong evidence for externalities to domestic R&D. There are well-known problems in measuring the contribution of research to productivity growth, as discussed by Griliches (1979). (See also the Appendix to Chapter 12.) Overall, though, studies have concurred in finding that social returns exceed even the high private returns often found in the literature. The survey by Griliches (1992) concludes that although work on R&D spillovers is often flawed and subject to a variety of reservations, the impression remains that externalities are significant and hence social returns may be very high.

The strength of international-research spillovers is more difficult to establish, but substantial progress has been made in an important paper by Coe and Helpman (1995). For each country, they construct measures of domestic and foreign R&D capital stocks, where the latter are weighted averages of

---

23. Slaughter (1997) develops this point in more detail.

the domestic stocks of trade partners. They find that foreign R&D appears to have a beneficial effect on domestic productivity, and that the effect increases in strength with the degree of openness. Hence, not only are there important spillovers, but there is also some evidence that these are mediated by trade (although some grounds for skepticism on this latter point have been raised by Keller 1996).

However, work at the aggregate level tends to run into an identification problem. Even if a correlation is observed between domestic productivity and foreign research, this may simply represent the outcome of common demand or input price shocks. Weighting the contribution of foreign research using data on bilateral trade flows, as in Coe and Helpman, is likely to mitigate this problem but will not overcome it altogether.

In another important paper, Branstetter (1996) argues that examination of intranational and international spillovers requires work at a more disaggregated level. The key advantage is that researchers can take into account the distance of firms from each other in "technology space," because this can be measured by the similarity of the fields in which firms patent, an approach due to Griliches (1979) and Jaffe (1986). The spillover variable for a particular firm is then the research of other firms, weighted by their distance away in technology space. Using this technique for a combined U.S. and Japanese data set, Branstetter finds that knowledge spillovers are primarily intranational. Although there is some (relatively weak) evidence that Japanese firms do benefit from U.S. research, there is little to suggest important flows of knowledge in the other direction.

The findings are supported in this respect by the aggregate study of Nadiri and Kim (1996), who conclude that the relative importance of domestic and foreign research seems to vary considerably across countries. Domestic research is much more important for the United States, but is dominated by the contribution of foreign research for countries like Italy and Canada. This is an intuitively plausible finding.

Overall, it may be difficult to generalize about the importance of spillovers between countries, but their existence within countries seems to be an increasingly well-established stylized fact. Hence theories in which comparative advantage is endogenous may have something useful to contribute, and the models of endogenous innovation are already providing a useful complement to previous work on learning by doing.

11.7   Conclusion

This chapter considers how the analysis of preceding chapters is affected by the introduction of international flows of goods, ideas, and financial assets between economies. Using the work of Grossman and Helpman (1991a) and

Young (1991), we have been able to demonstrate that many of the same tools and ideas discussed in previous chapters may be applied to an open economy.

The combination of endogenous growth models with international trade has some interesting consequences. It sheds light on the roles of trade and skill-biased technical progress in wage inequality. Although the existing literature has proposed these as competing explanations for rising inequality, Schumpeterian models in which the rate and direction of technological change are endogenous suggest that the two explanations may be complementary. Alternatively, it is possible that trade-induced shifts in the skilled wage lead in the long run to offsetting movements in the rate of technical progress.

Although the presumption must be that trade is beneficial for growth and welfare, perhaps the central finding discussed in this chapter is that free trade need not always be unambiguously good for long-run welfare. In some of these models, growth and welfare are dependent on the initial pattern of specialization. This can provide a justification for policies designed to work against the grain of comparative advantage, and instead encourage specialization in sectors where there may be dynamic gains through spillovers.

However, it is important to note that trade-based policies are often dominated by domestic instruments (e.g., R&D subsidies). In any case, the analysis certainly does not provide a blanket justification for interventionist trade policy. We have briefly discussed some of the qualifications, including the heavy demands made on policy-makers in terms of information gathering and expertise, and the potential for rent-seeking. A further qualification, which would be interesting to study in more detail, is that policies designed to shift comparative advantage may be ineffective if many countries try to adopt them simultaneously. Perhaps the most important counterarguments to intervention are provided by empirical studies. Much of this evidence suggests that governments that have tried to "close" their economies, and follow policies of import substitution, have done rather badly.

That said, several governments appear to have successfully combined open economies with interventionist industrial policies. Theoretical models of the kind presented by Krugman (1987), Grossman and Helpman (1991a), and Young (1991) do provide a potential justification for certain forms of intervention. It is clear that what is needed is more empirical evidence on the importance of spillovers, and more generally, work that deepens our understanding of the circumstances in which openness and industrial policy are beneficial.

11.8   Summary

This chapter considers how our main conclusions in previous chapters should be modified for open economies. Hence we discuss such issues as the relation between trade, competition, and growth. We also argue that the Schumpeterian framework provides some interesting insights into the much-studied issue of trade effects on wage inequality.

The chapter then concentrates on two particular aspects of the relationship between trade and growth: first, the effect of international trade in goods and flows of ideas between similar economies, where one abstracts from inter-industry trade and considerations of comparative advantage; and second, the relationship between international trade and economic growth, where there are several final goods, and endogenous technological change becomes a potential source of changes in comparative advantage.

The first issue was addressed within the framework of the Romer (1990a) model of endogenous growth through increasing specialization presented in Chapter 1. The introduction of international trade in intermediate inputs raises the market size for an individual researcher, but also increases the variety of intermediate inputs that may be employed in final-goods production. Together these effects raise the returns to labor in research and final-goods production by equiproportionate amounts, leaving the relative incentive to engage in research unchanged. Hence in this simple framework, for economies that are initially similar in knowledge stocks, growth is unaffected by trade.

In more general models, trade can play a role through increasing the extent of competition facing intermediate input producers. The analysis of Chapter 7 implies that the resulting effect on growth is ambiguous. If intermediate inputs are used in research, or countries differ in their initial stocks of knowledge, again trade will have ambiguous consequences for the rate of growth.

Now, if international flows of ideas are also allowed, labor's productivity in research is increased and the growth rate will unambiguously rise. The increased productivity of research raises growth directly, and indirectly by increasing the rate of return to research. This role for international spillovers of ideas does depend on ideas entering directly into the research technology; in other specifications of how research takes place, international spillovers may have no effect on growth.

International trade may also have important implications for economic growth through changes in the allocation of resources induced by comparative advantage. It is argued that the nature of these reallocative effects will depend crucially on whether knowledge spillovers are national or international in scope. The analysis began by considering the Grossman and Helpman (1991a) model of dynamic comparative advantage in which the Schumpeterian model of Chapter 2 is integrated into the traditional theory of international trade. If knowledge spillovers are *international* in scope, the equilibrium pattern of international trade is uniquely determined by factor endowments. In the free-trade equilibrium, both economies experience a common rate of innovation but differ in terms of the composition of output.

Specialization according to comparative advantage implies that the economy relatively well endowed with the factor of production used intensively in high-technology production will increase the quantity of resources devoted to such output, whereas the converse applies to the other economy. International trade has an ambiguous effect on each economy's rate of growth, and the economy relatively well endowed with human capital may experience dynamic welfare losses.

The case of *national* spillovers of technological knowledge is addressed by the Young (1991) model of endogenous growth through bounded learning by doing. With national knowledge spillovers, the pattern of comparative advantage at any one point in time becomes endogenous, and depends crucially on initial conditions. At the same time, the pattern of comparative advantage plays an important role in determining the rate of technological progress at any one point in time.

Considerations of comparative advantage imply that a less developed country (LDC) that begins with a lower level of technological knowledge will specialize in relatively unsophisticated goods with less potential for learning by doing. As a result, the LDC may experience a reduction in its rate of economic growth, which might translate into dynamic welfare losses from trade. In contrast, the DC with which it trades enjoys an increased rate of growth and dynamic welfare gains, which augment the standard static benefits from the exploitation of comparative advantage.

The analysis of both national and international knowledge spillovers suggests that although specialization according to comparative advantage certainly brings static welfare gains, it has an ambiguous effect on rates of economic growth (and may also have an ambiguous effect on intertemporal economic welfare). Interestingly, the prediction of which economy experiences dynamic welfare losses from trade differs substantially between the two cases of international and national knowledge spillovers. In the Grossman and Helpman model with international knowledge spillovers, it is the human capital-rich economy (which one would typically characterize as developed) that may experience dynamic welfare losses. In the Young model with national knowledge spillovers, it is the economy with the lower initial stock of technological knowledge (which one would typically think of as less developed).

Although the presumption is that free trade is beneficial for growth and welfare, the key finding of these new theories is that this need not always be the case. In certain circumstances (although there are many qualifications), the models discussed in the chapter can provide a potential justification for industrial policies and, to a lesser extent, for trade policy. The empirical evidence we briefly survey in the chapter suggests, however, that trade openness tends to be beneficial for growth: trade restrictions appear to be harmful. The evidence on the effectiveness of industrial policies is less clear-cut, and there is an obvious need for further work, to deepen our understanding of the circumstances in which openness and industrial policy may be welfare-enhancing.

Problems

Difficulty of Problems:

No star: normal

One star: difficult

Two stars: very difficult

1. A small open economy (based on Grossman and Helpman 1991a, chap. 6)

This problem presents a simple model of a small open economy, in which world product prices determine the amount of resources allocated to research and hence the growth rate of the economy.

Consider an economy that produces two final goods X and Y with the following constant returns to scale technologies:

$$Y = A_t x_y^\beta H_y^{1-\beta} \quad \text{and} \quad Z = A_t x_z^\beta L_z^{1-\beta}.$$

That is, the production of good Y uses intermediate goods and human capital, whereas that of good X uses intermediate goods and labor. Both sectors are competitive. A_t is the quality index for intermediate goods that behaves just as in Chapter 2, with each innovation raising productivity by a factor of γ. There is a fixed amount of labor, L, that is used only in the production of good Z. There is a given amount of human capital, H, that is employed in the production of Y and in the research sector. When H_R skilled workers are employed in research, innovations arrive randomly with a Poisson arrival rate λH_R.

The successful innovator becomes a monopolist who produces the latest vintage of the intermediate good. No other quality is used. The intermediate good is produced using the two final goods. There are fixed unit input coefficients, so that the constant unit cost depends only on the prices of Y and Z. Assume that for given input prices, the cost of each subsequent technology grows at the same rate as the quality of the intermediate good. That is, the unit cost is given by $A_t c(p_y, p_z)$, where p_y and p_z are respectively the prices of the two goods.

Final goods are traded, hence their prices p_y and p_z are given by world markets. No other good or factor is traded. There are no technology transfers.

a. Obtain the price of intermediate goods and the profits obtained by the successful innovator. What does the profit function depend on? What is the discounted expected payoff of an innovation?

b. Obtain the arbitrage equation, that is, the equilibrium condition for the human-capital market. Is there intertemporal dependence of research decisions as we saw in the basic Schumpeterian model?

c. From the arbitrage equation, explain the impact that opening up to trade would have on (i) an economy which is relatively abundant in human capital relative to world factor ratios, and (ii) an economy that is abundant in labor.

d. Consider a model with expanding product variety, where final outputs are produced according to

$$Y = H_y^{1-\beta} \int_0^n x_{jy}^\beta \, dj \quad \text{and} \quad Z = L_z^{1-\beta} \int_0^n x_{jz}^\beta \, dj.$$

Check that the effects of trade are the same as those found for the Schumpeterian model (not solved).

2. Factor price equalization and the time preference rate (based on Wälde 1994a,b)

The analysis of the dynamic comparative advantage model by Grossman and Helpman in section 11.4 has showed that one of the main results in international trade theory is robust to the introduction of Schumpetarian technical change: if countries are not too dissimilar in factor endowments and use identical technologies, factor prices equalize in the two economies through trade in goods. This result was shown by constructing the FPE equilibrium as illustrated in figure 11.1. If the endowment of countries as shown by point E lies in the cone of diversification $O^A N^A O^B N^B$, both countries produce both goods and factor prices equalize. However, casual observation shows that individuals differ in tastes, which suggests that countries might differ in "average" tastes as well. This problem addresses the question of whether factor price equalization still holds if the rate of time preference in country A is not identical to that in country B, though both countries' endowment point E still lies within the cone of diversification.

Consider the increasing specialization version of the model in section 11.4 as presented in Grossman and Helpman (1991a, section 7.1). Output of the single final good is now given by

$$Y_t = \int_0^n x_j^\alpha \, dj,$$

where n is the world number of varieties and x_j the amount of each variety produced. Assume that the two countries, $i = A, B$, produce different varieties, $n = n^A + n^B$. Expenditure, E, is normalized to one in each period, so the value of an innovation depends on how many intermediate goods are being used to produce a final output of value one ($E = 1$). In this setup, free entry into research implies

$$v^i = \frac{c_\gamma(w_L^i, w_H^i)}{n^A + n^B}, \tag{11.21}$$

which replaces equation (11.12) in the chapter. The equilibrium arbitrage condition becomes

$$\frac{\pi^i}{v^i} = r^i - \frac{\dot{v}^i}{v^i}. \tag{11.22}$$

Assume that countries differ in their rate of time preference. That is, $\rho^A \neq \rho^B$.

a. What is the steady-state interest rate in country A and country B? What should be assumed about international flows of financial capital for this to be an equilibrium?

b. Show that in steady state the value of a firm in country A falls at the same rate as the value of a firm in country B.

c. Let the cost of a unit of intermediate good be $c_x(w_L^i, w_H^i)$. Find the profits of an innovator in each period bearing in mind that expenditure in each period is normalized to one.

d. Using the arbitrage condition (11.22) show that different rates of time preference imply different factor rewards (prove by contradiction).

⋆ **3. Imitation and product cycles (based on Krugman 1979 and Grossman and Helpman 1991a, chap. 11)**

Here we show the existence of a product cycle in which new products are invented in the North (and initially produced there) and then imitated by the South (and production shifts to this area). The ideas brought about by the new growth theories can be used in this framework to examine what determines the rates of innovation and imitation.

Consider a model of North-South trade with endogenous rates of innovation and imitation that take the form of increasing product variety. The North country behaves, broadly, like the economy in the Romer (1990a) model of Chapter 1. The only input in the production of final goods are intermediate goods. Let

$$Y^N = \int_0^{A^N} x_j^\alpha dj, \tag{11.23}$$

where A^N is the number of varieties produced in the North. To produce one unit of the intermediate good, one unit of labor is required, which receives a wage w^N. Let L_1^N denote the level of employment in the North intermediate-goods sector. New varieties are discovered according to the production function

$$\dot{A} = \delta L_2^N A, \tag{11.24}$$

where A is total number of varieties already discovered, and L_2^N employment in research in the North.

The South country has the same production functions for final and intermediate goods, and it produces A^S varieties. It does not innovate. Instead, it can imitate some of the goods already discovered in the North, according to the function

$$\dot{A}^S = \eta L_2^S A^N. \tag{11.25}$$

The wage cost in the South is w^S, and we assume that it is sufficiently below the wage rate in the North for no good to be produced by both countries: that is, $\alpha w^N > w^S$. Then the number of goods produced in the North is $A^N = A - A^S$.

The price of the final good is one in both countries. Consumers have the same logarithmic utility function and the same rate of discount, ρ, in the North and the South. The supplies of labor in each country are given and are L^N and L^S, respectively.

a. Obtain the prices charged by intermediate goods firms in the North and in the South. Explain why the North will never produce a good that has been imitated by the South. Would prices in the South be different if $w^N > w^S > \alpha w^N$?

b. The conditional probability that one particular North producer has her variety copied is simply the rate of imitation, $\dot{A}^S$, divided by the number of varieties in the North that have not yet been imitated, A^N. That is, one particular North product is copied with a Poisson arrival rate of $\dot{A}^S / A^N$. Find the arbitrage (free entry) and the asset equations for the North and the South. Write down the labor-market equilibrium condition for each country (remember that labor is used in research and in the production of intermediate goods).

c. Find the rate of growth of the number of intermediate goods in the steady state, that is, when the rate of growth of the number of varieties manufactured by each of the two countries is the same, and production and consumption grow at the same rate. To do this, use the fact that the rate of imitation, $m \equiv \dot{A}^S / A^N$, will also be constant in the steady state.

★★ 4. Innovation, imitation, and intellectual property rights (based on Helpman 1993)

It has often been argued that lax intellectual property rights in less developed economies imply that innovating firms in industrial economies cannot fully appropriate the rents generated by their innovations, and hence reduce innovative effort. Here we show that this might not be the case.

Consider first the model in the previous section. The economy is identical except for the productivity parameter in the function that determines the number of new varieties in the South. This parameter is not constant, but it depends on the degree of intellectual property rights (IPR) protection. That is, $\eta = \bar{\eta} - \mu$, where $\bar{\eta}$ is a constant and μ the degree of IPR protection.

a. Examine whether or not a tightening of intellectual property rights increases the world's steady state rate of technical change. Find the impact on the rate of imitation and on the share of goods produced by the North and by the South.

In order to examine the welfare impact, let us consider a different model in which the rate of growth of the total number of products, g, and the rate of imitation by the South, $m = \bar{m} - \mu$, are both given. This way we can analyze the effects of intellectual property rights policies other than the growth effect. The utility function is logarithmic:

$$U = \int_0^\infty e^{-\rho t} \log u(t) dt. \tag{11.26}$$

Assume that the new types of goods enter directly into the instantaneous utility function, and that greater product variety increases utility just as it increases the level of output in the Romer model. That is,

$$u = \left[\int_0^A x_j^\alpha dj \right]^{1/\alpha}, 0 < \alpha < 1. \tag{11.27}$$

One unit of labor is required in order to produce one unit of any good.

In the North a manufacturer that invents a new variety (at no cost) becomes the monopolist producer until this good is imitated in the South. It therefore charges a price $p^N = w^N/\alpha$. When a product is imitated by the South, the technology is available to all South producers. Manufacturing is thus competitive, and the price charged is simply $p^S = w^S$. Assume that the wage rate is higher in the North.

b. Show that instantaneous utility is determined by a price index that depends on the shares of goods produced in each country, ξ^N and ξ^S, and on the prices in the two economies. Show that the terms of trade are given by the expression

$$\frac{p^N}{p^S} = \left[\frac{L^S}{L^N} \frac{\xi^N}{\xi^S} \right]^{1/\epsilon},$$

where $\epsilon = \frac{1}{1-\alpha} > 1$.

c. Let the rate of imitation be $m = \bar{m} - \mu$, where μ is the degree of intellectual property rights protection. Examine the effect of tighter rights on the share of goods manufactured by the North, both at the new steady state and on the path to it. Assume the economy was initially in a steady state. How are the terms of trade affected?

d. Express the instantaneous utility in each of the countries as a function of prices and output shares. What is the welfare effect on the North of tighter intellectual property rights?

e. Who loses from tighter intellectual property rights?

5. Bounded learning by doing and international trade (based on Young 1991)

Consider the Young model discussed in the chapter and in problem 5 of Chapter 6. Suppose economies A and B start trading, where A is the developed country (DC) and B the less developed country (LDC). Their levels of technological advance are denoted by S^A and S^B. Let $X = S^A - S^B > 0$ be the difference in the levels of technical knowledge. Thus, $a^A(s) < a^B(s)$ for all $s > S^B$, and $a^A(s) = a^B(s)$ for $s = S^B$. Let the wage in country B, w^B, be the numeraire, and define the relative wage as $\omega = w^A/w^B$. Suppose there is free trade in goods between the two countries.

a. For which values of unit costs $a^A(s)$ and $a^B(s)$ is good s produced in the LDC?

b. Let $M^A(M^B)$ be the lowest s consumed in the DC (LDC). Denote by GDC and GLDC the sets of goods produced in the DC and LDC, respectively. How are M^A and M^B determined, given GDC and GLDC?

c. What would occur if the relative wage were less than 1? If it were greater than e^{2X}?

d. Suppose $\omega = 1$. Find the range of goods consumed in each country. Find the range of goods produced by each country.

e. Suppose $\omega = e^{2X}$. Find the range of goods consumed in each country. Find the range of goods produced by each country.

A great deal of evidence has been produced in recent years casting doubt on endogenous growth theory. Mankiw, Romer, and Weil (1992) argue that the neoclassical growth model of Solow and Swan, with exogenous technological progress and diminishing returns to capital, explains most of the cross-country variation in output per person. Many writers have produced evidence to show that countries are converging[2] to parallel growth paths of the sort implied by the Solow-Swan model with a common worldwide technology level.[3] The "Schumpeterian" variant of endogenous growth theory that emphasizes technological progress, innovation, and R&D has come under particularly heavy fire. Growth-accounting exercises by Young (1995b) and Jorgenson (1995) portray technological progress as an unimportant source of economic growth relative to capital accumulation. According to Jones (1995), the fact that R&D inputs have increased enormously in the postwar period with no tendency for productivity to rise refutes existing Schumpeterian growth theories and supports alternatives in which the long-run growth rate is determined uniquely by the rate of population growth.

The main purpose of this chapter is to address these criticisms, in particular by showing that the simple Schumpeterian model of Chapter 3, which combines elements of the Solow-Swan neoclassical model of capital accumulation and the basic Schumpeterian model of Chapter 2, is broadly consistent with the critics' evidence as well as with other evidence that the Solow-Swan model cannot account for. At the same time, this Schumpeterian model with capital accumulation suggests a wealth of empirical implications that are potentially testable and that could conceivably refute it.

The chapter is organized as follows: In section 12.1 we outline the main empirical criticisms against endogenous growth theory. In section 12.2 we present a slightly extended version of the Schumpeterian model with capital accumulation developed in Chapter 3. In section 12.3 we use this extended model to confront two main empirical critiques of Schumpeterian growth theory, namely those based on growth accounting (Jorgenson 1995 and Young 1995b) and the Jones criticism. In section 12.4 we extend the model of section 12.2 into a multicountry model to address criticisms of endogenous growth theory based on cross-country evidence. In section 12.5 we put forward a number of testable implications that might be used to distinguish the Schumpeterian framework from competing approaches. Section 12.6 presents a first attempt—by Caballero and Jaffe—at testing a Schumpeterian model with creative destruction. Finally section 12.7 summarizes our findings in this chapter.

---

1. This chapter benefited from a fruitful collaboration with Jonathan Temple.

2. Barro and Sala-i-Martín (1995) survey work on conditional β-convergence. Evans (1996) shows more directly that per capita income levels among OECD countries don't diverge as predicted by earlier endogenous growth models.

3. See Chapter 1.

12.1   Some Criticisms of Endogenous Growth Theory

Our main focus in this chapter is on the empirical evidence questioning the Schumpeterian approach to growth. For an overview of the empirical debates raised by the AK model, in particular the Mankiw-Romer-Weil critique, we refer the reader to the first chapter of this book.

Growth Accounting

Since the early 1960s, several East Asian countries have grown at an unprecedented rate, especially the four "dragons" (Hong Kong, Singapore, South Korea, and Taiwan). The contribution made to this growth by improvements in total factor productivity (TFP) has been examined by Young (1995b) in an influential and much-discussed paper. Young uses growth accounting to show that much of East Asian growth can be attributed to capital accumulation, increased human capital, and increased labor force participation. Accordingly, Young finds that the role played by total factor productivity growth is a minor one.

Some figures may be helpful. In Hong Kong, GDP per capita grew by 5.7 percent per year over 1966–92. Over 1966–90, Singapore's GDP per capita grew at 6.8 percent per year, South Korea's also at 6.8 percent, and Taiwan's at 6.7 percent. Growth in GDP per worker was between one and two percentage points less, reflecting large increases in labor force participation. With just this simple adjustment, the growth rates begin to look less impressive, but are still very high by the standards of other developing countries.

Young (1995b) uses a translogarithmic aggregate production function to separate out the contributions to this growth of factor accumulation and TFP growth. Particular attention is paid to labor inputs. Census and survey data are used to estimate changes in the size and mix of the labor force, including improvements in the educational attainment of workers. Having made these adjustments, Young is able to derive estimates of the contribution made by TFP growth (the Solow residual). For the same time periods as before, he finds that TFP growth rates were 2.3 percent a year for Hong Kong, 0.2 percent for Singapore, 1.7 percent for South Korea, and 2.1 percent for Taiwan. Young argues that these figures are not exceptional by the standards of the OECD or several large developing countries.

That much of East Asian growth can be attributed to factor accumulation, in turn, seems to imply that technological progress is relatively unimportant as a source of growth.

Scale Effects and the Jones Critique

In a highly influential paper, Jones (1995) points out that OECD countries have seen permanent policy changes—trade liberalization, an increase in average years of schooling, increases in investment and, more directly relevant to the

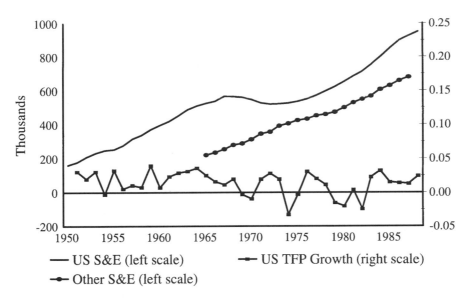

Figure 12.1
Scientists and engineers engaged in R&D and U.S. TFP growth. "Other S&E" is the sum of scientists and engineers engaged in R&D for France, West Germany, and Japan. Data provided by Charles Jones, as used in Jones (1995).

Schumpeterian approach, a substantial increase in R&D levels—that might have been expected to raise growth.[4] Yet there has been no apparent payoff in terms of faster growth. If anything, productivity growth has slowed, at least until recently (see figure 12.1). This apparent constancy of long-run growth, in the face of structural changes, calls into question the whole Schumpeterian approach. Well aware of this, Jones has used his findings to support a general critique of R&D–based models of growth, which we now discuss.

Consider the following reduced form of the Romer (1990a) model of endogenous technical change analyzed in Chapter 1. The aggregate flow of final output is equal to:

$$Y = K^\alpha (AL_1)^{1-\alpha}, \tag{12.1}$$

and the rate of growth of technical knowledge A is proportional to the current flow of research labor L_2:

$$\frac{\dot{A}}{A} = \delta L_2. \tag{12.2}$$

Total labor supply is constant and can be freely allocated between research and manufacturing:

---

4. Antweiler (1994) reinforces this by pointing out that there has been a fall in the costs of carrying out R & D, accompanied by a rise in research intensity, across the OECD.

$L = L_1 + L_2.$

In a steady state, the rate of growth of final output should be proportional to the steady-state share s^* of total labor force devoted to R&D:

$g_Y = g_A = \delta L_2 = \delta s^* L.$

However, while $L_2 = s^* L$ has substantially increased since the 1950s in all OECD countries, total productivity growth has shown no systematic upward trend. Jones argues that this is evidence of decreasing returns in the production of new knowledge, presumably because the more knowledge has already been accumulated, the harder it is to extend. To accommodate such decreasing returns, Jones proposes to modify equation (12.2) into:

$$\frac{\dot{A}}{A} = \delta L_2^\lambda A^{\phi-1} \tag{12.3}$$

with ϕ now being strictly less than 1, and $\lambda \le 1$. But then it is easy to see from (12.3) that the long-run growth rate becomes proportional to the rate of population growth, namely:

$$g = \frac{\lambda n}{1 - \phi}.$$

To summarize: there is evidence of decreasing returns in the production of new innovations, which according to Jones contradicts the view that long-run growth should be affected by structural parameters, other than ones usually taken as exogenous—the rate of labor force growth, and the productivity of knowledge in deriving new ideas. Instead, the Jones argument brings us back to the conclusions of the Solow model, in which long-run growth is independent of structural characteristics of the economy, and so independent of policy.

A Common Growth Rate?

Several empirical critiques have adduced cross-country evidence to argue that, contrary to what endogenous growth models predict, countries are converging toward a common growth rate in the long run. This is perhaps the central conclusion of Mankiw, Romer, and Weil (1992), although one that is rarely emphasized. More recently Evans (1996) has presented evidence that the advanced industrial countries, at least, are growing at the same rate. He claims that "either endogenous growth models are fundamentally flawed, or else the effects they predict must be relatively unimportant for the countries considered here."

The details of the argument are interesting. Evans points out that, if countries differ in their trend growth rates, the logarithms of their per capita incomes should wander away from each other over time. If, however, countries share the same long-run growth rate, the cross-country variance of log incomes should, to a first order, be stationary around a constant mean. Evans presents evidence for thirteen industrial countries that the variance has not trended upward and that, if anything, the reverse has occurred.

While the model in Chapter 3 cannot be used directly to confront cross-country evidence because it deals only with the case of a closed economy, a straightforward extension of that model—outlined in section 12.4—to a multicountry context reveals that endogenous growth theory can predict the sort of cross-country results that Evans and others have taken as evidence against endogenous growth theory.

12.2   An Augmented Schumpeterian Model

Consider the following variant of the Schumpeterian model with capital accumulation developed in Chapter 3. To confront the "scale effect" of Schumpeterian models, whereby a more populous economy ought to grow faster, we assume, following Young (1995a), that as population grows, so does the number of distinct products over which research must be spread.[5] More formally, there is a single final output, produced by labor and a continuum of intermediate goods, according to the production function:

$$Y_t = Q_t^{\alpha-1} \left(\int_0^{Q_t} A_{it} x_{it}^\alpha di \right) L_t^{1-\alpha}, \tag{12.4}$$

where Y_t is gross output at date t, Q_t is the measure of how many different intermediate products exist at t, $L_t = e^{g_L t}$ is labor input, assumed identical to the population that grows at the exogenous rate g_L, x_{it} is the flow output of intermediate product i, and A_{it} is a productivity parameter attached to the latest version of intermediate product i.

The presence of the factor $Q_t^{\alpha-1}$ in (12.4) eliminates any productivity gain resulting from the proliferation of products. This puts the model at the opposite extreme from the horizontal-innovation growth models of Romer (1990a) (see section 1.6) and others that portray expanding product variety as the main source of growth. We make this specification because although in reality both horizontal and vertical innovations occur, the productivity-enhancing effects of horizontal innovations are not as obvious as those of quality improvements. For while having more products definitely opens up more possibilities for specialization, and of having instruments more closely matched with a variety of needs, it also makes life more complicated and creates greater chance of error, especially when the different instruments are complementary. Moreover, even

---

5. Although Young's analysis implied that, as in the Jones model, the long-run growth rate would be independent of the incentive to innovate, the model presented below restores the role of innovation even in the long run.

if tailor-made goods are more useful than general-purpose ones, having a lot of the former, each produced in small quantities, raises thin-market transactions costs. Accordingly, we have specified a technology in which the advantages and disadvantages of product proliferation just cancel each other. As in the basic model of Chapter 2, all growth in this model is driven by vertical innovations that raise the quality of goods.[6]

The number of products does grow in the model, but only as a result of serendipitous imitation, not deliberate innovation.[7] Each imitation produces a new product whose productivity parameter is identical to that of a randomly chosen existing product. Each person in the economy has the same exogenous propensity to imitate. Hence the flow of imitation products can be written as: $\dot{Q}_t = \xi L_t$, $\xi > 0$. This implies asymptotic convergence of the number of workers per product to the constant $\ell = g_L/\xi$. To simplify the analysis, we assume that this convergence has already occurred when we start the analysis, so that $L_t = \ell Q_t$ for all t.[8]

Final output can be used interchangeably as a consumption or capital good, or as an input into a research technology. Each intermediate product is produced using capital alone, according to the production function: [9]

$$x_{it} = K_{it}/A_{it}, \tag{12.5}$$

where K_{it} is the input of capital in sector i. I divide K_{it} by A_{it} in (12.5) to indicate that successive vintages of the intermediate product are produced by increasingly capital-intensive techniques.[10]

---

6. Literally, the model implies that the optimal number of different products is vanishingly small. However, all the operationally meaningful properties of the model would be the same if we eliminated this counterintuitive welfare result by specifying the aggregate production function as:

$$Y_t = Q_t^{\alpha-1} \left(\int_0^{Q_t} A_{it} x_{it}^\alpha di \right) L_t^{1-\alpha} (Q_t/L_t)^\beta, 0 < \beta < 1,$$

where the last factor represents a benefit from variety that no individual producer can internalize. Expressing the benefit in terms of product variety *per person* might be justified by the fact that the variety of different tastes that *want to be* satisfied expands as people become more numerous, just as the variety of tastes that *can be* satisfied expands as products become more numerous, or by the fact that thin-market costs depend inversely upon the number of buyers per product.

7. The basic structure of the model would be the same if the horizontal innovations creating new products were motivated by the same profit-seeking objectives as the vertical quality-improving innovations, as long as horizontal innovations are relatively labor intensive. (See Howitt 1997.)

8. As will be clear soon, since ℓ is constant, the analysis applies directly to the case where there is no population growth and no imitation, in which case none of the assumptions we make in this section concerning the origins and consequences of expanding product variety have any effect on the results.

9. This assumption drastically simplifies the algebra of the model. However, it can be shown that the case in which both labor and capital are used to produce intermediate goods yields almost identical behavior.

10. With a Cobb-Douglas technology, this has no substantive implications.

Innovations are targeted at specific intermediate products. Each innovation creates an improved version of the existing product, which allows the innovator to replace the incumbent monopolist until the next innovation in that sector.[11] Likewise, a product-expanding imitation allows the imitator to monopolize that new sector until the next innovation in that sector. The incumbent monopolist of each good produces with a cost function equal to $\zeta_t K_{it} = \zeta_t A_{it} x_{it}$, where ζ_t is the cost of capital, and a price schedule given by the marginal product: $p_{it} = \alpha A_{it} x_{it}^{\alpha-1} \ell^{1-\alpha}$. Standard profit-maximization yields the implication that all intermediate sectors will supply the same quantity, namely:

$$x_{it} = x_t \equiv \ell \left(\zeta_t / \alpha^2 \right)^{\frac{1}{\alpha-1}}, \tag{12.6}$$

and that each local monopolist will earn a flow of profits proportional to its productivity parameter A_{it}, namely:

$$\pi_{it} = A_{it}\pi_t \equiv A_{it}\alpha \left(1 - \alpha\right) \ell^{1-\alpha} x_t^{\alpha}. \tag{12.7}$$

Assume that the cost of capital always adjusts so as to maintain equality between the supply of capital K_t and the demand:

$$K_t = \int_0^{Q_t} K_{it} di = x_t \int_0^{Q_t} A_{it} di = x_t Q_t A_t,$$

where A_t is the average productivity parameter across all intermediate products. Then the common output of all intermediate products will be:

$$x_{it} = x_t = K_t / A_t Q_t = k_t \ell, \tag{12.8}$$

where k_t ($\equiv K_t / A_t L_t$) is the capital stock per efficiency unit of labor. (By definition each unit of labor produces A_t efficiency units.) Substituting from (12.8) into (12.4) yields the Cobb-Douglas aggregate production function:

$$Y_t = K_t^{\alpha} \left(A_t L_t\right)^{1-\alpha} = A_t L_t f \left(k_t\right), \tag{12.9}$$

where:

$$f \left(k_t\right) \equiv k_t^{\alpha}. \tag{12.10}$$

Improvements in the productivity parameters come from an innovation process that uses final output as the only hired input.[12] The Poisson arrival rate ϕ_t of innovations in a sector to which R_t units of final output have been put into R&D is given by the function:

---

11. No innovations are done by incumbents because of the Arrow or replacement effect. (See Chapter 2.)

12. Or, equivalently, it uses intermediate goods and labor using the same technology as in the final goods sector. Barro and Sala-i-Martín (1995, chs. 6,7) make the same assumption.

$$\phi_t = \lambda \phi \left(R_t / A_t^{\max} \right); \ \ 0 < \lambda, \ \phi' > 0, \phi'' < 0, \phi\,(0) = 0; \tag{12.11}$$

where $A_t^{\max}$ is the "leading-edge technology parameter," that is, the maximal value of the productivity parameters A_{it} in the economy at date t, and λ is a parameter indicating the productivity of R&D. The function ϕ exhibits the decreasing returns that several studies[13] have found in R&D. We assume that it results from research congestion within a product. The appearance of the leading-edge parameter $A_t^{\max}$ in the right-hand side of (12.11) represents the force of increasing complexity; as technology advances, the resource cost of further advances increases proportionally.

The same amount of input (adjusted for the leading-edge productivity parameter) will be used in research in each intermediate sector, namely $n_t \equiv R_t / A_t^{\max}$, because the prospective payoff is the same in each sector. Specifically, each innovation at date t results in a new generation of that intermediate sector's product, which embodies the leading-edge productivity parameter $A_t^{\max}$. Thus the Poisson rate of innovation ϕ_t in each sector at date t will be:

$$\phi_t = \lambda \phi\,(n_t)\,. \tag{12.12}$$

The level of research will be determined by the arbitrage condition that the marginal cost of an extra unit of goods allocated to research equal the marginal expected benefit. In order to parameterize the incentive to innovate, we assume that research expenditures are subsidized at the proportional rate β_n. If we measure costs and benefits in units of final output, the marginal cost is $1 - \beta_n$, and the marginal benefit is the product of the value of an innovation V_t and the (private) marginal effect of research input in a sector on that sector's Poisson rate of innovation[14]: $\lambda \frac{\phi(n_t)}{n_t} / A_t^{\max}$. Hence we have the research arbitrage equation:

$$1 - \beta_n = \lambda \frac{\phi\,(n_t)}{n_t} v_t, \tag{12.13}$$

where v_t is the productivity-adjusted value of an innovation: $v_t = V_t / A_t^{\max}$.

We assume that with each innovation, the innovator enters into Bertrand competition with the previous incumbent in that sector, who by definition produces an inferior quality of good. Rather than face a price war with a superior rival, the incumbent exits. Having exited, the former incumbent cannot

---

13. For example, Arroyo, Dinopoulos, and Donald (1994) and Kortum (1993).

14. The assumption that diminishing returns result entirely from a congestion externality means that the private research firm sees itself as facing a constant arrival rate $\lambda \frac{\phi(n_t)}{n_t} n_{jt}$ per unit of R&D expenditure where n_{jt} is its own (productivity-adjusted) level of research expenditure and n_t is the research intensity of all others on the same product.

threaten to reenter. This is why the local monopolist can always charge the unconstrained monopolist price without worrying about competition from earlier vintages of the product.

Accordingly the value of an innovation at date t is the expected present value of all the future profits to be earned by the incumbent before being replaced by the next innovator in that product. Using (12.7) and (12.8) we can write the productivity-adjusted flow of profit per product π_t as:

$$\pi_t = \alpha \ (1 - \alpha) \ \ell k_t^{\alpha} \equiv \pi \ (k_t) \ \ell, \ \pi' > 0. \tag{12.14}$$

As in the model of Chapter 3, the productivity-adjusted value of an innovation at date t satisfies the asset equation:

$$\dot{v}_t = -\pi \ (k_t) \ \ell + (r_t + \phi_t) \ v_t, \tag{12.15}$$

where the instantaneous discount rate is the rate of interest r_t plus the rate of creative destruction ϕ_t.

Using the research-arbitrage equation (12.13) to express n_t as a function of v_t, we can rewrite (12.15) in terms of research intensity:

$$\dot{n}_t = \eta \ (n_t) \left[(r_t + \lambda \phi \ (n_t)) \ n_t - \lambda \ (1 - \beta_n)^{-1} \ \phi \ (n_t) \ \pi \ (k_t) \ \ell \right] \tag{12.16}$$

where

$$\eta \ (n_t) \equiv \left[1 - \phi' \ (n_t) \ n_t / \phi \ (n_t) \right]^{-1} > 0.$$

Growth in the leading-edge parameter $A_t^{\max}$ occurs as a result of the knowledge spillovers produced by innovations. That is, at any moment of time the leading-edge technology is available to any successful innovator, and this publicly available (but not costless) knowledge grows at a rate proportional to the aggregate rate of innovations. The factor of proportionality, which is a measure of the marginal aggregate impact of each innovation on the stock of public knowledge, is assumed to equal $\sigma / Q_t > 0$. We divide by Q_t to reflect the fact that as the economy develops an increasing number of specialized products, an innovation of a given size with respect to any given product will have a smaller impact on the aggregate economy.[15] Putting all this together yields a rate of technological progress equal to:

$$g_t = \dot{A}_t^{\max} / A_t^{\max} = \sigma \lambda \phi \ (n_t) . \tag{12.17}$$

Because the distribution of productivity parameters among new imitation products at any date is identical to the distribution across existing products

---

15. As with the lack of efficiency gain from product variety, this negative effect of Q_t on the economy does not affect any results in the case of zero population growth and no imitation.

at that date, one can show that the ratio of the leading edge to the average productivity parameter will converge monotonically to the constant[16] $1 + \sigma$. Thus we assume that $A_t^{\max} = A_t (1 + \sigma)$ for all t, so that the rate of growth of the average productivity parameter A_t will also be given by (12.17).

The rate of change of the capital stock per efficiency unit k_t is given by:

$$\dot{k}_t = f(k_t) - c_t - n_t (1 + \sigma) / \ell - (\delta + g_L + g_t) k_t, \tag{12.18}$$

where δ is the rate of capital depreciation and c_t is consumption per efficiency unit of labor. The first three terms on the right-hand side of (12.18) represent gross capital accumulation per efficiency unit, which is GDP minus consumption minus the resources used up in research, all expressed in efficiency units.[17] The remaining terms represent the reduction in the stock of capital per efficiency unit that takes place through depreciation and the increase in the number of efficiency units.

The growth rate G_t of real output per person is the growth rate of output per efficiency unit (that is, of k_t^α) plus the rate of technological progress:

$$G_t = \alpha \dot{k}_t / k_t + g_t. \tag{12.19}$$

We make the conventional assumption that saving is determined by intertemporal utility maximization on the part of a representative consumer, who has intertemporally additive preferences over consumption, a constant rate of time preference ρ, and a constant elasticity of marginal utility ε. As usual this implies that c_t must obey the Euler equation[18]:

$$\dot{c}_t = c_t \left[(r_t - \rho) / \varepsilon - g_t \right]. \tag{12.20}$$

We impose the following condition that for all feasible n the steady-state rate

---

16. By assumption, imitations do not affect the average A_t. Each innovation replaces a randomly chosen A_{it} with the leading edge $A_t^{\max}$. Since innovations occur at the rate $\mu_t / Q_t = \phi_t$ per product and the average change across innovating sectors is $A_t^{\max} - A_t$, we have:

$$\frac{dA_t}{dt} = \phi_t \left(A_t^{\max} - A_t \right).$$

This and equation (12.17) imply that the ratio $\Omega_t = A_t^{\max} / A_t$ evolves according to:

$$\frac{1}{\Omega_t} \frac{d\Omega_t}{dt} = \phi_t \sigma - \phi_t (\Omega_t - 1).$$

It follows that as long as ϕ_t is bounded above zero, Ω_t will converge asymptotically to $1 + \sigma$, as asserted in the text.

17. Because n_t is research input per line divided by $A_t^{\max}$, it must be multiplied by $\frac{1+\sigma}{l}$.

18. Since there is a continuum of sectors with independent risks of creative destruction, investing in research involves only diversifiable risk. Hence r_t is a risk-free rate.

of interest will exceed the rate of growth of aggregate output plus the capital subsidy rate:

$$\rho + \varepsilon g > g + g_L + \beta_k, \tag{12.21}$$

where g is the steady-state rate of technological progress. Since a rate of interest below the growth rate is not plausible empirically, this assumption amounts to ruling out a large subsidy to capital.

To parametrize the incentive to accumulate capital, we assume that capital is subsidized at the proportional rate β_k. The cost of capital ζ_t is the interest rate plus the depreciation rate minus the subsidy rate. Hence (12.6) can be rewritten, using (12.8) as:

$$r_t = \alpha^2 k_t^{\alpha-1} - \delta + \beta_k \equiv \alpha f'(k_t) - \delta + \beta_k, \tag{12.22}$$

Equation (12.22) expresses the intuitively obvious condition that the cost of capital must equal its marginal revenue product: $\alpha f'(k_t)$.

Equations (12.18) and (12.20) are the usual equations of the Cass-Koopmans-Ramsey model of optimal growth, modified to include labor-augmenting technological progress. The only difference is that the rate of technological progress g_t is no longer an exogenous constant but depends upon the research intensity n_t. These equations together with equation (12.16) can be reduced, with the aid of (12.17) and (12.22), to the three-dimensional system in capital intensity k_t, research intensity n_t, and consumption intensity c_t:

$$\dot{k}_t = f(k_t) - c_t - n_t(1+\sigma)/\ell - [\delta + g_L + \sigma\lambda\phi(n_t)]k_t \tag{12.23}$$

$$\dot{n}_t = \eta(n_t)\left[(\alpha f'(k_t) - \delta + \beta_k + \lambda\phi(n_t))n_t \right. \tag{12.24}$$

$$\left. - \lambda(1-\beta_n)^{-1}\phi(n_t)\pi(k_t)\ell\right]$$

$$\dot{c}_t = c_t\left[(\alpha f'(k_t) - \delta + \beta_k - \rho)/\varepsilon - \sigma\lambda\phi(n_t)\right] \tag{12.25}$$

The system's rest point $\left(\hat{k}, \hat{n}, \hat{c}\right)$ is a steady-state equilibrium with balanced growth in the usual sense. This steady state is locally stable, in the sense that for any initial capital intensity in a neighborhood of $\hat{k}$ there is a unique initial value of c and n that puts the system on a stable trajectory converging monotonically to the steady state.[19]

The steady-state values of capital intensity (k), research intensity (n), the rate of interest (r), the number of workers per product (ℓ) and the rate of growth of output per person (g) are defined by the following equations:

---

19. One can show that the linearized system around the steady state has one real negative root and two other roots with positive real parts, and that the stable manifold is not orthogonal to the capital axis.

$$\alpha f'(k) = r + \delta - \beta_k \tag{K}$$

$$1 - \beta_n = \lambda \frac{\phi(n)}{n} \frac{\pi(k)\ell}{r + \lambda\phi(n)} \tag{A}$$

$$r = \rho + \varepsilon g \tag{R}$$

$$\ell = g_L/\xi \tag{E}$$

$$g = \sigma\lambda\phi(n) \tag{G}$$

Equation (K) equates the cost of capital to its marginal revenue product. Equation (A) is the same equation that defines the steady-state research intensity in the model of Chapter 2. It equates the marginal cost of research (which was a productivity-adjusted wage in the model of Chapter 2, where labor was the only research input) to the expected discounted marginal benefit. Equation (R) is the familiar Fisher equation showing how the rate of interest rises with the growth rate of consumption. Equation (E) shows how the number of workers per product varies with the population growth rate, and equation (G) is the spillover equation determining the rate of technological progress and hence the steady-state rate of growth. Straightforward comparative-statics techniques yield the following proposition:

Proposition 12.1 The steady-state growth rate g depends positively upon the two subsidy rates (β_k, β_n), the population growth rate (g_L), the productivity of R&D (λ), and the size of innovations (σ); and negatively on the elasticity of marginal utility (ε), the rate of time preference (ρ), and the rate of depreciation (δ).

Most of the specific results of Proposition 12.1 are unremarkable, except for the positive effects of the capital subsidy rate and the population growth rate. To see more clearly how these work, use equations (R), (G), and (E) to eliminate r and ℓ from the first two equations. This leaves the two-dimensional system illustrated in figure 12.2. The capital curve (K) is downward sloping because higher research intensity raises the rate of growth, which raises the interest rate through the Fisher relation, which reduces the steady-state demand for capital. The research curve (A) is upward sloping because more capital raises the flow of profits $\pi(k)$ to a successful innovator.[20] An increase in the subsidy rate on capital shifts the capital curve to the right, raising the steady-state research intensity. An increase in the population growth rate raises the equilibrium number of workers per product, which also raises the steady-state

---

20. The fact that these two curves have opposite signed slopes guarantees uniqueness of the steady state.

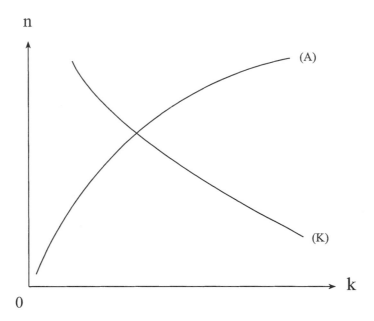

Figure 12.2

research intensity by shifting the research curve up. In both cases the steady-state growth rate increases according to the growth equation (G).

12.3   Back to the Empirical Critiques of Schumpeterian Growth Theory

12.3.1   Growth Accounting

Growth-accounting exercises of the sort performed by Jorgenson (1995) and Young (1995b) seem to imply that technological progress is relatively unimportant as a source of growth. The model presented above challenges this conclusion, because a growth-accounting exercise performed on an economy described by the model would "attribute" an even smaller fraction of growth to technological progress than Jorgensen does if the economy were in a steady state, and smaller still if the capital stock per efficiency unit of labor were below its steady-state value, as it clearly is in the newly industrialized countries studied by Young. However, the result does not imply that the innovation process is relatively unimportant for long-run growth. On the contrary, if innovation were shut down by a prohibitive tax, the economy would ultimately stop growing altogether.[21]

---

21. This is implied by equation (12.17) and the condition that $\phi\,(0) = 0$.

The result is a straightforward implication of the fact that aggregate output is given by a standard Cobb-Douglas production function with purely labor-augmenting technical progress. Consider the "residual":

$$\Phi_t = \frac{\dot{Y}_t}{Y_t} - \eta_n \frac{\dot{L}_t}{L_t} - \eta_k \frac{\dot{K}_t}{K_t} = (1 - \alpha)\left(\frac{\dot{L}_t}{L_t} + \frac{\dot{A}_t}{A_t}\right) + \alpha \frac{\dot{K}_t}{K_t} - \eta_n \frac{\dot{L}_t}{L_t} - \eta_k \frac{\dot{K}_t}{K_t}$$

where η_n and η_k are respectively the shares of labor and capital in GDP. Under the realistic assumption that the national accounts attribute all monopoly profits to capital, the share of capital implied by the above model is $\eta_k = \alpha$. Then as in any model describable by an aggregate production function, the residual will equal the rate of labor-augmenting technological progress times labor's share: $\Phi_t = (1 - \alpha)\frac{\dot{A}_t}{A_t} = (1 - \alpha) g_t$. Since the growth rate of output per person is: $G_t = g_t + \alpha \dot{k}_t / k_t$, therefore:

$$\Phi_t = \frac{1 - \alpha}{1 + \alpha \frac{\dot{k}_t / k_t}{g_t}} G_t. \tag{12.26}$$

Because capital includes both human and physical capital, the reasoning of Mankiw (1995) suggests that α is probably about 0.8. Thus if the economy were in a steady state, with $\dot{k}_t = 0$, the residual would be about 20 percent of the growth rate of output per person. This is even smaller than the estimate of Jorgenson and Fraumeni (1992), which yields a residual equal to 30 percent of the growth rate of output per hour worked in the United States from 1948 to 1986.[22] If the economy were below its steady state, with $\dot{k}_t > 0$, equation (12.26) indicates that the residual would be even less than 20 percent of the growth rate of output per person. This is what Young (1995b) finds for the East Asian countries in which capital is clearly being accumulated at more than a steady-state rate.

This illustrates the familiar general principle that accounting by itself cannot generate causal inferences. Finding that only a small fraction of growth is "accounted for" by technological progress does not imply that innovation is relatively unimportant in determining a country's growth rate. Indeed the model would yield a small residual even in the (admittedly unrealistic) case in which raw labor was the only input to research, where innovation is therefore the *only* determinant of long-run growth. (See section 3.2.3 above.)

---

22. Their table 5 indicates that on average output grew at a 2.93% rate and labor input (hours times quality) grew at a 2.20% rate. It also indicates that 58.1% of the contribution of labor input came from hours, implying an average growth rate in hours of (.581·2.20 =) 1.28% and an average growth rate in output per hour worked of (2.93-1.28 =) 1.65%. Their estimate of the residual was 0.50%, which is 30.3% of the growth rate of output per hour worked.

12.3.2   The Jones Critique

Jones (1995) has challenged endogenous growth theory by pointing out that the input to R&D, as proxied by the number of scientists and engineers engaged in R&D, has risen dramatically over the past half century, with no visible tendency for growth in output per person or in productivity to increase, in contradiction to simpler R&D–based models, including the model of Chapter 2. This finding does not, however, challenge the above extension of that model. For in the model's steady state, the total input to R&D must grow at the same rate as GDP, while the growth rates of productivity and of output per person are constant.

The reason rising R&D in a steady state does not cause the increase in the growth rate that simpler models predict is twofold. First, increasing complexity of technology makes it necessary to raise R&D over time just to keep the innovation rate constant for each product. (This is why we divided R_t by $A_t^{\max}$ inside the ϕ function.) Second, as the number of products increases, an innovation on any one product directly affects a smaller proportion of the economy, and hence has a smaller proportional spillover effect on the aggregate stock of knowledge. (This is why we assumed a spillover coefficient of σ/Q_t in deriving equation [12.17].)

Jones proposed a similar strategy for rescuing endogenous-innovation growth theory, but concluded that the result of such a rescue would be a model in which the long-run growth rate would cease to be affected by the incentive to innovate as well as by the incentive to accumulate capital, and would depend only on the rate of population growth. The method adopted above reaches the opposite conclusion, namely that the long-run growth rate is affected by incentives both to innovate and to accumulate capital. We have already discussed how growth would be affected by a capital subsidy.

The key difference between our model and Jones's is that we have taken into account that capital as well as labor is used in R&D. Jones's proposed research technology was:

$$\dot{A}_t/A_t = v\left(L_t^r\right)^\gamma A_t^{\psi-1},\ 0 < \psi < 1, v > 0, 0 < \gamma < 1,$$

where L_t^r is the total labor input to research. In a steady state, with L_t^r/L_t constant and $\dot{A}_t/A_t = g$, this equation implies:

$$g = \frac{\gamma g_L}{1 - \psi}.$$

Thus growth in the long run depends only on the rate of population growth and other parameters that one would normally consider invariant to policy intervention.

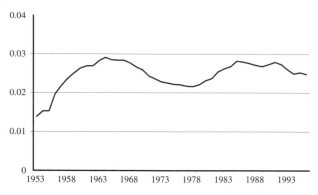

Figure 12.3
U.S. R&D expenditures as a fraction of GDP. Source: National Science Foundation (1996).

The research technology specified above is similar to Jones's. For example, in the special case where function $\phi(n) = n^\gamma$:

$$\dot{A}_t/A_t = v\,(R_t)^\gamma\,A_t^{\psi-1}, \tag{12.27}$$

where $v \equiv \sigma\lambda\,(1+\sigma)^{-\gamma}$ and $\psi = 1 - \gamma$, which differs from Jones's in that the input R_t includes capital as well as labor. Because R_t grows at the same rate as A_t in a steady state, equation (12.27) cannot be used to solve for the steady-state growth rate independently of the rest of the model.

Instead of predicting that the number of scientists and engineers engaged in R&D should remain constant during a period of relatively steady growth in output per person or in productivity, the present model predicts that the fraction (D_t/Y_t) of GDP allocated to R&D should remain constant. Figure 12.3, drawn from NSF data, shows that this does indeed seem to have been the case in the United States since the early 1950s. Total expenditure on R&D has remained between 2.2 percent and 2.9 percent of GDP in the U.S. economy every year between 1957 and 1996, with no apparent tendency to rise. In each of the three years from 1994 through 1996 it was 2.5 percent, which is the average figure for the years 1957 through 1962. Thus data on trends in U.S. R&D confirm endogenous-innovation growth theory rather than contradicting it.

It might be argued that the above model evades the scale effect at the root of Jones's criticism by assuming that horizontal innovations are just mechanical imitations. When horizontal innovations diffuse the scale effect in Alwyn Young's model, they do so in response to the same sort of profit opportunities as we have assumed drive vertical innovations, and they destroy the characteristic features of Schumpeterian growth theory—namely the positive effect on growth of such structural changes as a subsidy to innovation, the rents from which are dissipated by faster horizontal innovations.

It is easy to see, however, that the positive effect on the growth rate of a subsidy to vertical innovations does not depend critically on our simplifying assumption that horizontal innovations are automatically proportional to the population. Consider, for example, what would happen if horizontal innovations were driven by exactly the same considerations as vertical innovations. The successful horizontal innovator gets the same reward as the successful vertical innovator, except that instead of getting to implement a technology with the leading edge parameter $A_t^{\max}$, he or she gets a parameter drawn randomly from the existing cross-sectional distribution.

Suppose that the technologies for horizontal and vertical innovations are identical. Let $n_t^h = D_t^h / Q_t A_t$ be the (productivity adjusted) expenditure on horizontal innovation relative to the number of products, and suppose that the rate of horizontal innovation is:

$$\dot{Q}_t = \lambda \phi \left(n_t^h \right) Q_t.$$

That is, the flow of horizontal innovations is given by a constant-returns production function depending on the productivity-adjusted level of horizontal R&D $\left(D_t^h / A_t \right)$ and the number of existing products Q_t. The idea underlying this technology is that the more products there are, the easier it is to imitate one; but the more resources are devoted to R&D, the more congestion there is from duplication.

Suppose first that the same subsidy rate β_n must apply to vertical and horizontal innovations. Then instead of (A) above we have the pair:

$$1 - \beta_n = \lambda \frac{\phi\,(n)}{n} \frac{\pi\,(k)\,\ell}{r + \lambda \phi\,(n)}. \tag{A}$$

$$1 - \beta_n = \lambda \frac{\phi\left(n^h\right)}{n^h} \frac{\pi\,(k)\,\ell}{r + \lambda \phi\,(n)}. \tag{A^h}$$

Thus the two research intensities n and n^h would have to be equal. Their common value would be determined by the steady-state condition:

$$g_L = \phi\left(n^h\right) \tag{E$'$}$$

as a function of the population growth rate alone. As in the Jones model, the growth rate would depend only on the population growth rate ($g = \sigma \lambda g_L$), and as in the Young model a subsidy to innovation or to capital accumulation would be dissipated by a change in the number of workers per product, with no effect on the rate of growth.

If we suppose, however, that vertical innovations can be targeted, then the subsidy rate to innovation would affect growth as before (the LHS of (A^h)

would become unity), by inducing substitution away from horizontal innovations. Thus the scale effect can be eliminated using an argument much like Young's, and the Schumpeterian approach reconciled with the observations of Jones without destroying its essential characteristics. In particular, although the population growth rate has a positive effect on the steady-state rate of technological progress, it is not as Jones argued the only determinant of the steady-state rate of technological progress.

12.4   A Multicountry Model

In this section we shall try to address the empirical critiques of endogenous growth theory based on cross-country evidence, by amending the previous model to take into account a minimal degree of interaction between countries. Specifically, we follow Parente and Prescott (1994), Barro and Sala-i-Martín (1996), and our discussion in Chapter 11, in taking into account the mechanism of technology transfer, working through cross-country R&D spillovers of the sort that Coe and Helpman (1995) have argued are quite substantial among OECD countries and that Coe, Helpman, and Hoffmaister (1995) have shown also affect productivity growth in less developed countries. This extension to a multicountry context is just a first step. It ignores all aspects of international trade in goods. Yet even this simple extension reveals that endogenous growth theory predicts the sort of cross-country results that others have taken as evidence against endogenous growth theory. The theory also yields additional implications that should come from cross-country studies.

Specifically, the model as laid out below predicts that in the long run all countries should grow at the same rate, as is suggested by the evidence on conditional β-convergence and by the more direct evidence of Evans (1996) on σ-convergence. The long-run common world growth rate will be determined by the incentives to accumulate capital and to innovate in all countries.

The model provides a more complete account of cross-country differences in output per person than does the neoclassical growth model. For these differences depend upon differences in capital per effective worker and differences in productivity. The present Schumpeterian approach offers an explanation for both sets of differences, whereas the neoclassical approach must take the latter set as given.

Thus suppose that there are m different countries, each describable by the model above, but with possibly different parameter values and initial conditions. Suppose these countries have no interaction at the aggregate level, so all of domestic saving goes into domestic capital accumulation and R&D, and there is no tendency for the real return on capital to be equalized across countries. However, there are international R&D spillovers that make the parameter λ of the research technology in each country depend upon the cumulative R&D in all countries.

That is, let the value of this parameter λ^j in country j be a decreasing function of the relative productivity $z_t^j \equiv \ln A_t^j - \sum_1^m \omega^i \ln A_t^i$, where the weights ω^i are all positive and sum to unity. Each ω^i reflect the importance of country i as a source of new technological ideas for other countries.[23] A limiting case would be that in which country 1 is a "leader" to which the others are catching up: $\omega^1 = 1$, $\omega^i = 0$ for $i = 2 \ldots m$.

A country that is behind the average cannot catch up in one leap, but the speed with which it can gradually catch up is an increasing function of the gap to be made up. Specifically, each z_t^j will evolve according to:

$$\dot{z}_t^j = g_t^j - \sum_1^m \omega^i g_t^i = \sigma^j \lambda \left(z_t^j \right) \phi_j \left(n_t^j \right) - \sum_1^m \omega^i \sigma^i \lambda \left(z_t^i \right) \phi_i \left(n_t^i, \right), \quad (12.28)$$

where $\dot{g}_t^i = \dot{A}_t^i / A_t$ and $\lambda' < 0$. In addition, the consumption and capital per efficiency unit c^j, k^j and research intensity n_j will evolve according to country-specific versions of the system (12.23)–(12.25).

In a steady state, each z^j, k^j, c^j, n^j is constant. If follows from (12.28) that each country will have the same steady-state growth rate of output per person:

$$G = g = \sigma^j \lambda \left(z^j \right) \phi \left(n^j \right); \quad j = 1, \ldots, m. \quad (12.29)$$

Growth rates converge because a country whose productivity was growing more slowly than average would find that the productivity of its R&D was continually increasing, which would have the effect of inducing a faster rate of innovation and hence a faster rate of productivity growth. This process would continue to raise productivity growth until it caught up to the average growth rate.

A general characterization of the stability properties of this steady state seems out of reach except for the special case in which the spillovers work very slowly, that is, where the elasticity of the λ () function is very small. Suppose the elasticity is so small that the dynamics can be analyzed in two "runs." In the short run the relative productivity level z^j of a country is historically predetermined, and the variables (k_t^j, n_t^j, c_t^j) evolve according to the unconnected country-specific dynamical systems described by equations (12.23)–(12.25).

---

23. A more general analysis would allow the weights to vary by receiving as well as sending country. If the matrix of coefficients were decomposable, this would allow for convergence clubs to emerge.

Given the (local) stability of this system, each country will approach a "short-run equilibrium" defined by the steady state analyzed in the previous sections.

By Proposition 12.1, the growth rate g^j of country j in that short-run equilibrium will be a function of $\lambda^j = \lambda\left(z^j\right)$ and of the other country-specific parameters $\theta^j \equiv \left(\beta_k^j, \beta_n^j, g_L^j, \sigma^j, \varepsilon^j, \rho^j, \delta^j\right)$. Since λ^j depends inversely on z^j and, by Proposition 12.1, the growth rate g^j depends positively on λ^j, we can express the "short-run" equilibrium growth rate in country j as:

$$g^j = \tilde{g}\left(z^j, \theta^j\right), \qquad \frac{\partial \tilde{g}}{\partial z^j} < 0.$$

In the "long run," each z^j evolves according to equation (12.28). That is:

$$\dot{z}_t^j = \tilde{g}\left(z_t^j, \theta^j\right) - \sum_1^m \omega^i \tilde{g}\left(z_t^i, \theta^i\right); \quad j = 1, \ldots, m. \tag{12.30}$$

The steady state of this system can be shown to be globally stable by a straight-forward application of Lyapounov's second method.[24]

The structure of a stationary state in any economy j can be described in terms of the common world growth rate g, by equations (12.29) and:

$$\alpha f'\left(k^j\right) = r^j + \delta^j - \beta_k^j \tag{K^j}$$

$$1 - \beta_n^j = \frac{g}{\sigma^j n^j} \frac{\pi\left(k^j\right) \ell^j}{r^j + g/\sigma^j} \tag{A^j}$$

$$r^j = \rho^j + \varepsilon^j g \tag{R^j}$$

$$\ell^j = g_L^j/\xi \tag{E^j}$$

where (12.29) has been used to eliminate λ^j from (A^j) and (R^j). The capital equation (K^j) and the Fisherian interest equation (R^j) can be used to derive:

$$k^j = \tilde{k}\left(\rho^j + \varepsilon^j g + \delta^j - \beta_k^j\right), \qquad \tilde{k}' < 0. \tag{12.31}$$

Equations (12.31), (R^j), (E^j), and (A^j) can be used to solve for the steady-state research intensity:

$$n^j = \tilde{n}\left(\underset{(+)}{g} ; \underset{(+)}{\beta_k^j}, \underset{(+)}{\beta_n^j}, \underset{(+)}{g_L^j}, \underset{(-)}{\sigma^j}, \underset{(-)}{\varepsilon^j}, \underset{(-)}{\rho^j}, \underset{(-)}{\delta^j}\right), \qquad \frac{\sigma^j}{n^j}\frac{\partial \tilde{n}}{\partial \sigma^j} > -1 \quad \frac{g}{n^j}\frac{\partial \tilde{n}}{\partial g} < 1.$$

---

24. See Howitt 1997.

Substituting from this formula into the growth equation (12.29) and making use of the fact that, by (12.11), the elasticity of ϕ is less than one, yields the steady-state productivity difference:

$$z^j = \tilde{z} \left(\underset{(-)}{g} ; \underset{(+)}{\beta_k^j}, \underset{(+)}{\beta_n^j}, \underset{(+)}{g_L^j}, \underset{(+)}{\sigma^j}, \underset{(-)}{\varepsilon^j}, \underset{(-)}{\rho^j}, \underset{(-)}{\delta^j} \right). \tag{12.32}$$

The world growth rate g is determined as in the closed economy above, except that there are now some barriers between regions in the world economy that we did not take into account in the closed economy model. Specifically, the condition determining g is the adding-up constraint implied by the definition of the z^j's:

$$0 = \sum_1^m \omega^j z^j = \sum_1^m \omega^j \tilde{z} \left(g, \theta^j \right), \tag{12.33}$$

according to which the world growth rate is a function of the structural parameters within each country[25]:

$$g = \tilde{g} \left(\theta^1 \ldots \theta^m \right).$$

If follows from (12.32), (12.33), and Proposition 12.1 that any parameter change in country j that would have raised country j's growth rate according to the isolated-economy model of the previous sections, such as a subsidy to innovation or to capital accumulation, will raise country j's relative productivity parameter in this multicountry model and will also raise the world growth rate, although the effect on the world growth rate will be small if the country has a small spillover coefficient ω^j.

The empirical implications for cross-country income comparisons are straightforward. Suppose that all countries share the same underlying technology (12.4) for converting labor and intermediate products into final output. Then the difference in output per person between two countries i and j can be decomposed into differences in capital per effective worker and differences in relative productivity:

$$\ln \left(\frac{Y_t^i}{L_t^i} - \frac{Y_t^j}{L_t^j} \right) = \alpha \left(\ln k_t^i - \ln k_t^j \right) + \left(z_t^i - z_t^j \right).$$

In a steady state, this equation together with equations (12.31) and (12.32) imply that differences in output per person depend on differences in the

---

25. Because $\partial \tilde{z}/\partial g < 0$, the solution to (12.33), if it exists, is unique.

underlying parameters θ^i and θ^j that would determine the steady-state growth rates of the countries in isolation, and in the same direction, with some of the effects working just through the relative productivity level Δz and others working also through the relative capital stock Δk. For example, a subsidy to innovation will raise a country's relative productivity level but not its relative capital stock per effective worker.

Because each country has a Cobb-Douglas aggregate production function with the same coefficients, the model implies exactly the same steady-state equation that Mankiw, Romer, and Weil (MRW) find accounts for over three quarters of the variation across countries in income levels per capita in 1985:

$$\ln \frac{Y_t^j}{L_t^j} = \ln A_t^j + \frac{\alpha}{1-\alpha} \ln s^j - \frac{\alpha}{1-\alpha} \ln \left(\delta^j + g_L^j + g \right), \qquad (12.34)$$

where $s^j \equiv 1 - (c^j + n^j \frac{1+\sigma^j}{\ell^j})/f\left(k^j\right)$ is country j's investment rate. However, MRW assumed that the productivity levels $\ln A_t^j$ were randomly distributed across countries. Since the above model has endogenized relative productivity levels, it predicts that we should be able to do better than that. In particular, in a steady state:

$$\ln A_t^j = z^j + \ln \hat{A}_t,$$

where $\hat{A}_t \equiv e^{\sum_1^m \omega^i \ln A_t^i}$ is the world average productivity level.

Suppose we made the assumption that all countries shared the same "size" parameter σ and "imitation rate" ξ, and that they shared the same innovation function, of the form:

$$\phi\left(n\right) = n^\gamma, \ 0 < \gamma < 1, \ \text{for all } j = 1 \ldots m.$$

Suppose furthermore that the spillover function λ takes the form:

$$\lambda(z) = e^{-\lambda z}, \ 0 < \lambda.$$

Then from equation (12.29):

$$\lambda z^j = \gamma \ln n^j - \ln g + \ln \sigma.$$

Putting these equations together and making use of the fact that $n_t^j \equiv D_t^j / Q_t^j A_t^{\max, j}$, we arrive at the modified equation:

$$\ln \frac{Y_t^j}{L_t^j} = a + \frac{\lambda + \gamma}{\lambda} \left[\frac{\alpha}{1-\alpha} \ln s^j - \frac{\alpha}{1-\alpha} \ln \left(\delta^j + g_L^j + g \right) \right] \qquad (12.35)$$

$$+ \frac{\gamma}{\lambda} \ln \frac{D_t^j}{Y_t^j} + \frac{\gamma}{\lambda} \ln g_L^j,$$

where a is constant across countries. This equation is almost identical to the one (12.34) used by MRW except for the addition of one more explanatory variable, namely the fraction of GDP allocated to R&D.

12.5   The Main Observational Implications of Schumpeterian Growth Theory

In the previous sections we have tried to "reconcile" the empirical evidence on growth accounting, scale effects, and cross–country convergence in growth rates, with the view that long-run growth is *endogenous,* that is, dependant upon structural parameters of the economy.

It might be argued that any empirical refutation of the Schumpeterian model could be overcome by suitable modifications, in which case the practical value of the framework is called into question. It turns out, however, that the Schumpeterian approach can deliver a number of specific predictions that distinguish it from other approaches and make it potentially refutable.

These predictions concern the rate of growth as a function of various exogenous parameters (the rate of time preference, the endowment of skilled labor, R&D productivity, depreciation of physical capital) and of other endogenous variables such as market structure, unemployment, job creation and destruction, rates of entry and exit by firms, the rate of capital obsolescence, the level of R&D activity, and the rate of patenting. In this section, we would like to derive a potential set of observational implications that might be used to distinguish the Schumpeterian framework from competing approaches. The main conclusion of this exercise is that any serious empirical challenge to Schumpeterian models should go well beyond existing work. The testable implications are many, and as yet, empirical assessment of them has hardly begun.

More formally, we consider a Schumpeterian model essentially identical to the one analyzed in the previous section, except that:

a. we abstract from population growth and from the possibility of horizontal innovations, that is: $L_t \equiv L$ and $Q_t \equiv 1$.

b. both capital *and* labor are used as inputs in the production of intermediate goods. That is:

$$x_i = G(K_i/A_i, N_i), \tag{12.36}$$

where K_i and N_i are the inputs of capital and labor into production in sector i, and G is a regular constant-returns production function. We divide K_i by A_i in (12.36) to indicate that successive vintages of the intermediate good are produced by increasingly capital-intensive techniques.

Now, because we want to consider labor market effects of the kind analyzed in Chapter 4, we shall depart from Walrasian labor market clearing and instead assume the existence of labor market frictions stemming from positive hiring costs. More precisely, when determining the cost of labor, we assume that workers always bargain for a wage proportional to the leading-edge technology: $w_t = \omega A_t$, and that the firm must pay the setup cost ΓA_t each time it hires a worker.[26] There is an exogenous rate δ_w at which workers quit for non-economic reasons, as in the literature on job-matching (Pissarides 1990). Hence in steady state the cost of labor to the intermediate firm at any date s will be:

$$\bar{w}_s = A_s \bar{\omega} = A_s \left[\omega + (r + \delta_w + \phi_s - g)\Gamma \right], \tag{12.37}$$

where the creative destruction term $\phi_s = \lambda\phi(n_s)$[27] is offset by the capitalization term g, which exists because the setup cost of hiring labor rises at the rate g, and hence confers a steady capital gain to the firm on its stock of workers.[28]

It follows from the above equations and the fact that the intermediate firm's production function exhibits constant returns to scale that the unit cost of an intermediate firm with technology A_t at time s can be written in steady state as:

$$c_{s,t} = A_t C(\bar{r}, \bar{\omega} e^{g(s-t)}); \quad C_1 < 0, \quad C_2 < 0 \tag{12.38}$$

and the firms's profit and employment can be similarly expressed as:

$$\pi_{s,t} = A_t \hat{\pi}(\bar{r}, \bar{\omega} e^{g(s-t)}); \quad \hat{\pi} < 0, \quad \hat{\pi}_2 < 0, \tag{12.39}$$

where $\bar{r} = r + \phi$ is the cost of capital in steady state (when a monopolist is replaced, we assume that its capital has no second-hand value).

Assume that the production function G is Cobb-Douglas. Then the demand for labor by intermediate firms with technology A_t at date s is:

$$N_t = \hat{n}(\bar{r}, \bar{\omega} e^{g(s-t)}); \quad \hat{n}_1 < 0, \quad \hat{n}_2 < 0. \tag{12.40}$$

The value of an innovation at date t is equal to the expected present value of the rents that will accrue until the producer is replaced. The time until

---

26. This formulation of labor market frictions in terms of hiring costs turns out to be essentially equivalent to that in terms of matching functions used in Chapter 4, although the latter formulation is somewhat less handy for the comprehensive comparative statics exercise we perform in this section.

27. As in the previous sections, we let

$$n_s = \frac{R_s}{A_s^{\max}},$$

where R_s is the total amount of final output invested in R&D at date s and $A_s^{\max}$ is the leading-edge productivity parameter at that date.

28. Pissarides (1990, ch. 2) has an extensive discussion of the capitalization effect in a similar context.

replacement is distributed exponentially with parameter $\phi = \lambda\phi(n)$. Therefore:

$$V_t = \int_0^\infty e^{-(r+\phi)\tau} A_t \pi_{\tau,t} d\tau$$

$$\equiv A_t v(r+\phi, \overline{\omega}, g); \qquad v_i < 0, i = 1 \ldots 3$$

(12.41)

The negative dependency of V_t and therefore research on the growth rate arises because the value of any given vintage decreases as the equilibrium wage grows faster, that is, as the rate of technical progress is higher. (This negative feedback effect of growth on R&D is worth noting, especially in light of the Jones criticism.)

Finally, we assume that the economy is populated by infinitely lived individuals whose lifetime utility depends upon the path of consumption, c_t

$$U = \int_0^\infty e^{-\rho t} \frac{c_t^{1-\varepsilon} - 1}{1 - \varepsilon} dt. \quad \varepsilon \geq 0, \quad \varepsilon \neq 1$$

(12.42)

where ρ is the common rate of time preference and ε the common elasticity of marginal utility. (For simplicity, we were mainly considering the special case $\varepsilon = 0$ when introducing the Schumpeterian framework in Chapters 2 to 4.) It then follows from the Ramsey equation derived in Chapter 1 that in a steady state, with consumption growing at the rate g, the rate of interest must satisfy:

$$r = \rho + \varepsilon g.$$

(12.43)

12.5.1 Empirical Determinants of Growth

Using equations (12.37), (12.41), and (12.43) and taking the special case $\phi(n) \equiv n$ and $\beta_n = 0$, we can write the arbitrage equation (A) as:

$$1 = \lambda v(\rho + (\varepsilon + \frac{1}{\sigma})g, \omega + (\rho + (\varepsilon - 1 + \frac{1}{\sigma})g + \delta_w)\Gamma, g),$$

(A)

where the left-hand side of (A) is again the cost of research and the right-hand side is equal to the flow probability of innovating λ times the productivity-adjusted value v of an innovation.

This value is decreasing in ρ, δ_w, ω, and Γ, and therefore so will be the equilibrium amount of resources n invested in R&D. The steady-state growth rate, given by:

$$g = \sigma\lambda n,$$

(G)

will obviously also be a decreasing function of ρ, ε (and therefore of the interest rate r), of the quit rate parameter δ_w, and of the hiring cost Γ. The effect on g and n of an increase in the research productivity parameter λ is slightly more involved: to the extent that the equilibrium research investment

n is decreasing in g (which it will be if the capitalization effect is not too large: $\varepsilon - 1 + \frac{1}{\sigma} > 0$), a higher λ will indeed have an ambiguous effect on n. The overall effect on g, however, is unambiguously positive (by way of contradiction, suppose that $\frac{dg}{d\lambda} < 0$; this implies that $\frac{dn}{d\lambda} < 0$, which in turn could not happen unless increasing λ leads to a higher growth rate g. It is thus necessarily the case that $\frac{dg}{d\lambda} > 0$).

Thus by using the two basic equations of the model, namely (A) and (G), to solve simultaneously for the productivity-adjusted level of R&D and for the rate of growth g, we can derive our first "testable" proposition, which is essentially identical to Proposition 12.1.

Implication 1

a. The long-run growth rate g decreases with the interest rate, the quit rate, and hiring costs; on the other hand, long-run growth increases with respect to R&D productivity.

b. The productivity-adjusted level of R&D n displays basically the same comparative statics properties as the long-run growth rate g, except that the effect of an increase in R&D productivity on n becomes ambiguous.[29]

The negative dependency of growth on the taste parameters ρ and ε, and therefore on the interest rate r, does not distinguish this from other endogenous growth models, most of which use the same intertemporal-utility maximization by an infinitely lived representative consumer as the basis for saving decisions. The fact that the productivity λ of R&D has a positive effect on growth is also perhaps not surprising, but it does help to explain why it has been so hard to find cross-country evidence on the productivity of human capital. Specifically, to the extent that traditional empirical proxies for human capital such as years of schooling have a counterpart in the above model, it is in the supply of skilled workers. While the theory predicts that this variable has a positive effect on the growth of output, it does not necessarily imply a significant effect on the level of output, as it would if it entered an aggregate production function like any other factor of production.

Implication 1 also indicates that long-run growth will be affected, ceteris paribus, by various labor-market variables, such as the level of real wages, the quit rate, and the cost of hiring. An increase in any of these variables would reduce the profitability of monopolizing an intermediate good sector, which would reduce the profitability of R&D, the payoff to which is the prospect of gaining such a monopoly, and hence would reduce growth.

---

29. More formally, $\partial n / \partial \lambda$ has the same sign as one minus the (absolute) elasticity of the function:

$$V(g) \equiv v(\rho + (\varepsilon + \frac{1}{\sigma})g, \omega + (\rho + (\varepsilon - 1 + \frac{1}{\sigma})g + \delta_w)\Gamma, g).$$

The empirical implications of Schumpeterian theory are not exhausted by Implication 1, however, because the theory also has implications for how growth should covary with other endogenous variables.

There are three endogenous variables that the theory says should covary positively with growth because their values equal g in the theory. The first of those is the flow of new patents. According to this theory, each innovation is accompanied by a new patent, and the flow rate of innovations equals the long-run rate of growth. The second is the flow of entry of new firms. Each innovation is implemented by a new firm that takes over from the previous incumbent in one sector of the economy. The third is the flow of new products. (See Klenow 1994 for an empirical study based on this variable.) Each innovation introduces a new product.

Of course it is easy to see that even a slight generalization of the theory would destroy the exact identity between these three variables and the rate of growth, because not all industries and countries have the same propensity to patent, in practice some innovations are carried out by existing firms, and some innovations can take the form of new processes rather than new products. A weaker but more robust testable implication is that:

Implication 2   The long-run rate of growth should be positively correlated with the flow of patents, the flow of entry of new firms, and the flow of new product introduction.

The central role of creative destruction in Schumpeterian growth theory can be tested by looking at the correlation between growth and two other variables, the flow of exit of firms and the rate of obsolescence of capital. The former is identical to the flow of entry in a steady-state equilibrium, while the latter is the rate of arrival of new innovations, which we have seen is equal to the rate of growth. Hence:

Implication 3   The long-run rate of growth should be positively correlated with the flow of exit of firms and with the rate of obsolescence of capital.

12.5.2   Labor Market Variables

Implication 1 showed that a number of exogenous labor market variables should have a definite effect on the rate of growth. There are also a number of endogenous labor market variables that should be correlated in a definite manner with the growth rate. The first of these is the rate of job separation—the fraction of labor-market matches that break up per period. In the above model, this is just the fraction of those who leave for exogenous reasons δ_w plus the fraction working in firms that are replaced by an innovation. The latter is the fraction of sectors in which a new innovation arrives per period of time, which is just the rate of creative destruction: $\phi = \frac{g}{\sigma}$. (We are assuming that

δ_w is large enough that firms do not need to engage in layoffs in order to have employment decrease over time in response to the increase in real wages over time.) Because of this, we have:

Implication 4   The long-run rate of growth should be positively correlated with the rate of job separation.

Another key endogenous labor market variable is the gross flow of job creation. As measured by Davis and Haltiwanger (1992) this is just the rate at which new employment increases within production establishments with positive employment growth during the period. In the above model, the only firms that increase their employment are those that have just arrived with a new innovation. The rate at which they do so is the rate of new firm creation g/σ times the level of employment at each newly created firm $\widehat{n}(\overline{r}, \overline{\omega})$. (Recall (12.40).) We have:

Implication 5   The ratio of gross job creation to growth can be expressed as a function of the rate of growth and $\rho, \varepsilon, \delta_w, \omega, \Gamma$ and is decreasing in each argument.

Proof   From the preceding discussion, this ratio is $\sigma\widehat{n}(\overline{r}, \overline{\omega})$. (From (G), (12.37) and (12.43)

$$\widehat{n}(\overline{r}, \overline{\omega}) = \widehat{n}(\rho + (\varepsilon + \frac{1}{\sigma})g, \omega + (\rho + (\varepsilon - 1 + \frac{1}{\sigma})g + \delta_w)\Gamma).$$

From the sign restrictions in (12.40) we can rewrite this equation as:

$$\widehat{n}(\overline{r}, \overline{\omega}) = n^*(g; \rho, \varepsilon, \delta_w, \omega, \Gamma), \quad n_i^* < 0 \quad i = 1 \ldots 6. \quad \square$$

To discuss the rate of unemployment we need to make use of the fact that in this case the steady-state distribution of relative productivities

$$a = \frac{A_{it}}{A_t^{\max}}$$

is given by the density

$$h(a) = \frac{1}{\sigma} a^{\frac{1-\sigma}{\sigma}},$$

as analyzed in appendix 1 to Chapter 3.

From this, employment in the economy will be:[30]

$$N = \int_0^1 \widehat{n}[\rho + (\varepsilon + \frac{1}{\sigma})g, (\omega + (\rho + (\varepsilon - 1 + \frac{1}{\sigma})g + \delta_w)\Gamma)/a]h(a)da \quad (12.44)$$

---

30. To verify that the expression for the cost of labor in (12.44) is the same as in (12.40), note that at date s the vintage of firms for which $A_i/A = a$ is such that $e^{g(t-s)} = a$.

and the rate of unemployment will be

$$u = 1 - N/L, \tag{12.45}$$

where L is the exogenous supply of labor. It follows directly from (12.44), (12.45) and the sign restrictions in (12.40) that:

Implication 6   The rate of unemployment can be described as a function of the rate of growth and of ρ, ε, δ_w, ω, Γ. It is increasing in each argument.

The effect of growth on unemployment is a direct consequence of the creative destruction at the heart of the Schumpeterian model. When growth goes up, so does the cost of capital and labor. Even in the limiting case of infinite intertemporal substitution, where $\varepsilon = 0$ and there is no effect on the rate of interest, an increase in growth will raise the cost of capital by increasing the risk of creative destruction. Since labor and capital are complements in production (that is, $G_{12} > 0$ because of concavity and constant returns), therefore the increase in the cost of capital alone is enough (in the Cobb-Douglas case) to cause the demand for labor to decrease when growth rises.

It should be mentioned that a somewhat deeper analysis of the relationship between growth and unemployment, such as the one we conducted in Chapter 4, would allow the possibility for this effect of growth on unemployment to be offset by the capitalization effect. More specifically, the capitalization effect would no longer be offset by creative destruction in determining the cost of labor, if we allowed innovations to move faster through the list of potential techniques; that is if we had $\sigma > 1/(1 - \varepsilon)$ and $\varepsilon < 1$ in equation (G). Our earlier analysis, however, showed that there was always a range of growth rates over which creative destruction was the dominant force, and over which a rise in growth would lead to a rise in unemployment.

To summarize our analysis in this section, we have tried to identify a number of propositions arising from a general Schumpeterian model of endogenous growth. These propositions are testable, at least in principle, and we think they are likely to be robust to reasonable extensions of the model. One limitation is that they are all in the form of comparative-statics relationships across steady states, but we believe that similar results will come out of a more dynamic analysis. While preliminary research by various authors along these lines appears promising, much remains to be done.

12.6   A Preliminary Attempt at Testing the Schumpeterian Paradigm

In Chapter 6, we emphasized the potential importance of distinguishing between different types of knowledge-generating activity. This distinction is also relevant to the debate on scale effects. Consider, for instance, one of the key findings of Chapter 6: that the level of research can conceivably be pushed so far that the steady-state growth rate falls. In the long run, the rate of growth depends on the pattern of both fundamental and secondary innovations. If secondary innovations arise partly out of the experience of production, as seems likely, then too much research at the expense of production may ultimately be counterproductive. We are not advancing this as an explanation of postwar experience in the OECD: the key point is that the productivity of research can evolve in a variety of different ways, some of which may undermine the Schumpeterian paradigm, some of which definitely do not.

There has been one very interesting attempt to assess movements in research productivity using an endogenous growth model: we are thinking of Caballero and Jaffe (1993). They develop a new methodology for measuring the extent of creative destruction, knowledge obsolescence, and knowledge spillovers in the growth process, using U.S. data on patents and patent citations. They find an average annual rate of creative destruction (corresponding to the term "λn" in Chapter 2 and to the term "$\lambda n + \lambda n \frac{\alpha}{1-\alpha}$" in Chapter 3.1 of between 2 and 7 percent during the 1970s, with rates up to 25 percent in the pharmaceutical sector). Equally interesting, especially in light of Jones's criticism, is the estimation by Caballero and Jaffe of the equation describing the growth of general knowledge:

$$\dot{A} = \Gamma \cdot \lambda n_t,$$

where Γ denotes the current state of knowledge or what we called the "leading edge" in Chapter 3, and n_t is the current flow of research labor. The current state of knowledge Γ in turn is assumed to depend on the aggregate amount of diffused and not yet obsolete knowledge in the economy. More formally, if we consider the multisector model of Chapter 3, with:

$$y_t = \int_{-\infty}^{t} A_\tau(x_\tau^\alpha)d\tau,$$

then Γ is taken to be equal to the weighted sum of the contributions made by all existing vintages to current innovations. So, for example, an existing "idea" or "vintage" that has not had time to diffuse to researchers working on the *current* innovation will not be taken into account when evaluating Γ. Similarly, an old "idea" that has become obsolete is one that is too old for contributing significantly to current knowledge. More generally, the knowledge variable Γ is taken to be equal to the integral:

$$\int_{-\infty}^{t} a(t, s)\lambda n_s ds,$$

where:

$$a(t, s) = \delta \cdot e^{-\beta(A_t - A_s)} \cdot (1 - e^{-\gamma(t-s)}) \tag{12.46}$$

is the marginal contribution of a vintage s sector to current innovations, β is the rate at which an old idea becomes "obsolete" (i.e., useless in the production of new knowledge), and γ is the rate of diffusion of older ideas into current general knowledge.

This marginal contribution, in turn, is taken to be proportional to the *citation rate*:

$$a^*(t, s) = \frac{C_{t,s}}{S_t \cdot P_s},$$

where $C_{t,s}$ is the number of observed *citations* by current patents (of year t) of older patents of year s, P_s is the total number of patents of year s, $s < t$, and S_t is the number of sample patents in current year t.

While using as a working hypothesis the assumption that a^* is proportional to a, Caballero and Jaffe perform estimations that allow them to characterize the process of creative destruction. Particularly interesting are the following results from estimating the citation function $a(t, s)$:

1. Ideas diffuse rapidly, within one or two years.

2. The rate of ideas' obsolescence β has increased from 3 percent at the beginning of the century up to 12 percent in 1990, and it has averaged around 7 percent between 1975 and 1992.

3. The ratio $\dot{A}/n$, where $\dot{A}$ is measured by the number of new innovations, has decreased substantially between 1960 and 1990 (by $\sim$ 30 percent).

The latter result, which may reflect either a reduced spillover of older ideas on new knowledge (a decrease in δ) and/or an increased rate of obsolescence of old ideas (an increase in β) over the past years, suggests again that the empirical findings in Jones (1995) are not inconsistent with the Schumpeterian model. An interesting next step would be to try and reconcile the framework with microeconomic evidence on the returns to research. By bringing together a wide range of evidence, it may prove possible to calibrate a Schumpeterian model of the kind developed in the previous sections to match all the relevant stylized facts. Since the calibrated data could include the observed path of patents and patent citations, as well as microeconomic evidence on social returns, work along these lines would go significantly further than the existing empirical literature in assessing the consistency of endogenous growth models with the data.

12.7 Summary

In this chapter, we argued that Schumpeterian growth theory could be reconciled with several empirical findings that appeared at first sight to refute the very idea that growth should be "endogenous." Using a slightly modified version of the model of innovation and capital accumulation developed in Chapter 3, we confronted some of the main empirical challenges to endogenous growth theory: namely, the growth accounting exercises by Young (1995b) and Jorgenson (1995), which portray technological progress as a negligible source of economic growth relative to capital accumulation; the Jones (1995) critique of Schumpeterian models based on the observation that the number of scientists and engineers have tripled as a fraction of the labor force since 1950 without generating a corresponding increase in the rate of productivity growth; and finally cross-country evidence (e.g., by Evans 1996) showing that countries are converging to parallel growth paths of the sort implied by the Solow-Swan model.

While broadly consistent with the evidence put forward in all these critiques, the extended framework developed in this chapter also delivers a number of testable implications that can distinguish the Schumpeterian approach from alternative approaches to growth and thus could conceivably refute it. For example, the model predicts: (a) that the long-run growth rate should decrease with the interest rate and the depreciation rate for physical and human capital and with hiring costs, but that it should increase with respect to R&D productivity; (b) that the long-run rate of growth should be positively correlated with the flow of patents, the flow of entry of new firms, the flow of new product introduction, the flow of exit of firms, the rate of job separation, and the rate of capital obsolescence. These and other testable implications of Schumpeterian growth theory are still awaiting a serious empirical assessment. At this point, it might be worth mentioning the recent microeconomic studies of Blundell et al. (1994) and Nickell (1994), which provide tacit support for the Schumpeterian view that structural parameters can affect productivity growth. Using a U.K. firm-level data set covering the period between 1972 and 1982, Blundell et al. show that the arrival rate of innovations is significantly positively correlated with firms' market share and significantly negatively correlated with a measure of market concentration.[31]

In parallel work, using panel data from 600 British companies, Nickell (1996) presents evidence that competition, measured either by an increased number of competitors in the same industry or by lower levels of rents, is posi-

---

31. The knowledge stock in the industry, measured by the depreciated sum of past innovations in the same industry, is also a determinant factor in the probability of innovating.

tively correlated with productivity growth. As we have seen in earlier chapters, Schumpeterian models give ambiguous predictions on the relation between competition and growth. The key point for our present discussion is that the correlation, whatever its sign, appears to be statistically and quantitatively significant.

Appendix: On Some Problems in Measuring Knowledge-Based Growth[32]

Although there has been some progress in modeling knowledge at the theoretical level (so we hope to have convinced the reader by this point), less progress has been made at the empirical level. If knowledge is indeed different from other goods, then it must be measured differently from other goods, and its relationship to the price system must be different than that of other goods. But the theoretical foundation on which national income accounting is based is one in which knowledge is fixed and common, where all that need be measured are prices and quantities of commodities. Likewise, we do not have any generally accepted empirical measures of such key theoretical concepts as the stock of technological knowledge, human capital, the resource cost of knowledge acquisition, the rate of innovation, the rate of obsolescence of old knowledge, and so forth.

To some extent the situation is one of theory before measurement, to paraphrase one of the apostles of real business cycle theory (Prescott 1986). But to lay the blame on empirical economists or on data-gathering agencies would be disingenuous. It would be more accurate to say that formal theory is ahead of conceptual clarity. As the English side of the Cambridge capital controversy used to insist, the real question is one of meaning, not measurement. Only when theory produces clear conceptual categories will it be possible to measure them accurately.

The purpose of this appendix is to discuss some of these conceptual issues, to suggest ways in which they might be clarified, and to point out problems that they raise for the understanding of technical change and economic growth. The main point developed in what follows is that because of our inability to measure properly the inputs and outputs to the creation and use of knowledge, standard measures of GNP and productivity give a misleading picture. In particular, our failure to include a separate investment account for knowledge the way we do for physical capital means that much of an economy's annual output is simply missed.

These measurement problems have important implications for measuring growth even in a steady state. But they particularly distort standard measures of

---

32. This appendix is based on Howitt (1996).

growth during a period of transition such as we are going through now when the information revolution has greatly enhanced the opportunities for knowledge creation. In particular, they imply that GNP and productivity may appear to be slowing down when in fact they are surging. The discussion that follows is aimed at clarifying the nature of this measurement problem during such a period of transition as well as during periods of steady-state growth.

A.1   A Tentative Definition

We define knowledge in terms of potentially observable behavior, as the ability of an individual or group of individuals to undertake, or to instruct or otherwise induce others to undertake, procedures resulting in predictable transformations of material objects.[33] The knowledge can be codifiable, as when it can be transmitted by mathematical theorems or computer programs that can be reproduced through known procedures; or tacit, as when it exists only in the minds of particular individuals or in the established routines of organizations, and is not capable of routine transmission or reproduction.

This definition restricts knowledge to capabilities of individuals and organizations. One could alternatively define knowledge as being embedded in goods, as when a computer program is encoded in a file on a diskette. We prefer to think of such a diskette as a unique commodity that can be used in consumption or production, the creation of which required knowledge in the possession of some individual or group individuals. But there is probably nothing fundamental at stake here. One might just as well think of a properly inscribed diskette in the same terms as a properly indoctrinated graduate student. All that really matters at this stage is to be clear as possible.

The above definition also rules out knowledge in the abstract. Books, blueprints, and computer programs are instruments by which different people can create similar knowledge, not instruments by which they can merely use previously existing knowledge. This interpretation alters the usual distinction between the production and diffusion of knowledge, for it implies that the reader creates knowledge much as the writer did. What is different in the two cases is the process by which knowledge is created, and the degree to which the knowledge being created substitutes for preexisting knowledge. The writer probably took more time and effort, and the knowledge he created during the writing of the book had a greater scarcity value at the time of writing than

---

33. This definition is broad enough to include knowledge used in service industries, where the material objects can include such items as hair (in the case of hair-cutting services) or even electrons (in the case of many information services). When all that is received is advice, as in many business service industries, for example, the output of that industry is itself knowledge.

did the knowledge created by the millionth reader. One reason for defining knowledge this way is that much of what is commonly thought of as costless imitation in fact is a costly process that resembles in many ways the process of innovation. Any time an individual sets out to learn something, some of it will come from observing what others have done, and some of it will be novel.

There are many ways in which a piece of knowledge thus defined is like a capital good. It can be produced, exchanged, and used in the production of other goods, or in the production of itself. It can also be stored, although subject to depreciation, as when people forget or let their skills deteriorate, and subject also to obsolescence, as when new knowledge comes along to supersede it. In each of these cases, however, there are important differences between knowledge and capital goods, and the very features that make knowledge distinct from capital goods are what create measurement problems.

A.2   Measuring Output, Productivity, and Knowledge

Measuring knowledge-based growth appears to raise at least four major problems. The first is what we call a *"knowledge-input problem."* That is, the amount of resources devoted to the creation of knowledge is certainly underestimated by standard measures of R&D activity and resources used in the educational sector, which exclude a lot of informal activities routinely undertaken by firms and individuals, as well as much of the private cost of education borne by individuals. Many workers that are counted as engaged in production, management, or other nonresearch activities spend a considerable amount of their time and energy looking for better ways of producing and selling the output of the enterprise they are employed by, and hence their compensation should be counted, at least in part, as part of the cost of creating knowledge.

The second major measurement problem is what we call the *"knowledge-investment problem."* That is, the output of knowledge resulting from formal and informal R&D activities is typically not measured at all, because it does not result in an immediate commodity with a market price. From the Haig-Simons point of view, the creation of knowledge ought to be treated like the creation of capital goods, because in either case there is an expenditure of resources that could alternatively have been used to produce current consumption but that has instead been devoted to the enhancement of future consumption opportunities. Yet the national accounts include no category of final expenditure that would capture a significant amount of the annual increment to society's stock of knowledge the way it captures the annual increment to society's stock of capital, except for the output of the educational sector, and for R&D undertaken by or sold to the government sector. None of the new knowledge generated by R&D undertaken by business firms on their own account, which includes most of industrial R&D, results in a direct positive contribution to current GNP or to the current value added of that sector of the economy, as it would if the resources had instead been devoted to the creation of new capital goods.

To make this point more explicitly, consider the case of a firm that hires additional R&D workers at a cost of one million dollars during the current year, the only result of which is a new patent discovered at the very end of the year, which will enable the firm to earn additional profits in future years, whose expected discounted value is two million dollars. Because firms are not permitted to capitalize such R&D expenditures, this sequence of events will not result in any increase in output from that sector as far as the national income accounts are concerned. Likewise, from the income side of the accounts, although there has been additional one million in wages and salaries (assuming that the workers were hired from out of the labor force) there has been an exactly offsetting decrease in profits, because the expenditure by the firm resulted in no increased current revenue. If, instead of the patent, the workers had produced a machine worth two million dollars, GNP would have been higher by two million dollars.[34]

Of course, to the extent that R&D results in more or better goods being produced, it does eventually affect measured GNP. But new knowledge should also be counted as output when it is created, just as physical investment is counted when it is created even though it eventually has a further effect on GNP by increasing the potential to produce other goods. Furthermore, to the extent that R&D results in better goods, many of its future effects on GNP will not be measured, because of what we identify as the third major measurement problem, namely the "*quality-improvement problem.*" As many writers have observed, to the extent that knowledge creation within business firms results in improved goods and services, the practical difficulties of dealing with new goods and quality improvements in constructing price indices imply that much of the resulting benefit goes unmeasured.

The fourth problem is an "*obsolescence problem*". If standard measures of GNP ought to include a separate investment account for the production of knowledge, then by the same token, NNP and national income ought to include a deduction corresponding to the depreciation of the stock of knowledge that takes place as it is superseded, or otherwise reduced in value, by new discoveries and innovations. Furthermore, the creation of new knowledge also causes the depreciation of existing physical and human capital. Depreciation is a no-

---

34. The working group that produced the International System of National Accounts 1993 considered recommending the capitalization of R&D expenditures for just these reasons. In the end they decided to drop the recommendation, in view of the problems of measuring and evaluating such an intangible investment, although they did recommend the setting up of satellite R&D capital accounts on an experimental basis.

toriously difficult concept to account for in any case. The timing and extent of replacement investment are endogenous variables that the national income accountant can only capture in rough measure by applying simple mechanical formulas. But the problem becomes even more acute when a wave of innovations accelerates the rate of obsolescence of old knowledge and capital.

If an economy were in a steady state, the most serious of these measurement problems would be the quality-improvement problem. Much of the growth of productivity and output in the long-run is the result of product innovations that generate new and improved goods whose contributions to output are only partially measured. Robert Gordon (1990), for example, has estimated that correcting properly for quality improvements in capital goods alone would at least double the growth rate of aggregate real investment in the United States over the period 1947–83. Many of the gains from better capital goods do eventually get reflected in GNP growth when the improved capital goods boost output in other sectors. But even then the problem will distort measured productivity growth in different sectors, as when the airline industry is credited with productivity growth that actually occurred in the airframe and engine industries. Furthermore, to the extent that the improved capital goods allow other sectors to create new and improved products, the productivity gains may not even be measured in those sectors, as when more powerful computers allow banks to produce a better quality of service.[35]

By contrast, neither the knowledge-input problem nor the knowledge-investment problem would necessarily create distorted measures of growth in a steady state. Because productivity growth in all sectors would be the same and knowledge inputs would be growing at the same rate as production inputs, the failure to include the knowledge sector when measuring output would not create any distortion in growth rates. The effect on the level of output, however, would be potentially quite large. A country that devoted 2.5 percent of its inputs to R&D investment and 20 percent to physical investment would have to add 12.5 percent to the investment component of GNP investment to correct for this aspect of the knowledge investment problem if the two kinds of investment activities yielded the same rate of return. If, as many have argued, R&D investment has a social productivity much higher than that of physical investment, and if the level of knowledge input broadly conceived were much higher than 2.5 percent of total resources, then the unmeasured investment output would be correspondingly higher than 12.5 percent of measured investment.

By the same token, the obsolescence problem by itself would not cause any great distortions in a steady state, where the essential problem for the national

---

35. This point is made forcefully by Griliches (1994) in a paper summarizing a lifetime of research on the question of measuring the productivity gains from R&D and attributing them to the right sector.

income accountant would be to apply the right average rate of depreciation to each class of investment goods. This is of course a nontrivial problem, but it would exist even in the absence of new knowledge.

During a period of adjustment to a cluster of fundamental innovations, however (see Chapter 8), the combined effect of the four problems is probably to produce a downward bias in conventional measures of GNP growth and productivity growth. Consider first the quality-improvement problem. Just as it causes part of economic growth to go unmeasured in a steady state, so it will cause much of the surge of economic growth resulting from better computers and related goods to go unmeasured. Some of this problem has been dealt with by the adoption in the United States and Canada of hedonic measures of computer prices. But similar measures have not been undertaken in such areas as the electronic-equipment industry that manufactures chips.

Baily and Gordon (1988) have argued that the quality-improvement problem cannot account for a lot of the slowdown in productivity that took place in the late 1960s and early 1970s, mainly because the failure properly to measure quality improvements has been too steady over time. Griliches (1994) claims, however, that the fruits of the information revolution have been used disproportionately in sectors where quality improvements are next to impossible to measure. He estimates that over three quarters of the output of the computer industry is used in what he calls the unmeasurable sectors. Furthermore, the information revolution is contributing to an increase in the relative size of the unmeasurable sectors, which Griliches estimates now accounts for 70 percent of GNP in the United States.

Consider next the knowledge-input problem. When computers first started to change the way work is done throughout the economy, there was a long period of learning that had to be undertaken.[36] At first people looked for ways in which the new tool could simply replace old ones without a radical change in operating techniques. Although some gains were obtainable in that direction, the added cost of information services departments was often larger than the benefits. Gradually, through a process of trial and error, people are now beginning to exploit the enormous potential of computers, but for many years there were no visible productivity gains associated with the adoption of sophisticated information technologies.

From our point of view, part of the problem is that the time people spend learning to use computers efficiently, and all of the associated costs of training and experimentation, is unmeasured knowledge input. When the opportunities for such knowledge-creating activities are enhanced by the arrival of new fundamental technologies, workers spend less time producing output and more

---

36. David (1991) presents a provocative discussion of this problem.

time creating new knowledge. The fact that output does not seem to be rising as fast as before reflects this reduction in real production input but since there is no corresponding reduction in *measured* production input it appears as if productivity growth has slowed down. Indeed, from a broader perspective one might see the costly restructuring of firms and the sectoral reallocations involved in learning better to exploit fundamental technologies as an unmeasured knowledge input with similar effects on measured productivity growth.

Next, consider the knowledge-investment problem. Part of the effect of this problem during such a transitional period is just the other side of the knowledge-input problem. The learning and restructuring that goes on as people adjust to a new general-purpose technology have an unmeasured output, in the form of knowledge-accumulation. Even costly mistakes create knowledge of what not to do. If the output were properly measured, it would be seen to compensate for the fall in measured output that takes place when firms and workers start devoting more time to learning how to use their new tools.

Even beyond this, however, the reason why more workers go into knowledge-creating activities when new opportunities open up is that the return to these activities have risen by more than the return to production activities. Thus it seems likely that the knowledge-investment that goes unmeasured is even greater than the fall in output that is measured. So even if knowledge inputs were measured correctly, the knowledge-investment problem would imply that measured output and productivity growth would fail to reflect what has been in fact an increase in overall growth. For they would be counting neither the inputs nor the outputs of a sector whose productivity and output are growing faster than average.

Finally, consider the obsolescence problem. To some extent it moderates the distortions created by the knowledge-investment problem. For the net increase in society's stocks of capital and knowledge resulting from the information revolution would be overstated if the accelerated obsolescence of preexisting capital and knowledge were not taken into account. Thus if we were to solve the knowledge-investment problem without dealing with the obsolescence problem we would certainly overstate the gain in NNP and national income taking place during a technological transition, even though measures of GNP and gross productivity would not be affected by the omission.

Aside from this effect, however, the obsolescence problem generates a separate distortion that reinforces the understatement of productivity gains caused by the other problems during a wave of fundamental innovations. For to the extent that unmeasured obsolescence reduces the effective stock of capital, standard measures of TFP will overstate the capital services component of inputs to the production process, and will thereby understate the productivity of those inputs.

A.3   A Formal Model

To make these ideas more concrete, this section presents a simple abstract model, inspired from our analysis in Chapters 3 and 6, that highlights the four measurement problems identified above. The model abstracts from all aspects of human capital, and focuses only on the question of the creation of new knowledge by the business sector. It assumes for simplicity that there are only two sectors of the economy, one producing capital goods (sector K) and one producing consumption goods (sector C).

Aggregate output from sector C is governed by the technological relationship

$$C = Q_c(A_c)F_c(A_c, L_c^p, K), \tag{12.47}$$

where A_c represents the average stock of knowledge among firms in the C sector, F_c the measurable number of units of some standardized consumption good being produced, Q_c the average quality of these goods, L_c^p the input of production labor in C, and K the stock of capital. The stock of knowledge embodies both process and product innovations. The former are captured in the F_c function and the latter in the Q_c function.

The flow of aggregate gross output from sector K is governed by the technological relationship

$$I = Q_k(A_k)F_k(A_k, L_k^p), \tag{12.48}$$

where the technology is defined analogously to that of the first equation. For simplicity, and in order to highlight the use of computer capital in other sectors, we suppose that capital is used only in sector C.

The gross flow of new knowledge in the two sectors is governed by the relationships

$$B_k = \lambda A_k G_k(L_k^r) \tag{12.49}$$

$$B_c = H(A_c, A_k)G_c(L_c^r), \tag{12.50}$$

where the G functions represent the technology of knowledge creation, the L^r's represent labor input into knowledge creation in the two sectors, and λ is a parameter affecting the productivity of knowledge-creating activities in sector K. A wave of fundamental innovations such as those involved in the ongoing information revolution would be represented by an exogenous increase in λ. We suppose that the growth of knowledge in the two sectors is affected not only by current labor inputs but also by the accumulation of past knowledge. Knowledge in sector K is assumed to affect the growth of knowledge in sector C, because more sophisticated capital goods open up opportunities for more sophisticated applications in sector C, as when computers allow banks to invent new kinds of deposits.

In keeping with standard accounting procedures, we shall restrict attention to the special case where the rate of obsolescence of old capital and the rate of obsolescence of old knowledge remain constant and equal to the same known parameter δ. That is

$$\dot{K} = I - \delta K \tag{12.51}$$

and[37]

$$\dot{A}_i = B_i - \delta A_i; \quad i = c, k. \tag{12.52}$$

The final aggregate relationship is the market-clearing condition for labor:

$$L_k^p + L_c^p + L_k^r + L_c^r = L \tag{12.53}$$

where L is the aggregate supply of labor.

In order to operationalize the measurement problems discussed earlier, we will define growth in terms of GNP.[38] Ideally, GNP should include investment in all three categories: physical capital and the two kinds of knowledge:

$$Y \equiv C + \mu I + \mu_c B_c + \mu_k B_k, \tag{12.54}$$

where the μ's are shadow prices representing the value to society of incremental units of the respective stocks, in terms of the consumption good. In the standard theory of growth without technological change, there would be just the one μ representing the shadow price of capital, which would be Tobin's q.

The rate of growth is therefore

$$g = (\dot{C}/C)(C/Y) + (\dot{I}/I + \dot{\mu}/\mu)(\mu I/Y) + g_A, \tag{12.55}$$

where the term g_A represents the direct contribution of growth in investment in knowledge: $g_A \equiv \frac{1}{Y}\frac{d}{dt}(\mu_c B_c + \mu_k B_k)$. Total factor productivity growth τ is

---

37. We thus leave aside the *obsolescence problem,* which causes standard accounting procedures to miss the *accelerated* depreciation of capital and knowledge. In other words, to take full account of the obsolescence problem, we should have assumed something like:

$$\dot{K} = I - \delta(I, B_k)K,$$

with the depreciation rate on old capital being a nondecreasing function of the rate of gross investment (because it takes new investment to render old capital obsolete) and of the rate of creation of new knowledge in sector K. And similarly:

$$\dot{A}_i = B_i - \delta_i^a(B_i)A_i; \quad i = c, k,$$

with the rate of obsolescence of old knowledge also being a nondecreasing function of the rate of creation of that kind of knowledge.

38. See Usher (1980) for a comprehensive treatment of alternative measures of economic growth, including a discussion of the implications of different measures for the knowledge-investment problem.

g minus the contribution of increased inputs of capital and labor. The latter contributions are measured at market factor prices. The rental price of capital is taken to be the price of capital μ multiplied by the sum $r + \delta$, where r is the long-run average rate of interest and δ the long-run average rate of depreciation of capital. Hence

$$\tau = g - \frac{\mu(r + \delta)\dot{K} + w(\dot{L}_c^p + \dot{L}_k^p)}{Y}. \tag{12.56}$$

TFP growth in producing consumption goods is

$$\tau_c = \frac{\dot{C}}{C} - \frac{\mu(r + \delta)\dot{K} + w\dot{L}_c^p}{C}. \tag{12.57}$$

In what follows we denote measured labor, measured consumption, measured investment, and measured relative price respectively by Lm, Cm, Im and μm.

The knowledge-input problem can be captured simply by supposing[39] that the measured labor input into production in each sector includes a fraction ε_r of workers who are actually engaged in research:

$$Lm_i^p = L_i^p + \varepsilon_r L_i^r; \quad i = c, k \quad 0 < \varepsilon_r < 1. \tag{12.58}$$

The quality-improvement problem can be captured by supposing that the measured growth rate of quality improvement each period in each sector is only the fraction $1 - \varepsilon_q$ of the actual growth rate $d \ln(Q)/dt$. Assume there is some base year in which both actual and measured quality are defined to equal unity. Then measured consumption will differ from real consumption according to

$$Cm = Q_c(A_c)^{1-\varepsilon_q} F_c^p(A_c, L_c^p, K) = Q_c(A_c)^{-\varepsilon_q} C. \tag{12.59}$$

Likewise, under the same normalization assumption for the quality of capital goods,

$$Im = Q_k(A_k)^{1-\varepsilon_q} F_k^p(A_k, L_k^p) = Q_k(A_k)^{-\varepsilon_q} I. \tag{12.60}$$

Because the quality of capital and consumption goods are mismeasured, so are their total quantities, and also their relative price μ. Assume, however, that the total dollar values of consumption and investment can be measured every year. Then by dividing these two nominal quantities we get a measure of the relative values of the annual output from the two sectors, namely, $\mu I / C$. The measured relative price will be consistent with this magnitude. Hence

$$\mu m = \mu(I/Im)/(C/Cm) = (Q_k(A_k)/Q_c(A_c))^{\varepsilon_q}\mu. \tag{12.61}$$

---

39. Of course a statistical agency cannot make any such supposition. They do the best they can, which we suppose, for simplicity, leaves a constant fraction of research workers misrepresented as being engaged in production.

Hence, as Gordon has stressed, if quality improvements have been larger in capital goods than in consumption goods, then the relative price of capital goods will be overstated.

Under these assumptions measured output will equal

$$Ym = Cm + \mu m \cdot Im, \tag{12.62}$$

which differs from its real counterpart Y in (12.54) by (a) not including anything representing current investment in knowledge, (b) having measured instead of real consumption and investment, and (c) having a fixed measured relative price of capital instead of the current true relative price.

Note that, aside from the knowledge-investment problem, the only quality-measurement problem that would distort our measure of GNP is the problem of measuring the quality of *consumption* goods. Understatement of physical investment would be just offset by overstatement of the relative price of capital.

Corresponding to (12.62), the measured growth rate of GNP is:

$$gm = \left[c\frac{\dot{Cm}}{Cm} + (1-c)\frac{\dot{Im}}{Im} \right] = \left[c\frac{\dot{C}}{C} + (1-c)\frac{\dot{I}}{I} \right] - \varepsilon_q \left[c\frac{\dot{Q}_c}{Q_c} + (1-c)\frac{\dot{Q}_k}{Q_k} \right], \tag{12.63}$$

where c is the measured share of consumption in GNP. The measured rate gm differs from the actual growth rate g defined in (12.56) in four ways. First, c might not equal the actual share of consumption. Second, gm excludes the g_A term measuring the contribution of knowledge-investment. Third, gm makes no allowance for the changing relative price of investment. None of these would matter in a steady state with balanced growth. Fourth, the quality-improvement problem tends to make $gm < g$, because $\varepsilon_q > 0$. As we discussed, this last problem would exist even in a steady state with balanced growth.

To discuss the issue of productivity measurement, we first examine the special case in which the economy is in a steady state, where the rate of depreciation δ is constant and known. Then the measured capital stock will be

$$Km(t) = \int_0^t e^{-\delta(t-\tau)} Im(\tau)d\tau + e^{-\delta t} Km(0), \tag{12.64}$$

As time passes and the effect of the initial guess $Km(0)$ wears off, the fact that investment is underestimated will imply that the capital stock is also underestimated. Hence, the effects of mismeasurement that tend to underestimate the growth of output will be offset to some extent by underestimation of the growth of capital.

To be more precise, in a steady state with investment growing at the constant proportional rate g, and with the quality of capital goods Q_k growing at the proportional rate ηg (with $0 < \eta < 1$), the capital stock will be underestimated by proportionately less than investment. That is, in such a steady state:

$$\frac{Km(t)}{K(t)} = \frac{\int_0^\infty e^{-\delta s} I(t-s) Q_k(t-s)^{-\varepsilon_q} ds}{\int_0^\infty e^{-\delta s} I(t-s) ds} = \frac{Im(t) \int_0^\infty e^{-[\delta + g(1-\eta\varepsilon_q)]s} ds}{I(t) \int_0^\infty e^{-(\delta+g)s} ds}$$

$$> \frac{Im(t)}{I(t)}. \tag{12.65}$$

The reason behind this result is that the proportional measurement error in investment grows over time, and the capital stock, which is just a weighted sum of past investments, has a proportional measurement error which is a weighted sum of past proportional measurement errors.

Because the proportional measurement error on depreciation is the same as on the capital stock, it follows that the proportional measurement error on net investment in a steady state will exceed that on gross investment, because depreciation will not be understated by as much as will gross investment:

$$\frac{\dot{Km}(t)}{\dot{K}(t)} < \frac{\dot{Im}(t)}{\dot{I}(t)}. \tag{12.66}$$

Measured TFP growth will be

$$\tau m = gm - \frac{\mu m(r+\delta)\dot{Km}}{Ym} - \frac{w(1-\varepsilon_r)(\dot{L}_c^p + \dot{L}_k^p)}{Ym}. \tag{12.67}$$

In a steady state, the deduction for the growth in capital input in (12.67) will be understated. According to (12.61) the proportional measurement error for this deduction would have been the same as for consumption if gross investment had been used, but because net investment is used the error will be larger than this.

The error in the numerator is offset, however, by the fact that the denominator is also undermeasured. The analysis following (12.62) implies that the proportional measurement error of the denominator is also greater than that of consumption. Then in a steady state, where the last term in (12.67) vanishes, TFP growth will be underestimated by approximately the same amount as GNP growth, and both changes will be attributable to the quality-improvement problem. In transitional periods, however, as mentioned earlier, all four problems will interact to distort measured TFP growth.

Measured TFP growth in sector C will be

$$\tau m_c = \frac{\dot{Cm}}{Cm} - \frac{\mu m(r+\delta)\dot{Km}}{Cm} - \frac{w(\dot{L}_c^p + \varepsilon_r \dot{L}_c^r)}{Cm}. \tag{12.68}$$

Comparison of (12.57) and (12.68) shows that, contrary to the case of aggregate TFP growth, the steady-state mismeasurement of TFP growth in sector

C is likely to be less than that of GNP growth. For in this case the underestimate of the numerator in the deduction for growth in capital input is not fully offset by any underestimate in the denominator. That is, according to (12.61) and (12.66), the value of net investment will be underestimated relative to consumption.

During transitional periods the distortion of productivity growth in sector C will be more complicated. In particular, the information revolution is likely at first to create a bigger quality improvement problem for net investment than consumption, thus tending to create an overestimate of TFP growth in the consumption sector. But this will also be offset by the obsolescence problem, which will cause standard accounting procedures to miss the *accelerated depreciation of capital* (see note 37). Unmeasured knowledge-input growth in sector C induced by the radical change in capital inputs will also cause TFP growth in sector C to be understated.

A.4   Conclusion

If the critical component of our discussion in this appendix has been larger than the constructive component, this is mainly attributable to the fact that what is at issue is not something likely to be fixed by minor tinkering with national income accounting practices. The underlying problem is that the very conceptual foundations on which national income accounting is based assumes away the mainspring of long-term economic growth, by taking knowledge as unchanging and freely available. In such a world, market prices and quantities are all one needs to measure economic activity. In a world where growth is based on the creation, acquisition, and use of knowledge, however, we need to look at other magnitudes, and a better conceptual foundation is needed before we know just what magnitudes to look at and how.

This appendix suggests some general directions in which to look for better measures. First, to deal with the knowledge-input problem it would be helpful to ask business firms for more detailed information concerning their training, market research, brainstorming, exploration, and other activities, both formal and informal. At least some attempt could then be made to construct a more comprehensive measure of knowledge input, which could then be used to get better measures of productivity in knowledge creation, and could be subtracted from other inputs to get better measures of productivity in narrower production activities.

Better measures of knowledge input would also help in dealing with the knowledge-investment problem. One way of dealing at least imperfectly with this problem is simply to impute to the resources used in R&D an investment value equal to the value of the resources used. The characteristic uncertainty and externalities of knowledge investment makes this hazardous, because the value of knowledge will have a large random component, and even its expected social value will differ from the expected private value reflected in the value of R&D resources used.

In dealing with the knowledge-investment problem one can seek better measures of output as well as input. Thus data on patents and on the rate of introduction of new goods,[40] new firms, and new jobs all give clues to the extent of knowledge creation. These various quantitative measures have well known problems,[41] most notably that knowing how many goods, patents and the like have been created does not tell one directly what their social or even private value is. But it should be possible to use the sort of hedonic methods to attribute values to these characteristics of new knowledge that have been used since Griliches (1961) to assess the characteristics of new goods in dealing with the quality-adjustment problem.

The quality-improvement problem is perhaps the most susceptible to economic analysis, in as much as it has been recognized and dealt with for many years within the economics discipline. What is needed is a more systematic use of hedonic regressions among statistical agencies, as has been done in the case of computers, to deal with quality improvements in other industries. But the use of hedonic measures is itself subject to well-known problems, most notably that one's measures are crucially dependent on judgments as to how the prices of new goods affect those of old goods in imperfect competition, how the introduction of new goods hastens quality improvements in old goods,[42] and most important in this context, how the sort of deep structural change the world is now undergoing affects the relationships between particular characteristics and social value.[43]

Finally, the obsolescence problem would be mitigated by studies such as Caballero and Jaffé (1993), which has provided at least a preliminary estimate of the rate of obsolescence of patentable ideas. More frequently revised estimates of the rate at which old capital is scrapped would also be helpful, and should be fairly straightforward to obtain. The fact that a large fraction of current investment in recent years has been in new computers, whose rate of obsolescence continues to be much higher than that of the average piece of business equipment, creates an overstatement of net investment that could and should be corrected by surveying business enterprises on the frequency of replacement and incorporating the results rapidly into the computation of depreciation rates.

---

40. See Klenow (1994), for example.

41. See Griliches (1979), for example.

42. This is the famous "sailing ship" phenomenon that many economic historians have commented on.

43. See Jorgenson and Landau (1989) and Gordon (1990) for recent discussions of these problems.

13

The endogenous-growth models developed in the previous chapters can legitimately be criticized for their overly simplified representation of R&D activities. Indeed, except in Chapter 6 where we touched on the distinction between researchers and developers, we have otherwise taken R&D activities to be systematically performed by a single "aggregate" agent playing simultaneously the roles of *financier, creator, owner,* and *user* of the innovation.

In practice, however, R&D takes place either *within* firms where research employees are subject to assignment contracts with their employers and interact within prespecified hierarchical rules with other employees, or through contractual agreements *between* independent firms (e.g., through research joint ventures or licensing arrangements). In both cases, the provisions on how to allocate control over the R&D process, how to organize the communication channels among researchers (or between researchers and manufacturing units) within a firm, how to finance the research activities, and how to share property rights on innovations, are far more complex than the current aggregated view of the R&D process suggests.

Using both some of the existing *descriptive* literature on the organization of R&D and recent developments in the *theory of organizations*, this chapter will attempt (a) to summarize and organize current thinking about the management of R&D activities; (b) to suggest further work analyzing the interplay between the organization of R&D and the process of economic growth. (For example, we know from Chapter 2 that the long-run rate of productivity growth depends on the *frequency* and the *size* of innovations. As we shall see in this chapter, both turn out to be affected by the organizational form of research activities.) At the same time, we hope that the analysis in this chapter and the next will provide some useful (although quite preliminary) conceptual benchmarks, first to help build more efficient organization of research, and second to guide public intervention in the R&D sector (e.g., with regard to subsidy policies or to the design of patent legislation).

Although essentially descriptive and informal, the existing literature on the organization of R&D[2] addresses a broad range of interesting and relevant questions, such as

a. What is the most appropriate balance between basic and applied research?

---

1. This chapter borrows unrestrainedly from joint work with Jean Tirole (see Aghion and Tirole 1994a, 1994b, 1995). We are very grateful to Rebecca Henderson both for her precious advice on how to design this difficult chapter and also for providing us with many useful references. Unfortunately, due to space (and time) constraints, we could only deal with a small subset of those references, and we hope to have been accurately selective when choosing on which issues and papers to concentrate. Last but not least, Lucy White provided invaluable input to both this and the following chapter, and she also designed the problem sets and solutions to these last two chapters of the book.

2. Important papers in this field include Teece (1988), Kay (1988), Cohen and Levinthal (1989, 1990), Westney (1993), and Katz (1986).

b. Should research activities be vertically integrated with manufacturing activities?

c. Should the management of research within a firm be centralized or decentralized?

d. Should researchers interact "hierarchically" with other firm employees and divisions?

e. What are the costs and benefits of setting up research joint ventures?

f. How should research be rewarded and financed?

There is also a literature on the law and economics of R&D contracting,[3] which again is largely informal and descriptive but provides interesting insights and discussions on the role of various contractual restrictions in *research employment* relationships. For example, the so-called *trailer clauses*, which confer ownership of an innovation to the employer if the innovation is made by a breakaway research employee shortly after quitting the firm and to the employee otherwise.

The main purpose of this chapter is to provide the reader with a unified presentation of the currently miscellaneous literature (or literatures) on the organization of R&D and the management of innovation. Indeed, although somewhat disarticulated, the existing literature suggests that a unified theoretical framework, namely the incomplete contracts paradigm introduced by Grossman and Hart (1986), can be used to address many of the issues raised earlier.

13.1 Should Research Be Vertically Integrated?

Although *basic* (or fundamental) research activities used to be primarily conducted in universities or within independent research laboratories, industrial or *applied* research tends to be increasingly *vertically integrated*, that is, performed alongside production/marketing/distribution within the same business enterprise. Table 13.1 (drawn from Teece 1988) shows a dramatic decrease in the United States over the first half of the century of the fraction of independent research workers; this significant trend toward more integrated research activities has only been reinforced during the second half of this century.

How can one explain the reluctance of industrial firms to farm out their research activities and rely on external research facilities? Teece (1988) rightly points out that economies of scale cannot be the main reason, for nothing would prevent a manufacturing firm from "contracting R&D services from an established low-cost provider, just as for any other service or component." More

---

3. In particular, see Neumeyer (1971).

Table 13.1
Employment of scientific professionals in independent research organizations as a fraction of employment of scientific professionals in all in-house and independent research laboratories, 1921–46.

1921	15.2%
1927	12.9%
1933	10.9%
1940	8.7%
1946	6.9%

Source: Mowery (1983, chapter 2).

generally, if *complete contracts* could be written between researchers and users of the innovations (specifying how to use the innovations and how to share the revenues from the innovations in all possible states of nature), the issue of who owns the innovation and/or exerts authority over the research process would become irrelevant. Thus, if we are to explain why (and when) research activities tend to be vertically integrated, we need to make the working assumption that research contracts between inventors and customers (users, manufacturers, financiers) are *incomplete*. As Teece (1988) remarks, "It is inherent in an industry experiencing rapid technological improvement that a new product, incorporating the most advanced technology, cannot be contracted for by detailed specification of the final product. It is precisely the impossibility of specifying final product characteristics in a well-defined way in advance which renders competitive bidding impossible in the industry."

The incompleteness of research contracts, together with the limited ability of researchers to change developers ex-post (or for developers to switch to new technological sources),[4] in turn accounts for the need to allocate *property rights* on innovative activities and/or to allocate authority (i.e., decision rights) over the research process.

More formally, following the seminal work of Grossman and Hart (1986) on incomplete contracts and vertical integration, we can start by considering the basic contractual relationship between a researcher (or research unit) RU and a customer C. Customers are parties that directly benefit from the innovation: namely, the manufacturers who commercialize the innovation, the users who will purchase the resulting product, and the suppliers of complementary products or inputs used by the manufacturer (see von Hippel 1988). The research unit may or may not belong to the same firm as the customer, and it contributes its idea and knowledge whereas the customer contributes a capital investment.

---

4. This is referred to as "lock-in" betwen researchers and developers in Teece (1988).

The value of the innovation for the customer is denoted by $V > 0$. Let e denote the noncontractible research effort supplied by RU and E denote the investment provided by C, both at a linear cost. The probability of making the innovation is assumed to be increasing, strictly concave, and separable in (e, E), namely: $p(e, E) = q(e) + r(E)$. Both parties are risk-neutral and have reservation utility equal to zero. Then the socially optimal (or first-best) effort and investment are defined by

$$\max_{\{e,E\}} \{p(e, E) \cdot V - e - E\}$$

or

$$q'(e^*(V)) \cdot V = r'(E^*(V)) \cdot V = 1.$$

However, the first-best cannot be implemented in general, due to the incompleteness of the research contract. More specifically, the innovation cannot be described ex ante, so that the two parties cannot contract for delivery of a specific innovation. All that the contract can specify, therefore, is the allocation of *property rights* on any forthcoming innovation, a *sharing-rule* on the revenue (license fee) obtained by the research unit, and possibly (e.g., if it is monetary and verifiable by a third party) the customer's investment E.

13.1.1 Static Analysis

In the *integrated case* where property rights on the innovation are allocated to C, C can freely use the innovation. In that case RU receives no reward for innovating.[5] In the *non-integrated case* where RU owns his or her innovation, C and RU bargain over the licensing fee once the innovation has been made. For simplicity, we assume that the total pie V is equally split ex-post between the owner (RU) and the customer (C) so that RU gets a license equal to $\frac{V}{2}$.[6] (C's taking equity in RU has no economic effect,[7] nor does any sharing rule contracted upon ex ante.[8])

---

5. In practice successful research employees are rewarded ex-post through salary increases, cash awards, fringe benefits, stocks, or promotions. Such rewards are generally not commensurate with the value of the innovation.

6. The equal split outcome could result from a Rubinstein bargaining process with alternative offers by the two parties and no time delay between two successive offers. Focusing on the equal split case involves no loss of insights in this model where utility in the ex-post bargaining game is transferable in the relevant range (where RU's income is positive).

7. Indeed, either C has property rights and RU receives no licensing fee; or RU has property rights and the two parties then necessarily bargain over the *net* licensing fee, that is the formal fee minus the share that goes back to the customer through the equity participation.

8. Indeed, if $\alpha < \frac{1}{2}$ denotes RU's prespecified share of the innovation rents and if RU owns the innovation, then RU can always pretend that the prespecified innovation has not been discovered, and then renegotiate with C. The final shares will eventually depend only on ex-post bargaining and not upon the initial sharing rule. This reasoning makes use of the implicit assumption that

Now, let us compare the levels of aggregate utility, respectively when the customer and the research unit own the innovation, in other words, respectively when research is *integrated with* or *independent of* development activities.

Under *C-ownership*, *RU* receives no reward for innovating and therefore should supply no effort: $e = 0$. However, *C* is a residual claimant for *V* and therefore supplies the first-best investment level $E^*(V)$. Aggregate utility is then given by $U_{RU} + U_C = 0 + [p(0, E^*(V))V - E^*(V)]$.

Under *RU-ownership*, each party receives $\frac{V}{2}$ once the innovation occurs. This results in second-best effort and investment equal to $e^* \left(\frac{V}{2} \right)$ and $E^* \left(\frac{V}{2} \right)$ respectively. The corresponding aggregate utility level is

$$\widetilde{U}_{RU} + \widetilde{U}_C = p(e^* \left(\frac{V}{2} \right), E^* \left(\frac{V}{2} \right)) \frac{V}{2} \times 2 - e^* \left(\frac{V}{2} \right) - E^* \left(\frac{V}{2} \right).$$

Clearly, $\widetilde{U}_{RU} + \widetilde{U}_C > U_{RU} + U_C$ whenever the *marginal efficiency* of the research unit's effort is sufficiently large relative to that of the customer's investment; in that case non-integration yields a higher total surplus than integration (otherwise, integration may be more efficient).

In particular, to the extent that the marginal contribution of developers (customers) is significantly higher for *applied research* than for *basic research*, the former type of research activities should more often be *integrated* than the latter type. This is precisely what we commonly observe in practice, with industrial research taking place "in-house," and basic research tending to be conducted in universities or independent research laboratories.

Similarly, "systematic" innovations that require simultaneous updating of related equipment should more often be generated within an integrated firm than "autonomous" innovations that do not require complementary input adjustments.[9]

Let us now suppose that the customer's investment *E* is contractible (e.g., monetary), and consider a situation where *C-ownership* would be selected if the customer could finance $E^*(V)$ without going to the capital market. What happens if the customer has less than $E^*(V)$ and must now borrow on a credit market that is imperfect, say for informational reasons? External financing is then more costly than internal financing, and a move from *C*-ownership back to *RU*-ownership may become attractive because it reduces

---

C is the only potential purchaser of the innovation. The initial sharing-rule will however become relevant if the innovation developed by *C* and *RU* is aimed at a third party. (See later, where we discuss the benefits of vertical integration over research joint ventures.) □

9. Teece (1988) gives *instant photography* (which required the redesign of camera and film) and the *jet airliner* (which required new stress-resistant frame material) as examples of systematic innovations, in contrast to the *transistor* or the *discovery of faster microprocessors*, which are more *autonomous* innovations.

the customer's required investment from $E^*(V)$ to $E^* \left(\frac{V}{2} \right)$, and thus reduces the amount of cash C needs to borrow from the capital market. Financial constraints therefore bias the organizational form toward the use of creative inputs and away from capital expenditures. *An interesting implication of this analysis is the prediction that new firms or firms that have experienced hard times will tend to farm out their research activities more than established, healthy firms.* This is nothing but the well-known "long-purse" hypothesis proposed by Schumpeter, according to which a firm's R&D investment should be positively correlated with its assets.

Will the allocation of ownership rights (to RU or C) that emerges in equilibrium always be the efficient allocation, that is the allocation that maximizes aggregate utility? The answer is yes, *provided that none of the parties are cash-constrained* and both of them value monetary transfers. For example, if $\tilde{U}_{RU} + \tilde{U}_C > U_{RU} + U_C$, the customer will always agree to give ownership rights to RU in exchange for a transfer $T \geq U_C - \tilde{U}_C$. (Because $\tilde{U}_{RU} - U_{RU} > U_C - \tilde{U}_C$, RU will always gain in making such a transfer and thereby acquiring the ownership of the innovation.)

However, *if the research unit is cash-constrained*, then one may sometimes end up with *inefficient integration* in equilibrium. For example, suppose that the customer has all the bargaining power exante at the contracting stage, and therefore allocates the ownership rights on the innovation to himself, even though $\tilde{U}_{RU} + \tilde{U}_C > U_{RU} + U_C$. Unlike in the previous case, RU cannot make the necessary cash transfers that would induce C to give up its property rights on the innovation even when non-integration is the efficient organization form. The policy implications of the resulting inefficiency will be analyzed in section 13.4.

13.1.2   Integration as a Way to Facilitate the Communication of Knowledge

Our analysis of the costs and benefits of integrated research has so far remained essentially *static*, stressing the Grossman-Hart idea that property rights on the innovation should essentially be allocated to the party with the highest marginal efficiency of effort or investment. However, another important consideration underlying the choice between integrated and nonintegrated research turns out to be *dynamic* and has to do with the *transmission of proprietary information*.[10] Specifically, the out-sourcing of research may slow down the innovation process by preventing the transfer of information between research

---

10. "Because the knowledge acquired in the course of one project often has implications for the next round of R&D projects, it is important that the entity which is sponsoring the R&D activity keep a close liaison with the R&D unit, not only to access valuable technology and possibly firm-specific knowledge that the R&D unit will have generated, but also for reasons of preventing this from "spilling over" to competitors. Spillover would almost certainly occur if the R&D unit was free standing." (Teece 1988).

and manufacturing, in particular due the researchers' fear of losing proprietary knowledge and the corresponding additional rents from future innovations. For example, Frankel (1955) provides evidence on the fact that the insufficient degree of vertical integration in British industries such as textiles, iron, and steel in the early twentieth century was largely responsible for the low rate of diffusion of innovations in these sectors and eventually for the decay of the corresponding industries.

More formally, let us compare the non-integrated (e.g., research joint ventures[11]) and fully integrated research structures in the following (two-period) extension of the previous model. As before, we consider the relationship between RU and C, where C contributes capital and RU contributes "its knowledge" to the production of a current innovation aimed at a third party.[12] RU's decision whether to transfer ($e = 1$) or not to transfer ($e = 0$) its knowledge is noncontractible and must therefore be incentive-compatible from RU's perspective. This information transfer affects the probability of occurrence of the current innovation, that is, $p = q_0 e + r(E)$, $q_0 > 0$ (where E denotes C's capital investment as before).

If V_1 denotes the price at which the current innovation is sold ex-post to the third party and α_1 (resp. 1-α_1) denotes RU's (resp. C's) share of the resulting income, then technological diffusion yields a net benefit of $\alpha_1 q_0 V_1$ to RU in the absence of subsequent innovation.

Now let us introduce the possibility of a costless future innovation entirely based on RU's knowledge and with a value of V_2 to a third party.

Consider first a non-integrated structure (e.g., a research joint-venture). If RU does not transfer its technology to C in the first period, it remains full and exclusive owner of the future innovation and thus appropriates the whole value V_2; otherwise, if RU transfers its technology to C, it will have to compete with C on the product market. Assuming Bertrand competition ex-post, RU's second period payoff shrinks from V_2 to zero in the latter case. An information or (technology) transfer from RU to C in period 1 is thus incentive-compatible if and only if

$$\alpha_1 q_0 V_1 \geq V_2 \quad \text{or} \quad \alpha_1 \geq \frac{V_2}{q_0 V_1}.$$

---

11. A joint venture is typically defined as a temporary association among several parties to carry out a specific research program (Broadley 1982).

12. That a third party rather than C uses the innovation allows us to clearly identify the dynamic considerations behind the choice of ownership, because from a static viewpoint incentives are entirely provided by the rule for sharing the income from this third party and therefore ownership is irrelevant. One could reintroduce the static dimension of ownership by assuming, as in the previous subsection, that C is the only user of the innovation. However, this would only restrict the set of feasible sharing rules over the first innovation without adding any insight as to the basic tradeoffs governing the dynamic management of innovations.

Consider now a fully integrated structure where only C may commercialize the future innovation: RU gets $\frac{V_2}{2}$ if it has not transferred its knowledge to C in period 1, because despite being the owner C cannot dispense with RU's private knowledge ex-post. A technology transfer from RU to C is now incentive-compatible if and only if:

$$\alpha_1 q_0 V_1 \geq \frac{V_2}{2} \quad \text{or} \quad \alpha_1 \geq \frac{V_2}{2q_0 V_1}.$$

From this we can see that *the cost of technological diffusion* has two dimensions. First, α_1 must be higher to induce diffusion, resulting in reduced incentives for C to invest in the current innovation. Second, if ex-post competition cannot be prevented by an adequate patent system, future rents will be dissipated by competition between RU and C to produce the next innovation. Both these considerations suggest that the cost of technological diffusion is lower in the integrated case, that is, *within* rather than *between* organizations.

Now, if, as we have argued, research joint ventures tend to be dominated by more fully integrated structures with regard to the *cost of technological diffusion* from researchers to developers, why do we observe research joint ventures and other kinds of temporary collaborative ventures?

One reason has to do with our preceding analysis; namely, research joint ventures do presumably better at preserving the RU's entrepreneurial spirit and incentives to *produce* ideas and knowledge aimed at current and/or future innovations. In particular, the research unit will have more incentives to invest in the next product generation if it has the ability to develop it. This idea seems to be consistent with industry reasoning (for example, with the desire of pharmaceutical companies to keep an arms-length relationship with biotechnological firms.)

Another explanation, which lies more on the "ex-post" side of things, is that fundamental breakthroughs occur essentially in universities or independent research laboratories. Firms are then forced into collaborative ventures with the innovating laboratories in order to acquire the knowledge and basic skills necessary to develop the new paradigm. Interestingly, these collaborative ventures do often evolve toward more integrated structures.[13]

13.1.3   Are Integrated Firms Too Conservative?

Integrated firms have often been criticized for being too committed to their old technologies, in particular to preserve their technology-specific accumulated capital and also because of the replacement effect already discussed in

---

13. See Teece (1988), again with an example drawn from the biotechnology sector.

the previous chapters. This, in turn, should result in integrated firms' either delaying the adoption of new technologies or choosing to make more drastic (i.e., less incremental) innovations than independent research units. Both possibilities have natural implications for the growth process. Indeed, we have seen in the previous chapters that the long-run rate of productivity growth is increasing in both the *frequency* and the *size* of innovations. To the extent that organization considerations such as the integration of research activities affect either of these two components of innovations, they will eventually affect the overall process of growth.

To investigate the above conjecture somewhat further, consider the previous contracting model between RU and the customer C (whom we now refer to as the "incumbent"; other potential customers will be referred to as "potential entrants"). Let π_1^m denote the incumbent's profit when he obtains an exclusive license for the innovation, and let π_0^m denote the incumbent's (monopoly) profit in the absence of innovation; finally, let π_1 denote the profit of an entrant who has purchased an exclusive license. One has $\pi_1 \leq \pi_1^m$, with equality only if the innovation is drastic in the sense that the entrant owning the new technology is not constrained by the competitive pressure of the incumbent. We assume that the probability of innovation is linear in effort and investment ($q(e) \equiv e, r(E) \equiv E$) so that the effort/investment choices by RU and C amount to a zero-one decision on whether or not to develop the new technology.

Under C-ownership, the new technology will be adopted if and only if:

$$V^m = \underbrace{\pi_1^m - \pi_0^m}_{\substack{\text{value of innovation} \\ \text{for the incumbent}}} \geq \underbrace{1}_{\substack{\text{marginal cost} \\ \text{of investment}}}$$

In particular, the larger π_0^m, the less likely the adoption of a new technology by an integrated firm. This is nothing but Arrow's (1962) replacement effect.

Consider now *RU-ownership*. If the innovation is licensed to a potential entrant (instead of being licensed to the incumbent), the entrant can obtain a license fee equal to π_1. In other words, the research unit has an outside option to sell an exclusive license to an entrant at price π_1. A well-known result in bargaining theory (see Binmore et al, 1986) is then that under alternating-offer bargaining with this outside option, the research unit can obtain a license fee equal to $\max\left(\frac{V^m}{2}, \pi_1\right)$ from C, instead of $\frac{V^m}{2}$ in the absence of potential entrants. Now let us assume that π_0^m is sufficiently large that $V^m < 1$ (so that the integrated firm does not innovate). The independent research unit will still innovate whenever $\pi_1 > 1$. We can thus account for the possibility that, due to a strong replacement effect, the integrated firm does not innovate whereas the independent research laboratory does.

Our analysis so far has taken as given the "size" of the innovations, and therefore the value of the innovation V^m. Now, one could well imagine that integrated firms would respond to the replacement effect, not so much by delaying the adoption of the new technology but rather by pursuing more drastic innovations, that is innovations with higher size and therefore with higher net value V^m.

To investigate more formally the relationship between property rights and the size of innovations, let us ignore the inputs e and E and denote by $p(\gamma)$ the probability of discovery as a function of the size γ of the innovation ($\gamma \geq 1$, with $\gamma = 1$ if no innovation takes place). Let $\pi_1^m(\gamma)$ again denote the incumbent's profit when he implements the new innovation (under exclusive license); let $\pi_0^m = \pi_1^m(1)$ denote the incumbent's profit in the absence of innovation; and let $\pi_1(\gamma)$ denote the entrant's profit if he (rather than the incumbent) purchases the exclusive license for the innovation. Because γ indexes the size of innovations, $\pi_1^m(\cdot)$ and $\pi_1(\cdot)$ are both increasing in γ, and $\pi_1 \leq \pi_1^m$ because the entrant must compete with the incumbent's old technology.

We now compare the sizes γ_C and γ_{RU} of the innovation that obtain when C (respectively RU) has property rights on the innovation and chooses its size.

Under *C-ownership,* we have

$$\gamma_C = \arg\max_{\gamma > 1} p(\gamma)[\pi_1^m(\gamma) - \pi_0^m].$$

Note that γ_C is the efficient research line for the industry. By a revealed preference argument, the larger π_0^m, the more drastic the innovation. This is again Arrow's (1962) replacement effect. The incumbent prefers a lower probability/higher payoff research technology if its profit in the absence of innovation is high.

Consider now *RU-ownership.* Note that in the absence of potential entrants, the research unit gets a fraction of the value of the innovation in either case and therefore chooses the technology preferred by $C : \gamma_{RU} = \gamma_C$. This congruence between the research unit's and the incumbent's preference disappears, however, when the research unit can sell to an entrant.

More precisely, when it has the outside option to sell an exclusive license to an entrant at price $\pi_1(\gamma)$, we know from our previous analysis that the research unit can obtain a license fee equal to $\max\left(\frac{\pi_1^m(\gamma) - \pi_0^m}{2}, \pi_1(\gamma)\right)$ from C.

Suppose first that the optimal choice γ_{RU} by the research unit is such that

$$\frac{\pi_1^m(\gamma_{RU}) - \pi_0^m}{2} \geq \pi_1(\gamma_{RU}).$$

Then, the outside option of selling to an entrant is irrelevant and therefore, as in the absence of a potential entrant, the research unit chooses the same size of innovation as the incumbent customer: $\gamma_{RU} = \gamma_C$.

On the other hand, if $\pi_1(\gamma_{RU}) > \frac{\pi_1^m(\gamma_{RU}) - \pi_0^m}{2}$, the research unit's choice of size γ_{RU} will generally differ from the incumbent's γ_C because now the outside option of selling to an entrant becomes credible and the incumbent must pay $\pi_1(\gamma_{RU})$ to obtain the license. To compare the customer's and the research unit's preferred research lines, note that, by definition of γ_{RU} and γ_C,

$$p(\gamma_C)[\pi_1^m(\gamma_C) - \pi_0^m] \geq p(\gamma_{RU})[\pi_1^m(\gamma_C) - \pi_0^m]$$

and $p(\gamma_{RU})\pi_1(\gamma_{RU})$ $\geq p(\gamma_C)\pi_1(\gamma_C).$

Multiplying these inequalities, we obtain

$$\frac{\pi_1(\gamma_{RU})}{\pi_1^m(\gamma_{RU}) - \pi_0^m} \geq \frac{\pi_1(\gamma_C)}{\pi_1^m(\gamma_C) - \pi_0^m}.$$

In particular, we have established the following proposition:

Proposition 13.1   Interests may diverge as to the choice of the research line when there are potential entrants. Let $r(\gamma) \equiv \frac{\pi_1(\gamma)}{\pi_1^m(\gamma) - \pi_0^m}$ denote the appropriability ratio or relative willingness to pay of an entrant with respect to the incumbent for the innovation. Then:

$$\gamma_{RU} \begin{cases} \geq \gamma_C & \text{if } r \text{ is strictly increasing} \\ \leq \gamma_C & \text{if } r \text{ is strictly decreasing.} \end{cases}$$

In other words, if the relative willingness to pay of a potential entrant increases with the size of the innovation, then the research unit tends to choose a more drastic innovation than the incumbent, because by doing so it is able to appropriate a higher fraction of the incumbent's surplus. Similarly, if the relative willingness to pay of a potential entrant decreases with the size of the innovation, the research unit appropriates more of the surplus by choosing a less drastic innovation. In particular, when π_0^m is large (that is, when the replacement effect is strong), the appropriability ratio $r(\gamma)$ is always decreasing in γ and therefore, as conjectured above, research units will aim for less drastic innovations than the integrated firm. (Provided the replacement effect does not discourage the integrated firm from innovating at all!)

One special case where incumbent firms will always aim for more drastic innovations is the case of process innovations in a homogeneous good industry. Suppose, for example, that the incumbent monopolist produces at marginal cost c_0. The potential innovation is a process innovation that reduces the marginal cost to $c \leq c_0$. So $\gamma = c_0/c$. If an entrant purchases the exclusive license, the two firms wage Bertrand competition. Letting $D(p)$

denote the demand curve, one has (abusing notation slightly)

$$\pi_1^m(c) - \pi_0^m = \int_c^{c_0} D(p^m(x)) \, dx,$$

and $\pi_1(c) = \min\{D(c_0)(c_0 - c), D(p^m(c))(p^m(c) - c)\}.$

As we know, an entrant has more incentive to innovate than an incumbent due to the replacement effect, so $r > 1$. A fortiori, $\pi_1(c) > \frac{\pi_1^m(c) - \pi_0^m}{2}$, so that the outside option is binding regardless of the size of the process innovation. Furthermore, r decreases from $D(c_0)/D(p^m(c_0))$ to 1 as c decreases (γ increases). *In a homogenous good industry, an independent research unit will pursue less drastic innovations than an integrated one.* However, Aghion and Tirole (1993) analyzes two other standard models of industry behavior, respectively with horizontal and vertical product differentiation, that yield ambiguous conclusions as to the monotonicity of the appropriability ratio and therefore the comparison between γ_{RU} and γ_C.

13.2   The Organization of Research within Integrated Firms

For simplicity, we chose to model customer firms as "individuals" rather than "organizations" when addressing the issue of the costs and benefits of integrated research. At the same time, we chose to emphasize the allocation of ownership rights on the innovation rather than the allocation of authority (i.e., decision rights) over the research process itself. (In the stylized model of the previous section, both parties agree ex-ante on what the optimal research strategy, that is, the optimal effort-investment pair, should be, although they are unable to monitor each other's contribution to the research process.)

In other words, the previous model could not say much about the way in which R&D activities should be organized *within* an integrated firm: in particular, it could not account for the observed diversity of organizational patterns. Some firms *centralize* their R&D activities[14] while other (multidivisional)[15] firms *decentralize* their research activities, that is, *delegate* the control rights over these activities to downstream units (typically to divisional managers). Thus, even though the integrated firm's owner(s) formally holds the property

---

14. Although already multidivisional at the time, General Electric maintained its R&D activities centralized for a while after World War II.

15. Schematically, an organizational form whereby each agent specializes in only one kind of activity (e.g., production or marketing) corresponds to Chandler's (1962) definition of a "U-form"; by contrast, a multidivisional or "M-form" organization puts each agent in charge of a single good so the agent performs both the production and marketing of that good. See Williamson (1975) for a discussion of U- and M-forms.

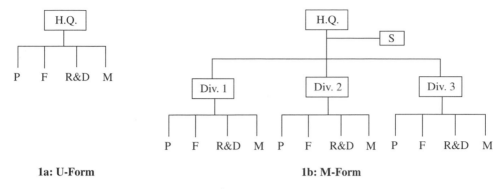

1a: U-Form   **1b: M-Form**

Figure 13.1
Basic hierarchies.

rights over the innovation(s) generated in-house, he or she may or may not find it profitable to reallocate the control rights over research (and other) activities to some of his or her subordinates.

Similarly, the previous model could not explain why firms that experience frequent innovations or that operate in a rapidly changing environment tend to organize research activities in a less *hierarchical* (or more "organic") fashion, allowing for lateral communication and the rotation of employees across tasks (with R&D personnel constantly rotating through marketing and manufacturing activities).

These and other aspects of the organization of R&D activities *within* industrial firms will now be taken up using some recent contributions to the theory of organizations.

13.2.1   Centralized versus Decentralized Research?

To illustrate the main trade-offs involved in the choice between centralized and decentralized R&D activities within an integrated firm, Kay (1988) considers the example of a multi-divisional (or "M-form") firm, organized as in figure 13.1. Where does R&D fit best within such an organization?

On the one hand, there are costs of having R&D performed at a divisional level. In particular: (a) R&D, and especially basic research, is largely product nonspecific, being mainly concerned with the invention or adaptation of new processes and products; (b) R&D exhibits substantial economies of scale and scope; (c) the objectives of divisional managers are not perfectly congruent with those of the headquarters. (Divisional managers are typically mobile within the organization and therefore would tend to operate their division or "profit center" on a short-run basis.) These considerations might explain why multidivisional companies such as General Electric or Du Pont chose, at least in the early postwar period, to centralize most of their R&D activities.

The flip side of centralized R&D, however, is that it may inhibit (or delay) some necessary adaptations of new designs to meet consumer requirements. Because of a greater experience of (and also a greater proximity to) consumers in their market, divisional managers may be quicker to understand or forecast the evolution of tastes and fashions. To put it another way, there are increasing returns from specialization. This, in turn, suggests that the most applied stages of R&D should be delegated to divisional managers. Doing so would reduce the overload experienced by the top managers and thus allow them to better concentrate on the more basic (product nonspecific) dimensions of research and development activities. This is precisely the trend we observe in most (if not all) multidivisional companies (including General Electric and Du Pont) during the past twenty-five years. This trend is a natural consequence of both company growth and industry growth, both of which had the effect of excessively expanding the range of horizontal activities those companies' headquarters had to be directly involved with. Headquarters' overload was increased beyond its efficiency limit, making it increasingly desirable for top managers to delegate some *vertical* activities, including research. Typically, top managers would retain authority over less product-specific research activities for which they have greater expertise, and they would delegate other more applied activities to downstream research employees or units.[16]

The decentralization of R&D activities in large multidivisional firms during recent decades thus points to an interesting feedback from growth to the organization of (R&D) activities within integrated firms.

13.2.2 Hierarchical versus Organic Research in Rapidly Changing Environments

When reading through the existing descriptive literature on the organization of R&D and the contrasted experience of U.S. and Japanese firms, one comes across the following idea. The hierarchical systems common to most large U.S. companies are ill suited to firms facing a rapidly changing technological environment that obliges them to innovate (or "imitate") *frequently*. A better system for such firms appears to be the so-called *organic* structure.[17] Here the existence of *lateral* channels of communication, together with the *limited degree of specialization* of employees (including R&D personnel) throughout the firm, and their *rotation* through various kinds of tasks (R&D, manufacturing, marketing) facilitates the rapid communication of new knowledge and the coordination both across and within the different subunits of the organization. Using the terminology of Cohen and Levinthal (1990), the reduction of

---

16. See the appendix for a formalization of this effect based on Aghion and Tirole's (1997) model of delegation of authority within organizations.

17. See Burns and Stalker (1966).

communication costs within the organization enhances the organization's *absorptive capacity*, that is, its ability to process new information quickly and thereby respond adequately to changes in the environment. The ability of the Japanese *organic* structures to achieve shorter product-development times is also emphasized by Westney (1993), who underlines the tradeoff between *communication and speed* in organic structures on the one hand and *specialization and depth* in hierarchical structures on the other hand.

To better understand why an organic structure can reduce processing delays and thereby increase the flow of innovations, consider the following formalization drawn from the recent literature on information processing and communication costs.[18]

The setup is one with an infinite horizon and continuous time. For simplicity, we abstract from incentive problems and concentrate entirely on the "operational research" problem of designing the optimal organizational structure that minimizes *delay*, that is the average processing time for each "innovation opportunity." An opportunity is assumed to arrive at equidistant dates $t = 1, 2, \ldots..$ in the form of "informational cohorts" composed of n items or projects each. A cohort is *processed* when at least one individual in the organization (say, the top manager) has absorbed all of the n items.

There are two ways in which individuals can acquire information about the projects (or items). They can either acquire the information directly, which takes $\tau > 0$ units of time per item (an overload constraint); or they can get the information secondhand by communicating with other agents. However, communication is also time consuming: it takes $\tau(\lambda + am)$ units of time to communicate m informational items.

Now, consider a new innovation opportunity comprising n items. If all the information processing is performed by a single individual, the total processing time will be $\tau \cdot n$, whereas, if the processing activity is split between say two individuals, with individual 1 processing $\frac{n}{2}$ items directly and learning about the remaining $\frac{n}{2}$ items through communication with individual 2, the total processing time will be $\tau \frac{n}{2} + \tau(\lambda + a\frac{n}{2})$. Delay will thus be reduced by having parallel processing whenever n is sufficiently large and/or there are enough economies of scale in communication (i.e., if a is sufficiently small). Note that the reduction in delay comes at the cost of more time being spent by the organization as a whole on each innovation opportunity.

To illustrate the comparative advantage of an *organic* structure over a *hierarchical* structure in reducing delay, consider the following example. Let $n = 20, a = 0, \tau = \lambda = 1$, so that it takes one period to process one item and

---

18. The following presentation is drawn from Bolton and Dewatripont (1995). Primary references in this literature include Radner (1993), Van Zandt (1994), and Bolton and Dewatripont (1994), (1995).

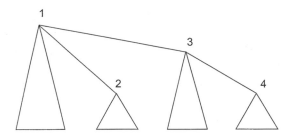

Figure 13.2

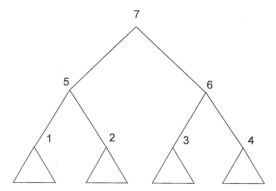

Figure 13.3

one period to communicate any number of items. The optimal structure is depicted in figure 13.2, and allows the whole innovation opportunity to be entirely
processed within seven periods and with only four individuals.[19]

In contrast, the minimum *hierarchical* structure required to process $n = 20$
items involves seven individuals and a nine-period delay.[20]

We have considered the case of a single research opportunity. Now in a repeated stationary environment where new research opportunities occur every
period, the optimal network can be shown to still look like figure 13.2, but
with a periodic rotation of individuals across innovation opportunities in order to equalize the average workload across individuals over time. We then

19. In period 7, individual 1 reads individual 3's report; in period 6, individual 1 reads from 2 and
3 reads from 4. Direct processing, which is equally divided between the four individuals, takes
place during the first $\frac{20}{4} = 5$ periods.

20. It takes the first five periods for the four downstream individuals to directly process the
twenty items. Plus two periods for 5 and 6 to learn about ten items each through downstream
communication. Plus two more periods for individual 7 to gather the whole information through
communicating with 5 and 6.

end up with an organic structure that closely fits the previous description of the Japanese system: lack of specialization,[21] lateral communication, and job rotations.

Although organic structures do comparatively better at reducing delays, hierarchical structures appear to be better suited to firms facing infrequent and/or predictable innovation opportunities, to the extent that they allow the organization to take better advantage of the existence of economies of scale in direct information processing.[22]

13.2.3 Law and Economics of Research Employment Contracts

Using the simple incomplete contracting model introduced in section 13.1, one can rationalize a number of common features of research employment contracts in industrial firms. Many research contracts between a customer firm (the employer) and its integrated research employees contain such restrictive clauses as, for example, (a) *"hired for"* clauses that confer ownership to the customer-employer for inventions that are "related" to the employer's business or make use of the employer's facilities or data, and to the research employee for inventions that pertain to other businesses; (b) *trailer clauses* that confer ownership to the customer-employer for innovations made by a breakaway researcher-employee *shortly* after quitting the firm and to the researcher-employee otherwise; (c) *shop rights,* which confer ownership to the research-employee while at the same time allocating a nonexclusive, nonassignable, and royalty-free license to use the innovation to the employer. Shop rights, "hired for" clauses, and rules governing breakaway research are instances of multiple, *split* property rights. We shall now try to rationalize these institutions by extending the basic framework of section 13.1 in order to account for the possibility of multiple innovations or the existence of multiple customers for the same innovation.

Breakaway and Trailer Clauses

Research contracts between a customer firm (employer) and its (integrated) research employees do often specify that an innovation made by the latter *after breakaway* belongs to the employer if made shortly after quitting the firm and to the research employees otherwise. An efficiency rationale for such "trailer clauses" can be easily obtained through the following extension of our basic framework, where *several* property rights (namely on the current innovation V_0, and on future innovations $V_t, t \geq 1$) are to be simultaneously allocated ex-ante between C and RU.

---

21. With most agents performing both processing and communication activities.

22. See Bolton and Dewatripont (1994) for an analysis of the information-processing problem when there are increasing returns from specialization.

Suppose that the effort e and the investment E produce a time sequence of innovations with value V_t in which the customer's marginal efficiency decreases over time:[23] $p(e, E, t) = q(e) + h(t)r(E), h'(t) < 0$. Let α_t denote RU's share of the return of the date t. Because both parties never have an incentive to overinvest,[24] an optimal contract maximizes the stake of one party (say, the customer) for a given value of the other party's stake:[25]

$$\max_{(\alpha_t)} \{\Sigma_t (1 - \alpha_t) h(t) V_t\}$$

$$s.t. \quad \Sigma_t \alpha_t V_t \geq V_{RU}^*.$$

The solution to this program satisfies

$$t < t_0 \Rightarrow \alpha_t = 0 \quad (C \text{ ownership})$$

$$t > t_0 \Rightarrow \alpha_t = 1 \quad (RU \text{ ownership})$$

The optimal policy is thus very similar to the trailer clauses observed in practice:[26] innovations occurring before sometime t_0 belong to C, and those occurring after t_0 belong to RU.

Contingent Property Rights and the "Hired for" Doctrine

Employment contracts and the law also allocate property rights on the basis of how much customer investment is used by the research unit and of whether the research unit has been hired for the innovation and made it during normal working hours. We argue that these contingent property rights stem from incentive considerations.

Suppose that the effort e and the investment E can yield one in a subset $T \subseteq \Re^+$ of types of innovation. With probability x_t and with $\sum_{t \in T} x_t = 1$, innovation t, with value V_t, is the relevant one. Some types of innovation are consumed by the customer; others are purchased at price V_t by alternative customers (so the "customer" can be both a customer and an investor in our terminology). Besides their value, types of innovation differ in the extent to which they make use of the customer's investment. In particular, we assume that the probability of discovery conditional on innovation t being the relevant one is $p(e, E, t) = q(e) + tr(E)$. We also assume that e and E are chosen before the parties know which innovation is relevant. Let α_t denote RU's share of the value of the innovation of type t. An optimal contract will again be solution of the program:

---

23. For example because RU has left the firm at date $t = 1$.

24. Because individual stakes never exceed $\sum_t V_t$ (we assume away discounting).

25. The optimal V_{RU}^* is determined by the same considerations (incentives, exante bargaining powers) as in section 13.1.

26. For example in research contracts used by Polaroid or Gulf Oil. (See Neumeyer 1971.)

$$\max \sum_{t \in T} x_t t (1 - \alpha_t) V_t$$

subject to

$$\sum_{t \in T} x_t \alpha_t V_t \geq V_{RU}^*$$

and

$$0 \leq \alpha_t \leq \overline{\alpha}_t,$$

where $\overline{\alpha}_t = 1/2$ if C consumes the innovation (recall that RU does not extract more than $V_t/2$ from C even if it owns the innovation) and $\overline{\alpha}_t = 1$ if an alternative customer uses the innovation. The solution to this program satisfies for some $t_0 \in T$:

$$t > t_0 \Rightarrow \alpha_t = 0 \qquad (C \text{ ownership})$$

$$t < t_0 \Rightarrow \alpha_t = \overline{\alpha}_t \qquad (\text{pure } RU \text{ ownership})$$

$$t = t_0 \Rightarrow 0 \leq \alpha_{t_0} \leq \overline{\alpha}_{t_0} (\text{sharing}).$$

If the innovation makes much use (resp. little use) of the customer's investment, the customer (resp. the research unit) will own the innovation. Presumably, the innovations for which the employee is hired make more use of the employer's investment and therefore should be owned by the employer. We have thus rationalized the so-called "hired for doctrine."

Multiple Users: A Rationale for Shop Rights

This last paragraph derives foundations for the observed practice of employers' allocating ownership to employees while keeping a royalty-free, nonassignable licence for themselves. Consider the following situation. An innovation designed and managed through a contract between a research unit RU and a customer C_1 can ex-post be sold to a second, yet unidentified customer C_2 as well as to C_1. C_1 and C_2 do not compete on the product market. Let V_1 and V_2 denote their valuations of the innovation where V_1 may reflect some non-contractible investment $\overline{E}$ by C_1, that increases C_1's willingness to pay for the innovation (e.g., $V_1 = V_0 + \overline{E}$, where V_0 is a constant). We adopt the convention that C_2 purchases the innovation at price V_2.

Let V_{RU} and V_{C_1} denote RU's and C_1's stakes in the innovation, that is the extra payoffs they obtain when innovation occurs. One has

$$V_{RU} + V_{C_1} = V_1 + V_2$$

and

$$V_{RU} \leq \frac{V_1}{2} + V_2.$$

Let α_1 and α_2 denote the RU's share of V_1 and V_2. When there is no customer investment in raising the value of innovation ($\overline{E} \equiv 0$), an optimal contract must solve

$$\max_{\alpha_1,\alpha_2}\{(1-\alpha_1)V_1 + (1-\alpha_2)V_2\}$$

subject to

$$\alpha_1 V_1 + \alpha_2 V_2 \geq V_{RU}$$

and

$$0 \leq \alpha_1 \leq \frac{1}{2}, \quad 0 \leq \alpha_2 \leq 1.$$

In this program α_1 is indeterminate, as both incentives depend only on RU's total share ($\alpha_1 V_1 + \alpha_2 V_2$). However, when C_1's investment affects not only the probability of discovery but also its own valuation V_1 for the innovation ($\overline{E} \geq 0$), the optimal contract must give maximal incentives to C_1 on its own use of the innovation. In particular $\alpha_1 = 0$ if $\alpha_2 < 1$. In other words, if C_1 can affect V_1 but not V_2, its relative share should be tilted as much as possible toward the first use. Indeed, if the optimal stake for the research unit, V_{RU}^* does not exceed V_2, the optimal contract gives a shop right to C_1 and allocates the licensing fees in proportions $\alpha_2^* \equiv V_{RU}^*/V_2$ to RU and $1 - \alpha_2^*$ to C_1. We thus obtain a rationale for shop rights.

We summarize our discussion in this subsection in the following proposition:

Proposition 13.2   In the presence of multiple users or multiple innovations, property rights may be split between the customer and the research unit. Each should get property rights on those activities for which it has a comparative advantage in creating value. This principle gives rise to shop rights, property rights based on the nature or the date of the innovation and to the "hired-for" doctrine.

13.3   Financing R&D

In section 13.1 we came across two sources of inefficiencies having to do with the existence of cash-constraints on researchers and/or customers. First, if only research units are cash-constrained and customers (manufacturers, suppliers, and so on) have ex-ante bargaining power (for example, because there is ex-ante competition between a large number of research labs), then ownership rights may end up being *inefficiently* allocated to the customer even in situations where the marginal efficiency of RU's research effort exceeds the marginal efficiency of C's investment. This, in turn, results in the research unit *underinvesting* in research effort. Second, if the customer is also cash-constrained, this inefficiency is magnified by the customer's inability to compensate for the underinvestment in research by more investment in capital.

A first question naturally raised by the above discussion is: Why not allow the customer to hold an equity share in the research unit? Indeed, while making RU-ownership of the innovation more attractive to the customer in situations where both C has the ex-ante bargaining power and the marginal efficiency of RU's research effort is high, holding equity shares in RU would also facilitate C's access to credit if C is also cash-constrained! It turns out that making C a shareholder in RU has no effect on the equilibrium outcome.

To see this, suppose that C is given $(1 - \alpha)$ shares in RU. The real license fee paid by C when both parties agree on a nominal license fee l is: $\bar{l} = l - (1 - \alpha)l = \alpha l$. The equilibrium level of $\bar{l}$ is, as before with l, driven by time preference only and not by the sharing rule $\left(\frac{\alpha}{2}, 1 - \frac{\alpha}{2}\right)$ implied by the initial contract. Therefore C's equity share in RU has no effect on the net license fee and is thus irrelevant. Put differently, the initial sharing rule cannot influence the ex-post bargaining game between RU and C because the object (innovation) to be traded ex-post is not contractible. And if the innovation is contractible (e.g., because it is aimed at a third party) then the specification of ex-ante sharing rules (which then become enforceable) in the contract between RU and C makes C's ownership in RU unnecessary.

Given that the above inefficiencies cannot be removed by making C a shareholder in RU, there is a role for third parties such as banks, venture capitalists or the government in *cofinancing* R&D activities. We first briefly discuss the role of *private* outside investors (banks, venture capitalists) and then touch on the delicate issue of *public R&D subsidies.*

13.3.1   Cofinancing by Private Outside Investors

Although existing high-tech firms rely substantially on internal financing (see Becchetti 1996), a significant share of firms' R&D in countries like the United States, Japan, and France is financed by outsiders. In Japan, the private outsiders are essentially *banks*, which either hold equity in the research firm or belong to the same holding company (*keiretsu*). In countries like the United Kingdom or the United States where financial markets are more developed, private outsiders are often *venture capitalists*, who typically hold concentrated equity positions and sit on the board of directors. Venture capital is typically used to finance start-up companies that are short of collateral and undertake risky projects (with a low probability of considerable profits); it is therefore hardly surprising to see that venture capital deals have been quite pervasive in highly innovative industries like biotechnology and software.[27]

Whether venture capital financing dominates the Japanese mode of bank financing (the two modes involve a combination of monitoring rights and equity participation) should depend both on the financial environment (market-oriented vs intermediated) and also on the type of innovation.[28]

Rather than pursue a detailed discussion of the comparative merits of various financing modes, we will now simply show that introducing third parties as co-owners of RU (and/or with an enforceable claim on RU's revenues) can help promote efficient RU-ownership in a situation where C has the bargaining power ex ante. More specifically, C may demand cofinancing E_I from an investor in exchange for that investor getting a claim of a fraction $(1 - \alpha)$ of RU's profits. As before RU and C bargain over the license fee after the innovation occurs and C must still pay a license fee equal to $\frac{V}{2}$ to RU's owners. However, the researchers themselves now receive a return of $\alpha \frac{V}{2}$ for the innovation, whereas the outside investors receive $(1 - \alpha)\frac{V}{2}$. Assuming ex-ante competition among outside investors leads to the following free-entry condition, where E_I (resp. E_C) denotes the outside investor(s)' (resp. the customer's) investment:

$$E_I = p(e^*(\alpha \frac{\alpha}{2}), E_I + E_C)(1 - \alpha)\frac{V}{2}.$$

C's profit is then

$$p(e^*(\alpha \frac{\alpha}{2}), E)\frac{V}{2} - E_C = p(e^*(\alpha \frac{\alpha}{2}), E)(1 - \frac{\alpha}{2})V - E,$$

where E is total investment. The optimal choice of α results from the following trade-off. First, a lower α increases cofinancing and thereby the rent that the customer can extract from RU under RU ownership $((1 - \frac{\alpha}{2})$ decreases with α); second, the dilution of RU's shares implied by a lower α reduces RU's incentives and therefore the probability of discovery p (the research effort $e^*(\alpha \frac{V}{2})$ and therefore p increases with α). The tradeoff between these "rent extraction" and "incentive" effects determines an optimal sharing coefficient α^* which is generally less than 1. So RU-ownership with cofinancing by a third party will generally dominate both pure RU-ownership and C-ownership, and this to a sufficient extent that it will also emerge as the equilibrium outcome in

---

27. "For instance Apple, Compaq, Intel, Lotus, and Microsoft initially received venture capital" (Tirole 1996).

28. Conventional bank-debt financing appears in any case to be rather unattractive for start-up firms implementing radical innovations, to the extent that such firms "are unlikely to generate positive cash-flows in the short-run and therefore would face a high probability of bankruptcy if submitted to short-term debt obligations" (Tirole 1996).

situations where inefficient C-ownership would have prevailed in the absence of outside investors.

13.3.2   The Scope for Public R&D Subsidies

The traditional approach to government intervention in the R&D sector (e.g., followed by the patent race or the endogenous-growth literatures) was formulated in purely *quantitative* terms: namely, from the point of view of allocative efficiency or optimal growth, should aggregate R&D investments be subsidized or taxed? The typical answer then would be that R&D investments should be subsidized whenever positive externality effects dominate and as a result growth under laissez-faire is suboptimal (see Chapter 1). However, R&D investments should be taxed either if too much "business-stealing" or creative destruction take place under laissez-faire (see Chapter 2) or if the innovating firms face *agency problems* that can be mitigated by reducing the amount of free-cash flow available to managers (see section 7.2.1).

In contrast, the preceding analysis points at the possibility of a more *targeted* or *qualitative* approach to public R&D financing. For example, should R&D subsidies be primarily targeted at integrated (C-owned) or non-integrated (RU-owned) research undertakings? Preliminary work with Jean Tirole on this issue suggests the following considerations. Suppose that C has the bargaining power ex-ante and farms out its R&D to one of several potential research units,[29] that C has no cash constraint, that there is a shadow cost of public funds so that the government wants to economize on R&D subsidies, and that participation in a government-sponsored R&D program is voluntary (so the customer is not hurt by the R&D program). Then it is optimal for the government to subsidize R&D if the shadow cost of public funds is under some threshold. This government intervention can take several forms.

One possibility consists in raising RU's incentives by reducing outside investors' share in the research unit. This takes the form of the government's buying up some of outside investor's shares in RU and turning them back for free to the research unit (either directly or in the form of fixed subsidies to the research unit) in exchange for the customer also contributing to this increase in RU's shareholding.

Another form of intervention consists in raising the customer's contractible investment by subsidizing it (again, in exchange of the customer's also contributing to the increase in RU's shareholding). Subsidizing customers, however, again raises the issue of monitoring the use of government funds. What

---

29. As we showed above, C may also inefficiently perform R&D internally. In this case the government may want to subsidise the farming out of R&D by providing direct subsidies to C in exchange for RU being granted the property rights over the innovation. The costs and benefits of such a policy are discussed briefly below.

guarantees that R&D subsidies to industries will not be diverted into other activities, including the setting up of entry barriers to new innovators in competing sectors and/or products? Such an agency problem between government and industries (which often reflects agency problems *within* the industrial firms themselves, e.g., of the kind of analyzed in Chapter 7) appears to be a real concern in practice.[30]

More generally, the issue of how to organize R&D subsidies to industries and that of designing adequate support and protection to innovations remain largely open to future research, although there already exists an interesting literature on the subject, to which we turn in our final chapter.

13.4   Summary

In this chapter we use the *incomplete contracts* approach to analyze the best way to organize research and development activity within and between firms. Should a firm hire the services of an independent research unit, or should it have its own research department? The central issue is how this will affect the incentives for innovation and the transfer of information. If it were possible to write a *complete* contract specifying the actions of the firm and the research unit in every contingency, then it would not matter whether research was conducted in-house or externally, because each party would always act exactly as the contract specified. But in reality such a contract would be far too complicated to write and enforce. For example, it would be very difficult to describe the exact nature of the innovation in advance, so that if either party wanted to breach the contract they could simply claim that the innovation that occurred was not the one to which the contract applied, and it would be very difficult for a court to rule on such a case. As a result, the integration decision is particularly important in an R&D context where outcomes are uncertain. We begin by considering under what conditions research ought to be *integrated*. We then consider how research should be organized *within* an integrated firm, and the impact of integration on the *size* and *probability* of innovation. Finally, we consider what implications this approach has for the *financing* of R&D.

The basic question in deciding whether a firm should integrate or "farm out" its R&D activity is whether the input of the customer or the research unit is more important in producing results. An independent research unit owns any innovation it makes. By contrast, when the research unit is simply a department of a customer firm, the customer owns the innovation. Therefore, under

---

30. It has, for example, been raised by the French government agency ANVAR, in charge of providing R&D subsidies to industries.

integration the research unit receives relatively little reward for innovating and puts in little effort, but the customer firm receives more and so is prepared to invest more. So whether integration is good or bad depends on whose investment is more important. For applied research, the customer firm's input may be relatively more important, which suggests that integration might be better. For basic research, the reverse may be true.

We can use the same principle in the presence of multiple users or multiple innovations. Each party should get property rights on those activities for which it has a comparative advantage in creating value. In this case, it may be feasible to split property rights between the customer firm and the research unit. This idea provides a rationale for shop rights, property rights based on the nature or date of the innovation, and the "hired-for" doctrine we observe in research employees' contracts.

Because information transfer is also difficult to dictate contractually, it is probable that the integration decision will affect not only the relative rewards for innovation, but also the incentive to transfer knowledge. If the probability of innovation depends heavily on the diffusion of information between the research unit and the customer, integration may be desirable. In the absence of integration, one party may want to use his private information later to make another innovation and to prevent his collaborator from doing the same. He will not be so reluctant to release information when the two firms are integrated, in as much as integration makes future competition much less likely.

Even within an integrated firm, it is possible to structure the firm in such a way that the transmission of information is improved. It is clear that if information can be transferred laterally as well as vertically within an organization, it is often possible to reduce information-processing costs. So a rigidly hierachical organization (where information flows only up and down) can be slow to absorb information and respond to change.

In considering how research activities should be organized within an integrated firm, there are two additional questions: to what extent research decisions should be delegated rather than centralized, and which activities should be delegated.

First, as detailed in the appendix to this chapter, delegating research decisions involves the following tradeoff. Subordinates care about which new projects the firm undertakes, but their preferences may not be perfectly congruent with the profits of the firm. So when authority is delegated, subordinates have more incentive to gather information, thereby easing headquarters' workload. But decentralization increases the chance that a project that is suboptimal for the firm as a whole will be chosen.

Second, if headquarters has only a limited amount of time to spend in monitoring research activities, it must also decide which research activities to monitor. Other things being equal, it should specialize in monitoring those activities it finds less costly to monitor. For example, headquarters may monitor basic (non-product specific) research and delegate the monitoring of applied (product-specific) research.

Turning to the impact of integration on the nature of innovations, the perennial question is whether integrated firms are too conservative. Here we can consider the *probability* and the *size* of innovations. The probability of innovation depends on the familiar Arrow replacement effect. Because an integrated firm is already enjoying a stream of profits, the increment it gains by innovating may be relatively small. So an integrated firm may not innovate, whereas a disintegrated structure (which can sell to potential entrants) would do so.

By contrast, when there are no other potential customers, integration is irrelevant for the size of the innovation because the research unit makes most money by producing the customer firm's preferred size. When there are other firms for the research unit to sell to, however, it may decide to improve its bargaining position with the customer firm by producing an innovation of a different size; whether it chooses to aim at one which is larger or smaller will depend on the exact details of the market into which it sells.

Finally, we consider the delicate issue of *financing* R&D. When the research unit is cash-constrained, the customer firm may find it optimal to integrate with it, even though integration is inefficient because it reduces the research unit's incentives. It would be better for a third party to take equity in the research unit, because then the research unit's incentives are at least partially maintained. This explains the phenomenon of cofinancing of R&D by banks and venture capitalists. It also points to an important role for the government in subsidizing R&D: buying up outside equity in independent research units and turning it over to them would increase research efforts and output, as would subsidizing contractible investment. Moreover, the government clearly has a very important role in enforcing property rights, which have been crucial to the analysis of this chapter. It is to these issues that we turn in the next chapter.

Appendix: Growth and the Decentralization of Activities within Firms

A.1   Modeling the Allocation of Authority within an Organization

In the simplest hierarchy, the firm's owner, or "principal" (P), hires a research employee, or "agent" (A), to implement a project. There are n potential and a priori identical projects, whose payoffs are ex-ante unknown to both parties. A research activity consists precisely in finding out which of these n projects should be implemented. Project k ($1 \leq k \leq n$) yields monetary benefit B_k to the principal and private benefit b_k to the agent.[31] The reservation payoffs of both parties in the case when no project ("project 0") is implemented are set equal to zero, that is, $B_0 = b_0 = 0$.

Let V (resp. b) denote the principal's (resp. the agent's) highest possible benefit among the n projects. Both V and b are assumed to be known ex-ante, even though the parties do not ex-ante know which projects yield these maxima.[32] Let αV, where $0 \leq \alpha \leq 1$, denote the principal's expected benefit when the agent's preferred project (yielding b to the agent) is implemented. Similarly, βb, where $0 \leq \beta \leq 1$, is the agent's expected benefit when the principal's preferred project (yielding V to the principal) is implemented. The parameters α and β are congruence parameters.

We assume that the random choice of a project by uninformed parties yields very negative expected utilities to both. This property, together with the fact that each party when uninformed will prefer to rubber-stamp the other informed party's suggestions rather than do nothing ($\alpha \geq 0$, $\beta \geq 0$), implies that privately held information about payoffs confers control over decision making to the informed party.

Throughout this section we shall assume that the principal is risk-neutral and the agent is infinitely risk-averse with respect to income, so that the agent does not respond to monetary incentives. The agent receives a fixed wage, normalized at zero.

The relationship between the owner and the research employee is described by the following four-stage game.

Stage 1: The principal allocates authority to herself or to the agent. The holder of authority has the right to pick a project or to do nothing.

Stage 2: The two parties acquire information about the project's payoffs.[33] At private (increasing and convex) cost $g_p(E)$, the principal learns her payoffs from all projects with probability E, and learns nothing at all with probability $1 - E$. Similarly, at private (increasing and convex) cost $g_A(e)$, the agent learns his payoff structure perfectly with probability e, and remains completely uniformed with probability $1 - e$.

---

31. In the main part of the chapter, we normalize these private benefits to be equal to zero. More generally, these benefits include reputation and/or perks on the job and they typically entail conflicts of interest over the best research strategy.

32. Using the terminology of incomplete contract theory, the exact choice of projects is not describable and thus not contractible ex-ante. All that the contract between P and A can do is allocate control rights (or authority) over the ex-post choice of project to either party.

33. Information collection is here assumed to be simultaneous. We could alternatively assume that the principal investigates only after the agent has made a suggestion.

Stage 3: The party who does not have formal authority suggests a project (or nothing) to the other party.

Stage 4: The party who has formal authority rubber-stamps the other party's suggestion, or selects an alternative project, or decides to do nothing.

A.2 The Basic Trade-off between the Principal's Loss of Control and the Agent's Initiative

Consider first the case where the principal has authority, that is control rights over the research activity. The two parties' expected utilities are

$$u_P = EV + (1 - E)e\alpha V - g_P(E) \qquad \text{and}$$

$$u_A = E\beta b + (1 - E)eb - g_A(e). \tag{13.1}$$

That is, with probability E, P becomes informed about her payoffs, imposes her preferred project, and obtains the monetary payoff V. This project will yield expected private benefit of only βb to the agent. With probability $(1 - E)$, P remains uniformed and loses control over the choice of project. Then, either the agent acquires information (which occurs with probability e) in which case he can impose his preferred project to the principal, or the agent also remains uniformed, in which case no project is implemented.

On the other hand, the two parties' payoffs when the agent has authority are given by

$$\widehat{u}_P = e\alpha V + (1 - e)EV - g_P(E) \qquad \text{and}$$

$$\widehat{u}_A = eb + (1 - e)E\beta b - g_A(e). \tag{13.2}$$

When the principal retains formal authority, the reaction curves in information gathering for the principal and the agent are respectively defined by the first-order conditions

$$(1 - \alpha e)V = g'_P(E) \tag{13.3}$$

and

$$(1 - E)b = g'_A(e). \tag{13.4}$$

The more the principal supervises, the lower the agent's effort. And the more the agent demonstrates initiative and/or the higher the congruence parameter, the lower the principal's interference.

We assume that the two equations $\{(13.3).(13.4)\}$ have a unique stable intersection (E, e).[34]

---

34. That is, $\alpha b V < g''_P(E)g''_A(e)$.

When formal authority is delegated to the agent, the reaction curves of the principal and the agent become respectively

$$(1 - e)B = g'_P(E) \tag{13.5}$$

and

$$(1 - \beta E)b = g'_A(e). \tag{13.6}$$

Assuming again that $\{(13.5).(13.6)\}$ yields a unique stable equilibrium (E^d, e^d), one can show that

$$E > E^d \quad \text{and} \quad e < e^d.$$

Delegating authority to the agent will thus have two effects: on the one hand, it fosters the agent's *initiative* as measured by e (the agent will not be overruled by the principal and therefore has more incentive to search for new projects). This *initiative effect* will in turn have a positive impact on the principal's payoff. On the other hand, by delegating authority to the agent the principal faces a higher risk of having to endorse suboptimal projects.[35] The trade-off between these *initiative* and *loss of control* effects determines the optimal scope of centralization versus delegation in the organization. This is equally true in the context of *multiple* research activities where the principal can only devote *limited attention* to each activity due to his *overload constraint* (i.e., to the increasing marginal learning cost $g'_p(E)$).

A.3   The Optimal Scope of Centralization

We now extend the previous analysis to the case of a *continuum* of research activities. We index these activities by the principal's degree of expertise θ at performing each of them. More precisely, we consider the special case where the principal's monitoring decision on each research activity is *discrete*

---

35. For example, when there are two relevant projects ($\alpha = \beta$) and costs are quadratic, with $g_P(E) = \frac{E^2}{2}$ and $g_A(e) = \frac{e^2}{2}$, one has:

$$E = \frac{V(1 - \alpha\beta)}{1 - \alpha bV}, \quad e = \frac{b(1 - V)}{1 - \alpha bV},$$

and

$$E^d = \frac{V(1 - b)}{1 - \alpha bV}, \quad e^d = \frac{b(1 - \alpha V)}{1 - \alpha bV}.$$

Hence

$$u_P - u_P^d = \frac{V^2 b(1 - \alpha)}{(1 - \alpha bV)^2}[1 - \frac{b}{2}(1 + \alpha) - \alpha(1 - \alpha bV)].$$

Principal authority is optimal for low levels of congruence (α small), and agent-authority dominates when preferences almost concide (α close to 1). Indeed, there is a cutoff value $\alpha^* \in (0, 1)$ such that principal authority is optimal if and only if $\alpha < \alpha^*$.   □

$(E \in \{0, 1\})$ and where $\varphi = \frac{1}{\theta}$ is the "time" the principal must spend in order to monitor a research activity for which her ability is θ. *Typically, lower φ's refer to more basic (non-product specific) research whereas higher φ's correspond to more applied (product specific) R&D.* Let $h(\varphi)d\varphi$ denote the mass of research activities in the interval $[\varphi, \varphi + d\varphi]$. Let $x(\varphi) = 1$ if the principal chooses to have control over activities of type φ and $x(\varphi) = 0$ if she chooses to delegate authority over those activities.

The principal's overall cost of monitoring is modeled as a time-constraint:[36]

$$\int E(\varphi)\varphi h(\varphi)d\varphi \leq \overline{T},$$

where $\overline{T}$ reflects the principal's overload (a lower $\overline{T}$ corresponding to a higher degree of overload).

Let employee's cost function g_A be quadratic, with $g_A(e) = \frac{1}{2}e^2$. Thus we know from (13.4) and (13.6) that the employees reaction curves, respectively for centralized and delegated research activities, will be simply defined by:

$$e(\varphi) = \begin{cases} b(1 - E(\varphi)) & \text{if } x(\varphi) = 1 \\ b(1 - \beta E(\varphi)) & \text{if } x(\varphi) = 0. \end{cases}$$

Let

$$\pi(\varphi) = E(\varphi)V + (1 - E(\varphi))e(\varphi)\alpha V \quad (\text{where } e(\varphi) = b(1 - E(\varphi))) \qquad \text{and}$$

$$\widehat{\pi}(\varphi) = e(\varphi)\alpha V + (1 - e(\varphi))E(\varphi)V \quad (\text{where } e(\varphi) = b(1 - \beta E(\varphi)))$$

denote the principal's expected monetary return from research activity of type φ respectively under centralization and decentralization. The optimal scope of centralization is then defined by the solution of the following program

$$\max_{\{x(\cdot), E(\cdot)\}} \int_0^\infty [(\pi(\phi).x(\phi) + \widehat{\pi}(\phi) \cdot (1 - x(\phi))h(\phi)d\phi]$$

$$s.t. \int_0^\infty E(\phi).\phi h(\phi)d\phi \leq \overline{T}.$$

---

36. That is, we consider the special case where the principal's monitoring cost function is defined by:

$$g_P(E) = \begin{cases} 0 & \text{for } E \leq \overline{T} \\ +\infty & \text{for } E > \overline{T}, \end{cases}$$

where

$$E = \int E(\varphi)\varphi h(\varphi)\, d\varphi$$

The analysis in this section can naturally be extended to the case of more general convex g_P - functions (see Aghion and Tirole 1995).

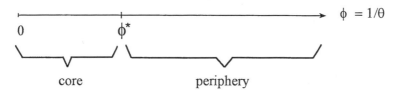

Figure 13.4

Let us assume that $\int_0^\infty \varphi h(\varphi)d\varphi > \overline{T}$, so that the principal cannot monitor *all* research activities within her time-constraint. We can immediately establish:

Proposition 13.3 There exists a cut-off value $\varphi^* > 0$ such that: $\varphi \leq \varphi^* \Rightarrow x(\varphi) \equiv 1$ and $\varphi > \varphi^* \Rightarrow x(\varphi) \equiv 0$. Furthermore φ^* is increasing in $\overline{T}$.

In other words, the principal will retain authority over those research activities (less product-specific) for which she has greater expertise and she will delegate the other (more applied) activities to her research employees.

Proof of Proposition 13.3 A first observation is that the principal will never delegate an activity φ that she plans to monitor anyway, for $\pi(\varphi) > \widehat{\pi}(\varphi)$ if $E(\varphi) = 1$. On the other hand, she will always delegate activities φ which she does not plan to monitor, for $\pi(\varphi) < \widehat{\pi}(\varphi)$ if $E(\varphi) = 0$. Now let us reason by contradiction and suppose that there exists φ and φ' such that: $\varphi < \varphi'$ and $x \equiv 0$ around φ while $x \equiv 1$ around φ'. The principal can then do strictly better by delegating activities in the neighborhood of φ' while taking on activities in a neighborhood of φ. Indeed, by delegating activities in the interval $[\varphi', \varphi' + d\varphi']$, the principal saves the amount of time $\varphi' \cdot h(\varphi')d\varphi'$. Having thus relaxed her overload constraint, the principal can take on and monitor a positive mass of research activities in the neighborhood of φ, namely up to an interval $[\varphi, \varphi + d\varphi]$ where:

$$h(\varphi) \cdot \varphi \cdot d\varphi = h(\varphi') \cdot \varphi' \cdot d\varphi'. \tag{13.7}$$

The net profit gain of such a reallocation of decision rights is

$$[V - b\alpha V]h(\varphi)d\varphi + [b\alpha V - V]h(\varphi')d\varphi',$$

which is unambiguously positive since

$$\varphi' > \varphi \quad \text{and} \quad (13.7) \Rightarrow h(\varphi')d\varphi' < h(\varphi)d\varphi.$$

This establishes the proposition. □

Consider now a *growth in research opportunities*, modeled as a local increase in h around some φ. Then the cutoff value φ^* will either remain constant or decrease in order not to violate the principal's time constraint while guaranteeing that only those research activities for which the principal has more expertise will be kept centralized.

Similarly, an *increase in the headquarters' overload* (i.e., a decrease in $\overline{T}$) due to an expansion of its *horizontal* activities will make it desirable to delegate some *vertical* activities, including research, that is again to lower the cut-off point φ^*. The increasing decentralization of R&D activities in multidivisional firms like General Electric during the last decades provides a good illustration of such development, and thus points to an interesting feedback from growth to the organization of R&D activities.

Problems

Difficulty of Problems:

No star: normal

One star: difficult

Two stars: very difficult

1. Ownership rights in innovations (based on Aghion and Tirole 1994b)

Consider two contracting parties, a research unit (RU) and a customer (C). RU contributes a research effort e and has no cash. C provides capital investment E, which we shall also assume not to be contractible. C is assumed to be the only purchaser for the innovation and V denotes the value of the innovation for the customer. Let $p(e, E)$ denote the probability of discovery; p is assumed to be increasing, concave, and separable in e and E:

$$p(e, E) = \alpha\sqrt{e} + \beta E.$$

Both parties are risk-neutral, and have reservation utility zero. We assume linear costs of effort and investment ($c_{RU}(e) = e, c_e(E) = E$).

a. Derive the first-order conditions for the socially optimal levels of effort and investment.

b. *Contractual incompleteness:* we assume that the two parties cannot specify the innovation ex-ante; thus, all that the initial contract can do is allocate property rights on the forthcoming innovation.

i. Under C-ownership, C can freely use the innovation and RU receives no reward for innovation. Derive the equilibrium values of e and E.

ii. Under RU-ownership, C and RU bargain over the license fee after the innovation occurs. Assuming a symmetric Nash bargaining outcome with each party getting $\frac{V}{2}$, derive the equilibrium values of e and E in that case.

c. Under what condition on α and β does the social outcome under RU-ownership dominate that under C-ownership?

d. Assume that C has the bargaining power ex-ante at the contracting stage. Keeping in mind that RU has no cash to compensate C for transferring ownership to him or her, for which values of α and β will C consent to offer a contract that allocates ownership of the innovation to RU? Compare this latter condition to that derived in question c and conclude.

e. *Schumpeterian hypotheses*: these hypotheses state that a firm's R&D inputs (expenditure, personnel) and R&D output ("number" of significant innovations) increase with scale and with the market power of the customer firm. That is, the equilibrium values of e, E, and $p(e, E)$, should all increase with V. Show that this is true in our model provided the ownership form (to C or RU) remains fixed. Show however that this ceases to be true once the ownership form is endogenous and determined by ex-ante contracting.

f. *Trailer clauses:* suppose that RU's effort e and the customer's investment E generate a sequence of innovations V_t (where t is the date of innovation) which are to be simultaneously allocated between C and RU. Suppose also that the customer's marginal efficiency decreases with t, that is

$$p(e, E, t) = \alpha \sqrt{e} + e^{-\lambda t} E, \quad \text{where} \quad \lambda > 0.$$

Then show that it is optimal to allocate ownership of innovation t to C for $t \leq t_0$ and to RU for $t > t_0$, for some $t_0 > 0$. Calculate t_0.

g. *Property rights and the size of innovations:* Consider again a single innovation, but now assume that the probability of discovery is $p(\gamma)$, where γ denotes the *size* of innovation and $p'(\gamma) < 0$. (You may ignore e and E.] Let $\Pi_1^m(\gamma)$ denote the incumbent customer's (i.e., C's) profit when she obtains an exclusive license for the innovation. Let $\Pi_0^m = \Pi_1^m(1)$ denote C's profit in the absence of innovation. The value of innovation is then equal to: $V(\gamma) = \Pi_1^m(\gamma) - \Pi_0^m$.

i. Show that in the absence of other customers for the innovation, the optimal size γ^* is the same under RU-ownership as under C-ownership: $\gamma_{RU} = \gamma_C$.

ii. Now suppose that there is another potential customer (entrant) to whom RU could sell the innovation at price $\Pi_1(\gamma)$, provided RU owns the innovation. Following Binmore, Rubinstein, and Wolinski (1986) on bargaining with outside options, we assume that under RU-ownership RU gets $\max(\frac{V(\gamma)}{2}, \Pi_1(\gamma))$. Let $r(\gamma) = \frac{\Pi_1(\gamma)}{V(\gamma)}$. Then using a revealed preference argument show that $\gamma_{RU} \geq \gamma_C$ if r is increasing in γ. What is the intuition for this result?

2. The Schumpeterian hypothesis (based on Aghion and Tirole 1994b)

This problem considers the effect of the value of innovation on organizational form, and the implications of this for the Schumpeterian hypothesis. A research unit RU performs research for a customer C. The value of innovation for the customer is $V > 0$. The probability of discovery $p(e, E)$ depends on the noncontractible effort cost e by RU and the investment E by C. Suppose $p(e, E) = q(e) + r(E)$.

a. Suppose that the probability of discovery depends only on RU's effort: $r(E) = r_0 > 0$ for all E. Suppose that the efficacy of RU's effort is given by $q(e) = 2e/V_0$ for $0 \leq e \leq 1$, and $q(e) = 2/V_0$ for $e \geq 1$.

i. Consider the case of RU ownership. How does the probability of discovery depend on V?

ii. Show that C prefers C-ownership to pure RU-ownership or cofinancing when $V < V_0$.

iii. Show that for $V > V_0$, C prefers RU-ownership to C-ownership if r_0 is sufficiently small.

iv. Suppose that C has the bargaining power ex ante. How does the probability of innovation depend on the value of V?

b. Now suppose that the customer has to make a nonmonetary and noncontractable investment E. Let $r(E) = 2\mu\sqrt{E}$ and $q(e) = 2eV_0$ for $e \leq V_0/4$ and $q(e) = \frac{1}{2}$ for $e \geq V_0/4$. Suppose $V > V_0$. Show that as V grows, C ownership becomes more desirable for C. How does the probability of discovery change as V grows?

c. What do you conclude about the Schumpeterian hypothesis (relationship between V and p) in this framework?

d. How would allowing the possibility of cofinancing affect the model?

★ **3. Cooperative R&D joint ventures (based on Katz 1986)**

An industry consists of n symmetric firms competing in a product market in which the representative firm i has profits (gross of R&D costs) given by

$$V^i(c_i, \Omega(c_1, c_2, \cdots, c_n))$$

Costs $c(z_i)$ can be reduced through R&D. Each firm i can choose its own level of R&D spending, r_i, but can also benefit from spillovers from other firms' R&D spending. In the absence of a cooperative R&D agreement, such spillovers occur at rate $\phi \geq 0$, but if k $(0 < k \leq n)$ firms decide to set up a "joint venture" they can agree to share more of their R&D output, choosing the rate ϕ^k $(\underline{\phi} \leq \phi^k \leq \overline{\phi} \leq 1)$ at which spillovers occur within the group. Thus the "effective R&D" of an individual firm is

$$z_i = r_i + \underline{\phi} \sum_{j \neq i} r_j$$

for a nonmember and

$$z_i = r_i + \underline{\phi} \sum_{j \notin A} r_j + \phi^k \sum_{j \in A, j \neq i} r_j$$

for a member of the agreement A.

Member firms may also decide to share the cost of their R&D, setting a sharing rule so that each firm bears a fraction $s^k (0 \leq s^k \leq \bar{s})$ of its own R&D costs and $(1 - s^k)/k$ of its rivals':

$$\text{Member firm } i\text{'s R&D expenditure} = s^k r_i + \frac{(1 - s^k)}{k - 1} \sum_{j \in A, j \neq i} r_j.$$

Thus firms play the following four stage game:

i. Individual firms decide whether to join an R&D joint venture.

ii. The joint venture decides on (a) a linear symmetric rule s^k for sharing the costs of R&D or (b) the level of spillover of knowledge ϕ^k.

iii. The individual firms choose their level of R&D spending given ϕ^k and s^k.

iv. The firms compete on the product market given costs $c_i(z_i)$, to make profit $V^i(c_i, \Omega)$.

a. Suppose that all n firms are in the cooperative agreement. Find the first-order condition for the choice of R&D level in a symmetric equilibrium, given the prior choice of ϕ^n and s^n. Find also the first-order condition for the case where there is no cooperative agreement. Show that R&D is higher with an industry-wide cooperative agreement than without if

$$(1 - s^n)\{1 + (n - 1)\phi^n \rho(cz_0)\} + (\phi^n - \underline{\phi})s^n(n - 1)\rho(cz_0) > 0,$$

where $\rho(c_1, \cdots c_n) = (\partial V^i / \partial c_j)/(\partial V^i / \partial c_i)$, $j \neq i$. How do the cost and output-sharing rules affect the likelihood of an agreement raising R&D?

b. Suppose now that firms do form an industry-wide agreement in equilibrium. At what level will they set s^n and ϕ^n :

i. If an industry-wide increase in R&D reduces net profits?

ii. If industry-wide R&D can increase net profits?

iii. Interpret your result from (ii) if $\bar{\phi} = 1$.

iv. How might allowing independent R&D (i.e., outside the scope of the joint venture's cost and output sharing schemes) affect the outcome in part (i)?

v. Suppose that the cooperative agreement does reduce effective R&D. Is it necessarily against the public interest?

c. Let $\rho(c) = \rho$, a constant, invariant to c. Using your results from (a) and (b), show that if R&D raises profits, the sign of $z^n - z^0$ is given by the sign of

$$\frac{\overline{\phi}}{[1 + \underline{\phi} + (n - 1)\overline{\phi}]} + \rho$$

d. Summarize your results. When are industry-wide R&D joint ventures most likely to be beneficial, and when harmful? What additional considerations are raised by the case where only $k < n$ firms join the coalition?

14 Organizing R&D II: Public Aid to Innovation[1]

The previous chapters have pointed to various sources of inefficiency in the *level* and *allocation* of R&D investments. In particular, we have discussed the pervasiveness of knowledge spillovers, the complementarity between fundamental and applied research (or between *research* and *development* activities), the credit constraints faced by research firms, and the contractual incompleteness induced by the impossibility of describing the characteristics of an innovation in advance. All of these have the mutually reinforcing effect of discouraging R&D investments and the diffusion of new knowledge to future potential innovators. This obviously suggests a role for public intervention both in subsidizing R&D activities and also in allocating and enforcing property rights to innovations.

As it turns out, government intervention in the R&D sector is quite marked throughout the developed world, and to a comparable extent in countries like France or Japan where governments are generally more interventionist, as it is in countries like the United States that have traditionally advocated laissez-faire policies. For example, Adam and Farber (1987, 1988) report that the government's share of total R&D spending is currently about 50 percent in the United States[2] and France, 33 percent in Germany, and 20 percent in Japan. Public intervention also affects the allocation and legal enforcement of property rights on innovations.

The main motivations for public intervention in the R&D sector should be transparent to the reader at this stage, but the particular form that such an intervention should take remains unclear, and also highly controversial among policy makers. Should public intervention be centralized or decentralized? Should it emphasize the provision of R&D subsidies or instead should it confine itself to the design and enforcement of patent legislation? Should R&D subsidies be targeted to particular sectors, industries, or firms, or instead should R&D subsidies be provided on a nondiscriminatory basis? Should public financial participation in R&D investments take the form of direct subsidies (e.g., tax subsidies or government transfers) or instead should it involve the government's participation as a creditor and/or as a shareholder?[3] And so on.

R&D subsidies have been heavily criticized in various countries for being wasteful and unnecessary, and are also subject to political lobbying in a context of widespread informational asymmetries, especially between research firms, government agencies, politicians at various levels of responsibility, and the electorate. Incentive problems and the difficulties involved in combining so many instruments (taxes, subsidies, direct transfers, financial participations,

---

1. The first two sections of this chapter borrow heavily from lecture notes prepared by J. Tirole for the Centre Nationale d'Études en Télécommunications.

2. Katz and Ordover (1990) report a 47 percent subsidy rate for private sector research in the United States in 1988.

3. We have already touched on this question; see section 13.5.

development banking, patent design, and so on) into a coherent and efficient policy have contributed greatly to divide public opinion and politicians on the form and scope of public intervention in the R&D sphere.

Without entering into the controversy between the ultraliberals advocating a complete withdrawal of the state from the R&D sector and the proponents of systematic and unconditional R&D subsidies, we shall restrict our discussion in this chapter to three main aspects of government intervention to support innovative activities: first, the design and use of *direct* and *targeted* subsidies; second, the use and design of *untargeted* subsidies, both ex-ante at the investment stage and ex-post at the patenting stage; and third, the design of patent legislation.

14.1   Targeted R&D Subsidies

Government subsidies that are deliberately aimed at particular sectors or firms are known as *targeted* subsidies. For example, when the government sets aside funds to finance defense R&D, it has chosen a particular sector (and often a particular firm and a particular innovation that is desires), so this kind of R&D subsidy is targeted. Such targeted subsidies are common in developed countries and may take various forms including public investments in state-owned laboratories, research grants, participation in R&D funds, subsidies to enterprises (e.g., input subsidies or procurement contracts in sectoral development programs),[4] credit guarantees,[5] and public investment in high-technology industries.[6]

Targeted R&D subsidies are often criticized for being arbitrary and discretionary in the choice of beneficiary. Discretion and arbitrariness are indeed somewhat inevitable with targeted subsidies, because by definition it is the government rather than a properly functioning market that decides who will receive funding. This means that there is always room for genuine mistakes on the government's part, as well as incentives on the firms' side to waste resources lobbying for lucrative contracts. Moreover, the problem is particularly severe compared with other branches of government decision making for several reasons. First, knowledge externalities (the possibility of "spill-over") are

---

4. For example, 74 percent of R&D spending in the U.S. aircraft sector is financed by the U.S. government. Government participation to R&D investments is also important in sectors like defense, space, nuclear energy, electronics.

5. For example, the French government agency ANVAR uses both input subsidies (in cash or in the form of expertise and services) and subsidized loans to confinance R&D expenses by small and medium size enterprises.

6. For example the U.S. consortium Sematech was created in 1987 with a $100 million capital endowment contributed by the U.S. government and another $100 million being put up by fourteen private semiconductor firms.

particularly hard to identify and measure adequately, as are the various market imperfections that motivate intervention in the R&D sector. Second, "picking winners" is always hazardous, especially in the R&D sector whose activities are often unpredictable. Even if the government makes the right decision ex-ante, it may *appear* to be a bad decision ex-post if the project fails. Third, there are severe informational asymmetries between the government and potential beneficiaries regarding the measurement of R&D inputs and the impact (or "additionality") of R&D subsidies.[7]

In analyzing targeted R&D subsidies, we will assume that in choosing to target the government has solved the difficult problem of *which* firms to subsidize (otherwise untargeted subsidies might be more appropriate, see the next section). The question then remains as to how large a subsidy the government should provide, and whether it should pay firms up front, or only on successful completion of the project. To explore this issue, consider the following simple model of R&D investment. The government targets a firm whose R&D investment I at the beginning of the period will yield both a monetary benefit I to the firm and a knowledge externality $E > 0$ if the innovation succeeds; the investment yields zero otherwise. The probability of success is given by $p(e)$[8] where e is a non-observable monetary R&D effort put up by the firm, with cost

$$\psi(e) = \frac{1}{2}ce^2.$$

The parameter $c \in \{c_1, c_h\}$, $c_1 < c_h$ is private information to the firm; the government believes that $proba(c = c_1) = q = 1 - proba(c = c_h)$.

Suppose that the shadow cost of public funds to the government λ is zero (i.e., there is no welfare loss from making transfers to the firm). It has two possible instruments that it can use: an ex-post subsidy S paid contingent on the success of the project, and an ex-ante subsidy s paid regardless of whether the project succeeds or fails. The government wants to maximize the expected gain from innovation minus the effort and investment cost for whichever type of firm it faces:[9]

$$\max_e p(e)(R + E) - \frac{1}{2}c_1e^2 - I, \quad \text{if} \quad c = c_1$$

or

$$\max_e p(e)(R + E) - \frac{1}{2}c_he^2 - I, \quad \text{if} \quad c = c_h.$$

---

7. The additionality of an R&D subsidy is how much the R&D subsidy generates in addition to what would have been undertaken without the subsidy.

8. Where $p(e)$ is concave (so that second-order conditions will automatically be satisfied), and $p(0) = 0$, $p(\infty) = 1$.

9. Because the shadow cost of public funds is zero, the transfers s and S do not appear in the government's objective function.

Notice that the firm will choose effort such that

$$e^*(c_1) = \arg\max \ p(e)(R + S) - \frac{1}{2}c_1 e^2 - I - s \quad \text{if it has } c = c_1$$

$$e^*(c_h) = \arg\max \ p(e)(R + S) - \frac{1}{2}c_h e^2 - I - s \quad \text{if it has } c = c_h$$

Thus the government can achieve the first-best result by simply paying over the amount of the externality $S = E$ to the firm if it succeeds.[10] In this way the firm completely internalizes the externality and therefore chooses the right effort. By contrast, the ex-ante subsidy s is completely useless in stimulating effort because it is independent of whether success occurs.[11]

Because it is generally true that rather than giving a particular subsidy s ex-ante the government can better tackle moral hazard problems by giving the same expected sum $S = s/p$, one wonders why in fact ex-ante subsidies are so common. One obvious possibility is that because banks view R&D as risky and difficult to monitor, R&D firms are *credit-constrained* ex-ante, making them simply unable to undertake worthwhile projects unless the government provides funds up front. R&D firms may also be more *risk-averse* than the government, and unwilling to take on an uncertain project without a sure subsidy. The *nonverifiability* of innovations ex-post could also preclude the use of ex-post subsidies by preventing the government from promising to pay only if the project is successful.

A more subtle argument is that when there are limited public funds available — that is, the cost of public funds λ is strictly positive — the government may want to try to target its subsidies to the type of firm where they will have more effect on effort and the probability of success, namely, the low-cost ($c = c_1$) firm. However, because it does not know whether the firm is low-cost or high-cost, it must offer a choice ("a menu")[12] of different subsidies so that each type of firm will choose a different contract. The choice between ex-ante and ex-post subsidies could be used to "sort" firms in this way, because

---

10. Indeed, this reward will make the innovator fully internalize the knowledge externality E from his or her innovation. Here, we implicitly assume that the policy $S = E$ satisfies the individual rationality constraint of the firm, that is,

$$e^*(E + R) - \frac{1}{2}c(e^*)^2 > I \quad \text{for} \quad c = c_\ell.$$

11. Indeed, in the absence of ex-post reward, the firm will choose e to maximize $\{eR - \psi(e)\}$, i.e., the second-best effort $\widehat{e} = {\psi'}^{-1}(R)$, whatever the ex-ante subsidy s. Still, in case $\widehat{e}R - \psi(\widehat{e}) - I < 0$, providing an ex-ante subsidy $s \geq I + \psi(\widehat{e}) - \widehat{e}R > 0$ to the enterprise will dominate a fully non-interventionist policy ($s = S = 0$), in as much as the subsidy will at least get the project started by making it individually rational to the firm.

12. See problems 1, 2, and 3.

more efficient firms have a higher probability of success and will prefer ex-post subsidies, whereas less efficient firms will prefer ex-ante subsidies. We refer the reader to Laffont and Tirole (1993) for a systematic treatment of this kind of problem. However, we note that in this context, optimal ex-ante subsidies are very likely to be negative; public funds are costly, so the government taxes up front to recoup some of the large subsidies that it plans to give ex-post. So it is again difficult to justify the use of ex-ante subsidies even in tandem with expost subsidies unless there are problems of risk-aversion, credit constraints, or nonverifiability.

14.2   Untargeted Subsidy Policies

Untargeted subsidies are subsidies not aimed at any particular firm, industry, or project, and are another important instrument of policy intervention in the R&D sector. Such subsidies include research tax credits, accelerated amortisements, tax deductions on stock options, tax deductions for firms that invest in joint R&D funds, credit guarantees, subsidized insurance for risky capital investments, and the like.

Being less subject to political lobbying, untargeted R&D subsidies also tend to be more *redundant* than their targeted counterparts. That is, precisely because they are not aimed toward projects known to be marginal, untargeted subsidies can end up being "wasted" in financing inframarginal investment. For example, tax credits of the kind mentioned earlier may often end up financing investments that would have taken place anyway.[13]

This latter concern does not apply as much to government support to *fundamental* research[14] (i.e., essentially to *universities*), because often this research lacks direct profit opportunities and is likely to be marginal. But it may be important in relation to industrial firms involved in various kinds of investments that they can easily *cross-subsidize.*

Thus a difficult issue when dealing with *applied* (industrial) research is the following. On one hand, a centralized ("top-down") policy would lack flexibility and also would end up giving too much authority to institutions (like the government and parliament) that are uninformed about the R&D needs of the various industries. On the other hand, giving full discretion to industries as to the use of R&D subsidies would further increase the concern that these

---

13. In France and several other OECD countries, more than 50 percent of R&D-motivated fiscal deductions are considered redundant.

14. Whether peer-review systems as exemplified by the U.S. National Science Foundation or the British ESRC provide the appropriate model for government support to fundamental research is an interesting but as yet largely open question.

subsidies be diverted into other types of (non-innovative) investments (such as advertising or entry-deterrent activities). The following proposal, recently put forward by Paul Romer (1993), is a first attempt to strike the right balance between these two extremes.

14.3   Delegating the Financing of R&D Inputs to Industries

The driving idea behind this "bottom-up" proposal is that firms can take the initiative of creating "industry investment boards" aimed at subsidizing R&D investments and, conditionally upon contributing to the financing of such boards, they can benefit from government subsidies in the form of tax exemptions. More precisely, the timing of events can be described as follows:

1. Firms (individually or collectively) submit investment proposals (and/or an application for the creation of an investment board to the government).

2. The relevant government authority examines the application and decides to accept it whenever there is evidence first, that the investments envisaged by the firms are of sufficient public good, and second, that these investments do not involve highly negative externalities on other sectors and industries.

3. Once the application has been accepted by the relevant government authority, it is submitted to a vote among firms in the industry. The application becomes operational once it is approved by a qualified majority of firms (e.g., those representing y percent of total industry sales). Once operational, the approved investment projects will be financed by a special tax (or tariff) on the consumption of the firms' output.

Firms' investment proposals may typically involve the financing of research activities within the industry, the financing of fundamental research (e.g., within universities) that is relevant to the industry, or human capital investments (such as training and education) that will help in the implementation of new technologies by the industry.

Investment projects would always be managed by investment boards, and firms could allocate their tax revenues to one or several boards, depending on how many investment projects they wished to push forward. Finally, the research output generated by these investment projects would have to be disclosed and diffused in a *nondiscriminatory* fashion (in contrast to the innovative output of a research joint venture).

Undoubtedly stimulating and thought-provoking, this proposal raises a number of delicate issues. First, how does one define an "*industry*," and, in particular, can this proposal adequately deal with R&D investments that are relevant to *several* industries, or with innovative activities that lead to the emergence of *new* products and industries? Being managed by existing industries, the proposal appears in essence to be biased toward incumbent firms. This in turn may induce some technological bias (e.g., in favor of drastic but low-frequency innovations[15]), and also encourage collusive behavior[16] among groups of firms in a given sector.

Second, who controls the investment boards? And who monitors investment board-managers? With regard to the latter question, there is clearly the temptation for each individual firm that contributes to the financing of the Board to *free-ride* on its partners' monitoring efforts. As to the control issue this becomes particularly problematic when firms within the industry are *heterogenous* or have different views as to what the priority investments should be. This heterogeneity may be of a strategic nature (e.g., linked to the choice of a technological standard) or it may simply reflect a diversity of market conditions within the industry (e.g., between export-oriented and inward-looking firms, or between firms facing a greater and a lesser threat from competing foreign firms).

Third, Romer's proposal is subject to the same objections as against any other policy which amounts to providing *ex ante* targeted subsidies to R&D. (See section 14.1 and problems 1 and 2.) The most compelling argument in favor of ex-ante subsidies appears to hinge on the existence and importance of credit market imperfections. However, whether this proposal can mitigate the informational problems underlying these imperfections remains a largely open question.

More generally, whether these considerations are sufficiently serious to override the potential advantage of having R&D subsidies to industries managed by the industries themselves is the subject of an important policy debate which goes beyond the scope of this book.

14.4   Using the Existing Patent System to Optimally Reward R&D Output

Michael Kremer (1996) has recently proposed a mechanism, based on ex-post reward, for inducing the socially optimal amount of R&D. The basic idea of this mechanism is to make use of the information conveyed by the *laissez-faire* patent price V[17] in order to fix the optimal price at which the social planner (government) will *repurchase* the innovations to put them in the public domain.

---

15. See our discussion in section 13.2.

16. Having joint R&D investments be financed by a proportional consumption tax can only encourage the enforcement of (implicit) price agreements among the participating firms.

17. Where

$$V = \frac{\gamma \cdot \frac{1-\alpha}{\alpha}(N - \widehat{n})}{r + \lambda \widehat{n}}$$

in Chapter 2.

Putting innovations in the public domain in turn removes the (static) monopoly distortion created by patents.

Directly inspired by the mechanism-design literature,[18] the Kremer "scheme" can be described as follows:

1. The innovator obtains a patent for his or her innovation, as in Chapter 2.

2. The ("laissez-faire") price of the patent is revealed through an *auction* for the exclusive right to implement the innovation. Suppose that the laissez-faire value V emerges as the equilibrium price in this (say, first-price) auction; that is, $p_0 = V$.

3. With probability $(1 - \varepsilon)$, the government repurchases the innovation from the inventor at a price $p_1 = m \cdot V$ that tries to approximate the social value of innovation V^*. With probability ε, the patent remains in the hands of the winner of the auction, Note that ε needs to be strictly positive in order for private bidders to find it worth their while to come and participate to the auction. However, ε should not be too large in order for innovation incentive to remain socially optimal and also for (static) monopoly distortions to be largely removed. The multiplier $m = \frac{p_1}{V}$ should typically be greater than 1. For example, in the case of pharmaceutical innovations, Kremer estimates at about 2 the average value of m.

What makes the above scheme attractive in our view is first that it is truly untargeted (no particular line or domain of research is being privileged by the scheme); second, that it does better than other proposals at eliciting information about the value of innovations; and third, that insofar as ε remains small, the scheme removes all incentives to engage in (duplicative) imitation activities while at the same time eliminating the (static) monopoly distortions generated by innovations in the absence of imitations.

However, and this is somewhat unavoidable for any scheme that might appear simple enough to implement in practice, the Kremer proposal raises a number of questions.

First, how to *compute the multiplier m*? The value of m will typically depend on parameters (such as the productivity of research λ and the elasticity parameter α), about which the government is unlikely to have perfect information. And even if the government can in principle compute m, how should it proceed in delicate situations, for example when, due to an overriding business-stealing

---

18. In particular by the literature on Nash and subgame perfect implementation under *symmetric* information. (Primary references in this literature are Maskin 1977 and Moore and Repullo 1988.)

19. Where

$$V^* = \frac{\gamma \cdot \frac{1-\alpha}{\alpha}(N - n^*)}{r + \lambda n^* - \lambda n^* \gamma}$$

in Chapter 2.

effect, $V^* < V$ (then m should in theory be less than 1; is this enforceable?); or, in the opposite case where the innovation is in fact an "imitation" in the sense of Grossman and Helpman (1991a), which essentially results in reducing monopoly profits in the industry down to zero (then $V = 0$, so that m should theoretically be infinite?).[20]

Second, what guarantees that the equilibrium price that emerges in the auction is actually equal to the *true* value of the innovation under laissez-faire (i.e., equal to V)? In particular, when ε is small, will private bidders still have adequate incentive to acquire *information* about V?

Third, what would prevent the innovator from *colluding* with potential bidders in order to (artificially) increase the auction price p_0 far above the true (private) value of the innovation V? Well aware of this latter problem, the author proposes to use not the winning bid, but the third or fourth bid price as the basis for computing the multiplier. But then, the above concern about information acquisition by private bidders might end up being dramatically reinforced.

Fourth, is the scheme adapted to the case of multiple *successive* innovations? There are actually several aspects to this question. One aspect has to do with the relationship between *fundamental research* and *development*, already considered in Chapters 6 and 13: to the extent that subsequent (applied) innovations may contribute to enhancing the value of the fundamental innovation, how should m be computed for each successive innovation? In particular, how can the government make sure that by putting a first (fundamental) innovation in the public domain "too soon" it will not discourage other researchers from engaging in the development activities that are required in order to give (full) value to that innovation?[21]

Another aspect of the same question about successive innovations has to do with the case where subsequent innovations may *substitute* (rather than complement) the first innovation.[22] For example, what should happen in the case where subsequent innovations, especially when put in the public domain, reduce the (laissez-faire) value of the current innovation?[23]

---

20. Based on empirical work by Mansfield et al. (1977), Nadiri (1993), Trajtenberg (1990), and others, Kremer argues that a reasonable value of the mark-up for the pharmaceutical sector should be 2.

21. On the other hand, the proposed mechanism would ensure that potential inventors of subsequent complementary innovations will assume that the earlier good is being sold at marginal cost.

22. In particular, this system may fail to provide adequate incentives for the invention of durable goods. This is because the expectation that future substitutes will be placed in the public domain, and hence sold at marginal cost, may reduce current demand for durable patented goods.

23. Here, Kremer suggests that the government repurchase the first innovation at its private value $p_0 = V$ and then later resume the auction process for the overall package of innovations. But this in turn presupposes that the government will know *in advance* whether the first innovation is to be substituted for by subsequent innovations, and that it also knows *how many* successive innovations of this kind are to take place in the future: two heroic assumptions!

This said, the Kremer proposal is certainly interesting, if only because it forces R&D and growth specialists to get better acquainted with the virtues and techniques of mechanism design, and in particular with the auction mechanism, which has recently proved to be quite operational.[24] We are sympathetic to the view that most of these queries are likely to be less dramatically important in the pharmaceutical sector where Michael Kremer suggests that his proposal be tried first.[25] If adequate modifications and/or additions to the scheme could make it become practical in *all* sectors, then the government would be able to achieve social efficiency (i.e., both to eliminate static deadweight losses and to provide the efficient incentives for research and innovations) independently of the particular patent legislation in place. For example, the determination of the optimal duration and breadth of patents would simply become irrelevant insofar as policy-makers can make full use of mark-up policy.[26] However, our discussion suggests that the stage where all the intricacies of patent legislation design could be fully dispensed with still lies ahead of us as quite a remote prospect. This brings us naturally to the last section of this book.

14.5   On the Design of Patent Legislation

An important aspect of the organization of R&D has to do with the allocation and enforcement of intellectual property rights on innovations. Throughout the previous chapters we have implicitly assumed that innovations (no matter what their size) were systematically protected by a system of infinitely lived patents. And in the previous sections of this and the former chapter we have concentrated on situations where property-right allocations could always be achieved through *private* contracting, taking the total value of innovations (V) as given. In this section, we will briefly touch on the issue of the optimal design of legal patent protection. In particular, we will analyze how various features of patent legislation (namely patent *duration*, *breadth,* or *depth*) will affect R&D incentives and aggregate welfare (which reflect respectively the private and social values of innovations).

The theoretical literature on optimal patent legislation was initiated by Nordhaus (1969) and Scherer (1972), who derived a theory of the optimal *duration* of patents based on the trade-off between the dynamic incentive effect and the static deadweight loss involved in increasing the duration of patents. Subse-

24. See Milgrom (1997).

25. First, in the United States the FDA approval process generates information about the effects of new pharmaceuticals, which should make it easier for private bidders to estimate the value of new pharmaceutical inventions. Second, pharmaceuticals are not durable, so the problems discussed in note 22 could largely be avoided. Third, the strong government intervention in the pharmaceutical sector should reduce the scope for collusion.

26. Although given a fixed markup, the duration and breadth of patents will not be neutral.

quent contributions by Klemperer (1990) and Gilbert and Shapiro (1990) have extended the analysis by associating the issue of duration with that of the optimal *breadth* of a patent, where breadth is defined as the degree of horizontal (or vertical) differentiation which a new product must satisfy vis-à-vis an existing patented product in order to avoid infringement of the patent. More recently, Cornelli and Schankerman (1996) have analyzed the issue of optimal patent renewals in a context of adverse selection where innovators have private information about their R&D productivities. All of these models are *static* in that they consider a single innovation over time.

Other papers (including Green and Scotchmer 1995, Chang 1995, O'Donoghue, Scotchmer, and Thisse 1995, and Hunt 1995) have taken up the issue of optimal patent design in a *dynamic* context closer to the Schumpeterian paradigm, where innovations are sequential and cumulative. In contrast to the static case, the *statutory* duration of an innovation no longer coincides with its *effective* duration because any non-infringing new innovation may nevertheless displace the existing patent. In that case, the *effective* duration of a patent will eventually depend on both its statutory duration *and* its breadth.

The following two subsections, respectively dealing with the static and dynamic aspects of optimal patent design, briefly introduce the reader to the main issues and tradeoffs analyzed by the theoretical literature on patent legislation, and also suggest some implications of patent design for growth.

14.5.1   Patent Duration and Patent Breadth in the Static Case

Consider the following framework, developed by Klemperer (1990): a patentholder produces a single good for which the aggregate demand per unit of time would be $F(p)$ if no other product varieties were available (for example this would be the case in a homogeneous product market). Let w denote the breadth of the patent: that is, competing firms must locate at a minimum distance of w from the patentholder's product, otherwise they infringe on the patent. Suppose that each consumer incurs a (different) transportation cost t per unit distance when substituting away from the patentholder's good, where t is distributed according to the cumulative distribution function $H(t) = 1 - G(t)$. Then, if the patentholder sets price p, the actual demand for his or her product will be $F(p) \cdot G(p/w)$, in that all consumers with transport cost less than p/w will prefer to buy from a non-infringing competitor at the patent boundary[27] at price 0 rather than from the patentholder. (These consumers will incur total transport costs $t.w$ in the former case, which is less than p if $t < \frac{p}{w}$.)

Faced with the demand curve $F(p)G(p/w)$, the patentholder will, at each point in time, choose price p to maximize his or her profit flow. Let

---

27. Free entry is assumed to drive the competitive price down to marginal cost, which we assume to be zero without loss of generality.

$$\pi(w) = \max_{p} \{pF(p)G(p/w)\}$$

denote the equilibrium profit flow, achieved for $p = p^*(w)$. The corresponding deadweight loss is

$$D(w) = \int_0^{p^*(w)} F(p)G(p/w)dp - \pi(w).$$

Assuming that the innovation will occur if and only if the innovator obtains an expected discounted profit at least equal to $\underline{V} > 0$,[28] the social planner's problem becomes one of choosing a duration T and a breadth w for the patent, which minimize the intertemporal deadweight loss subject to the innovation not being deterred. More formally, the social planner will choose T and w to

$$\min_{w,T} \int_0^T D(w)e^{-rt}\,dt$$

$$\text{s.t.} \quad \int_0^T \pi(w)e^{-rt}\,dt = \underline{V}.$$

(IC)

Notice that $\int_0^T D(w)e^{-rt}dt = D(w)\frac{1-e^{rT}}{r}$, and that $\int_0^T \pi(w)e^{-rt}dt = \pi(w)\frac{1-e^{rT}}{r} = \underline{V}$, so that $D(w)\frac{1-e^{rT}}{r} = \frac{D(w)}{\pi(w)}.\underline{V}$. Then, one immediately sees that the optimal patent policy (w^*, T^*) can be derived in two steps. First, the optimal breadth w^* minimizes the deadweight loss/profit ratio $\frac{D(w)}{\pi(w)}$; and second, the patent duration T^* satisfies the innovator's IC-constraint with equality for $w = w^*$. Let us now characterize the optimal solution (w^*, T^*) in two important special cases.

All Consumers Have the Same Transportation Cost t_0

In this case $G(p/w) = 0$ if $p/w > t_0$ and $= 1$ if $p/w \le t_0$. The ratio $\frac{D(w)}{\pi(w)}$ is then simply reexpressed as:

$$\frac{D(w)}{\pi(w)} = \frac{\int_0^{p^*(w)} F(p)dp}{p^*(w)F(p^*(w))} - 1 = \frac{1}{p^*(w)} \int_0^{p^*(w)} \left(\frac{F(p)}{F(p^*(w))} - 1\right) dp.$$

This average value is obviously minimized (at zero) for $w = 0$, because as $w \to 0$, $p^*(w) \to 0$. We thus have $w^* = 0$ and $T^* = \infty$.

Intuitively, as Klemperer writes, "since a narrower patent constraints the patentholder to lower prices, the narrowest possible patent is the most cost-effective way of awarding profits to the innovation." As in the homogenous product case analyzed by Gilbert and Shapiro (1990), in the differentiated

---

28. This will be the case for example if innovating is a zero-one decision ($e \in \{0, 1\}$), with $c(0) = 0$ and $c(1) = \underline{V}$. Or alternatively, the innovation technology is linear, with $\underline{V}.e$ being the cost of innovating with probability $e \in [0, 1]$.

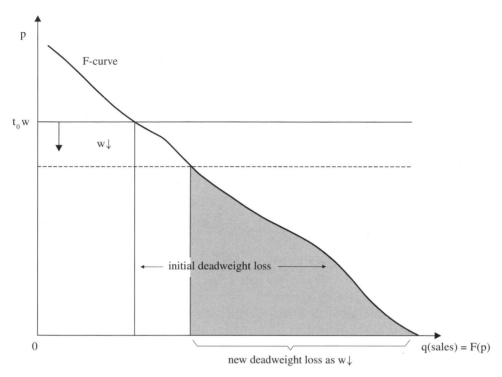

Figure 14.1

product case where all consumers have the same transportation cost, no consumer will ever substitute away from the patented product (obviously $p^*(w) \leq t_0 w$), and therefore the only source of deadweight loss is the monopoly-price distortion incurred by all (nontraveling) consumers. This loss in turn is minimized for $w = 0$. Hence the somewhat surprising result that the optimal duration of patents is *infinite*. (In particular, this conclusion is at odds with the earlier results of Nordhaus and Scherer, but remember that duration of patents was the *only* policy instrument considered by these two authors.)

Figure 14.1 depicts the case where all consumers have the same transportation cost. The deadweight loss is obviously minimized when patent breadth w is reduced down to zero.

The Aggregate Demand Curve $F(p)$ is Infinitely Elastic

Here, we consider the polar case where all consumers have the same reservation price for the patentholder's good while differing in transportation costs. In that case, the aggregate demand curve is defined by:

$$F(p) = \begin{cases} 1 & \text{if } p \leq v \\ 0 & \text{otherwise.} \end{cases}$$

and the monopoly price $p^*(w)$ is thus less than or equal to v. Assume $p^*(w) = v$ without loss of generality.

The social planner will then choose the breadth parameter w to solve

$$\min_{w} \left\{ \frac{\int_0^v G(p/w)dp}{v \cdot G(v/w)} - 1 \right\},$$

or equivalently, to solve

$$\min_{w} \left\{ \frac{1}{v} \int_0^v \left(\frac{G(p/w)}{G(v/w)} - 1 \right) dp \right\}.$$

As $w \to \infty$, $G(p^*(w)/w) \to G(0) = 1$, so that the ratio $\frac{G(p/w)}{G(v/w)}$ converges to 1 for all p and therefore this deadweight loss/profit ratio becomes arbitrarily close to zero.

Hence $w^* = \infty$ and $T^* < +\infty$. Intuitively, choosing a finite breadth would allow potential competitors to enter the market. But then, consumers with low transportation costs ($t < \frac{v}{w}$) would travel away from the patentholder and switch to the competitors. This, in turn, would entail an additional welfare loss equal to the total transport cost incurred by all travelling consumers. Choosing an infinite breadth for the patent is socially optimal in this case because it removes potential competition and therefore the motive for socially wasteful travelling. At the same time, because aggregate demand is infinitely elastic, there is no deadweight loss to be incurred by the (nontraveling) consumers.

Figure 14.2 depicts the case where the demand curve F is infinitely elastic. As w increases the G-curve pivots rightward, thereby reducing the deadweight loss (which in this case is simply equal to the total traveling cost incurred by consumers who purchase from the competitive fringe, that is, whose unit transport cost t is less than $\frac{\bar{v}}{w}$). In the limit, when $w = +\infty$, and the G-curve is vertical, the deadweight loss simply disappears.[29]

Remark: This analysis and, more generally, the theoretical literature on the design of patent legislations concentrates on a small number of prespecified policy instruments, namely the breadth and duration of patents. However, one could well imagine the government using (nonlinear) fees and subsidies schedules instead when seeking to maximize social welfare subject to the innovators' incentive-constraint. Now, what may limit the use of direct fees and subsidies are again observability and/or verifiability problems (e.g., profits may not be verifiable and innovators are protected by limited liability).

---

29. "More generally, a narrow patent is desirable when it causes relatively few consumers to substitute, that is, when demand is relatively inelastic in substitution cost. When demand is relatively inelastic in reservation price, on the other hand, controlling price is relatively less important, and so broader patents are optimal" (Klemperer 1990).

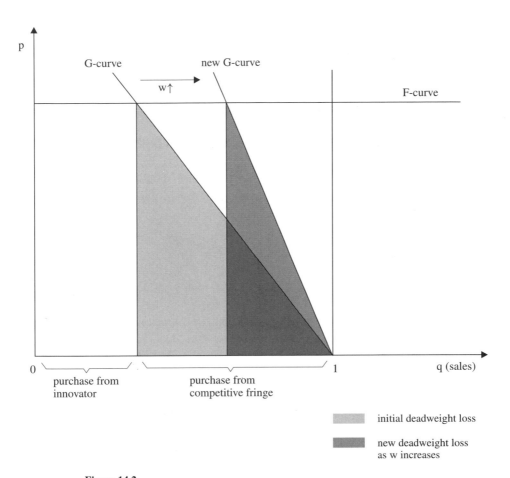

Figure 14.2

Our analysis so far has been entirely conducted in a context of ex-ante *symmetric* information between the government and the patentholders. An interesting paper by Cornelli and Schankerman (1996) shows that the duration of patents (and more specifically the renewal policy) may serve as a useful screening device in situations of ex-ante asymmetric information, where, for example, the R&D productivity of patentholders is private information. Let us briefly sketch the argument.

As before there is only one innovation occurring over time, but the (vertical) quality μ of the new product depends on the research effort incurred by the innovator. Thus the researcher's incentive problem becomes continuous, namely that of choosing the quality (or size) μ in order to maximize his or her discounted innovation rents net of R&D costs.

For given quality μ, the innovator faces a demand curve $Q(p \mid \mu)$ and therefore obtains a profit flow equal to

$$\pi = \pi(\mu) = \max_{p} p.Q(p \mid \mu).$$

Assuming that $\frac{d\pi}{d\mu} > 0$, one can invert the above relationship between π and μ and use π as the quality parameter.

Now, let us simply assume that by exerting R&D effort equal to z (which involves a non-monetary cost equal to $\psi(z) = \frac{1}{2}z^2$), the innovator can achieve the quality level $\pi = \theta \cdot z$ (where $\theta > 0$ measures the R&D productivity of the innovator). Then if the government knew the true parameter θ it could compute the first-level R&D effort, namely,

$$z^{**}(\theta) = \arg \max_{z} \left\{ \int_0^\infty S(\theta z)e^{-rt}dt - \psi(z) \right\},$$

where $S(\theta z) = \int_0^\infty Q(p \mid \theta z)dp$ is the total consumer surplus when the patented good is of quality θz.

Now, let us assume that the government does *not* know θ. The patentholder's value of making an innovation of size $\pi = \theta z$ is equal to

$$\pi(\theta z, T) = \int_0^T \theta z e^{-rt}dt - \psi(z),$$

and the corresponding optimal choice of R&D by the patentholder will be

$$z^*(\theta, T) = \arg \max_{z} \pi(\theta z, T) = \frac{\theta}{r}(1 - e^{-rT}),$$

which is obviously increasing in θ and T.

Note that the optimal choice of effort z^* satisfies the Spence-Mirrlees condition $\frac{\partial^2 z}{\partial \theta \partial T} > 0$; that is, the more productive innovators will be more responsive to an increase in the duration of their patents. But then, it is certainly not optimal for the government to set a *uniform* patent length when designing the legislation that maximizes intertemporal social surplus: with uniform T, the government will provide too little incentive to highly productive firms and too much incentive to low-θ firms! Rather, the government should design an incentive structure that shifts the distribution of R&D efforts towards higher θ's. In particular the government should offer a schedule $(T(\widehat{\theta}), f(\widehat{\theta}))$ where $\widehat{\theta}$ is the productivity parameter *announced* by the patentholder[30]; $T(\widehat{\theta})$ is the corresponding patent length, which is obviously nondecreasing in $\widehat{\theta}$; and $f(\widehat{\theta})$ is a

---

30. By virtue of the *revelation principle* in the theory of mechanism design, there is no loss of generality in restricting ourselves to *direct* mechanisms where T and f depend directly on the productivity $\widehat{\theta}$ announced by the patent holder. (See problem 3.)

fee schedule that guarantees incentive compatibility, namely that a low-θ innovator will not overstate its productivity by announcing $\widehat{\theta} > \theta$. (In the absence of such a fee, innovators would always announce the maximum value of θ in order to be granted a more generous duration of their patent.)

This above analysis thus indicates that the optimal patent fee should rise with the corresponding patent duration. This prediction appears to be consistent with the existing evidence on statutory-renewal fee schedules, as estimated by Schankerman and Pakes (1986), even though the analysis in Cornelli and Schankerman (1996) suggests that the optimal renewal fees should rise much more sharply with patent length than the existing statutory fee schedules.

14.5.2   Patent Duration and Patent Breadth in the Dynamic Case

Once we take into account the multiplicity and sequentially of innovations over time, the interaction between the duration and breadth of a patent becomes more involved. To begin with, when innovations are sequential and cumulative, the statutory duration of a patent becomes somewhat irrelevant, in as much as the incumbent innovator may now be displaced by a new innovation *before* the patent expires. (This was indeed the case in the Schumpeterian models analyzed in the previous chapters, where the statutory length of patents was implicitly infinite and still the *effective* average duration of a patent was finite and equal to $1/\lambda n$.)

In fact, a solution to the problem of having effective patent lives too short is actually to increase the *breadth* (or "depth") of the patent. In other words, when innovations are cumulative, breadth and duration must work together to achieve an adequate *effective* patent duration. One may want to distinguish here between lagging breadth, which protects an innovator from inferior imitations, from leading breadth, which protects him from innovations that are superior but insufficiently large. It is clear that when innovations arrive frequently, an innovator who is protected only by lagging breadth and no leading breadth may have insufficient incentives to do R&D because he knows that he will soon be displaced. Here, the effective patent life is short, even if statutory life is infinite. The courts can remedy the situation by providing leading breadth through the doctrine of "anticipation." If a patentholder clearly anticipates certain developments of his product, he may be granted rights over them even if he has not yet developed them.

Another instrument the government may use with the same object is the so-called patentability requirement. Rather than, or as well as, granting the patent holder some leading breadth, the government may require further innovations to have some minimum size before they can be granted patents of their own. This discourages small innovations and prolongs market incumbency and innovation profits. Notice that leading breadth can be larger or smaller than the patentability requirement so that new products that infringe may or may not be patentable in their own right.

To see how setting a patentability requirement can affect growth, consider for example the following extension of the basic Schumpeterian model of Chapter 2, directly inspired by Hunt (1995).

As before, innovations arrive sequentially according to a linear Poisson technology with parameter $\lambda \cdot n$, where n is the current flow of research labor. However, the size of innovations is now randomly distributed in the interval $[0, \overline{\gamma}]$, with density function $f(\gamma)$ and cumulative distribution function $F(\gamma)$.

Let s denote the "patentability requirement," that is, the minimum size of innovation for which the patent office is willing to grant a new patent[31] (the minimum degree of "non-obviousness"), and suppose that there is zero leading breadth. Then an innovator will obtain patent protection only with exante probability $1 - F(s)$, but, as in the previous chapters, the statutory duration of patents is assumed to be infinite. Assuming for simplicity that in the absence of a patent the new innovation is not implemented, the growth-adjusted value of an innovation is now expressed as

$$V = \frac{\int_s^{\overline{\gamma}} \pi(\gamma) f(\gamma) d\gamma}{r + (1 - F(s))\lambda n}, \tag{14.1}$$

where $\pi(\gamma)$ is the growth-adjusted profit flow generated by an innovation of size γ.

Looking at equation (14.1), one can immediately see two main effects of tightening the size (or "non-obviousness") requirement, that is of an increase in s. First, a negative "profitability" effect, which is captured by the term in the numerator of (14.1). An increase in s reduces the likelihood that the next discovery will be patentable. This profitability effect will tend to discourage R&D and growth. Second, a positive "dynamic" effect, which is captured by the second term in the denominator of (14.1): an increase in s will make subsequent innovations also less likely, thereby reducing the probability of creative destruction. This dynamic effect will thus tend to stimulate R&D and growth.

Which of these two effects dominates will depend on λ, n, and the initial value of s. In particular, the dynamic effect is more likely to dominate in rapidly innovating industries (large values of $\lambda \cdot n$) or for small initial values of s (see Hunt 1995): then, increasing the breadth of patents will stimulate R&D and growth. On the other hand, in infrequently innovating industries and for large

---

31. This type of size-contingent clause is currently observed in practice. Hunt (1995) gives the example of the U.S. Semiconductor Chip Protection Act, enacted in 1984, which obliges firms that reverse-engineer other firms' products to pay royalties unless they have developed "a sufficiently better product than the original."

initial values of s, increasing the breadth of patents will rather discourage R&D and growth. Whether it is socially efficient to increase the growth rate will in turn depend on which of the welfare effects of technological change (intertemporal spillover and consumer surplus versus business-stealing) dominates at the initial rate of growth.

One could perform a similar analysis setting s as the leading breadth of patents, excluding ex-ante agreements between firms, and assuming that the incumbent has sufficient bargaining power ex-post that no firm would want to produce an infringing product. The exact relation between leading breadth and patentability requirements is investigated by O'Donoghue, Scotchmer, and Thisse (1995) and by O'Donoghue (1996) (see problem sets 4 and 5). The issue of direct licensing agreements between successive innovators, conversely, is the main focus of the paper by Green and Scotchmer (1995). The main idea is that the statutory breadth of a patent determines a starting point for subsequent bargaining between the patentholder and the subsequent innovator(s). The framework developed by Green and Scotchmer has two innovators inventing in sequence but with no time lag between the two innovations. The statutory duration T of the first patent will thus equally apply to the second innovation and therefore determines the total amount of profits to be shared among the two innovators when (ex-ante) agreements are allowed between them. The problem for the government is to maximize social surplus, which involves providing the adequate research incentives to *both* innovators. Here comes the complementarity of roles for duration and breadth: although the statutory breadth will affect the *division* of profits among the two innovators by determining a starting point for negotiation over the licensing agreement, the duration of the patent will adjust total profits so as to guarantee a minimal level of rents to the first innovator for him to cover his innovation cost. (One might think of the two innovations either as purely substitutable, as in the basic Schumpeterian model of Chapter 2, or as complementary, as in the research and development model of Chapter 6. Both cases are actually covered by Green and Scotchmer 1995.)

Let γ denote the size of the second innovation; let $\pi_1(T)$ and $\pi_{1+\gamma}(T)$ be the discounted value of profits *respectively* when only the first innovation *and* when both innovations are being marketed (jointly) by the patentholder, that is, by the first innovator; and finally let c_i denote the cost of innovation $i \in \{1, 2\}$.[32] Three main insights come out of Green and Scotchmer's analysis. First, unless the patent breadth s is set equal to $(+\infty)$, the *duration* of the first innovator's patent will have to exceed the deadweight loss minimizing T_0 defined by $\pi_{1+\gamma}(T_0) = c_1 + c_2$, in order for the first innovator to always

---

32. R&D efforts are again assumed to be *discrete*, with c_i being the cost of agent i innovating (i.e., $\psi_i(0) = 0$, $\psi_i(1) = c_i$).

cover his or her innovation cost c_1 no matter the size γ of the subsequent innovation. The reason for this is that, as in the previous model, the size γ is assumed to be randomly distributed, say on the interval $(0, \infty)$. If the breadth of the first patent is finite, then whenever $\gamma > s$ the second innovator will not infringe on the first patent and thus can threaten the first innovator with ex-post competition when negotiating over the licensing agreement. This threat of competition may in turn reduce the expected discounted profit the first innovator gets from agreement. Because his or her R&D cost c_1 is already sunk, it is possible for bargained profits to fall below costs, unless the duration of the patent T is adequately adjusted upward.

Second, setting $s = +\infty$ is indeed the optimal policy when ex-ante agreements between the two innovators are allowed. Indeed, choosing an infinite breadth boils down to making the first innovator the residual claimant over the total net profits from the two innovators. The first innovator will then automatically induce the second innovation and make the required side transfer c_2 to the second innovator whenever this latter innovation involves a net increase in total net profits, that is, whenever $\pi_{1+\gamma}(T_0) - \pi_1(T_0) > c_2$.

Third, an infinite patent breadth policy may become suboptimal when ex-ante agreements between the two innovators are precluded (e.g., because of antitrust considerations). In this case the second innovator may sometimes find himself unable to cover his R&D cost c_2 even where the second innovation has a positive net value added (i.e., $\pi_{1+\gamma}(T) > \pi_1(T) + c_2$). Because ex-ante agreements between the two innovators are now precluded, the R&D cost c_2 has to be entirely born by the second innovator, and may be expropriated ex-post by the first innovator. Hence the need in this case to reduce lower the patent breadth s in order to satisfy the incentive constraint of the second innovator.

14.6   Summary

We have already seen in the previous chapters that invention is typically associated with both positive and negative externalities. (For example, there is a positive intertemporal spillover and a negative business-stealing effect in the basic Schumpeterian model of Chapter 2.) To the extent that the net externality is positive, the government may wish to encourage R&D. In this chapter we consider the best way for the government to do this. There are essentially two means available (which are not necessarily mutually exclusive). The government can subsidize R&D directly by giving money to the firms concerned, or the government can confer property rights on the innovation once made, allowing the firms involved to earn monopoly rents as a reward for innovation.

We begin by considering the first of these options. Supposing that the government intends to subsidize directly R&D, how should it choose which potential R&D projects should benefit? One way is to *target* R&D subsidies: to aim them at particular projects, firms, or sectors. Another is to "let the market decide" by offering *untargeted* subsidies to those that take them up. Which is better depends essentially on how much information the government has. If the government is not well informed about which projects have large positive externalities, then targeted subsidies risk being awarded arbitrarily; but indiscriminate untargeted subsidy can be wasteful if some projects would have been undertaken without a subsidy. On this basis, the government is likely to find targeted subsidies useful in certain key sectors where it has expertise (e.g., defense, where it is a large buyer), and to use untargeted subsidies elsewhere. In this chapter we consider how both targeted and untargeted subsidy schemes should be designed.

When considering targeted subsidies, one relevant question is whether the subsidy should be paid up front (ex-ante) or only in case of success (ex-post). It is clear that if the beneficiary has to make some uncontractable costly effort toward the success of the project, the same expected sum given ex-post will be much better from a moral hazard point of view. When public funds are costly and there is adverse selection as well as moral hazard, the government can benefit from offering a "menu" from which firms choose a combination of ex-post and ex-ante rewards, because this will enable it to direct funds more cost effectively. However, optimal ex-ante subsidies may be negative in this case: the government should tax firms ex-ante to recoup some of the large reward that it plans to give ex-post. The value of ex-ante subsidies therefore depends on R&D firms facing credit-constraints or being risk-averse, or alternatively upon it being difficult to verify whether a project is successful (as in Chapter 13).

When untargeted subsidies are used, the government does not have enough information to explicitly direct them, so the essential problem is ensuring that the right firms nevertheless get the right amount. Here two proposals have received much attention.

Romer (1993) suggests that industry boards might be set up to direct R&D investment, in as much as industrialists will have a better idea of which R&D projects are useful. The inevitable tradeoff, of course, it that what is good for the industry may not be good for social welfare; would such a scheme deal appropriately with new entrants to an industry, or with the interests of consumers? It could easily become a vehicle for constructing barriers to entry, or for facilitating collusion. The form of financing of R&D projects is another issue here. Direct subsidy is unattractive if the government has little information, in that very low value projects might end up being financed. But the suggested option of a tax on the final product is problematic in being a form of ex-ante subsidy (because it is allowed whether or not the R&D is successful.)

A more radical proposal due to Kremer (1996) is that an auction might be used to help determine the private value of innovations. The government could then use the revealed private value to help it determine the social value of an innovation, which could then be paid over to the innovator. Assuming that the government performs this calculation correctly, the innovator would then have the correct incentives to innovate. Moreover once the government has purchased the patent, the government could place it in the public domain, eliminating monopoly distortions and thus any rent to be gained through costly imitation. However, working out the ratio of private to social value is potentially a highly controversial issue because theoretically this relationship depends on many factors such as the rate of innovation subsequently, the elasticity of demand, and the effectiveness of patent protection (see below), all of which are likely to vary across industries and even across firms and innovations. Even given the unreliability of the private value of a patent as a measure of its social value, the elicitation of the true private value through auction could cause further problems, because it must be juggled with the fact that (presumably) very few patents will actually be sold to the highest bidder. This combination may result on the one hand in few bidders entering the auction, facilitating collusion between bidders and the inventor; and on the other hand with the patents which are sold into private hands being seriously undervalued due to competition from publicly owned patents.

Finally, we consider the case where the only way in which innovation is rewarded is through reaping monopoly profit from the innovation. Notice that if there are positive externalities associated with the project, this reward is lower than the first-best, but may be socially optimal if the cost of public funds is very high compared to the cost of monopoly pricing, or if as in Klemperer (1990), the effort decision is zero-one. In this case, we can suppose that a potential innovator will bother to make the effort to innovate if and only if the reward to innovation is at least V. The question is then what is the best way to let the innovator reap monopoly profits V, because these could be given either by giving him a patent that lasts a long time, or one that is shorter but broader, that is, provides more protection from competing products during its lifetime. Klemperer finds that which of these two alternatives is better depends on the details of the market, but that in general extreme solutions are likely. The idea is to design the patent to minimize the deadweight losses of consumers switching to less-preferred imitating products. For products where customers have similar propensities to substitute to imitating products, the innovator will price to prevent this, so a long narrow patent should be issued; where consumers differ in their utilities for substitutes, a short broad patent should be used to reduce substitution.

If the productivity of research firms differs, however, Cornelli and Shankerman show that rather than setting the same patent life for all innovations, governments should (and generally do, though not a sufficient extent) charge higher fees for longer patents. Such an incentive system efficiently gives more encouragement to high productivity firms to conduct research.

So far we have considered only the case where innovations can be imitated but not improved. When innovations can be improved, the length and breadth of patents are no longer substitutes. Suppose that there is a basic technology, and an accessory for it or an improvement or application is developed by a different firm. Then the *length* of the patent determines the *total profit* to be divided between the two firms, whereas patent *breadth,* by affecting relative bargaining positions, can be used to determine its *division* between the two firms. When there is a long sequence of improving innovations (a quality ladder), each innovator plays both the roles of first and second firm, so patent length and breadth must work together to ensure sufficient profit. The reason is that it then becomes necessary to distinguish between the *statutory length* of a patent and its *effective length*, because unless a patent is broad as well as long, it will become effectively worthless before its legal expiration date.

Problems

Difficulty of Problems:

No star: normal

One star: difficult

Two stars: very difficult

1. Targeted subsidies and participation constraints

Consider a firm that can make non-observable effort e ($0 \leq e \leq 1$) to try to make a discovery which if it occurs will generate revenues R for the firm and an externality E to other firms and consumers. The probability of discovery is $p(e) = e$, and the cost of effort is $\psi(e) = \frac{1}{2}ce^2$. Suppose that the parameter c is common knowledge between the government and the firm, as are the parameters R and E. (Assume that $(R + E)/c < 1$ so that $p < 1$.)

a. Write down the firm's individual rationality (IR) constraint supposing that the project costs the firm I to set up. Suppose that the government can only give ex-ante subsidies. Under what conditions might it be a good idea for the government to target the firm with an ex-ante subsidy s? How large a subsidy should it give?

b. Let us ignore the firm's IR constraint for the moment (e.g., suppose $I = 0$), and suppose that the government is free to choose between using ex-post and ex-ante subsidies. Assume that the government is not allowed to tax the firm (i.e., that s, $S \geq 0$). What are the optimal ex-ante subsidy s and ex-post subsidy S if the shadow cost of public funds is $\lambda \geq 0$? Interpret your result.

c. Now reintroduce the firm's IR constraint and suppose that it is binding: the government must give an ex-ante subsidy s to make up for any excess of costs over benefits for the firm after the ex-post subsidy is chosen, in order to ensure that the project is undertaken. Suppose that the government chooses its ex-post subsidy S with this in mind.

i. Use the IR constraint to derive an expression for the ex-ante subsidy s in terms of the ex-post subsidy S.

ii. Substitute for s in the expression for social welfare which you used in (b), and maximize over S to find the optimal ex-post and ex-ante subsidies in this situation.

iii. Show (by substituting back into your expression for social welfare and rearranging) that when s and S are chosen optimally, social welfare is given by $-(1 + \lambda)s$.

iv. What do you conclude about the usefulness of ex-ante subsidies from your answers to this and parts (a) and (b)?

2. Targeted subsidies and the sorting of firms I: the discrete case

Use the same model as in problem 1 above, but now suppose that there are two possible cost levels for the firm, low or high: $c \in \{c_L, c_H\}$. The government does not know the firm's cost (this is private information to the firm), so it will try to separate the two "types" of firms by offering a choice of contracts. It offers the firm a choice from a menu $\{(s_L, S_L), (s_H, S_H)\}$, where the former pair of ex-ante and ex-post subsidies is supposed to attract the low-cost firm, and the latter the high-cost firm. Also suppose that the government is allowed to tax or subsidize the firms ex-ante or ex-post (so s_L, s_H, S_L, and S_H could be positive or negative), subject to their still being willing to join the scheme $\{(s_L, S_L), (s_H, S_H)\}$. The shadow cost of public funds is $\lambda > 0$.

a. Work out how much effort each type of firm will exert, assuming that it chooses the contract intended for it.

b. Use your expression for effort (and hence probability of success) to write down the government's objective function in terms of s_L, S_L, s_H, and S_H, given that the prior probability of a firm being of the high cost type is α_H, and of the low cost type $\alpha_L = 1 - \alpha_H$.

c. Why is there no loss of generality in supposing that the government wants both types of firms to join the scheme $\{(s_L, S_L), (s_H, S_H)\}$?

d. What is the rent of the high cost firm when it does not join the scheme ("its reservation utility")? Write down the high-cost firm's individual rationality constraint. Why will this hold with equality; that is, why will the government want to give it the same rent if it does join the scheme? Use this fact to derive an expression for s_H in terms of S_H.

e. Suppose from now on that the high cost type would still operate the project even if it did not join the scheme. Why will the individual rationality constraint of the low-cost firm not bind? Write down the incentive compatibility constraint for the low-cost firm. Why will the low-cost firm be tempted to choose the high-cost firm's contract, but not vice versa? Use your result to find an expression for s_L in terms of S_L, s_H, and S_H.

f. Use your answers to (d) and (e) to substitute in the government's objective function from (b). Now maximize with respect to S_L and S_H.

g. What do you find about the signs of s_L, s_H, S_L, and S_H? How do the firms' incentives to exert effort compare with the first best? Give some intuition for your results.

h. Imagine that there had been two types of firm in problem (1) but that the government had chosen not to separate them (i.e., to offer only one type of contract, as was done there). How do you think social welfare under the policies used here and in problem 1 will compare?

** **3. Targeted subsidies and the sorting of firms II: the continuous case (based on Laffont and Tirole 1993, chap. 1)**

This problem considers how one might organize targeted R&D subsidies when it is possible to describe in advance the innovation required, and the government is ill-informed only about costs. Suppose, in particular, that the government has a deterministic R&D project that it wants to realize, and that there is only one firm capable of realizing the project. Suppose for simplicity that the project will generate social surplus S but no revenues for the firm (if it does, these can be easily dealt with, essentially by subtracting them from the transfer). Thus the government must pay for the firm to realize the project, which it does by making a transfer T to the firm. The problem is that the government does not know ex-ante how much the project will cost the firm to realize, although it can observe the cost ex-post. The cost of the project to the firm is given by $C = \beta - e$, where β is private information of the firm (e.g., relating to the efficiency of the firm, or the difficulty of the project), and e is the unobservable nonmonetary effort which the firm puts in to keep costs down. The government knows that the firm's "type" β is distributed on $[\underline{\beta}, \overline{\beta}]$ with cumulative distribution $F(\beta)$ and density $f(\beta)$, and that the cost of effort to the firm is $\psi(e)$ with $\psi'(e)$, $\psi''(e)$, $\psi'''(e) > 0$. All parties are risk-neutral, so the firm's utility as a function of its private information β is given by

$$U(\beta) = T(\widehat{\beta}) - C(\widehat{\beta}) - \psi(e).$$

The firm has reservation utility equal to zero. The government has to choose how large a transfer T to make to the firm given its reported type $\widehat{\beta}$, and its observed cost C.

a. Explain why the Revelation Principle tells us that there is no loss of generality in assuming that the government's optimal scheme induces each type of firm to report its true type to the government.

b. Write down the individual rationality (IR) and incentive compatibility constraints of a firm of type β in terms of its costs and transfers. Explain why only the least efficient type $\overline{\beta}$ will have an IR that binds at the optimum.

c. Suppose that the government has a shadow cost of public funds $\lambda > 0$. Write down the government's objective function and the associated constraints. Substitute out for costs and transfers, so that the control variable is $e(\cdot)$.

d. Solve the government's problem of maximizing with respect to $e(\beta)$. Compare your solution to the first-best effort level for type β. Interpret your result.

e. Show that the optimal net transfer t^* to the firm (that is, the optimal gross transfer T net of costs: $t^* = T^* - C^*$) is a convex function of C. Sketch a graph of $t^*(C)$ and the indifference curves for different types of firms and hence deduce that the government can implement the solution to its problem using a series of linear contracts $t = a - bC$.

f. What problems might there be with implementing such a scheme for R&D finance in reality?

⋆ 4. The patentability requirement (based on O'Donoghue 1996)

Consider the following model: There are N identical firms $i \in I$ ($I = \{1, 2, \ldots, i, \ldots, N\}$) with unit cost c, which at any moment in time compete on price to sell products in the output market. At all times the output market consists of a mass one of identical consumers, with each consumer receiving utility $q - p$ from consuming at most one unit of the product at price p with quality q. The quality of product received by consumers depends on the concurrent innovative activity of the firms, which engage in successive patent races for the next innovation. During each race firm i has Poisson arrival rate λ^i, with independence between firms, so that the industry arrival rate is $\Sigma_{i=1}^{N} \lambda^i$. Suppose that at each stage each firm can choose both its level of R&D spending, x, and the size of innovation which it will achieve if it wins the race, Δ, such that $\lambda^i(x^i, \Delta^i) = h(x)g(\Delta)$ with $h' > 0, h'' < 0, g' < 0$ and $g'' < 0$. These races result in an infinite sequence of innovations that repeatedly increase the maximum technologically feasible quality. If the tth innovation is of size Δ_t, then $q_t = q_{t-1} + \Delta_t$. After t innovations firms can produce any feasible quality ($q \leq q_t$) unless prohibited from doing so by patents. Moreover, in racing to make the next innovation, firms all build on the same current base level q_t.

a. Explain why dynamic social welfare in a stationary equilibrium (x, Δ) of this model is given by

$$DSW = \Omega(x, \Delta) = -\frac{Nx}{r} + \frac{N\lambda(x, \Delta)}{t} \times \frac{\Delta}{r}.$$

Use this expression to calculate the first order conditions for a social planner directing firms in their choice of x and Δ. Denote the first-best choices of x and Δ by x^* and Δ^* respectively.

b. Suppose that patent policy will provide complete lagging breadth, so that if a firm wins the tth patent race with an innovation of size Δ_t to become the market leader, then the other firms—the market followers—can produce only products with quality no greater than $q_{t-1} = q_t - \Delta_t$. Suppose that all innovations are nondrastic. Argue that there exists an equilibrium where all firms (market leaders and followers) take the same action (x^e, Δ^e) at all times. Why is there no replacement effect in this model?

c. Use your results from (a) and (b) to show that when patents have infinite life but zero leading breadth, firms in this model will target the first-best innovation size, but spend too little. Explain why this should be so. (Assume that $\lambda(0, \Delta^*) > r/\Delta^*$ so firms spend a strictly positive amount.)

d. Consider the introduction of a patentability requirement such that firms can patent only innovations above size $P > \Delta^*$. Show that this can increase spending and hence dynamic social welfare.

e. Consider an alternative policy of giving patents leading breadth strong enough to protect the innovator during the whole life of his patent. (So the patent lasts for T years rather than until a firm manages to produce an innovation larger than the patentability requirement.) Thus innovators must reach licensing agreements with current patentholders to market an innovation. Suppose that in bargaining they can only capture a fraction α of their total contribution to industry profit. Show that firms target the first best innovation size, but spend too little. Show that provided $\alpha > r/(r + (N - 1)\lambda)(1 - e^{-rT})$, increasing the length of the patent can increase spending and hence dynamic social welfare.

f. Discuss the relative advantages and disadvantages of the policies suggested in parts (d) and (e). Which is superior? How might your answer change if output demand were not inelastic or if firms competed in quantities not prices?

⋆⋆ 5. The length and breadth of patents (based on O'Donoghue, Scotchmer, and Thisse 1995)

Consider the following model, which investigates the tradeoff between the length and breadth of patents. As in the previous problem, firms' products are differentiated only by quality q, but now consumers are heterogeneous, so that more than one firm can survive in the market at once. Firms compete to sell their products in a "natural oligopoly," where only two firms can profitably produce at any one time. Denote the summed willingness to pay of consumers who buy the higher quality product in the market θ_H and that of consumers who buy the lower quality product $\theta_L > 0$. Let the sales revenue of the market leader and follower after the tth innovation be $\pi_H(\Delta_t)$ and $\pi_L(\Delta_t) > 0$ respectively. That is, suppose that as in the previous problem, profits are increasing only in the size of the market gap, and are independent of the overall level of quality; let $\pi_H(\Delta_1 + \Delta_2) = \pi_H(\Delta_1) + \pi_H(\Delta_2)$. A very large number of firms collectively are continually (and costlessly) receiving "ideas" for quality improvements, according to a Poisson process with parameter λ. Since the number of firms is large, the probability that a firm currently producing makes the next innovation is negligible. Each idea (Δ, c) is received by a single randomly chosen firm, and consists of an increment Δ to the current highest quality, and an investment cost of implementing the idea c. If an idea is not implemented, it is lost. Suppose that all ideas have the same cost of implementation, c, but that the size of the quality improvement is distributed on $[0, \Delta^{\max}]$ with distribution F. The strategy of each firm consists in choosing a minimum size Δ (the cutoff point) for ideas which it will implement.

a. Explain intuitively why in this model, unlike in the previous problem, investment can be undesirably high when there is complete lagging breadth but zero leading breadth. Why is this not the case if ideas arrive frequently?

b. Consider the patent policy (K, ∞), where the patentholder is granted leading breadth K forever.

i. Denote by S^K the addition to the profit surplus of licensors when an infringing innovation is licensed. Suppose that only infringing innovations can be licensed (the others must be marketed competitively) and that the marginal idea to be licensed is that for which $S^K = 0$. Define $\Delta^*(0, \lambda)$ as the cutoff point when there is zero leading breadth. Describe the equilibrium cutoff point $\Delta^K(K, \lambda)$ of the game for different patent widths K, where $K \in [\Delta^*, \Delta^{\max}]$. Show that moderate leading breadth can reduce growth below the level with either zero or large leading breadth.

ii. What is the average effective patent life (time until the next non-infringing innovation) under the policy (K, ∞) if the cut-off is Δ^K?

iii. Find an expression for S^K. (Hint: the profit from being a follower can be ignored here. Why?)

c. Now consider an alternative policy (∞, T), where the patentholder is granted infinite leading breadth for time T. Growth under this policy is given by:

$$\int_H \left[\int_{\Delta T}^{\Delta \max} \Delta dF \right] dG(h; T, \lambda)$$

where Δ^T is the equilibrium cut-off in the game, which depends on $G(h; T, \lambda)$, the cumulative probability distribution on H (the set of possible patenting histories h) induced by this policy.

i. Explain intuitively why the cut-off point will vary over time according to the history of innovation.

ii. Find an expression for S^T, the addition to the profit surplus of licensors when an infringing innovation is licensed under this policy. (Hint: the gross revenues contain two parts, the increment to the profit of the market leader, and the incremental licensing income that can be earned from innovations made between t and $t + T$, which you may denote $L(T, h, \lambda)$).

d.

i. Suppose again that the marginal innovation to be licensed is that for which profit surplus is zero. Using your results from (b)(ii) and (iii) and (c)(ii), show that for a given growth rate, average effective patent life is shorter under the policy (∞, T) than under for the policy (K, ∞). (Hint: you will need to use the Taylor Series Expansion $e^{-rt} \approx 1 - rt$.) Why is this so?

ii. Find an expression for social welfare gross of development costs for the policies (K, ∞) and (∞, T). Using your result from (e)(i) show that this is larger under the policy (∞, T) than under the policy (K, ∞).

e. Explain intuitively why for a given growth rate development costs will be nevertheless higher under the policy (∞, T). (Hint: A time-varying equilibrium cutoff implies a larger number of innovations to achieve the same growth rate. Why is this so?)

Chapter 1

1. Utility functions

The problem faced by agents is

$$\max \int_0^\infty u(c_t)e^{-\rho t}dt$$

subject to $\quad \dot{k}_t = f(k_t) - c_t.$

Solving this program we obtain the optimal path for consumption, as a function of the marginal product of capital, the rate of time discount and the intertemporal elasticity of substitution,

$$\frac{\dot{c}}{c} = \frac{f'(k) - \rho}{-u''(c)c/u'(c)}.$$

In the standard Ramsey-Cass-Koopmans model with zero long-run growth, the shape of the utility function was irrelevant, as the steady state was simply determined by the condition $f'(k) = \rho$. However, in the endogenous growth models with constant returns, the term $f'(k) - \rho$ will be a nonzero constant. Consequently, the intertemporal elasticity of substitution must be constant too. That is, $-u''(c)c/u'(c) = \varepsilon$. Solving this differential equation we get precisely the CES function, $(c^{1-\varepsilon} - 1)/(1 - \varepsilon)$.

⋆ 2. Convergence in the neoclassical model and the "augmented Solow" model (based on Mankiw, Romer, and Weil 1992 and the mathematical appendix in Barro and Sala-i-Martín 1995)

a. Define all the variables in terms of "efficiency units of labor," that is, $y_t = Y_t/(A_t L_t)$ and $k_t = K_t/(A_t L_t)$, so that the production function can be written as

$$y_t = k_t^{1-\alpha}. \tag{S1.1}$$

The budget constraint of the economy is then

$$\dot{k}_t - s y_t \quad (x + n + \delta)k_t. \tag{S1.2}$$

In steady state the rate of growth of k must be zero; thus we have the equilibrium stock of capital per efficiency unit of labor,

$$k^* = \left(\frac{s}{x+n+\delta}\right)^{\frac{1}{\alpha}}. \tag{S1.3}$$

The steady state level of income (in efficiency units) is then

$$y^* = \left(\frac{s}{x+n+\delta} \right)^{\frac{1-\alpha}{\alpha}}. \tag{S1.4}$$

From (S1.1), the rate of growth of output is proportional to the rate of growth of the stock of capital, $g_y = (1-\alpha)g_k$. Substituting the budget constraint into this expression and using (S1.1) and (S1.4) we find that the rate of growth of output is

$$\frac{\dot{y}_t}{y_t} = (1-\alpha)(x+n+\delta) \left(\left(\frac{y^*}{y_t} \right)^{\frac{\alpha}{1-\alpha}} - 1 \right). \tag{S1.5}$$

Equation (S1.5) implies that the farther an economy is from its steady state, the faster it will be growing.

To find the speed of convergence to the steady state we log-linearize the rate of growth. Recall that $\dot{y}_t/y_t = d(\log y_t)/dt$. Doing a Taylor's expansion around the steady-state value of $\log y$, we have

$$\frac{d \log y_t}{dt} = \left. \frac{d \log y_t}{dt} \right|_{y^*} + \left. \frac{d \left(d \log y_t/dt \right)}{d \log y_t} \right|_{y^*} \left(\log y_t - \log y^* \right).$$

The first term is zero, as income does not change in the steady state. To obtain the second term we differentiate (S1.5) with respect to $\log y_t$ and evaluate it at y^*. We then have

$$\frac{d \log y_t}{dt} = \alpha(x+n+\delta) \left(\log y^* - \log y_t \right). \tag{S1.6}$$

Hence the speed of convergence, that is, the rate at which the level of income approaches its steady state is $\phi = \alpha(x+n+\delta)$. The convergence coefficient, β, is defined as the proportional change in the growth rate caused by a change in the initial level of income. We can obtain it from equation (S1.5). The convergence coefficient is then

$$\beta = -\frac{d \left(d \log y_t/dt \right)}{d \log y_t} = \phi \left(\frac{y^*}{y_t} \right)^{\frac{\alpha}{1-\alpha}}. \tag{S1.7}$$

The differential equation (S1.6) implies $\log y_{t+T} = \left(1 - e^{-\phi T} \right) \log y^* + e^{-\phi T} \log y_t$. Hence

$$\log \frac{y_{t+T}}{y_t} = \left(1 - e^{-\phi T} \right) \log \frac{y^*}{y_t}.$$

The average growth rate between period t and $t+T$ can be obtained from the preceding equation,

$$\frac{1}{T} \log \frac{y_{t+T}}{y_t} = -\frac{1 - e^{-\phi T}}{T} \log y_t + \frac{1 - e^{-\phi T}}{T} \log y^*. \qquad (S1.8)$$

We can rewrite this expression as

$$\frac{1}{T} \log \frac{y_{t+T}}{y_t} = -\frac{1 - e^{-\phi T}}{T} \log y_t + \frac{1 - e^{-\phi T}}{T} \frac{1 - \alpha}{\alpha} \left[\log s - \log(x + n + \delta) \right],$$

which in turn can be expressed as equation (1.6) in the chapter for the purpose of empirical estimation.

b. Clearly, convergence is conditional on the steady state of the economy. Equation (S1.6) implies that poor economies grow faster than rich ones if both share the same parameters that determine the steady state. Hence, we must interpret this equation as saying that an economy grows faster the farther it is from its steady state, not as saying that it grows faster the poorer it is.

c. Again we define all the variables in terms of efficiency units of labor, so that the production function can be written as

$$y_t = k_t^\alpha h_t^\beta, \qquad (S1.9)$$

where $h_t = H_t / (A_t L_t)$, and y_t and k_t are defined as before. There are two restrictions governing the accumulation of physical and human capital,

$$\dot{k_t} = s_k y_t - (x + n + \delta) k_t \qquad (S1.10)$$

and

$$\dot{h_t} = s_h y_t - (x + n + \delta) h_t. \qquad (S1.11)$$

If we divide these two equations by k and h respectively, we see that the only possible constant growth rate occurs when there is zero growth per efficient unit of labor, as there are diminishing returns to the two cumulable factors together. Hence, we can obtain the steady-state values of physical capital, human capital and income (all expressed in efficiency units of labor). That is,

$$k^* = \left(\frac{s_k^{1-\beta} s_h^\beta}{x + n + \delta} \right)^{\frac{1}{1-\alpha-\beta}}, \quad h^* = \left(\frac{s_k^\alpha s_h^{1-\alpha}}{x + n + \delta} \right)^{\frac{1}{1-\alpha-\beta}},$$

and

$$y^* = \left(\frac{s_k^\alpha s_h^\beta}{(x + n + \delta)^{\alpha+\beta}} \right)^{\frac{1}{1-\alpha-\beta}}.$$

Because y^* is constant, output per capita must grow at the exogenous rate of technical change, just as in the neoclassical model.

Using the same method as in section (a), we find that the rate of growth of output (in efficiency units) is

$$\frac{d \log y_t}{dt} = \lambda \left(\log y^* - \log y_t \right),$$
(S1.12)

where $\lambda = (1 - \alpha - \beta)(x + n + \delta)$ is the speed of convergence. The average rate of growth between periods t and $t + T$ is then given by

$$\frac{1}{T} \log \frac{y_{t+T}}{y_t} = -\frac{1 - e^{-\lambda T}}{T} \log y_t +$$

$$\frac{1 - e^{-\lambda T}}{T} \frac{1}{1 - \alpha - \beta} \left[\alpha \log s_k + \beta \log s_h - (\alpha + \beta) \log(x + n + \delta) \right].$$

3. The AK model with an exogenous saving rate (based on Barro and Sala-i-Martín 1995)

a. We solve the model as the standard neoclassical model with a constant savings rate. The equation defining the evolution of the stock of capital per worker is

$$\dot{k} = sk^\alpha A^\eta - (n + \delta)k,$$

as all firms are identical. Substituting for the level of technology and dividing this expression by k, we get that the rate of growth of the capital stock is given by

$$\frac{\dot{k}}{k} = sA_0^\eta k^{\alpha+\eta-1} - (n + \delta).$$

We normalize the initial level of technology, $A_0 = 1$.

b. We can represent this solution graphically for the three cases. The growth rate is the distance between the term $sf(k)/k$ and the horizontal line defined by $n + \delta$. We are, thus, interested in the shape of the function $f(k)/k$. When there are diminishing returns it is decreasing and convex, when there are increasing returns it is increasing. The first case is the standard neoclassical model in which the growth rate converges to zero at a positive value of the capital stock. In figure S1.1 we can see that in the case of increasing returns, the $sf(k)/k$ function crosses the $n + \delta$ line, resulting in an unstable equilibrium with positive k. Hence, the growth rate will either explode or converge to a zero-growth/zero-capital equilibrium, depending on whether the initial value of k is such that it implies a positive or a negative growth rate (that is, whether the initial value is to the right or the left of the unstable equilibrium). Only in the case in which $\alpha + \eta$ is exactly 1 is the rate of growth constant and positive. If the sum of the coefficients differs, no matter how little, from unity, the growth rate will go to infinity or to zero. This has been termed the "knife-edge

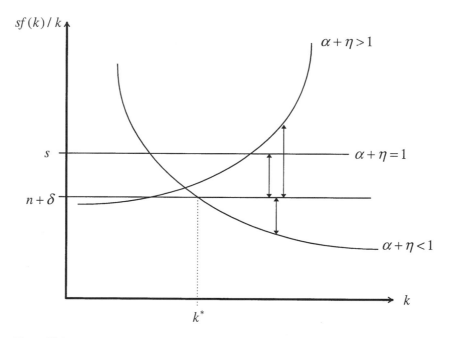

Figure S1.1
Source: Barro and Sala-i-Martín (1995), p. 23.

property" of the endogenous growth models, on the sense that the prediction of a constant long-run growth rate is not robust to small changes in parameter values

c. From the figure we can see that a higher saving rate will shift upward the curve $sf(k)/k$. For the cases of increasing and decreasing returns, the long-run growth rate will be unaffected. However, when there are constant returns, a higher s implies a faster rate of growth.

d. When there are decreasing returns, we have the standard results from the neoclassical model. As part of the capital stock is destroyed, the growth rate accelerates until the steady state value of the capital stock is reached again. The only possible steady state is again zero growth, and at this equilibrium the capital stock and income levels are exactly those in the preshock steady state. There are, thus, no long-run effects on the level of income.

When there are increasing returns, the reduction in the capital stock implies that the growth rate in the periods immediately after the shock will be reduced. If the new capital stock is to the right of the unstable equilibrium, as k increases growth accelerates and tends to infinity in the long-run, just as if there had been no shock. If the shock reduces the capital stock enough to make the growth rate negative, the growth rate would start to decrease and the economy would move toward a point where the capital stock is zero.

In the case where $\alpha + \eta = 1$, the growth rate does not change no matter what the capital stock is. Consequently, even immediately after the shock the economy grows at the steady-state rate. This implies that the loss of capital, and of income, is permanent. To see this, note that because the growth rate is constant, we can write the level of income in period t as $y_t = y_0 e^{gt}$. If there were an earthquake in period 0 that halved the capital stock, and thus y_0, the level of income t periods after the shock would be $y_t = y_0 e^{gt}/2$. That is, it would be half the income that the economy would have enjoyed had there been no shock.

Hence, one of the most important differences between models with constant returns to scale and those with increasing or decreasing returns is that it is only in the former that shocks have permanent effects.

4. Justification for the AK model: human capital

The introduction of human capital has been one of the most important ways of obtaining constant returns to an aggregate measure of capital. Note, however, that having human capital as a factor of production per se does not generate an AK type of function, as we saw in the augmented Solow model of problem 2.

a. The equations describing the accumulation of the two types of capital are

$$\dot{K} = s_k Y - \delta_k K \quad \text{and} \quad \dot{H} = s_h Y - \delta_h H. \tag{S1.13}$$

Savings can thus be invested in either of these two assets. In equilibrium, the return to both, and hence their net marginal product, must be the same. That is,

$$\alpha \left(\frac{K}{H} \right)^{1-\alpha} - \delta_h = (1 - \alpha) \left(\frac{H}{K} \right)^{\alpha} - \delta_k,$$

which yields

$$\left(\frac{K}{H} \right)^{-\alpha} \left(\frac{K}{H} - \frac{1-\alpha}{\alpha} \right) = \frac{\delta_h - \delta_k}{\alpha}. \tag{S1.14}$$

This arbitrage equation implies that the physical to human capital ratio is a constant. Denote it by κ . There may be more than one solution. In the case where both types of capital depreciate at the same rate, we get

$$\frac{K}{H} = \frac{1-\alpha}{\alpha}. \tag{S1.15}$$

Note that in this case we need a restriction on the saving rates for a balanced growth path to exist. Because the physical to human capital ratio is constant, both types of capital must grow at the same rate. That is, $\dot{K}/K = \dot{H}/H$.

Using (S1.13) and given that both types of capital depreciate at the same rate, $\dot{K}/K = \dot{H}/H$ implies $s_k/s_h = K/H$. Hence it must be that the savings rates satisfy $s_k/s_h = (1-\alpha)/\alpha$.

b. We can express the production function as $Y = (K/H)^\alpha \, K$, and substitute for the ratio of the two types of capital,

$$Y = \kappa^\alpha K. \tag{S1.16}$$

The rate of growth of output is given by

$$\frac{\dot{Y}}{Y} = \alpha \frac{\dot{H}}{H} + (1-\alpha)\frac{\dot{K}}{K},$$

which, substituting for the rates of accumulation of H and K as given by equations (S1.13) and for the physical to human capital ratio, gives us the following rate of growth:

$$\frac{\dot{Y}}{Y} = \alpha(s_k \kappa^{-\alpha} - \delta_k) + (1-\alpha)(s_h \kappa^{1-\alpha} - \delta_h).$$

The rate of growth is thus constant and depends on model parameters, such as the saving rates and the depreciation rates. The difference with the augmented Solow model is that in that setup there were decreasing returns to a combined measure of capital that included human and physical capital. As a result, there were diminishing returns to the accumulation of factors and the growth rate tended to zero. Conversley, the model we have just seen exhibits constant returns to all cumulable factors.

5. Justification for the AK model: government expenditure (based on Barro 1990)

a. Individuals face the following problem

$$\max_{c_t} \int_0^\infty \frac{c_t^{1-\varepsilon} - 1}{1-\varepsilon} e^{-\rho t} dt \tag{S1.17}$$

s.t. $\dot{k}_t = (1-\tau)A k_t^{1-\alpha} \gamma_t^\alpha - c_t.$

Optimizing, we obtain that the Euler equation for consumption is

$$\frac{\dot{c}}{c} = \frac{(1-\tau)A(1-\alpha)(\gamma/k)^\alpha - \rho}{\varepsilon}. \tag{S1.18}$$

(The time subscripts have been suppressed for notational simplicity.) We can find the ratio of government expenditure to private capital expenditure from the government's budget constraint. The budget constraint simply requires that per worker expenditure be equal to per worker revenue. That is,

$$\gamma = \tau y = \tau A k^{1-\alpha} \gamma^{\alpha}.$$

Hence

$$\frac{\gamma}{k} = A^{1/(1-\alpha)} \tau^{1/(1-\alpha)}. \tag{S1.19}$$

Substituting (S1.19) in equation (S1.18), we obtain the growth rate as a function of model parameters and policy variables only,

$$g = \frac{\dot{c}}{c} = \frac{(1-\alpha)A^{\frac{1}{1-\alpha}}(1-\tau)\tau^{\frac{\alpha}{1-\alpha}} - \rho}{\varepsilon}. \tag{S1.20}$$

The steady state growth rate is thus constant.

b. To obtain the total impact of capital accumulation on the level of output, we simply substitute the government budget constraint as expressed in equation (S1.19) in the production function, $y = Ak(\gamma/k)^{\alpha}$, to get

$$y = A^{1/(1-\alpha)} \tau^{\alpha/(1-\alpha)} k. \tag{S1.21}$$

We thus have an AK function.

c. The growth rate, as expressed by equation (S1.20), is a concave function of the tax rate. Concavity is due to two opposing effects. On the one hand, a higher tax rate reduces the post-tax return to capital. This in turn reduces the incentives to save, and consequently the accumulation of capital (as seen in equation (S1.18)). On the other, a higher tax rate permits the provision of more of the public good, thus increasing the productivity of private investment, and hence inducing more capital accumulation.

Maximizing g as given by (S1.20) with respect to τ, we get that the highest growth rate is obtained when the government sets $\tau = \alpha$. If there were no taxation, there would be no provision of the public good, and hence no production is possible (think of a country without roads!). If the tax rate were one, all the returns to savings would be appropriated by the state, and there would be no incentive to save and hence no private capital. Again, nothing could be produced. Moreover, note that at very high or very low tax rates, the growth rate could be negative.

d. The competitive equilibrium will not achieve the social optimum if there is an externality of some sort. In this setup, the external effects stem from the fact that by investing in capital, an agent also increases tax revenue and therefore the amount of the public good that can be financed. This in turn raises the productivity of all inputs in the economy. Competitive agents ignore such effect, and hence underinvest in capital.

Formally, a social planner faces the following problem:

$$\max_{c_t} \int_0^\infty \frac{c_t^{1-\varepsilon} - 1}{1-\varepsilon} e^{-\rho t} dt \tag{S1.22}$$

s.t. $\dot{k}_t = (1-\tau)A^{1/(1-\alpha)}\tau^{\alpha/(1-\alpha)}k_t - c_t$.

That is, she maximizes the discounted sum of utility subject to the social constraint, which takes into account the fact that public expenditure is a function of the capital stock. Solving this problem, we find that the planner chooses a faster rate of growth of consumption,

$$g = \frac{A^{\frac{1}{1-\alpha}}(1-\tau)\tau^{\frac{\alpha}{1-\alpha}} - \rho}{\varepsilon}. \tag{S1.23}$$

Hence, the competitive equilibrium is not socially optimal. Note, however, that the tax rate that maximizes growth in a planned economy is precisely the one that would maximize growth in the competitive economy.

6. The Cass-Koopmans-Ramsey model: the golden rule and dynamic inefficiency

a. From the chapter we know that the dynamic equations of the competitive economy are

$$\frac{\dot{c}_t}{c_t} = \frac{f'(k_t) - \rho - \delta}{\varepsilon},$$

$$\dot{k}_t = f(k_t) - c_t - (\delta + n)k_t.$$

We can represent the $\dot{c}$- and the $\dot{k}$-schedules in the (c, k)-space. The $\dot{k} = 0$ schedule has an inverted-U shape. It is initially increasing, when k is small and the marginal product of capital large, and becomes decreasing as the marginal product of capital falls. The $\dot{c} = 0$ schedule is a vertical line. As we saw in the chapter, the steady-state capital stock is then given by the so-called modified golden rule, $f'(k^*) = \rho + \delta$, that is, $k^* = (\alpha/(\rho + \delta))^{1/(1-\alpha)}$.

b. The golden rule of capital accumulation maximizes consumption when $\dot{k}_t = 0$. From the budget constraint, this means that it is given by the solution to

$$\max_k c = f(k) - (\delta + n)k.$$

Hence, the golden rule is $f'(k^{GR}) = \delta + n$, which implies $k^{GR} = (\alpha/(n + \delta))^{1/(1-\alpha)}$. We can see in figure S1.2 that this is the maximum of the $\dot{k}$-schedule.

c. All those points to the left of k^{GR} are dynamically efficient. An increase in steady-state consumption requires more capital and hence a temporary

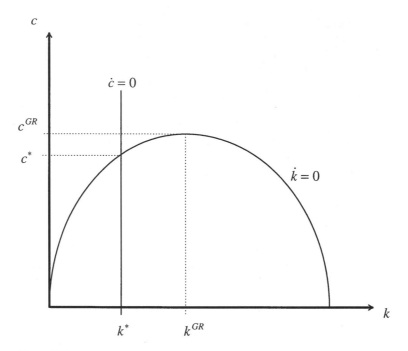

$\dot{c} = 0$

c^{GR}

c^*

$\dot{k} = 0$

k^* k^{GR}

k

c

Figure S1.2

reduction in consumption, thus there is no possible change in the stock of capital that would be a Pareto improvement. Those points to the right of k^{GR} are dynamically inefficient, as an *increase* in consumption would reduce the capital stock and result in higher steady consumption, thus increasing utility both in the steady state and during the transition. Because $\rho > n$, then $f'(k^*) > f'(k^{GR})$, which implies that the stock of capital in the competitive economy is below that associated with the golden rule, $k^* < k^{GR}$. Thus the economy can never be dynamically inefficient.

★★ **7. Dynamic inefficiency and fiscal policy in the neoclassical versus the AK models (based on Blanchard 1985, Saint-Paul 1992, and Barro and Sala-i-Martín 1995)**

a. Maximizing (1.40) subject to (1.41), we obtain that the dynamic equation for consumption in the competitive economy is

$$\frac{\dot{c}(t)}{c(t)} = r - \rho. \tag{S1.24}$$

(the probability p has canceled out as it affects equally the rate of return and the rate of time preference).

The transversality condition is now

$$\lim_{t\to\infty} \left[e^{-(r+p)(t-s)} \cdot w(t,s) \right] = 0. \tag{S1.25}$$

Equations (1.41) and (S1.25) imply that the agent's lifetime budget constraint is

$$\int_s^\infty c(t,s) e^{-(p+r)(t-s)} dt = w(s,s) + h(s,s), \tag{S1.26}$$

where $h(t,s) = \int_t^\infty (\beta + p)\omega(v) e^{-\beta(v-s)} e^{-(p+r)(v-t)} dv$ is the present value of labor income or human wealth at time t of an individual born at s. We can now use (S1.24) and (S1.26) to determine consumption as a function of human and financial wealth,

$$c(t,s) = (\rho + p)(w(t,s) + h(t,s)), \tag{S1.27}$$

which implies a constant marginal propensity to consume out of wealth.

b. The aggregate magnitudes are obtained by adding across cohorts, where each cohort is given a weight corresponding to its size. Then aggregate consumption and wealth are

$$C(t) = \int_{-\infty}^t c(t,s) \cdot e^{-p(t-s)} ds, \tag{S1.28}$$

$$W(t) = \int_{-\infty}^t w(t,s) \cdot e^{-p(t-s)} ds, \tag{S1.29}$$

and the aggregate present value of wages is

$$H(t) = \int_{-\infty}^t \left[\int_t^\infty (\beta + p)\omega(v) e^{-\beta(v-s)} e^{-(p+r)(v-t)} dv \right] \cdot e^{-p(t-s)} ds$$

$$= \int_t^\infty \omega(v) \cdot e^{-(p+r+\beta)(v-t)} dv. \tag{S1.30}$$

The aggregate consumption function can be obtained from equations (S1.27) and (S1.28)–(S1.30) as

$$C(t) = (\rho + p)(H(t) + W(t)). \tag{S1.31}$$

Equation (S1.31) then implies that the rate of growth of aggregate consumption depends on the change in both aggregate labor income and aggregate wealth. Differentiating (S1.29) with respect to time, we have

$$\dot{W}(t) = w(t,t) - pW(t) + \int_{-\infty}^t \dot{w}(t,s) \cdot e^{-p(t-s)} ds, \tag{S1.32}$$

where the first term is the wealth of the newly born, the second the wealth of those who die, and the third the change in wealth of those alive. Using (1.41) to substitute for the last term in (S1.32), we get

$$\dot{W}(t) = rW(t) + \omega(t) - C(t). \tag{S1.33}$$

Individual wealth accumulates at a rate $(r + p)$, but aggregate wealth accumulates at a rate r, the reason being that the amount pW received by individuals is a net transfer from those who die to those that stay alive. Similarly, human wealth accumulates according to

$$\dot{H}(t) = (r + p + \beta)H(t) - \omega(t). \tag{S1.34}$$

Aggregate consumption is then characterized by equations (S1.31), (S1.33) and (S1.34). Differentiating (S1.31) and substituting for $\dot{H}$ and $\dot{W}$, we have

$$\dot{C}(t) = (r + \beta - \rho)C(t) - (p + \beta)(p + \rho)W(t). \tag{S1.35}$$

The dynamic equations describing the behavior of the economy are thus (S1.33) and (S1.35). If agents have finite horizons, $p = 0$, and labor endowments are constant, $\beta = 0$, the system reduces to the Cass-Koopmans-Ramsey setup examined in the chapter, in which both individual and aggregate consumption are constant when $r = \rho$. In this model, if $r = \rho$ individual consumption would be constant, but aggregate consumption would in general vary.

c.

i. The dynamic equations are

$$\dot{C}/C = r(K) - (\rho - \beta) - (p + \beta)(p + \rho)K/C, \tag{S1.36}$$

$$\dot{K} = F(K) - \delta K - C, \tag{S1.37}$$

where the interest rate is equal to the net marginal product of capital, $r(K) = F'(K) - \delta$.

You can represent these two equations graphically on the (C, K)-space just as we did in figure S1.2. The $\dot{K}$-schedule has the same inverted-U shape as in figure S1.2. However, the $\dot{C}$-schedule is no longer a vertical line, in as much as now aggregate steady-state consumption increases with the capital stock, as

$$C = \frac{(p + \beta)(p + \rho)}{r(K) - (\rho - \beta)} K. \tag{S1.38}$$

The $\dot{C}$-schedule is increasing, goes through the origin, is convex and has an asymptote at $\hat{K}$, where $r\left(\hat{K}\right) = \rho - \beta$. There is a unique steady state, (K^*, C^*), determined by the intersection of the $\dot{K}$- and the $\dot{C}$-schedules, and this equilibrium is saddle-path stable.

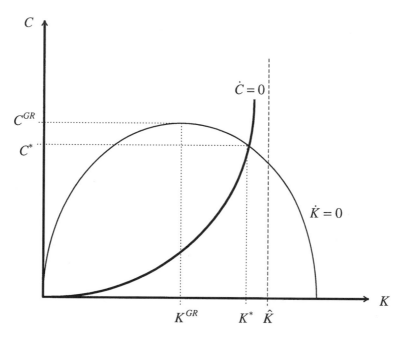

Figure S1.3
Source: Blanchard (1985), p. 237.

ii. To find the golden rule stock of capital we simply maximize $C = F(K) - \delta K$ with respect to K, to get $F'(K^{GR}) = \delta$.

iii. Suppose $r(K^*) = r^* > p + \rho$. Then, $(r^* - \rho + \beta)C^* > (p + \beta)C^*$. From (S1.36) and $\dot{C} = 0$, $(r^* - \rho + \beta)C^* = (p + \beta)(p + \rho)K^*$, and hence $(p + \rho)K^* > C^*$. From (S1.37) and $\dot{K} = 0$, we have $C^* = F(K^*) - \delta K^*$. Thus $(p + \rho + \delta)K^* > F(K^*)$, which implies $r^* + \delta > F(K^*)/K^*$, which is not possible as $F'(K) = \alpha K^{\alpha-1} < K^{\alpha-1} = F(K)/K$. This result, together with the fact that the $\dot{C}$-schedule has an asymptote, implies that the equilibrium marginal product of capital lies in the interval $[\delta + \rho - \beta, \delta + \rho + p]$.

We can see in two ways that the economy can exhibit dynamic inefficiency. If $\rho < \beta$, the equilibrium interest rate could be smaller than the golden rule $F'(K^{GR}) = \delta$, hence the equilibrium stock of capital could be to the right of K^{GR} and the economy could be dynamically inefficient. Alternatively, we can ask whether the necessary and sufficient condition, $F'(K) - \delta > g$, holds. Note that if $\rho < \beta$, the interest rate could be negative and hence lower than the rate of growth, $g = 0$. Saving in order to provide for old-age consumption can result in the overaccumulation of capital.

iv. The overaccumulation of capital implies that all agents can be better off if the capital stock per worker is reduced. The social security system does precisely that. A lower $\bar{\beta}$ shifts the $\dot{C}$-schedule upward (as can be seen differentiating equation (S1.38) and using the fact that $r^* < (p + \rho)$, which implies a lower equilibrium capital stock (draw it and check for yourself). Hence it is less likely that the economy is dynamically inefficient. If labor endowments were constant over the lifetime of individuals, $\bar{\beta} = 0$, the equilibrium marginal product of capital would lie in the interval $[\delta + \rho, \delta + \rho + p]$. Because the lower bound implies that the equilibrium marginal product of capital is greater than the golden rule, $F'(K^{GR}) = \delta < \delta + \rho$, the equilibrium capital stock would be below the golden rule and the economy would not be dynamically inefficient.

v. When the government holds a balanced budget, the dynamic equations of the economy are

$$\dot{C} = (r(K) - (\rho - \beta))C - (p + \beta)(p + \rho)K,$$

$$\dot{K} = F(K) - \delta K - G - C.$$

The tax rate on labor income has no effect on any decisions, in as much as individuals take their labor income as given. Hence increasing the tax rate has no effect on the equilibrium capital stock. When the government issues debt, financial wealth can be held in either of two assets, physical capital or government debt. Then

$$\dot{C} = (r(K) - (\rho - \beta))C - (p + \beta)(p + \rho)(D + K),$$

$$\dot{K} = F(K) - \delta K - G - C,$$

$$\dot{D} = r(K)D + G - T,$$

where T denotes aggregate tax revenue, $T = \tau \omega$.

We can draw a graph on the (C, K)-space similar to figure S1.3. Note that in the steady state $\dot{D} = 0$. The interest rate (and the capital stock) are therefore determined by the dynamic equations for consumption and physical capital, whereas the government dynamic budget constraint determines the tax rate. The $\dot{K}$-schedule has the standard inverted-U shape, and is the same before and after debt was introduced. The $\dot{C}$-schedule is upward-sloping. Moreover, given its initial position for $D = 0$, issuing debt shifts it to the left, hence reducing the equilibrium capital stock. If the economy was initially to the left of the golden rule, this reduction in K^* implies higher consumption for current generations (while K is falling) but lower consumption for future ones (as the steady-state level of consumption is lower). However, if the economy was initially dynamically inefficient, issuing debt implies higher consumption for both current generations (while K is falling) and for future ones, as a lower stock of capital permits higher steady state consumption. It is therefore Pareto efficient.

d.

i. With an AK production function, the interest rate is $r_t = \alpha A_t K_t^{1-\alpha} \quad \delta$, which substituting for A_t implies $r = \alpha A - \delta$. That is, the rate of interest is constant and the economy will therefore grow at a positive rate. The dynamic equations can now be expressed as

$$\frac{\dot{C}}{C} = (\alpha A - (\delta + \rho - \beta)) - (p + \beta)(p + \rho)\frac{K}{C}, \tag{S1.39}$$

$$\frac{\dot{K}}{K} = A - \delta - \frac{C}{K}. \tag{S1.40}$$

In steady state all variables, except the interest rate, must grow at the same rate, g. From (S1.40) we have $g = A - \delta - C/K$. Equation (S1.31) implies that consumption is $C = (p + \rho)(H + K)$. Equation (S1.34) gives $\omega/H = (r + p + \beta - g)$, which together with the fact that the wage rate is $\omega = (1 - \alpha)AK$ yields $H/K = (1 - \alpha)A/(r + p + \beta - g)$. Substituting these two expressions into (S1.40), we get that the equilibrium growth rate is given by the solution to

$$g = A - \delta - (p + \rho)\left(1 + \frac{(1 - \alpha)A}{r + p + \beta - g}\right). \tag{S1.41}$$

ii. In this case the marginal product of capital is $F'(K) = A$; that is, the relevant rate in order to establish the efficiency of the economy is the social interest rate. Because both consumption and the capital stock are positive, equation (S1.40) implies that the growth rate is less than the net social marginal product of capital, $g < A - \delta$, implying that the economy cannot exhibit dynamic inefficiency. Why is this so? Dynamic inefficiency in the standard neoclassical model stems from the fact that when the stock of capital is large, and therefore has a low productivity, the cost in terms of forgone consumption of replacing the capital that depreciates is actually larger than the amount produced by that capital. Clearly, if there are constant returns to capital this would not occurs as all units of machinery are equally productive (as long as $A > \delta$).

iii. Because there is no dynamic inefficiency, a social security system will not generate the Pareto improvement that occurred in the neoclassical model. Moreover, such a system has a negative effect on the growth rate, as the benefits in old age discourage capital accumulation. To see this note, that the growth rate is now given by equation (S1.41) but with $\bar{\beta}$ instead of β. The tax has no impact because since $(1 - \tau) = (p + \bar{\beta})/(p + \beta)$, aggregate net earnings are equal to the gross wage bill. That is,

$$\int_{-\infty}^{t} (1 - \tau)\omega(t)(p + \beta)e^{-\bar{\beta}(t-s)}e^{-p(t-s)}ds = \omega(t).$$

Then $dg/d\bar{\beta} > 0$, which implies that the social security system reduces the growth rate.

iv. When the government issues debt, we have

$$\dot{C} = (\alpha A - (\delta + \rho - \beta))C - (p + \beta)(p + \rho)(D + K),$$

$$\dot{K} = A - \delta - G - C,$$

$$\dot{D} = (\alpha A - \delta)D + G - T.$$

The steady state growth rate can then be expressed as

$$g = A - \delta - (p + \rho)\left(1 + \Delta A + \frac{(1 - \alpha)(1 - \tau)A}{r + p + \beta - g}\right),$$

where Δ is the (constant) ratio of government debt to aggregate income, $D/(AK)$. In steady state, debt and government expenditure also grow at rate g. Hence the dynamic government budget constraint implies $\tau = ((r - g)\Delta + \gamma)/(1 - \alpha)$, where γ is the (constant) ratio of government expenditure to aggregate income, $G/(AK)$. Substituting for τ in our expression for the growth rate, we have

$$g = A - \delta - (p + \rho)\left(1 + \frac{(1 - \alpha) + (p + \beta)\Delta - \gamma}{r + p + \beta - g}A\right). \tag{S1.42}$$

Assume that $\Delta > -(1 - \alpha)/(p + \beta)$; that is, the government does not hold financial assets whose value is greater than the human wealth of current generations. Then the derivative of the growth rate with respect to the debt ratio can be shown to be negative. That is, the introduction of public debt reduces the growth rate.

Now suppose that the economy is initially in a steady state with a positive debt ratio. From equation (S1.42), a reduction in the debt ratio increases the rate of growth, and this will benefit future generations. However, current generations would be harmed. The reason is that as long as the interest rate is unaffected by the policy (which is our case, as the technology is AK), the welfare of a generation depends only on their permanent income. A higher permanent income would in turn imply higher consumption. But for the growth rate to increase, current generations must reduce their consumption. Hence their permanent income cannot be higher. Overall, no change in the government debt ratio can result in a Pareto improvement when the technology is AK. (See Caballé 1995 for an analysis of dynamic inefficiency in an overlapping-generations endogenous growth model.)

⋆ **8. Welfare analysis when there is product diversity (based on Romer 1990a)**

The problem faced by the social planner is

$$\max_{C} \int_0^\infty \frac{C^{1-\varepsilon} - 1}{1 - \varepsilon} e^{-\rho t} dt$$

subject to

$$\dot{K} = K^\alpha A^{1-\alpha} L_1^{1-\alpha} - C \tag{S1.43}$$

$$\dot{A} = \delta A L_2 \tag{S1.44}$$

$$L \geq L_1 + L_2. \tag{S1.45}$$

The Hamiltonian of this problem is

$$H(C, L_2, K, A, t, \lambda, \mu) = \frac{C^{1-\varepsilon} - 1}{1 - \varepsilon} e^{-\rho t} + \mu \delta A L_2$$

$$+ \lambda \left(K^\alpha A^{1-\alpha} (L - L_2)^{1-\alpha} - C \right),$$

which implies the following first-order conditions:

$$\frac{\partial H}{\partial C} = 0 \Rightarrow C^{-\varepsilon} e^{-\rho t} = \lambda \tag{S1.46}$$

$$\frac{\partial H}{\partial L_2} = 0 \Rightarrow \lambda (1 - \alpha) \frac{\Delta}{L - L_2} = \mu \delta A \tag{S1.47}$$

$$\frac{\partial H}{\partial K} = -\dot{\lambda} \Rightarrow -\dot{\lambda} = \lambda \alpha \frac{\Delta}{K} \tag{S1.48}$$

$$\frac{\partial H}{\partial A} = -\dot{\mu} \Rightarrow -\dot{\mu} = \lambda (1 - \alpha) \frac{\Delta}{A} + \mu \delta L_2, \tag{S1.49}$$

where $\Delta \equiv A^{1-\alpha} (L - L_2)^{1-\alpha} K^\alpha$. We can rewrite (S1.47) as

$$\frac{\lambda}{\mu} = \frac{\delta}{1 - \alpha} \frac{A^\alpha (L - L_2)^\alpha}{K^\alpha},$$

and take logs and differentiate to get

$$\frac{\dot{\lambda}}{\lambda} - \frac{\dot{\mu}}{\mu} = \alpha \frac{\dot{A}}{A} - \alpha \frac{\dot{K}}{K}. \tag{S1.50}$$

Because K and A grow at the same rate (as $K = xA$), equation (S1.50) implies that

$$\frac{\dot{\lambda}}{\lambda} = \frac{\dot{\mu}}{\mu}. \tag{S1.51}$$

From equation (S1.46) we have the dynamic equation for the shadow price of capital

$$\frac{\dot{\lambda}}{\lambda} = -\rho - \varepsilon \frac{\dot{C}}{C}. \tag{S1.52}$$

In the steady state, consumption must grow at the same rate as the level of technology, A. Thus, substituting for equation (S1.44) in the preceding expression, we have

$$\frac{\dot{\lambda}}{\lambda} = -\rho - \varepsilon \delta L_2. \tag{S1.53}$$

From (S1.49) we get the dynamic equation for the shadow value of designs

$$-\frac{\dot{\mu}}{\mu} = \delta L_2 + \frac{\lambda}{\mu}(1 - \alpha)\frac{\Delta}{A},$$

where we can substitute equation (S1.47) to obtain

$$-\frac{\dot{\mu}}{\mu} = \delta L. \tag{S1.54}$$

Last, using (S1.51), (S1.53) and (S1.54) we get the optimal level of employment in the research sector,

$$L_2^{**} = \frac{\delta L - \rho}{\delta \varepsilon}, \tag{S1.55}$$

and the rate of growth

$$g^{**} = \frac{\delta L - \rho}{\varepsilon}. \tag{S1.56}$$

Recall from the text that the level of employment in the research sector and the growth rate in the competitive economy are

$$L_2^* = \frac{\delta L - \rho/\alpha}{\delta(1 + \varepsilon/\alpha)} \quad \text{and} \quad g^* = \frac{\delta L - \rho/\alpha}{1 + \varepsilon/\alpha},$$

which clearly are smaller than L_2^{**} and g^{**}. That is, the social planner chooses a higher level of employment in the research sector than the competitive economy. There are two sources of market failure that give rise to this divergence. First, there is the fact that the intermediate-goods sector is monopolistic. The term $1/\alpha$ is precisely the monopoly markup, and it is absent from L_2^{**} and g^{**}. The planner would choose to produce more units of each type of capital good than the monopolist, and hence the value of the design would be greater. This induces a higher level of employment in research. Second, there is the intertemporal spillover effect. The competitive economy discounts more heavily, as captured by the one in the denominator, because it does not take into account the fact that a new design increases the productivity of all future researchers. Because knowledge spillovers are not appropriable, private firms will not internalize this effect of their research, and hence invest a suboptimal amount.

⋆ **9. The role of the linear R&D function (based on Jones 1995)**

a. The equation for the rate of growth of the stock of knowledge is

$$\frac{\dot{A}}{A} = \delta \frac{L_2^{\lambda-1}}{A^{1-\phi}} L_2. \tag{S1.57}$$

In steady state, the rate of growth of designs is constant. Hence, if we take logs and differentiate equation (S1.57) with respect to time, we obtain that the steady-state rate of growth of the stock of designs is

$$g \equiv \frac{\dot{A}}{A} = \frac{\lambda}{1-\phi} \frac{\dot{L_2}}{L_2}. \tag{S1.58}$$

We can now proceed as usual. As in the chapter, we have that the level of x is such that

$$r = \alpha^2 \left(\frac{L_1}{x}\right)^{1-\alpha}, \tag{S1.59}$$

and the value of the patent is

$$P_A = \frac{1-\alpha}{\alpha} x. \tag{S1.60}$$

What changes is the labor-market equilibrium equation, which, from the production function and equation (S1.57) (taking the productivity of researchers as given), yields

$$\delta L_2^{\lambda-1} A^\phi P_A = (1-\alpha) L_1^{-\alpha} x^\alpha A. \tag{S1.61}$$

We rearrange equation (S1.61) and substitute into it (S1.59) and (S1.60), to get

$$\frac{L_1}{L_2} = \frac{r}{\alpha} \frac{1}{\delta L_2^\lambda A^{\phi-1}}, \tag{S1.62}$$

and, using (S1.57),

$$\frac{L_1}{L_2} = \frac{r}{\alpha} \frac{1}{g}. \tag{S1.63}$$

Because in steady state the interest rate and the growth rate are constant, this expression implies that a constant proportion, s, of the labor force is employed the research sector. That is,

$$\frac{L_2}{L} = s, \quad \text{where } s = \frac{1}{1+\varphi} \text{ and } \varphi = \frac{r}{\alpha}\frac{1}{g}.$$

Research employment is proportional to the stock of labor; therefore it must grow at the same rate as the population. Hence, from equation (S1.58) we have that the growth rate of the stock of designs is

$$g = \frac{\lambda n}{1 - \phi}. \tag{S1.64}$$

This expression pins down all growth rates in the model. It is straightforward to show that the steady-state growth rates of per capita consumption, per capita income, and per capita capital must be equal to g.

To obtain the value of φ, we use the Ramsey-Cass-Koopmans equation for the rate of growth of consumption, $\dot{c}/c = (r - \rho)/\varepsilon$ and substitute for the growth rate as defined by equation (S1.64). Then

$$\varphi = \frac{1}{\alpha}\left(\varepsilon + (1 - \phi)\frac{\rho}{\lambda n}\right). \tag{S1.65}$$

b. Let us examine (S1.64), which tells us what the steady-state growth rate is. First of all, note that when $\phi = 1$, as in the Romer model, no balanced growth path exists because the population is growing. This is solved by assuming that $\phi < 1$. Second, note that the scale effects have disappeared, and that the growth rate depends on the *rate of growth* of the labor force, instead of on its *level*. The implications of the Romer (and other) growth models that tax policy, and in particular R&D subsidies, or the level of education of the labor force can affect the growth rate have now disappeared. The rate of growth of the stock of designs is determined by the rate of population growth, and the degree of spillovers and duplication in the research process. Equation (S1.65) tells us that the share of labor devoted to R&D depends on various model parameters, but the difference is that causality now runs from the growth rate, as determined by n, to R&D, and not vice versa.

On this sense what we have is what Jones calls a "semi-endogenous" growth model. There is a research sector that generates new designs, and on this sense the rate of technological change is endogenously determined within the model. However, what determines the rate of technical change are parameters that are generally viewed as invariant to government policy decisions.

c. The problem faced by the social planner is

$$\max_{C} \int_0^\infty \frac{C^{1-\varepsilon} - 1}{1 - \varepsilon} e^{-\rho t} dt$$

subject to

$$\dot{K} = K^\alpha A^{1-\alpha} L_1^{1-\alpha} - C$$

$$\dot{A} = \delta A^\phi L_2^\lambda$$

$$L \geq L_1 + L_2$$

Setting up the Hamiltonian and optimizing (see problem 8) we obtain that the rates of growth of income, consumption and capital are all equal to the rate of growth of the stock of designs, as given by equation (S1.64). This means that the social planner chooses the same rate of growth as the competitive economy, despite the presence of externalities. However, the proportion of the labor force engaged in research differs in the two cases due to the presence of imperfect competition and the intertemporal spillover effect. (Check for yourselves that the social planner would choose a constant L_2/L.)

The absence of monopoly implies that the term $1/\alpha$ representing the monopoly markup disappears from the expression determining the share of labor devoted to research. A second difference is that the planner would take into account the effect of duplication, and hence the labor-market equilibrium equation is

$$\lambda \delta L_2^{\lambda-1} A^\phi V_A = (1 - \alpha) L_1^{-\alpha} x^\alpha A, \tag{S1.66}$$

where V_A is the value of the innovation. The socially optimum x is determined at the point where marginal benefit is equal to marginal cost. That is, it is given by the expression

$$r = \alpha L_1^{1-\alpha} x^{\alpha-1}.$$

The value of the innovation is then $V_A = L_1^{1-\alpha} x^\alpha / r - x = (1 - \alpha) L_1^{1-\alpha} x^\alpha$. Substituting for the value of the innovation in equation (S1.66), we have that the level of employment in research is

$$\frac{L_2}{L} = \frac{1}{1 + \varphi^{**}},$$

where

$$\varphi^{**} = \frac{1}{\lambda} \left(\varepsilon + (1 - \phi) \frac{\rho}{\lambda n} - \phi \right). \tag{S1.67}$$

The steady-state share of labor devoted to R&D differs from the competitive outcome for three reasons: the monopoly markup term disappears, the intertemporal spillover effect is internalized, and the effect of duplication that led the competitive economy to overinvest in research is taken into account (as represented by the term $1/\lambda$). The first two effects imply that there is too little research employment in a competitive economy, the third that too much is undertaken. Either effect can in principle dominate.

Chapter 2

1. Innovation by the leader (based on Barro and Sala-i-Martín 1995)

a. The monopolist employs n workers in research. Thus, her objective function is

$$\max_{n} \lambda n_t V_{t+1} - w_t n_t,$$

which yields the same arbitrage equation we had in the text.

The discounted expected payoff to the $(t+1)^{th}$ innovation differs from the one when there are many innovators for two reasons. First, the monopolist subtracts the rents that she was obtaining from the previous innovation, and only values the *increase* in profits. Second, she takes into account the fact that the discovery brings about the possibility of moving up the quality ladder and discover quality $(t+2)^{th}$. Hence, the asset equation is

$$r V_{t+1} = \pi_{t+1} - \pi_t - \lambda n_{t+1} V_{t+1} + \lambda n_{t+1} V_{t+2}.$$

The monopoly profit is exactly as derived before, that is, $\pi_t = (1-\alpha)\omega x A_t/\alpha$. The expected discounted payoff to the $(t+2)^{th}$ innovation is simply γV_{t+1}, because (in steady state) the economy reproduces itself after each innovation, except that all costs and payoffs are increased by a factor of γ. Substituting for π_{t+1} and V_{t+2}, we can express V_{t+1} as

$$V_{t+1} = \frac{1-\alpha}{\alpha} \frac{(\gamma-1)\omega x A_t}{r - \lambda n_{t+1}(\gamma-1)}.$$

Using the arbitrage equation and the fact that $x = L - n$, we get that the equation defining the steady-state level of research is

$$1 = \frac{1-\alpha}{\alpha} \frac{\lambda(\gamma-1)(L-n)}{r - \lambda n(\gamma-1)}.$$

Recall from the text that the equilibrium conditions for the competitive economy and for the planned economy were, respectively,

$$1 = \frac{1-\alpha}{\alpha} \frac{\lambda\gamma(L-\hat{n})}{r + \lambda\hat{n}} \quad \text{and} \quad 1 = \frac{1}{\alpha} \frac{\lambda(\gamma-1)(L-n^*)}{r - \lambda n^*(\gamma-1)}.$$

Clearly, the n chosen by a monopolist with no competition in research is somewhere in between that of the laissez-faire and the planned economy. The monopolist can only appropriate part of the (static) consumer surplus, thus she will value the innovation less than the planner does and consequently employs fewer researchers. This is reflected by the term $(1 - \alpha)$ in the numerator. The monopolist's behavior mimics that of the planner in two aspects. First, she takes into account creative destruction, in as much as it is her own rents from the tth innovation that are destroyed when the next vintage is discovered. Second, because the monopoly is permanent, the incumbent internalizes the intertemporal externality, in as much as finding a new quality gives her the possibility of discovering the next one up the quality ladder. These effects are captured by the term $(\gamma - 1)$ in the numerator and the denominator, respectively.

b. The expected benefit accruing from a research project is $\lambda z V_{t+1}$, where z is the number of researchers employed by a firm and V_{t+1} is the value of the innovation to an outside firm (i.e., any firm but the incumbent monopolist). The arbitrage equation is thus

$$w_t = \lambda V_{t+1}.$$

The incumbent takes into account that her own rents are being destroyed. The value of discovering the next quality is $V_{t+1} - V_t = (1 - 1/\gamma)V_{t+1}$, which is less than V_{t+1}. If $\lambda_l = \lambda$, the expected payoff of the innovation, $\lambda \frac{\gamma-1}{\gamma} V_{t+1}$, is less than the wage, $w_t = \lambda V_{t+1}$. Hence, if the incumbent had the same probability of success as all other firms, she would not invest in R&D.

Now suppose that the incumbent has a greater probability of success. The incumbent takes the amount of research done by other firms, and hence the competitive wage, as given. In order to assess whether or not she will engage in research, we compare the marginal product of researchers working for the incumbent, $\lambda_l \frac{\gamma-1}{\gamma} V_{t+1}$ to the wage, $w_t = \lambda V_{t+1}$. The incumbent monopolist invests in R&D if and only if

$$\lambda_l \frac{\gamma - 1}{\gamma} \geq \lambda,$$

that is, if her probability of success is sufficiently larger than that of outsiders. Note that the greater γ (the larger the increase in profits), the more likely it is that the incumbent does research for any given difference in the Poisson probabilities, λ_l/λ. The intuition for this result is that a larger γ implies a larger gain for any given loss of profits; hence the current monopolist is more willing to do research.

2. Welfare and patent auctions (based on Kremer 1996)

a. Recall from the text that in a competitive economy the private value of an innovation (in steady state) is given by

$$V_{t+1}^P(n_{t+1}) = (1 - \alpha) \frac{\alpha(L - n_{t+1})^\alpha}{r + \lambda n_{t+1}} \gamma A_t, \tag{S2.1}$$

where n_{t+1} is the level of employment the period during which the innovation is being used. Recall that the monopolist chooses to produce an amount $x_t = (\alpha^2/\omega_t)^{1/(1-\alpha)}$, hence the productivity-adjusted wage at time t is $\omega_t = \alpha^2 x_t^{-(1-\alpha)}$. The equilibrium condition determining the aggregate amount of research undertaken at period t is then

$$(L - n_t)^{-(1-\alpha)} = \gamma\lambda\frac{1-\alpha}{\alpha}\frac{(L - n_{t+1})^\alpha}{r + \lambda n_{t+1}}. \tag{S2.2}$$

The resulting steady state is

$$1 = \gamma\lambda\frac{1-\alpha}{\alpha}\frac{L - \hat{n}}{r + \lambda\hat{n}}. \tag{S2.3}$$

For the social planner, the choice of the amount of each intermediate good produced is a static problem that can be determined from the inverse demand for intermediate goods, $p_t = \alpha\, A_t\, x^{\alpha-1}$. Allocative efficiency requires marginal cost pricing. Since producing a unit of the intermediate good requires one unit of labor, the unit cost is the wage rate. Then we have $x_t = (\alpha/\omega_t)^{\frac{1}{1-\alpha}}$. The resulting net benefit from an innovation, or "profits", to the planner is $\pi_t = A_t x_t^\alpha - x_t w_t$, which given the amount of each intermediary produced yields $\pi_t = (1-\alpha)\, A_t x_t^\alpha$. The social obsolescence-adjusted interest rate is $r - \lambda\, n(\gamma - 1)$, hence the social value of an innovation is

$$V_{t+1}^S(n_{t+1}) = (1-\alpha)\frac{(L - n_{t+1})^\alpha}{r - \lambda(\gamma - 1)n_{t+1}}\gamma A_t. \tag{S2.4}$$

In the text we saw that the equilibrium condition determining the level of R&D expenditure that maximizes social welfare is

$$1 = \frac{(\gamma - 1)\lambda}{\alpha}\frac{L - n^*}{r - \lambda n^*(\gamma - 1)}. \tag{S2.5}$$

The markup, m, should be the ratio of the social value of the innovation to its private value as revealed in the auction (which should be equal to (S2.1) above). Hence, if n_{t+1} workers are employed in research in period $t + 1$, the ratio of the social to the private value of the innovation in period t is

$$m(n_{t+1}) = \frac{V_{t+1}^S}{V_{t+1}^P} = \frac{1}{\alpha}\frac{r + \lambda n_{t+1}}{r - \lambda(\gamma - 1)n_{t+1}} > 1.$$

A higher n_{t+1} increases the mark-up for two reasons. First, it reduces the private value of the innovation as it increases the arrival rate. Second, it increases the social value of the innovation, as the next quality will arrive sooner.

b. For all those innovations that are placed in the public domain there is perfect competition. Firms manufacturing the highest quality of a good engage in marginal cost pricing and therefore the optimal amount of x is produced. Only in those cases in which the patent is sold to the highest bidder, there is static inefficiency as a result of monopoly pricing.

Suppose all patents were bought by the government at the private cost revealed in the auction times $m(n_{t+1})$. Then the innovator that sold her patent would get exactly the social value of the innovation. As a result the R&D decision problem of a firm is given by

$$\max_{n} \lambda n_t \cdot m(n_{t+1}) V_{t+1}^P(n_{t+1}) - w_t(n_t) \cdot n_t,$$

which implies the first-order condition $\lambda m(n_{t+1}) V_{t+1}^P(n_{t+1}) = w_t(n_t)$. The first-order condition defines the level of R&D employment $n_t = \phi(m, n_{t+1})$, which depends on the markup and on the level of research employment next period through its effect on $V_{t+1}^P(n_{t+1})$. It is straightforward to check that the partial derivatives are such that $\phi_m > 0$ and $\phi_n < 0$. That is, the larger the markup and the lower next period's R&D employment are, the higher is the level of research employment today. Denote by $\bar{n}$ the steady-state level of research under the patent buy-out system. Then

$$\frac{d\bar{n}}{dm} = \phi_m + \phi_n \frac{d\bar{n}}{dm},$$

which implies

$$\frac{d\bar{n}}{dm} = \frac{\phi_m}{1 - \phi_n} > 0. \tag{S2.6}$$

There is a positive direct effect of the patent buy-out system on research, and a negative indirect effect caused by the fact that since steady-state research increases the arrival rate is larger (the private value of the innovation falls). Since the denominator in equation (S2.6) is greater than one, an increase in the mark-up increases steady-state research by less than it would be suggested if one ignored the impact of future research on current R&D.

In our particular case, we can substitute for $V_{t+1}^P(n_{t+1})$ and the productivity-adjusted wage $\omega_t = \alpha^2 x_t^{-(1-\alpha)}$ into the first-order condition to get

$$(L - n_t)^{-(1-\alpha)} = \lambda \gamma \frac{1 - \alpha}{\alpha} m(n_{t+1}) \frac{(L - n_{t+1})^\alpha}{r + \lambda n_{t+1}}.$$

Comparing this expression with the equilibrium condition (S2.2), we can see that since $m(n_{t+1}) > 1$, the level of research at time t is greater than in the absence of patent buy-outs *for any given* n_{t+1}. A higher level of research employment next period has two effects. First, it reduces both the profits from the innovation (as wages are higher) and the period during which these profits are enjoyed, thus reducing n_t. Second, it increases the mark-up, which has a positive impact on current research. Substituting in for $m(n_{t+1})$ and imposing the steady-state condition $n_t = n_{t+1}$, we find that the equilibrium level of research is given by

$$1 = \lambda\gamma\frac{1-\alpha}{\alpha^2}\frac{L-\bar{n}}{r-\lambda(\gamma-1)\bar{n}}. \qquad (S2.7)$$

Comparing this expression to equation (S2.3) we can immediately see that the equilibrium research expenditure would be greater than under the standard patent system (graphic analysis can help to see this). This means that the markup chosen by the government must be greater than the ratio of the public to private value of the innovation before the system was introduced. Whether or not the chosen level of research is greater than the socially optimum depends on parameter values. Only if $\gamma = \alpha/(2\alpha-1)$ will $\bar{n}$ be equal to n^*, and thus the patent buy-out system would achieve dynamic efficiency. Solving (S2.5) and (S2.7) for n and comparing them, we find that the auction mechanism leads to a level of research employment below the socially optimal one whenever $\lambda(\gamma-1)L > r$.

So far we have supposed that all patents were bought and put in the public domain. However, in order to induce truthful revelation in the auction, some of the patents have to be sold to the highest bidder. Since this situation implies the possibility that a bidder actually gets the patent, it prevents agents from making offers that they would not be willing to pay. Suppose that a proportion q of all patents is sold to the highest bidder at a price equal to the private value (equivalently, it remains in the hands of the inventor). Then the R&D decision is the solution to the problem

$$\max_n \lambda n_t\left(qV^P_{t+1} + (1-q)m(n_{t+1})V^P_{t+1}\right) - w_t n_t.$$

The arbitrage condition is $\lambda\left(qV^P_{t+1} + (1-q)m(n_{t+1})V^P_{t+1}\right) = w_t$, which yields

$$1 = \lambda\gamma\frac{1-\alpha}{\alpha}\left[q\frac{L-\bar{n}}{r+\lambda\bar{n}} + \frac{1-q}{\alpha}\frac{L-\bar{n}}{r-\lambda(\gamma-1)\bar{n}}\right].$$

This equation determines $\bar{n}$. Once again, the solution to this equation ensures that the level of research expenditures is greater than that under the standard patent system.

c. If the level of research in the competitive economy were greater than the social optimum, the auction system could still be used to place new discoveries in the public domain and thus induce allocative efficiency. In order to reduce the incentive to innovate, the lifetime of patents could be reduced, so that it expired before the next quality was discovered. As a result the private value of the innovation would be lower.

★ **3. Financial intermediation and growth (based on Berthelemy and Varoudakis 1996)**

a. This is a standard Ramsey-Cass-Koopmans problem where the rate of growth of consumption is given by

$$\frac{\dot{c}}{c} = \frac{r - \rho}{\sigma},$$

which implies an elasticity of savings with respect to the interest rate of $1/\sigma$.

b. In the research sector the level of employment is chosen so as to maximize the expected present value of an innovation, $\lambda n_t V_{t+1}$, minus the present value of the cost, $w_t n_t (1 + i_t)$. The resulting arbitrage equation is

$$\lambda V_{t+1} = w_t (1 + i_t). \tag{S2.8}$$

The intermediate-good producer maximizes profits, which are given by $\pi_t = \alpha A_t x_t^\alpha - w_t (1 + i_t) x_t$. The resulting level of intermediate good is $x_t = \left(\alpha^2 / ((1 + i_t) \omega_t) \right)^{1/(1-\alpha)}$, and profits in period t are given by

$$\pi_t = A_t \frac{1 - \alpha}{\alpha} \omega_t (1 + i_t) x_t.$$

The asset equation is identical to that in the chapter; hence we can obtain the value of the innovation and substitute it in (S2.8) to express the arbitrage equation as

$$A_t \omega_t = \frac{1 - \alpha}{\alpha} A_t \lambda \gamma \frac{\omega_{t+1} x_{t+1}}{r + \lambda n_{t+1}} \frac{1 + i_{t+1}}{1 + i_t}. \tag{S2.9}$$

It therefore depends on the cost of intermediation.

c. In this section we ignore the t subscripts in as much as all decisions in the sector are relevant only during the period for which the current quality is used. The present value of the bank's profits is given by

$$\Pi_j = (1 + i) f(v_j) S_j - S_j - v_j w. \tag{S2.10}$$

The bank maximizes this expression with respect to S_j and v_j. The first-order condition $\partial \Pi_j / \partial S_j = 0$ implies

$$(1 + i) f(v_j) - 1 + f(v_j) S_j \frac{\partial (1 + i)}{\partial r} \frac{\partial r}{\partial S} \frac{\partial S}{\partial S_j} = 0,$$

where S are aggregate savings, $S \equiv \sum_j S_j$. Recall that $(1 + i) = R/r$, hence $\partial (1 + i) / \partial r = -R/r^2$. Because all banks are symmetric, $S_j = S/B$. From (a), $(\partial S / \partial r)(r/S) = 1/\sigma$. Hence the first-order condition $\partial \Pi_j / \partial S_j = 0$ gives

$$1 + i = \frac{1}{\left(1 - \frac{\sigma}{B}\right) f(v)}. \tag{S2.11}$$

The equilibrium intermediation margin depends negatively on the extent of competition in the sector, represented by the number of banks, on the intermediation function, and on the interest-rate elasticity of the savings function. The first-order condition with respect to employment yields

$$w = (1+i) f'(v) \frac{S}{B}. \tag{S2.12}$$

To complete the equilibrium decisions of banks we need the free-entry condition, which is simply $\Pi = 0$, where the profit function is given by (S2.10). This condition, together with equation (S2.12) and the assumption that $f(v) = v^\varepsilon$, implies

$$1 + i = \frac{1}{(1-\varepsilon) f(v)}. \tag{S2.13}$$

Once we know the value of the intermediation coefficient we can substitute it in the first-order condition (S2.11) and get the number of banks in the economy

$$B = \frac{\sigma}{\varepsilon}. \tag{S2.14}$$

The number of banks is inversely related to both the elasticity of savings with respect to the interest rate and the elasticity of the intermediation function.

d. The market clearing condition simply requires that the aggregate amount of savings lent by the banks be equal to the total amount borrowed by firms, that is,

$$f(v_t) S_t = w_t (n_t + x_t). \tag{S2.15}$$

e. We can now compute the equilibrium of the economy. There are four variables in the model, x_t, n_t, v_t, and S_t, which are simultaneously determined by the arbitrage equation, the expression determining the wage in the financial sector, and the market-clearing conditions in the lending and the labor markets. The latter can be expressed as

$$L = x_t + n_t + B v_t. \tag{S2.16}$$

Combining (S2.12) and (S2.15) we have

$$(1 + i_t) \frac{\varepsilon}{v_t} \frac{n_t + x_t}{B_t} = 1, \tag{S2.17}$$

which determines the level of employment in the financial sector as a function of employment in research. Substituting for $(1 + i)$ and B from (S2.13) and (S2.14), we get that the level of employment in the financial sector is

$$v_t = \left(\frac{n_t + x_t}{\sigma} \frac{\varepsilon^2}{1 - \varepsilon} \right)^{\frac{1}{1+\varepsilon}}. \tag{S2.18}$$

We can now obtain the two equations determining the steady state growth rate. In steady state, equation (S2.9) becomes

$$1 = \lambda \gamma \frac{1 - \alpha}{\alpha} \frac{\hat{x}}{r + \lambda \hat{n}}, \tag{S2.19}$$

which is identical to the equilibrium condition of the Schumpeterian model in the chapter. Because the intermediation cost affects in the same way the cost of doing research and the profitability of an innovation, their ratio is not affected. However, the level of research employment, $\hat{n}$, is lower. The reason is that the labor-market clearing condition has now changed to take into account the fact that some resources are being devoted to financial intermediation. This condition has become

$$L = \hat{x} + \hat{n} + \frac{\sigma}{\varepsilon} \left(\frac{\hat{n} + \hat{x}}{\sigma} \frac{\varepsilon^2}{1 - \varepsilon} \right)^{\frac{1}{1 + \varepsilon}}.$$

Note how parameters in the financial sector affect the equilibrium level of research (and thus the growth rate). For example, a greater interest elasticity of savings, $1/\sigma$, would result in more employment in research. A higher $1/\sigma$ implies that there are fewer banks, each employing more workers. The overall effect is to reduce the total number employed by the sector, hence increasing n.

4. Multidimensional quality ladder model (based on Li 1996b)

a. Total profits are $\pi = A[(1 - \alpha)/\alpha]\omega_L x$, where $\omega_L = w_L/A$ and w_L is the wage of unskilled workers. Hence innovators who improve γ_1^i and γ_2^j earn

$$\pi_1 = \kappa \pi, \quad \pi_2 = (1 - \kappa) \pi. \tag{S2.20}$$

b. Use V_1 to denote the value of innovation, which increases the quality index from $\gamma_1^i \gamma_2^j$ to $\gamma_1^{i+1} \gamma_2^j$. It must satisfy the following recursive equation:

$$V_1 = \pi_1 d\tau + (1 - rd\tau) (1 - \lambda_1 H_1 d\tau) V_1,$$

in that the innovator earns π_1 for the time interval $d\tau$, and achieves V_1 at the end of this interval with probability of $1 - \lambda_1 H_1 d\tau$. Note that V_1 is independent of $\lambda_2 H_2$, because the innovator continues to earn royalty π_1 even if other entrepreneurs succeed in raising the quality index in γ_2. Following the same logic, we can write a similar recursive equation for V_2. Rearranging this equation and letting $d\tau \to 0$, we obtain the value of innovation

$$V_k = \frac{\pi_k}{r + \lambda_k H_k}, \quad k = 1, 2. \tag{S2.21}$$

c. As we saw in the chapter, free entry in R&D implies

$$V_k \lambda_k = A \omega_H, \quad k = 1, 2, \tag{S2.22}$$

where $\omega_H = w_H/A$ and w_H is the wage of skilled workers. In a stochastic steady state, ω_H is constant. For two types of R&D to be conducted simultaneously, researchers (or investors) must be indifferent between them. This is ensured by the research-arbitrage condition, which is obtained by equating the left-hand sides of the free-entry conditions (S2.22) for both types of R&D:

$$V_1 \lambda_1 = V_2 \lambda_2. \tag{S2.23}$$

Using (S2.20), (S2.21), (S2.22), (S2.23), and the skilled workers full-employment condition $H = H_1 + H_2$, we can express the research arbitrage condition as

$$\frac{\kappa \lambda_1}{r + \lambda_1 H_1} = \frac{(1 - \kappa)\lambda_2}{r + \lambda_2 (H - H_1)}. \tag{S2.24}$$

The left-hand side is decreasing in H_1 and the right-hand side is increasing in H_1, giving rise to a unique equilibrium.

d. Taking the expectation of the production function, we have

$$E[y] = E\left[\gamma_1^i \gamma_2^j\right] L^\alpha = e^{[(\gamma_1 - 1)\lambda_1 H_1 + (\gamma_2 - 1)\lambda_2 H_2]\tau} L^\alpha.$$

The second equality arises by using the Poisson density functions of $(\lambda_1 H_1 \tau)^i e^{-\lambda_1 H_1 \tau}/i!$ and $(\lambda_2 H_2 \tau)^j e^{-\lambda_2 H_2 \tau}/j!$. This leads to the expected growth rate

$$g = (\gamma_1 - 1)\lambda_1 H_1 + (\gamma_2 - 1)\lambda_2 (H - H_1). \tag{S2.25}$$

Thus an isogrowth contour is monotonically increasing in H_1 for $(\gamma_1 - 1)\lambda_1 > (\gamma_2 - 1)\lambda_2$, decreasing for $(\gamma_1 - 1)\lambda_1 < (\gamma_2 - 1)\lambda_2$, or horizontal for $(\gamma_1 - 1)\lambda_1 = (\gamma_2 - 1)\lambda_2$. Observe that g is maximized if $H_1 = H$ for $(\gamma_1 - 1)\lambda_1 > (\gamma_2 - 1)\lambda_2$ and if $H_2 = H$ for $(\gamma_1 - 1)\lambda_1 < (\gamma_2 - 1)\lambda_2$. The growth rate is independent of the resource allocation if $(\gamma_1 - 1)\lambda_1 = (\gamma_2 - 1)\lambda_2$.

e. It follows that if the laissez-faire economy allocates resources such that H_1 and H_2 are positive, it grows too slowly, apart from the "knife-edge" case $(\gamma_1 - 1)\lambda_1 = (\gamma_2 - 1)\lambda_2$. It cannot grow excessively, as in the one-dimensional quality ladder model. This is because of the assumption that skilled workers are used only for R&D, not for manufacturing, as a result of which the business-stealing effect (and the monopoly-distortion effect) does not affect the optimal allocation of skilled labour. But the intertemporal spillover effect exists within each type of R&D and across different types of research activities. In the social optimum, the rent sharing parameters κ and $1 - \kappa$ are not present, and $\gamma_1 - 1$ and $\gamma_2 - 1$ take their places, as the social planner takes into account not only profits but the entire surplus created by the innovation.

It is often argued that in order to achieve the socially optimal level of R&D expenditure an R&D subsidy should be introduced. But it is usually assumed to be financed by an unrealistic lump-sum tax that creates no distortions. This model suggests an alternative method: the patent policy affecting κ. For example, if $(\gamma_1 - 1)\lambda_1 > (\gamma_2 - 1)\lambda_2$, all the government has to do is to raise κ so that $v_1\lambda_1 > v_2\lambda_2$, which results in $H_1 = H$ and $H_2 = 0$.

Chapter 3

1. Intermediate goods in research in a one-sector model

a. Research firms now maximize $\{\lambda n_t V_{t+1} - n_t A_t\}$, where $n_t \equiv N_t/A_t$. The resulting arbitrage equation is then, $\lambda V_{t+1} = A_t$. The value of the innovation is, just as in the basic Schumpeterian model,

$$V_{t+1} = \frac{A_{t+1}\tilde{\pi}(\omega)}{r + \lambda n_{t+1}},$$

where $\tilde{\pi}(\omega) = (1 - \alpha)\omega \cdot x(\omega)/\alpha$, and $x(\omega) = (\alpha^2/\omega)^{1/(1-\alpha)}$. The arbitrage equation thus reads

$$1 = \lambda\gamma \frac{\alpha(1 - \alpha)x^\alpha}{r + \lambda n_{t+1}}. \tag{S3.1}$$

The labor-market clearing condition is now simply $L = x(\omega)$. Substituting for x in the arbitrage equation, we get that the steady-state level of research is

$$n = \gamma\alpha(1 - \alpha)L^\alpha - \frac{r}{\lambda}. \tag{S3.2}$$

b. Just as in Chapter 2, the rate of growth of A_t is $g = \lambda n \log \gamma$.

c. The goods-market equilibrium condition implies that total output of the final good has to be equal to the amount consumed plus the amount employed in research,

$$C_t + N_t = A_t x_t^\alpha.$$

Dividing by A_t, and using the labor-market condition to substitute for x, we get $C_t/A_t = L^\alpha - n$. Because the right-hand side is constant in the steady state, so is the left-hand side, which implies that consumption and the level of technology grow at the same rate.

d. The Ramsey equation for consumption defines the rate of interest as a function of the growth rate, $r = \rho + \sigma g$. Substituting for r into equation (S3.2) and using the fact that $g = \lambda n \log \gamma$, we get that the equilibrium level of research expenditures and the growth rate are respectively

$$n^* = \frac{\alpha\gamma(1-\alpha)L^\alpha - \rho/\lambda}{1 + \sigma \log \gamma}, \tag{S3.3}$$

$$g^* = \frac{\lambda\gamma\alpha(1-\alpha)L^\alpha - \rho}{1 + \sigma \log \gamma} \log \gamma. \tag{S3.4}$$

The negative effect of a higher γ on n is due to the fact that a higher γ implies a larger growth rate, which in turn leads to a larger interest rate. Future profits are hence discounted more heavily and the level of R&D investment falls. The positive effect is standard: greater quality increases profits.

e. The social planner faces the following problem:

$$\max_c \int_0^\infty c_\tau e^{-r\tau} d\tau$$

subject to

$$c_\tau + n_\tau = x^\alpha \left[\sum_{t=0}^\infty \frac{(\gamma\lambda n\tau)^t}{t!} e^{-\lambda n\tau} \right],$$

where the term under the summation sign is the probability of innovating t times between time τ and $\tau + 1$, and the term in brackets is the expected number of innovations. We then have

$$\max_n \int_0^\infty \left[x^\alpha e^{\gamma\lambda n\tau} e^{-\lambda n\tau} - n \right] e^{-r\tau} d\tau = \frac{L^\alpha}{r - \lambda(\gamma - 1)n} - \frac{n}{r},$$

where n is constant over time (as we are interested in a steady state solution) and x is equal to L. Maximizing with respect to n we obtain

$$\lambda \frac{(\gamma - 1)L^\alpha}{(r - \lambda(\gamma - 1)n)^2} = \frac{1}{r},$$

which we rearrange to get equation (3.10). If we compare equations (3.10) and (S3.1) we can see the welfare effects discussed in Chapter 2: the social planner takes into account the rents destroyed by an innovation, values the fact that a higher quality creates the possibility of advancing one step farther up the quality ladder, and includes the entire consumer surplus generated by the innovation and not only the monopoly profits. There is a new term on the left-hand side of equation (3.10), which represents the consumption forgone when an amount n is invested in R&D. In the model in Chapter 2 forgone consumption was captured by the fact that $x = L - n$, that is, workers that could have been employed in production were employed in research. Now all labor is employed in research, but part of the final good is invested in R&D rather than consumed.

★ **2. The multisector economy with a nonconstant Poisson arrival rate (based on Barro and Sala-i-Martín 1995, chap. 7; see also Grossman and Helpman 1991, chap. 4)**

a. Differentiating the production function with respect to each type of capital, we have that the inverse demand for an intermediate good is

$$p_{it} = \alpha A q_{it}^{\alpha} x_{it}^{\alpha-1}. \tag{S3.5}$$

If the producer of the latest vintage is a monopolist, it maximizes $\pi_{it} = (p_{it} - 1)x_{it}$. It is straightforward to check that profits are maximized when she charges a price $1/\alpha$. γ units of the intermediate good of previous vintage are needed in order to provide the same services as one unit of the state-of-the-art technology. Hence the previous-vintage producer cannot charge a price greater than $1/(\alpha\gamma)$. If this price is less than the unit cost, that is, $\alpha\gamma \geq 1$, the previous vintage producer would make negative profits, and would choose not to offer the good. Only the state-of-the-art technology would be produced, and it would be sold at the monopoly price $1/\alpha$. If $\alpha\gamma < 1$, that is, the price that the previous-vintage producer can charge is greater than the unit cost, it is possible for this firm to make positive profits. Because firms engage in price (Bertrand) competition, prices would be pushed down until the highest cost producer makes zero profits. That is, the price for an intermediate good of quality $t - 1$ would be 1, and that for a good of quality t would be γ. Moreover, the state-of-the-art producer would limit price (charging a price just below γ), and drive the previous quality out of the market.

b. Consider the case where $\alpha\gamma \geq 1$ and the monopoly price is $1/\alpha$. Just as in section 3.1.1, we can get the amount of each type of capital produced from the inverse demand function,

$$x_{it} = \left(\alpha^2 A q_{it}^{\alpha}\right)^{\frac{1}{1-\alpha}}. \tag{S3.6}$$

The resulting profit flow to the only producer of the latest quality of good i is then $\pi_{it} = (1 - \alpha)x_{it}/\alpha$. Note that the amount of the good produced is larger the higher the quality that has been reached. In the alternative scenario, the only change would be the value of the profit flow, which would be given by $\pi_{it} = (\gamma - 1)x_{it}$, where $x_{it} = \left(\alpha A q_{it}^{\alpha}/\gamma\right)^{1/1-\alpha}$. We can define the aggregate quality index,

$$Q \equiv \sum_{i=1}^{I} q_{it}^{\frac{\alpha}{1-\alpha}},$$

and, using (S3.6), express aggregate output as $Y = \left(\alpha^{2\alpha} A\right)^{\frac{1}{1-\alpha}} Q$.

Just as in the chapter, the discounted value of the innovation is given by $V_{it} = \pi_{it}/(r + \lambda(t_i)N_{it})$, which together with the profit function determines the payoff to the successful innovator. The level of R&D effort is chosen to maximize expected net profits, $\{\lambda(t_i)N_{it}V_{it+1} - N_{it}\}$, which gives the arbitrage condition $\lambda(t_i)V_{it+1} = 1$. Hence the equilibrium equation that determines the level of research in the sector is

$$r + \lambda(t_i + 1)N_{it+1} = \frac{1 - \alpha}{\alpha}\lambda(t_i)\left(\alpha^2 A q_{it+1}^{\alpha}\right)^{\frac{1}{1-\alpha}}. \tag{S3.7}$$

c. Equation (S3.7) implies that the probability of going a step farther up the quality ladder, $\lambda(t_i + 1)N_{it+1}$, depends in two ways on the technological level already achieved. First, there is a positive effect operating through the profitability of the innovation: the higher the quality level, the larger the profit flow from the production of intermediate goods is. Second, for a given level of R&D expenditure, the probability of innovating is lower the more advanced the sector is, as we have assumed that innovations are increasingly difficult ($\lambda'(t_i) < 0$). If the first effect dominates, the right-hand side of equation (S3.7) is higher the more advanced the sector is, which implies that the probability of innovating is greater in those sectors that are high up in the quality ladder. Advanced sectors grow faster than retarded ones, and the average growth rate increases over time. If the second effect dominates, the opposite occurs. Advanced sectors grow more slowly, and the average rate of growth falls over time as the technological level improves.

When $\lambda(t_i) = q_{it+1}^{-\alpha/(1-\alpha)}$, the right-hand side of (S3.7) is constant, which implies that the probability of innovating is the same in all sectors. This probability is given by

$$q_{it+2}^{-\frac{\alpha}{1-\alpha}} N_{it+1} = \frac{1-\alpha}{\alpha}\left(\alpha^2 A\right)^{\frac{1}{1-\alpha}} - r. \tag{S3.8}$$

Hence all sectors grow at the same rate, which is the (constant) growth rate of the economy. Note, however, that because innovating becomes harder and harder, an equal success probability implies that more advanced sectors have to devote more resources to R&D. That is,

$$N_{it+1} = q_{it+2}^{\frac{\alpha}{1-\alpha}}\left(\frac{1-\alpha}{\alpha}\left(\alpha^2 A\right)^{\frac{1}{1-\alpha}} - r\right). \tag{S3.9}$$

d. The rate of growth of output is given by the evolution of the aggregate quality index, $Q \equiv \sum_{i=1}^{I} q_{it}^{\frac{\alpha}{1-\alpha}}$. If all sectors innovate at the same rate, we have that $Q_{t+1} = \gamma^{\frac{\alpha}{1-\alpha}} Q_t$. The probability of inventing is the same in all sectors, and it is given by equation (S3.8). Hence, using the same argument as in the chapter, we have that the expected rate of output growth is

$$E\left(\ln Q(t+1) - \ln Q(t)\right) = \left(\frac{1-\alpha}{\alpha}\left(\alpha^2 A\right)^{\frac{1}{1-\alpha}} - r\right)\ln\gamma^{\frac{\alpha}{1-\alpha}}. \qquad (S3.10)$$

Intertemporal utility maximization implies that the rate of growth of consumption is given by $g = r - \rho$. We use this expression together with (S3.10) to get

$$\hat{g} \simeq \left(\frac{1-\alpha}{\alpha}\left(\alpha^2 A\right)^{\frac{1}{1-\alpha}} - \rho\right)\left(1 - \gamma^{-\frac{\alpha}{1-\alpha}}\right). \qquad (S3.11)$$

(We have used the approximation $\ln(1+a) \simeq a$.)

⋆ 3. Welfare analysis in the multisector economy (based on Barro and Sala-i-Martín, section 7.5)

a. We first calculate the social surplus delivered by an innovation. Allocative efficiency requires marginal cost pricing. Given the inverse demand function, $p_i = \alpha A q_{it}^\alpha x_{it}^{\alpha-1}$, and because the unit cost of production of intermediaries is one, we have $x_{it} = (\alpha A q_{it}^\alpha)^{\frac{1}{1-\alpha}}$. The social benefit, or "profits" to the planner, is the entire social surplus, $\pi_t^s = A q_{it}^\alpha x_{it}^\alpha - x_{it}$, which, given the amount of each intermediary produced, yields

$$\pi_{it}^s = \frac{1-\alpha}{\alpha}\left(\alpha A q_{it}^\alpha\right)^{\frac{1}{1-\alpha}} . \qquad (S3.12)$$

This expression is clearly greater than the profits of a private firm, which we obtained in the previous problem, $\pi_{it} = \alpha^{\frac{1}{1-\alpha}}\pi_{it}^s < \pi_{it}^s$. The social value of an innovation is then (see the welfare analysis in Chapter 2, section 2.3)

$$V_{it}^s = \frac{1-\alpha}{\alpha}\frac{\left(\alpha A q_{it}^\alpha\right)^{\frac{1}{1-\alpha}}}{r - \lambda(t_i)N_{it}(\gamma-1)}. \qquad (S3.13)$$

b. The level of output chosen by a planner is $Y = (\alpha^\alpha A)^{\frac{1}{1-\alpha}}Q$, where Q is the quality index defined in the previous problem $Q \equiv \sum_{i=1}^{I} q_{it}^{\frac{\alpha}{1-\alpha}}$. The expected change in this index is

$$E\left(Q(t+1) - Q(t)\right) = \sum_{i=1}^{I}\left(q_{it+1}^{\frac{\alpha}{1-\alpha}} - q_{it}^{\frac{\alpha}{1-\alpha}}\right)P_{it}, \qquad (S3.14)$$

where P_{it} is the probability of innovating in sector i during the period, and it is given by $N_{it}q_{it+1}^{-\frac{\alpha}{1-\alpha}}$. Substituting for P_{it} in the above expression and because $q_{it+1} = \gamma q_{it}$ we get

$$E\left(Q(t+1) - Q(t)\right) = \left(1 - \gamma^{-\frac{\alpha}{1-\alpha}}\right) N_t \tag{S3.15}$$

where N_t is the aggregate level of R&D spending, $N_t \equiv \sum_{i=1}^{I} N_{it}$.

c. The social planner maximizes $\int_0^\infty \log c_t e^{-\rho t} dt$, subject to the aggregate budget constraint, $Y_t = c_t + X_t + N_t$, and to the dynamic equation for the quality index as given by (S3.15). X_t is the total amount of intermediaries in the economy, which can be expressed as $X_t = (\alpha A)^{\frac{1}{1-\alpha}} Q_t$. Substituting for X_t and Y_t, we can reexpress the budget constraint as

$$\frac{1-\alpha}{\alpha}(\alpha A)^{\frac{1}{1-\alpha}} Q_t = c_t + N_t.$$

The Hamiltonian is then

$$H(c, N, Q, \mu, \nu, t) = e^{-\rho t} \log c_t + \mu \left(1 - \gamma^{-\frac{\alpha}{1-\alpha}}\right) N_t$$

$$+ \nu \left(\frac{1-\alpha}{\alpha}(\alpha A)^{\frac{1}{1-\alpha}} Q_t - N_t - c_t\right).$$

The first-order conditions are as follows (for simplicity we omit the time subscripts):

$$e^{-\rho t}\frac{1}{c} - \nu = 0, \tag{S3.16}$$

$$-\nu + \mu \left(1 - \gamma^{-\frac{\alpha}{1-\alpha}}\right) = 0, \tag{S3.17}$$

$$\frac{1-\alpha}{\alpha}(\alpha A)^{\frac{1}{1-\alpha}} Q - N - c = 0, \tag{S3.18}$$

$$\nu \frac{1-\alpha}{\alpha}(\alpha A)^{\frac{1}{1-\alpha}} = -\dot{\mu}. \tag{S3.19}$$

Equation (S3.16) implies the usual relation $\dot{c}/c = -\dot{\nu}/\nu - \rho$. Using (S3.17) and (S3.19) together we get an expression for $-\dot{\nu}/\nu$, which, when substituted it in the dynamic equation for consumption, yields

$$g^* = \frac{1-\alpha}{\alpha}(\alpha A)^{\frac{1}{1-\alpha}}\left(1 - \gamma^{-\frac{\alpha}{1-\alpha}}\right) - \rho. \tag{S3.20}$$

Recall from the previous problem that the rate of growth in the competitive economy was

$$\hat{g} = \frac{1-\alpha}{\alpha}(\alpha^2 A)^{\frac{1}{1-\alpha}}\left(1 - \gamma^{-\frac{\alpha}{1-\alpha}}\right) - \rho\left(1 - \gamma^{-\frac{\alpha}{1-\alpha}}\right). \tag{S3.21}$$

The first term is larger in the case of the socially optimal growth rate because of the appropriability effect. The second term is also larger for the planned economy (making the optimal growth rate smaller) because of the business-stealing effect. As in the one-sector model, either effect could dominate. g^* is greater than $\hat{g}$ if the following condition holds:

$$\left(1 - \alpha^{\frac{1}{1-\alpha}}\right)(1-\alpha)(\alpha^\alpha A)^{\frac{1}{1-\alpha}}\left(\gamma^{\frac{\alpha}{1-\alpha}} - 1\right) > \rho. \tag{S3.22}$$

A sufficiently large size of the quality increases implies that the competitive growth rate is smaller than the social optimum. The first term in brackets on the left-hand side denotes the difference in growth rates due to monopoly pricing. Large monopoly power (α small) or a large discount rate imply that the competitive growth rate is excessive.

4. Capital income taxation and growth (based on Uhlig and Yanagawa 1996)

a. An equilibrium are sequences $(c_{y,t}, c_{o,t}, k_t, y_t, x_t, w_t, R_t, r_t)_{t=1}^{\infty}$, where r_{t+1} and R_{t+1} are, respectively, the before-tax and after-tax returns on savings, so that

i. The consumption bundle solves

$$\max U = \log(c_{y,t}) + \log(c_{o,t+1})$$

s.t. $c_{y,t} + \dfrac{c_{o,t+1}}{R_{t+1}} = (1 - \tau_L)w_t,$

given the after-tax return R_{t+1} on savings, wages w_t, and labor tax rate τ_L. The initial old eat the initial return on capital, $c_{o,1} = R_1 k_1$. This problem implies that consumption when young is

$$c_{y,t} = (1 - \tau_L)\frac{w_t}{2}. \tag{S3.23}$$

ii. Markets clear. The market-clearing conditions are that the stock of capital at time $t + 1$ be equal to the savings of the generation born at t, and the aggregate resource constraint. Respectively,

$$k_{t+1} = s_t, \tag{S3.24}$$

$$y_t = c_{y,t} + c_{o,t} + x_t. \tag{S3.25}$$

iii. The before-tax return to capital is equal to a fraction θ of the capital output ratio, plus the revenue from the sale of the capital stock (net of depreciation) to the next generation. We also have the following relations

$$r_t = \theta A + 1 - \delta,$$

$$R_t = (1 - \tau_K)r_t,$$

$$w_t = (1 - \theta)y_t.$$

Because the capital stock is equal to savings, we have

$$k_{t+1} = (1 - \tau_L)w_t - c_{y,t}. \tag{S3.26}$$

Substituting for $c_{y,t}$ and w_t in equation (S3.26) and dividing by k_t gives the growth rate g,

$$g = \frac{k_{t+1}}{k_t} - 1 = \frac{(1-\theta)A}{2}(1 - \tau_L) - 1. \tag{S3.27}$$

That is, the higher the tax rate on labor income, the less agents save and the lower the growth rate is.

b. The government budget constraint is simply

$$\gamma y_t = h_t = \tau_K r_t k_t + \tau_L w_t, \tag{S3.28}$$

and the aggregate resource constraint changes to

$$y_t = c_{y,t} + c_{o,t} + x_t + h_t.$$

Dividing equation (S3.28) by y_t and solving for τ_L, we find

$$\tau_L = \frac{\gamma}{1-\theta} - \frac{\theta A + 1 - \delta}{(1-\theta)A}\tau_K. \tag{S3.29}$$

A rise in the capital income tax rate results in a fall in the labor income tax rate, because government consumption as a fraction of output is fixed.

c. Equations (S3.27) and (S3.29) together then imply that the growth rate is decreasing in τ_L, and hence increasing in τ_K. That is, the growth rate is higher the higher the tax rate on capital income, contrary to the "conventional wisdom." Note what is driving the result: the labor income tax has a direct effect on growth, whereas the capital income tax has none (because of the assumption of intertemporal elasticity of substitution equal to one). An increase in the (nondistortionary) capital tax rate reduces the (distortionary) labor tax rate required to keep a balanced budget.

d. The consumer's problem is now

$$\max U = \frac{c_{y,t}^{1-1/\sigma} - 1}{1 - 1/\sigma} + \beta \frac{c_{o,t+1}^{1-1/\sigma} - 1}{1 - 1/\sigma}$$

s.t. $c_{y,t} + \dfrac{c_{o,t+1}}{R_{t+1}} = (1 - \tau_L)w_t.$

A bit of calculation shows that now the solution for the maximization problem of the agent implies savings

$$s_t = \frac{\beta^{1/\sigma} R_{t+1}^{1/\sigma-1}}{1 + \beta^{1/\sigma} R_{t+1}^{1/\sigma-1}}(1 - \tau_L)w_t.$$

That is, savings are a fraction, $s(R)$, of the net wage. If $\sigma > 1$, the savings rate is decreasing in the net interest rate, R, whereas if $\sigma < 1$, it is increasing. Going through the same logic as above with the right-hand side of equation (S3.26) replaced by $s(R)(1 - \tau_L)w_t$, we find

$$g = (1 - \theta)A(1 - \tau_L)\frac{\beta^{1/\sigma}R^{1/\sigma-1}}{1 + \beta^{1/\sigma}R^{1/\sigma-1}} - 1.$$

Thus, an increase in the capital income tax rate works in the same direction on both τ_L as well as $s(R)$ for $\sigma > 1$. In other words, if the utility function is characterized by a constant intertemporal elasticity of substitution of unity or higher, $\sigma \geq 1$, then a higher capital income tax rate will unambiguously result in a higher growth rate. If $\sigma < 1$, an increase in the capital income tax rate works in opposite directions for τ_L vis-à-vis $s(R)$: whether a higher capital income tax rate will result in lower or in higher growth will depend on the relative magnitude of the two effects.

e. Even though the lifecycle analysis at the basis of this exercise is well understood in public finance and elsewhere, the "conventional wisdom" has focused on the results obtained for infinitely lived individuals as in Chamley (1986). As we have seen, when agents live for two periods, the effect of labor and capital income taxation on the incentives to save is reversed. This issue is examined in Uhlig-Yanagawa (1996) as well as Bertola (1996).

⋆ **5. Physical capital obsolescence and the lock-in effect (based on Redding 1996c)**

a. The inverse demand is, as usual, $p_{m,t,1} = \gamma^m \alpha x_{m,t,1}^{\alpha-1}$. Because there is perfect competition in the production of x, both labor and capital are paid their marginal value product, that is

$$w_{m,t,1} = \alpha(1 - \beta)\gamma^m L^{\alpha(1-\beta)-1}K_{m,t,1}^{\alpha\beta},$$

$$r_{m,t,1} = \alpha\beta\gamma^m L^{\alpha(1-\beta)}K_{m,t,1}^{\alpha\beta-1}.$$

The level of output is

$$Y_{m,t,1} = \gamma^m L^{\alpha(1-\beta)}K_{m,t,1}^{\alpha\beta} \tag{S3.30}$$

b. Because the technology level is the same, the price of the intermediate good is $p_{m,t,2} = \gamma^m \alpha x_{m,t,2}^{\alpha-1}$, where the level of $x_{m,t,2}$ is determined by the stock of capital, $K_{m,t,2} = K_{m,t,1} + sY_{m,t,1}$. The wage and the interest rate are as above, except that the stock of capital is now larger,

$$w_{m,t,2} = \alpha(1 - \beta)\gamma^m L^{\alpha(1-\beta)-1}K_{m,t,2}^{\alpha\beta}, \tag{S3.31}$$

$$r_{m,t,2} = \alpha\beta\gamma^m L^{\alpha(1-\beta)}K_{m,t,2}^{\alpha\beta-1}.$$

c. If an innovation occurs, the inverse demand for an intermediate good of higher quality is $p_{m+1,t,2} = \alpha \gamma^{m+1} \cdot x^{\alpha-1}_{m+1,t,2}$, where $x_{m+1,t,2}$ is the amount of intermediate good produced with the capital stock $K_{m+1,t,2} = (1-\theta)K_{m,t,1} + sY_{m,t,1}$. The innovator can attract all capital and all labor by paying them their external options, that is, their rewards if they were employed by the competitive firms producing intermediate goods of the previous vintage, given by (S3.31). Hence, the innovator's profits are

$$\pi_{m+1,t} = p_{m+1,t,2} \cdot x_{m+1,t,2} - w_{m,t,2} \cdot L - r_{m,t,2} \cdot K_{m,t,2}$$

$$= \alpha \gamma^{m+1} \cdot x^{\alpha}_{m+1,t,2} - \alpha(1-\beta)\gamma^m \cdot x^{\alpha}_{m,t,2} - \alpha\beta\gamma^m \cdot x^{\alpha}_{m,t,2}.$$

This profit function can be written as

$$\pi_{m+1,t} = \left(\gamma \left(\frac{K_{m+1,t,2}}{K_{m,t,2}} \right)^{\alpha\beta} - 1 \right) \alpha\gamma^m x^{\alpha}_{m,t,2}. \tag{S3.32}$$

If the term in brackets is negative, an innovator would not make positive profits and the new innovation would not be adopted. Note that $K_{m+1,t,2}/K_{m,t,2}$ is equal to $\left(1 - \theta K_{m,t,1}/K_{m,t,2}\right)$, which from (3.13) and (S3.30) can be expressed as

$$\frac{K_{m+1,t,2}}{K_{m,t,2}} = 1 - \frac{\theta}{1 + s\gamma^m L^{\alpha(1-\beta)} K^{\alpha\beta-1}_{m,t,1}}. \tag{S3.33}$$

This expression is decreasing in the existing stock of capital and increasing in the level of technology, m. Equations (S3.32) and (S3.33) together determine whether or not the innovation is adopted. Equation (S3.33) implies that $\pi_{m+1,t}$ is more likely to be negative the larger the stock of capital is, for a given level of technology. That means that if two economies have the same technological level but one has accumulated more capital than the other, the former is less likely to introduce a higher quality of intermediate goods, in as much as the cost in terms of lost capital stock is larger. It will stay locked in the old technology, and lag behind the capital-poor economy.

Chapter 4

1. First elementary look (based on Blanchard et al. 1996)

a. A rise in productivity, which leaves output unchanged (or increases output by less than productivity), leads to a fall in employment. One can think of firms investing to increase capacity or to reduce costs for a given level of capacity. In the latter case it is possible that if production is constrained by the capacity restriction, a fall in costs leads to a rise in productivity but leaves output unchanged.

This effect will be examined in problems 4 and 5, which consider the effect on employment of technical change that increases productivity by reducing fixed costs while leaving marginal costs and output unchanged.

b. The firm solves $max_x\{x^{-(1-\alpha)}x - \delta x\}$. Denote the profit-maximizing output level by $x(\delta)$. The first order condition implies $x(\delta) = (\alpha/\delta)^{1/(1-\alpha)}$. Hence employment equals $\delta x(\delta) = \alpha^{1/(1-\alpha)}\delta^{-\alpha/(1-\alpha)}$. As δ is reduced, employment $\delta x(\delta)$ rises. The intuition is that a labor-saving innovation that reduces δ leads to a fall in the firm's price and therefore to a rise in the amount of output demanded. The effect on employment of the rise in production outweighs the effect of a fall in labor per unit produced, if demand is sufficiently elastic.

c. The problem is that the price elasticity of an economy-wide aggregate-demand function is not well defined. Hence the result in (b) at the individual firm level does not apply immediately at the economy wide level. However, there is a general equilibrium effect caused by the cost of reallocation and its effect on the labor market (see (d)).

d. In the chapter, when one firm innovates this happens at the expense of an older firm that goes bankrupt. It then takes time for the workers of the obsolete firm to be reallocated to new starting firms. The faster growth is, the more firms go bankrupt per period and hence more workers need to be reallocated. If reallocation takes time (as it does in the chapter), this rise in reallocation activity increases unemployment.

2. Search and matching with high implementation costs (based on Mortensen and Pissarides 1995)

a. If at each moment in time $m(v, u)$ unemployed workers are matched with a job, while u workers are unemployed, then the job arrival rate for one unemployed worker equals $m(v, u)/u = m(\theta, 1)$, because $m(., .)$ is homogenous of degree 1 in its two arguments. Similarly, on the firm side of the market, the match arrival rate for a particular firm equals $m(v, u)/v = m(\theta, 1)/\theta$.

b. The value of a job vacancy at time t, $V(t)$, is made up of three components. First, there is the change in value $J(t) - V(t)$ if the vacancy is matched with a worker minus the cost of creating the new job, pK. This happens with arrival rate $m(\theta, 1)/\theta$. Second there is the cost of posting the vacancy, pc. Finally there is the change in value V over time if the firm is not matched with a worker.

If there is free entry into job creation, entry will continue until $V(t) = 0$, and hence $dV(t)/dt = 0$ for each t. Substituting this into the Bellman equation yields equation (4.24).

c. The value at $t + s$ (with $s \geq 0$) of a job created at time t equals $p(t)x - w(t + s)$. The discounted value equals $e^{-(r+\delta)s}[p(t)x - w(t + s)]$. Payoffs are discounted at a rate $r + \delta$, where r is the discount rate conditional on survival and δ is the exogenous Poisson arrival rate of bankruptcy. Finally, if the firm has not gone bankrupt it will cease production once $p(t)x - w(t + s) \leq 0$. Hence the life span T is chosen to maximize the discounted sum of payoffs, which is precisely what equation (4.25) says.

d. We can rewrite (4.25) as

$$J(t) = \max_{T \geq 0} \int_0^T [p(0)e^{gt}x - w_0 p(0)e^{g(t+s)}]e^{-(r+\delta)s}ds.$$

Letting $p(0) = 1$, we have

$$J(t) = e^{gt} \max_{T \geq 0} \int_0^T [xe^{-(r+\delta)s} - w_0 e^{-(r+\delta-g)s}]ds$$

$$= e^{gt} \left\{ \max_T \frac{x}{r + \delta}\left(1 - e^{-(r+\delta)T}\right) - \frac{w_0}{r + \delta - g}\left(1 - e^{-(r+\delta-g)T}\right)\right\}$$

From the first order condition for T it follows that $T^* = [ln(x/w_0)]/g$.

Hence we find that $J(t) = e^{gt}J$ with

$$J = \left\{\frac{x}{r + \delta}\left(1 - e^{-(r+\delta)T^*}\right) - \frac{w_0}{r + \delta - g}\left(1 - e^{-(r+\delta-g)T^*}\right)\right\}.$$

Substituting this in (4.24), we get that $\theta c/m(\theta, 1) + K = J$.

e. As the growth rate g rises, equation (4.26) is unaffected and equation (4.27) shifts to the left. A rise in the growth rate leads to a sharper rise in wages over time thereby reducing per period profits and the life span T^* of firms. Consequently, a rise in g leads to a fall in the value of a created job J^*. As J^* falls, fewer firms enter the job-creation business and hence less vacancies are posted. This reduces the labor market tightness measure, θ^*.

f. Each period there are $m(v, u)$ matches, hence $m(v, u) = m(\theta, 1)u$ jobs are created. Each period δ firms employing $(1 - u)$ workers go bankrupt exogenously. Further, there is the endogenous bankruptcy of the firms that have reached the end of their life span T^*. There are $e^{-\delta T^*}$ of such firms.

In steady state we get $m(\theta, 1)u = \delta(1 - u) + m(\theta, 1)ue^{-\delta T^*}$. Solving this for unemployment u yields

$$u = \frac{\delta}{\delta + m(\theta^*, 1)\left(1 - e^{-\delta T^*}\right)}$$

g. A rise in the growth rate reduces the life span of firms T^*; this is the direct creative destruction effect. Further, it also reduces the number of vacancies

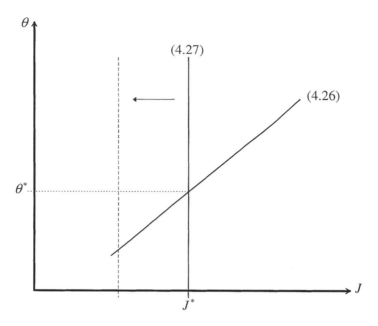

Figure S4.1

posted, reducing θ^*, thereby increasing u. This is the indirect creative destruction effect.

3. Search and matching with zero implementation costs (based on Mortensen and Pissarides 1995)

a. This is obvious because nothing has changed in the job-creation business.

b. As firms can continuously update their equipment with the latest technology at zero implementation costs, the payoff at time $t + s$ (with $s \geq 0$) of a firm that started production in period t equals $p(t + s)x - w(t + s)$, which is positive for each period $t + s$. Hence, the value of a job created at time t equals $J(t) = \int_0^\infty [e^{g(t+s)}x - w_0 e^{g(t+s)}]e^{-(r+\delta)s}ds$ which is equivalent to $J(t) = e^{gt}(x - w_0)/(r + \delta - g) = e^{gt}J$ with $J = (x - w_0)/(r + \delta - g)$.

c. As growth g rises, J^* increases because firms benefit from faster rising prices $p(t)$. Such an increase in the value of a created job attracts more entrants into the job-creation business. This leads to a rise in labor market tightness θ^*.

d. The reasoning is the same as in section (f) of problem 2, except now there is no endogenous bankruptcy in the JD equation.

In steady state we get $m(\theta, 1)u = \delta(1 - u)$. Solving this for the unemployment rate u yields $u = \delta/[m(\theta^*, 1) + \delta]$. As the growth rate increases, it becomes more profitable to post vacancies, hence more firms enter the

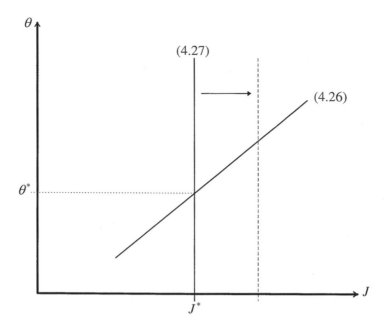

Figure S4.2

job-creation business. This leads to a rise in labor market tightness θ^* and a fall in steady state unemployment.

⋆ **4. Form of technological progress and unemployment (based on Boone 1996a)**

a. In the second period firm a chooses x_a to solve $max_x\{\gamma Ax^{-(1-\alpha)}x - wx\}$. The first order condition can be written as $\alpha\gamma Ax^{-(1-\alpha)} = w$ and x_a equals $x_a = (\alpha\gamma A/w)^{1/(1-\alpha)}$. Substituting this value of x_a in the demand function $p_a(x_a)$ yields $p_a = w/\alpha$. A similar derivation for good r yields $x_r = (\alpha RA/w)^{1/(1-\alpha)}$ and $p_r = w/\alpha$. The price cost margin for firm a equals $(p_a - w)/p_a = 1 - \alpha$. As α falls, firm a's monopoly power increases and its price cost margin rises. Last, firm a's share in the economy equals

$$s_a = \frac{\left(\frac{\alpha\gamma A}{w}\right)^{\frac{1}{1-\alpha}}}{\left(\frac{\alpha\gamma A}{w}\right)^{\frac{1}{1-\alpha}} + \left(\frac{\alpha RA}{w}\right)^{\frac{1}{1-\alpha}}} = \frac{\gamma^{\frac{1}{1-\alpha}}}{\gamma^{\frac{1}{1-\alpha}} + R^{\frac{1}{1-\alpha}}}.$$

b. Firm a's second period profits as a function of a's first-period choice variables (γ, f) equal $\pi(\gamma, f) = p_a x_a - w x_a - wf = w(1/\alpha - 1)(\alpha\gamma A/w)^{1/(1-\alpha)} - wf = w(1 - \alpha)/\alpha(\alpha\gamma A/w)^{1/(1-\alpha)} - wf$.

The marginal rate of substitution in (γ, f) space can be found as follows. As firm a takes A as given, it can be verified that $d\pi/df = -w$ and $d\pi/d\gamma =$

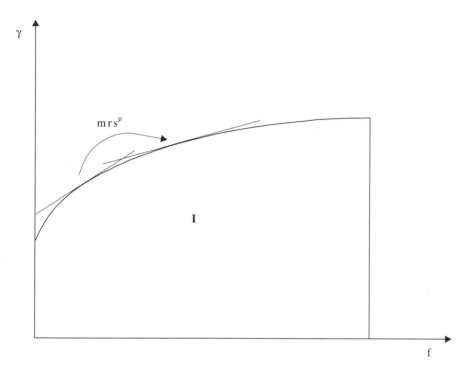

Figure S4.3

$(w/\alpha)\gamma^{1/(1-\alpha)}(\alpha A/w)^{1/(1-\alpha)}$. Substituting into $d\pi/d\gamma$ the expression for A given in the text with $p_a = p_r = w/\alpha$ yields

$$\frac{d\pi}{d\gamma} = \frac{w}{\alpha}\gamma^{\frac{\alpha}{1-\alpha}}\left(\frac{\alpha}{w}\frac{\left(\frac{w}{\alpha}\right)^{\alpha}}{\left(\gamma^{\frac{1}{1-\alpha}} + R^{\frac{1}{1-\alpha}}\right)^{1-\alpha}}\right)^{\frac{1}{1-\alpha}} = \frac{1}{\gamma}s_a.$$

Hence $mrs^p = -(d\pi/df)/(d\pi/d\gamma) = \gamma w/s_a$. If w is low in period 2, the mrs^p is lower for each value of (γ, f) and the firm chooses higher values of f and γ as illustrated in figure S4.3. If wages are lower in period 2, the firm has less incentive to cut fixed costs f because this yields w per unit reduction in f.

c. A rise in unemployment weakens the bargaining position of the labor unions, thereby reducing the wage rate. The parameter θ denotes the union's bargaining power for a given level of unemployment. One can think of θ as being determined by factors like the unemployment benefit paid by the government and other institutional features that determine the union's bargaining position vis-à-vis the firms.

Total labor demand equals $\lambda^d = x_a + x_r + f = (\alpha\gamma A/w)^{1/(1-\alpha)} + (\alpha R A/w)^{1/(1-\alpha)} + f$. Substituting into this the expression for A given in the text with $p_a = p_r = w/\alpha$ yields $\lambda^d = (\alpha/w)s_a + (\alpha/w)(1 - s_a) + f = \alpha/w + f$. Substituting this into the wage equation gives $w = \theta b(1 - \lambda^d) = \theta b \left(1 - \frac{\alpha}{w} - f\right)$.

d. To find $\partial u/\partial \alpha$, first derive $\partial w/\partial \alpha$ as follows: $\partial w/\partial \alpha = \theta b'(\cdot)[(\alpha/w^2) (\partial w/\partial \alpha) - 1/w]$, or equivalently $\partial w/\partial \alpha = \theta[-b'(\cdot)]/(w + \theta[-b'(\cdot)]\alpha/w) > 0$, because $b'(.) < 0$. Because a rise in α increases the equilibrium wage, it must be the case that a rise in α reduces unemployment, that is $\partial u/\partial \alpha < 0$. If the economy is more competitive in the sense that α is higher, firms produce higher output levels, which increases labor demand.

Similarly, first derive $\partial w/\partial f = \theta[-b'(\cdot)]/(1 + \theta[-b'(\cdot)]\alpha/w^2) > 0$ to find that $\partial u/\partial f < 0$. So if firm a invests in reducing fixed costs f, it increases unemployment in the second period.

A labor-saving innovation that reduces marginal labor costs as in problem 1(b) increases employment. But a labor-saving innovation that reduces fixed labor costs increases unemployment. The point is that a reduction in fixed costs f leaves firm a's output level unaffected. Hence there is no compensating output-expansion effect.

e. The effect of α on firm a's choice of $(\gamma, f) \in I$ in period 1 is determined by α's effect on mrs^p. One can check that $\partial mrs^p/\partial \alpha > 0$ because $\partial w/\partial \alpha > 0$ as shown under (d). Also

$$\partial s_a/\partial \alpha = \frac{\partial \left(\left(1 + (R/\gamma)^{\frac{1}{1-\alpha}}\right)^{-1}\right)}{\partial \alpha} < 0$$

because $R > \gamma$ by assumption. As a rise in α increases mrs^p, firm a chooses lower values for γ and f. The intuition is that a rise in α, increases total output, thereby increasing employment and the wage rate. The higher wage rate makes it more attractive for firms to reduce fixed costs. Second, a rise in α by reducing monopoly power makes it harder for firm a to capture the consumer surplus associated with an increase in quality. Therefore as α rises, the firm is less inclined to invest in increasing quality γ.

In other words, the static effect of more competition, or a reduction in monopoly power $(1 - \alpha)$, is higher output levels and hence higher employment. However, the dynamic innovation effect of a rise in competition is that firm a is more inclined to reduce fixed costs, thereby increasing unemployment in period 2. The overall effect of a rise in competition on unemployment in period 2 depends on the shape of the innovation possibility set I.

A rise in θ, increases labor-union bargaining power and hence increases the wage rate. This leads to a rise in the mrs^p. Hence firm a will invest more to reduce fixed costs f and invest less to increase quality γ.

★ 5. Form of technological progress and unemployment: welfare analysis (based on Boone 1996a)

a. Using the expression for output x_a, x_r found in problem 4(a) together with the given expression for A and $p_a = p_r = w/a$, yields:

$$W(\gamma, f) = \frac{1}{\alpha} \ln \left(\gamma \left[\frac{\alpha}{w} \frac{\gamma^{\frac{1}{1-\alpha}}}{\gamma^{\frac{1}{1-\alpha}} + R^{\frac{1}{1-\alpha}}} \right]^\alpha + R \left[\frac{\alpha}{w} \frac{R^{\frac{1}{1-\alpha}}}{\gamma^{\frac{1}{1-\alpha}} + R^{\frac{1}{1-\alpha}}} \right]^\alpha \right)$$

This can be rewritten as

$$W(\gamma, f) = \ln(\alpha) - \ln(w) + \frac{1-\alpha}{\alpha} \ln(\gamma^{1/(1-\alpha)} + R^{1/(1-\alpha)}).$$

b. First, $dW(\gamma, f)/df = -(1/w)dw/df$. Second, one can verify that

$$\frac{dW}{d\gamma} = \frac{1-\alpha}{\alpha} \frac{1}{\gamma^{\frac{1}{1-\alpha}} + R^{\frac{1}{1-\alpha}}} \frac{1}{1-\alpha} \gamma^{\frac{\alpha}{1-\alpha}} = \frac{s_a}{\alpha\gamma}.$$

Combining these two results yields $mrs^s = [(dw/df)/w]\gamma\alpha/s_a$.

c. If w solves $\alpha/w + f = 1$, then dw/df satisfies $dw/df = w^2/\alpha$. Substituting this into the expression for mrs^s yields $mrs^s = \gamma w/s_a$, which is identical to the expression for mrs^P found in problem 4(b). So in this case $mrs^s/mrs^P = 1$. The intuition is that if the wage clears the labor market the wage coincides with the shadow price of labor. Hence the social planner's incentive to reduce fixed costs f coincides with the private incentive. On the γ dimension of the innovation, the social planner's and private incentives coincide as well, in as much as the appropriability effect and the business-stealing effect exactly cancel out in this model. Therefore in the market clearing case we find $mrs^s/mrs^P = 1$.

d. The expression for dw/df is derived in problem 4(d) to show that $\partial u/\partial f < 0$. Substituting this expression for dw/df into mrs^s yields

$$mrs^s = \frac{\gamma}{s_a} \frac{[-b'(.)]\frac{\alpha}{w}}{1 + [-b'(.)]\frac{\alpha}{w}}.$$

It follows that

$$mrs^s/mrs^P = \frac{[-b'(.)]\frac{u}{w^2}}{1 + [-b'(.)]\frac{\alpha}{w^2}} < 1,$$

because $b'(.) < 0$. Hence in the social optimum the mrs is smaller than in the private outcome. In other words, the point of tangency of the isowelfare line with the boundary of the innovation set I occurs at a point to the right and above the private outcome, as illustrated in figure S4.3. Thus the social planner invests less in reducing fixed costs and more in increasing quality than the private outcome. This leads to higher welfare and lower unemployment in the social outcome as compared with the private outcome.

The laissez-faire economy can thus choose a form of technological progress that leads to higher unemployment and lower welfare. The intuition for the market's overinvestment in reducing fixed costs is as follows. With labor union bargaining there is equilibrium unemployment. Consequently the wage rate is above the shadow price of labor. This gives firm a higher incentive to reduce fixed costs than it does the social planner.

Chapter 6

1. Learning by doing has no effect on general knowledge

a. Let us rewrite the research arbitrage equation (6.10) and the growth equation (6.31) as

$$g = R\left(H^r\right), \qquad g = G\left(H^r\right) \equiv \lambda^r H^r,$$

respectively. Given that $R(0) = -\infty$ and $G(0) = 0$ and $R', G' > 0$, a unique (interior) equilibrium arises if $R(H^r = H) > G(H^r = H)$. This implies that, at the equilibrium $\widehat{H}^r$,

$$R'(\widehat{H}^r) > G'(\widehat{H}^r). \tag{S6.1}$$

b. We apply Cramer's rule to the system of equations (6.10) and (6.31). The determinant of the Jacobian matrix is

$$J = \sigma \frac{1-\alpha}{\alpha} \frac{H}{(H^r)^2} - \lambda^r.$$

Because we are concerned with small changes near the steady state, and we know $R'(\widehat{H}^r) > G'(\widehat{H}^r)$, the Jacobian is positive. Then,

$$\frac{dg}{d\rho} = -\frac{\lambda^r}{J} < 0, \quad \frac{dg}{dH} = \sigma \frac{1-\alpha}{\alpha} \frac{\lambda^r}{H^r J} > 0, \quad \frac{dg}{d\alpha} = -\frac{\sigma \lambda^r}{\alpha^2} \frac{H-H^r}{H^r J} < 0,$$

$$\frac{dg}{d\sigma} = \frac{\lambda^r(\rho-g)}{\sigma J} > 0, \quad \frac{dg}{d\lambda^r} = \sigma \frac{1-\alpha}{\alpha} \frac{H}{H^r J} > 0, \quad \frac{dg}{d\lambda^d} = 0,$$

where $\rho > g$ is assumed. Similarly,

$$\frac{dH^r}{d\rho} = -\frac{1}{J} < 0, \quad \frac{dH^r}{dH} = \sigma \frac{1-\alpha}{\alpha} \frac{1}{H^r J} > 0, \quad \frac{dH^r}{d\alpha} = -\frac{\sigma}{\alpha^2} \frac{H-H^r}{H^r J} < 0,$$

$$\frac{dH^r}{d\sigma} = \frac{\rho-g}{\sigma J} > 0, \quad \frac{dH^r}{d\lambda^r} = \frac{H^r}{J} > 0, \quad \frac{dH^r}{d\lambda^d} = 0.$$

Note that g and H^r are independent of λ^d. Chapter 6 shows that λ^d positively affects the growth rate through equation (6.11). These results indicate that the growth rate does not vary with the productivity of learning by doing if it does not expand general knowledge. Whether learning by doing contributes to long-run economic growth depends on whether or not it increases general knowledge. The qualitative results carry over to the R&D model with internalized learning by doing with equation (6.31) for the growth of general knowledge.

2. Welfare analysis when learning by doing has no effect on general knowledge

We first derive the equations of motion, subject to which the social planner maximizes the utilitarian social welfare function. First, note that $Z_0 = 0$ and $dZ_{t-\tau}/dt = dZ_a/da$ in (6.13), because $a = t - \tau$. Bearing them in mind and differentiating the aggregate output (6.1) with respect to t, we obtain

$$\dot{Y}_t = K_t - \alpha\sigma Y_t \qquad (S6.2)$$

where

$$K_t = \int_{-\infty}^{t} \lambda^d \lambda^r H_\tau^r A_\tau \, (\ell_0)^{1-\nu+\alpha} \, e^{-\phi(t-\tau)} d\tau$$

and $\phi = \sigma(1 - \nu + \alpha)$. Differentiating this equation leads to

$$\dot{K}_t = \lambda^d \lambda^r H_t^r A_t \, (\ell_0)^{1-\nu+\alpha} - \phi K_t. \qquad (S6.3)$$

In the labor market, there is a flow of workers, $\sigma(H - H_t^r)$, who are upgraded and have the choice to enter into production or research at each instant. Of those, the number of workers who move into production is given by $\lambda^r H_t^r \ell_0$, as $\lambda^r H_t^r$ of new production lines are created at time t. Thus, the change in the number of workers in R&D is

$$\dot{H}_t^r = \sigma\left(H - H_t^r\right) - \lambda^r H_t^r \ell_0. \qquad (S6.4)$$

The social planner's problem is to maximize $\int_0^\infty e^{-\rho t} Y_t dt$ subject to (6.31), (S6.2), (S6.3), and (S6.4). The current-value Hamiltonian is

$$\mathfrak{H} = Y_t + \mu_t^A \lambda^r H_t^r A_t + \mu_t^Y \left(K_t - \alpha\sigma Y_t\right) + \mu_t^K \left(\lambda^d \lambda^r H_t^r A_t \, (\ell_0)^{1-\nu+\alpha} - \phi K_t\right)$$

$$+ \mu_t^r \left[\sigma\left(H - H_t^r\right) - \lambda^r H_t^r \ell_0\right].$$

The first-order conditions are

$$\dot{\mu}_t^A = \rho\mu_t^A - \mu_t^A \lambda^r H_t^r - \mu_t^K \lambda^d \lambda^r H_t^r \, (\ell_0)^{1-\nu+\alpha} \qquad (S6.5)$$

$$\dot{\mu}_t^Y = \rho\mu_t^Y - 1 - \mu_t^Y \alpha\sigma \qquad (S6.6)$$

$$\dot{\mu}_t^K = \rho\mu_t^K - \mu_t^Y + \mu_t^K \phi \qquad (S6.7)$$

$$\dot{\mu}_t^r = \rho\mu_t^r - \mu_t^A \lambda^r A_t - \mu_t^K \lambda^d \lambda^r A_t \, (\ell_0)^{1-\nu+\alpha} \qquad (S6.8)$$
$$+ \mu_t^r(\sigma + \lambda^r \ell_0)$$

$$0 = \mu_t^K \lambda^d A_t \, (\ell_0)^{-\nu+\alpha} \, (1 - \nu + \alpha) - \mu_t^r. \qquad (S6.9)$$

We are interested in a steady state where $\dot{A}/A = g$, $\dot{H}^r = 0$, and all μ's grow at constant rates (possibly zero). (S6.6) implies $\dot{\mu}^Y = 0$; this and (S6.7) imply $\dot{\mu}^K = 0$; this and (S6.5) imply $\dot{\mu}^A = 0$; this and (S6.9) imply $\dot{\mu}^r/\mu^r = g$. Combining these results with (S6.5), (S6.8), and (S6.9), we obtain

$$\rho = \lambda^r H_t^r + \frac{\mu^K}{\mu^A} \lambda^d \lambda^r H_t^r \, (\ell_0)^{1-\nu+\alpha} \tag{S6.10}$$

$$\rho + \sigma - g = \frac{\mu^K}{\mu^r} \lambda^d \lambda^r A_t \, (\ell_0)^{1-\nu+\alpha} - \lambda^r \ell_0 + \frac{\mu^A}{\mu^r} \lambda^r A_t \tag{S6.11}$$

$$\mu^r = \mu^K A_t \lambda^d \, (\ell_0)^{-\nu+\alpha} \, (1 - \nu + \alpha) \tag{S6.12}$$

Using (S6.10), (S6.12), and (S6.4) with $\dot{H}^r = 0$, equation (S6.11) can be rewritten as

$$\rho + \sigma - g = \sigma \frac{\nu - \alpha}{1 - \nu + \alpha} \frac{H - H^r}{H^r} + \Gamma \tag{S6.13}$$

where $\Gamma = \sigma \lambda^r (H - H^r)/(\rho - g)(1 - \nu + \alpha) > 0$, because we have assumed $\rho > g$. This is the social-research arbitrage condition. Compare it with the market-research arbitrage condition (6.15). The two conditions are identical except for a positive term Γ on the right-hand side of (S6.13). It follows immediately that the social-research arbitrage condition lies everywhere to the right of the private arbitrage curve in (g, H^r) space. Given the same equation (6.31) for the growth of general knowledge, it is obvious that the steady-state level of research under laissez-faire is less than the social optimum, that is, the market economy grows too slowly. To understand why the equilibrium always involves too little research, note that the production of general knowledge is a purely external benefit of R&D. Everyone takes the time path of general knowledge as given, even though their collective innovative activities are what make it grow.

★ 3. Arrow's learning by doing (based on d'Autume and Michel 1993)

a. Because final output firms do not waste any input with a positive price, they must operate at a point where

$$Y(t, v) = aI(v) = (a/b) K(v)^\alpha L(t, v). \tag{S6.14}$$

b. Using (S6.14), we obtain the labor demand, $L(t, v) = bK(v)^{-\alpha} I(v)$. The oldest equipment still in use was introduced at time $t - T(t)$. Thus, (S6.14) implies that the full employment of labor requires

$$L = \int_{t-T(t)}^{t} bK(v)^{-\alpha} I(v) \, dv. \tag{S6.15}$$

Moreover, performing the change of variables $S = K(v)$ which implies

$$dS = I(v)\,dv, \tag{S6.16}$$

from equation (6.33), we can rewrite (S6.15) as $L = \int_{M(t)}^{K(t)} bS^{-\alpha}dS$. Upon integration, it gives (6.34).

c. Total output in the economy is

$$Y(t) = \int_{t-T(t)}^{t} aI(v)dv = a\left[K(t) - M(t)\right]$$

where we have performed the change of variables using (S6.16) to obtain the second equality. Using (6.34), this equation can be rearranged to give (6.35).

d. A constant saving rate implies $\dot{K}(t) = sY(t)$, which, together with (6.35), yields

$$\frac{\dot{K}(t)}{K(t)} = \begin{cases} sa\left[1 - \left(1 - \frac{1-\alpha}{b}\frac{L}{K(t)^{1-\alpha}}\right)^{1/(1-\alpha)}\right] & \text{if } \alpha \neq 1 \\ sa\left(1 - e^{-L/b}\right) & \text{if } \alpha = 1. \end{cases}$$

i. For $1 > \alpha > 0$, the term inside the square bracket tends to zero, as $K(t)$ rises, i.e., $\lim_{t\to\infty} \dot{K}(t)/K(t) = 0$.

ii. For $\alpha = 1$, $\dot{K}(t)/K(t)$ is constant. Moreover, $\dot{Y}(t)/Y(t) = \dot{K}(t)/K(t)$ for $\alpha = 1$ from (6.35).

iii. When $\alpha > 1$, the term inside the square bracket tends to one as $K(t)$ increases, i.e., $\lim_{t\to\infty} \dot{K}(t)/K(t) = sa$.

Thus, whether $K(t)$ grows exponentially in the long run crucially depends on the value of α.

e. Equation (6.35) says that for $\alpha = 1$, $Y(t) = AK(t)$, $A = a(1 - e^{-L/b})$, which is equivalent to the AK–type production function discussed in Chapter 1. The social planner solves

$$\max \quad \int_{0}^{\infty} e^{-\rho t}\frac{C(t)^{1-\sigma} - 1}{1 - \sigma}dt$$

s.t. $\quad \dot{K}(t) = AK(t) - C(t), \quad \dot{K}(t) \geq 0.$

The solution to this problem is equation (6.36).

f.

i. Future quasi-rent per unit of equipment at $\tau \geq t$ is $\pi(\tau, t) = [Y(\tau, t) - w(\tau)L(\tau, t)]/I(t)$, which equals $a - bK(t)^{-1}w(\tau)$, using (S6.14). Note that the equilibrium wage rate must ensure that the quasi-rent of equipment on the marginal generation is zero at time t, i.e., $a = bK(t - T(t))^{-1}w(t)$, which leads to $\pi(\tau, t) = a[1 - K(\tau - T(\tau))/K(t)]$. But in the long run with

$K(t) = K_0 e^{gt}$, $M(t) = K_0 e^{g(t-T)}$, and constant T, this equation can be rewritten as $\pi(\tau, t) = a[1 - e^{g(\tau - T - t)}]$.

ii. (6.34) gives $L/b = \ln K(t)/M(t)$. But $M(t) = K_0 e^{g(t-T)} = K(t)e^{-gT}$. Combining them yields $gT = L/b$.

iii. In equilibrium, investment is made if the discounted value of future quasi-rents is equal to the value of the investment:

$$\int_t^{t+T} e^{-r(\tau - t)} \pi(\tau, t)\, d\tau = 1.$$

Using $\pi(\tau, t) = a[1 - e^{g(\tau - T - t)}]$ and $gT = L/b$, this is re-expressed as the first equation in (6.37). The other equilibrium condition comes from the consumers' intertemporal utility maximization:

$$\max \quad \int_0^\infty e^{-\rho t} \frac{c(t)^{1-\sigma} - 1}{1 - \sigma}\, dt$$

s.t. $c(t) + \dot{a}(t) = w(t) + r(t)a(t)$, a_0 is given

where $a(t)$ and $c(t)$ are the consumer's asset holding and consumption. Solving this problem, we obtain the second equation in (6.37).

iv. Combining the two equations in (6.37) gives

$$\int_t^{t+L/(bg)} e^{-(\rho + \sigma g)(\tau - t)} a[1 - e^{g(\tau - t) - L/b}]\, d\tau = 1,$$

The left-hand side is decreasing in g. It is also decreasing in b, ρ and σ and increasing in a and L. Therefore, g is decreasing in b, ρ, and σ and increasing in a and L.

g. First consider the social optimum. The equilibrium condition is given by (6.36), which can be interpreted as implying a rate of return to investment $r = \psi(g) \equiv \rho + \sigma g$, where $r = A$. If you draw a figure with the horizontal and vertical axes representing g and r respectively, the $r = \psi(g)$ curve is upward-sloping and the $r = A$ schedule is horizontal. The optimal growth rate is given by their intersection point, assuming $A > \rho$. For the market economy, the equilibrium conditions are given in (6.37). The second equation is equivalent to $r = \psi(g)$, and the first equation can be reexpressed implicitly as $r = \phi(g)$. Implicitly differentiating it, we find that the $r = \phi(g)$ schedule is downward-sloping. Moreover, when $g = 0$, it collapses to $\int_t^\infty e^{-r(\tau - t)} A\, d\tau = 1$, that is, $r = A$. Thus, the $\phi(g)$ schedule is downward-sloping starting from $r = A$. It follows that this curve intersects the $r = \psi(g)$ schedule below $r = A$, establishing that a market economy grows too slowly. The reason is that learning by doing is an unappropriable activity for private agents, whereas the social planner internalizes it.

* **4. Bounded learning by doing (based on Young 1991, 1993a)**

a. Consider two goods indexed by $S(t) - \Delta$ and $S(t) + \Delta$:

$$a\left(S\left(t\right) + \Delta, t\right) = e^{-[S(t)+\Delta]-2S(t)} = e^{-S(t)-\Delta} = a\left(S\left(t\right) - \Delta, t\right).$$

This implies that $a(s, t)$ is U-shaped with $a(S(t), t)$ being the lowest unit labor requirement.

b. Because all markets for consumption goods are perfectly competitive, marginal cost pricing implies

$$p\left(s, t\right) = w\left(t\right) a\left(s, t\right). \tag{S6.17}$$

c. The slope of an indifference curve between any two goods associated with the utility function (6.38) is given by

$$\frac{\partial x\left(s, t\right)}{\partial x\left(v, t\right)} = \frac{x\left(s, t\right) + 1}{x\left(v, t\right) + 1}, \qquad s \neq v.$$

This slope is $x(s, t) + 1$ for $x(v, t) = 0$ and $1/[x(v, t) + 1]$ for $x(s, t) = 0$. Thus an indifference curve intersects the vertical and horizontal axes in $(x(s, t), x(v, t))$ space, which implies that corner solutions (i.e., either $x(s, t) = 0$ or $x(v, t) = 0$) are possible if the price of either of the goods is sufficiently high. Generalizing this logic, a consumer consumes only a limited range of intermediate goods whose prices are sufficiently low, for $\lim_{x(s,t) \to 0} \partial u / \partial x(s, t) < \infty$. This implies that the goods that are actually consumed are located around $S(t)$, and that $p(S(t), t)$ is the lowest price at t.

d.

i. A representative consumer's problem is to maximize (6.38) subject to her budget constraint $w(t) = \int_{M(t)}^{N(t)} p\left(s, t\right) x\left(s, t\right) ds$. Combining any two first-order conditions gives

$$[x\left(s, t\right) + 1] a\left(s, t\right) = [x\left(v, t\right) + 1] a\left(v, t\right) \tag{S6.18}$$

for $s, v \in [M(t), N(t)]$. But $x(N(t), t) = x(M(t), t) = 0$. Hence (S6.18) implies $x(s, t) = a(M(t), t)/a(s, t) - 1$. This together with equation (6.39) and the fact that $S(t) = (M(t) + N(t))/2$, gives (6.41).

ii. Consider two goods indexed by $S(t) - \Delta$ and $S(t) + \Delta$. From (a) we know that $a(S(t) - \Delta) = a(S(t) + \Delta)$. Hence (S6.18) implies

$$x\left(S\left(t\right) - \Delta, t\right) = x\left(S\left(t\right) + \Delta, t\right).$$

Moreover, (6.41) implies that $x(s, t)$ increases in s for $M(t) < s < S(t)$ and decreases for $S(t) < s < N(t)$, giving a $\cap$-shape.

iii. The consumer's budget constraint implies

$$1 = \int_{M(t)}^{N(t)} a(s,t)x(s,t)ds.$$

Substituting for $a(s,t)$ and $x(s,t)$ and integrating we obtain $1 = 2e^{-S(t)} - 2e^{-M(t)} + (N(t) - M(t))e^{-M(t)}$. Rearranging this expression and using the definition of $\tau(t)$ gives (6.42).

e.

i. Because $a(s,t)$ and $x(s,t)$ are symmetric around $S(t)$, $L(s,t) = a(s,t)x(s,t)$ must be so. This implies $\int_{S(t)}^{N(t)} L(s,t)ds = L/2$. Substituting into (6.40) yields equation (6.43).

ii. (6.39) implies $-\frac{da(s,t)/dt}{a(s,t)} = 2\dot{S}(t)$ for $S(t) < s < N(t)$. But learning occurs for only half the industries. Thus, the average proportionate rate of changes in $a(s,t)$ is

$$g = \text{average}\left\{-\frac{da(s,t)/dt}{a(s,t)}\right\} = \frac{1}{2} \cdot 2\dot{S}(t) = \frac{\Psi L}{2}.$$

f. The full-employment condition in the steady state is $L = L_R + L_M$, where L_M denotes the number of workers employed in manufacturing consumption goods. Because $N(t) \leq A(t)$, the production and learning structure is still the same as before. Hence the long-run equilibrium requires $g = \dot{S}(t) = \Psi L_M/2$. Besides, R&D technology implies $g = L_R/a_R$ in the long run. Combining these equations gives (6.44).

⋆⋆ 5. Learning by doing in a small open economy (based on Lucas 1993)

a. Because the value of each product is $e^{\mu s}x(s,t)$, the value of total production is

$$y(t) = \int_0^{\lambda t} e^{\mu s}x(s,t)\, ds. \tag{S6.19}$$

b. At any point in time T, such that $\tau \leq T \leq t$ equation (6.46) holds (because τ is the period when the sth product was first introduced). Rearrange it as $z(s,T)^{-\alpha}dz(s,T) = \varphi(T-\tau)dT$. Integrating both sides from τ to t, we obtain

$$z(s,t) = \left[z(s,\tau)^{1-\alpha} + (1-\alpha)\left(1 - e^{-\sigma(t-\tau)}\right)\right]^{\frac{1}{1-\alpha}}. \tag{S6.20}$$

c. From (6.47), it is obvious that $\partial z(s,t)/\partial s < 0$ for $s > \lambda t$. This and (6.46) imply that the unit cost of more advanced goods (higher s) is higher. Moreover, we have

$$1 = \delta \int_0^{\lambda t} e^{-\delta(\lambda t-u)}z(u,t)\, du, \tag{S6.21}$$

because the right-hand side of (6.47) is equal to 1 for $s = \lambda t$. It follows that the right-hand side of (6.47) for $s > \lambda t$ is smaller than 1, and therefore, products are introduced into the economy sequentially from less advanced goods.

d. When the sth product is first introduced into the economy, the right-hand side of (6.47) equals 1. Thus, $z(s, \tau) = 1$ must hold. Using this, (S6.20) becomes

$$z(s,t) = \left[1 + (1 - \alpha) \left(1 - e^{-\sigma(t-s/\lambda)} \right) \right]^{\frac{1}{1-\alpha}} \tag{S6.22}$$

where we have used the fact that $s = \lambda \tau$. Substituting this equation into (S6.21), performing the change of variables with $v = t - s/\lambda$ and letting $t \to \infty$ for the long-run analysis, we obtain (6.48).

e. First let us rewrite (6.48) as

$$1 = \int_0^\infty f(v) \chi(v) \, dv, \tag{S6.23}$$

where $f(v) = \delta \lambda e^{-\delta \lambda v}$ and $\chi(v) = [1 + (1 - \alpha)(1 - e^{-\sigma v})]^{\frac{1}{1-\alpha}}$. Integrating by parts, we obtain

$$1 = (2 - \alpha)^{\frac{1}{1-\alpha}} - \int_0^\infty \left(1 - e^{-\delta \lambda v} \right) \chi'(v) \, dv. \tag{S6.24}$$

Equation (S6.24) implies that the right-hand side is decreasing in λ and δ, and (S6.23) implies that the right-hand side is increasing in σ. It follows that λ is decreasing in δ and increasing σ.

f. Using (6.45) and (S6.22), we can rewrite (S6.19) as

$$y(t) = \int_0^{\lambda t} e^{\mu s} k \sigma e^{-\sigma(t-s/\lambda)} \left[1 + (1 - \alpha) \left(1 - e^{-\sigma(t-s/\lambda)} \right) \right]^{\frac{\alpha}{1-\alpha}} ds,$$

which is reexpressed by changing variables with $v = t - s/\lambda$ as

$$y(t) = e^{\mu \lambda t} \int_0^t \lambda k \sigma e^{-(\mu \lambda + \sigma)v} \left[1 + (1 - \alpha) \left(1 - e^{-\sigma v} \right) \right]^{\frac{\alpha}{1-\alpha}} dv.$$

This leads to

$$\frac{\dot{y}(t)}{y(t)} = \mu \lambda + \frac{\lambda k \sigma e^{-\sigma t} \left[1 + (1 - \alpha) \left(1 - e^{-\sigma t} \right) \right]^{\frac{\alpha}{1-\alpha}}}{y(t)}.$$

As $t \to \infty$, the second term vanishes, and hence $\lim_{t \to \infty} \dot{y}(t)/y(t) = \mu \lambda$. The asymptotic growth rate is higher, as workers are more concentrated on more advanced goods, in that a higher σ implies a higher λ. It suggests that differences in growth rates among countries can be explained, at least partly, by how they allocate resources among different sectors with different learning possibilities, as Lucas (1993) argues.

g. Equations (6.45) and (6.46) imply

$$\frac{dz(s,t)/dt}{z(s,t)} = z(s,t)^{-(1-\alpha)}$$

and

$$\frac{dx(s,t)/dt}{x(s,t)} = \alpha \frac{dz(s,t)/dt}{z(s,t)},$$

using $\varphi(t-\tau) = 1$. Combining them yields

$$\frac{dx(s,t)/dt}{x(s,t)} = \alpha z(s,t)^{-(1-\alpha)},$$

which asymptotically converges to zero. Note that this is because of $1 > \alpha > 0$, that is, the learning effect is subject to diminishing returns. On the other hand, if $\alpha = 1$, that is, the learning effect had constant returns, the economy would grow at the rate of 1. This shows that when the learning externality is limited, introducing new goods with large scope for learning is one way to sustain growth in the long run.

★★ 6. Technological "lock-in" (based on Jovanovic and Nyarko 1994)

a. First take expectation of (6.49). But $E_t[q_{mt} - z_t]^2 = E_t[q_{mt}^2] - (E_t[q_{mt}])^2 + (E_t[q_{mt}] - z_t)^2$ by expanding and factorizing it again for a given z_t. It implies that $E_t[y_t]$ is maximized for $z_t = E_t[q_{mt}] = E_t[\theta_m]$, where (6.50) has been used for the second equality.

b. Substituting $z_t = E_t[\theta_m]$ and (6.50) into (6.49) generates

$$E_t\left[y_t\right] = \gamma^m \left\{1 - E_t\left[\theta_m - E_t\left[\theta_m\right]\right]^2 - E_t\left[w_{mt}^2\right]\right\},$$

which is equivalent to (6.52).

c.

i. The use of technology γ^m at t reduces the prior variance from x_{mt} to x_{mt+1}, and (6.52) implies that the expected output approaches to $\gamma^m[1 - \sigma_w^2]$ as learning exhausts. Thus, growth is bounded in this case.

ii. Because γ is larger than one, (6.52) implies that growth is unbounded.

d. Suppose that the agent used γ^m at t and he upgrades it to γ^{m+1} at $t+1$. His prior variance of θ_{m+1} at $t+1$ is calculated by using (6.51):

$$\text{Var}_{t+1}\left(\theta_{m+1}\right) \equiv x_{m+1t+1} = \alpha h_{mt} + \sigma_\varepsilon^2. \tag{S6.25}$$

If $\alpha = 1$ and $\sigma_\varepsilon^2 = 0$, human capital is general and freely transferable across technologies. If $\alpha = 0$, human capital is technology-specific and no transfer occurs, that is, successive technologies are not related. (S6.25) can be rewritten as

$$\frac{1}{h_{mt}} - \frac{1}{x_{m+1t+1}} = \frac{1}{h_{mt}} - \frac{1}{\alpha h_{mt} - \sigma_\varepsilon^2}. \tag{S6.26}$$

The left-hand side of (S6.26) represents the part of human capital that is not transferred from γ^m to γ^{m+1}. It is increasing in α, because a higher α hastens the depreciation of human capital when it is transferred. The same interpretation applies to σ_ε^2.

e. (6.52) implies that if the agent sticks to γ^m at t, expected net output is $\pi(x_{mt+1}, m) = \gamma^m[1 - x_{mt+1} - \sigma_w^2]$. But $x_{mt+1} = h_{mt}$. Thus, expected net output if the agent continues to use γ^m at $t + 1$ is given by (6.53). If the agent switches to γ^{m+1}, the expected net output at $t + 1$ is $\pi(x_{m+1t+1}, m + 1) = \gamma^{m+1}[1 - x_{m+1t+1} - \sigma_w^2]$ from (6.52). Using (S6.25), we can reexpress this expression as equation (6.54).

f.

i. Let us compare the expected payoffs in the two cases:

$$\pi(h_{mt}, m + 1) - \pi(h_{mt}, m) = \gamma^m \left[\gamma \left(1 - \sigma_\varepsilon^2 - \sigma_w^2 \right) \right.$$
$$\left. - \left(1 - \sigma_w^2 \right) + (1 - \gamma\alpha) h_{mt} \right] \tag{S6.27}$$

It follows that a sufficient condition for the agent to upgrade his technology in every period is

$$\frac{1}{\alpha} \geq \gamma \geq \frac{1 - \sigma_w^2}{1 - \sigma_\varepsilon^2 - \sigma_w^2}.$$

ii. Using (S6.27) again, a sufficient condition for the agent to be locked into the initial technology γ is

$$\frac{1 - \sigma_w^2}{1 - \sigma_\varepsilon^2 - \sigma_w^2} \geq \gamma \geq \frac{1}{\alpha}.$$

g. Define $\Delta = \pi(h_{mt}, m + 1) - \pi(h_{mt}, m)$. Equation (S6.27) implies

$$\frac{\partial \Delta}{\partial \alpha} < 0, \quad \frac{\partial \Delta}{\partial \sigma_\varepsilon^2} < 0, \quad \frac{\partial \Delta}{\partial \sigma_w^2} < 0, \quad \frac{\partial \Delta}{\partial \gamma} \gtreqless 0, \quad \frac{\partial \Delta}{\partial h_{mt}} \gtreqless 0.$$

Δ is decreasing in α and σ_ε^2, for they positively affect the depreciation of human capital when it is transferred across technologies, making technology upgrading less profitable. Δ is also decreasing in σ_w^2. Its higher value makes the continual use of the same technology in every period less attractive to the agent, but it is dominated by the negative effect on the incentive to switch. As regards γ, its effect on Δ depends on the value of h_{mt}, that is, the level of human capital. A higher γ raises the incentive for technological upgrading at a high human capital level (a small h_{mt}) and lowers it at a lower human capital level (a large h_{mt}). Last, Δ increases with h_{mt} for $1 > \gamma\alpha$, but decreases for $1 < \gamma\alpha$. Thus if successive technologies are closely linked (a high α), a higher stock of human capital level is more likely associated with technological updating and fast growth.

⋆ **7. "Penalty" to a pioneer (based on Redding 1996c)**

a.

i. The inverse demand is

$$p_{1t}(x_t) = \alpha \cdot F_{1t} \cdot S_{1t} \cdot x_t^{\alpha-1}, \tag{S6.28}$$

and the wage

$$w_{1t} = \alpha \cdot F_{1t} \cdot S_{1t} \cdot x_t^{\alpha-1}. \tag{S6.29}$$

ii. If there is no innovation (i.e., with probability $(1 - \lambda \cdot n_t)$), we have

$$p_{2t}(x_t) = (1 + \theta) \cdot p_{1t}(x_t), \tag{S6.30}$$

$$w_{2t} = (1 + \theta) \cdot w_{1t}. \tag{S6.31}$$

iii. Differentiating (6.55) and using (S6.28),

$$\begin{aligned} p_{2t}(x_t) &= \alpha \cdot \gamma \cdot F_{1t} \cdot S_{1t}^{\sigma} \cdot x_t^{\alpha-1} \\ &= \gamma \cdot S_{1t}^{\sigma-1} \cdot p_{1t}(x_t). \end{aligned} \tag{S6.32}$$

iv. Comparing (S6.30) and (S6.32), final-goods producers will employ the state-of-the-art technology if $\gamma \cdot S_{1t}^{\sigma-1} > (1 + \theta)$. We assume this parameter restriction is satisfied.

v. If an innovation is introduced, the innovating monopolist pays workers in production their outside option. That is, workers receive $w_{2t} = (1 + \theta) \cdot w_{1t}$ with probability $\lambda \cdot n_t$. The second-period wage is therefore independent of whether or not there is an innovation. Hence the value of a lifetime in production is

$$V_{xt} = \left(1 + \frac{1+\theta}{1+\rho}\right) \cdot w_{1t}. \tag{S6.33}$$

b. In subperiod 1, a researcher has no profits. If she succeeds, she obtains $\pi_{2t} = p_{2t}(x_t) \cdot x_t - w_{2t} \cdot x_t$. Substituting for $p_{2t}(x_t)$ and w_{2t}, we get

$$\pi_{2t} = \left[\gamma \cdot S_{1t}^{\sigma-1} - (1 + \theta)\right] \cdot w_{1t} \cdot x_t, \tag{S6.34}$$

where the labor market clearing condition implies $x_t = L - n_t$. Because the probability of success for an individual producer is λ,

$$V_{rt} = \frac{\lambda}{1+\rho} \cdot \left[\gamma \cdot S_{1t}^{\sigma-1} - (1+\theta) \right] \cdot w_{1t} \cdot (L - n_t), \tag{S6.35}$$

where w_{1t} depends on the stock of secondary knowledge inherited by generation t.

c. In equilibrium $V_{xt} = V_{rt}$, which from (S6.33) and (S6.35) implies

$$(1 + \rho) + (1 + \theta) = \lambda(L - n_t) \left[\gamma \cdot S_{1t}^{\sigma-1} - (1+\theta) \right], \tag{S6.36}$$

where the left-hand side is the marginal cost of research, and the right-hand side the marginal benefit, which depends negatively on research employment (as a higher n_t implies a lower x_t and hence lower profits). Then

$$\widehat{n}_t = \frac{\left[\gamma \cdot S_{1t}^{\sigma-1} - (1+\theta) \right] L - (2 + \rho + \theta)/\lambda}{\gamma \cdot S_{1t}^{\sigma-1} - (1+\theta)}. \tag{S6.37}$$

Because by assumption $\gamma \cdot S_{1t}^{\sigma-1} > (1 + \theta)$, for an interior solution to exist we require that $\lambda \left[\gamma \cdot S_{1t}^{\sigma-1} - (1+\theta) \right] L > 2 + \rho + \theta$.

d. Taking logs of the production function we have

$$E[\ln y_{t+1}] = E[\ln S_{1t+1}] + E[\ln F_{1t+1}] + \alpha \ln x_{1t},$$

where $E[\ln S_{1t+1}]$ is the expected level of secondary innovations and $E[\ln F_{1t+1}]$ the expected number of fundamental innovations at time $t + 1$. Because an innovation occurs with probability $\lambda\widehat{n}_t$, we have

$$E[\ln y_{t+1}] = \lambda\widehat{n}_t \cdot \ln S_{1t}^{\sigma} + (1 - \lambda\widehat{n}_t) \ln(1+\theta)S_{1t}$$
$$+ \lambda\widehat{n}_t \ln(\gamma \cdot F_{1t}) + (1 - \lambda\widehat{n}_t) \ln F_{1t} + \alpha \ln x_{1t},$$

which can be expressed as

$$E[\ln y_{t+1}] = \ln[S_{1t} \cdot F_{1t} \cdot x_{1t}^{\alpha}] - \lambda\widehat{n}_t(1 - \sigma) \ln S_{1t} \tag{S6.39}$$
$$+ (1 - \lambda\widehat{n}_t)\ln(1+\theta) + \lambda\widehat{n}_t \ln \gamma.$$

The first term on the left-hand side is simply $\ln y_t$. Hence rearranging (S6.39) gives (6.57).

e. The latecomer grows faster for two reasons, both due to the fact that it has accumulated less secondary knowledge. First, a lower stock of secondary knowledge reduces the loss of productive knowledge when a new innovation arrives, thus raising the payoff to research and increasing the number of agents working in R&D (see equation (S6.37)). Second, there is a direct effect on the growth rate, in as much as for any given number of researchers a higher level of secondary knowledge reduces the increase in the level of output stemming from an innovation, as we can see in (6.57).

Chapter 7

1. Example of product market competition

a. As α increases, goods become closer substitutes. This implies that firms 1 and 2 are more exposed to each others' actions: a rise in production level x_i affects firm j ($\neq i$) more as α is higher.

b. To solve the consumer's optimization problem, we write the Lagrangian as $\max_{x_1, x_2} \{(x_1^\alpha + x_2^\alpha)^{1/\alpha} - \lambda(p_1 x_1 + p_2 x_2 - y)\}$.

The first-order condition for x_i can be written as (i) $x_i^{\alpha-1}(x_1^\alpha + x_2^\alpha)^{(1-\alpha)/\alpha} = \lambda p_i$. Dividing equation $(i = 1)$ by $(i = 2)$ and adding 1 on both sides of the equation yields

$$\frac{x_1^\alpha + x_2^\alpha}{x_2^\alpha} = \frac{y}{p_2 x_2}.$$

This can be rewritten as

$$p_2(x_1, x_2) = \frac{y/x_2^{1-\alpha}}{x_1^\alpha + x_2^\alpha}.$$

And a similar expression can be derived for firm 1.

To find the Cournot-Nash equilibrium, solve simultaneously the first-order conditions for profit maximization for firms $i = 1, 2 : \max_{x_i} \{y x_i^\alpha / (x_1^\alpha + x_2^\alpha) - c_i x_i\}$, where the first-order condition can be written as $\alpha y x_i^{\alpha-1}/(x_1^\alpha + x_2^\alpha)^2 = c_i (i = 1, 2)$. Solving these two equations for x_i yields

$$x_i(c_1, c_2; \alpha) = \frac{y}{c_i} \frac{\alpha \left(\frac{c_i}{c_j}\right)^\alpha}{\left(1 + \left(\frac{c_i}{c_j}\right)^\alpha\right)^2} \text{ for } i, j = 1, 2 \text{ and } i \neq j.$$

Finally substituting these results into the expression for i's profits yields

$$\pi_1(c_1, c_2; \alpha) = y \frac{1 + (1 - \alpha)\left(\frac{c_i}{c_j}\right)^\alpha}{\left(1 + \left(\frac{c_i}{c_j}\right)^\alpha\right)^2}$$

c. Choosing $i = 1$ without loss of generality, we have $\gamma = c_1/c_2$ and profits can be written as

$$\pi_1(c_1, c_2; \alpha) = y \frac{1 + (1 - \alpha)(\gamma)^\alpha}{(1 + (\gamma)^\alpha)^2}.$$

Then one can easily verify that $d\pi_1/d\alpha < 0 <=> (1 + \gamma^\alpha)[-\gamma^\alpha + (1 - \alpha)(\ln \gamma)\gamma^\alpha] - 2[1 + (1 - \alpha)\gamma^\alpha](\ln \gamma)\gamma^\alpha < 0$. The latter can be rewritten as

$$(-ln\gamma) < (1 + \gamma^\alpha)/[(1 + a) + 2(1 - \alpha)\gamma^\alpha]. \tag{S7.1}$$

i. If $c_1 = c_2$ then $\gamma = 1$ and (S7.1) holds, that is, $d\pi_i/d\alpha < 0$ for both firms. In other words, both firms lose as PMC increases.

ii. If $c_1 > c_2$ then firm 1 is the follower and 2 is the leader. Then $\gamma > 1$ and (S7.1) holds, that is, the follower always loses as PMC is increased.

iii. This claim is incorrect, as can be seen as follows. If $c_1 < c_2$, firm 1 is the leader, and firm 1 is far enough ahead of firm 2 in the sense that $\gamma < 1$ is close enough to 0, the inequality in equation (S7.1) is reversed. In other words, if the leader is far enough ahead of its opponent, a rise in PMC leads to an increase in the leader's profits. The intuition is that if the leader is far enough ahead, a rise in PMC makes it easier for the leader to marginalize its opponent.

d. Total production employment equals $c_1 x_1 + c_2 x_2 = y[\alpha\gamma^\alpha/(1 + \gamma^\alpha)^2 + \alpha\gamma^{-\alpha}/(1 + \gamma^{-\alpha})^2] = 2y\alpha\gamma^\alpha/(1 + \gamma^\alpha)^2$, where $\gamma = c_1/c_2$ and we assume $\gamma > 1$, without loss of generality.

Then one can verify that $d(c_1 x_1 + c_2 x_2)/d\alpha > 0$ if and only if $\alpha(\ln \gamma) < (1 + \gamma)/(\gamma^\alpha - 1)$, that is, if $\gamma > 1$ is close enough to 1. The intuition is that a rise in PMC spurs firms to produce more, which increases total labor demand if firms are roughly equally efficient. However if one firm is far more efficient than the other one, a rise in competition will shift production from the inefficient to the efficient firm, thereby reducing industry demand for labor.

Hence if firms are close together, a rise in competition draws labor away from R&D, and thereby lowers growth. If one firm is far more efficient than its opponent, a rise in competition lowers industry labor demand, more labor is left for R&D, and this general equilibrium effect leads to faster growth.

2. Product market competition and concentration

a. As travel costs fall, consumers tend more and more to buy from the cheapest firm instead of the closest firm. That is, differences in firms' prices become more important as travel costs fall.

b. At given prices p_A and p_B, the consumer at position $x \in [0, 1]$ is indifferent between buying from firm A or B, if and only if x satisfies $tx + p_A = t(1 - x) + p_B$. That is $x = 1/2 + (p_B - p_A)/(2t)$. Because firm A is on the left of the beach at position 0, we find $q_A = 1/2 + (p_B - p_A)/(2t)$ and $q_B = 1/2 + (p_A - p_B)/(2t)$.

Solving for the Bertrand-Nash equilibrium, consider firm i's optimization problem: $\max_{p_i}(p_i - c_i)[1/2 + (p_j - p_i)/(2t)]$. The first-order condition for firm i can be written as $1/2 + (p_j - p_i)/(2t) - (p_i - c_i)/(2t) = 0$ for $i, j = A, B$, and $i \neq j$.

Solving the first-order conditions for firms A and B simultaneously yields $p_i = (3t + 2c_i + c_j)/3$. Substituting this into the equations for firms' output levels given the prices p_A and p_B, yields $q_i = 1/2 + (c_j - c_i)/(6t)$, $i, j = A, B$, and $i \neq j$.

c. Because the total market is fixed in this example on 1, one can measure concentration here simply as q_A/q_B where we assume without loss of generality that $c_A \leq c_B$.

If $c_A = c_B$ then $q_A = q_B = 1/2$ and concentration is unaffected by travel costs t. However, if $c_A < c_B$, then firm A can exploit its cost advantage better if t is lower. Consequently, more competition in the sense of lower travel costs leads to higher concentration levels.

⋆ **3. Product market competition and the speed of technological progress (based on Boone 1996b)**

a. Firm i's valuation of c_0 is highest, if $\pi_i(c_i, c_0, c_k; t)$ is lowest. Because π_i is increasing in $\Sigma_{j \neq i} c_j$, profits π_i are smallest if both opponents have low costs. That is, if firm k with $c_k > c_j$ buys c_0.

The intuition is that if i's high cost opponent buys c_0, firm i faces two low-cost opponents. If i's low-cost opponent buys c_0, i has one opponent with costs c_0 and one with relatively high costs. Firm i's profits are higher in the latter case.

b. Firm 1's valuation of the innovation equals $V_1(t) = \pi_1(c_0, c_2, c_3; t) - \pi_1(c_1, c_2, c_0; t)$. Using the expression for $\pi_i(.)$ and the values for c_i given in the text, one finds $V_1(t) = [(5t + c_2 + c_3 - 2c_0)^2 - (5t + c_2 + c_0 - 2c_1)^2]/(25t) = (90t + 99)/(25t)$. Similarly, one derives for firms 2 and 3 that $V_2(t) = (130t + 39)/(25t)$ and $V_3(t) = (170t - 153)/(25t)$.

Then at $t = 4$, we find that $V(4) = \max\{V_1(4), V_2(4), V_3(4)\} = \max\{459/100, 559/100, 527/100\} = 559/100 = V_2(4)$. And at $t = 10 : V(10) = \max\{999/250, 1339/250, 1547/250\} = 1547/250 = V_3(10)$.

The valuation of an innovation consists of two effects. First there is the strategic effect that makes low-cost firms want to prevent high-cost firms from coming close to them. This works in the direction of low-cost firms being willing to pay more for an innovation than high-cost firms. Second, there is the direct cost effect, which says that the cost reduction to c_0 is bigger for a high-cost firm than for a low-cost firm. This works in the direction of high-cost firms being willing to pay more for an innovation than low-cost firms.

If travel costs are high, firms are more or less isolated from each other and the strategic effect is weak. Then the direct cost effect, dominates the strategic effect, and high-cost firm 3 buys c_0.

c. At $t = 4$, one finds $dV(t)/dt = dV_2(t)/dt = [130(25t) - 25(130t + 39)]/(25t)^2 < 0$. While at $t = 10$, it is the case that $dV(t)/dt = dV_3(t)/dt = [170(25t) - 25(170t - 153)]/(25t)^2 > 0$.

So an increase in PMC, here modeled as a reduction in travel costs t, leads to a rise in the value of the innovation at $t = 4$. However, at $t = 10$ an increase in

PMC leads to a reduction in the value of c_0. Hence the relation between PMC and the prize in the research laboratories' patent race is nonmonotone. In other words, there is no simple monotone relation between PMC and the speed of technological progress.

⋆⋆ **4. Product market competition and the socially optimal allocation of labor (based on Stokey 1995)**

a. The linearity of the function $f(.)$ follows from the homogeneity of $u(.)$ as the following steps show: $f(\lambda) = \max_x\{u(x)|\Sigma x_i \leq \lambda\} = \max_x\{\lambda u(x/\lambda)|\Sigma x_i \leq \lambda\} = \lambda \max_{x/\lambda}\{u(x/\lambda)|\lambda\Sigma(x_i/\lambda) \leq \lambda\} = \lambda \max_y\{u(y)|\Sigma y_i \leq 1\} = a\lambda$ where $a = \max_y\{u(y)|\Sigma y_i \leq 1\}$.

b. The social valuation of z labor units allocated to research consists of two parts. First, allocating z labor to research leaves $(L - z)$ labor for producing consumption goods. This yields a level of utility $([\gamma^n a(L - z)]^{1-\sigma} - 1)/(1 - \sigma)$ this period. This is the first part on the right-hand side of the Bellman equation. Second, allocating z labor to research yields a new $(n + 1)th$ technology next period with probability $\Theta(z)$. With probability $1 - \Theta(z)$, no new technology is found and social welfare next period equals $W(n)$. This is the second (discounted) part on the right-hand side of the Bellman equation.

c. The Bellman equation under (b) shows that the socially optimal allocation of labor over research and production is independent of PMC as modeled by α. So although the market allocation of labor over research and production changes with PMC, the socially optimal allocation does not.

5. Market structure and firms' investments in R&D

a. The first-order condition for firm i can be written as $1 - \Sigma_{j \neq i} q_j - 2q_i - c_i = 0$. One can check that the first-order condition for each firm i is satisfied if $q_i = (1 - nc_i + \Sigma_{j \neq i} c_j)/(n + 1)$. Substituting this result in the expression for firm i's profits yields $\pi_i(c_1, \ldots, c_n) = [(1 - nc_i + \Sigma_{j \neq i} c_j)/(n + 1)]^2$.

b. Firm i chooses c_i to solve

$$\max_c\{[(1 - nc + \Sigma_{j \neq i} c_j)/(n + 1)]^2 - \psi(c)\}. \tag{S7.2}$$

Free entry means that the last firm to enter makes zero profits:

$$\max_c\{[(1 - nc + \Sigma_{j \neq i} c_j)/(n + 1)]^2 - \psi(c)\} = 0. \tag{S7.3}$$

The first-order condition for (S7.2) evaluated at the symmetric Nash equilibrium can be written as $2n(1 - c)/(n + 1)^2 = -\psi'(c)$. The free-entry condition (S7.3) evaluated at the symmetric Nash equilibrium can be written as $[(1 - c)/(n + 1)]^2 = \psi(c)$. Finally, one can easily check that in the symmetric equilibrium the Herfindahl index equals $H = 1/n$.

Therefore, dividing the two equations found above yields

$$H = 2\psi(c)/[-\psi'(c)(1-c)].$$ (S7.4)

c. With this specification of $\psi(.)$, the first derivative equals $\psi'(c) = -\psi_1\psi_0(1-c)^{\psi_1-1}$. Substituting this in equation (S7.4) yields $H = 2/\psi_1 \iff n = \psi_1/2$. Using the free-entry condition (S7.3), yields

$$1 - c = \cfrac{1}{\left(\psi_0\left(\tfrac{1}{2}\psi_1 + 1\right)^2\right)^{\frac{1}{\psi_1-2}}}.$$

Consequently, $dn/d\psi_1 > 0$ and $dc/d\psi_0 > 0$, because $\psi_1 > 2$. As ψ_0 rises, reducing costs becomes more expensive and hence equilibrium cost levels are higher. As ψ_1 increases, total development costs $\psi(c)$ fall, as $(1-c) < 1$. Hence more firms can enter the industry.

d. The results of such regressions are not very meaningful, for both c_k and H_k are endogenously determined in equilibrium. By appropriately changing ψ_0 and ψ_1, a given value of c can be made compatible with any value of H. Similarly, a given value of H can be made compatible with any value of c by changing ψ_0.

6. A simple patent race

a. Firm i chooses x_i to solve $\max_x\{p_i(x_1,\dots,x_{i-1},x,x_{i\mid 1},\dots,x_n)V - x\}$. The first-order condition can be written as $\partial p_i(.)/\partial x_i V = 1$. A change in $x_j(j \neq i)$ affects i's investment x_i in the following way: $\partial^2 p_i(.)/\partial x_i^2(dx_i/dx_j) + \partial^2 p_i(.)/\partial x_i x_j = 0$. Using $\partial^2 p_i(.)/\partial x_i^2 < 0$, one finds $sign(dx_i/dx_j) = sign(\partial^2 p_i(.)/\partial x_i x_j)$.

Hence a rise in rivalry x_j increases x_i if $\partial^2 p_i(.)/\partial x_i \partial x_j > 0$, that is, if investments interact as strategic complements. A rise in rivalry x_j reduces x_i if investments interact as strategic substitutes.

b. The social valuation V^s exceeds the market valuation V due to the intertemporal spillover effect and the appropriability effect. The market valuation is bigger than the social valuation due to the business-stealing effect.

c. In the market equilibrium, firm i solves $\max_x\{xV\Theta(X)/X - x\}$ taking X as given. This leads only to a finite positive investment level if $V\Theta(X)/X = 1$ or equivalently $\Theta(X)/X = 1/V$. If this holds the expected payoff to each firm equals zero, hence the free-entry condition is satisfied as well.

d. The social planner is not interested in which firm innovates, only in the overall probability of an innovation. Hence X^s solves $\max_X\{V^s\Theta(X) - X\}$, where the first-order condition can be written as $\Theta'(X^s) = 1/V^s$.

e. If $V = V^S$, then X^m and X^s satisfy $\Theta'(X^s) = \Theta(X^m)/X^m$. By the concavity of $\Theta(.)$ and $\Theta(0) = 0$, this implies $X^m > X^s$: the market overinvests in research. This is caused by the common "pool externality": in choosing its R&D level, a firm does not take into account the negative effect on its rivals' chances of innovating first.

★★ **7. The evolution of duopoly (based on Budd, Harris, and Vickers 1993)**

a. Define s as $s \equiv \ln(c_A/c_B)$. Then the profits of firm A equal

$$\pi(s) = y\frac{1 + (1-\alpha)e^{\alpha s}}{(1 + e^{\alpha s})^2},$$

while B's profits equal $\pi(-s)$.

b. Firm A's normalized discounted payoff starting from state s can be written as the sum of the direct payoff plus the discounted value function in the next period. That is,

$$(1/r)V(s) = [\pi(s) - x(s)^2/2]dt + e^{-rdt}(1/r)V(s + ds). \tag{S7.5}$$

Linearizing e^{-rdt} around $dt = 0$ yields $(1 - rdt)$. This is in fact a good approximation because dt is very small. Further, the function $V(s + ds)$ can be approximated by $V(s) + V'(s)ds$ with $ds = [x(s) - y(s)]dt$. Substituting this into equation (S7.5) and again using the fact that $(dt)^2$ is approximately zero yields

$$\frac{V(s)}{r} = \left[\pi(s) - \frac{x(s)^2}{2}\right]dt + \frac{1 - rdt}{r}V(s) + \frac{x(s) - y(s)}{r}V'(s)dt$$

or, equivalently, $V(s)dt = (\pi(s) - x(s)^2/2)dt + (1/r)V'(s)[x(s) - y(s)]dt$. Rearranging this expression and dividing by dt, we can express it as: $rV(s) = r(\pi(s) - x(s)^2/2) + V'(s)[x(s) - y(s)]$. Now $x(s)$ is A's optimal strategy if and only if it solves

$$rV(s) = \max_x\{r(\pi(s) - x^2/2) + V'(s)[x - y(s)]\}. \tag{S7.6}$$

c. The first-order condition for this optimization problem (S7.6) can be written as

i. $x(s) = V'(s)/r$. Substituting $V'(s) = rx(s)$ into (S7.6) yields

ii. $V(s) = \pi(s) - x(s)^2/2 + x(s)(x(s) - y(s))$.

The equations (7.13) and (7.14) follow in a similar fashion keeping in mind that B's value function $W(s)$ is decreasing in s.

d. Substituting the approximations of $x(s)$ and $V(s)$ into equation (7.11) yields: $\{x_0(s) + r^{-1}x_1(s) + \cdots\} = (1/r)\{V_0(s) + r^{-1}V_1(s) + \cdots\}$. Equating terms of the order 0 in r gives us $x_0(s) = 0$. The intuition is that for very high values of r, the future benefit of an increase in state s equals zero. Hence for a high enough discount rate r, firm A is not willing to spend $x^2/2$ now to receive a future rise in s.

Similarly, $y_0(s) = 0$.

e. Substituting the approximations for $V(s), x(s)$ and $y(s)$ into equation (7.12) we get $\{V_0(s) + r^{-1}V_1(s) + \cdots\} = \pi(s) - \{r^{-1}x_1(s) + r^{-2}x_2(s) + \cdots\}^2/2 + \{r^{-1}x_1(s) + r^{-2}x_2(s) + \cdots\}$ $(\{r^{-1}x_1(s) + r^{-2}x_2(s) + \cdots\} - \{r^{-1}y_1(s) + r^{-2}y_2(s) + \cdots\})$. Equating terms of order zero in r yields $V_0(s) = \pi(s)$. If r is very high, firms do not invest ($x_0(s) = 0$) and do not value the future. Hence the value function equals current payoff $\pi(s)$.

f. Substituting the approximations found for $x(s)$ and $V(s)$ into equation (7.11) yields $\{r^{-1}x_1(s) + r^{-2}x_2(s) + \cdots\} = \{\pi'(s) + r^{-1}V_1(s) + \cdots\}/r$, because $V_0'(s) = \pi'(s)$. Equating terms of order one in r, we get $x_1(s) = \pi'(s)$. Similarly, for firm B, one gets $y_1(s) = \pi'(-s)$.

Because $x_0(s) = y_0(s) = 0$, the principal contribution to $x(s) - y(s)$ is of order one and equals $x_1(s) - y_1(s) = \pi'(s) - \pi'(-s) = \partial(\pi(s) + \pi(-s))/\partial s$.

This result says that firm A invests more than B ($x_1(s) - y_1(s) > 0$) if and only if a rise in s increases joint profits for A and B, $\pi(s) + \pi(-s)$. Similarly, firm B invests more than A if and only if a fall in s increases joint profits. Hence over time the industry moves in the direction that maximizes joint profits.

8. Product market competition and the identity of the innovator

a. If travel costs are so high that some consumers in the middle of the beach do not buy any product, then the markets of firms A and B are completely isolated. In this case firms are unaffected by each other's actions. If, covnersely, travel costs go to zero, only the most efficient firm survives and serves the whole market. If both firms are equally efficient, they set their price equal to marginal costs and earn zero profits.

b. The low-cost firm's valuation equals $\pi(c_0, c_2; \theta) - \pi(c_1, c_0; \theta)$. And the high-cost firm's valuation equals $\pi(c_0, c_1; \theta) - \pi(c_2, c_0; \theta)$. The former exceeds the latter if and only if $\pi(c_2, c_0; \theta) + \pi(c_0, c_2; \theta) \geq \pi(c_1, c_0; \theta) + \pi(c_0, c_1; \theta)$.

In words, joint profits are higher if the low-cost firm buys c_0 than if the high-cost firm buys c_0. This is the joint profit effect of the previous exercise.

c. Each of the three terms in { }-brackets on the left-hand side depends on a change in the opponent's cost level. Hence for $\theta = 0$ these terms all disappear. If $\pi(c_1, c_1; \theta) > 0$ then $\pi(c_1, c_1; \theta) - \pi(c_2, c_1; \theta) > 0$ by the assumption that $\partial\pi(c_i, c_j; \theta)/c_i < 0$. Hence at $\theta = 0$, the high-cost firm innovates.

For $\theta \to \infty$, both terms on the right-hand side of the inequality go to zero. Further, for $\theta > 0$ the left-hand side is strictly positive by the assumptions that

$\partial \pi (c_i, c_j; \theta)/\partial c_j|_{\theta > 0} > 0$ and $\partial^2 \pi (c_i, c_j; \theta)/\partial c_i \partial c_j|_{\theta > 0} < 0$. Hence for high values of θ, the low-cost firm innovates.

The intuition for these results is as follows. There are two effects determining the identity of the innovator. On one hand, there is the direct cost effect which says that the follower is willing to pay to catch up with the leader. This effect is represented by $\pi (c_1, c_1; \theta) - \pi (c_2, c_1; \theta) > 0$ on the right hand side of the inequality. The idea is that the fall in cost level for the high-cost firm 2 is bigger than for low-cost firm 1. This effect works in the direction of the high-cost firm being willing to pay more for c_0 than the low-cost firm. On the other hand, there are the strategic considerations of the leader who wants to prevent the follower from coming close. These strategic effects are on the left-hand side of the inequality. For $\theta = 0$ the strategic effects disappear and the follower leapfrogs. For $\theta \to \infty$ competition is intense and the strategic effects dominate the direct cost effect. In this case the leader increases its dominance.

d. In that case it is always the follower that leapfrogs.

Chapter 8

1. Obsolescence and GPT in neoclassical models (based on Howitt 1998)

a. With a constant saving rate, the equation governing the accumulation of capital is $\dot{K}_t = sY_t - [\delta + \beta(g)]K_t$. Given the definition of k_t, we know $\dot{K}_t/(e^{gt}L_t) = \dot{k}_t + (n + g)k_t$, hence

$$\frac{\dot{k}_t}{k_t} = sk_t^{-(1-\alpha)} - [\delta + n + g + \beta(g)]. \tag{S8.1}$$

b. Because the first term on the right-hand side of (S8.1) falls as the economy accumulates capital per efficiency unit of labor, it eventually reaches a steady state where $\dot{k}_t = 0$ and the equilibrium stock of capital is

$$k^* = \left(\frac{s}{\delta + n + \beta(g) + g} \right)^{\frac{1}{1-\alpha}}.$$

Equation (8.26) implies that per capita output is given by

$$y_t = e^{gt}k_t^{\alpha}. \tag{S8.2}$$

Its long-run growth rate is

$$g_y^* \equiv \left(\frac{\dot{y}}{y} \right)^* = g, \tag{S8.3}$$

because $\dot{k}_t = 0$ in steady state.

c. Equation (S8.2) implies that

$$g_{y_t} = g + \alpha \frac{\dot{k}_t}{k_t}, \tag{S8.4}$$

as k_t is changing off the steady state. Substituting (S8.1) into it, we obtain equation (8.27). This expression is decreasing in k_t.

d. First consider the long-run growth rate. From (S8.3), we have $\partial g_y^*/\partial g = 1$. An increase in g has a one-for-one positive effect on the long-run growth rate. The short-run growth rate is given by (8.27), which implies

$$\frac{\partial g_{y_t}}{\partial g}\bigg|_{\text{given } k_t} = (1 - \alpha) - \alpha\beta'(g) \gtreqless 0. \tag{S8.5}$$

Consider the first term, $(1 - \alpha)$, which captures the direct effect of a change in g on the growth rate and is smaller than the long-run impact, 1. The term $-\alpha$ appears due to the fact that a rise in g reduces the available stock of capital per efficiency unit of labor in the short run. This direct effect is not strong enough to offset the positive long-run effect, as $(1 - \alpha) > 0$. Now consider the indirect effect through obsolescence. Because the rate of obsolescence rises due to more rapid technological changes, that is, $\beta' > 0$, the rate at which the stock of capital is diminished (the second term in (S8.1)) increases. If the negative effect of obsolescence is sufficiently large, the short-run growth rate can actually decrease because of higher technological advance. This happens if the elasticity of β with respect to g is larger than $(1 - \alpha)g/(\alpha\beta)$.

e.

i. Equation (8.28) can be reexpressed

$$U = \int_0^\infty e^{-[\rho - n]t} \frac{e^{(1-\sigma)gt}(c_t)^{1-\sigma} - 1}{1 - \sigma} dt,$$

where we assume that $\rho > n + (1 - \sigma)g$, and $c_t \equiv C_t/(e^{gt}L_t)$. Consumers maximize this expression subject to the budget constraint

$$\dot{k}_t = k_t^\alpha - c_t - [\delta + n + g + \beta(g)]k_t. \tag{S8.6}$$

The first-order condition is

$$\frac{\dot{c}_t}{c_t} = \frac{\alpha k_t^{-(1-\alpha)} - \rho - \delta - \beta(g) - \sigma g}{\sigma}. \tag{S8.7}$$

If you draw a figure with the vertical and horizontal axes representing c and k, respectively, the $\dot{c}_t = 0$ schedule is a vertical line at k^* and the $\dot{k}_t = 0$ schedule looks like a parabola starting from the origin. It can be easily checked that the intersection point (c^*, k^*) of the two schedules is stable with a positively sloping saddle path.

ii. When g rises, the $\dot{c}_t = 0$ line shifts leftward and the $\dot{k}_t = 0$ curve shifts downward. A new steady state is established at the intersection point (c^{**}, k^{**}) where $c^{**} < c^*$ and $k^{**} < k^*$. In a steady state, per capita output is still given by (S8.2) and its growth rate by (S8.3). Thus, a rise in g due to a new GPT generates a one-to-one impact just as in the model without consumers' optimization.

Turning to the short run, we have from equations (S8.4) and (S8.6)

$$g_{y_t} = g + \alpha \left\{ k_t^{-(1-\alpha)} - \frac{c_t}{k_t} - [\delta + n + g + \beta\,(g)] \right\}.$$

Differentiating this expression with respect to g gives

$$\left.\frac{\partial g_{y_t}}{\partial g}\right|_{\text{given } k_t} = (1 - \alpha) - \alpha\beta'\,(g) - \frac{\alpha}{k_t}\frac{\partial c_t}{\partial g} \gtreqless 0.$$

Comparing it with (S8.5), there is an extra term $(\alpha/k_t)(\partial c_t/\partial g)$ here. In general, c_t can rise or fall for a given k_t immediately after a rise in g. If consumption increases, the short-run growth rate is more likely to fall.

★ 2. The effects of fluctuations on growth (based on Aghion and Saint-Paul 1991)

a. Use $r > 0$ to denote the rate at which the firm discounts its future profits. The value functions V_i, $i = E, R$ will satisfy the following Bellman equations:

$$V_E\,(x) = \max_v \left\{ h\,(v)\,e^x y_E dt + (1 - r dt) \right. \tag{S8.8}$$

$$\times \left\{ V_E\,(x + v dt)\,(1 - \gamma dt) + V_R\,(x + v dt)\,\gamma dt \right\} \right\}$$

$$V_R\,(x) = \max_v \left\{ h\,(v)\,e^x y_R dt + (1 - r dt) \right. \tag{S8.9}$$

$$\times \left\{ V_R\,(x + v dt)\,(1 - \varepsilon dt) + V_E\,(x + v dt)\,\varepsilon dt \right\} \right\}$$

Consider (S8.8). If the firm is currently in an expansion and devotes the fraction $1 - h(v)$ of its current profits $y_E e^x$ to R&D during the time interval dt, then it earns $h(v)e^x y_E dt$. At the end of this time interval, the firm will have reached the technological level $x + dx = x + v dt$. Furthermore, by then, the economy will have switched to a recessionary phase with probability γdt and remained in expansion with the complementary probability. The second Bellman equation (S8.9) is identically interpreted, except that the two states E and R must be permuted and the transition probability γ must be replaced by ε.

b. Differentiating the right-hand sides of the preceding Bellman equations and letting $dt \to 0$ implies

$$e^x y_i h'\,(v_i) + V_i'\,(x) = 0, \quad i = E, R.$$

Rearranging them with $h(v) = 1 - v^2$ and $V_i(x) = V_i^0 e^x$ (which holds in equilibrium) gives (8.29).

c.

i. Rearranging the Bellman equations (S8.8) and (S8.9) and letting $dt \to 0$ yields

$$0 = h(v_E) e^x y_E - (r + \gamma) V_E(x) + \gamma V_R(x) + v_E V_E'(x) \tag{S8.10}$$

$$0 = h(v_R) e^x y_R - (r + \varepsilon) V_R(x) + \varepsilon V_E(x) + v_R V_R'(x) \tag{S8.11}$$

where we have used the fact that $\lim_{s_i \to 0} v_i [V_i(x + s_i) - V_i(x)]/s_i = v_i V_i'(x)$, $s_i = v_i dt$.

ii. Using $h(v) = 1 - v^2$ and $V_i(x) = V_i^0 e^x$, equations (S8.10) and (S8.11) can be reexpressed

$$v_R = -\frac{\theta \left[v_E^2 - 2(r + \gamma) v_E + 1 \right]}{2\gamma} \Rightarrow v_R = \psi(v_E) \tag{S8.12}$$

$$v_E = -\frac{v_R^2 - 2(r + \varepsilon) v_R + 1}{2\varepsilon\theta} \Rightarrow v_R = \phi(v_E) \tag{S8.13}$$

where $\theta = y_E/y_R > 1$. Their slopes in (v_R, v_E) space are given by

$$\psi' = \theta \left(1 + \frac{r - v_E}{\gamma} \right) > \theta \left(1 + \frac{r - v_R}{\varepsilon} \right)^{-1} = \phi'.$$

Thus, because $\psi(0) < \phi(0)$, there is a unique equilibrium.

iii. Using (8.31) and $V_i(x) = V_i^0 e^x$, equations (S8.10) and (S8.11) can be rewritten as

$$r + \gamma \left(1 - \frac{V_R^0}{V_E^0} \right) = \frac{2v_E^2 + 1}{2v_E} \equiv f(v_E), \tag{S8.14}$$

$$r - \varepsilon \left(\frac{V_E^0}{V_R^0} - 1 \right) = \frac{2v_R^2 + 1}{2v_R} \equiv f(v_R). \tag{S8.15}$$

Because $V_R^0 < V_E^0$, the left-hand side of (S8.14) is strictly larger than that of (S8.15), implying $f(v_E) > f(v_R)$. Moreover, $f'(v_i) < 0$ for $v \in (0, 1)$. This implies $v_E < v_R$, that is, the productivity improvements of the firm are countercyclical.

iv. Recessions tend to increase the rate of productivity growth because of an intertemporal substitution effect: the opportunity cost in terms of forgone profits of investing part of the labor resources in technological improvements or in managerial reorganizations is lower during depression phases, and the more so when the discrepancy between booms and slumps is large.

v. The random process generated by this economy is Markovian with transition probabilities γ and ε, respectively, from expansion to recession and vice versa. Thus the firm will spend on average a fraction $\gamma/(\gamma + \varepsilon)$ of its lifetime in recession and the remaining fraction $\varepsilon/(\gamma + \varepsilon)$ in an expansion. Moreover, productivity grows at the rates of v_R and v_E in recession and expansion, respectively. Thus, the average growth rate of the firm's productivity is given by (8.32).

⋆⋆ 3. Obsolescence and GPT in R&D-based model (based on Howitt 1998)

a.

i. The demand curve for intermediate goods is $p_{it} = \alpha \gamma^{m_{it}} x_{it}^{\alpha-1}$. Using this and (8.32), profit maximization leads to

$$x_t = x_{it} = \left(\frac{\alpha^2}{\omega_t} \right)^{1/(1-\alpha)} \tag{S8.16}$$

$$\pi_{it} = \gamma^{m_{it}} \alpha (1 - \alpha) x_t^\alpha \tag{S8.17}$$

where ω_t is the cost of capital.

ii. Taking into account the probability of a product becoming obsolete, the asset equation for innovation at t is given by

$$\dot{V}_{it} = -\pi_{it} + (r_t + \phi_{it})\, V_{it}. \tag{S8.18}$$

The expected benefit arising from R&D is $V_{it}\phi_{it} - R_{it}$. Free entry implies that this should be zero. That is,

$$V_{it}\lambda = \gamma^{m_{it}}. \tag{S8.19}$$

iii. Equation (S8.19) implies $\dot{V}_{it} = 0$ for a given m_{it}. Using this relationship, (S8.16), (S8.17), and (S8.19), equation (S8.18) becomes

$$\lambda\alpha\,(1 - \alpha)\, x_t^\alpha - r_t = \phi_{it}. \tag{S8.20}$$

Because the left-hand side is independent of i, so is the right hand side, that is, $\phi_{it} = \phi_t$ for all i.

iv. From (8.32) the aggregate capital stock is $K_t = \int_0^1 K_{it}di = x_t A_t$, giving (8.34).

v. The cost of capital can be expressed as

$$\alpha^2 k_t^{\alpha-1} = r_t + (1 - \eta)\, \phi_t,$$

using (8.34) and (S8.16). Substituting this into (S8.20) generates (8.35).

b.

i. Gross investment consists of net investment $\dot{K}$ plus the value of obsolescent capital. The rate of obsolescence per unit of time per unit of capital is the flow probability that the unit of capital will be scrapped, ϕ_t, times the loss in value $(1 - \eta)$ when scrapped, so that the value of total obsolescent capital is given by $(1 - \eta)\phi_t K_t$. It follows that the income identity is

$$\dot{K}_t = y_t - c_t - (1 - \eta)\,\phi_t K_t \qquad (S8.21)$$

where c_t is aggregate (or per capita) consumption.

ii. Equations (8.31) and (8.34) imply (8.36).

iii. A_t can be interpreted as the average quality index across industries: $A_t = \sum_{m=0}^{\infty} \Pr(m; t)\,\gamma^m$, where $\Pr(m; t) = (\int_0^t \phi_\tau d\tau)^m \exp(-\int_0^t \phi_\tau d\tau)/m!$ is the Poisson probability distribution of m innovations occurring during the time interval t. Hence $A_t = \exp[(\gamma - 1)\int_0^t \phi_\tau d\tau]$, and

$$\frac{\dot{A}_t}{A_t} = (\gamma - 1)\,\phi_t. \qquad (S8.22)$$

iv. First divide both sides (S8.21) by A_t. From equation (8.36) $(y_t - c_t)/A_t = sk_t^\alpha$, and $\dot{K}_t/A_t = \dot{k}_t + k_t \dot{A}_t/A_t$. Substituting these equations and (S8.22) into the income identity (S8.21) yields (8.37).

c. Substituting (8.35) into (8.37) gives

$$\dot{k}_t = k_t^\alpha \left\{ s - (\gamma - \eta)\frac{\alpha}{\eta}\left[\lambda(1 - \alpha)k_t - \alpha\right] \right\}. \qquad (S8.23)$$

The unique solution for $\dot{k} = 0$ gives the steady-state stock of capital and the arrival rate

$$k^* = \frac{1}{\lambda(1 - \alpha)}\left[\frac{s\eta}{(\gamma - \eta)\alpha} + \alpha\right],$$

$$\phi^* = \frac{s}{(\gamma - \eta)(k^*)^{1-\alpha}}.$$

The differential equation (S8.23) implies that $\dot{k}_t > 0$ for $k_t < k^*$ and $\dot{k}_t < 0$ for $k_t > k^*$. Thus the economy always converges to the steady state.

d. Equation (8.36) implies $\dot{y}_t/y_t = \dot{A}_t/A_t + \alpha \dot{k}_t/k_t$. Substituting (S8.22) and (8.37) into this expression yields the short-run growth rate

$$\frac{\dot{y}_t}{y_t} = (\gamma - 1)\,\phi_t + \alpha\left[sk_t^{-(1-\alpha)} - (\gamma - \eta)\,\phi_t\right]. \qquad (S8.24)$$

In the long run, the second term vanishes, so that the economy grows at the rate of

$$\frac{\dot{y}}{y} = (\gamma - 1)\,\phi^*. \tag{S8.25}$$

e.

i. Differentiating (S8.25) with respect to λ gives $\partial(\dot{y}/y)/\partial\lambda > 0$.

ii. The short-run rate of technological progress is given by (S8.22), where ϕ_t is given by (8.35). Then

$$\left.\frac{\partial(\dot{A}_t/A_t)}{\partial\lambda}\right|_{\text{given } k_t} = \frac{\alpha\,(1-\alpha)\,(\gamma-1)\,k_t^\alpha}{\eta} > 0. \tag{S8.26}$$

iii. Differentiating (S8.24) with respect to λ for a given k_t yields

$$\left.\frac{\partial(\dot{y}/y)}{\partial\lambda}\right|_{\text{given } k_t} = -\left[1 - (1-\alpha)\,\gamma - \alpha\eta\right](\gamma-1)\left.\frac{\partial(\dot{A}_t/A_t)}{\partial\lambda}\right|_{\text{given } k_t}.$$

Assuming $1 > (1-\alpha)\,\gamma$, the bracketed term is more likely to be positive with lower η. That is, the growth rate of per capita output is more likely to fall in the short run, as η becomes lower. The reason for this result is the same as the one given in the previous question with the neoclassical growth model.

⋆ **4. Unequal technological opportunities (based on Cheng and Dinopoulos 1992)**

a. Because the production function (8.38) is linear in x, breakthrough and improvement innovations are necessarily "nondrastic" ($\alpha = 1$ in the Cobb-Douglas case; see Chapter 2). Thus monopoly producers charge the price of

$$p_B = \gamma_B w_B, \qquad p_I = \gamma_I w_I, \tag{S8.27}$$

so that profits are

$$\pi_B = (\gamma_B - 1)\,w_B x_B, \qquad \pi_I = (\gamma_I - 1)\,w_I x_I. \tag{S8.28}$$

First consider breakthrough innovations. Profits π_B are earned in phase B during which w_B and x_B are constant. Phase B ends when an improvement over the existing good occurs with a Poisson arrival rate of $\lambda_I n_I$. Therefore, the value of a breakthrough innovation is given by

$$V_B = \frac{\pi_B}{r + \lambda_I n_I}. \tag{S8.29}$$

Similarly, the value of an improvement innovation is

$$V_I = \frac{\pi_I}{r + \lambda_B n_B}. \tag{S8.30}$$

b. The expected "profits" from engaging in breakthrough and improvement R&D are $V_B \lambda_B n_B - w_I n_B$ and $V_I \lambda_I n_I - w_B n_I$, respectively. Hence free entry implies

$$V_B \lambda_B = w_I, \quad \text{and} \quad V_I \lambda_I = w_B. \tag{S8.31}$$

c. Consider phase I. In this state, intermediate goods that embody the latest improvement are manufactured and breakthrough R&D is conducted. Thus the full employment of workers in phase I requires

$$N = n_B + x_I. \tag{S8.32}$$

Following the same procedure, we have the condition

$$N = n_I + x_B \tag{S8.33}$$

for phase B.

d. Combining (S8.29), (S8.33) and the first equations of (S8.28) and (S8.31) gives

$$r + \lambda_I n_I = \lambda_B (\gamma_B - 1) \frac{w_B}{w_I} (N - n_I). \tag{S8.34}$$

To derive the reduced form of w_B/w_I, recall that the profit maximization of the final output producers gives the first-order condition $p_x = A$. Using this, we can write $\gamma_B w_B = \gamma_B^{i+1} \gamma_I^j$ and $\gamma_I w_I = \gamma_B^i \gamma_I^j$, because w_B is wage after breakthroughs occur. Those two equations give $w_B/w_I = \gamma_I$, and (S8.34) can be rearranged to give the first equation of (8.39).

Using (S8.30), (S8.32) and the second equations of (S8.28) and (S8.31), we obtain

$$r + \lambda_B n_B = \lambda_I (\gamma_I - 1) \frac{w_I}{w_B} (N - n_B). \tag{S8.35}$$

Because, following the above argument, $w_I/w_B = \gamma_B$, equation (S8.35) can be reexpressed as the second equation of (8.39).

e.

i. From (S8.32) and (S8.33), $n_I - n_B = x_I - x_B$. Using (8.39), we have

$$x_I - x_B = \lambda (\gamma_B - \gamma_I)(\lambda N + r) > 0.$$

The economy exhibits cycles such that $n_I > n_B$ and $x_I > x_B$ due to uneven technological opportunities $\gamma_B > \gamma_I$.

ii. Suppose that the economy is phase I with output of $y_I = \gamma_B^i \gamma_I^j x_I$. In the following phase B, output is given by $y_B = \gamma_B^{i+1} \gamma_I^j x_B$. Then we have

$$y_B - y_I = \frac{\gamma_B^i \gamma_I^j \, (\lambda N + r) \, (\gamma_I - 1) \, (\gamma_B^2 - \gamma_B - 1)}{\lambda \left[1 + (\gamma_I - 1) \, \gamma_B \right] \left[1 + (\gamma_B - 1) \, \gamma_I \right]},$$

using (8.39), (S8.32), and (S8.33). Recessions can occur in phase B if $\gamma_B^2 - \gamma_B - 1 < 0$, that is, the economy exhibits cycles of booms and slumps for $\gamma_B \in (1, \frac{1}{2}(1 + \sqrt{5}))$. The intuition is that when there is a technological breakthrough, output increases by a factor γ_B, other things held constant. But in phase B the labor demand in improvement R&D is so large that x_B dramatically decreases to the extent that it more than offsets the increase of output caused by the breakthrough.

f. Consider the difference in output levels between phase I and the next phase I:

$$\ln \gamma_B^{i+1} \gamma_I^{j+1} x_I - \ln \gamma_B^i \gamma_I^j x_I = \ln \gamma_B \gamma_I.$$

The expected time between these two phases is of $1/\lambda_B n_B + 1/\lambda_I n_I = (\lambda_B n_B + \lambda_I n_I)/\lambda_B n_B \lambda_I n_I$. Its inverse gives the expected number of increases in the size of $\ln \gamma_B \gamma_I$ in a unit time interval. Therefore, the expected growth rate is given by (8.40). Note that this is independent of whether slump occurs in phase B or not.

★ **5. Technology specific machines (based on Felli and Ortalo-Magné 1997)**

a. The representative agent's behavior in this economy is characterized by the following maximization problem:

$$\max_{k_{i,t}} \sum_{t=0}^{\infty} \frac{1}{(1+r)^t} c_t$$

(S8.36)

$$\text{s.t.} \quad \sum_{t=0}^{\infty} \frac{1}{(1+r)^t} c_t \leq \sum_{t=0}^{\infty} \frac{1}{(1+r)^t} \max \{\theta_0, \pi_{1,t}, \pi_{2,t}\}$$

where $\pi_{i,t}$ denotes the period t profit accruing to the agent from using technology i, $i \in \{1, 2\}$. This period t profit can be defined as the difference between the period t revenues accruing to the agent from the use of machine $k_{i,t}$ and the user costs of the same machine:

$$\pi_{i,t} = \theta_i k_{i,t}^\alpha - u_{i,t} k_{i,t}$$

(S8.37)

where $u_{i,t}$ denotes the per-unit user cost of machine $k_{i,t}$:

$$u_{i,t} = q_{i,t} - \frac{(1-\delta)}{(1+r)} q_{i,t+1}$$

(S8.38)

From the solution of program (S8.36), using (S8.37) and (S8.38), we obtain the following demand for machines of type i at time t:

$$k_{i,t} = \left(\frac{\alpha \theta_i}{u_{i,t}} \right)^{\frac{1}{1-\alpha}}. \tag{S8.39}$$

The agent at each instant of time t will demand only one type of machine. This type is going to be $i \in \{1, 2\}$ if $\pi_i > \theta_0$ and, for $i \neq j$, $\pi_i > \pi_j$. This last inequality can be rewritten as:

$$\frac{u_{i,t}}{u_{j,t}} < \left(\frac{\theta_i}{\theta_j} \right)^{\frac{1}{\alpha}}. \tag{S8.40}$$

b. The steady-state equilibrium of the economy before the discovery, (q_1^*, k_1^*), is characterized by the following two equilibrium conditions:

$$\mu_1 \left(q_1^* - q_1^{\min} \right) = \delta k_1^* \tag{S8.41}$$

and

$$k_1^* = \left(\frac{\alpha \theta_1}{(r + \delta) q_1^*} \right)^{\frac{1}{1-\alpha}}. \tag{S8.42}$$

To guarantee that in such a steady state the agent will never prefer to be a worker, we need $\pi_1 > \theta_0$, can be rewritten as:

$$\theta_1^{\frac{1}{1-\alpha}} \left[(r + \delta) q_1^* \right]^{\frac{\alpha}{\alpha-1}} \alpha^{\frac{\alpha}{1-\alpha}} (1 - \alpha) > \theta_0 \tag{S8.43}$$

c. We have to distinguish two cases.

If $q_{2,t_s} > q_1^{\min} (\theta_2/\theta_1)^{1/\alpha}$, then the unique steady-state equilibrium is such that the representative agent will not use any machine of type 2. This equilibrium is fully characterized by the equations (S8.41), (S8.42), and (S8.43).

Conversely, if $q_{2,t_s} < q_1^{\min} (\theta_2/\theta_1)^{1/\alpha}$, then there exists a continuum of steady-state equilibria such that the representative agent uses machines of type 2. This continuum of steady-state equilibria (q_1^{**}, k_1^{**}) satisfies the following conditions:

$$q_{2,t_s} \left(\frac{\theta_1}{\theta_2} \right)^{\frac{1}{\alpha}} \leq q_1^{**} \leq q_1^{\min} \tag{S8.44}$$

and

$$k_1^{**} = 0, \tag{S8.45}$$

as long as the representative agent prefers to be an entrepreneur rather than a worker. That is, as long as

$$\theta_2^{\frac{1}{1-\alpha}} \left[(r+\delta)q_{2,t_d} \right]^{\frac{\alpha}{\alpha-1}} \alpha^{\frac{\alpha}{1-\alpha}} (1-\alpha) > \theta_0 \tag{S8.46}$$

is satisfied.

d. Let

$$q_{2,t_s} < q_1^s \left(\frac{\theta_2}{\theta_1} \right)^{\frac{1}{\alpha}}. \tag{S8.47}$$

Condition (S8.47) guarantees that the scrap value of a machine of type 1 is in the set of the steady-state equilibria characterized by (S8.44) and (S8.45). It follows from $q_1^s < q_1^{\min}$ that $q_1^{**} = q_1^s$ and $k_1^{**} = 0$ is a steady-state equilibrium.

To prove that the announcement is followed by a recession, we proceed in three steps. First, we show that the sequence of prices $\{q_{1,t}\}_{t=t_d}^{\infty}$ is *non-increasing*. Second, we prove that $q_1^* \geq q_{1,t_d}$. Third, we demonstrate that such properties of $\{q_{1,t}\}_{t=t_d}^{\infty}$ imply a declining sequence of equilibrium quantities of machines of type 1 before agents adopt machines of type 2.

Denote by $\bar{t}$ the date at which all agents adopt the machines of type 2. This date $\bar{t} \in [t_d, t_s]$ *does* exist by condition (S8.47). The first-order conditions for the representative agent imply for every $t \in \left[t_d, \bar{t} - 1 \right]$:

$$q_{1,t} = \sum_{\tau=t}^{\bar{t}-1} (1+r)^{-(\tau-1)} \alpha \theta_1 k_{1,\tau}^{\alpha-1} + (1+r)^{-(\bar{t}-t)} q_1^s \tag{S8.48}$$

which is a sequence of prices non-increasing in t that converges to q_1^s.

Assume by way of contradiction that $q_1^* < q_{1,t_d}$, then from (S8.41):

$$\kappa_1(q_1^*) < \kappa_1(q_{1,t_d}) \tag{S8.49}$$

However, $q_1^* < q_{1,t_d}$, combined with equations (S8.48), and $\{q_{1,t}\}_{t=t_d}^{\infty}$ non-increasing, implies:

$$\alpha \theta_1 (k_1^*)^{\alpha-1} < \alpha \theta_1 k_{1,t_d}^{\alpha-1} \tag{S8.50}$$

which is equivalent to $k_1^* > k_{1,t_d}$. This inequality contradicts equation (S8.49), by market clearing of type 1 machines.

The equilibrium condition of the market for the machines of type 1 is:

$$k_{1,t} = \kappa(q_{1,t}) + (1-\delta)k_{1,t-1}. \tag{S8.51}$$

Because the equilibrium supply $\kappa(q_{1,t})$ is upward sloping and the stock of existing machines is depreciating through time, the sequence $\{q_{1,t}\}_{t=t_d}^{\infty}$ is associated in equilibrium with a non-increasing sequence of quantities of machines of type 1 $\{k_{1,t}\}_{t=t_d}^{\infty}$ converging to $k_1^{**} = 0$.

Given that for every $t \in [t_d, \bar{t} - 1]$, no agent adopts machines of type 2, then the decreasing set of quantities of machines used in equilibrium $\{k_{1,t}\}_{t=t_d}^{\bar{t}-1}$ generates a set of equilibrium levels of output decreasing over time.

By definition, at time $\bar{t}$ all agents adopt the machines of type 2, which generates a sudden increase in the level of output produced.

We still need to prove that the dynamic process described before cannot converge to any steady-state equilibrium other than the one characterized by (S8.44) and (S8.45). Assume by way of contradiction that the dynamic process converges to a steady-state equilibrium characterized by

$$q_1^{**} \neq q_1^s \tag{S8.52}$$

where

$$q_{2,t_s} \left(\frac{\theta_1}{\theta_2} \right)^{\frac{1}{\alpha}} \leq q_1^{**} \leq q_1^{\min} \tag{S8.53}$$

and

$$k_1^{**} = 0 \tag{S8.54}$$

Consider the behavior of a representative agent at the date $\bar{t}$ in which he decides to adopt the machines of type 2. Because all the agents in the economy are identical, at that date, all want to sell their type 1 machines. Hence, there is no demand for type 1 machines. So the only equilibrium price for these machines is their scrap value q_1^s. This contradicts the fact that the price $q_1^{**} \neq q_1^s$ equilibrates the market for the machines of type 1. Notice, finally, that once the value of the price $q_{1,\bar{t}}$ is determined, equation (S8.48) identifies the values of all the prices $q_{1,t}$ where $t \in [t_d, \bar{t} - 1]$.

★ **6. Creative destruction versus the cycle (based on Canton and Uhlig 1996)**

a. To define and calculate the steady-state equilibrium, we normalize by dividing through the growth trends, obtaining two aggregate states s: $s = r$ for "recession" ($B_r = 1$) and $s = b$ for "boom" ($B_b = \delta > 1$). Let ρ be the discount factor in the utility function. An equilibrium comprises numbers $(w_s, \pi_s, V_s, L_s, n_s)_{s \in \{r,b\}}$ so that

i. Given the state s and the wage w_s for skilled labor, the leading monopolist maximizes profits,

$$\pi_s = \max_L \alpha B_s^\alpha L^\alpha - w_s L.$$

Note that we have already substituted out the final goods production sector for simplicity. Let L_s denote the value that maximizes π_s.

ii. The value V_s of a leading firm in state s at some date t is given by the profits received between t and $t + dt$ and the expected, discounted value of the firm at time $t + dt$.

$$V_r = \pi_r dt + e^{-\rho dt} \left[(\mu dt) V_b + (1 - \mu dt - \lambda n_r dt) V_r \right]$$

with a similar equation for V_b. Sorting terms, dropping squares of dt, and dividing by dt, the equilibrium conditions are

$$\pi_r = (\mu + \lambda n_r + \rho) V_r - \mu V_b, \qquad (S8.55)$$

$$\pi_b = (\mu + \lambda n_b + \rho) V_b - \mu V_r. \qquad (S8.56)$$

iii. The arbitrage equation is

$$w_s = \gamma \lambda V_r \quad \text{for } n_s > 0, \qquad (S8.57)$$

$$w_b = \gamma \lambda V_b \quad \text{for } n_b > 0. \qquad (S8.58)$$

iv. $n_s \geq 0$, $L_s \geq 0$ and $n_s + L_s = N$ (market clearing).

b. To compute the equilibrium, note that the first equilibrium condition implies

$$L_s = \left(\frac{\alpha^2 B_s^\alpha}{w_s} \right)^{\frac{1}{1-\alpha}}, \qquad \pi_s = \frac{1 - \alpha}{\alpha} L_s w_s \qquad (S8.59)$$

The second equilibrium condition can be viewed as two equations in the two unknowns V_r and V_b. Solving for V_r yields

$$V_r = \frac{(\mu + \lambda n_b + \rho) \pi_r + \mu \pi_b}{(\mu + \lambda n_b + \rho)(\mu + \lambda n_r + \rho) - \mu^2}$$

For the third and forth equilibrium condition, one must now distinguish three cases.

Case I: There is always positive R&D. That is, $n_s > 0$, $s = r, b$. The third equilibrium condition thus implies

$$w_s = w_r = w = \gamma \lambda V_r. \qquad (S8.60)$$

This equation together with equation (S8.59) implies $L_h > L_r$. Furthermore, proceeding from equation (S8.60), substituting out V_r, then π_r and π_b and finally L_r and L_b, one obtains

$$1 = \gamma \lambda (1 - \alpha) \alpha^{\frac{1+\alpha}{1-\alpha}} \frac{\left((\mu + \lambda n_b + \rho) + \mu \delta^{\frac{\alpha}{1-\alpha}} \right) w^{-1/(1-\alpha)}}{(\mu + \lambda n_b + \rho)(\mu + \lambda n_r + \rho) - \mu^2} \qquad (S8.61)$$

Let $\zeta = w^{-1/(1-\alpha)}$ and note that with the first and the forth equilibrium conditions, π_s and n_s are affine-linear functions of ζ. Thus, equation (S8.61) can be rewritten as a quadratic equation in ζ and solved in the usual way. Given ζ, everything else can be computed. One finds that only the larger of the two roots of the quadratic equation for ζ is relevant, because one will otherwise always get negative R&D intensity. To validate the solution, one needs to check that the inequalities in the equilibrium conditions (S8.57) and (S8.58) are satisfied. In particular, one needs to check that $L_b < N$.

Case II: There is positive R&D in only one of the two states. Because Case I leads to $L_b > L_r$, one can quickly see that we must have $L_b = N > L_r$ and $w_b \geq w_r = \gamma \lambda V_r$ in case II. The first equilibrium condition implies

$$w_b = \alpha^2 \delta^\alpha N^{\alpha-1}, \quad \pi_b = (1-\alpha)\alpha\delta^\alpha N^\alpha.$$

Proceeding similarly to Case I, one obtains

$$w_r = \gamma \lambda \frac{(\mu + \rho)\pi_r + \mu\pi_b}{(\mu + \rho)(\mu + \lambda n_r + \rho) - \mu^2}, \tag{S8.62}$$

where, as before, π_r and n_r are affine linear functions of $w_r^{-1/(1-\alpha)}$. For, say, $\alpha = 1/2$, equation (S8.62) can be written as a third-order polynomial in w_r and solved in closed form with the appropriate formulas from calculus books. In general, however, one needs to obtain the solution numerically. Once w_r is obtained, all other variables can be calculated easily. To validate the solution, one needs to check once more that the inequalities in (S8.57) and (S8.58) are satisfied.

Case III: Zero R&D in all states. Using the first and second equilibrium conditions with $L_r = L_b = N$, solve for w_s, w_b, and V_r. Check that the inequalities in the third and fourth equilibrium condition are satisfied.

c. Check Case I above: because $L_b > L_r$, we have $n_r > n_b$, that is, R&D activity is higher in recession states, making a leapfrogging jump more likely there.

d. This is either Case II or an extreme version of Case I with $L_b = N$. Taking the latter perspective and using the formulas obtained for Case I, pick, for example, $\alpha = 1/2$, $N = 1 = L_b$, $\delta = 16$, so that $w = 1$ (see the first equilibrium condition), $n_b = 0$ and $n_r = 15/16$. Substituting everything into equation (S8.62) yields

$$1 = \frac{\gamma \lambda}{16} \frac{(\mu + \rho) + 16\mu}{(\mu + \rho)(\mu + 15\lambda/16 + \rho) - \mu^2}.$$

Hence, pick any positive values for μ, ρ and λ and adjust γ to assure equality. Because for fixed $\lambda > 0$ and μ, ρ converging to zero, one obtains γ converging to infinity, it is not hard to find constellations that result in $\gamma > 1$, needed for a "sensible" equilibrium. One finally needs to check that $w = 1$ is indeed the larger root of the quadratic equation mentioned above when solving Case I.

e. Recessions seem to be good for growth in the context of this model, because it is in recessionary states that R&D activity is the highest. We also obtained the same result in problem 2. However, one needs to be careful with this interpretation. First, if the probability of leaving a recession μ is very small, the leading monopolist will tend to stay for a long time in the initial recessionary state, depressing the value of being the leading monopolist. This, in turn, depresses the incentives for doing R&D. Second, from a social planner's perspective, it clearly must be preferable to always be in a boom state rather than a recessionary state. From that perspective, recessions are too costly as a tool to induce growth: better market arrangements would be preferable.

⋆ 7. Endogenous GPT (based on Li 1997)

a. Because the production function (8.42) is linear in x, monopoly intermediate producers charge the price of

$$p_x = \gamma w. \tag{S8.63}$$

(See question 4(a)). Thus the total profits generated by the state-of-the-art product are $\pi = (p_x - w)x = (1 - 1/\gamma)p_x x$. The first-order condition of profit maximization of the final output producers is $p_x = p_y \gamma^m$. Multiplying both sides by x gives $p_x x = p_y y$. Because $p_y y$ is a numeraire, then

$$p_x x = 1. \tag{S8.64}$$

Thus we have $\pi = 1 - 1/\gamma$, and profits earned by the GPT and intermediate innovators are given by (8.43).

b. Equations (S8.63) and (S8.64) imply $x_k = 1/(\gamma w_k)$, $k = G, I$. Hence full-employment in phases G and I requires

$$L = \frac{1}{\gamma w_k} + \xi_k, \quad k = G, I. \tag{S8.65}$$

c. Consider phase I when GPT_m is currently available but GPT_{m-1} is actually used and entrepreneurs are aiming at inventing an input that implements GPT_m. Define $t_{G_{m+1}}$ and $t_{I_{m+1}}$, $t_{G_{m+1}} < t_{I_{m+1}}$, as the instants when GPT_{m+1} and its compatible input are invented, respectively. Remember that $t_{G_{m+1}}$ and $t_{I_{m+1}}$ are both stochastic. An intermediate innovator for GPT_m earns profits until $t_{I_{m+1}}$, and V_I is the expected present value of profits up to $t_{I_{m+1}}$. Now define V_I^1 as the expected present value of profits from $t_{G_{m+1}}$ to $t_{I_{m+1}}$. Then for the time interval between t and $t + dt$, V_I must satisfy the following recursive equation:

$$V_I = \pi_I dt + (1 - r dt)\left[V_I (1 - \xi_G dt) + V_I^1 \xi_G dt\right], \tag{S8.66}$$

because an innovator earns π_I during this time period and, at the end of this interval, achieves V_I with probability of $1 - \xi_G dt$ and V_I^1 with $\xi_G dt$.

Rearranging the terms and letting $dt \to 0$, we obtain

$$rV_I = \pi_I - \xi_G \left(V_I - V_I^1 \right). \tag{S8.67}$$

Turning to the value of V_I^1, for the time interval between $t + dt$, it must satisfy the value function

$$V_I^1 = \pi_I dt + (1 - rdt)(1 - \xi_I dt) V_I^1, \tag{S8.68}$$

because an innovator gains π_I during dt and achieves V_I^1 at the end of this time interval with probability of $1 - \xi_I dt$. (S8.68) becomes

$$rV_I^1 = \pi_I - \xi_I V_I^1. \tag{S8.69}$$

Combining (S8.67) and (S8.69) yields (8.44). Free entry in intermediate R&D ensures

$$V_I = w_I. \tag{S8.70}$$

d. Consider phase G when GPT$_m$ is currently used and entrepreneurs are aiming at inventing GPT$_{m+1}$. Denote $t_{I_{m+1}}$ as the instant when an intermediate product which implements it is introduced. Similarly use $t_{G_{m+2}}$ and $t_{I_{m+2}}$ for the instants when GPT$_{m+2}$ and its compatible input are invented respectively. Thus, $t_{I_{m+1}} < t_{G_{m+2}} < t_{I_{m+2}}$. A GPT innovator does not earn profit until $t_{I_{m+1}}$, simply because his technology cannot be used by final output producers without its compatible intermediate good. Now define V_G^1 as the expected present value of profits from $t_{I_{m+1}}$ to $t_{I_{m+2}}$. Then, V_G must satisfy the following equation:

$$V_G = (1 - rdt) \left[V_G (1 - \xi_I dt) + V_G^1 \xi_I dt \right], \tag{S8.71}$$

because the GPT innovator attains V_G with $1 - \xi_I dt$ or V_G^1 with $\xi_I dt$ at the end of time interval dt. This equation gives rise to

$$rV_G = -\xi_I \left(V_G - V_G^1 \right), \tag{S8.72}$$

after letting $dt \to 0$. Turning to V_G^1, it must satisfy

$$V_G^1 = \pi_G dt + (1 - rdt) \left[V_G^1 (1 - \xi_G dt) + V_G^2 \xi_G dt \right]$$

$$V_G^2 = \pi_G dt + (1 - rdt)(1 - \xi_I dt) V_G^2$$

where V_G^2 is the expected present value of profits from $t_{G_{m+2}}$ to $t_{I_{m+2}}$. The interpretation of these two equations are similar to the one given for (S8.71), except that profits are now included. Rearranging them and letting $dt \to 0$, we obtain

$$rV_G^1 = \pi_G - \xi_G \left(V_G^1 - V_G^2 \right), \tag{S8.73}$$

$$rV_G^2 = \pi_G - \xi_I V_G^2. \tag{S8.74}$$

Combining (S8.72), (S8.73), and (S8.74) leads to (8.45). Free entry in R&D for GPT implies

$$V_G = w_G. \tag{S8.75}$$

e. Using (8.45), (S8.65), (S8.70), and (S8.75), equations (8.44) and (8.45) can be reexpressed as

$$\frac{1}{(1-\kappa)(\gamma-1)} = \frac{(r+\xi_G+\xi_I)(L-\xi_I)}{(r+\xi_G)(r+\xi_I)}, \tag{I}$$

$$\frac{1}{\kappa(\gamma-1)} = \frac{\xi_I(r+\xi_G+\xi_I)(L-\xi_G)}{(r+\xi_G)(r+\xi_I)^2}. \tag{G}$$

(I) and (G) are the equilibrium conditions in phases I and G respectively. Let us rewrite them in an implicit form as $\xi_G = I(\xi_I)$ and $\xi_G = G(\xi_I)$. If you draw a figure with the vertical and horizontal axes for ξ_G and ξ_I respectively, the intersection point(s) of two curves representing $\xi_G = I(\xi_I)$ and $\xi_G = G(\xi_I)$ give(s) an equilibrium (or multiple equilibria). $\xi_G = I(\xi_I)$ is strictly decreasing in ξ_I at a decreasing rate and it cuts the horizontal axis. The intuition is that as ξ_G rises, a next generation GPT$_{m+1}$ arrives more quickly on average, and R&D for an intermediate good associated with GPT$_{m+1}$ starts earlier than otherwise. It leads to the reduction of the value of intermediate innovation, discouraging the current intermediate R&D intensity ξ_I. On the other hand, $\xi_G = G(\xi_I)$ is increasing for small ξ_I but decreasing for large ξ_I after reaching a maximum, and it never cuts the horizontal axis. We can identify two opposing effects. First, as ξ_I increases, the period during which an GPT innovator earns a stream of profits arrives earlier on average. This tends to raise the value of GPT innovation, tending to increase ξ_G. Second, as ξ_I rises, an intermediate product that implements the innovator's GPT will be more likely to be replaced by a next generation intermediate good. This tends to decrease the value of GPT innovation, tending to reduce ξ_G. In general, there are odd numbers of equilibria, including a unique equilibrium.

f. Let us write output associated with γ^m in phase G as $y_m = \gamma^m x_G$. Output increases to $y_{m+1} = \gamma^{m+1} x_G$ in the following phase G. That is, $\ln y_{m+1} - \ln y_m = \ln \gamma$. The expected time length of phases G and I are $1/\xi_G$ and $1/\xi_I$ respectively. It follows that the expected time length between y_m and y_{m+1} is $1/\xi_G + 1/\xi_I = (\xi_G + \xi_I)/\xi_G \xi_I$. Therefore, the expected growth rate is

$$g = (\ln \gamma) \frac{\xi_G \xi_I}{\xi_G + \xi_I}.$$

Turning to the time profile of final output y, (8.44) and (S8.65) imply

$$\frac{y_G}{y_I} = \frac{L - \xi_G}{L - \xi_I} \gtreqless 1$$

where y_k, $k = G, I$ is output in phase k. This compares output levels within cycle. We have three cases. (i) If $\xi_G/\xi_I < 1$, then output falls in phase I compared to phase G, that is, output falls before it increases by more than $\ln \gamma$. (ii) If $\xi_G/\xi_I > 1$, then output rises in phase I, hence when a new intermediate input is invented output increases less than $\ln \gamma$. (iii) If $\xi_G/\xi_I = 1$, the time profile of $\ln y_m$ is the same as that of the standard quality ladder model in Chapter 2. (i) is the most interesting case, as we have seen in Chapter 8 that an introduction of GPT may initially negatively affect output. When does it happen in this model? The restriction $\xi_G/\xi_I < 1$ implies that GPT research is conducted less intensively than intermediate R&D.

Chapter 9

1. The incentive effect and intergenerational redistribution

a. An agent with initial endowment smaller than φA_t faces the following problem:

$$\max_e \left\{ e \left(\sigma A_t (1 - \tau) - \rho \left(\varphi A_t - s A_t - w_t^i \right) \right) - A_t \frac{e^2}{2} \right\}.$$

She then chooses the following level of effort:

$$e_t^i = \sigma (1 - \tau) - \rho \left(\varphi - s - \varepsilon_t^i \right). \tag{S9.1}$$

An agent with an initial endowment high enough to finance the fixed investment cost, $w_t^i \geq \varphi A_t$, chooses

$$e_t^i = \arg\max \left\{ e \sigma A_t (1 - \tau) - A_t \frac{e^2}{2} \right\} \tag{S9.2}$$

$$= \sigma (1 - \tau).$$

b. The government taxes all the old, but subsidizes only those young agents that cannot fully fund a project. Let q_t be the proportion of young individuals that receive the subsidy. That is, $q_t = \int_0^{\varphi A_t} di$. Total revenue is given by $\tau_t y_{t-1}$. Hence the balanced-budget constraint reads $q_t s_t A_t = \tau_t A_t$. Suppose that the government sets the same tax rate in all periods. Then, the balanced-budget condition defines the equilibrium subsidy

$$\int_0^\varphi s^* di = \int_0^{\bar\varepsilon} \tau di. \tag{S9.3}$$

c. When there are no taxes, the effort of an individual who cannot finance a project from her wealth is $e_t^i(0) = \sigma - \rho(\varphi - \varepsilon_t^i)$. Comparing it with the effort under the tax-subsidy system as given by (S9.1), we have that the effort level is raised by the tax-subsidy system if $\rho s^* > \sigma \tau$. Equation (S9.3) implies that this inequality is satisfied (that is, $e_t^i(\tau) > e_t^i(0)$) whenever

$$\rho > \int_0^\varphi \sigma \, di. \tag{S9.4}$$

That is, if the borrowing rate is sufficiently high relative to the productivity parameter, or the number of rich individuals large enough (i.e., φ is not too close to $\bar\varepsilon$).

d. When there are no taxes, total effort is given by

$$e_t(0) = \int e_t^i(0) \, di = \sigma - \rho \int_0^\varphi (\varphi - \varepsilon_t^i) \, di, \tag{S9.5}$$

whereas under a positive tax, total effort is

$$e_t(\tau) = \sigma - \rho \int_0^\varphi (\varphi - \varepsilon_t^i) \, di + \int_0^\varphi \rho s^* \, di - \int_0^{\bar\varepsilon} \sigma \tau \, di. \tag{S9.6}$$

Total effort is greater under a positive tax whenever the increase in incentives due to the subsidy to the young is larger than the reduction due to the tax payed when old. Using (S9.3), we obtain that the last two terms in (S9.6) are simply

$$\int_0^{\bar\varepsilon} \tau(\rho - \sigma) \, di.$$

Then, the tax-subsidy system results in a gain in effort if $\rho > \sigma$. That is, the smaller the return to investment is, the more likely it is that total effort increases as the loss is small. The larger the borrowing rate is, the more the effort of those constrained in their borrowing is increased, and the more likely it is that total effort increases under the tax-subsidy system.

2. Complementarities in production and skill-biased technical change (based on Krusell, Ohanian, Ríos-Rull, and Violante 1996)

a. If $\sigma = \rho = 0$, then $f(.)$ would simply be a Cobb-Douglas function of the three inputs. If the parameters are above zero, then there is greater substitutability than under Cobb-Douglas. If $\sigma > \rho$, then equipment capital is more complementary with skilled labor than with unskilled workers. The opposite would hold if $\sigma < \rho$.

b. Differentiating (9.29) we have that the skill premium, defined as $\omega_t \equiv w_t^s / w_t^u$, is

$$\omega_t = \frac{(1-\mu)(1-\lambda)}{\mu} \left(\lambda \left(\frac{q_t k_t}{s_t} \right)^\rho + (1-\lambda) \right)^{\sigma/\rho - 1} \left(\frac{u_t}{s_t} \right)^{1-\sigma}. \qquad (S9.7)$$

To find the impact of a change in the amount of equipment used or its quality, differentiate equation (S9.7) to get

$$\frac{\partial \omega_t}{\partial k_t} = (\sigma - \rho) \frac{\omega_t}{k_t} \left(1 + \frac{1-\lambda}{\lambda} \left(\frac{s_t}{q_t k_t} \right)^\rho \right)^{-1}, \qquad (S9.8)$$

$$\frac{\partial \omega_t}{\partial q_t} = (\sigma - \rho) \frac{\omega_t}{q_t} \left(1 + \frac{1-\lambda}{\lambda} \left(\frac{s_t}{q_t k_t} \right)^\rho \right)^{-1}. \qquad (S9.9)$$

It is clear from equations (S9.8) and (S9.9) that the effect of an increase in the amount of equipment or its quality on the skill premium depends on the complementarity of the latter with the two types of labor. If it is more complementary with skilled labor, that is $\sigma > \rho$, then the preceding derivatives are positive, implying that more or better equipment increases the wage of skilled workers by more than it increases the wage of unskilled workers. If $\sigma < \rho$, then more or better equipment reduces ω_t.

c. Taking logarithms of equation (S9.7) and using the approximation $\log(1 + x) \simeq x$, we get

$$\log \omega_t \simeq + \frac{\sigma - \rho}{\rho} \lambda \left(\left(\frac{q_t k_t}{s_t} \right)^\rho - 1 \right) + (1-\sigma) \log \left(\frac{u_t}{s_t} \right) + \theta,$$

where θ is a constant that depends on μ and λ. Using again the approximation $x - 1 \simeq \log(x)$, the growth rate of the skill premium can be written as

$$g_{\omega t} \simeq (1-\sigma)(g_{ut} - g_{st}) + \lambda(\sigma - \rho)(g_{kt} + g_{qt} - g_{st}). \qquad (S9.10)$$

The rate of growth of the skill premium depends on the relative growth rates of the supplies of the two types of labor, g_{ut} and g_{st} (standard effect). Because $1 > \sigma$, faster (relative) growth of skilled labor reduces the skill premium. There is also a term capturing the capital-skill complementarity. If $\sigma > \rho$, faster growth of either the amount of equipment or its quality, for a given rate of growth of the stock of skilled labor, raises the skill premium. Hence, technical change that raises the quality of equipment (as in the basic Schumpeterian model) or the amount of capital (as in the Romer model or the extended Schumpeterian model of Chapter 3) is skill-biased.

⋆ 3. The factor distribution of income and economic growth (based on Alesina and Rodrik 1994)

a. The growth rate of the consumption of capitalists is simply $g \equiv \dot{c}^k / c^k = r - \tau - \rho$. It is straightforward to show that the rates of growth of the capital stock and workers' consumption have to be equal to g, that is $\dot{k}/k = \dot{c}^l / c^l = \dot{c}^k / c^k = g$.

Differentiating (9.29) and using (9.30) to substitute for γ, we get

$$r = \alpha A[(1 - \lambda)\tau]^{1-\alpha} = r(\lambda, \tau) \tag{S9.11}$$

$$w = (1 - \alpha)A[(1 - \lambda)\tau]^{1-\alpha}k = \omega(\lambda, \tau)k. \tag{S9.12}$$

We can substitute for the interest rate and express the growth rate as

$$g = g(\lambda, \tau) = \alpha A[(1 - \lambda)\tau]^{1-\alpha} - \tau - \rho. \tag{S9.13}$$

b. Differentiating g, we find $\partial g / \partial \lambda < 0$ for all λ. That is, the growth rate is strictly decreasing in the fraction of revenue devoted to transfers. The growth rate is increasing in τ for values greater than $[\alpha(1 - \alpha)(1 - \lambda)^{1-\alpha}A]^{1/\alpha}$, and decreasing for smaller values of τ. Hence, the growth rate is maximized when $\lambda = 0$ and $\tau = \tau^*$, where

$$\tau^* \equiv [\alpha(1 - \alpha)A]^{1/\alpha}. \tag{S9.14}$$

c. The government's problem is

$$\max_{\lambda, \tau} W = \int_0^\infty \log c^k e^{-\rho t} dt$$

s.t. $c^k = [r(\lambda, \tau) - \tau]k - g(\lambda, \tau)k.$

The latter can be rewritten as

$$\max_{\lambda, \tau} W = \int_0^\infty \log \rho k e^{-\rho t} dt$$

s.t. $\dot{k} = g(\lambda, \tau)k.$

The Hamiltonian of this problem is

$$H = \log[\rho k]e^{-\rho t} + \mu g(\lambda, \tau)k$$

where μ is the (positive) costate variable. Differentiating with respect to λ and τ, we find that welfare is maximized when the rate of growth is maximized, that is when $\lambda = 0$ and $\tau = \tau^*$.

d. If the government cares about the welfare of workers, its maximization problem is given by

$$\max_{\lambda, \tau} W = (1 - \beta) \int_0^\infty \log c^k e^{-\rho t} dt + \beta \int_0^\infty \log c^l e^{-\rho t} dt$$

s.t. $c^k = \rho k$

$c^l = \omega(\lambda, \tau)k + \lambda \tau k$

$\dot{k} = g(\lambda, \tau)k$

$\lambda \geq 0.$

The Hamiltonian is

$$H = (1 - \beta) \log[\rho k]e^{-\rho t} + \beta \log[\omega(\lambda, \tau)k + \lambda \tau k]e^{-\rho t} + \mu g(\lambda, \tau)k,$$

which implies the following first-order conditions:

$$\beta \left(\frac{\partial \omega(\lambda, \tau)}{\partial \tau} + \lambda \right) \frac{ke^{-\rho t}}{c^l} + \mu \frac{\partial g(\lambda, \tau)}{\partial \tau} k = 0 \tag{S9.15}$$

$$\beta \left(\frac{\partial \omega(\lambda, \tau)}{\partial \lambda} + \tau \right) \frac{ke^{-\rho t}}{c^l} + \mu \frac{\partial g(\lambda, \tau)}{\partial \lambda} k = 0 \tag{S9.16}$$

$$(1 - \beta) \frac{e^{-\rho t}}{k} + \beta \frac{e^{-\rho t}}{k} + \mu g(\lambda, \tau) = -\dot{\mu}. \tag{S9.17}$$

From (S9.15) we immediately see that the tax rate chosen is smaller than the one that maximizes the growth rate. We know that $\partial \omega / \partial \tau > 0$, hence as long as β is positive, the first term in equation (S9.15) is positive. Because $\mu > 0$, a necessary condition for an optimum is that $\partial g / \partial \tau < 0$, which implies that $\tau > \tau^*$. The reason why the chosen tax rate is greater than the one that maximizes growth is that, starting from τ^*, an increase in the tax rate has a first-order effect on the consumption of workers (as there is a larger transfer), but only a second-order effect on the growth rate.

If we solve equations (S9.15), (S9.16), and (S9.17) for λ and τ, we get that the optimal values are given by

$$\lambda^{**} = 1 - \frac{[(1 - \alpha)A]^{1/\alpha}}{\beta \rho} \quad \text{and} \quad \tau^{**} = \beta \rho.$$

However, λ has to be nonnegative. Hence, these values are an optimum only if $\beta \rho \geq [(1 - \alpha)A]^{1/\alpha}$. In this case, $\tau^{**} > \tau^* = [\alpha(1 - \alpha)A]^{1/\alpha}$, which implies that the chosen tax rate is larger than the one that maximizes growth.

If the restriction $\beta\rho \geq [(1-\alpha)A]^{1/\alpha}$ is not satisfied, the optimal level of transfers is $\lambda^{**} = 0$, and the tax rate is implicitly given by

$$\tau^{**}[1 - \alpha(1-\alpha)A\tau^{**}] = (1-\alpha)\beta\rho,$$

which again is greater than τ^*.

⋆ 4. Majority voting, the distribution of factor endowments, and economic growth (based on Alesina and Rodrik 1994)

a. From the previous problem we know the wage rate and the interest rate. The income of agent i is given by $y^i = \omega(\tau)kl^i + [r(\tau) - \tau]k^i = \omega(\tau)k^i\sigma^i + [r(\tau) - \tau]k^i$. Hence agents i's maximization problem is

$$\max_{c^i} U = \int_0^\infty \log c^i e^{-\rho t} dt \tag{S9.18}$$

s.t. $\quad \dfrac{dk^i}{dt} = \omega(\tau)k^i\sigma^i + [r(\tau) - \tau]k^i - c^i.$

We obtain that the rate of growth of the consumption (and of the capital stock) of agent i is $g^i(\tau) = r(\tau) - \tau - \rho$, which is clearly the same for all agents, and hence is the growth rate of the economy. Note that this implies: (i) the growth rate is independent of the distribution of endowments, for any given tax rate, (ii) the distribution of relative endowments does not change over time.

b. Substituting for $r = \alpha A\tau^{1-\alpha}$ and differentiating $g(\tau)$ with respect to the tax rate, we obtain that the value of τ that maximizes growth is $\tau^* = [\alpha(1-\alpha)A]^{1/\alpha}$.

c. Substituting for the rate of growth of capital $dk^i/dt = [r(\tau) - \tau - \rho]k^i$ into the budget constraint in (S9.18), we can express individual consumption as $c^i = [\omega(\tau)\sigma^i + \rho]k^i$. This equation says that in any given period, the agent consumes all her labor income plus a fraction of her capital stock. The preferred tax rate is given by the solution to the following problem:

$$\max_{\tau} U = \int_0^\infty \log c^i e^{-\rho t} dt$$

s.t. $\quad c^i = [\omega(\tau)\sigma^i + \rho]k^i$

$\qquad dk^i/dt = g(\tau)k^i$

$\qquad dk/dt = g(\tau)k.$

The solution to this problem implicitly defines the preferred tax rate

$$\tau^i[1 - \alpha(1-\alpha)A(\tau^i)^{-\alpha}] = (1-\alpha)\rho\theta^i(\tau^i), \tag{S9.19}$$

where

$$\theta^i(\tau^i) = \omega(\tau^i)\sigma^i / [\omega(\tau^i)\sigma^i + \rho]. \tag{S9.20}$$

$\theta^i(\tau^i)$ is the share of the labor-income component in consumption, and it is increasing in σ^i. An agent with no labor income ($\sigma^i = 0$) consumes a constant fraction of her capital stock; hence she benefits from the tax rate only in so far as it increases the growth rate. She would choose $\tau^i = \tau^*$. An agent with labor income also experiences a level effect, as a higher tax increases the level of output and therefore her wage. Consequently she prefers a higher tax rate than τ^*. Check for yourself (from (S9.19) and (S9.20)) that the tax rate is monotonically increasing in σ^i.

d. If the tax rate were chosen by majority voting, the outcome would be the tax rate preferred by the median voter, denoted by τ^m, and given by (S9.19) and (S9.20). This implies that the greater σ^m, that is, the more unequal the distribution of capital is, the higher the tax rate is, and the lower the rate of growth.

⋆ 5. R&D and the distribution of firm sizes (based on García-Peñalosa 1996a)

a. Because borrowing is costly, firms prefer to use their own profits to fund research, rather than borrow. Consider a large firm that has enough profits to finance its R&D project. The cost of undertaking the project is $wh_i(1+r)$. The firm chooses to employ the number of researchers that maximizes its expected profits, that is

$$\max_{h_i} \lambda DP \log(q_i h_i) - wh_i(1+r), \tag{S9.21}$$

which yields the optimal level of employment

$$h_0 = \frac{\lambda DP}{w(1+r)}. \tag{S9.22}$$

All firms with profits large enough to finance this level of employment, do not borrow. That is, those for which $PD_i/r \geq wh_0 = \lambda DP/(1+r)$. Hence any firm of size $\delta_1 \equiv \lambda r/(1+r)$ or greater can hire the optimal level of researchers h_0.

Consider a firm of size δ_i, less than δ_1. It can invest PD_i/r from its own profits, and needs to borrow the rest at rate R. Hence, its optimization problem is

$$\max_{h_i} \lambda \left[DP \log(q_i h_i) - \left(wh_i - \frac{PD_i}{r} \right)(1+R) \right] - (1+r)\frac{PD_i}{r}. \tag{S9.23}$$

If the project succeeds, the firm obtains enough profits to repay the bank, thus paying the entire cost of the project. If it fails, the amount paid is only the profits that were invested, and is therefore less than the total cost of the project. The first-order condition gives the level of employment,

$$h_m = h_0 \frac{1+r}{\lambda(1+R)}. \tag{S9.24}$$

b. A firm δ_i larger than δ_1 wants to engage in research only if the maximum in equation (S9.21) is greater than zero, $\lambda DP \log(q_i h_0) - w h_0 (1+r) \geq 0$. That is, if its quality is at least q_0, where

$$q_0 = \frac{w(1+r)e}{\lambda DP}. \tag{S9.25}$$

Any firm with quality above q_0 invests in R&D, those with quality below it do not. Note that $q_0 = e/h_0$. A firm smaller than δ_1 invests only if the maximum in (S9.23) is greater than zero. That is, if its quality is at least $q_m(\delta)$, where

$$q_m(\delta) = q_0(1+\alpha) Exp\left[-\alpha \frac{\delta}{\delta_1}\right], \tag{S9.26}$$

and $\alpha \equiv \lambda (1 + R) / (1 + r) - 1 > 0$. The threshold quality now depends on the size of the firm. There is a tradeoff between size and the minimum project quality required: the smaller the firm is, the greater the cost of employing a certain number of researchers is, and hence it requires a higher quality in order to make the project profitable.

c. The minimum quality is given by the function $q(\delta)$, which is a piecewise function taking the value $q_m(\delta)$ for all $\delta \leq \delta_1$, and q_0 for firms greater than δ_1. Differentiating, we have that $q'_m = -\alpha q_m < 0$ and $q''_m = \alpha^2 q_m > 0$. The minimum quality is a function of firm size, which is decreasing and convex in the size of the firm for firms smaller than δ_1, and constant for firms lager than this threshold value. It is also continuous. To see this note that $q_m(\delta_1) = q_0(1+\alpha)e^{-\alpha}$. Because α is small, $\log(1+\alpha) \simeq \alpha$. Then, $q_m(\delta_1) \simeq q_0$. All those firms with quality greater than $q(\delta)$ invest in R&D, those with lower quality do not. The size distribution of firms affects the density at each point on the (q, δ)-space and hence the number of firms that do research and the quality of the projects.

d. A firm's market share is, δ/N. We can then express the Herfindahl index as

$$H = \frac{1}{N} \int_0^N \delta^2 d\Phi(\delta).$$

Because δ^2 is a convex function, we know, that the value of the index is increased by an MPS (see Chapter 9, note 6). That is, market concentration, as measured by the Herfindahl index, is greater the more dispersed firm sizes are.

e. Let $\bar{q}_t$ be the expected average quality of research projects at period t. We obtain it by integrating over q and δ,

$$\bar{q}_t = \int_0^N \int_{q(\delta)}^1 q \, dq \, d\Phi_t(\delta)$$

$$= \int_0^N \frac{1 - q(\delta)^2}{2} \, d\Phi_t(\delta).$$

For any $\delta \geq \delta_1$, $\left(1 - q(\delta)^2\right)$ is constant. For $\delta < \delta_1$, it is concave as the second derivative of $\left(1 - q_m^2\right)$ is $-2\left(q_m'q_m' + q_m q_m''\right)$, which is negative as $q_m'' > 0$. Thus $\left(1 - q(\delta)^2\right)$ is concave, and an MPS reduces the average quality of research.

The expected rate of growth of the stock of designs is given by

$$g_t = \int_0^N \int_{q(\delta)}^1 \lambda \log(qh(\delta)) \, dq \, d\Phi_t(\delta)$$

$$= \int_0^N \lambda \left[q \left(\log(qh(\delta)) - 1 \right) \right]_{q(\delta)}^1 d\Phi_t(\delta).$$

Substituting in for $q(\delta)$ and $h(\delta)$, we can express g_t as

$$g_t = \lambda \int_0^N f(\delta) \, d\Phi_t(\delta),$$

where $f(\delta)$ takes the form

$$f(\delta) = \begin{cases} -\log q_0 - \log(1 + \alpha) + \alpha\delta q_m(\delta) & \text{if } \delta < \delta_1 \\ -\log q_0 & \text{if } \delta \geq \delta_1. \end{cases}$$

Because q_0 lies between zero and one, $-\log q_0$ is positive. It is precisely the growth rate if all firms could borrow at the risk-free rate, and is independent of the distribution of firm sizes. For large firms, q_0 does not depend on firm size as changes in the size of the firm do not affect $f(\delta)$. For small firms ($\delta < \delta_1$), the second derivative of $f(\delta)$ is negative, $d^2 f(\delta)/d\delta^2 < 0$. Consequently $f(\delta)$ is concave, and an MPS reduces the expected rate of technical change. Hence, an increase in market concentration, as measured by the Herfindahl index, implies a lower rate of technical change.

6. Vested interests with no learning externalities

Let us represent the game in the following way

	t	
$t+1$	1	0
1	$(1-\alpha)\gamma^{v+1}$	$(1-\alpha)\gamma^{v+1}$
0	γ^{v}	γ^{v}

The process to find the equilibrium if the old decide and there are no learning externalities is the same as in the appendix.

Step 1. $\binom{0}{0}$ is an equilibrium if $1 > (1-\alpha)\gamma$.

The payoff to the old from innovating or not is independent of what happened in the previous period, as there is no learning. It is also independent of what will happen in the next period, as they will not be around. If $1 > (1-\alpha)\gamma$, the payoff from innovating, $(1-\alpha)\gamma^{v+1}$, is smaller than that from not innovating, γ^{v}. Hence the old always vote against innovating.

Step 2. $\binom{1}{1}$ is an equilibrium if $1 < (1-\alpha)\gamma$.

In this case, $\gamma^{v} < (1-\alpha)\gamma^{v+1}$. Hence the old get a higher payoff when they vote for an innovation this period.

Step 3. $\binom{0}{1}$ and $\binom{1}{0}$ are not an equilibrium.

The reason is that, because what strategy gives a higher payoff is independent of what occurred in the previous period, if the old of generation t prefer a certain outcome, so will the old of all other generations. Switching is not an equilibrium.

Chapter 10

⋆ 1. Growth driven by the accumulation of human capital (based on Uzawa 1965, and Lucas 1988)

a. The problem faced by agents is

$$\max \int_0^\infty \frac{c^{1-\sigma}-1}{1-\sigma} e^{-\rho t} dt \tag{S10.1}$$

subject to

$$\dot{k} = Ak^\beta (uh)^{1-\beta} h_a^\gamma - c - nk, \tag{S10.2}$$

$$\dot{h} = \delta(1-u)h. \tag{S10.3}$$

The Hamiltonian is

$$H(c, u, k, h, \lambda, \mu, t) = \frac{c^{1-\sigma}-1}{1-\sigma} e^{-\rho t} + \lambda(Ak^\beta (uh)^{1-\beta} h_a^\gamma - c - nk)$$
$$+ \mu(\delta(1-u)h),$$

from where we obtain the following first order conditions:

$$\frac{\partial H}{\partial c} = 0 \Rightarrow c^{-\sigma} e^{-\rho t} = \lambda \tag{S10.4}$$

$$\frac{\partial H}{\partial u} = 0 \Rightarrow \lambda (1 - \beta) A k^{\beta} u^{-\beta} h^{1-\beta+\gamma} = \mu \delta h \tag{S10.5}$$

$$\frac{\partial H}{\partial k} = -\dot{\lambda} \Rightarrow -\dot{\lambda} = \lambda \left(A \beta k^{\beta-1} u^{1-\beta} h^{1-\beta+\gamma} - n \right) \tag{S10.6}$$

$$\frac{\partial H}{\partial h} = -\dot{\mu} \Rightarrow -\dot{\mu} = \lambda (1 - \beta) A k^{\beta} u^{1-\beta} h^{-\beta+\gamma} + \mu \delta (1 - u), \tag{S10.7}$$

where we have used the fact that the average level of human capital h_a has to be equal to that of the individual, as all agents are identical. The last two expressions determine the rates of change of the shadow prices of the two types of capital. Equations (S10.2)–(S10.7), together with the transversality conditions, implicitly define the optimal trajectories of $k(t)$ and $h(t)$.

b. To find the growth rate we start by obtaining the rate of growth of consumption from equations (S10.4) and (S10.6). That is,

$$\frac{\dot{c}}{c} = \frac{A\beta(uh/k)^{1-\beta}h^{\gamma} - \rho - n}{\sigma}. \tag{S10.8}$$

The next step is to find the relationship between the steady-state rate of growth of consumption, the capital stock and the level of human capital. In the steady state, the rate of growth of all these variables is constant, and u, the fraction of time spent at work is also constant (if it grew, even at a constant rate, it would reach either 0 or 1, which would imply either no production or no investment in human capital). Denote by g_c^* the steady-state rate of growth of consumption. Substituting (S10.8) into equation (S10.2) we get

$$g_k^* = \frac{\sigma g_c^* + \rho + n}{\beta} - \frac{c}{k} - n, \tag{S10.9}$$

where g_k^* is the steady-state rate of growth of the capital stock. Because g_c^* and g_k^* are constant, then c/k must be constant, which implies that consumption and the capital stock grow at the same rate, $g_c^* = g_k^*$.

Let g_h^* be the steady-state rate of growth of human capital. We take logs and differentiate equation (S10.8), to get

$$g_k^* = \frac{1 - \beta + \gamma}{1 - \beta} g_h^*. \tag{S10.10}$$

That is, the rate of growth of physical capital is proportional to the rate of growth of human capital. The rate of growth of the stock of human capital plays the same role in determining the path of consumption and capital as the rate of exogenous technological change in the Solow model, as the evolution of h determines the productivity of factors at each point in time.

c. To find the rate of growth of output, we rewrite equation (S10.5) as

$$\frac{\lambda}{\mu} = \frac{\delta}{(1-\beta)A} k^{-\beta} u^{\beta} h^{\beta-\gamma}. \tag{S10.11}$$

Take logs, differentiate with respect to time, and use equation (S10.10) to get

$$\frac{\dot{\lambda}}{\lambda} - \frac{\dot{\mu}}{\mu} = -\frac{\gamma}{1-\beta} g_h^*. \tag{S10.12}$$

To obtain the dynamic equations for the shadow prices we use equation (S10.4) to get

$$\frac{\dot{\lambda}}{\lambda} = -\sigma g_c^* - \rho, \tag{S10.13}$$

and equation (S10.7) to obtain

$$-\frac{\dot{\mu}}{\mu} = \delta(1-u) + \frac{\lambda}{\mu}(1-\beta)Ak^{\beta}u^{1-\beta}h^{-\beta+\gamma}. \tag{S10.14}$$

Using (S10.11) to substitute for the ratio of the shadow prices of the two types of capital, equation (S10.14) becomes

$$-\frac{\dot{\mu}}{\mu} = \delta. \tag{S10.15}$$

We can now use (S10.10), (S10.12), (S10.13), and (S10.15) to get

$$g_h^* = \frac{1-\beta}{\sigma(1-\beta+\gamma)-\gamma}(\delta-\rho). \tag{S10.16}$$

That is, there is a constant rate of growth of human capital, determined by the parameters of the model. This growth rate, in turn, defines the rate of growth of physical capital, consumption and output, all of which are proportional to it.

d. From (S10.10) and the aggregate production function we have that

$$g_y^* = g_c^* = g_k^* = \frac{1-\beta+\gamma}{\sigma(1-\beta+\gamma)-\gamma}(\delta-\rho). \tag{S10.17}$$

Last, we need to find the division of time between the two activities, production and education. Equations (S10.3) and (S10.16) imply that the steady-state proportion of time devoted to education is

$$1-u^* = \frac{1-\beta}{\sigma(1-\beta+\gamma)-\gamma}\frac{\delta-\rho}{\delta}, \tag{S10.18}$$

which is determined by the model parameters. Note that if $\gamma = 0$, $1 - u^* = (\delta - \rho)/\delta\sigma$, and the growth rate is simply $g = \delta(1 - u^*)$, as was argued in the chapter.

e. In the model there is an externality arising from the fact that the average level of human capital affects the overall level of productivity and thus the return to the two types of capital. A social planner would take this effect into account and choose a higher rate of investment in human capital.

For the planner, equation (S10.7) is substituted by

$$\frac{\partial H}{\partial h} = -\dot{\mu} \Rightarrow -\dot{\mu} = \lambda(1 - \beta + \gamma)Ak^\beta u^{1-\beta}h^{-\beta+\gamma} + \mu\delta(1 - u), \qquad \text{(S10.7')}$$

which implies

$$-\frac{\dot{\mu}}{\mu} = \delta(1 - u) + \frac{1 - \beta + \gamma}{1 - \beta}\delta u. \qquad \text{(S10.15')}$$

We can now use (S10.12), (S10.13), and (S10.15') and get

$$-\frac{\gamma}{1-\beta}g_h^{**} = \delta + \frac{\gamma}{1-\beta}\delta u - \sigma\frac{1-\beta+\gamma}{1-\beta}g_h^{**} - \rho,$$

where g_h^{**} is the steady-state rate of growth of human capital chosen by the planner. Using equation (S10.3) to substitute for u, we find that the socially optimal rate of growth of human capital and level of investment in it are

$$g_h^{**} = \frac{1}{\sigma}\frac{(\delta - \rho)(1 - \beta) + \gamma\delta}{1 - \beta + \gamma} \qquad \text{(S10.16')}$$

and

$$1 - u^{**} = \frac{1}{\sigma\delta}\frac{(\delta - \rho)(1 - \beta) + \gamma\delta}{1 - \beta + \gamma}, \qquad \text{(S10.18')}$$

both of which are greater than the corresponding values for the competitive economy if $\gamma > 0$. Only when $\gamma = 0$, that is, when there are no spillovers between workers, is the competitive outcome socially optimal.

There is another externality in the model, as the level of human capital today affects the return to subsequent investments in this production factor. This intertemporal spillover effect is in fact what makes unbounded growth possible. In the Ramsey-Cass-Koopmans world, infinitely lived agents internalize the externality and their investment in human capital is the optimal one. However, if individuals had finite lives, they would not fully internalize the impact that their investment has on the human capital of the next generation, and there would be a further divergence between the competitive equilibrium and the social optimum.

f. The budget constraint is now $\dot{k} = (1 - \tau)Ak^{\beta}(uh)^{1-\beta}h^{\gamma} - c - nk$. The first-order conditions from the resulting Hamiltonian are (S10.4) and

$$\mu\delta h = \lambda(1 - \beta)(1 - \tau)Ak^{\beta}u^{-\beta}h^{1-\beta+\gamma}, \tag{S10.5''}$$

$$-\dot{\lambda} = \lambda((1 - \tau)A\beta k^{\beta-1}u^{1-\beta}h^{1-\beta+\gamma} - n), \tag{S10.6''}$$

$$-\dot{\mu} = \lambda(1 - \beta)(1 - \tau)Ak^{\beta}u^{1-\beta}h^{-\beta+\gamma} + \mu\delta(1 - u). \tag{S10.7''}$$

The rate of growth of consumption is then

$$\frac{\dot{c}}{c} = \frac{A(1 - \tau)\beta(uh/k)^{1-\beta}h^{\gamma} - \rho - n}{\sigma}. \tag{S10.8''}$$

However, you can check that neither equation (S10.9) nor (S10.10) change, so the relation between the rate of growth of physical and human capital is unaffected by the tax. From equation (S10.5'') we have

$$\frac{\lambda}{\mu}(1 - \tau) = \frac{\delta}{(1 - \beta)A}k^{-\beta}u^{\beta}h^{\beta-\gamma}, \tag{S10.11''}$$

which, taking logs and differentiating with respect to time gives equation (S10.12). Equation (S10.13) is not changed either, as it is derived from (S10.4). From (S10.7'') we obtain

$$-\frac{\dot{\mu}}{\mu} = \delta(1 - u) + \frac{\lambda}{\mu}(1 - \tau)(1 - \beta)Ak^{\beta}u^{1-\beta}h^{-\beta+\gamma}. \tag{S10.14''}$$

Using (S10.11'') to substitute for $\lambda(1 - \tau)/\mu$, equation (S10.14'') becomes equation (S10.15). Since the growth rate is determined by equations (S10.10), (S10.12), (S10.13), and (S10.15), none of which is affected by the tax, the economy grows at the same rate as in the absence of the income tax.

2. The Lucas model with physical capital in the accumulation of human capital (based on Rebelo 1991)

a. Efficiency requires that the marginal value product of the two inputs be equal across sectors. Differentiating (10.16) and (10.17) with respect to physical capital and to human capital, we have

$$\beta A_1\left(\frac{uh}{\phi k}\right)^{1-\beta} = q\gamma A_2\left(\frac{(1 - u)h}{(1 - \phi)k}\right)^{1-\gamma} \tag{S10.19}$$

$$(1 - \beta)A_1\left(\frac{\phi k}{uh}\right)^{\beta} = q(1 - \gamma)A_2\left(\frac{(1 - \phi)k}{(1 - u)h}\right)^{\gamma}. \tag{S10.20}$$

These two equations together yield

$$\frac{1-\beta}{\beta}\frac{\phi k}{uh} = \frac{1-\gamma}{\gamma}\frac{(1-\phi)k}{(1-u)h} \tag{S10.21}$$

b. The rate of return to capital employed in final-good production is

$$r = \beta A_1(\phi k)^{\beta-1} (uh)^{1-\beta} . \tag{S10.22}$$

Alternatively, one could accumulate $1/q$ units of human capital, which yield a return in the human-capital accumulation sector of

$$r^h = (1-\gamma)A_2((1-\phi)k)^\gamma((1-u)h)^{-\gamma} + \frac{\dot{q}}{q}, \tag{S10.23}$$

where the last term in (S10.23) represents the "capital gain" from investing in human capital. At the optimum both should be equal, that is, $r = r^h$. In the steady state, equation (S10.19) (or equivalently (S10.20)) imply that q is constant. Then

$$\beta A_1 \left(\frac{\phi k}{uh}\right)^{\beta-1} = (1-\gamma)A_2 \left(\frac{(1-\phi)k}{(1-u)h}\right)^\gamma . \tag{S10.24}$$

(We could alternatively have equated the return to physical capital in the human-capital accumulation sector to the return to human capital in the final-good sector.)

c. We can solve equations (S10.21) and (S10.24) together for the capital-labor intensities, and obtain

$$\frac{\phi k}{uh} = \left(\frac{A_1}{A_2}\frac{\beta}{1-\gamma}\right)^{v/\gamma} \left(\frac{1-\gamma}{\gamma}\frac{\beta}{1-\beta}\right)^v,$$

$$\frac{(1-\phi)k}{(1-u)h} = \left(\frac{A_1}{A_2}\frac{\beta}{1-\gamma}\right)^{v/\gamma} \left(\frac{1-\gamma}{\gamma}\frac{\beta}{1-\beta}\right)^{-v(1-\beta)/\gamma} .$$

The capital-labor intensities are constant in the two sectors. Substituting them into either (S10.22) or (S10.23) we find the steady-state interest rate,

$$r^* = A_1^v A_2^{1-v}\Psi^v, \tag{S10.25}$$

where $\Psi = \beta^\beta(1-\beta)^{1-\beta}\gamma^{1-\beta}(1-\gamma)^{(1-\beta)(1-\gamma)/\gamma}$. The rate of interest is therefore a constant that depends only on model parameters, and not on the level of either the stock of human or physical capital.

d. Because the rate of growth of consumption is given by $g = (r-\rho)/\sigma$, in steady state we have

$$g = \frac{A_1^v A_2^{1-v} \Psi^v - \rho}{\sigma}. \tag{S10.26}$$

The crucial aspect is the interplay between the two types of capital. The accumulation of human capital increases the marginal product of physical capital, and hence induces its accumulation. But this in turn increases the marginal product of human capital, and more resources are invested in it. Although there are diminishing returns to each factor, there are constant returns to all cumulable factors taken together, which prevent the marginal product from falling as inputs are accumulated and induce continuous investment and hence sustained growth.

e. The static efficiency condition is not affected by the tax. Equality between the (net) marginal value product of the two inputs implies

$$(1 - \tau)\beta A_1 \left(\frac{uh}{\phi k}\right)^{1-\beta} = q\gamma A_2 \left(\frac{(1 - u)h}{(1 - \phi)k}\right)^{1-\gamma},$$

$$(1 - \tau)(1 - \beta)A_1 \left(\frac{\phi k}{uh}\right)^{\beta} = q(1 - \gamma)A_2 \left(\frac{(1 - \phi)k}{(1 - u)h}\right)^{\gamma},$$

which together yield equation (S10.21). The net rate of return to capital employed in final-good production is

$$r = (1 - \tau)\beta A_1 (\phi k)^{\beta - 1} (uh)^{1-\beta}, \tag{S10.22''}$$

whereas the return to $1/q$ units of human capital is given by (S10.23). It is then straightforward to show that the steady-state rate of interest is

$$r^* = (1 - \tau)^v A_1^v A_2^{1-v} \Psi^v, \tag{S10.25''}$$

and the growth rate is lower than that in equation (S10.26). The tax on income leads to a reduction in the capital/labor intensity in both sectors, substituting away from the input whose production is taxed (physical capital). Note that if there were no such substitution away from physical capital, the interest rate would be $r^* = (1 - \tau)A_1^v A_2^{1-v} \Psi^v$, and the fall in the growth rate would be larger.

3. Growth and the level of human capital (based on Romer 1990a)

We proceed as in Chapter 1 to get the labor-market equilibrium condition for skilled workers, which now is

$$P_A = \frac{\alpha}{\delta} \frac{x^{1-\alpha-\beta} L^\beta}{H_1^{1-\alpha}}. \tag{S10.27}$$

Differentiate the aggregate production function with respect to x_i to obtain the inverse demand for capital goods

$$p(x) = (1 - \alpha - \beta)H_1^\alpha L^\beta x^{-\alpha-\beta}, \tag{S10.28}$$

in a symmetric equilibrium. This expression implies an elasticity of demand of $1/(\alpha + \beta)$. The revenue function for the intermediate goods producer is $R(x) = p(x)x$. Profits are maximized when marginal revenue is equal to the marginal cost, r. This implies

$$x = \left(\frac{(1 - \alpha - \beta)^2}{r} H_1^\alpha L^\beta \right)^{1/(\alpha+\beta)}. \tag{S10.29}$$

Profits are given by $\pi = x(p - r)$, which imply that the price at which the patent for the new design can be sold is

$$P_A = \frac{\alpha + \beta}{(1 - \alpha - \beta)} x. \tag{S10.30}$$

Using equations (S10.27), (S10.29), and (S10.30), we get the level of employment in the manufacturing sector

$$H_1 = \theta \frac{r}{\delta}, \quad \text{where } \theta = \frac{\alpha}{(\alpha + \beta)(1 - \alpha - \beta)}. \tag{S10.31}$$

The rate of output growth is given by $g = \delta(H - H_1)$, which together with (S10.31) and the dynamic equation for consumption, $g = (r - \rho)/\sigma$, gives the steady state growth rate,

$$g = \frac{\delta H - \rho\theta}{1 + \theta\sigma}. \tag{S10.32}$$

The rate of growth exhibits again scale effects, but they are caused by the stock of human capital and not by the supply of unskilled labor.

Why does the supply of unskilled labor have no effect on the growth rate? A greater stock of labor raises the productivity of human capital in the final-goods sector. Thus, it should result in a shift of employment from research to manufacturing. However, a larger L also affects the productivity of capital goods, increasing their marginal value product and hence the value of the innovation. Consequently, the marginal product of skilled workers in research also rises. With our particular specification, the two effects exactly cancel out. This is not a robust feature of the model, and under different functional forms the stock of unskilled labor may affect (increase or decrease) the allocation of human capital between the production and the research sector. For example, suppose that unskilled labor and capital goods were substitutes, whereas human capital was complementary with either of the two. Then, a larger value of L would increase the marginal product of skilled labor, whereas it would reduce the number of capital goods employed. This second effect would in turn reduce the value of patents, and the desired level of employment in research. Hence, an increase in the stock of labor would unambiguously lead to fewer researchers and a slower growth rate. Such a result may help understand why we observe that countries like India have not grown fast despite having a large population.

4. Income distribution, education, and growth (based on Galor and Zeira 1993)

a. The utility of an individual who does not invest in education is

$$U_u(x) = \log\left[w_u + (x + w_u)(1 + r)\right] + \beta, \tag{S10.33}$$

where $\beta \equiv \alpha \log \alpha + (1 - \alpha) \log(1 - \alpha)$. This individual is a lender and leaves a bequest of

$$b_u(x) = (1 - \alpha)\left[w_u + (x + w_u)(1 + r)\right]. \tag{S10.34}$$

An individual with inheritance $x \geq h$ invests in education, and her utility and bequest are given by

$$U_s(x) = \log\left[w_s + (x - h)(1 + r)\right] + \beta, \tag{S10.35}$$

$$b_s(x) = (1 - \alpha)\left[w_s + (x - h)(1 + r)\right]. \tag{S10.36}$$

Last, the utility and bequest of an agent who borrows in order to invest in education $(x < h)$ are respectively

$$U_s(x) = \log\left[w_s + (x - h)(1 + i)\right] + \beta, \tag{S10.37}$$

$$b_s(x) = (1 - \alpha)\left[w_s + (x - h)(1 + i)\right]. \tag{S10.38}$$

If condition (10.23) does not hold, all agents would prefer to work as unskilled. If it does, all those that can afford education without borrowing invest. Those who have to borrow choose to study if their utility from doing so is greater that their utility from remaining unskilled, $U_s(x) \geq U_u(x)$. Comparing (S10.33) and (S10.37) we have that the individual invests if

$$x \geq f \equiv \frac{w_u(2 + r) + h(1 + i) - w_s}{i - r}, \tag{S10.39}$$

that is, if inheritance is "large enough."

b. By definition D_t satisfies $L = \int_0^\infty dD_t(x_t)$. Then, D_t determines the number of skilled and unskilled workers in dynasty t,

$$L_t^s = \int_f^\infty dD_t(x_t) \quad \text{and} \quad L_t^u = \int_0^f dD_t(x_t),$$

and hence the level of output. Note that the social optimum would be for all agents to invest (from condition (10.23)), and that this would be achieved under perfect capital markets.

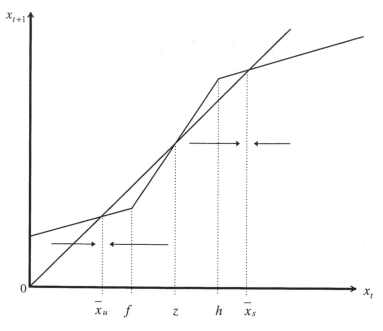

Figure S10.1
Source: Galor and Zeira (1993), p. 41.

c. From equations (S10.34), (S10.36), and (S10.38), next period's distribution of inheritances is given by

$$x_{t+1} = \begin{cases} (1-\alpha)\left[w_u + (x_t + w_u)(1+r)\right] & \text{if } x_t < f \\ (1-\alpha)\left[w_s + (x_t - h)(1+i)\right] & \text{if } f \leq x_t < h \\ (1-\alpha)\left[w_s + (x_t - h)(1+r)\right] & \text{if } h \leq x_t. \end{cases}$$

Figure S10.1 depicts this function. It is a piecewise function that, under the assumption that $(1-\alpha)(1+r) < 1$, intersects the 45° line three times. These three intersections determine the two steady-state equilibria, $\bar{x}_s$ and $\bar{x}_u$, and the critical point z. $\bar{x}_s$ and $\bar{x}_u$ correspond to locally stable equilibria, whereas z does not. All dynasties who inherit less than f work as unskilled and converge to

$$\bar{x}_u = \frac{1-\alpha}{1 - (1-\alpha)(1+r)}(2+r)w_u. \tag{S10.40}$$

Their descendants will always choose not to invest in education. Dynasties who can study without borrowing converge to

$$\bar{x}_s = \frac{1-\alpha}{1 - (1-\alpha)(1+r)}\left[w_s - h(1+r)\right], \tag{S10.41}$$

and their children will always study. Now consider an individual who chooses to invest in education but needs to borrow to do so. The intersection point z is given by the intersection of the corresponding bequest function with the 45° line. That is, $z = (1 - \alpha)\left[w_s + (z - h)(1 + i)\right]$. This expression defines z as given in equation (10.24). If her initial inheritance is greater than z, she bequeaths to her child more than she inherited. Hence her child will also prefer to study, and will also leave a bequest greater than the one received. The dynasty eventually converges to $\bar{x}_s$. However, if her inheritance was less than z, she bequeaths less than she inherited. Eventually this will take her dynasty to a point below f, where it is no longer optimal to invest in education. The dynasty will then converge to $\bar{x}_u$.

d. The number of skilled workers in the long run is given by the number of individuals who received a bequest greater than z in the first period, t. That is

$$L_\infty^s = L_t^s = \int_z^\infty dD_t(x_t).$$

The long-run level of average wealth can then be expressed as

$$\bar{x} = \bar{x}_u + (\bar{x}_s - \bar{x}_u)\frac{L_t^s}{L},$$

which depends on the initial distribution of bequests. That is, there are multiple long-run equilibria, and the one that the economy converges to depends on the initial distribution of wealth. A country that is initially poor will have a low level of wealth in the long run as few agents were above the threshold value z in period t. Now consider a rich country. If wealth is initially very concentrated in the hands of few dynasties, L_t^s is small, and long-run average wealth is low. However, if wealth is initially spread so that many individuals are above the z threshold, the economy will converge to a higher level of wealth. That is, a large middle class is beneficial for growth.

5. Education and unemployment (based on Acemoglu 1996)

a. The expected profit from entering equals $m(\theta, 1)/\theta[p(y + a)/2 + (1 - p)y/2] - \gamma$ because:

• with probability $m(\theta, 1)/\theta$ the firm is matched with a worker,

• with probability p it is matched with a skilled worker and the firm earns $(y + a)/2$,

• with probability $(1 - p)$ it is matched with an unskilled worker and the firm earns $y/2$,

• the entry cost equals γ.

Free entry implies that the expected profit from entering equals zero. This can be written as $m(\theta, 1)/\theta[p(y + a) + (1 - p)y] = 2\gamma$.

b. The benefit for a worker to acquire skills equals $a/2$ conditional on being matched with a firm. Hence the expected revenue of acquiring skills equals $m(\theta, 1)a/2$. The worker is willing to invest c in education if and only if $m(\theta, 1)a/2 - c > 0$ or, equivalently, $m(\theta, 1)a > 2c$.

c.

i. If no worker acquires skills ($p_1 = 0$), firms only get half of the minimum total surplus y and not many firms will enter, that is, θ_1 will be low. If θ_1 is low, it is not profitable for workers to acquire skills. Hence this is a Nash equilibrium.

ii. In this equilibrium p_2 workers acquire skills. The firms expect a total surplus of $y + p_2 a$ and more firms enter than under (i). Because this increases the probability of being matched with a firm as compared to (i), some workers are indeed willing to acquire skills.

iii. Here all workers acquire skills and firms anticipate a total surplus of $y + a$. This attracts enough firms to make it worthwhile for all workers to acquire skills. So this is a Nash equilibrium.

d. As p and θ increase, total welfare is increased. The reason why the economy will not always attain the efficient outcome is a coordination failure among workers. If almost no worker decides to invest in education, very few firms will enter and indeed the best a worker can do is not to invest in education. If, however, a lot of workers invest in education, this attracts a lot of firms, making it worthwhile for other workers to acquire skills as well. The government can try to coordinate workers by making it cheaper for them to acquire skills (i.e., by subsidizing education).

e. As a increases, more workers will invest in education and more firms will enter. This will reduce unemployment. So in this context of coordination failures, technological progress may spur workers to become educated. This rise in education makes it more profitable for firms to enter, which in turn reduces unemployment.

⋆ **6. School ownership, competition, and efficiency (based on Bolton and Xu 1996)**

a. The Nash bargaining solution implies that each party gets $v(k)/2$. Hence, in stage one the teacher chooses the level of investment in knowledge that maximizes her net payoff. That is,

$$\max_k \left\{ \frac{v(k)}{2} - k \right\} \tag{S10.42}$$

which gives the first order condition

$$\frac{v'(k^n)}{2} = 1, \tag{S10.43}$$

where k^n is the solution to the teacher's maximization problem when there are no schools. The first-best solution would be the one that maximizes the total net value,

$$\max_k \{v(k) - k\} \Rightarrow v'(k^*) = 1. \tag{S10.44}$$

b. The Shapley-value implies that the outsider gets $(V(k) - v(k))/3$, and the teacher and the government (students) $(V(k) - v(k))/3 + v(k)/2$ each. The teacher then maximizes her net payoff, which implies

$$\frac{V'(k^O) - v'(k^O)}{3} + \frac{v'(k^O)}{2} = 1, \tag{S10.45}$$

where $V' = f' \cdot v'$, and k^O is the level of investment chosen by the teacher under outsider ownership. Comparing equations (S10.43) and (S10.45), we find that k^O is greater than k^n if and only if $f'(v(k)) > 1$. The presence of the school can therefore be damaging from an ex-ante perspective, as it may reduce the teacher's incentive to invest in knowledge. However, this only occurs when knowledge and the school facilities are not sufficiently complementary (i.e., if $f'(v(k)) < 1$).

c. The outsider gets nothing, while the teacher and the government (students) get $V(k)/2$ each. The teacher's optimization problem yields

$$\frac{V'(k^g)}{2} = 1. \tag{S10.46}$$

This investment is greater than the one implied by equation (S10.45) if and only if $f'(v(k)) > 1$. Hence, teacher or government ownership is optimal (induces higher investment in knowledge) whenever the teacher-school complementarities are large enough ($f' > 1$). Otherwise ($f' < 1$) outsider ownership is better. In this case, the level of investment will be below that of the no-school case, but the overall benefit, $V(k) - k$, may still be higher as the school increases the value of the teacher's knowledge to the student ($V(k) > v(k)$).

⋆ **7. Competition among teachers within one school (based on Bolton and Xu 1996)**

a. The social planner wants to maximize the expected payoff of education. Hence her ex-ante investment problem is

$$\max_{k_1, k_2 \geq 0} \left\{ \frac{1}{2}\lambda \log(1 + k_1) + \frac{1}{2}\lambda \log(1 + k_2) - k_1 - k_2 \right\},$$

which implies that the first-best investment levels are

$$k_1^* = k_2^* = \frac{\lambda}{2} - 1,$$

which, under the assumption that $\lambda > 2$, are positive.

b. The students' outside payoff from the bargaining game is $\underline{V}$. To see this, note that the bad teacher makes no socially valuable contribution; hence she is willing to compete away her entire surplus by offering it to the government. When bargaining with the good teacher, there are two possible outcomes. If $\underline{V} < \bar{V}/2$, the social surplus will be evenly divided between the two parties, so that the government and the good teacher get $\bar{V}/2$ each. If $\underline{V} > \bar{V}/2$, then the good teacher has to offer the students a payoff of $\underline{V}$. Because we have assumed that $\underline{V} > \bar{V}/2$, the students will get $\underline{V}$, the good teacher $\bar{V} - \underline{V}$, and the bad teacher zero. Thus, under government ownership the ex-ante expected gross payoff is $(\bar{V} - \underline{V})/2$. Hence the teachers choose their investments to solve

$$\max_{k_i \geq 0} \left\{ \frac{1}{2} \left[\lambda \log(1 + k_i) - \log(1 + k_j) \right] - k_i \right\},$$

which gives the following (symmetric) Nash-equilibrium investment levels:

$$k_1^g = k_2^g = \frac{\lambda}{2} - 1.$$

That is, under government or student ownership the investment incentives for teachers yield first-best levels of investment.

c. Under outsider ownership, the outside option for the students is the value of education obtained outside the school, $\max\{\bar{v}/2, \underline{v}\}$. Under our assumption that $\underline{V} > \bar{V}/2$, we also have $\underline{v} > \bar{v}/2$. The government's outside option is then $\underline{v}$, the good teacher's outside option is $\bar{v} - \underline{v}$, and that of the bad teacher is zero. Suppose the outside options are binding (that is, $\bar{V}/3 < \underline{v}$). Then the government gets $\underline{v}$, the good teacher $\bar{v} - \underline{v}$, and the outsider $\bar{V} - \bar{v}$. Given this ex-post bargaining solution, the teachers' ex-ante maximization problem is

$$\max_{k_i \geq 0} \left\{ \frac{1}{2} \left[\alpha \lambda \log(1 + k_i) - \alpha \log(1 + k_j) \right] - k_i \right\},$$

which yields (symmetric) Nash-equilibrium investment levels equal to

$$k_1^O = k_2^O = \frac{\alpha \lambda}{2} - 1.$$

d. Under joint teacher ownership, the two teachers bargain ex-post over the residual value of the school, $\bar{V} - \underline{v}$. Hence each gets a gross payoff of $(\bar{V} - \underline{v})/2$. The government gets the outside option, $\underline{v}$. Each teacher then chooses an investment to solve

$$\max_{k_i \geq 0} \left\{ \frac{1}{4} \left[\lambda \log(1 + k_i) - \alpha \log(1 + k_j) \right] \right.$$

$$\left. + \frac{1}{4} \left[\lambda \log(1 + k_j) - \alpha \log(1 + k_i) \right] - k_i \right\}.$$

which implies

$$k_1^T = k_2^T = \max \left\{ 0, \frac{\lambda - \alpha}{4} - 1 \right\}.$$

Outsider ownership induces higher levels of investment than joint teacher ownership whenever $\lambda(2\alpha - 1) > -\alpha$. That is, if the value added by the school is small (α large) or the difference between the good and the bad teacher is big (λ large).

e. Ex-ante allocation of the school to one of the teachers introduces competition. Since the two teachers are ex-ante identical, it does not matter to whom the school is allocated. Suppose, without loss of generality, that T_1 owns the school. If T_1 is the best teacher, then the students get their outside option $\underline{v}$, teacher T_1 gets $\bar{V} - \underline{v}$, and teacher T_2 gets zero. If teacher T_1 is the bad teacher, the students outside option is what they could get in the school with the bad teacher, $\underline{V}$; teacher T_2 could provide education outside the school, offer students $\underline{V}$, and get $\bar{v} - \underline{V}$. If the outside options are not binding, the bargaining solution would give $\bar{V}/3$ to each of the two teachers and to the students. Consider the more interesting case in which the difference between teachers is very large so that outside options are binding, $\bar{v} - \underline{V} \geq \bar{V}/3$, which will happen when the difference between teachers is large and/or when the value added of the school is small. Then, teacher T_2 gets her outside option $\bar{v} - \underline{V}$, the students get $\underline{V}$, and teacher T_1 gets $\bar{V} - \bar{v}$. Hence T_1's expected ex-ante payoff is

$$\frac{1}{2} \left[\bar{V}(k_1) - \underline{v}(k_2) \right] + \frac{1}{2} \left[\bar{V}(k_2) - \bar{v}(k_2) \right]$$

$$= \frac{1}{2} \bar{V}(k_1) + \frac{1}{2} \left[\bar{V}(k_2) - \bar{v}(k_2) - \underline{v}(k_2) \right],$$

and T_2's expected ex-ante payoff is $(\bar{v}(k_2) - \underline{V}(k_1))/2$. Then T_1 chooses her investment to solve

$$\max_{k_1 \geq 0} \left\{ \frac{1}{2} \left[\lambda \log(1 + k_1) + (\lambda - \lambda\alpha - \alpha) \log(1 + k_2) \right] - k_1 \right\},$$

and T_2 solves

$$\max_{k_2 \geq 0} \left\{ \frac{1}{2} \left[\alpha\lambda \log(1 + k_2) - \log(1 + k_1) \right] - k_2 \right\}.$$

The solutions under T_1-ownership are then

$$k_1^1 = \frac{\lambda}{2} - 1,$$

$$k_2^1 = \frac{\alpha\lambda}{2} - 1.$$

We thus have that: government ownership achieves the first-best; both outsider ownership and joint teacher ownership give rise to underinvestment, and their relative efficiencies depend on the value added of the school and the ex-post difference between teachers; ownership by one teacher creates competition among the teachers that induces the first-best on the part of the owner but a suboptimal investment by the nonowner.

Chapter 11

1. A small open economy (based on Grossman and Helpman 1991a, chap. 6)

a. From the production functions for the two goods we have that the inverse demands for intermediate goods are

$$p(x_{y,t}) = \beta A_t x_{y,t}^{\beta-1} H_{y,t}^{1-\beta} p_y \tag{S11.1}$$

and

$$p(x_{z,t}) = \beta A_t x_{z,t}^{\beta-1} L^{1-\beta} p_z. \tag{S11.2}$$

The monopolist chooses the amount of intermediate good that maximizes its profits from the two sectors

$$\max_{x_y, x_z} \pi_t = \left[p(x_{y,t})x_{y,t} + p(x_{z,t})x_{z,t} - A_t c(p_y, p_z)(x_{y,t} + x_{z,t}) \right].$$

The resulting monopoly price is simply $p_{x,t} = A_t c(p_y, p_z)/\beta$, and the demands for the intermediate input in the two sectors are

$$x_{y,t} = \left(\beta^2 \frac{p_y}{c(p_y, p_z)} \right)^{\frac{1}{1-\beta}} H_{y,t} \tag{S11.3}$$

and

$$x_{z,t} = \left(\beta^2 \frac{p_z}{c(p_y, p_z)} \right)^{\frac{1}{1-\beta}} L. \tag{S11.4}$$

We can then obtain the profit function,

$$\pi_t = \frac{1-\beta}{\beta} A_t \cdot c(p_y, p_z) \left(\frac{\beta^2 \cdot p_y}{c(p_y, p_z)}\right)^{\frac{1}{1-\beta}} \left(H_{y,t} + L\left(\frac{p_z}{p_y}\right)^{\frac{1}{1-\beta}}\right) \quad \text{(S11.5)}$$

$$= A_t \bar{\pi} \left(c_t(p_y, p_z), p_y, p_z, H_{y,t}\right),$$

which depends on the productivity adjusted cost of the intermediate good, the prices of the two final goods and the level of employment in the sector producing Y.

The payoff to an innovation is given by the asset equation,

$$V_{t+1} = \frac{\pi_{t+1}}{r + \lambda H_{R,t+1}}$$

$$= A_t \frac{\gamma \bar{\pi}(p_y, p_z, H_{y,t+1})}{r + \lambda H_{R,t+1}}. \quad \text{(S11.6)}$$

b. Differentiating the production function for Y with respect to human capital, $H_{y,t}$, and substituting in for x_y, we get that the wage in the Y sector is

$$w_{Ht} = (1-\beta)A_t \left(\frac{\beta^2}{c(p_y, p_z)}\right)^{\frac{\beta}{1-\beta}} p_y^{\frac{1}{1-\beta}}. \quad \text{(S11.7)}$$

The wage in the R&D sector is simply

$$w_{Ht} = \lambda V_{t+1}. \quad \text{(S11.8)}$$

Equating these two expressions and using equations (S11.5) and (S11.6), gives us the arbitrage equation

$$\frac{\beta \lambda \gamma}{r + \lambda H_{R,t+1}} \left(H_{y,t+1} p_y^{\frac{1}{1-\beta}} + L p_z^{\frac{1}{1-\beta}}\right) = p_y^{\frac{1}{1-\beta}}. \quad \text{(S11.9)}$$

Together with the human capital market-clearing condition, $H_{R,t+1} + H_{y,t+1} = H$, this arbitrage equation defines the equilibrium of the model. Note that, in contrast with the basic Schumpeterian model, this equation does not imply a relation between employment decisions on two subsequent periods. The reason is that in this setup, the wage of human capital in period t is fixed by model parameters (see equation (S11.7)), just as it happened in the Romer (1990a) model of Chapter 1.

c. We can use the arbitrage equation to assess the effect that opening up to trade would have on a previously closed small economy. The effect is going to depend crucially on whether the economy is labor-abundant or human capital-abundant compared to the rest of the world.

Consider first an economy that has a higher H/L ratio than the rest of the world. Then, opening up to trade results in an increase in the price of good Y and reduces that of good Z, as compared to the autarchy case. Equation (S11.9) implies that this change in goods prices has two effects. First, it increases the marginal value product of human capital in the Y sector and thus its wage (the right-hand side of equation (S11.9)). This reduces the demand for researchers, for any given value of the innovation. Second, from the left-hand side of (S11.9), we see that the value of the innovation changes. The new prices imply that more of good Y is produced, thus the demand for intermediate inputs in this sector increases, and fewer units of Z are manufactured, hence reducing x_z. The overall effect on the value of the innovation is in principle ambiguous.

In our particular model, the effect of a higher wage is strong enough to offset any possible increase in the value of the innovation. We can rewrite the arbitrage condition as

$$r + \lambda(1 + \gamma\beta)H_{R,t+1} = \lambda\gamma\beta H + \lambda\gamma\beta L \left(\frac{p_z}{p_y}\right)^{\frac{1}{1-\beta}}, \tag{S11.10}$$

which implies that a higher relative price of good Y results in a lower level of employment in research and hence slower growth. What is happening is that the change in prices increases the relative productivity of human capital in production and reduces (or increases by less) its productivity in research. Consequently, resources are shifted away from the R&D sector, and the rate of technical change falls.

If the economy were abundant in labor relative to world supplies, free trade results in a lower relative price of Y. The wage of researchers falls, whereas the effect on the value of the innovation is ambiguous. In this model, the wage effect would be strong enough to ensure that employment in R&D always rises, as seen in (S11.10), thus inducing faster technical change.

2. Factor price equalization and the time preference rate (based on Wälde 1994a,b)

a. As in the chapter, normalized expenditure does not grow in the steady state, $\dot{E}^i/E^i = 0$. Equation (11.8) then implies that the steady-state nominal interest rate in country i is given by the time preference rate, $r^i = \rho^i$. Clearly, for this to be an equilibrium, there must not be any international flows of financial capital.

b. In a steady state, factor prices are constant. Differentiating (11.21) with respect to time implies that

$$\frac{\dot{v}^i}{v^i} = -\frac{\dot{n}}{n}.$$

c. Expenditure in final output is normalized, that is, $E = p_y \cdot Y = p_y \cdot x^\alpha \cdot n$. This implies that the price of the final good falls as the number of intermediaries increases, $p_y = 1/(x^\alpha \cdot n)$. Profits are given by

$$\pi^i = \alpha x^\alpha p_y^i - c_x(w_L^i, w_H^i) p_y^i x.$$

Maximizing with respect to x gives $p_x^i = p_y^i \cdot c_x(w_L^i, w_H^i)/\alpha$ and $x^i = (\alpha^2/c_x(w_L^i, w_H^i))^{1/(1-\alpha)}$. Profits are then,

$$\pi^i = \frac{(1-\alpha)\alpha}{n^A + n^B}.$$

d. Because $r^i = \rho^i$, the no-arbitrage condition (11.22) reads

$$\frac{\pi^i}{v^i} = \rho^i - \frac{\dot{v}^i}{v^i},$$

which, together with $\dot{v}^i/v^i = -\dot{n}/n$, gives the following relationship between profitability and the rates of time preference:

$$\frac{\pi^A}{v^A} - \frac{\pi^B}{v^B} = \rho^A - \rho^B. \tag{S11.11}$$

Substituting into (S11.11) equation (11.21) and the expression for profits, we get

$$\frac{(1-\alpha)\alpha}{c_\gamma(w_L^A, w_H^A)} - \frac{(1-\alpha)\alpha}{c_\gamma(w_L^B, w_H^B)} = \rho^A - \rho^B. \tag{S11.12}$$

Assume that factor prices equalize. Then the left-hand side of (S11.12) is zero, which contradicts $\rho^A \neq \rho^B$. Hence factor prices must differ.

★ **3. Imitation and product cycles (based on Krugman 1979, and Grossman and Helpman 1991a, chap. 11)**

a. A North firm that is the only producer of a variety charges a price $p^N = w^N/\alpha$ and obtains profits

$$\pi^N = (1-\alpha)p^N x^N \tag{S11.13}$$

per unit of time. Because imitation is costly, only one South firm spends resources in imitating each particular intermediate good. An imitator would choose to charge the monopoly price $p^S = w^S/\alpha$. If $\alpha w^N > w^S$, this price is less than the marginal cost of producing the good in the North, and hence the South firm is the sole producer of that variety. Its profits would be

$$\pi^S = (1-\alpha)p^S x^S \tag{S11.14}$$

If the difference in costs were not sufficiently large for the monopoly price to drive the North firm out of the market, the South producer would set the limit price $p^S = w^N$, which would make it, again, the only producer of the good. The South firm would have lower profits, $\pi^S = (1 - w^S/w^N) p^S x^S$.

b. From equation (11.24) we have that the cost of producing a new design for an intermediate good is $1/\delta A$ units of labor. Then the free-entry condition in the R & D sector implies

$$V^N = \frac{w^N}{\delta A}, \tag{S11.15}$$

where V^N is the value of a North variety that has not been copied by the South. Similarly, the arbitrage equation for the South is

$$V^S = \frac{w^S}{\eta A^S}. \tag{S11.16}$$

The asset equation for a South firm is simply that the value of the variety be equal to the discounted profit flow,

$$r^S V^S = \pi^s. \tag{S11.17}$$

(Note that this expression is like the one used in the Romer model in Chapter 1.) In the case of a North firm, we have to take into account the fact that the rents disappear when the variety is imitated. Any North product is copied with a Poisson arrival rate of $\dot{A}^S/A^N$. Hence the asset equation is

$$V^N = \frac{\pi^N}{r^N + \dot{A}^S/A^N}. \tag{S11.18}$$

(Note the similarities with the asset equation used in the Schumpeterian model of Chapter 2.)

   The last equilibrium conditions that we need are the labor market equilibrium equations. They simply require that the sum of employment in the two sectors be equal to the total supply, that is,

$$\frac{\dot{A}}{\delta A} + A^N x^N = L^N \tag{S11.19}$$

and

$$\frac{\dot{A}^S}{\eta A^S} + A^S x^S = L^S. \tag{S11.20}$$

c. In a steady state, the number of varieties manufactured by the two countries grow at the same rate, g. Denote the share of each country in the total number of products as $\xi^i \equiv A^i/A$, $i = N, S$. In the steady state, this share remains constant. That is, $g = \dot{A}/A = \dot{A}^N/A^N = \dot{A}^S/A^S$. Define also the rate of imitation as $m \equiv \dot{A}^S/A^N$. Differentiating $\xi^S A = A^S$ with respect to time we find that

$$\xi^S = \frac{m}{m + g} \tag{S11.21}$$

in the steady state. This expression tells us that the higher the rate of imitation and the lower the rate of growth are, the greater the steady-state proportion of goods manufactured by the South is.

We also know that consumer preferences imply that the rate of growth of consumption in country i is given by $r^i - \rho$. Because both economies grow at the same rate, in the steady state the interest rate must be $r = g + \rho$ in the two countries. To find the steady state in the North, substitute for the steady state interest rate in (S11.18) and rewrite it as

$$\frac{\pi^N}{V^N} = \rho + g + m. \qquad \text{(S11.22)}$$

Now substitute the labor-market equilibrium condition (S11.19) and the pricing rule into the expression for profits, (S11.13), to get

$$\pi^N = \frac{1-\alpha}{\alpha} \frac{w^N}{\delta A} \frac{\delta L^N - g}{1 - \xi^s}. \qquad \text{(S11.23)}$$

Using (S11.15), (S11.21), (S11.22), and (S11.23) we obtain the following equilibrium condition that relates the rates of innovation and imitation:

$$\frac{1-\alpha}{\alpha} \left(\delta L^N - g\right) \frac{g+m}{g} = \rho + g + m. \qquad \text{(S11.24)}$$

The left-hand side represents the profit rate, that is, the inverse of the price earning ratio. On the right-hand side we have the effective cost of capital, including a premium for the risk of being imitated by the South. (As an extra exercise, graph the equilibrium relationship between the rates of innovation and imitation and discuss its shape.)

Similarly, we can rewrite (S11.17) as

$$\frac{\pi^S}{V^S} = \rho + g, \qquad \text{(S11.25)}$$

and obtain the steady-state expression for profits in the South country using (S11.14) and (S11.20)

$$\pi^s = \frac{1-\alpha}{\alpha} \frac{w^S}{\eta A^S} \left(\eta L^S - g\right). \qquad \text{(S11.26)}$$

These two equations together with the arbitrage equation (S11.16) give us the equilibrium relationship

$$\frac{1-\alpha}{\alpha} (\eta L^S - g) = \rho + g. \qquad \text{(S11.27)}$$

Equations (S11.24) and (S11.27) give the combinations of steady-state rates of innovation and imitation that are consistent with pricing behavior, asset market equilibrium, and labor market equilibrium. In fact (S11.27) defines the growth rate as a function of the parameters of the economy,

$$g = (1 - \alpha)\eta L^S - \alpha\rho. \tag{S11.28}$$

The rate of imitation can then be obtained from (S11.24),

$$m = g\frac{(1 - \alpha)(\eta L^S - \delta L^N)}{\alpha\rho - (1 - \alpha)(\eta L^S - \delta L^N)}. \tag{S11.29}$$

Note that the growth rate is determined by parameters in the South, not by those in the country that innovates. The greater the capacity to imitate in the South (as determined by the parameter η and the labor supply), the faster technological change is, as North firms have to keep inventing new products in order not to be driven out of the market by the lower-cost South firms. The rate of imitation itself depends on labor supplies and the productivity of researchers in both economies.

⋆⋆ 4. Innovation, imitation, and intellectual property rights (based on Helpman 1993)

a. We can use the results we obtained in the previous problem and simply differentiate with respect to η. From equation (S11.28) we have that the growth rate is $g = (1 - \alpha)\eta L^S - \alpha\rho$. That is, it depends positively on the "productivity" of researchers who engage in imitation in the South. Tighter IPR (a larger μ) implies a reduction in η, and hence a slower rate of growth. The reason is that since the rate of imitation is now lower, due to a greater difficulty of copying, firms in the North enjoy the profits from a new product for a longer period before they are displaced by South firms. As a result, they do not have to innovate as much in order to keep producing.

To check that the rate of imitation falls, recall that

$$m = g\frac{(1 - \alpha)(\eta L^S - \delta L^N)}{\alpha\rho - (1 - \alpha)(\eta L^S - \delta L^N)}.$$

This expression is strictly increasing in η, which means that m is lower the greater IPR protection is. The proportion of goods manufactured by the South is given by $\xi^S = m/(m + g)$, which, substituting for g and m, gives

$$\xi^S = \frac{1 - \alpha}{\alpha}\frac{\eta L^S - \delta L^N}{\rho}.$$

The proportion of goods manufactured in the North can be expressed as $\xi^N = 1 - \xi^S$. A tightening of intellectual property rights then leads to a reduction in the proportion of goods manufactured by the South and an increase of the share produced in the North.

b. With homothetic preferences we can derive the demand functions directly from individual preferences. The resulting aggregate demand function is

$$x_j = p_j^{-\epsilon} \frac{E}{P^{1-\epsilon}}, \tag{S11.30}$$

where E is aggregate world expenditure on consumer goods and P is the weighted price index

$$P \equiv \left[\int_0^A p_j^{1-\epsilon} dj \right]^{1/1-\epsilon}. \tag{S11.31}$$

The indirect utility function of an individual in country i can then be written as

$$\log u^i = \log \frac{E^i}{L^i} - \log P, \tag{S11.32}$$

where E^i/L^i is per capita expenditure in country i. There are only two prices, those set in the North and those set in the South. Hence the price index can be expressed as

$$P = A^{1/1-\epsilon} \left[\xi^N \left(p^N \right)^{1-\epsilon} + \xi^S \left(p^S \right)^{1-\epsilon} \right]^{1/1-\epsilon}. \tag{S11.33}$$

To obtain relative prices we use the labor-market clearing conditions $A^N x^N = L^N$ and $A^S x^S = L^S$. These two equations and the demand functions in (S11.30) give us the terms of trade

$$\frac{p^N}{p^S} = \left[\frac{L^S}{L^N} \frac{\xi^N}{\xi^S} \right]^{1/\epsilon}. \tag{S11.34}$$

Changes in the share of manufacturing taking place in each region affect the terms of trade: the greater the proportion of goods that a country is manufacturing, the greater its relative prices will be.

c. By definition $\xi^N = A^N/A$. Differentiating, we have that, at any point in time, the fraction of goods that have not been imitated is given by $\dot{\xi}^N = g - (g + m)\xi^N$. The solution to this equation is

$$\xi^N(t) = \bar{\xi}^N + \left[\xi^N(0) - \bar{\xi}^N \right] e^{-(g+m)t} \tag{S11.35}$$

where $\bar{\xi}^N = g/(m + g)$ is the steady-state value of the share of goods manufactured in the North. Because the rate of growth is given, we have that the steady-state share of the North increases as IPR are tightened, $d\bar{\xi}^N/d\mu > 0$. The effect on the out-of-steady-state share is given by

$$\frac{d\xi^N(t)}{d\mu} = \left[1 - e^{-(g+m)t}\right]\frac{d\bar{\xi}^N}{d\mu} + \left[\xi^N(0) - \bar{\xi}^N\right]te^{-(g+m)t}, \tag{S11.36}$$

which, if the economy was initially in a steady state, is always positive. That is, starting from a steady state situation, tighter intellectual property rights increase the share of goods manufactured in the North. Given that $\xi^S = 1 - \xi^N$, the share produced by the South decreases. It follows from equation (S11.34) that the terms of trade improve for the North and deteriorate for the South.

d. To find the effect of the policy on utility we have to find the value of expenditure in each economy. Income per capita in country i is given by the value of production, $p^i x^i A^i$, divided by L^i, which, using the labor-market clearing conditions, is simply p^i. Hence per capita expenditure is p^N in the North and p^S in the South. We can use equations (S11.32) and (S11.33) to express instantaneous utility in the two countries as

$$\log u^N = \frac{1}{\epsilon - 1}\log A + \frac{1}{\epsilon - 1}\log\left[\xi^N + \xi^S\left(\frac{p^N}{p^S}\right)^{\epsilon-1}\right], \tag{S11.37}$$

$$\log u^S = \frac{1}{\epsilon - 1}\log A + \frac{1}{\epsilon - 1}\log\left[\xi^N\left(\frac{p^S}{p^N}\right)^{\epsilon-1} + \xi^S\right] \tag{S11.38}$$

Clearly for given terms of trade, $p^N/p^S > 1$, an increase in the proportion of goods manufactured in the North reduces welfare in both countries, in as much as there is a reallocation effect that leads to a higher share of goods being manufactured at a high cost. The change in terms of trade (a higher relative price of North products) benefits the North and hurts the South. Thus, welfare in the South is always reduced, whereas in the North it might or not fall.

To find the welfare effect of changes in intellectual property rights policies in the North economy we calculate the change in total lifetime utility

$$\frac{dU^N(0)}{d\mu} = \int_0^\infty e^{-\rho t}\frac{d\log u^N(t)}{d\mu}dt.$$

Differentiating and using (S11.34), (S11.36), and (S11.37) we get

$$\frac{dU^N(0)}{d\mu} = \frac{1}{K}\left[1 - \left(1 - \frac{\alpha}{\bar{\xi}^N}\right)\left(\frac{L^S}{L^N}\frac{\bar{\xi}^N}{1 - \bar{\xi}^N}\right)^\alpha\right], \tag{S11.39}$$

where $K = (\epsilon - 1)\rho(\rho + g + m)\left[1 + (\bar{\xi}^S/\bar{\xi}^N)^{1-\alpha}(L^S/L^N)^\alpha\right] > 0$. The last term in parenthesis in equation (S11.39) is always greater than one, as our assumption on wages implies that prices in the North are greater than those in the South (see equation (S11.34)). If $\alpha/\bar{\xi}^N$ is greater than one, the whole expression is positive. As this term falls the overall effect will be reduced and at some point become negative. Note that $\alpha/\bar{\xi}^N = \alpha(g + m)/g$. The impact of tighter intellectual property rights will therefore be related to the initial rate of imitation. If it were very small, $\alpha/\bar{\xi}^N$ would be close to α, and both regions would be hurt by a tighter policy. If, on the other hand, imitation is initially large, it is in the interest of the North to tighten intellectual property rights. The optimum is achieved when the derivative in (S11.39) equals zero.

e. In order to extract policy recommendations one would have to also take into account the growth effect examined in section (a). There are thus three effects in operation. First, there is a growth effect arising from the fact that the overall rate of technical change slows down. Second, there is a misallocation of resources, as production shifts away from the country with lower costs. The more goods that the North manufactures, the more inefficient the interregional allocation of production is. These two effects imply that tighter IPR hurt both countries. Third, there is a change in the terms of trade. As production shifts to the North, demand for its production factor increases, while demand declines in the South. The North experiences an improvement of its terms of trade while the South sees them worsen. On this account, the North benefits from tighter IPR, while the South is worse off. Overall, tighter IPR always have a negative effect on the welfare of the South, whereas they may or may not increase welfare in the North, depending on the relative strength of the various effects.

5. Bounded learning by doing and international trade (based on Young 1991)

a. Because there is perfect competition, the prices of good s are $p^A(s) = \omega \cdot a^A(s)$ and $p^B(s) = a^B(s)$. Hence good s is produced in the LDC if $a^B(s) < \omega \cdot a^A(s)$, and vice versa, because only the lower-cost producer can sell its good.

b. As we saw in Chapter 6, problem 5, the range of goods consumed in the economy is determined by the budget constraint. That is, M^A is determined by the budget constraint in the LDC,

$$\omega = \int_{s \in GDC} p(s) \cdot x^A(s)ds + \int_{s \in GLDC} p(s) \cdot x^A(s)ds$$

where $x^A(s) = p(M^A)/p(s) - 1$. Similarly, M^B is determined by the budget constraint in the DC,

$$1 = \int_{s \in GDC} p(s) \cdot x^B(s)ds + \int_{s \in GLDC} p(s) \cdot x^B(s)ds$$

where $x^B(s) = p(M^B)/p(s) - 1$.

c. If $\omega < 1$ and $X > 0$, all goods would be cheaper to produce in the DC, and none would be manufactured in the LDC. If $\omega > e^{2x}$, all goods would be cheaper to produce in the LDC.

d. Because $\omega = 1$ implies both economies have the same budget constraints, then the range goods consumed in both is the same. That is, $M^A = M^B$ and $N^A = N^B$. In this equilibrium, $p^A(s) = a^A(s) < p^B(s) = a^B(s)$ for all $s > S^B$. Thus the LDC produces no goods above S^B. Lower s goods are produced by either or both of the two countries.

e. The highest possible wage is $\omega = e^{2X}$, for otherwise all goods would be produced in the LDC. Consider goods $s \geq S^A$. The price in the LDC is $p^B = a^B(s) = e^{s-2S^B}$. The price in the DC is

$$p^A = \omega \cdot a^A(s) = e^{2X} \cdot e^{s-2S^A} = e^{s-2S^B}.$$

Hence, for goods $s \geq S^A$, the cost of production is the same in both countries. All other goods are produced more cheaply in the LDC.

The greater income (wage) in the DC allows the residents there to consume both a greater variety ($N^A > N^B$ and $M^B < M^A$) and a greater amount of each type of good (as $x^A(s) = p(M^A)/p(s) - 1 > p(M^B)/p(s) - 1 = x^B(s)$). All goods $s < S^A$ are produced in the LDC, all goods $s \geq S^A$ can be produced in either economy. Hence, the LDC produces more goods but consumes fewer than the DC.

Chapter 13

1. Ownership rights in innovations (based on Aghion and Tirole 1994)

a. The first-best effort e^* and investment E^* are defined as the solution to the maximization program:

$$\max_{e,E}\{(\alpha\sqrt{e} + \beta E)V - e - E\}.$$

The first-order condition for e^* is:

$$\frac{\alpha V}{2\sqrt{e}} = 1,$$

that is:

$$e^* = \left(\frac{\alpha V}{2}\right)^2$$

and

$$E^* = 1 \quad \text{if} \quad \beta V \geq 1$$
$$= 0 \quad \text{if} \quad \beta V < 1.$$

b.

i. Under C-ownership, C gets the whole value V. Hence:

$$E^C = \arg\max\{\beta V E - E\} = E^*$$

and $e^C = 0$.

ii. Under RU-ownership, RU and C obtain $\frac{V}{2}$ each. Thus

$$e^{RU} = \arg\max\left\{\alpha\sqrt{e}\frac{V}{2} - e\right\}$$

$$= \left(\frac{\alpha V}{4}\right)^2$$

and

$$E^{RU} = 1 \quad \text{if} \quad \frac{\beta V}{2} \geq 1$$

$$= 0 \quad \text{if} \quad \frac{\beta V}{2} < 1.$$

c. The social outcome W is defined as the sum of RU's utility and of C's utility in equilibrium. Thus:

• under C-ownership:

$$W^c = \underbrace{0}_{RU'\text{s utility}} + \underbrace{\max(\beta V - 1, 0)}_{C'\text{s utility}}$$

• under RU-ownership:

$$W^{RU} = \underbrace{\frac{\alpha V}{4} \cdot \alpha \cdot \frac{V}{2} - \left(\frac{\alpha V}{4}\right)^2}_{RU'\text{s utility}} + \underbrace{\max(\beta \frac{V}{2} - 1, 0)}_{C'\text{s utility}}$$

$$= \left(\frac{\alpha V}{4}\right)^2 + \max(\beta \frac{V}{2} - 1, 0).$$

Thus $W^{RU} > W^C$ if:

• $\beta\frac{V}{2} > 1$ and $\alpha^2\frac{V}{8} > \beta$

• $\beta\frac{V}{2} < 1$ but $\beta V > 1$ and $\left(\frac{\alpha V}{4}\right)^2 \geq \beta V - 1$

• $\beta V < 1$

d. C will consent to grant ownership of the innovation to RU if and only if C's utility under RU-ownership is greater or equal to her utility under

C-ownership (since RU has no cash to compensate C). That is, if and only if:

$$\max(\beta V - 1, 0) \leq \max(\beta \frac{V}{2} - 1, 0)$$

which in turn can only be satisfied when $\beta V < 1$. This means that when C has the bargaining power ex-ante, she will *not* grant ownership of the innovation when $\beta V > 1$ although it might have been efficient to do so in that case if $\alpha^2 \frac{V}{8} > \beta$ and $\left(\frac{\alpha V}{4}\right)^2 \geq \beta V - 1$ (as we saw in question (c)).

e. If we fix the ownership structure, then the equilibrium values of e and E are increasing in V: indeed E is more likely to be equal to 1 the higher V; and whenever positive the equilibrium research effort e is equal to $\left(\frac{\alpha V}{4}\right)^2$ which is clearly increasing in V.

However, if ex-ante contracting determines the ownership structure and, say if C has the ex-ante bargaining power, we know from the previous questions that:

$$\beta V < 1 \implies RU\text{-ownership} \implies e = \left(\frac{\alpha V}{4}\right)^2$$

$$\beta V > 1 \implies C\text{-ownership} \implies e \equiv 0$$

Thus as V increases from $\frac{1}{\beta} - \varepsilon$ to $\frac{1}{\beta} + \varepsilon$, the equilibrium e *decreases* down to 0!

f. Let s_t denote RU's share of the innovation discovered at date t. Because neither party has an incentive to overinvest, an optimal contract maximizes the stake of one party (say, the customer C) for a given value of the other party's stake:

$$\max_{s_t} \underbrace{\left(\sum_t (1 - s_t)e^{-\lambda t} V_t\right)}_{\substack{C's \text{ marginal value} \\ \text{of investment}}}$$

s.t. $\quad \sum_t s_t V_t \geq \overline{U}$

and

$$0 \leq s_t \leq \frac{1}{2} \text{ for all } t.$$

Let

$$\mathcal{L} = \sum_t ((1 - s_t)e^{-\lambda t} + \mu s_t) V_t$$

denote the Lagrangian for this maximization program. We have:

$$\frac{\partial \mathcal{L}}{\partial s_t} = \mu - e^{-\lambda t},$$

which is necessarily positive for t sufficiently large. Thus, there exists $t_0 \geq 0$ such that:

$t < t_0 \Rightarrow s_t^* = 0$ (i.e., innovation t belongs to C)

$t > t_0 \Rightarrow s_t^* = \dfrac{1}{2}$ (i.e., innovation t belongs to RU).

The optimal t_0 will make the RU's incentive constraint binding, that is:

$$\sum_t s_t^* = \sum_{t_0}^{\infty} \frac{V_t}{2} = \overline{U}.$$

g.

i. In the absence of other customers for the innovation, C and RU bargain as before over the value of innovation $V(\gamma) = \Pi_1^m(\gamma) - \Pi_0^m$. Under C-ownership, C gets the whole value $V(\gamma)$ and therefore will choose $\gamma = \gamma_c$ to maximize $p(\gamma) \cdot V(\gamma)$. Under RU-ownership, RU gets $\frac{V(\gamma)}{2}$ (like C) and therefore RU will choose $\gamma = \gamma_{RU}$ to maximize $p(\gamma) \cdot \frac{V(\gamma)}{2}$. But

$$\arg\max_{\gamma} \, p(\gamma) V(\gamma) = \arg\max_{\gamma} \, p(\gamma) \cdot \frac{V(\gamma)}{2},$$

or equivalently, $\gamma_C = \gamma_{RU}$!

ii. Under RU-ownership, RU will now get $\max(\frac{V(\gamma)}{2}, \Pi_1(\gamma))$ instead of $\frac{V(\gamma)}{2}$. So, whilst γ_C remains the same as before, γ_{RU} now maximizes the product $p(\gamma) \cdot \max(\frac{V(\gamma)}{2}, \Pi_1(\gamma))$. Suppose first that the optimal choice γ_{RU} by the research unit is such that:

$$\frac{\pi_1^m(\gamma_{RU}) - \pi_0^m}{2} \geq \pi_1(\gamma_{RU}).$$

Then, the outside option of selling to another customer is irrelevant and therefore, as in the absence of such a customer, the research unit chooses the same technology (or technologies if there are multiple optima) as the incumbent customer: $\gamma_{RU} = \gamma_C$.

On the other hand, if $\pi_1(\gamma_{RU}) > \frac{\pi_1^m(\gamma_{RU}) - \pi_0^m}{2}$, the research unit's choice γ_{RU} will generally differ from the incumbent's γ_C since now the outside option of selling to another customer becomes credible and the incumbent must pay $\pi_1(\gamma_{RU})$ to obtain the license. To compare the customer's and the research unit's preferred research lines, note that, by revealed preference, and by definition of γ_{RU} and γ_C,

$$p(\gamma_C)[\pi_1^m(\gamma_C) - \pi_0^m] \geq p(\gamma_{RU})[\pi_1^m(\gamma_{RU}) - \pi_0^m]$$

and $p(\gamma_{RU})\pi_1(\gamma_{RU}) \qquad \geq p(\gamma_C)\pi_1(\gamma_C).$

Multiplying these two inequalities, we obtain:

$$r(\gamma_{RU}) = \frac{\pi_1^m(\gamma_{RU})}{\pi_1^m(\gamma_{RU}) - \pi_0^m} \geq \frac{\pi_1(\gamma_C)}{\pi_1^m(\gamma_C) - \pi_0^m} = r(\gamma_C),$$

where $r(\gamma)$ denotes the relative willingness to pay of another customer with respect to the incumbent customer. Then

$$\gamma_{RU} = \begin{cases} \geq \gamma_C & \text{if } r \text{ is strictly increasing, and} \\ \leq \gamma_C & \text{if } r \text{ is strictly decreasing.} \end{cases}$$

In other words, if the relative willingness to pay of another customer increases with the size of the innovation, then the research unit tends to choose a more drastic innovation than the incumbent, since by doing so he is able to appropriate a higher fraction of the surplus of the incumbent. Similarly, if the relative willingness to pay of the other customer decreases with the size of the innovation, the research unit appropriate more of the surplus by choosing a less drastic innovation.   □

2. The Schumpeterian hypothesis (based on Aghion and Tirole 1994)

a. $p(E, e) = r_0 + 2e/V_0$ for $0 \leq e \leq 1$ and $p(E, e) = r_0 + 2/V_0$ for $e \geq 1$.

i. C makes no investment ($E = E^* = 0$) no matter how the firm is owned, in as much as its investment does not affect the probability of discovery. RU owns the firm, so if it makes a discovery with value V it bargains with C to get $V/2$; C also gets $V/2$. Therefore RU's payoff is given by

$$p(E, e)V/2 - e = \begin{cases} (r_0 + 2e/V_0)V/2 - e & \text{for } 0 \leq e \leq 1 \\ (r_0 + 2/V_0)V/2 - e & \text{for } e \geq 1. \end{cases}$$

Clearly RU never sets $e > 1$. Indeed, the choice of e is zero-one according to whether V/V_0 is less than or greater than one. Thus as the value V increases, we have that the probability of discovery is

$$p = \begin{cases} r_0 & \text{for } V < V_0 \\ r_0 + 2/V_0 & \text{for } V \geq V_0 \end{cases}$$

The probability of discovery is weakly increasing in V given RU ownership.

ii. If $V < V_0$, we know from (i) that neither C nor RU makes any effort under RU ownership. Similarly, under C ownership, neither will make any effort, because RU receives no reward and C's investment is worthless. Thus for $V < V_0$, the probability of discovery is r_0 regardless of whether we have pure RU or pure C ownership. But under C ownership, C has the property rights on the innovation, so his payoff in the case of discovery is V, compared to only $V/2$ when RU held the property rights. Hence C prefers C ownership for $V < V_0$.

iii. If $V \geq V_0$, then we know from part (i) that RU sets $e = 1$ under RU ownership. Under C ownership, RU will set $e = 0$ because he receives no reward for effort. Thus C's expected payoff for $V \geq V_0$ is given by

$$
\begin{aligned}
p(e)V/2 &= (r_0 + 2/V_0)V/2 \quad \text{under } RU \text{ ownership} \\
p(e)V &= r_0 V_0 \quad\quad\quad\quad\;\; \text{under } C \text{ ownership.}
\end{aligned}
$$

If r_0 is sufficiently small, (in particular, $r_0 < 2/V_0$), C prefers pure RU ownership to C ownership for $V \geq V_0$.

iv. For $V < V_0$, we will have C ownership; whereas for $V \geq V_0$ and r_0 sufficiently small we will have RU ownership. Thus the probability of discovery is given by

$$
p(\text{ownership}) = \begin{cases} r_0 & \text{for } V < V_0 \\ (r_0 + 2/V_0) & \text{for } V \geq V_0. \end{cases}
$$

The probability of discovery is weakly increasing in V.

b. Under RU ownership, the parties share the reward V equally in the case of discovery. So RU's reward is

$$
p(E, e)V/2 - e = \begin{cases} (2\mu\sqrt{E} + 2e/V_0)V/2 - e & \text{for } e \leq V_0/4 \\ (2\mu\sqrt{E} + 1/2)V/2 - e & \text{for } e \geq V_0/4. \end{cases}
$$

RU never sets $e > V_0/4$. Because $V/V_0 > 1$, RU sets $e = V_0/4$, (he sets $e = 0$ otherwise). C's reward is

$$
p(E, e)V/2 - E = (2\mu\sqrt{E} + 2e/V_0)V/2 - E \quad (\text{for } e \leq V_0/4).
$$

So C sets $E = V^2\mu^2/4$ (by differentiating and finding a maximum for E).
   Thus the value of the project to C under RU ownership is

$$
p(E, e)V/2 - E = (2\mu\sqrt{E} + 2e/V_0)V/2 - E
$$

where $E = V^2\mu^2/4$ and $e = V_0/4$,

$$
\Rightarrow p(E, e)V/2 = \mu^2 V^2/4 + V/4 \quad \text{(by substituting in).}
$$

Under C ownership, RU receives no reward and makes no effort. C's payoff is given by

$$
p(E, 0)V - E = (2\mu\sqrt{E})V - E.
$$

So he sets $E = \mu^2 V^2$. The value of the project to C is thus

$$
\begin{aligned}
p(E, e)V - E &= (2\mu\sqrt{E})V - E \quad \text{where } E = \mu^2 V^2 \\
&= \mu^2 V^2.
\end{aligned}
$$

Compare the values of the project to C under C and RU ownership. As V becomes very large, the terms in V^2 will dominate, so that C ownership will become more desirable.

The probability of discovery under RU ownership is

$$p(E, e \mid RU) = (\mu^2 V + 1/2) \quad \text{(because } e = V_0/4,\ E = V^2\mu^2/4\text{)},$$

whereas under C ownership,

$$p(E, e \mid C) = 2\mu^2 V \quad \text{(because } e = 0,\ E = V^2\mu^2\text{)}.$$

For any given ownership type, the probability of innovation grows with V. Endogenizing the ownership decision, we have seen that assuming that C has the bargaining power ex-ante, RU ownership is desirable for low V, whereas for high V, C ownership is desirable. At $V^* = 1/3\mu^2$, the payoffs from the two ownership structures are just equal. Notice that here the probability of innovation under RU ownership is 5/6, whereas under C ownership it is only 2/3. So with endogenous ownership there is a discrete fall in the probability of innovation as V rises above V^*.

c. When ownership is held constant, raising the value of the project V obviously (weakly) increases incentives to innovate, and hence effort and the probability of innovation p. When ownership is endogenized, however, the relationship between V and p is no longer straightforward. We saw in part (b) that the probability of innovation could fall when the value of innovation increased because of the change in ownership, whereas in part (a) it increased. Moreover, the examples make clear that one cannot judge a priori the likely direction of the ownership change: it all depends on how the relative efficiency of each party's investment changes as V grows.

d. In both parts (a) and (b), C prefers cofinancing by a third party to pure RU ownership. The third party takes a share $(1 - \alpha)$ in RU in exchange for making an investment E_I — it pays this lump sum directly to C. The third party expects to gain a share $(1 - \alpha)$ of RU's license fee $V/2$ if discovery occurs, so with free entry of investors, $E_I = p(e, E)(1 - \alpha)V/2$. Because the transfer C receives is increasing in third party's share, C would like to set α as low as possible subject to maintaining RU's incentives. When V is close to V_0, any nonnegligible amount of cofinancing will destroy RU's incentives, but as V grows, more cofinancing becomes feasible. However, because in the models discussed here RU's choice of effort is zero-one and the third party's investment does not affect the probability of discovery, ruling out cofinancing does not affect the basic results. The relationship between V and p is unchanged; it is merely the distribution of rent between RU and C that is altered by the possibility of cofinancing.

⋆ **3. Cooperative R&D joint ventures (based on Katz 1986)**

a. Firm i's total profit net of R&D costs is given by

$$\pi_i = V^i(c_i, \Omega(c_1, c_2 \cdots c_n)) - s^n r_i - \frac{(1 - s^n)}{n - 1} \sum_{j \in A, j \neq i} r_j.$$

Differentiating π_i with respect to i's level of R&D spending, r_i, to find a maximum, we have

$$\frac{dV}{dc_i} \cdot \frac{dc_i}{dr_i} + \sum_{j \neq 1} \frac{dV^i}{dc_j} \cdot \frac{dc_j}{dr_i} - s^n.$$

Notice that the terms in dr_j/dr_i drop out because we suppose each firm decides while taking the R&D of the others as given. Thus the first-order condition for R&D choice is

$$V_i^i c'(z^n)\{1 + (n - 1)\rho(c(z^n))\phi^n\} - s^n \leq 0, \tag{S13.1}$$

where the subscript denotes the partial derivative of V^i with respect to i's cost. Similarly, in the absence of a cooperative agreement we have first-order condition

$$V_i^i c'(z^0)\{1 + (n - 1)\rho(c(z^0)\underline{\phi}\} - 1 \leq 0, \tag{S13.2}$$

with strict inequality in each case only if we have a corner solution at $r_i = 0$. If both these conditions hold with equality, then r_i and hence z must be larger when there is a cooperative agreement if and only if cooperating firms would want to increase their R&D from the level z^0. That is, $z^n - z^0$ is positive if and only if, substituting z^n into the first order condition for z^0, we have

$$V_i^i c'(z^0)\{1 + (n - 1)\rho(c(z^0))\phi^n\} - s^n \geq 0.$$

Using the first-order condition for z^0 (S10.2), we know that $V_i^i c'(z^0) = 1/\{1 - (n - 1)\rho(c(z^0))\underline{\phi}\}$. Substituting in gives $z^n \geq z^0$ if and only if

$$\{1 + (n - 1)\rho(c(z^0))\phi^n\} - s^n\{1 + (n - 1)\rho(c(z^0))\underline{\phi}\} \geq 0.$$

We know from the first-order conditions that both the expressions in curly brackets are positive. Thus equilibrium-effective R&D is likely to be higher in the presence of a cooperative agreement if members have to bear a smaller share of their own R&D costs; and if spillovers are high both in the presence and absence of an agreement. Rearranging this expression shows that the sign of $z^n - z^0$ is given by the sign of

$$\{1 + (n - 1)\rho(c(z^0))\phi^n\}(1 - s^n) - s^n(n - 1)\rho(c(z^0))\{\phi^n - \underline{\phi}\}. \tag{S13.3}$$

b.

i. If profits fall when the industry collectively reduces its costs (because the benefits are passed on to consumers through competition and lower prices) then the industry will set s^n and ϕ^n as high as possible (i.e. $s^n = s$ and $\phi^n = \phi$), because we know from part (a) that this will reduce R&D. The joint venture thus functions as kind of "collusive" agreement to reduce R&D. If $\bar{s} = 1$ and $\bar{\phi} = 1$, then the firms will effectively sign royalty-free cross-licensing agreements—they can use the results of each others' R&D without contributing to the costs.

ii. Because firms are symmetric, an industry-wide agreement will set ϕ^n and s^n with the aim of maximizing industry profits. Firstly, firms will set $\phi^n = \bar{\phi}$ for efficiency reasons. If $\phi^n < \bar{\phi}$, then, holding other things equal, ϕ^n could be set higher to give each firm more effective R&D at no extra cost. Of course, firms will want to reduce their R&D when ϕ^n is increased, but this effect can be offset by reducing s^n. Thus unless $\phi^n = \bar{\phi}$, effective R&D can be held constant while collective R&D cost is reduced.

Turning to the industry-profit maximizing choice of s^n, we have that industry profits are

$$\sum_{i=1}^{n}(V_i - r_i).$$

We can differentiate to find the first-order condition for the optimal (symmetric) r_i

$$\underbrace{\frac{dV^i}{dc_i} \cdot \frac{dc_i}{dr_i}}_{\substack{\text{effect on } i\text{'s cost} \\ \text{and hence } i\text{'s profit}}} + \underbrace{\sum_{j \neq 1} \frac{dV^i}{dc_j} \cdot \frac{dc_j}{dr_i}}_{\substack{\text{effect on } j\text{'s cost} \\ \text{and hence } i\text{'s profit}}} + \underbrace{\sum_{j \neq i} \frac{dV^j}{dc_j} \cdot \frac{dc_j}{dr_i}}_{\substack{\text{effect on } j\text{'s cost} \\ \text{and hence } j\text{'s profit}}}$$

$$+ \underbrace{\sum_{j \neq i} \frac{dV^j}{dc_i} \cdot \frac{dc_j}{dr_i}}_{\substack{\text{effect on } i\text{'s cost} \\ \text{and hence } j\text{'s profit}}} + \underbrace{\sum_{j \neq i} \frac{dV^j}{dc_j} \cdot \frac{dc_k}{dr_i}}_{\substack{\text{effect on } k \neq i\text{'s cost} \\ \text{and hence } j \neq i\text{'s profit } (k \neq j)}} \leq 0.$$

Substituting in and then simplifying gives

$$V_i^i c'(z^n)1 + V_j^i c'(z^n)(n-1)\phi^n + (n-1)V_i^j c'(z^n)1$$

$$+ (n-1)V_j^j \phi^n + (n-2)V_k^j c'(z^n)(n-1)\phi^n\} - 1 \leq 0.$$

Because symmetry implies $V_i^i = V_j^j$, $V_i^j = V_j^i$, and so on, we can express this as

$$1 \geq V_i^i c'(z^n)\{1 + \rho(z^n)(n-1)\}\{1 + (n-1)\phi^n\}. \tag{S13.4}$$

Compare this with the individual firm's first-order condition (S13.1). It is clear that setting $s^n = \{1 - (n-1)\rho(c(z^n))\phi^n\} / [\{1 + \rho(c(z^n))(n-1)\}\{1 + (n-1)\phi^n\}]$ will make the individual maximization condition coincide with the jointly optimal one. However, it is possible that this choice for s is greater than the maximum feasible s. Thus the firms will set $\phi^n = \overline{\phi}$ and

$$s = \min \left\{ \overline{s}, \frac{1 - (n-1)\rho(c(z^n))\phi^n\}}{[\{1 + \rho(c(z^n))(n-1)\}\{1 + (n-1)\phi^n\}]} \right\}$$

iii. If $\overline{\phi} = 1$, we have $\phi^n = 1$ and $s^n = 1/n$: the firms in effect set up a joint research laboratory and instruct it to do the optimal amount of R&D. They share its costs equally, and all enjoy its output.

iv. Allowing independent R&D would undermine the firms' ability to restrict equilibrium R&D by setting ϕ^n and s^n high. If they tried to set effective R&D lower than in the no-agreement equilibrium, individual firms would have incentives to conduct additional R&D outside the auspices of the joint venture. Even though they would pay for it themselves and not share the output so that $\phi = \underline{\phi}$ and $s = 1$, this would be profitable if effective R&D were lower than the no-agreement equilibrium. It follows that if independent R&D is allowed, industry-wide cooperative agreements can reduce neither effective R&D nor welfare.

v. Because firms always set ϕ^n as high as possible (whether it is their intention to increase or reduce R&D), joint ventures that reduce effective R&D are not necessarily a bad thing. The higher level of spillovers under a joint venture reduces the R&D cost of attaining any given level of effective R&D, which may offset the welfare losses from reducing effective R&D.

c. From (a) we have that the sign of $z^n - z^0$ is given by equation (S13.3). Substituting for s^n and ϕ^n from part (b), and letting $\rho(c(z^0)) = \rho(c(z^n)) = \rho$, gives that $z^n - z^0$ is positive if and only if

$$\frac{[\{1 + (n-1)\rho)(1 + (n-1)\overline{\phi} - (1 + (n-1)\rho\underline{\phi})\}}{\{1 + (n-1)\rho\}\{1 + (n-1)\overline{\phi}\}}$$

$$+ \frac{(1 + (n-1)\rho\underline{\phi}) - (\overline{\phi} - \underline{\phi})(1 + (n-1)\rho\phi(n-1)\rho]}{\{1 + (n-1)\rho\}\{1 + (n-1)\overline{\phi}\}} \geq 0$$

We can multiply this expression through by $\{1 + (n-1)\rho\}\{1 + (n-1)\overline{\phi}\}/(1 + (n-1)\rho\phi)$. We know this is positive because $(1 + (n-1)\rho) > 0$ is necessary for R&D to increase industry profits (see equation (S13.4)). Then the sign of $z^n - z^0$ is given by the sign of

$$(1 + (n-1)\rho)(1 + (n-1)\overline{\phi}) - (1 + (n-1)\rho\underline{\phi}) - (\overline{\phi} - \underline{\phi})(n-1)$$

which, rearranging and dividing by $(n-1)$ gives:

$$\frac{\overline{\phi}}{(1 + \underline{\phi} + (n-1)\overline{\phi}} + \rho. \tag{S13.5}$$

An industry-wide agreement is more likely to increase effective R&D when spillovers in the absence of an agreement ($\underline{\phi}$) are low, and when product market competition is not too intense (that is, ρ is not too negative).

d. Industry-wide R&D joint ventures are most likely to be beneficial when they increase effective R&D. This is ensured if independent R&D is feasible (from (b)(iii)). But if independent R&D is not allowed, industry-wide R&D joint ventures may still be beneficial (from (b)(iv)) if it is possible to arrange both large spillovers ($\overline{\phi}$ high) and cost-sharing between members (from (b)(ii),(c)). Allowing large spillovers without cost-sharing will, however, reduce effective R&D (see (ii)(a)). R&D joint ventures are also more beneficial when spillovers in the absence of an agreement ($\underline{\phi}$) are high, in that in the absence of an agreement strong spillovers will discourage R&D. They are most likely to be harmful when product market competition is strong (ρ high); then firms may wish to restrict R&D because the benefits are passed on to consumers.

When only $k < n$ firms join the coalition, most of the same results can be proved with additional assumptions on the slope of the reaction functions (see Katz 1986). An additional consideration is that when firms within the coalition choose their effective R&D level, they ignore not only the externality they have on consumers, but also that on the firms outside the coalition. Firms outside the coalition may reduce their equilibrium R&D in response to an increase in the coalition's effective R&D; thus even if effective R&D rises within the coalition, it is not clear that it rises overall. Moreover, it is not clear that it is desirable for "total" effective R&D to increase, in that the firms inside the coalition have incentives to do R&D merely to steal business from outside firms; this familiar business-stealing effect means that R&D could be socially too high.

Chapter 14

1. Targeted subsidies and participation constraints

a. The firm's individual rationality constraint requires that the expected ex-post rent of firm be greater than the investment cost,

$$p(e^*)R - \psi(e^*) \geq I - s,$$

where

$$e^* = \arg\max_e \{p(e)R - \psi(e)\}.$$

That is, unless the firm at least covers its investment cost it will not undertake the project. Substituting for $p(e)$ and $\psi(e)$ we obtain that the effort level chosen by the firm is $e^* = R/c$, which gives the IR constraint as

$$\frac{R^2}{2c} \geq I - s.$$

Suppose this constraint is violated for $s = 0$, but the externality associated with the project is large. Then the government may still want the project to go ahead. In order to persuade the firm to invest, the government will have to give a subsidy s^* just large enough to satisfy the firm's IR constraint,

$$s^* = I - \frac{R^2}{2c}.$$

The social benefit associated with the project under subsidy s^* and given that the shadow cost of public funds is λ, is

$$
\begin{aligned}
\text{social benefit} &= p(e^*)[E + R] - \psi(e^*) - I - \lambda s^* \\
&= \frac{RE}{c} + \frac{R^2}{2c}(1 + \lambda) - I(1 + \lambda).
\end{aligned}
$$

The government should give the subsidy only if this expression is positive, which occurs if

$$E \geq (1 + \lambda)\left[\frac{c}{R}I - \frac{1}{2}R\right].$$

That is, if the externality associated with the project is sufficiently large compared to its cost and the cost of public funds.

b. The government's problem is

$$\max_{s,S} \left\{p(e^*)(E + R) - \psi(e^*) - I - \lambda[s + p(e)S]\right\} \tag{S14.1}$$

subject to

$$e^* = \arg\max_e\{p(e)[R + S] - \psi(e)\} \tag{IC}$$

$$p(e^*)(S + R) - \psi(e^*) - I + s \geq 0. \tag{IR}$$

Substituting and solving for effort, we have $e^* = (S + R)/c$. Ignoring the IR constraint for the time being, the government's problem reduces to

$$\max_{s,S} \left\{\frac{S + R}{c}(E + R) - \frac{(S + R)^2}{2c} - I - \lambda\left[s + \frac{(S + R)}{c}S\right]\right\}. \tag{S14.2}$$

Differentiating with respect to S gives the optimal ex-post subsidy S^*,

$$S^* = \frac{E - \lambda R}{1 + 2\lambda}.$$

Notice that if the shadow cost of public funds is zero, $\lambda = 0$, then we have $S^* = E$: the government pays over the whole amount of the externality to the firm, so that the firm completely internalizes it.

Differentiating with respect to s, we find that because s only appears negatively in the expression for social welfare, $s^* = 0$. Provided that the firm's individual rationality constraint is satisfied when the optimal S^* is given, there is no need to give an ex-ante subsidy s, as it affects neither whether the project is undertaken nor the incentives for effort.

c. We now investigate the more complex case where the firm's individual rationality constraint (IR) is binding in the absence of an ex-ante subsidy. That is, $(S + R)p(e^*) - \psi(e^*) \geq I$, which substituting for the optimal effort level, implies

$$\frac{(S + R)^2}{2c} \geq I. \tag{S14.3}$$

In this case the government must set $s = I - (S + R)^2/2c$ in order to ensure that the project is undertaken. Substituting this extra constraint into the government's maximand (S14.2), and proceeding as before we have

$$\max_{S} \left\{ \frac{S + R}{c}(E + R) - \frac{(S + R)^2}{2c} - I - \lambda \left[I - \frac{(S + R)^2}{2c} + \frac{(S + R)}{c}S \right] \right\}.$$

Differentiating and simplifying gives first-order condition

$$S^* = \frac{E}{1 + \lambda}$$

and the associated ex-ante subsidy is

$$s^* = I - \frac{\left(\frac{E}{1+\lambda} + R \right)^2}{2c},$$

which from (S14.3) is positive.

We now investigate whether the need to satisfy a firm's individual rationality constraint in this way can provide an argument for the use of ex-ante subsidies. In other words, whether social welfare is improved by such a scheme. Substituting the optimal s and S under this scheme back into the government's maximand (S11.2) gives that the social welfare is simply $-(1 + \lambda)s^*$. Because s^* is positive, social welfare is negative under this scheme. The government could do better by providing no subsidies at all, in which case social welfare would be zero because the project would not be undertaken.

In conclusion, we have seen in parts (a), (b) and (c) that the need to induce firms to undertake expensive projects with large spillovers does not provide an argument in favor of the use of *ex-ante* subsidies when ex-post subsidies are available. Ex-ante subsidies are an inferior policy instrument because, unlike ex-post subsidies, they do not provide incentives to extra effort. In this context ex-ante subsidies are not even useful as a complementary policy instrument, because if a project is not profitable when the optimal ex-post subsidy is given, it will not be socially beneficial to undertake the project. When the optimal ex-post subsidy is given, it is as if the firm already internalizes all the externalities involved in the project (including those associated with public funding); if the project is still unprofitable, it should not be allowed to go ahead. Thus, unless the firm is credit-constrained and needs money up-front to undertake the project, or unless ex-post subsidies are infeasible (e.g., because of difficulties in verifying success), *ex-ante subsidies should never be used.*

2. Targeted subsidies and the sorting of firms I: the discrete case

a. Assuming that it decides to invest in the project, a firm of cost type $i \in \{L, H\}$ solves the following problem

$$\max_{e} \left\{ e(R + S_i) - \frac{1}{2}c_i e^2 + s_i \right\}.$$

From the first-order condition we therefore have that

$$e_i^* = \frac{R + S_i}{c_i}.$$

b. The government's objective is to maximize the expected gains from success net of the costs of effort and of public funds

$$\max_{s_L, S_L, s_H, S_H} \{\alpha_H[p(e_H^*)(R + E) - \psi_H(e_H^*) - I - \lambda[p(e_H^*)S_H + s_H]]$$

$$+ \alpha_L[p(e_L^*)(R + E) - \psi_L(e_L^*) - I - \lambda[p(e_L^*)S_L + s_L]]\},$$

which can be re-expressed as

$$\max_{s_L, S_L, s_H, S_H} \left\{ \alpha_H \left[\frac{(R + S_H)}{c_H}(R + E) - \frac{(R + S_H)^2}{2c_H} - \right. \right.$$

$$I - \lambda \left[S_H \frac{(R + S_H)}{c_H} + s_H \right] \right] + \alpha_H \left[\frac{(R + S_L)}{c_L}(R + E) - \right.$$

$$\left. \frac{(R + S_L)^2}{2c_L} - I - \lambda \left[S_L \frac{(R + S_L)}{c_L} + s_L \right] \right] \right\}.$$

c. There is no loss of generality in supposing that the government wants both types of firm to join the scheme because it can always set s_H and S_H equal to zero (which is equivalent to the high cost type not joining the scheme) if it turns out to be welfare-maximizing to do so.

d. Assuming that it still operates the project, the rent of the high-cost firm when it does not join the scheme is

$$\underbrace{\frac{R}{c_H}}_{\text{prob. of success}} \cdot R - \underbrace{\frac{c_H}{2}\left(\frac{R}{c_H}\right)^2}_{\text{effort cost}} - \underbrace{I}_{\text{investment cost}} = \frac{R^2}{2c_H} - I.$$

If the firm does not choose to operate the project when it does not join the scheme, it has zero profits. Thus in general its rent outside the scheme is $\max\left\{0, R^2/(2c_H) - I\right\}$.

The high-cost firm's individual rationality constraint is therefore

$$\frac{(R+S_H)^2}{2c_H} - I + s_H \geq \max\left\{0, \frac{R^2}{2c_H} - I\right\}.$$

The government will want to set s_H and S_H so that this expression holds with equality, because if the left-hand side strictly exceeded the right-hand side it could reduce s_H and still induce the firm to invest. This would not have any effect on effort incentives, and would reduce transfers to the firm, and hence the associated deadweight loss. We can then solve for s_H in terms of S_H,

$$s_H = I - \frac{(R+S_H)^2}{2c_H} + \max\left\{0, \frac{R^2}{2c_H} - I\right\}.$$

e. The individual rationality constraint of the low cost firm will not bind as long as the high-cost firm operates the project. This is because the low-cost firm can always duplicate the behavior of the high-cost firm, and make larger expected profits. As we saw in section (c), if the high-cost firm would operate the project even without the scheme, the government will set $\{s_H, S_H\}$ so that it is just indifferent about whether it joins the scheme or not. Under such circumstances the low-cost firm would strictly prefer to join the scheme, so its individual rationality constraint will not bind.

By contrast, the low-cost firm's incentive compatibility constraint will bind, in that the contract $\{s_L, S_L\}$ has to be made sufficiently attractive that it does not want to "mimic" the high-cost firm in this way. The IC constraint of the low-cost firm is given by

$$\frac{(R+S_L)^2}{2c_L} + s_L \geq \frac{(R+S_H)^2}{2c_L} + s_H.$$

Given that the contract $\{s_L, S_L\}$ is designed to make the low-cost firm just indifferent between $\{s_H, S_H\}$ and $\{s_L, S_L\}$, the high-cost firm will not be tempted to choose the low-cost firm's contract instead of its own. The reason for this is that for any given contract, the low-cost firm will always find it profitable to make more effort than the high-cost firm would. Because this is socially efficient, the government can encourage it by giving the low-cost type a larger ex-post subsidy (so $S_L > S_H$). Then if the low-cost firm is just indifferent between a high ex-ante/low ex-post subsidy combination $\{s_H, S_H\}$, and a low ex-ante/high ex-post combination $\{s_L, S_L\}$, the high-cost firm will always prefer the former because it makes a lower effort, so has a lower probability of success and hence of claiming the ex-post reward.

Because the IC constraint of the low-cost firm is binding, one can rearrange it to yield an expression for s_L,

$$s_L = \frac{(R + S_H)^2 - (R + S_L)^2}{2c_L} + s_H.$$

Writing down the IC constraint of the high-cost type and substituting in for s_L shows that indeed it does not bind as long as $S_L > S_H$. We will now solve the government's maximization problem and show that this is indeed the case.

f. Because we have assumed that the high-cost firm operates the project in the absence of subsidies, we have $R^2/(2c_H) - I > 0$ so $s_H = -\frac{1}{2}S_H(2R + S_H)$. Substituting this into our expression for s_L and then putting s_L and s_H into the government's maximization problem and rearranging terms we have

$$\max_{S_L, S_H} \left\{ \frac{\alpha_H}{c_H} \left[(R + S_H)\frac{R + 2E - S_H}{2} - \lambda\frac{S_H^2}{2} \right] \right.$$

$$+ \frac{\alpha_L}{c_L} \left[(R + S_L)\frac{R + 2E - S_L}{2} - \lambda \left[S_L(R + S_L) \right. \right.$$

$$\left. \left. \left. + \frac{(R + S_H)^2}{2} - \frac{(R + S_L)^2}{2} - \frac{c_L}{c_H}\frac{(2R + S_H)}{2}S_H \right] \right] - I. \right\}$$

Differentiating with respect to S_L and rearranging gives

$$S_L^* = \frac{E}{1 + \lambda}.$$

Maximizing over S_H and rearranging gives

$$S_H^* = \frac{E}{1 + \lambda + \beta} - \beta\frac{R}{1 + \lambda + \beta},$$

where $\beta \equiv \lambda(\alpha_L/\alpha_H)((c_H - c_L)/c_L) > 0$.

g. Notice first that $S_L^* > 0$ and that $S_L^* > S_H^*$. It is also very likely that $S_H^* > 0$ and thus that s_H and s_L are both *negative*. Because public funds are costly government *taxes* up front to recoup some of the rewards it plans to give ex-post. Thus once again it is difficult to find a role for ex-ante subsidies:

as a sorting instrument ex-ante *taxes* are preferable because they reduce the transfers the government must make to the firm.

Both types of firms make less than first-best effort because their ex-post rewards are less than the full amount of the externality E. The low-cost firm's effort is distorted only by the fact that transfers to and from the firm are costly. (If λs_L were not lost, the government could tax the firm more ex-ante and raise its ex-post reward to E). The high-cost type's effort is additionally distorted by the incentive-compatibility constraint of the low-cost type. Inducing more effort from the high-cost type necessitates giving more rent to the low-cost type, who would otherwise choose the high-cost contact, and rents are socially costly.

The trade-off between giving rents to the low type and inducing effort from the high type depends on their relative probabilities α_L and α_H, and their relative efficiencies, c_L and c_H. If the high type is very unlikely or very inefficient, inducing effort from it becomes less important compared to extracting rents from the low-cost type.

h. One would expect social welfare to be higher under the policies used in question (2) than under those used in question (1) for two reasons. The first is that we have allowed the government the freedom to set negative ex-ante subsidies, and we have seen that these are useful in trading off between inducing effort and avoiding giving large rents to firms. Second, allowing the government to separate the two types of firms will generally be beneficial in that it can then *target* subsidies to induce more effort from the type for which effort is less costly. In general, the government has more instruments in question (2), so we would expect it do better.

** 3. Targeted subsidies and the sorting of firms II: the continuous case (based on Laffont and Tirole 1993, chap. 1)

a. Suppose the optimal scheme has the firm lie to the government about it's type, so that instead of reporting β, a firm of type β reports $L(\beta)$. Then instead of offering the scheme $T(\widehat{\beta}), C(\widehat{\beta})$, the government can offer the scheme $T(L(\widehat{\beta})), C(L(\widehat{\beta}))$ (i.e., distort the firm's report for it). Then the firm will have an incentive to tell the truth, but the outcome in terms of which firms get what contracts will be the same. Thus any scheme which has the firm distort it's type can be replicated by one in which the firm tells the truth, so there is no loss of generality in searching for an optimal contract among the class of contracts that induce truth-telling. This idea is known as the Revelation Principle.

b. The IR constraint for a firm of type β is

$$U(\beta) = T(\beta) - C(\beta) - \psi(\beta - C(\beta)) \geq 0.$$

The reason that the IR constraint will bind only for $\overline{\beta}$ is that all firms can potentially mimic the behavior of this type, achieving the same cost and receiving the same transfer, but making less effort. If their IC constraints are satisfied, they prefer not to do so, however, so they must receive at least as much utility from the strategy they do follow. Thus if the highest-cost type receives just its reservation utility, all other types will receive a "rent" (i.e., strictly positive utility). The government will set the utility of the lowest type equal to its reservation utility, because the positive shadow cost of public funds makes it costly to give the firm rents.

The IC constraint for a firm of type β contemplating making a false report β' is

$$U(\beta, \beta) = T(\beta) - C(\beta) - \psi(\beta - C(\beta))$$
$$\geq T(\beta') - C(\beta') - \psi(\beta - C(\beta')) = U(\beta', \beta)$$

for all $\beta' \neq \beta$. It must similarly be true that a firm of type β' prefers to make a true report

$$U(\beta', \beta') = T(\beta') - C(\beta') - \psi(\beta' - C(\beta'))$$
$$\geq T(\beta) - C(\beta) - \psi(\beta' - C(\beta)) = U(\beta, \beta')$$

for all $\beta' \neq \beta$. Adding up these two constraints gives

$$\psi(\beta - C(\beta)) + \psi(\beta' - C(\beta')) \leq \psi(\beta - C(\beta')) + \psi(\beta' - C(\beta)).$$

So if $\beta > \beta'$, then $C(\beta) \geq C(\beta')$, and the incentive compatibility constraint requires that $C(\cdot)$ is nondecreasing.

Another way of writing the IC constraint is to note that in order for truthtelling to be optimal $\widehat{\beta} = \beta$ must maximize the firm's utility, $U(\widehat{\beta}, \beta)$. Hence

$$\beta = \arg \max_{\widehat{\beta}} U(\widehat{\beta}, \beta),$$

where $U(\widehat{\beta}, \beta) = T(\widehat{\beta}) - C(\widehat{\beta}) - \psi(\beta - C(\widehat{\beta}))$. Then $dU(\widehat{\beta}, \beta)/d\widehat{\beta} = 0$ implies

$$T'\left(\widehat{\beta}\right) - C'\left(1 + \psi'(\beta - C\left(\widehat{\beta}\right)\right) = 0, \quad \text{when } \widehat{\beta} = \beta. \tag{S14.4}$$

Thus, in order for the scheme $[T(\beta), C(\beta)]$ to be incentive compatible, the necessary (and sufficient) conditions are $C'(\cdot) \geq 0$ and $T'(\beta) = (1 + \psi'(\beta - C(\beta))C'(\beta)$.

c. The government's objective is

$$\max_{C(\beta), T(\beta)} \int_{\underline{\beta}}^{\overline{\beta}} [S - C(\beta) - \psi(\beta - C(\beta)) - \lambda T(\beta)]dF(\beta)$$

$$\begin{aligned}
\text{subject to} \quad & U(\beta) \geq 0 && (IR) \\
& T'(\beta) = (1 + \psi'(\beta - C(\beta))C'(\beta) && (IC1) \\
& C'(\beta) \geq 0. && (IC2)
\end{aligned}$$

However, because of the relation between $T(\cdot)$ and $C(\cdot)$ given by (IC1), the government cannot really treat them as independent instruments. It turns out to be easier to solve the problem by substituting them out, and choosing the effort level for each type β. This effort level will then be induced by appropriate choice of $T(\beta)$ and $C(\beta)$. Thus substituting for $T(\beta) = U(\beta) - C(\beta) - \psi(e(\beta))$ and $C(\beta) = (\beta - e(\beta))$, we have

$$\max_{e(\beta)} \int_{\underline{\beta}}^{\overline{\beta}} [S - (\beta - e(\beta)) - \psi(e) - \lambda(U(\beta) - (\beta - e(\beta)) - \psi(e(\beta)))] dF(\beta)$$

subject to
$$\begin{array}{ll} U(\beta) \geq 0 & (IR) \\ U'(\beta) = -\psi'(e(\beta)) & (IC1) \\ e'(\beta) \leq 1. & (IC2) \end{array}$$

Simplifying the problem further, we know that (IR) and (IC1) will hold with equality, so we can combine them to give us an expression for the utility of type β, which we can then substitute into the objective function

$$\begin{aligned} U(\beta) &= U(\overline{\beta}) - \int_{\beta}^{\overline{\beta}} U'(\widetilde{\beta}) d\widetilde{\beta} \\ &= \int_{\beta}^{\overline{\beta}} \psi'(e(\widetilde{\beta})) d\widetilde{\beta} \end{aligned}$$

Hence

$$\int_{\underline{\beta}}^{\overline{\beta}} U(\beta) dF(\beta) = \int_{\underline{\beta}}^{\overline{\beta}} \int_{\beta}^{\overline{\beta}} \psi'(e(\widetilde{\beta})) d\widetilde{\beta} dF(\beta),$$

which integrating by parts yields

$$\int_{\underline{\beta}}^{\overline{\beta}} U(\beta) dF(\beta) = \int_{\underline{\beta}}^{\overline{\beta}} \frac{F(\beta)}{f(\beta)} \psi'(e(\beta)) dF(\beta).$$

The government's problem thus reduces to

$$\max_{e(\beta)} = \int_{\underline{\beta}}^{\overline{\beta}} \left[S - (1+\lambda)[\beta - e(\beta) - (1+\lambda)\psi(e(\beta))] \right. $$
$$\left. - \lambda \frac{F(\beta)}{f(\beta)} \psi'(e(\beta)) \right] dF(\beta) \quad \text{(S14.5)}$$

s.t. $e'(\beta) \leq 1$

d. Let us ignore the remaining constraint $e'(\beta) \leq 1$ (we can check that it holds afterward). For each β, we can maximize over $e(\beta)$ to get

$$\psi'(e(\beta)) = 1 - \frac{\lambda}{1+\lambda} \frac{F(\beta)}{f(\beta)} \psi''(e(\beta)). \quad \text{(S11.6)}$$

Effort is less than the first-best effort for type β, $\psi'(e(\beta)) = 1$, as a result of two effects. The first of these is that it is costly for the government to give rents to the firms, represented by the fact that $\lambda > 0$. The government could make each type of firm achieve its first-best cost level if it were willing to give up a lot of rent to each type of firm, but when transfers are costly this is not optimal. The second influence is that whenever the government gives more rent to a particular type β, it must give more rent to all types more efficient than β in order to maintain incentive compatibility. The extent to which the government wants to give up rent in order to reduce costs for each type of firm β depends on the relative frequency of that type of firm (given by $f(\beta)$) compared to more efficient types (given by $F(\beta)$). Notice that this implies that more efficient types will be induced to make more effort than less efficient types, because the former have fewer more efficient types below them.

To be more specific, raising effort of types in $[\beta, \beta + d\beta]$ by de increases productive efficiency by $[1 - \psi'(e)]de$ for these types, yielding social gain $(1 + \lambda)[1 - \psi'(e)]f(\beta)d\beta de$ (marginal benefit of raising $e(\beta)$). But the cost is that types in $[\underline{\beta}, \beta]$ gain an increase in rent $\psi''(e(\beta))d\beta de$, with social cost $\lambda F(\beta)\psi''(e(\beta))\overline{d}\beta de$. Equating the marginal social benefit with the marginal social cost gives (S14.6).

We need to check the second order condition by differentiating (S14.5) again. Doing so shows we have a maximum if and only if the so-called monotone hazard rate property is satisfied, $d(F(\beta)/f(\beta))/d\beta \geq 0$. If it is, the firm's IC constraint $e'(\beta) \leq 1$ also holds.

e. The firm is offered a choice of contract of the form: "Achieve cost $C(\beta)$; receive compensation for your costs and net transfer $t(\beta)$, that is, total transfer $T(\beta) = C(\beta) + t(\beta)$." It then chooses a contract by choosing its effort level and hence its cost. (The net transfer can be thought of as the "reward for truth-telling" or "informational rent".) The net transfer as a function of the firm's type is given by

$$t(\beta) = T(\beta) - C(\beta)$$
$$= U(\beta) + \psi(\beta - C(\beta)). \tag{S14.7}$$

But how does the optimal net transfer t^* depend on observed cost? Because $C^*(\beta)$—the optimal cost for type β within the incentive scheme—is strictly increasing, we can invert it to give $\beta^*(C)$: the type of a firm which reports cost C. We can then see how the optimal net transfer varies with observed cost (with the type of the firm implicit in the observed cost)

$$\frac{dt^*}{dC} = \frac{dt^*}{d\beta} \frac{1}{dC^*/d\beta}$$

$$= \frac{1}{C^{*\prime}(\beta)}[-\psi'(\beta^*(C) - C) + \psi'(\beta^*(C) - C)(1 - C^{*\prime}(\beta))],$$

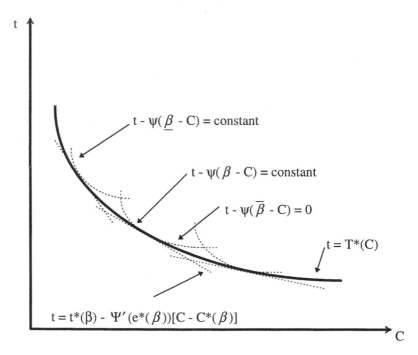

Figure S14.1
Source: Laffont and Tirole (1993), p. 69.

which yields $dt^*/dC = -\psi'(\beta^*(C) - C)$. Differentiating again

$$\frac{d^2 t^*}{dC^2} = -\psi''(\beta^*(C) - C)\frac{e^{*\prime}(\beta)}{C^{*\prime}(\beta)} \geq 0,$$

because $e'(\beta) \leq 0$ (from part (d) above), $C'(\beta) > 0$ (from part (b)), and $\psi'' > 0$.

Because t^* is convex in C it can be replaced by the family of its tangents, as shown in figure S14.1. Also depicted on the diagram are the indifference curves for a firm of a given type β, which from (S14.7) can be defined as $U(t^*, C; \beta) = t^*(C) - \psi(\beta - C) = \text{constant}$. Because $\psi', \psi'' > 0$, these are also convex in C. It is thus clear that the firm can optimally be offered a choice among the "menu" of linear contracts that are the tangents of t^*. In particular, the linear contract designed for type β should give a net transfer of $t^*(\beta) - \psi'(e^*(\beta))(C - C^*(\beta))$. Faced with such a menu, the firm of type β then chooses its contract (implicitly by choosing a report $\widehat{\beta}$) and its effort level by solving the following problem:

$$\max_{\widehat{\beta}, e} U = t^*(\widehat{\beta}) - \psi'(e^*(\widehat{\beta})) \left(\beta - e - C^*(\widehat{\beta})\right) - \psi(e) \tag{S14.8}$$

The first-order condition for contract choice/report of type $\widehat{\beta}$ is

$$t^{*\prime}(\widehat{\beta}) - \psi''(e^*(\widehat{\beta}))e^{*\prime}(\widehat{\beta})\left(\beta - e - C^*(\widehat{\beta})\right) \tag{S14.9}$$
$$- \psi'(e^*(\widehat{\beta})) + \psi'(e^*(\widehat{\beta})C^{*\prime}(\widehat{\beta}) = 0.$$

Differentiating the indifference curve, we have

$$t^{*\prime}(\widehat{\beta}) - \psi'\left(\widehat{\beta} - C^*(\widehat{\beta})\right) = -\psi'(e^*(\widehat{\beta}))C^{*\prime}(\widehat{\beta}).$$

We substitute this expression into the first-order condition, and (S14.9) becomes

$$\psi''(e^*(\widehat{\beta})e^{*\prime}(\widehat{\beta})\left(\beta - e - C^*(\widehat{\beta})\right) = 0,$$

which implies $\widehat{\beta} = \beta$. The first-order condition for effort e is

$$\psi'(e^*(\beta)) - \psi'(e) = 0,$$

which implies $e = e^*(\beta)$. Thus given a menu of contracts of this form, the firm selects the correct contract for its type, $\widehat{\beta} = \beta$, and chooses the correct effort level, $e = e^*(\beta)$. Notice that in this case $C - C^*(\beta) = 0$ and the firm ends up receiving a net transfer t^*.

f. This R&D subsidy is targeted at a single firm, so that all the criticisms regarding targeted R&D subsidies discussed in the chapter apply. Here politicians or civil servants do not have to know the cost of carrying out the project, but they need to know the distribution of cost types $F(\beta)$ and the effort function $\psi(\cdot)$ for reducing costs. The fact that the optimal solution can be implemented using a menu of linear contracts is attractively simple, but not particularly robust to perturbations such as risk-aversion and credit-constraints that are likely to be found in real-world R&D situations. (See Laffont and Tirole 1993, chap. 1 for more discussion.)

However, even if the information required is known by the policy-makers, we have the following difficulty. The private information of the firm about its cost means that any firm participating in such a scheme will gain rents (unless it is of type $\overline{\beta}$). Consequently, it will be difficult to determine whether rather than acting optimally, government agencies have instead been "captured" by firms, in as much as government-sponsored contracts will in any case be lucrative. Even if agencies have not been captured, it may appear that they have been, perhaps resulting in political pressure to reduce participating firms' rents. This in turn could give the government difficulty in *committing* to the menu of contracts, which of course it must do if the scheme is to be incentive-compatible. (If firms anticipate having their rents taken from them at a later date, they will make less effort to reduce costs.) Last, the optimality of the scheme assumes that the firms' rents are social gains—to the firms at least. But it is easy to foresee that firms may waste these rents in advance of receiving them in lobbying to get the government to target their particular firm in the first place.

★ **4. The patentability requirement (based on O'Donoghue 1996)**

a. The measure of dynamic social welfare give the social benefit of R&D net of R&D costs is

$$DSW = \Omega(x, \Delta) = -\frac{xN}{r} + \frac{N\lambda(x, \Delta)\Delta}{r^2}.$$

The first term represents discounted industry R&D costs, which are x for each of the N firms. The second term represents the benefits of R&D, where Δ/r is the value of an innovation (because consumers receive the improved quality forever) and $N\lambda(x, \Delta)$ the expected arrival rate, so that over time the total benefit is $\int_0^\infty N\lambda(x, \Delta)e^{-rt}(\Delta/r)dt = N\lambda(x, \Delta)/r \times \Delta/r$.

Assume that the number of firms active in the industry is given. The first-order conditions for maximization of dynamic social welfare with respect to x and Δ are

$$\frac{dDSW}{dx} = 0 \quad \Rightarrow \quad -1 + \frac{\lambda_x(x^*, \Delta^*)\Delta^*}{r} = 0,$$

$$\frac{dDSW}{d\Delta} = 0 \quad \Rightarrow \quad \lambda_\Delta(x^*, \Delta^*)\Delta^* + \lambda(x^*, \Delta^*) = 0. \tag{S14.10}$$

b. In the race for the tth innovation, all firms aim to make improvements on the *same* base quality q_{t-1}. By assumption, their *probabilities* of success given their action (x, Δ) are equal and independent, and do not depend on their identities, or how much they have spent in the past (because of the assumption of a stationary Poisson process). Thus in order to show that all firms take the same action at all times, it suffices to show that the *reward* to innovation is the same for all firms at all times.

Because the innovation is nondrastic and firms compete on price, at any time the most recent innovator—the market leader—will charge $p = c + \gamma$ and supply the whole market, earning flow profit γ, where $\gamma = q^L - q^F$ is the "market gap" or difference between the qualities of the market leader and the market followers (the $N - 1$ other firms). When patents have complete lagging but zero leading breadth, the quality gap is equal to the size of the most recent innovation, $\gamma = \Delta_t$. For a follower the profit from innovation will be Δ until the next firm innovates. The same is true for a market leader: each new innovation $t + j$ allows him to raise his price above the competition by a further Δ_{t+j}, giving an incremental gain of Δ_{t+j} until the next firm innovates. Thus there is no replacement effect. Moreover because all firms choose their actions simultaneously, there is no strategic advantage to being market leader in the symmetric equilibrium. Thus all firms are identical and face identical reward structures, and hence take the same action.

Why is there no replacement effect in this model? Although the leader enjoys a flow profit from his current product, this is not "replaced" when he innovates again, but rather added to, or "built upon," with exactly the increment that market followers would receive if they were to innovate. This result depends on innovations' being nondrastic, and the fact that the increment received by the leader and followers is exactly the same is a rather special feature of the model, resulting from price competition and unidimensional differentiation. In models where the innovation is drastic, such as the basic model of Chapter 2, the profits that one can make with a given innovation size (γ in their model) are fixed, whereas here profits depend on "how far away" the competition is.

c. Consider firm i taking action (x^i, Δ^i) when all other firms are taking the symmetric equilibrium action (x^e, Δ^e) resulting in combined arrival rate $\Lambda^{-i} = \Sigma_{j\neq i}\lambda^j = (N - 1)\lambda^j$. Firm i's flow R&D cost is x, and it has instantaneous probability of successful innovation $\lambda(x, \Delta)$. Thus firm i's expected flow profits are $[\lambda(x, \Delta)\Delta/(r + \Lambda^{-i}) - x]$, which gives its total expected discounted profits as

$$V^i(x, \Delta; \Lambda^{-i}) = \frac{1}{r}\left[\frac{\lambda(x, \Delta)\Delta}{r + \Lambda^{-i}} - x\right]. \tag{S14.11}$$

Differentiating $V^i(x^i, \Delta^i; \Lambda^{-i})$ with respect to x and Δ gives the first order conditions

$$-1 + \frac{\lambda_x(x^i,\Delta^i)\Delta^i}{r+\Lambda^{-i}} = 0,$$

$$\lambda_\Delta(x^i, \Delta^i)\Delta^i + \lambda(x^i, \Delta^i) = 0. \tag{S14.12}$$

Assuming the equilibrium is symmetric and comparing with (S14.10), we can see that the second first-order condition is the same in both cases, whereas the first one differs. In particular, given Δ, $\lambda_x(x^i, \Delta^i) > \lambda_x^*(x, \Delta)$, which implies x^i is smaller than a social planner would choose. Firms spend too little because they do not take into account the fact that the surplus from their innovation lasts forever (the familiar intertemporal spillover effect). However, they target the correct innovation size because the size of their innovation does not affect their ability to extract the surplus it creates. Given the multiplicative separability of λ, we have that $\lambda_\Delta(x^i, \Delta^i)\Delta^i + \lambda(x^i, \Delta^i) = 0$ implies $\lambda_\Delta(x^*, \Delta)\Delta + \lambda(x^*, \Delta) = 0$, so $\Delta^i = \Delta^*$. Further, unlike in Aghion-Howitt, for example, there is no "business-stealing" effect to encourage firms to make innovations too small: when a firm innovates, it does not get any of the surplus enjoyed by the previous market leader, the whole of which is transferred to the consumers in the form of lower prices.

d. Firms will not aim at innovation sizes that they cannot patent, so they will not choose innovation sizes less than P. Thus firms face the problem of maximizing profits, given in (S14.11), subject to $\Delta \geq P$. Suppose that the patentability requirement is set such that $P > \Delta^*$ to have any effect on the equilibrium in (c). Then, the constraint will be binding, so we can substitute $\Delta^i = P$ into (S14.11),

$$V^i(x, \Delta; \Lambda^{-i}) = \frac{1}{r}\left[\frac{\lambda(x, P)P}{(r + \Lambda^{-i})} - x\right]. \tag{S14.13}$$

Differentiating with respect to x gives first order condition

$$1 = \frac{\lambda_x(x^P, P)P}{r + \Lambda^{-i}}. \tag{S14.14}$$

Notice that

$$\frac{dV^i(x^P, \Delta; \Lambda^{-i})}{d\Delta^i} = \frac{1}{r(r + \Lambda^{-i})}\left[\lambda_\Delta(x^P, P)P + \lambda(x^P, P)\right] < 0$$

so innovations are socially too large.

To determine what happens to spending we totally differentiate the first-order condition $V_x = 0$ with respect to P,

$$V_{xx}\left(\frac{dx}{dP}\right) + V_{xP} + V_{x\Lambda^{-i}}\left[\frac{\partial\Lambda^{-i}}{\partial P} + \frac{\partial\Lambda^{-i}}{\partial x}\frac{dx}{dP}\right] = 0,$$

which, rearranged, gives

$$\frac{dx}{dP} = \frac{V_{xP} + V_{x\Lambda^{-i}}\partial\Lambda^{-i}/\partial P}{-V_{xx} - V_{x\Lambda^{-i}}\partial\Lambda^{-i}/\partial x}. \tag{S14.15}$$

We then have,

$$V_{xx} = \frac{1}{r}\lambda_{xx}\frac{P}{r + \Lambda^{-i}} < 0, \text{ because } \lambda_{xx} < 0$$

$$\frac{\partial\Lambda^{-i}}{\partial P} = (N - 1)\lambda_\Delta < 0$$

$$V_{x\Lambda^{-i}} = -\frac{1}{r}\lambda_x P\frac{1}{(r + \Lambda^{-i})^2} < 0$$

$$\frac{\partial\Lambda^{-i}}{\partial x} = (N - 1)\lambda_x > 0$$

$$V_{xP} = \frac{1}{r}\frac{1}{r + \Lambda^{-i}}\frac{\lambda_x}{\lambda}(\lambda + \lambda_\Delta P)$$

where we have used the fact that λ is multiplicatively separable to get the last line. Substituting these in (S14.15) gives $dx/dP > 0$. This increase in spending can increase dynamic social welfare

$$\frac{dDSW}{dx} = \Omega_x(x(\Delta), \Delta) \cdot \frac{dx}{d\Delta} + \Omega_\Delta(x(\Delta), \Delta).$$

In the original equilibrium, $\Omega_x(x^e(\Delta), \Delta) > 0$, there is too little spending. But equally we know that at $\Delta = \Delta^*$, $\Omega_\Delta(x(\Delta), \Delta) = 0$. Thus there is some P greater than but sufficiently close to Δ^* that will increase spending and hence social welfare. Intuitively, because at the initial equilibrium without the patentability requirement, innovation size was undistorted whereas spending was suboptimal, one can raise welfare by distorting size somewhat in order to reduce the distortion in spending. Around the optimum size, the welfare effects of changing size will be second-order, whereas raising spending has first-order effects because this was initially-suboptimal.

e. If the patent lasts for T years then the total contribution of an innovation of size Δ to industry profits is $\int_0^T \Delta e^{-rt} dt = \Delta(1 - e^{-rT})/r$, of which the innovator receives a fraction α in bargaining. Thus the discounted value of a firm's profits is

$$V = \frac{1}{r} \left[\frac{\alpha \lambda \Delta(1 - e^{-rT})}{r} - x \right].$$

The firm maximizes this expression with respect to x and Δ, which yields the first-order conditions

$$
\begin{aligned}
0 &= -1 + \lambda_x \left(\frac{\alpha \Delta(1 - e^{rT})}{r} \right) \\
0 &= \lambda_\Delta \Delta + \lambda
\end{aligned}
$$
(S14.16)

Comparing the first-order conditions with those in (S14.10), we can see that firms target the best innovation size ($\Delta = \Delta^*$), but spend too little ($\lambda_x > \lambda_x^*$), because they are unable to appropriate the whole of the surplus they create in bargaining.

Comparing the first-order conditions with those in (S14.12), we can see that firms will spend more under the policy of strong leading breadth and licensing than in the absence of leading breadth and licensing if and only if

$$\frac{\alpha \Delta(1 - e^{-rT})}{r} > \frac{\Delta}{(r + \Lambda^{-i})},$$

which, rearranging and exploiting symmetry, yields

$$\alpha > \frac{r}{(r + (N - 1)\lambda)(1 - e^{-rT})}.$$

If α satisfies this condition, the policy of strong leading breadth and licensing entails more spending than in the absence of leading breadth and licensing, yet (as we have already seen) less spending than the first best. Hence a move to a policy of strong leading breadth and licensing will increase welfare in these circumstances.

f. Evidently, the policy of strong leading breadth plus licensing is worse if bargaining inefficiencies are large (i.e., if α is small). However, in this model the problem can be partially overcome by lengthening the life of the patent, which has no offsetting costs: T should be set equal to ∞ to limit the extent of underspending on R&D due to intertemporal spillovers. Leaving this aside, the main advantage of using the policy of strong leading breadth is that unlike the use of a patentability requirement, it does not distort innovation size; such a distortion could be costly if λ_Δ is quite large around the optimum. The disadvantage of such a policy in a more general model is that allowing licensing increases the market gap between leader and followers, so potentially increasing *static* inefficiency. There is no static inefficiency associated with a large market gap here, but one could arise if innovations were drastic and market demand not inelastic (so too few consumers receive the new product), or firms competed in quantities, not prices. In such a model $T < \infty$ will generally be desirable, and the question of which policy is superior will depend on the relative sizes of bargaining and static inefficiency (see O'Donoghue 1996).

⋆⋆ 5. The length and breadth of patents (based on O'Donoghue, Scotchmer, and Thisse 1995)

a. In the previous question, growth was always too low because of the intertemporal spillover effect that implied that firms could not capture all the profit from entry. In the current model, firms have another source of profit from entry: profit from being a market follower. This extra source of profit will encourage entry, potentially to an excessive extent. Because profits depend only on the size of the market gap, the size of one's own innovation determines one's profits only when one is the market leader. A follower's profits are determined by the size of the *next* innovation. Consequently, firms may pay the development cost for innovations that are very small (in the limit, equal to zero), even though the gap whilst leader will be very small (zero in the limit). This is because if the *next* innovation is quite large, the profits whilst market follower may be large enough to cover the development cost. We can call this the "foot in the door effect."

If ideas arrive very frequently, the length of market incumbency both as leader and follower becomes very short. Firms will not be willing to pay the development cost for small ideas in as much as they will not be able to recoup their costs. The intertemporal spillover effect then implies that firms spend too little, that is, they invest in too few ideas. So if the arrival rate of ideas is high,

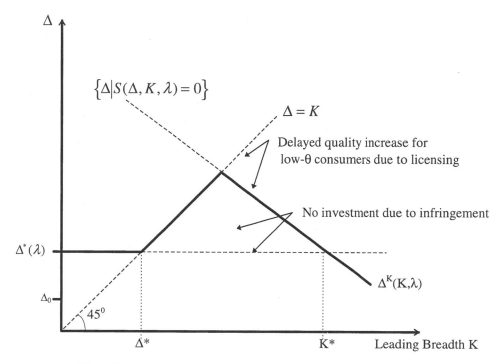

Figure S14.2
Source: O'Donoghue, Scotchmer, and Thisse (1995), p. 19.

increasing leading breadth from zero may improve welfare by lengthening market incumbency.

b.

i. Firms' optimal policy in this model is to invest only in ideas that exceed a minimum improvement size. If $K \leq \Delta^*(\lambda)$, the equilibrium cut-off $\Delta^K(K, \lambda)$ is given by $\Delta^K(K, \lambda) = \Delta^*(\lambda)$. Leading breadth will affect the equilibrium only if K exceeds the minimum improvement size $\Delta^*(\lambda)$ that firms would otherwise choose. If $K \geq \Delta^*(\lambda)$ and $S(K, K, \lambda) < 0$, then $\Delta^K(K, \lambda) = K$. Here leading breadth is large enough to affect the equilibrium, but the profit surplus from licensing an infringing innovation (which rises in the size of the innovation) is negative. So only non-infringing innovations will be invested in: the marginal innovation size is thus $K = \Delta^K$, such that $S(\Delta^K, K, \lambda) = 0$. If $K \geq \Delta^*(\lambda)$ and $S(K, K, \lambda) \geq 0$, then it is profitable to license infringing innovations. The minimum innovation that it is profitable to license is that for which the profit surplus $S(\Delta^K, K, \lambda)$ is zero.

The result is shown in figure S14.2. Obviously the cutoff point is higher for K between Δ^* and K^* than without leading breadth, or with leading breadth larger than K^*, reducing growth.

ii. If the number of occurrences of an event in a given unit of time has a Poisson distribution with parameter λ, then the time t between successive occurrences of the event will have an exponential distribution: $\lambda e^{-\lambda t}$. In this case the number of occurrences of ideas that are non-infringing and in which there is subsequently investment has a Poisson distribution with parameter $\lambda(1 - F(K))$ (assuming $K \geq \Delta^*$; it would be $(\lambda(1 - F(\Delta^*))$ otherwise). Hence the length of time between sequential innovations has distribution $\lambda(1 - F(K))e^{-\lambda(1-F(K))t}$, with mean $1/(\lambda(1 - F(K)))$.

iii. When an infringing innovation of size $\Delta < K$ is licensed, it costs c to produce and adds $\pi_H(\Delta)$ to the market leader's profits, until the next non-infringing innovation occurs. A licensee's innovation adds nothing to the licensor's profits as a market follower because the licensor will eventually become market follower anyway. When he does his profits depend positively on the size of the market gap, so he would prefer not to use the licensee's innovation. Thus S^K is given by the addition to the leader's profits until the next non-infringing innovation:

$$
\begin{aligned}
S^K &= \int_0^\infty \lambda(1 - F(K))e^{-\lambda(1-F(K))t}\pi_H(\Delta)e^{-rt}dt - c \\
&= \frac{\pi_H(\Delta)}{r+\lambda(1-F(K))} - c.
\end{aligned}
\tag{S14.17}
$$

c.

i. It is more attractive to develop an idea when there are fewer previous patentholders to bargain with, and when existing patents are near the end of their term. These things vary over time.

ii. As before, we ignore the profit earned as market follower. Therefore the profit surplus on an infringing innovation at time t is the addition to market leader profits during the life of the patent, plus the incremental licensing income that can be earned from innovations between t and $t + T$, less the implementation cost,

$$
S^T = \frac{\pi_H(\Delta)(1 - e^{-rT})}{r} + L(T, h, \lambda) - c.
\tag{S14.18}
$$

d.

i. Growth under the two policies is the same if the average cut-off under the two policies is the same

$$
\int_{\Delta^K}^{\Delta^{\max}} \Delta dF = \int_H \left[\int_{\Delta^T}^{\Delta^{\max}} \Delta dF \right] dG(h; T, \lambda).
\tag{S14.19}
$$

Suppose that for every history the profit surplus from the marginal innovation is the same (zero) under both policies. Then we have $S^K = S^T$, which from (S14.17) and (S14.18) implies

$$\frac{\pi_H(\Delta^K(K,\lambda))}{r+\lambda(1-F(K))} = \frac{\pi_H(\Delta^T(T,h,\lambda))(1-e^{-rt})}{r} + L(T,h,\lambda). \qquad (S14.20)$$

Dropping the licensing income $L(T,h,\lambda)$ from this expression yields a weak inequality. To simplify further, consider equation (S14.19). If the growth rates are the same, the average cutoff values must be the same; yet we know that Δ^T varies over time. Consequently here must exist a history h such that $\Delta^T \geq \Delta^K$, so that $\pi_H(\Delta^K(K,\lambda)) \leq \pi_H(\Delta^T(T,h,\lambda))$. Because the equality of profit surpluses holds for every history, it must hold for this particular history h, so that, dividing through by $\pi_H(\Delta^K(K,\lambda))$ on the left-hand side of (S14.20) and by $\pi_H(\Delta^T(T,h,\lambda))$ on the right-hand side, and, using the approximation $e^{-rt} \approx 1 - rT$, we have

$$\frac{1}{r+\lambda(1-F(K))} > \frac{(1-(1-rT))}{r} = T.$$

Because (from (b)(ii)) effective patent life under the policy (K,∞) is given by $1/\lambda(1-F(K))$, which is greater than $1/(r+\lambda(1-F(K)))$, it follows that average effective patent life is longer under the policy (K,∞) than under the policy (∞,T).

ii. Social welfare under policy (K,∞) is given by:

$$W^K(K,\lambda) = \int_0^\infty \left[\int_{\Delta^K}^{\Delta^{\max}} \theta_H \Delta dF \right] e^{-rt} dt$$

$$+ \int_0^\infty \lambda(1-F(K)) e^{-\lambda(1-F(K))t} \left[\int_{\Delta^K}^{\Delta^{\max}} \theta_L \Delta dF \right] e^{-rt} dt$$

because high-θ consumers receive quality improvements as soon as they are implemented, whereas low θ consumers receive them only after their patent has run out—that is, after there has been an innovation of size K.

Similarly social welfare under policy (∞,T) is given by:

$$W^T(T,\lambda) = \int_0^\infty \left[\int_{\Delta^K}^{\Delta^{\max}} \theta_H \Delta dF \right] dG(h;T,\lambda) e^{-rt} dt$$

$$+ \int_T^\infty \int_H \left[\int_{\Delta^K}^{\Delta^{\max}} \theta_L \Delta dF \right] dG(h;T,\lambda) e^{-rt} dt$$

because under this policy high θ consumers receive quality improvements immediately that they are implemented, whereas low θ consumers receive them only after their patent has run out—that is, after T periods.

To shorten the notation, let

$$\psi = \int_{\Delta^K}^{\Delta^{\max}} \Delta dF,$$

so that from equation (S14.19) we have

$$\int_H \left[\int_{\Delta^T}^{\Delta^{\max}} \Delta dF \right] dG(h; T, \lambda) = \psi.$$

Also, let $\Omega(K, T, \lambda) \equiv W^T(K, \lambda) - W^T(T, \lambda)$ be the difference between gross social welfare under the two policies. Then

$$\Omega(K, T, \lambda) = \theta_L \left[\int_0^\infty \lambda(1 - F(K))e^{-\lambda(1-F(K))t} \psi \; e^{-rt} dt \right.$$

$$\left. - \int_T^\infty \psi e^{-rt} dt \right]$$

$$= \theta_L \psi \left[\frac{\lambda(1 - F(K))}{r + \lambda(1 - F(K))} - e^{-rT} \right]$$

$$\approx -\theta_L \psi \left[\frac{rT(r + \lambda(1 - F(K))) - r}{r + \lambda(1 - F(K))} \right] < 0.$$

Gross social welfare is higher under the policy (∞, T) than under the policy (K, ∞). This is simply because if you can sustain the same growth rate with a shorter patent life, the growth gets passed on more quickly to the low-θ consumers, increasing social welfare.

The reason why the effective patent life necessary to sustain a given growth rate is higher under the policy (K, ∞) than under the policy (∞, T) is the following. Policy (∞, T) has some "extra profit" compared to the policy (K, ∞). Previous patents that are infringed expire before this one, so some future innovations will infringe this patent but not previous ones, leading to licensing income. This income does not arise under the policy (K, ∞) because the probability of innovations arising that infringe on the current patent is the same as the probability of innovations arising that infringe on the current and licensee's patents, conditional on the licensee's having innovated. By contrast, there is no clear distinction between infringing and non-infringing ideas under the scheme (∞, T); each idea typically infringes for part of its life, but collects licensing income for the remainder. So profit is directed away from marginal ideas under the scheme (K, ∞) compared with the scheme (∞, T). Consequently, to achieve the same growth rate (i.e., the same marginal idea), one must compensate by a longer patent life (and hence more static inefficiency) in the (K, ∞) case.

e. Each idea developed costs c no matter what its size, so the costs of development are proportional to the number of ideas developed. A nonconstant cutoff point for ideas implies that on average a larger number of ideas must be developed in order to achieve the same growth rate, and hence costs of development to achieve a given growth rate are greater. The intuition for this is as follows. Sometimes the cutoff is higher under the policy (∞, T) than under the policy (K, ∞), and sometimes it is lower. But when the cutoff point Δ^T is higher than Δ^K, relatively small innovations are gained. Thus if Δ^T varied symmetrically around Δ^K, the average idea implemented would be smaller than (∞, T) than under (K, ∞), and the growth rate would be correspondingly lower. To make the growth rate the same under the two policies, we have to compensate for the fact that the cutoff point varies under the policy (∞, T) by having a relatively large number of innovations (or lower average cutoff, i.e., $\Delta^T < \Delta^K$ on average). This results in a higher development cost for the same growth rate than the policy (K, ∞).

References

Acemoglu, D. 1994. "Search in the Labor Market, Incomplete Contracts, and Growth." CEPR Discussion Paper no. 1026.

Acemoglu, D. 1996. "A Microfoundation for Social Increasing Returns in Human Capital Accumulation." *Quarterly Journal of Economics* 111(3)*:* 779–804.

Acemoglu, D. 1997. "Training and Innovation in an Imperfect Labor Market." Forthcoming in the *Review of Economic Studies.*

Acemoglu, D., and Zilibotti, F. 1997. "Agency Costs in the Process of Development." MIT Mimeo.

Adam, M.-C., and Farber, A. 1987. "Le Financement de l'Innovation Technologique. Premiere partie: Les caracteristiques de l'investissement novateur." *Cahiers Économiques de Bruxelle* 116: 323.

Adam, M.-C., and Farber, A. 1988. "Le Financement de l'Innovation Technologique. Deuxieme partie: L'apport de la theorie financiere." *Cahiers Économiques de Bruxelle* 117: 3–36.

Aghion, P., Banerjee, A., and Piketty, T. 1996. "Dualism and Macroeconomic Volatility." University College London Mimeo.

Aghion, P., and Bolton, P. 1997. "A Trickle-Down Theory of Growth and Development with Debt Overhang." *Review of Economic Studies* 64(2), no. 219: 151–172.

Aghion, P., Dewatripont, M., and Rey, P. 1994. "Renegotiation Design with Unverifiable Information." *Econometrica* 62(2): 257–282.

Aghion, P., Dewatripont, M., and Rey, P. 1997a. "Competition, Financial Discipline and Growth." Mimeo.

Aghion, P., Dewatripont, M., and Rey, P. 1997b. "Agency Costs, Firm Behavior, and the Nature of Competition." University College London Mimeo.

Aghion, P., Harris, C., and Vickers, J. 1995. "Competition and Growth with Step-by-Step Technological Progress." Mimeo.

Aghion, P., and Howitt, P. 1988. "Growth and Cycles through Creative Destruction." MIT Mimeo.

Aghion, P., and Howitt, P. 1992a. "A Model of Growth through Creative Destruction." *Econometrica* 60: 323–51.

Aghion P., and Howitt, P. 1992b. "Growth and Unemployment." University of Western Ontario, unpublished.

Aghion, P., and Howitt, P. 1994. "Growth and Unemployment." *Review of Economic Studies* 61: 477–494.

Aghion, P., and Howitt, P. 1996a. "The Observational Implications of Schumpeterian Growth Theory.*" Empirical Economics* 21(1): 13–25.

Aghion, P., and Howitt, P. 1996b. "Research and Development in the Growth Process." *Journal of Economic Growth* 1: 49–73.

Aghion, P., and Saint-Paul, G. 1991. "On the Virtue of Bad Times: An Analysis of the Interaction Between Economic Fluctuations and Productivity Growth." CEPR Working Paper no. 578.

Aghion, P., and Saint-Paul, G. 1993. "Uncovering Some Causal Relationships between Productivity Growth and the Structure of Economic Fluctuations: A Tentative Survey." NBER Working Paper no. 4603.

Aghion, P., and Tirole, J. 1993. "The Management of Innovation." IDEI, Toulouse Mimeo.

Aghion, P., and Tirole, J. 1994a. "Opening the Black Box of Innovation." *European Economic Review* 38(3-4): 701-710.

Aghion, P., and Tirole, J. 1994b. "The Management of Innovation." *Quarterly Journal of Economics* 109: 1185–1209.

Aghion, P., and Tirole, J. 1995. "Some Implications of Growth for Organizational Form and Ownership Structure." Mimeo.

Aghion, P., and Tirole, J. 1997. "Formal and Real Authority in Organizations." *Journal of Political Economy* 105(1): 1-29.

Alesina, A., and Rodrik, D. 1994. "Distributive Politics and Economic Growth." *Quarterly Journal of Economics* 109(2): 465–490.

Antweiler, W. 1994. "International Differences in R&D: An Empirical Investigation of a 'Quality Ladder' Implication." University of Toronto, unpublished.

Arrow, K. J. 1962. "The Economic Implications of Learning-by-Doing." *Review of Economic Studies* 29(1): 155–173.

Arroyo, C. R., Dinopoulos, E., and Donald, S. G. 1994. "Schumpeterian Growth and Capital Accumulation: Theory and Evidence." Unpublished.

Arrow, K J., and Kurz, M. 1970. *Public Investment, the Rate of Return, and Optimal Fiscal Policy.* Baltimore: The Johns Hopkins University Press.

Atkeson, A., and Kehoe, P. 1993. "Industry Evolution and Transition: The Role of Information Capital." Federal Reserve Bank of Minneapolis Staff Report: 162.

Atkinson, A. 1996. "Bringing Income Distribution in from the Cold." Presidential address to the Royal Economic Society, Swansea.

Azariadis, C., and Drazen, A. 1990. "Threshold Externalities in Economic Development." *Quarterly Journal of Economics* 105(2): 501–526.

Baily, M. N., and Gordon, R. J. 1988. "The Productivity Slowdown, Measurement Issues, and the Explosion of Computer Power." *Brooking Papers on Economic Activity 2:* 347–420.

Baldwin, R. 1989. "The Growth Effects of 1992." *Economic Policy* 9: 247–281.

Barnett, H. J., and Morse, C. 1963. *Scarcity and Growth: The Economics of Natural Resource Availability.* Baltimore: The Johns Hopkins University Press.

Barro, R. J. 1990. "Government Spending in a Simple Model of Endogenous Growth." *Journal of Political Economy* 98(5), part 2: 103–125.

Barro, R. J., and Sala-i-Martín, X. 1994. "Quality Improvements in Models of Growth." NBER Working Paper no. 4610.

Barro, R. J., and Sala-i-Martín, X. 1995. *Economic Growth.* New York: McGraw-Hill.

Barro, R. J., Mankiw, N. G., and Sala-i-Martín, X. 1995. "Capital Mobility in Neoclassical Models of Growth." *American Economic Review* 85(1): 103–115.

Bartel, A., and Lichtenberg, F. 1987. "The Comparative Advantage of Educated Workers in Implementing New Technology." *Review of Economics and Statistics* 69(1): 1–11.

Bean, C. 1990. "Endogenous Growth and the Procyclical Behaviour of Productivity." *European Economic Review* 34(2-3): 355–363.

Becchetti, L. 1996. "Finance, Investment and Innovation Under Asymmetric Information: A Theoretical and Empirical Analysis." Ph.D. dissertation.

Becker, G. 1964. *Human Capital.* New York: Columbia University Press.

Becker, G., Murphy, K., and Tamura, R. 1990. "Human Capital, Fertility and Economic Growth." *Journal of Political Economy* 98(5), part 2: S12–S37.

Beltratti, A. 1995. "Growth with Natural and Environmental Resources." Fondazione ENI Enrico Mattei Working Paper no. 58.95.

Benabou, R. 1996a. "Inequality and Growth." In B. S. Bernanke and J. Rotemberg, eds., *NBER Macroeconomics Annual* 11. MIT Press.

Benabou, R. 1996b. "Heterogeneity, Stratification, and Growth: Macroeconomic Implications of Community Structure and School Finance." *American Economic Review* 86(3): 584–609.

Benassy, J-P. 1997. "Is There Always Too Little Research in Endogenous Growth with Expanding Product Variety?" Forthcoming in the *European Economic Review.* In Press.

Ben-David, D. 1993. "Equalising Exchange: Trade Liberalization and Income Convergence." *Quarterly Journal of Economics* 108(3): 653–679.

Ben-David, D. 1996. "Trade and Convergence Among Countries." *Journal of International Economics* 40(3-4): 279–298.

Benhabib, J., and Day, R.H. 1981. "Rational Choice and Erratic Behaviour." *Review of Economic Studies* 48(3): 459–472.

Benhabib, J., and Jovanovic, B. 1991. "Externalities and Growth Accounting." *American Economic Review* 81(1): 82–113.

Benhabib, J., and Spiegel, M. M. 1994. "The Role of Human Capital in Economic Development: Evidence from Aggregate Cross-Country Data." *Journal of Monetary Economics* 34(2): 143–173.

Berthelemy, J-C., and Varoudakis, A. 1996. "Economic Growth, Convergence Clubs, and the Role of Financial Development." *Oxford Economic Papers* 48: 300–328.

Bertola, G. 1996. "Factor Shares in OLG Models of Growth." *European Economic Review* 40: 1541–1560.

Binmore, K., Rubinstein, A. and Wolinsky A. 1986. "The Nash Bargaining Solution in Economic Modeling." *Rand Journal of Economics* 17: 176–188.

Blanchard, O. 1985 "Debt, Deficits and Finite Horizons." *Journal of Political Economy* 93: 223–247.

Blanchard, O., Solow, R., and Wilson, B. A. 1996. "Productivity and Unemployment." MIT Mimeo

Blundell, R., Griffith, R., and Van Reenen, J. 1995. "Dynamic Count Data Models of Technological Innovation." *Economic Journal* 105(429): 333–344.

Bolton, P., and Dewatripont, M. 1994. "The Firm as a Communication Network." *Quarterly Journal of Economics* 109: 809–839.

Bolton, P., and Dewatripont, M. 1995. "The Time and Budget Constraints of the Firm." *European Economic Review* 39: 691–699.

Bolton, P., and Xu, C. 1997. "Ownership and Competition: An Application to Schools." ECARE, Brussels Mimeo

Boone, J. 1996a. "Technological Progress and Unemployment." Nuffield College, Oxford University Mimeo.

Boone, J. 1996b "R&D, Intensity of Competition, and the Schumpeterian Trade Off." Mimeo, Nuffield College, Oxford University Mimeo.

Borjas, G. J., Freeman, R. B., and Katz, L. F. 1992. "On the Labor Market Effects of Immigration and Trade." In G. J. Borjas and R. B. Freeman, eds., *Immigration and the Workforce: Economic Consequences for the United States and Source Areas*. Chicago: University of Chicago Press.

Bound, J., and Johnson, G. 1992. "Changes in the Structure of Wages in the 1980's: An Evaluation of Alternative Explanations." *American Economic Review* 82(3): 371–392.

Bourguignon, F., and Morrisson, C. 1992. "The Kuznets Curve and the Recent Evolution of Income Inequality in Developed Countries." Delta, Paris Mimeo.

Bovenberg, A. L., and Smulders, S. 1995. 'Environmental Quality and Pollution-Augmenting Technological Change in a Two-Sector Endogenous Growth Model." *Journal of Public Economics* 57: 369–391.

Branstetter, L. 1996. "Are Knowledge Spillovers International or Intranational in Scope? Microeconometric Evidence from the U.S. and Japan." NBER Working Paper no. 5800.

Braudel, F. 1979. *The Wheels of Commerce.* New York: Harper and Row.

Brewer, A. 1991. "Economic Growth and Technical Change: John Rae's Critique of Adam Smith." *History of Political Economy* 23: 1–11.

Brezis, E., Krugman, P., and Tsiddon, D. 1993. "Leapfrogging in International Competition: A Theory of Cycles in National Technological Leadership." *American Economic Review* 83(5): 1211–1219.

Broadley, J. 1982. "Joint Ventures and Anti-Trust Policies." *Harvard Law Review* 95: 1523–1590.

Bruno, M., and Easterly, W. 1995. "Inflation, Crises and Long-Run Growth." NBER Working Paper no. 5209.

Budd, C., Harris, C., and Vickers, J. 1993. "A Model of the Evolution of Duopoly: Does the Asymmetry Between Firms Tend to Increase or Decrease?" *The Review of Economic Studies* 60: 543–573.

Burns, T., and Stalker, G. 1966. *The Management of Innovation.* London: Tavistock.

Burnside, C., Eichenbaum, M., and Rebelo, S. 1995. "Labor Hoarding and the Business Cycle." *Journal of Political Economy* 101(2): 245–273.

Burtless, G. 1995. "International Trade and the Rise in Earnings Inequality." *Journal of Economic Literature* 33: 800–816.

Caballé, J. 1995. "Endogenous Growth, Human Capital and Bequests in a Life-Cycle Model." *Oxford Economic Papers* 47(1): 156–181.

Caballero, R. J. 1993. "Discussion of the Bean-Pissarides Paper." *European Economic Review* 37: 855–859.

Caballero, R. J., and Hammour, M. 1994. "The Cleansing Effects of Recessions." *American Economic Review* 84: 1350–1368.

Caballero, R. J., and Jaffe, A. B. 1993. "How High Are the Giant's Shoulders: An Empirical Assessment of Knowledge Spillovers and Creative Destruction in a Model of Economic Growth." *NBER Macroeconomics Annual,* 15–74. Cambridge, MA: MIT Press.

Cameron, G. 1996. "Catch-up and Leap-frog between the U.S.A. and Japan." Nuffield College, Oxford University Mimeo.

Campbell, J., and Mankiw, G. N. 1987. "Are Output Fluctuations Transitory?" *Quarterly Journal of Economics* 102(4): 857–880.

Cannon, E. 1995. "Endogenous Growth and Depreciation of Physical Capital." Nuffield College, Oxford University Mimeo.

Canton, E., and Uhlig, H. 1996. "Growth and the Cycle: Creative Destruction versus Entrenchment." CentER, Tilburgy University, unpulished.

Cappelli, P., and Daniel, K. 1995. "Technology, Work Organization and the Structure of Wages." University of Pennsylvania Mimeo

Card, D., and Krueger, A. 1992. "Does School Quality Matter? Returns to Education and the Characteristics of Public Schools in the United State's", *Journal of Political Economy* 100: 1–40.

Caroli, E., Greenan, N., and Guellec, D. 1997. "Organizational Change, Human Capital Accumulation and Wage Inequality." Mimeo.

Caselli, F., Esquivel, G., and Lefort, F. 1996. "Reopening the Convergence Debate: A New Look at Cross-Country Growth Empirics," *Journal of Economic Growth* 1: 363–389.

Cass, D. 1965. "Optimum Growth in an Aggregative Model of Capital Accumulation." *Review of Economic Studies* 32: 233–240.

Chamley, C. 1986. "Optimal Taxation of Capital Income in General Equlibrium with Infinite Lives." *Econometrica* 54: 607–622.

Chandler, A. 1962. *Strategy and Structure: Chapters in the History of the Industrial Enterprise.* Cambridge, Mass.: MIT Press.

Chang, H. F. 1995. "Patent Scope, Antitrust Policy and Cumulative Innovation." *Rand Journal of Economics* 26(1): 34–57.

Cheng, L. K., and Dinopoulos, E. 1992. "Schumpeterian Growth and Stochastic Economic Fluctuations." University of Florida Mimeo.

Cho, D., and Graham, S. 1996. "The Other Side of Conditional Convergence." *Economics Letters* 50: 285–290.

Clarke, G. R. G. 1995. "More Evidence on Income Distribution and Growth", *Journal of Development Economics* 47: 403–427.

Coe, D. T., and Helpman, E. 1995. "International R&D Spillovers." *European Economic Review* 39(5): 859–887.

Coe, D. T., and Helpman, E., and Hoffmaister, A. W. 1995. "North-South Research and Development Spillovers." NBER Working Paper no 5048.

Cohen, D. 1995. *The Misfortunes of Prosperity.* Cambridge, Mass.: MIT Press.

Cohen, W. M., and Levinthal, D. A. 1989. "Innovation and Learning: The Two Faces of R&D." *The Economic Journal* 99(397): 569–596.

Cohen, W. M. and Levinthal, D. A. 1990. "Absorptive Capacity: A New Perspective on Learning and Innovation." Cornell University Mimeo.

Common, M. S., and Perrings, C. 1992. "Towards an Ecological Economics of Sustainability." *Ecological Economics* 6: 7–34.

Cooper, R.W., and Haltiwanger, J. 1993 "The Aggregate Implications of Machine Replacement: Theory and Evidence." *American Economic Review* 83(3): 360–382.

Cooper, R.W., and John, A. 1988. "Coordinating Coordination Failures in Keynesian Models." *Quarterly Journal of Economics* 103: 441–463.

Copeland, B. R. and Taylor, M.S. 1994. "North-South Trade and the Environment." *Quarterly Journal of Economics* 109(3): 755–787.

Cornelli, F. and Schankerman, M. 1996. "Patent Renewals and R&D Incentives." Mimeo.

Crafts, N. B. 1996. "Economic History and Endogenous Growth." In D. Kreps and K. Wallis, eds., *Advances in Economics and Econometrics: Theory and Applications.* Cambridge: Cambridge University Press.

D'Autume, A., and Michel, P. 1993. "Endogenous Growth in Arrow's Learning by Doing Model." *European Economic Review* 37: 1175–1184.

D'Autume, A., and Michel, P. 1994. "Education et Croissance." *Revue d'Économie Politique* 104: 457–499.

Dasgupta, P. 1994. "Optimal Development and the Idea of Net National Product." In I. Goldin and L. A. Winders, eds., *The Economics of Sustainable Development.* Cambridge: Cambridge University Press.

Dasgupta, P., and Stiglitz, J. 1980. "Industrial Structure and the Nature of Innovative Activity." *The Economic Journal* 90: 266–293.

David, P. 1990. "The Computer and the Dynamo: An Historical Perspective on the Productivity Paradox." *American Economic Review* 80: 355–361.

David, P. 1991. "Computer and Dynamo: The Modern Productivity Paradox in a Not-too-Distant Mirror." In *Technology and Productivity.* Paris: Organization for Economic Cooperation and Development.

Davis, S. J., and Haltiwanger, J. 1992. "Gross Job Creation, Gross Job Destruction, and Employment Reallocation." *Quarterly Journal of Economics* 107: 819-864.

Dearden, L., Ferri, J. and Meghair, C. 1997. "The Effects of School Quality on Educational Attainment and Wages." UCL Mimeo.

Dellas, H. 1993. "Recessions and Ability Discrimination." University of Maryland Mimeo.

DeLong, B. J., and Summers, L. H. 1991. "Equipment Investment and Economic Growth." *Quarterly Journal of Economics* 106(2): 445–502.

Den Haan, W. J. 1995. "Convergence in Stochastic Growth Models: The Importance of Understanding Why Income Levels Differ." *Journal of Monetary Economics* 35(1): 65–82.

Devereux, M. B., and Lapham, B J. 1994. "The Stability of Economic Integration and Endogenous Growth." *Quarterly Journal of Economics* 109(1): 299–308.

Diamond, P. 1965. "National Debt in a Neoclassical Growth Model." *American Economic Review* 55(5): 1126–1150.

Diamond, D. 1984. "Financial Integration and Delegated Monitoring." *Review of Economic Studies* 51(3): 393–419.

Dinopoulos, E. 1993. "Schumpeterian Growth Theory: An Overview." University of Florida, unpublished.

Dixit, A. 1988. "A General Model of R&D Competition and Policy." *Rand Journal of Economics* 19: 317–326.

Dixit, A., and Norman, V. D. 1980. *Theory of International Trade*. Cambridge: Cambridge University Press.

Dixit, A., and Pindyck, R. S. 1994. *Investment under Uncertainty.* Princeton, N. J.: Princeton University Press.

Dixit, A., and Stiglitz, J. E. 1977. "Monopolistic Competition and Optimum Product Diversity." *American Economic Review* 67(3): 297–308.

Domar, E. 1946. "Capital Expansion, Rate of Growth, and Employment." *Econometrica* 14(2): 137-47.

Domar, E. 1947. "Expansion and Employment." *American Economic Review* 37(1): 34-55

Eaton, J., and Kortum, S. 1994. "International Patenting and Technology Diffusion." NBER Working Paper no. 4931.

Edwards, S. 1993. "Openness, Trade Liberalization, and Growth in Developing Countries." *Journal of Economic Literature* 31(3): 1358–1393.

Ethier, W. J. 1982. "National and International Returns to Scale in the Modern Theory of International Trade." *American Economic Review* 72: 389–405.

Evans, P. 1996. "Using Cross-Country Variances to Evaluate Growth Theories." *Journal of Economic Dynamics and Control* 20: 1027–1049.

Feenstra, R. C. 1996. "Trade and Uneven Growth." *Journal of Development Economics* 49: 229–256.

Felli, L., and Ortalo-Magné, F. 1997. "Technological Innovations: Recessions and Booms." London School of Economics Mimeo.

Fernandez, R., and Gali, J. 1996. "To Each According To ...?" New York University Mimeo.

Fischer, S. 1977. "Long Term Contracts, Rational Expectations and the Optimal Money Supply." *Journal of Political Economy* 85(1): 191–206.

Frankel, J. A., Romer, D., and Cyrus, T. 1996. "Trade and Growth in East Asian Countries: Cause and Effect?" NBER Working Paper no. 5732.

Frankel, M. 1955. "Obsolescence and Technological Change in a Maturing Economy." *American Economic Review* 55(3): 296–319.

Frankel, M. 1962. "The Production Function in Allocation and Growth: A Synthesis." *American Economic Review* 52: 995–1022.

Freeman, C., and Perez, C. 1988. "Structural Crises of Adjustment, Business Cycles and Investment Behaviour." In G. Dosi, C. Freeman, R. Nelson, G. Silverberg, and L. Soete, eds., *Technical Change and Economic Theory*. London: Pinter Publishers.

Frydman, R. and Phelps, E. S., eds 1983. *Individual Forecasting and Aggregate Outcomes: "Rational Expectations" Examined.* New York: Cambridge University Press.

Gali, J., and Hammour, M. 1991. "Long-Run Effects of Business Cycles." University of Columbia Mimeo.

Galor, O., and Tsiddon, D. 1994. "Human Capital Distribution, Technological Progress, and Economic Growth." Brown University Mimeo.

Galor, O., and Zeira, J. 1993. "Income Distribution and Macroeconomics." *Review of Economic Studies* 60: 35–52.

García-Peñalosa, C. 1995a. "The Paradox of Education or the Good Side of Inequality." *Oxford Economic Papers* 47: 265-285.

García-Peñalosa, C. 1995b. "Distribution and Growth: Essays on Human Capital, R&D and Skill Differentials." Nuffield College, Oxford University Ph.D. dissertation.

García-Peñalosa, C. 1996a. "Small Is Beautiful: Intentional R&D and the Role of Firm Size." Nuffield College, Oxford University Mimeo.

García-Peñalosa, C. 1996b. "Trade and Skill-Biased Technical Change." Nuffield College, Oxford University Mimeo.

Gastaldo, S., and Ragot, L. 1995. "Croissance Endogène et Pollution: une Approche Fondée sur le Comportement du Consommateur." Ecole Centrale de Paris, unpublished.

Gastaldo, S., and Ragot, L. 1996. "Sustainable Development Through Endogenous Growth Models." INSEE, unpublished.

Gavin, M., and Hausmann, R. 1996. "Securing Stability and Growth in a Shock-Prone Region: The Policy Challenge for Latin America." Inter-American Development Bank Working Paper.

Gilbert, R., and Shapiro, C. 1990. "Optimal Patent Length and Breadth." *Rand Journal of Economics* 21: 106–112.

Glomm, G., and Ravikumar, B. 1992. "Public vs Private Investment in Human Capital: Endogenous Growth and Income Inequality." *Journal of Political Economy* 100(4): 818–834.

Goodwin, R. M. 1967. "A Growth Cycle." In C. H. Feinstein ed., *In Socialism, Capitalism and Economic Growth: Essays presented to Maurice Dobb.* Cambridge: Cambridge University Press: 54–58.

Gordon, R. J. 1990. *The Measurement of Durable Goods Prices*: Chicago: University of Chicago Press.

Gordon, R. J. 1993. "One Big Wave?" Northwestern University Mimeo.

Grandmont, J.-M. 1985. "On Endogenous Competitive Business Cycles." *Econometrica* 53(5): 995–1045.

Green, J., and Scotchmer, S. 1990. "Antitrust Policy, the Breadth of Patent Protection and the Incentive to Develop New Products." University of California, Berkeley GSPP Working Paper no. 172.

Green, J., and Scotchmer, S. 1995. "On the Division of Profit in Sequential Innovation." *Rand Journal of Economics* 26: 20–33.

Greenwood, J., and Jovanovic 1990. "Financial Development, Growth and the Distribution of Income." *Journal of Political Economy* 98: 1076–1107.

Greenwood, J., and Yorukoglu, M. 1996. "1974." University of Rochester, unpublished.

Griliches, Z. 1961. "Hedonic Price Indexes for Automobiles: An Econometric Analysis of Quality Change." In *The Price Statistics of the Federal Government,* Report of the Price Statistics Review Committee, General Series No.73 NBER.

Griliches, Z. 1979. "Issues in Assessing the Contribution of R&D in Productivity Growth." *Bell Journal of Economics* 10: 92–116.

Griliches, Z. 1989. "Patents: Recent Trends and Puzzles." *Brookings Papers on Economic Activity: Microeconomics*, 291–330.

Griliches, Z. 1992. "The Search for R&D Spillovers." *Scandinavian Journal of Economics* 94: 29–47.

Griliches, Z. 1994. "Productivity, R&D, and the Data Constraint." *American Economic Review* 84: 1–23

Grossman, S., and Hart, O. 1986. "The Costs and Benefits of Ownership: A Theory of Lateral and Vertical Integration." *Journal of Political Economy* 94: 691–719.

Grossman G. M., and Helpman, E. 1990. "Comparative Advantage and Long-Run Growth." *American Economic Review* 80: 796–815.

Grossman, G. M., and Helpman, E. 1991a. *Innovation and Growth in the Global Economy*. Cambridge, Mass.: MIT Press.

Grossman, G. M., and Helpman, E. 1991b. "Trade, Knowledge Spillovers and Growth." *European Economic Review* 35: 517–526.

Grossman, G. M., and Helpman, E. 1991c. "Quality Ladders and Product Cycles." *Quarterly Journal of Economics* 106: 557–586.

Grossman, G. M., and Helpman, E. 1996. "Technology and Trade." In G. Grossman and K. Rogoff, eds., *Handbook of International Economics*, vol. III. Amsterdam: North Holland.

Hall, R. E. 1991. "Recessions as Reorganizations." *NBER Macroeconomics Annual.*

Harrison, A. 1996. "Openness and Growth: A Time-Series, Cross-Country Analysis for Developing Countries." *Journal of Development Economics* 48: 419–447.

Harrod, R. 1939. "An Essay in Dynamic Theory." *Economic Journal* 49(193): 14–33.

Hanushek, E. 1986. "The Economics of Schooling: Production and Efficiency in Public Schools." *Journal of Economic Literature* 24: 1141–1177.

Helpman, E. 1993. "Innovation, Imitation, and Intellectual Property Rights." *Econometrica* 61: 1247–1280.

Helpman, E., and Trajtenberg, M. 1994. "A Time to Sow and a Time to Reap: Growth Based on General Purpose Technologies." Centre for Economic Research Policy, Working Paper no. 1080.

Henderson, R. 1991. "Successful Japanese Giants: A Major Challenge to Existing Theories of Technological Capability." MIT Mimeo

Hernandez, F. 1996. "Essays on the Economics of Corporate Control: Applications to Internal Labour Markets and Corporate Finance." Nuffield College, Oxford University Ph.D. dissertation.

Hicks, J. R. 1950. *A Contribution to the Theory of the Trade Cycle.* New York: Oxford University Press.

Holmstrom, B., and Tirole, J. 1993. "Market Liquidity and Performance Monitoring." *Journal of Political Economy* 101: 678–709.

Howitt, P. 1996. "On Some Problems in Measuring Knowledge-Based Growth." In P. Howitt, ed., *The Implications of Knowledge-Based Growth for Micro-Economic Policies.* Calgary: University of Calgary Press.

Howitt, P. 1997. "Capital Accumulation and Innovation in Endogenous Growth: Confronting the Facts." Ohio State University Mimeo.

Howitt, P. 1998. "Measurement, Obsolescence, and General Purpose Technologies." In Elhanan Helpman, ed., *General Purpose Technologies and Economic Growth*. Cambridge, Mass.: MIT Press.

Hung, V. T. Y., Chang, P., and Blackburn, K. 1993. "Endogenous Growth, Environment and R&D." Fondazione ENI Enrico Mattei Working Paper no. 23.93.

Hunt, R. M. 1995. "Nonobviousness and the Incentive to Innovate: An Economic Analysis of Intellectual Property Reform." Mimeo.

Ishaq, M., and Nadiri, S. K. 1996. "International R&D Spillovers, Trade and Productivity in Major OECD Countries." NBER Working Paper no. 5801.

Islam, N. 1995. "Growth Empirics: A Panel Data Approach." *Quarterly Journal of Economics* 110(4): 1127–1170.

Jacobs, J. 1969. *The Economy of Cities.* New York: Random House.

Jaffe, A. B. 1986. "Technological Opportunity and Spillover of R&D: Evidence from Firms' Patents, Profits, and Market Value." *American Economic Review* 76: 984–1001.

Jensen, M. 1986. "Agency Costs of Free Cash Flow, Corporate Finance and Takeovers." *American Economic Review* 76(2): 323–329.

Jones, C. I. 1995. "R&D-Based Models of Economic Growth." *Journal of Political Economy* 103: 759–84.

Jones, C. I., and Williams, J. C. 1996. "Too Much of a Good Thing? The Economics of Investment in R&D." Stanford University, unpublished.

Jones, L. E., and Manuelli, R. E. 1990. "A Convex Model of Equilibrium Growth: Theory and Policy Implications." *Journal of Political Economy* 98(5), part 2: 1008–1038.

Jorgenson, D. W. 1995. *Productivity.* Cambridge, Mass.: MIT Press.

Jorgensen, D. W., and Fraumeni, B. M. 1992. "Investment in Education and US Economic Growth." *Scandinavian Journal of Economics* 94: S51–S70.

Jorgenson, D. W. and Landau, R. 1989. *Technology and Capital Formation.* Cambridge, Mass.: MIT Press.

Jovanovic, B., and Nyarko, Y. 1994. "The Bayesian Foundations of Learning by Doing." NBER Working Paper no. 4739.

Jovanovic, B., and Rob, R. 1990. "Long Waves and Short Waves: Growth through Intensive and Extensive Search." *Econometrica* 58: 1391–1409.

Jovanovic, B., and Yaw, N. 1996. "Learning by Doing and the Choice of Technology." *Econometrica* 64: 1299–1310.

Juhn, C., Murphy, K., and Pierce, B. 1993. "Wage Inequality and the Rise in Returns to Skill." *Journal of Political Economy* 101(3): 410–442.

Kaldor, N. 1956. "Alternative Theories of Distribution." *Review of Economic Studies* 23: 83–100.

Kaldor, N. 1957. "A Model of Economic Growth." *Economic Journal* 57: 591–624.

Kaldor, N. 1961. "Capital Accumulation and Economic Growth." In F. A. Lutz and D. C. Hague, eds. *The Theory of Capital*. London: Macmillan.

Kamien, M. I., and Schwartz, N. L. 1981. *Dynamic Optimization: The Calculus of Variations and Optimal Control in Economics and Management*. New York: North-Holland.

Katz, M. L. 1986. "An Analysis of Cooperative Research and Development." *Rand Journal of Economics* 17: 527-543.

Katz, L. F., and Murphy, K. M. 1992. "Changes in Relative Wages, 1963–1987: Supply and Demand Factors." *Quarterly Journal of Economics* 107: 35–78.

Katz, M. L., and Ordover, J. A. 1990. "R&D Cooperation and Competition." *Brookings Papers on Economic Activity:* Special Issue: 137–91.

Kay, N. 1988. "The R&D Function: Corporate Strategy and Structure." In G. Dosi, *Technical Change and Economic Theory*. London: Pinter Publishers.

Keller, W. 1996. "Are International R&D Spillovers Trade-related? Analyzing Spillovers Among Randomly Matched Trade Partners." Unpublished.

Kelly, M. 1992. "On Endogenous Growth with Productivity Shocks." *Journal of Monetary Economics* 30(1): 47–56.

Ketels, C. 1997. "International Competition and the Efficient Choice of Technology." CEPR, LSE Mimeo.

King, R. G., and Levine, R. 1993a. "Finance and Growth: Schumpeter Might be Right." *Quarterly Journal of Economics* 108(3): 717–737.

King, R. G., and Levine, R. 1993b. "Finance, Entrepreneurship and Growth: Theory and Evidence." *Journal of Monetary Economics* 32: 513–542.

King, R. G., and Levine, R. 1994. "Capital Fundamentalism, Economic Development, and Economic Growth." *Carnegie-Rochester Conference Series on Public Policy* 40: 259–292.

King, R. G., Plosser, C. I., and Rebelo, S. 1988. "Production, Growth, and Business Cycles." *Journal of Monetary Economics* 21: 309–341.

King, R. G., and Rebelo, S. 1986. "Business Cycles with Endogenous Growth." Mimeo.

King, R. G., and Rebelo, S. 1993. "Transitional Dynamics and Economic Growth in the Neoclassical Model." *American Economic Review* 83(4): 908–931.

Klemperer, P. 1990. "How Broad Should the Scope of Patent Protection Be?" *The Rand Journal of Economics* 21(1): 113–130.

Klenow, P. J. 1994. "New Product Innovations." Unversity of Chicago, unpublished.

Kocherlakota, N. R. and Yi, K.-M. 1995. "Can Convergence Regressions Distinguish Between Exogenous and Endogenous Growth Models?" *Economics Letters* 49: 211–215.

Koopmans, T. C. 1965. "On the Concept of Optimal Economic Growth." In *The Econometric Approach to Development Planning*, Amsterdam: North-Holland.

Kortum, S. 1993. "Equilibrium R&D and the Patent-R&D Ratio: U.S. Evidence.' *American Economic Review* 83: 450–457.

Kortum, S. 1994. "A Model of Research, Patenting and Productivity Growth." NBER Working Paper no. 4646.

Kremer, M. 1996. "A Mechanism for Encouraging Innovation." MIT Mimeo.

Kremer, M., and Maskin, E. 1994. "Segregation by Skills and the Rise in Inequality." MIT Mimeo.

Krugman, P. 1979. "A Model of Innovation, Technology Transfer, and the World Distribution of Income." *Journal of Political Economy* 87: 253–266.

Krugman, P. 1987. "The Narrow Moving Band, the Dutch Disease, and the Competitive Consequences of Mrs. Thatcher: Notes on Trade in the Presence of Dynamic Scale Economies." *Journal of Development Economics* 27: 41–55.

Krugman, P. 1995. "Growing World Trade: Causes and Consequences." *Brookings Papers on Economic Activity* 1: Cambridge, Mass.: 327–362.

Krugman, P. 1996. *Pop Internationalism.* Cambridge, Mass.: MIT Press.

Krusell, P., and Ríos-Rull, J.-V. 1996. "Vested Interests in a Positive Theory of Stagnation and Growth." *Review of Economic Studies* 63: 301–329.

Krusell, P., Ohanian, L., Ríos-Rull, J.-V., and Violante, G. L. 1996. "Capital-Skill Complementarity and Inequality." University of Rochester Mimeo..

Kuznets, S. 1950. "Schumpeter's Business Cycles." *American Economic Review* 30: 257–271.

Kuznets, S. 1955. "Economic Growth and Income Inequality." *American Economic Review* 45: 1–28.

Kydland, F. E., and Prescott, E. C. 1982. "Time to Build and Aggregate Fluctuations." *Econometrica* 50: 1345–1370.

Laffont, J.-J. and Tirole, J. 1993. *A Theory of Incentives in Procurement and Regulation*. Cambridge, Mass.: MIT Press.

Lawrence, R. Z,. and Slaughter, M. J. 1993. "International Trade and American Wages in the 1980s: Giant Sucking Sound or Small Hiccup?" *Brookings Papers on Economic Activity* 2: 161–210.

Lee, K., Pesaran, M. H., and Smith, R. 1996. "Growth and Convergence in a Multi-Country Empirical Stochastic Solow Model." Cambridge University, unpublished.

Lee, T., and Wilde, L. L. 1980. "Market Structure and Innovation: A Reformulation." *Quarterly Journal of Economics* 94: 429–436.

Legros, P., and Newman, A. 1994. "Wealth Effects, Distribution, and the Theory of Organization." Cornell and Columbia University Mimeo.

Leung, C., and Quah, D. T. 1996. "Convergence, Endogenous Growth, and Productivity Disturbances." *Journal of Monetary Economics* 38(3): 535-547.

Levine, R., and Renelt, D. 1992. "A Sensitivity Analysis of Cross-Country Growth Regressions", *American Economic Review* 82(4): 942–963.

Levine, R., and Zervos, S. J. 1996. "Stock Market Development and Long Run Growth." *World Bank Economic Review* 10(2): 323–339.

Li, C.-W. 1996a. "Scientific Progress, Limited R&D Learning and Growth with Schumpeterian Cycles." University of Glasgow Mimeo.

Li, C.-W. 1996b. "Knowledge Structure, Multiple Equilibria and Growth with Heterogeneous R&D." University of Glasgow Mimeo.

Li, C.-W. 1996c. "Some Extensions of Quality Ladder Model." University of Glasgow, unpublished.

Li, C.-W. 1997. "Patents, Multiple Equilibria and Growth." University of Glasgow Mimeo.

Lipsey, R., and Bekar, C. 1995. "A Structuralist View of Technical Change and Economic Growth." In T. Courchene, ed., *Technology, Information and Public Policy*. Kingston, Ont: John Deutsch Institute for the Study of Economic Policy.

Little, I. M. D., Scitovsky, T., and Scott, M. 1970: *Industry and Trade in Some Developing Countries*. London: Oxford University Press.

Long, J., and Plosser, C. 1983. "Real Business Cycles." *Journal of Political Economy* 91(1): 39–69.

Loury, G. C. 1979. "Market Structure and Innovation." *Quarterly Journal of Economics* 93(3): 395–410.

Lucas, R. E. 1972. "Expectations and the Neutrality of Money." *Journal of Economic Theory* 4: 103–124.

Lucas, R. E. 1988. "On the Mechanics of Economic Development." *Journal of Monetary Economics* 22(1): 3–42.

Lucas, R. E. 1993. "Making a Miracle." *Econometrica* 61: 251–272.

Mankiw, N. G. 1995. "The Growth of Nations." *Brookings Papers on Economic Activity 25:* 275–310.

Mankiw, N. G., Romer, D., and Weil, D. N. 1992. "A Contribution to the Empirics of Economic Growth." *Quarterly Journal of Economics* 107(2): 407–437.

Mansfield, E. 1977. *The Production and Application of New Industrial Technology.* New York: W. W. Norton.

Manzocchi, S., and Martin, P. 1996. "Are Capital Flows Consistent with the Neoclassical Growth Model? Evidence from a Cross-Section of Developing Countries." CEPR Discussion Paper no. 1400.

Martin, P., and Rogers, C. A. 1995. "Long-Term Growth and Short-term Economic Instability." CEPR Discussion Paper no. 1281.

Maskin, E. 1977. "Nash Equilibrium and Welfare Optimality." Mimeo.

McCallum, B. T. 1996. "Neoclassical vs. Endogenous Growth Analysis: An Overview." NBER Working Paper no. 5844.

Michel, P., and Rotillon, G. 1996. "Disutility of Pollution and Endogenous Growth." GREQAM, University of Aix Marseille, and MO DEM, University of Paris X, unpublished.

Milgrom, P. 1998. *Auction Theory for Privatization.* New York: Cambridge University Press.

Mirrlees, J. 1971. "An Exploration in the Theory of Optimum Income Taxation." *Review of Economic Studies* 38: 175–208.

Mokyr, J. 1990. *The Lever of Riches: Technological Creativity and Economic Progress.* New York: Oxford University Press.

Mokyr, J. 1992. "Is Economic Change Optimal?" *Australian Economic History Review* 32: 3–23.

Moore, J., and Repullo, R. 1988. "Subgame Perfect Implementation." *Econometrica* 56: 1191–1220.

Mortensen, D. T., and Pissarides, C. A. 1995. "Technological Progress, Job Creation and Job Destruction." CEPR Discussion Paper no. 264.

Murphy, K., and Topel, R. 1987. "The Evolution of Unemployment in the United States." *NBER Macroeconomic Annual* 1: 11–69.

Murphy, K., and Welch, F. 1992. "The Structure of Wages." *Quarterly Journal of Economics* 107: 285–326.

Musu, I. 1994. "On Sustainable Endogenous Growth." Fondazione ENI Enrico Mattei Working Paper no. 11.94.

Nadiri, M. I. 1993. "Innovations and Technological Spillovers." NBER Working Paper no. 4423.

National Science Foundation 1996. *National Patterns of Research and Development Resources* Washington.

Nelson, C., and Plosser, C. 1982. "Trends and Random Walks in Macroeconomic Time Series." *Journal of Monetary Economics* 10: 139–162.

Nelson, R., and Phelps, E. 1966. "Investment in Humans, Technological Diffusion, and Economic Growth." *American Economic Review* 61: 69–75.

Neumeyer, F. 1971. *The Employed Inventor in the United States: R&D Policies, Law, and Practice.* Cambridge, Mass.: MIT Press.

Nickell, S, J. 1996. "Competition and Corporate Performance." *Journal of Political Economy* 104(4): 724–46.

Nickell, S. J., and Bell, B. 1995. "The Collapse in Demand for the Unskilled and Unemployment across the OECD." *Oxford Review of Economic Policy* 11(1): 40–62

Nickell, S., Wadhwani, S., and Wall, M. 1992. "Productivity Growth in UK Companies, 1975–1986." *European Economic Review* 36: 1055–1085.

Nickell, S. J., Nicolitsas, D., and Dryden, N. 1997. "What Makes Firms Perform Well?" *European Economic Review* 41(3-5): 783–796.

Nordhaus, W. D. 1969. *Invention, Growth and Welfare.* Cambridge, Mass.: MIT Press.

North, D. 1989. "Institutions and Economic Growth: An Historical Introduction." *World Development* 17(9): 1319–1322.

North, D. 1990. *Institutions, Institutional Change and Economic Performance.* Cambridge: Cambridge University Press.

Obstfeld, M., and Rogoff, K. 1996. *Foundations of International Macroeconomics.* Cambridge, Mass.: MIT Press.

O'Donoghue, T. 1996. "Patent Protection when Innovation is Cumulative." Berkeley Mimeo

O'Donoghue, T., Scotchmer, S., and Thisse, J.-F. 1995. "Patent Breadth, Patent Life and the Pace of Technological Progress." University of California, Berkeley Working Paper no 45–242.

OECD. 1989. *Science and Technology Indicators.* Paris.

Olson, M. 1982. *The Rise and Decline of Nations.* New Haven: Yale University Press.

Parente, S. L., and Prescott, E. C. 1994. "Barriers to Technology Adoption and Development." *Journal of Political Economy* 102(2): 298-321

Pearce, D., Barbier, E., and Markandya, A. 1990. *Blueprint for a Green Economy*. London: Earthscan Publications.

Perotti, R. 1993. "Political Equilibrium, Income Distribution, and Growth." *Review of Economic Studies* 60: 755–776.

Perotti, R. 1996. "Growth, Income Distribution, and Democracy: What the Data Say." *Journal of Economic Growth* 1(2): 149–187.

Persson, T., and Tabellini, G. 1994. "Is Inequality Harmful for Growth?" *American Economic Review* 84(3): 600–621.

Piketty, T. 1996. "Inegalites et Redistribution: Developements theoriques recents." *Revue d'Économie Politique.* 104(6): 769–800.

Piore, M. 1988. "Corporate Reform in American Manufacturing and the Challenge to Economic Theory." MIT Working Paper no. 533.

Pissarides, C. A. 1990. *Equilibrium Unemployment Theory*. Oxford: Basil Blackwell.

Porter, M. 1990. *The Competitive Advantage of Nations*. New York: Free Press.

Prescott, E. C. 1986: "Theory Ahead of Business Cycle Measurement." In *Carnegie-Rochester Conference Series on Public Policy* 25: 11–44.

Pritchett, L. 1996. "Measuring Outward Orientation in LDCS: Can It Be Done?" *Journal of Development Economics* 49: 307–335.

Qian, Y. 1994. "Incentives and Loss of Control in an Optimal Hierarchy." *Review of Economic Studies* 61: 527–544.

Quah, D. 1996. "Convergence Empirics Across Economies with Some Capital Mobility." *Journal of Economic Growth* 1(1): 95–124.

Rae, J. 1834. *Statement of Some New Principles on the Subject of Political Economy*. Boston: Hilliard, Gray, and Co.

Radner, R. 1993. "The Organization of Decentralized Information Processing." *Econometrica* 62: 1109–1146.

Ramey, G. and Ramey, V. A. 1995. "Cross-Country Evidence on the Link Between Volatility and Growth." *American Economic Review* 85: 1138–1151.

Ramsey, F. 1928. "A Mathematical Theory of Saving." *Economic Journal* 38: 543–559.

Rebelo, S. 1991. "Long-Run Policy Analysis and Long-Run Growth." *Journal of Political Economy* 99: 500–521.

Redding, S. 1996a. "Low-Skill, Low-Quality Trap: Strategic Complementarities between Human Capital and R&D." *Economic Journal* 106: 458–470.

Redding, S. 1996b. "Dynamic Comparative Advantage and the Welfare Effects of Trade." Nuffield College, Oxford University Mimeo.

Redding, S. 1996c. "Is There a Penalty to Being a Pioneer?" Nuffield College, Oxford University Working Paper no. 109,.

Reinganum, J. F. 1989. "The Timing of Innovation: Research, Development and Diffusion." In R.Schmalensee and R. D. Willig, eds., *Handbook of Industrial Organization* vol. 1. New York: North-Holland

Rivera-Batiz, L., and Romer, P. 1991: "Economic Integration and Endogenous Growth." *Quarterly Journal of Economics* 106(2): 531–555.

Romer, P. M. 1986. "Increasing Returns and Long Run Growth." *Journal of Political Economy* 94(5): 1002–1037.

Romer, P. M. 1987. "Growth Based on Increasing Returns Due to Specialization." *American Economic Review Papers and Proceedings* 77(2): 56–72.

Romer, P. M. 1990a. "Endogenous Technological Change." *Journal of Political Economy* 98(5) part 2: 71–102.

Romer, P. M. 1990b. "Capital, Labor and Productivity." *Brookings Papers on Economic Activity, Microeconomics Special Issue*: 337–367.

Romer, P. M. 1993. "Implementing a National Technology Strategy with Self-Organizing Industry Investment Boards." NBER Reprint no. 1870.

Romer, P. M. and Sasaki, H. 1986. "Scarcity and Growth Reinterpreted: Endogenous Technological Change and Falling Resource Prices." Rochester Center for Economic Research Working Paper no. 19.

Rosenberg, N. 1963. "Technological Change in the Machine Tool Industry, 1840–1910." *Journal of Economic History* 23(4): 414–443.

Rosenberg, N., and Birdzell, L. E., Jr. 1986. *How the West Grew Rich*. New York: Basic Books.

Sachs, J. D., and Shatz, H. J. 1994. "Trade and Jobs in U.S. Manufacturing." *Brookings Papers on Economic Activity* 1: 1–69.

Sachs, J. D., and Warner, A. 1995. "Economic Reform and the Process of Global Integration." *Brookings Papers on Economic Activity* 1: 1–95.

Saint-Paul, G. 1991. "Unemployment and Productivity Growth in OECD Countries." Unpublished.

Saint-Paul, G. 1992. "Fiscal Policy in an Endogenous Growth Model." *Quarterly Journal of Economics* 107: 1243–1259.

Saint-Paul, G. 1993a. "Productivity Growth and the Structure of the Business Cycle." *European Economic Review* 37(4): 861–883.

Saint-Paul, G., and Verdier, T. 1993b. "Education, Democracy and Growth." *Journal of Development Economics* 42(2): 399–407.

Samuelson, P. 1949. "International Factor-Price Equalization Once Again." *Economic Journal* 59(234): 181-197.

Samuelson, P. 1988. "Mathematical Vindication of Ricardo on Machinery." *Journal of Political Economy* 96: 274–282.

Schankerman, M., and Pakes, A. 1986. "Estimates of the Value of Patent Rights in European Countries During the Post-1950 Period." *The Economic Journal* 96: 1052–1076.

Scherer, F. 1972. "Nordhaus Theory of Optimal Patent Life: A Geometric Reinterpretation." *American Economic Review* 62: 422–427.

Scherer, F., and Huh, K. 1992. "Top Managers' Education and R&D Investment." *Research Policy* 21: 507–511.

Schumpeter, J. A. 1934. *The Theory of Economic Development*. Cambridge, Mass.: Harvard University Press.

Scott, M. F. 1989. *A New View of Economic Growth*. Oxford: Clarendon Press.

Scott, E., O'Shaugnessy, K., and Cappelli, P. 1996. "Management Jobs in the Insurance Industry: Organisation, Deskilling and Rising Pay Inequality." University of Pennsylvania Mimeo.

Segerstrom, P. 1991. "Innovation, Imitation and Economic Growth." *Journal of Political Economy* 99(4): 807–827.

Segerstrom, P. S., Anant, T., and Dinopoulos, E. 1990, "A Schumpeterian Model of the Product Life Cycle." *American Economic Review* 80: 1077–1092.

Shell, K. 1967. "A Model of Inventive Activity and Capital Accumulation." In K. Shell, ed., *Essays on the Theory of Optimal Economic Growth*. Cambridge, Mass.: MIT Press.

Shell, K. 1973. "Inventive Activity, Industrial Organization, and Economic Activity." In J. Mirrlees and N. Stern,. eds., *Models of Economic Growth*. London: Macmillan.

Shleifer, A. 1986. "Implementation Cycles." *Journal of Political Economy* 94: 1163–1190.

Slaughter, M. J. 1997. "Per Capita Income Convergence and the Role of International Trade." NBER Working Paper no. 5897.

Smulders, S. A. 1994a. "Environmental Issues in Models of Endogenous Growth." Paper presented to the 50th Congress of the International Institute of Public Finance.

Smulders, S. A. 1994b. *Growth, Market Structure and the Environment: Essays on the Theory of Endogenous Economic Growth*. Hilvarenbeek: J. A. Smulders.

Solow, R. M. 1956. "A Contribution to the Theory of Economic Growth." *Quarterly Journal of Economics* 70(1): 65–94.

Solow, R. M. 1957. "Technical Change and the Aggregate Production Function." *Review of Economics and Statistics* 39: 312–320.

Solow, R. M. 1993. "Sustainability: An Economist's Perspective." In R. Dorfman and S. Dorfman, eds., *Economics of the Environment: Selected Readings*. 3rd ed. New York: Norton.

Stadler, G. W. 1990.: "Business Cycles Models with Endogenous Technology." *American Economic Review* 80(4): 763–778.

Stern, N. 1989. "The Economics of Development: A Survey." *Economic Journal* 99: 597–685.

Stiglitz, J. E. 1993. "Endogenous Growth and Cycles." NBER Working Paper no. 4286.

Stokey, N. L. 1991. "Human Capital, Product Quality and Growth." *Quarterly Journal of Economics* 106(2): 587–616.

Stokey, N. L. 1995. "R&D and Economic Growth." *The Review of Economic Studies* 62: 469–489.

Stokey, N. L. 1996. "Are There Limits to Growth?" University of Chicago, unpublished.

Stole, L., and Zwiebel, J. 1996. "Intra-Firm Bargaining under Non-Binding Contracts." *Review of Economic Studies* 63: 375-410.

Swan, T. W. 1956. "Economic Growth and Capital Accumulation." *Economic Record* 32: 334–361.

Symposia in the *Journal of Economic Perspectives* 1994. 8(1-4).

Symposium on School Quality and Educational Outcomes. 1996. *The Review of Economics and Statistics* 78(4): 559–752.

Takayama, A. 1974. *Mathematical Economics*. Hinsdale, IL: The Dryden Press.

Taylor, J. 1980. "Aggregate Dynamics and Staggered Contracts." *Journal of Political Economy* 88: 1–24.

Teece, D. 1988. "Technological Change and the Nature of the Firm." In G. Dosi, ed., *Technical Change and Economic Theory*. London: Pinter Publishers: 256–281.

Tirole, J. 1988. *The Theory of Industrial Organisation*. Cambridge, Mass.: MIT Press.

Tirole, J. 1996. "Lecture Notes on Public Aid to Innovation." Unpublished.

Trajtenberg, M. 1990. *Economic Analysis of Product Innovation: The Case of CT Scanners*. Cambridge, Mass.: Harvard University Press.

Trefler, D. 1993. "International Factor Price Differences: Leontief Was Right!" *Journal of Political Economy* 101: 961–987.

Trefler, D. 1995. "The Case of Missing Trade and Other Mysteries." *American Economic Review* 85: 1029–1046.

Tybout, J. R. 1992. "Linking Trade and Productivity: New Research Directions." *The World Bank Economic Review* 6(2): 189–211.

Uhlig, H. and Yanagawa, N. 1996. "Increasing the Capital Income Tax May Lead to Faster Growth." *European Economic Review* 40: 1521–1540.

U.S. Department of Commerce. 1994. "A Satellite Account for Research and Development." *Survey of Current Business:* 37-71.

Usher, D. 1980. *The Measurement of Economic Growth*. New York: Columbia University Press.

Uzawa, H. 1965. "Optimum Technical Change in an Aggregative Model of Economic Growth." *International Economic Review* 6: 18–31.

van Elkan, R. 1996. "Catching Up and Slowing Down: Learning and Growth Patterns in an Open Economy." *Journal of International Economics* 41: 95–111.

van Hippel, E. 1988. *The Sources of Innovation*. New York: Oxford University Press.

van Zandt, T. 1990. "The Structure and Returns to Scale of Organizations that Process Information with Endogenous Agents." Princeton Mimeo.

Ventura, J. 1997. "Growth and Interdependence." *Quarterly Journal of Economics* 112(1): 57–84.

Verdier, T. 1993. "Environmental Pollution and Endogenous Growth: A Comparison Between Emission Taxes and Technological Standards. Fondazione ENI Enrico Mattei Working Paper no. 57.93.

Vernon, R. 1966. "International Investment and International Trade in the Product Cycle." *Quarterly Journal of Economics* 80: 190–207.

Violante, G. L "Equipment Investment and Skill Dynamics: A Solution to the Wage Dispersion Puzzle?" University of Pennsylvania Mimeo.

Wälde, K. 1994a. "On an Additional Condition for Factor-Price Equalization in Intertemporal Heckscher-Ohlin Models." *Economic Letters* 44: 411– 414.

Wälde, K. 1994b. "Unequal Factor Rewards and Incomplete Specialization in a Heckscher-Ohlin Model of Endogenous Growth." *Journal of Economics* 59: 311–323.

Westney, E. 1993. "Country Patterns in R&D Organization: The United States and Japan." In Bruce Kogut, ed., *Country Competitiveness: Technology and the Organizing of Work*. New York: Oxford University Press, 36–53.

Williams, J. 1995. "The Limits to 'Growing an Economy.'" Federal Reserve Board Discussion Paper no. 95-30.

Williamson, O. E. 1975. *Markets and Hierarchies: Analysis and Antitrust Implications* New York: Free Press.

Wood, A. 1994. *North-South Trade, Employment and Inequality: Changing Fortunes in a Skill Driven World.* Oxford: Clarendon Press.

World Bank. 1992. *World Development Report: Development and Environment.* Oxford: Oxford University Press.

World Commission on Environment and Development. 1987. *Our Common Future.* Oxford: Oxford University Press.

Young, A. 1928. "Increasing Returns and Economic Progress." *Economic Journal* 38(152): 527–542.

Young, A. 1991. "Learning by Doing and the Dynamic Effects of International Trade." *Quarterly Journal of Economics* 106(2): 369–406.

Young, A. 1992. "A Tale of Two Cities: Factor Accumulation and Technical Change in Hong Kong and Singapore." NBER Macroeconomics Annual: 13–54.

Young, A. 1993a. "Invention and Bounded Learning by Doing." *Journal of Political Economy* 101(3): 443–472.

Young, A. 1993b. "Substitution and Complementarity in Endogenous Innovation." *Quarterly Journal of Economics* 108(3): 775-807.

Young, A. 1995a. "Growth Without Scale Effects." NBER Working Paper no. 5211.

Young, A. 1995b. "The Tyranny of Numbers: Confronting the Statistical Realities of the East Asian Growth Experience." *Quarterly Journal of Economics* 110: 641–680.

Index